150 COFFEE SHOPS YOU NEED TO VISIT BEFORE YOU DIE

By Léa Teuscher

Lannoo

The best Maxim I know in this life is, to drink your Coffee when you can...

— Jonathan Swift

Let me start with an apology: very sorry, but your favourite café will probably not be included in this book. Humanity drinks around two billion cups of coffee every day. In the UK alone, there are over 12,000 independent coffee shops, plus about the same number of outlets of big coffee brands... So, far from a definitive list, this book is a snapshot of some of the cafés that stand out from the crowd.

Many follow the new international coffee bar style – tattooed baristas, industrial fittings and colourful merch – but there are also outliers, including historic cafés, high-tech roasteries and bohemian coffee lounges. From Arabic to Vietnamese coffee, and from cascara drinks in Costa Rica to dirty coffee in Beijing, you might even discover your new favourite order.

It's fair to say that the little coffee bean has been on quite a journey. Legend has it that Ethiopian goatherd Kaldi discovered it in Kaffa after seeing his four-legged friends get pretty excited by some strange leaves. It then took off from the Arabic Peninsula, via Turkey, Venice and Austria, to the rest of the world.

Throughout the centuries, great thinkers have been energised by the potent dark brew and the people they met at their favourite café. From London's 'penny universities' to Paris, Vienna and Addis Ababa, coffee houses have been hotspots for new ideas and even revolutions. 'It has been the world's most radical drink in that its function has always been to make people think,' wrote William Ukers in his classic *All About Coffee*. No wonder England's Charles II tried to ban coffee houses, the 'great resort of idle and disaffected persons'.

Since then, the waves have kept rolling in, turning the tide and leading the way in terms of fair trade and sustainability: coffee making is now a precious craft focused on growers and the environment. Baristas have become artists and stars, and as for the cafés, they are not so much countercultural but the culture itself: third spaces found from Shanghai to Seattle, where you can set up your laptop or have a chat with friends in real life.

OVERVIEW

AFRICA AND THE MIDDLE EAST

THE AMERICAS

OVERVIEW

ASIA

OVERVIEW

EUROPE

OVERVIEW

01 CAFÉ CONTINENT

Galerie Square Centre, rue Clément Ader, Zone 03,
Abidjan, Côte d'Ivoire

TO VISIT
BEFORE YOU DIE
BECAUSE

Discover some of Côte d'Ivoire's lesser-known beans at this beautiful contemporary café, a cultural hub for speciality coffee in Africa.

This smart café located in Abidjan's Zone 03 was opened in 2021 by speciality coffee aficionado Hadi Beydoun, the first and – to date – only certified arabica Q Grader in West Africa. Designed by Paul Kaloustian Architect in collaboration with Rym Beydoun, the minimalist space features a Portuguese marble-top bar where treats such as marbled cake, pastries and cookies are neatly displayed; white banquettes where you can relax with a cup of freshly roasted coffee sourced from Kenya to Côte d'Ivoire; and long wooden benches to perch on while thinking about your next move on the chessboard. 'We proudly source and roast coffees grown locally across Africa, celebrating the richness and diversity of its terroirs while working hand in hand with farmers,' says Hadi. Customers call it a 'true coffee library', and enjoy local beans including Biankouma, Danané and Man, grown in the lush mountains of western Côte d'Ivoire. Beyond serving coffee, Café Continent also offers certified training courses, workshops and masterclasses for both professionals and enthusiasts.

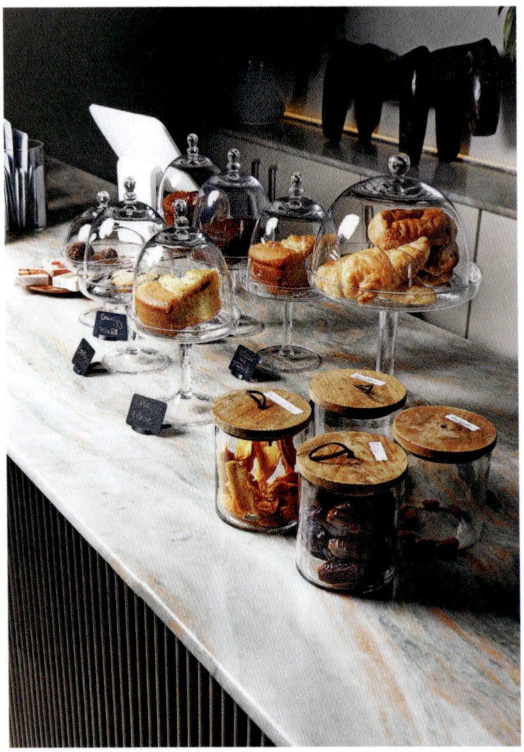

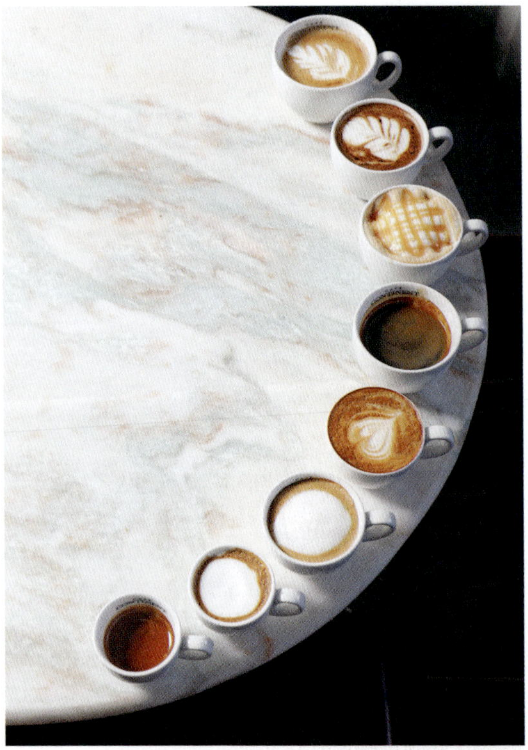

@cafecontinent

+225 05 07 48 6982

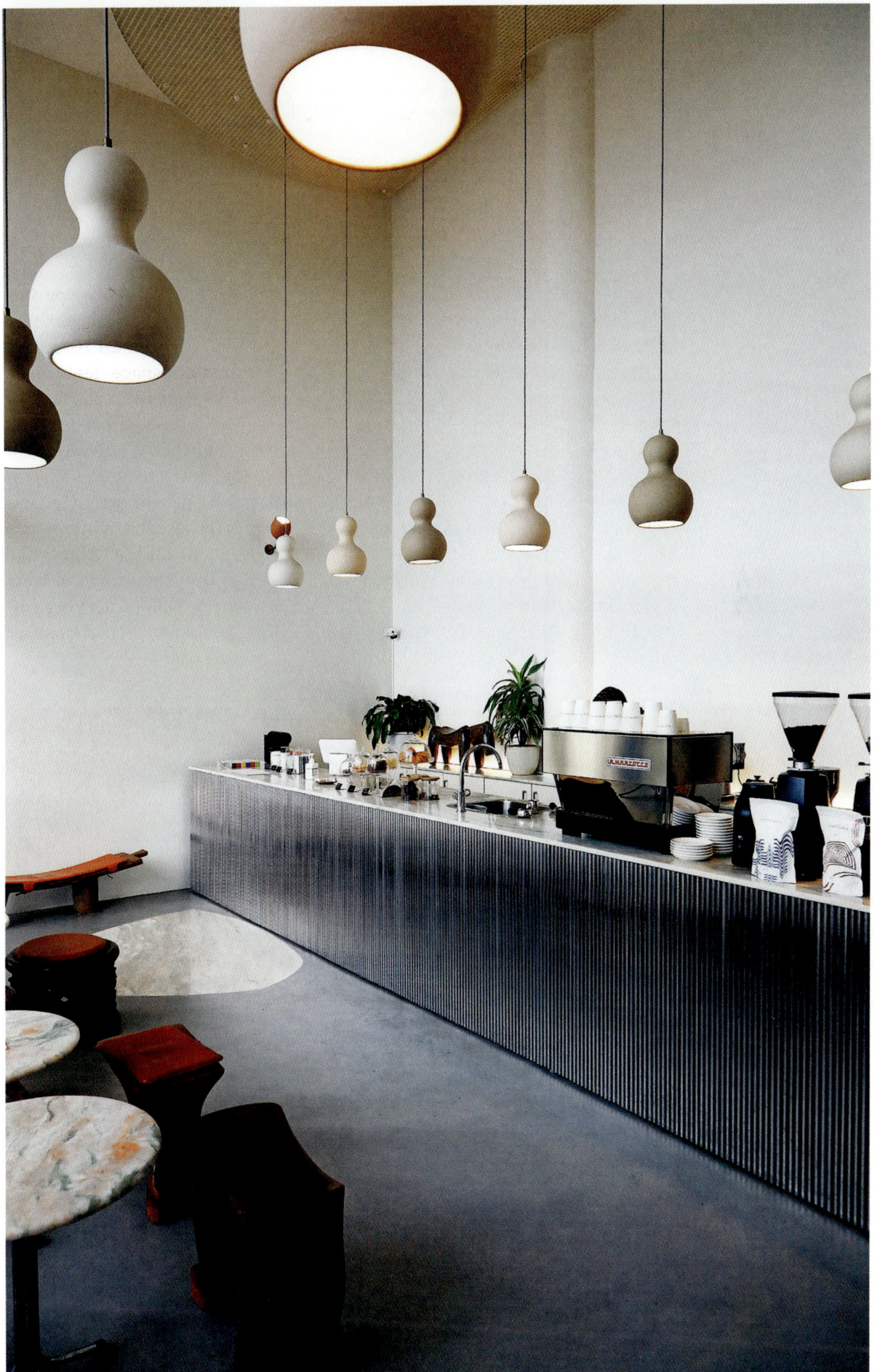

02 TOMOCA

Wawel St, Addis Ababa, Ethiopia

TO VISIT BEFORE YOU DIE BECAUSE

Taste a bit of history and some of the best beans from Ethiopia, the birthplace of coffee, at one of the oldest coffee shops in town.

Ethiopia is known for its exquisite traditional coffee ceremony, involving the roasting of beans on hot coals, the addition of frankincense, and three rounds of coffee served with snacks like popcorn. A symbol of hospitality, community and respect, it can last for hours. But there's a quicker way to get your caffeine fix in Addis Ababa, thanks to the widely used espresso machine – its adoption by locals being the only silver lining of the brutal 1930s Italian occupation. All these stories come together at this historic wood-panelled café, opened in 1953 by Tomoca (short for Torrefazione Moderna Café), a family-owned company who pioneered the meticulous roasting of arabica beans from Ethiopia's Kaffa region. Here, surrounded by vintage coffee grinders, conversations among friends and new acquaintances continue over a cup of Ethiopian macchiato (a sort of layered latte) and Tomoca Cravate (sweetened black coffee). Make sure to try the surprising Tomoca Sprice, a mix of sweetened black coffee and tea.

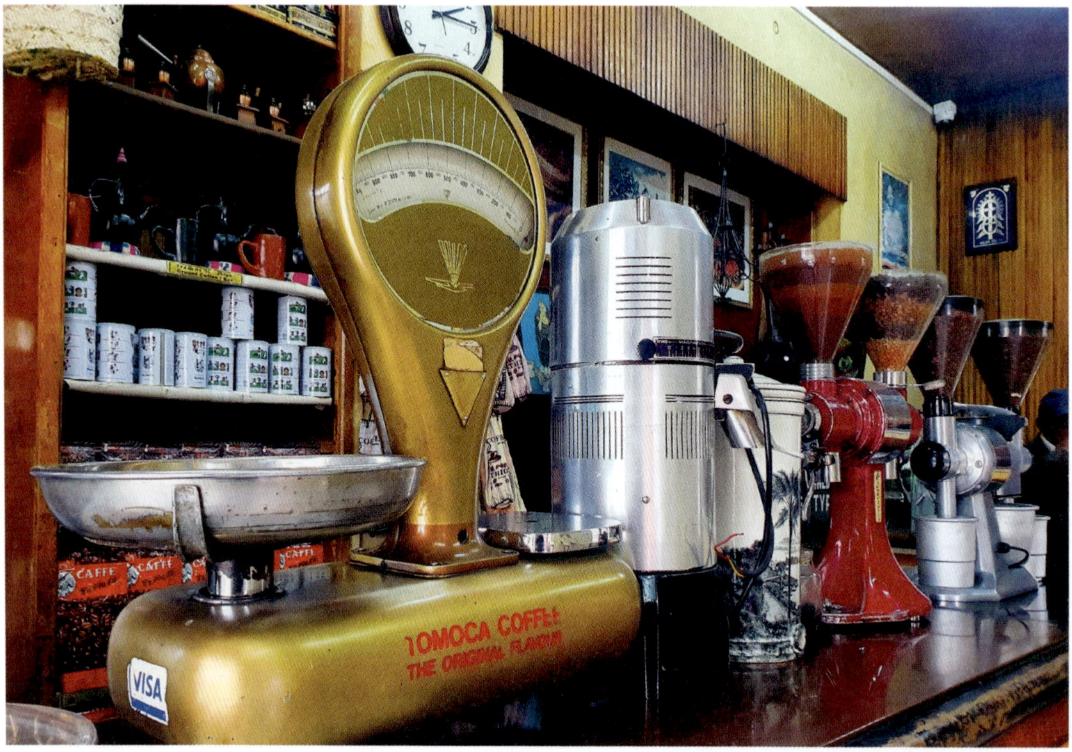

tomocacoffeeafrica.com

+254 110 097 919

03 KAHAWA COFFEE SHOP

Arusha Coffee Lodge, Old Dodoma Rd, Burka Coffee Estate, Arusha, Tanzania

TO VISIT
BEFORE YOU DIE
BECAUSE

The journey from bean to cup has never been shorter than at the café of this Tanzanian coffee plantation, set in a lush garden.

Most people visit Tanzania on a safari, but the country is also Africa's fourth biggest coffee producer, known for its mild arabica often grown in high-altitude fields and shaded by banana trees. Located in one of Tanzania's largest coffee plantations, this coffee shop is part of the Arusha Coffee Lodge, a stylish resort by Elewana featuring spacious suites and rooms overlooking the surrounding berry-laden coffee fields. A peaceful retreat surrounded by greenery, the lodge's Kahawa café and bakery is the best place to sample the local produce after joining one of the plantation's bean-to-coffee tours, which are open to both guests and visitors. Here, on a terrace in the garden, you can try the plantation's coffee, available in a variety of roasts and served by a team of friendly baristas, as well as specialities including Kahawa's signature coffee martini and coffee-infused cakes. For a truly reinvigorating coffee experience, pair this with a birdwatching tour, an afternoon spent observing the playful resident monkeys, or a spa session.

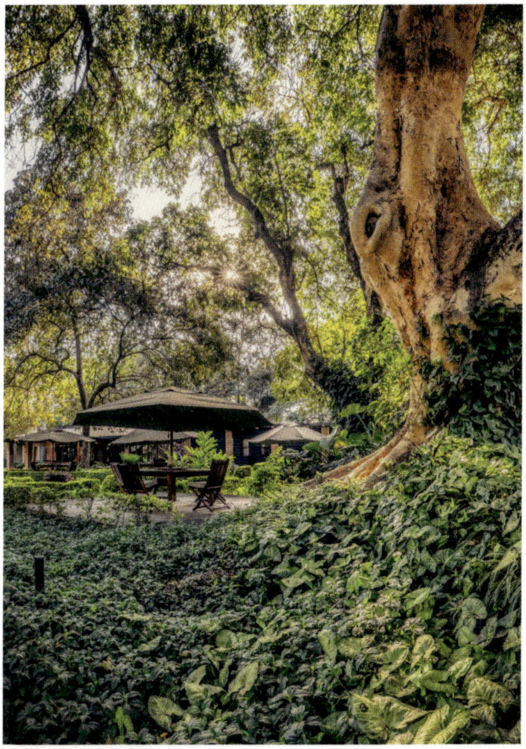

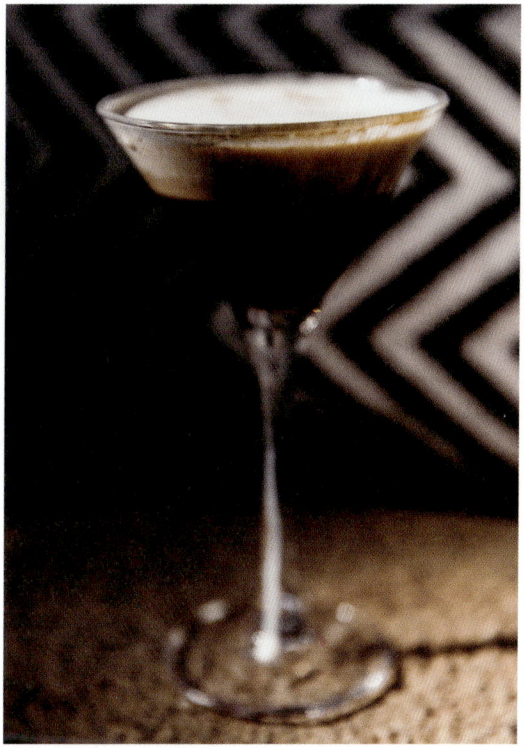

elewanacollection.com

+254 730 127 000

04 KALEI RAS BEIRUT

Rue Mansour Jurdak, Beirut, Lebanon

TO VISIT
BEFORE YOU DIE
BECAUSE

Everybody is welcome at this peaceful café, a true community hub opened by the country's first speciality roastery.

Originally founded in 2015 as an online shop, Lebanese roastery Kalei now has two beautiful cafés in the capital. Housed in an atmospheric Ottoman-era townhouse, its Ras Beirut roastery is arranged around a central bar and features a peaceful garden with plenty of outdoor seating and visiting stray cats. 'When we opened, we were the first speciality coffee roastery in Lebanon,' explains co-founder Dalia Jaffal, whose time working in East Africa inspired her to open the roastery. 'We source our own green beans, a lot of which we get via direct trade, then roast on two different roasters for use in the two cafés, or to sell as retail and wholesale coffees.' Popular drinks include the batch brew, cappuccino, and the bright and refreshing espresso lemonade – 'an all-time favourite'. Meanwhile the menu includes great breakfast and brunch items, including a freekeh salad and a chicken sandwich with homemade kimchi. It's also worth visiting Kalei's Mark Mikhael outpost, a beautifully restored 1950s house with a stunning garden, where you can sip your coffee among the tree trunks.

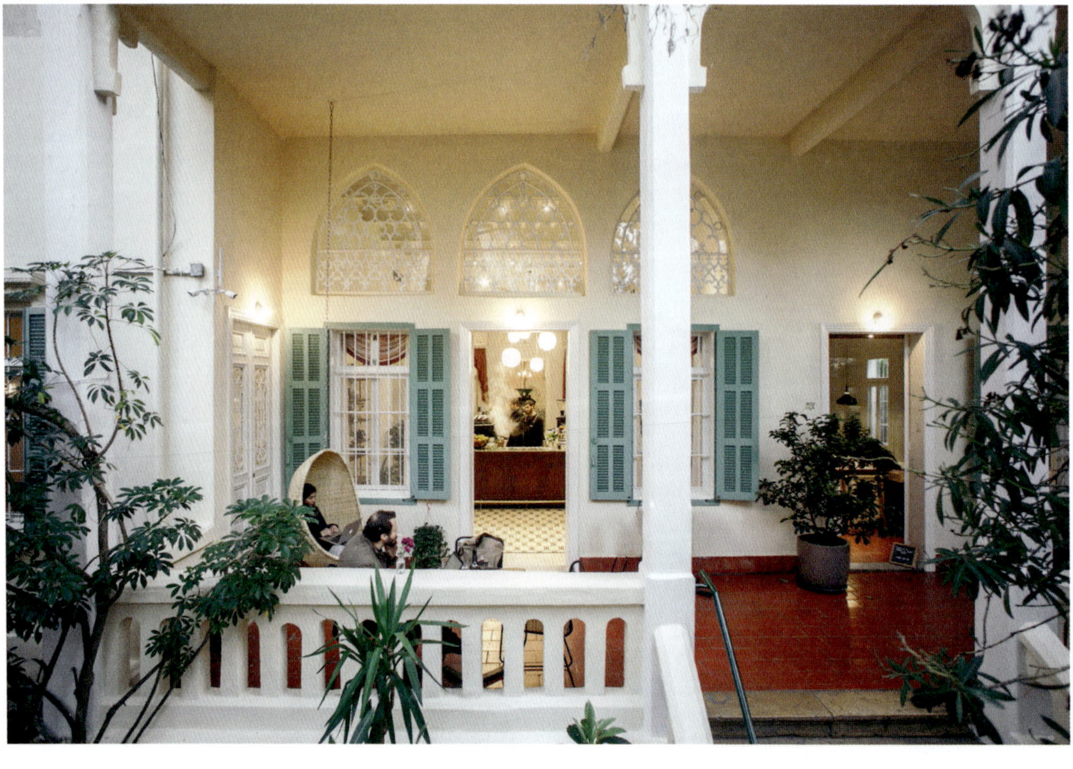

kaleicoffee.com @kaleicoffee.co +961 1 752 001

05 30 NORTH COFFEE

Grand Egyptian Museum, Kafr Nassar, Al Haram, Giza Governorate 3513204, Egypt

TO VISIT BEFORE YOU DIE BECAUSE

At this 30 NORTH outpost you can try the largest selection of speciality coffee in Egypt, in the country's most magnificent museum.

A truly pharaonic project that has been years in the making, the Grand Egyptian Museum in Cairo was certainly worth the wait. Not only does it offer views over the Pyramids of Giza and countless ancient treasures inside, but it also boasts a branch of the country's leading speciality coffee purveyors, 30 NORTH (nickname: 'the gem at the GEM'). Founded by Amr El-Khazindar and Noha Khattab in 2017, 30 NORTH offers carefully selected coffees – or *ahwah*, as Egyptians say – from around the world as well as six different brewing methods. It's an ideal spot to take a break away from the crowds between visits to the museum's galleries. Sit by the window to admire the monumental statues of Ramses, Hatshepsut and others towering in the museum's entrance hall and grand staircase, and enjoy a cup of cappuccino with latte art flourish – if you're in luck you might get a foam seahorse. Then head into town to continue your Cairo coffee experience with a stop at one of the many lovely coffee shops in Zamalek or Maadi, or the historic El Fishawy café in the Khan el-Khalili market.

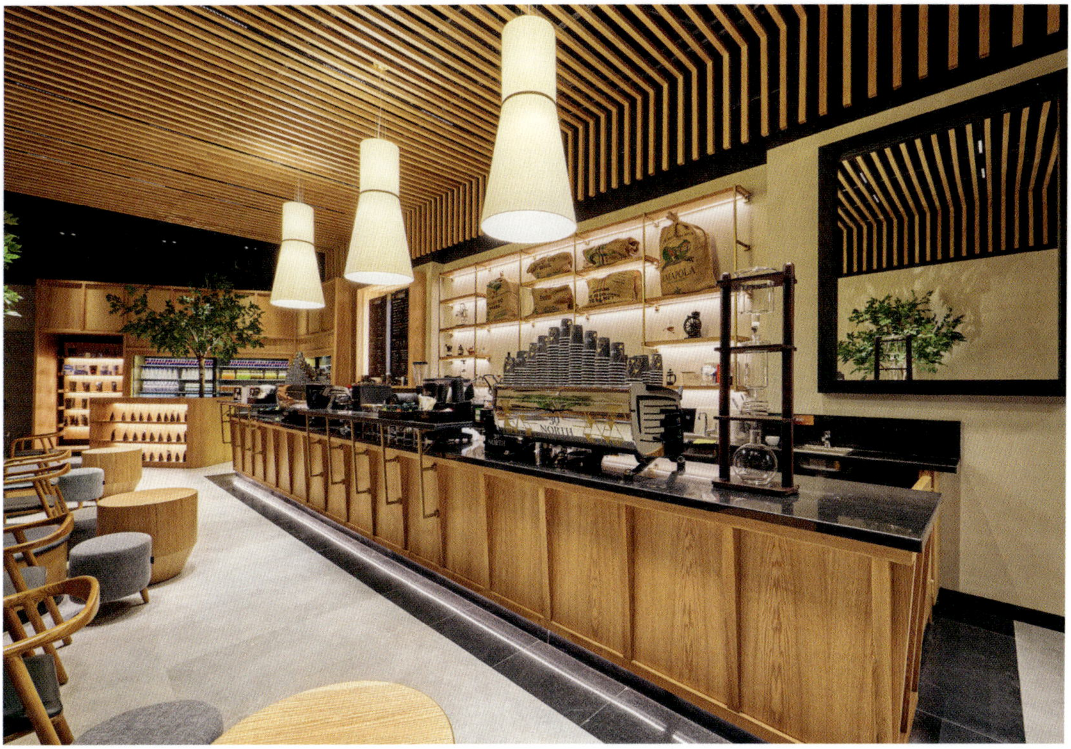

@30northcoffee

06 ROSETTA ROASTERY

97 Bree St, C/o Bree St and Shortmarket St,
Cape Town 8001, South Africa

TO VISIT
BEFORE YOU DIE
BECAUSE

This highly praised café takes you on a journey of discovery through the world's best coffee lots.

Both a multi-award-winning roastery and a friendly corner café in the heart of Cape Town's culinary district, Rosetta on Bree Street is a bright and airy space co-founded in 2010 by Jono Le Feuvre. 'Coffee is an organic product. It doesn't stay static, it's a living thing,' he says. Which is why Rosetta's filter brew bar highlights seasonal single origins and a rotating choice of two single-origin espresso coffees. 'At the core of what we do is a hands-on approach: we source and carefully roast all our own coffees, ensuring that each origin's character is expressed with clarity and integrity,' says roastery manager Shannen Mackay. Try some of the world's best speciality-grade coffees, from Colombia to Indonesia; stop for a Taisho- or Kyoto-style iced coffee on a hot day; or come early to grab a seat and catch up with your friends over an espresso, freshly baked pastries or a slice of banana bread.

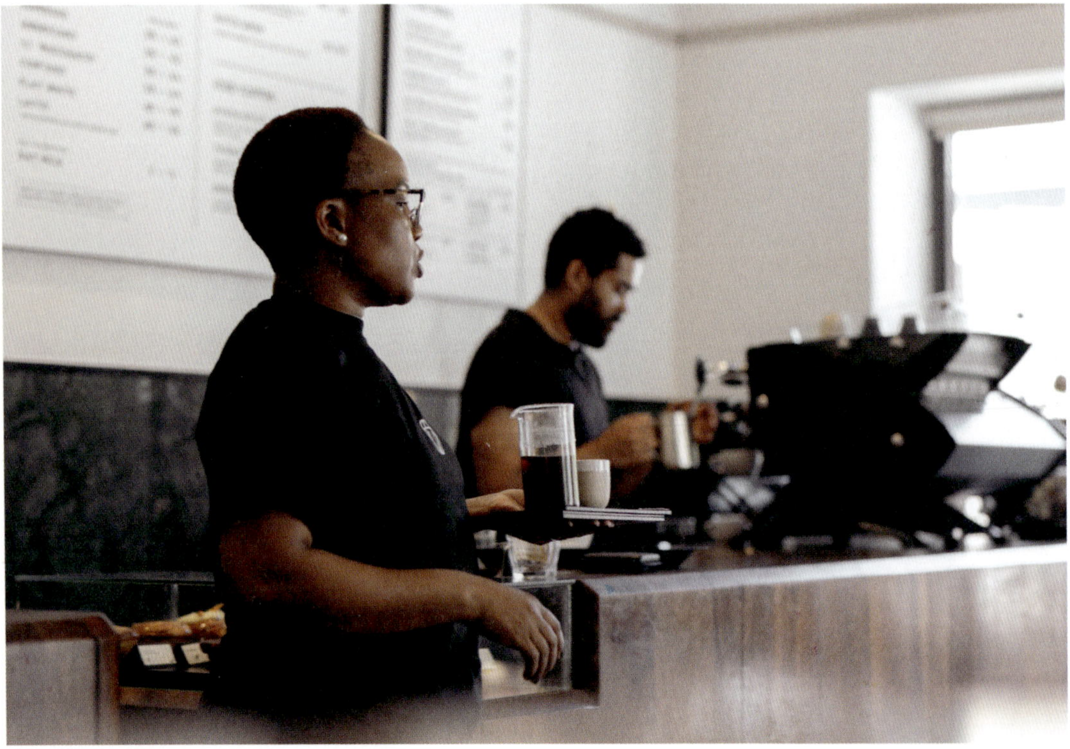

rosettaroastery.com

+27 21 447 4099

07 TRUTH COFFEE

36 Buitenkant St, Cape Town 8000, South Africa

TO VISIT BEFORE YOU DIE BECAUSE

Put your goggles on and suspend your disbelief at this steampunk-themed café housed in a three-storey historic warehouse.

A huge metal machine with clunky pipes, wheels and burners; steam and hisses coming out of strange valves; the deafening noise of a spinning drum... It's obvious that classic coffee roasters and espresso machines were tailor-made for the steampunk universe. At Truth Coffee, the 'colossus', a vintage coffee roaster, takes centre stage in a retro-futuristic sci-fi interior by Haldane Martin, with wraparound Victorian-style steel shelving, a leather-top bar and cog-shaped stools. Sit at the communal table to enjoy a cup of the house's Resurrection or Deep, Dark & Twister espresso blends, and let your imagination take you to a world of steam-powered flying machines. 'At Truth Coffee, it's not just about sourcing unique and delicious coffees and roasting them for exquisite flavour in the roaster that we have built our café around,' says founder David Donde. 'It is about delighting our guests, creating moments within the steampunk aesthetic. It is also about creating joy – all this in a space that gives a breather and pause to your every day.'

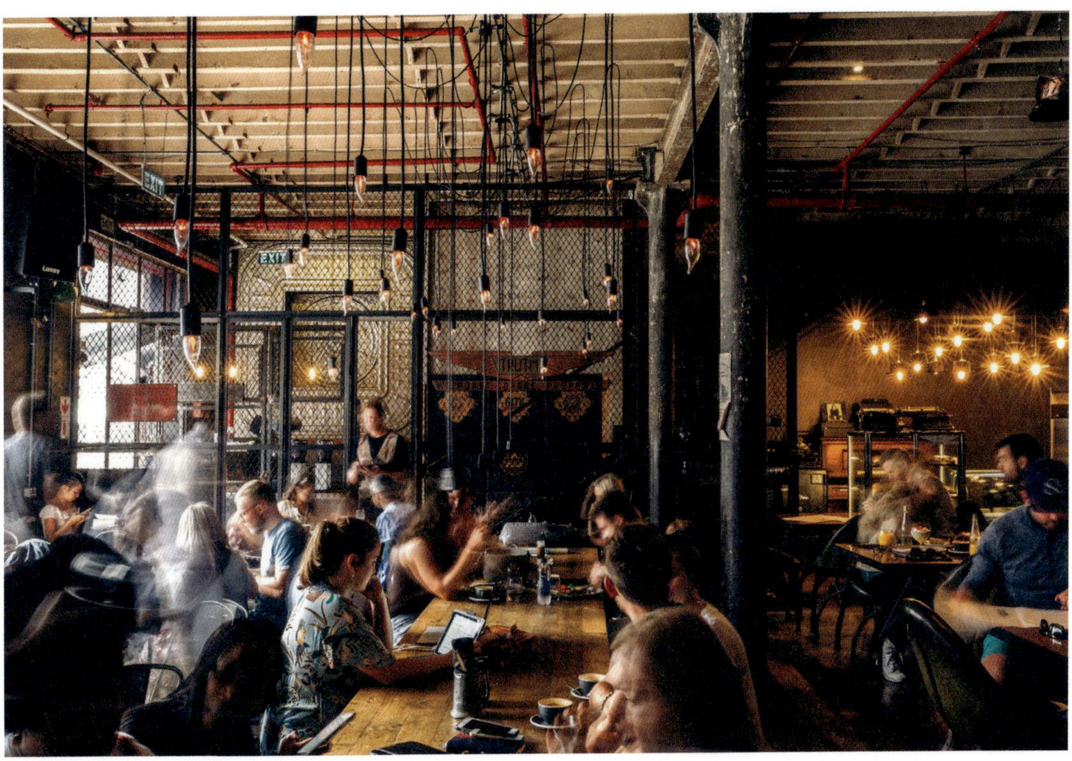

truth.coffee

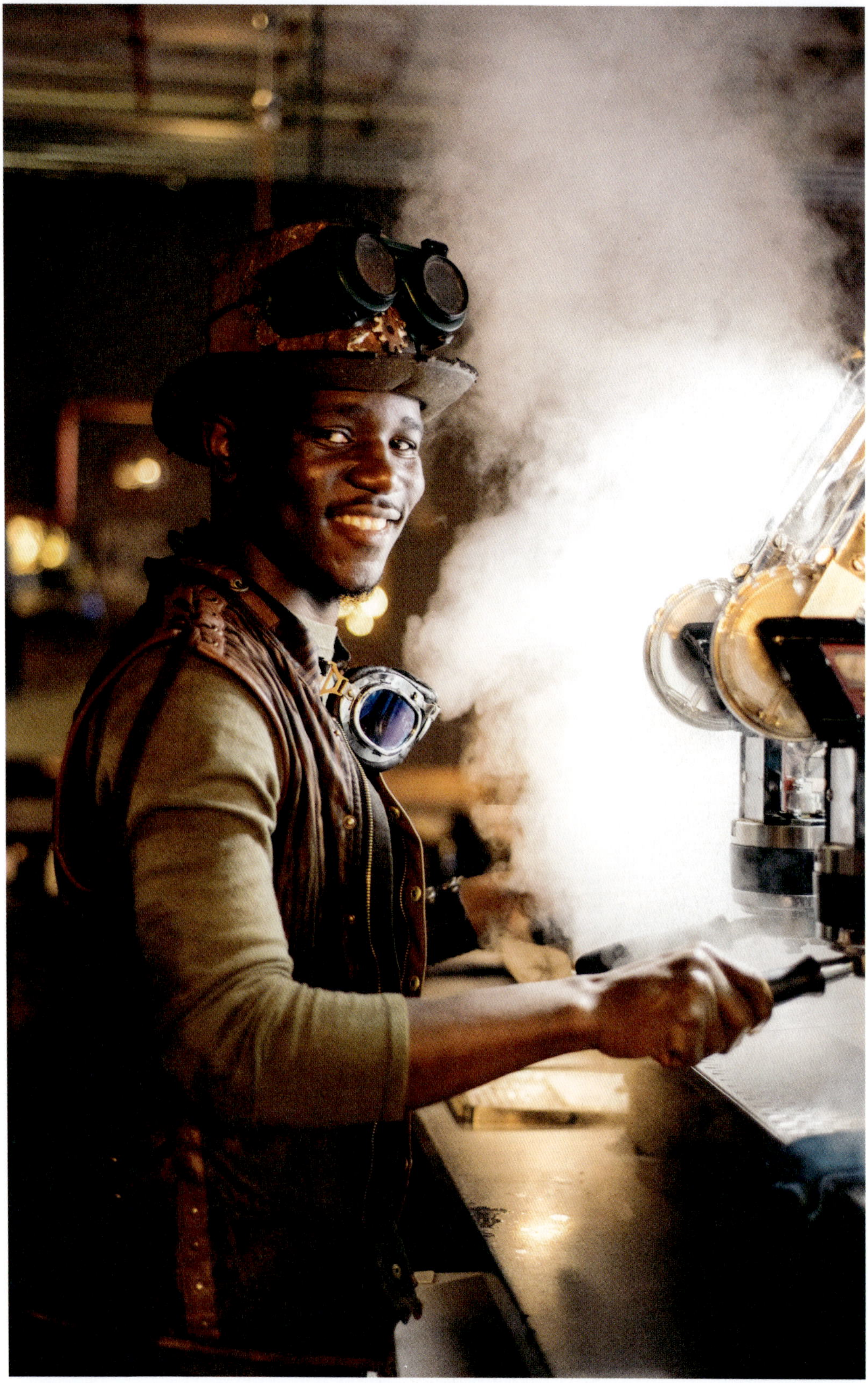

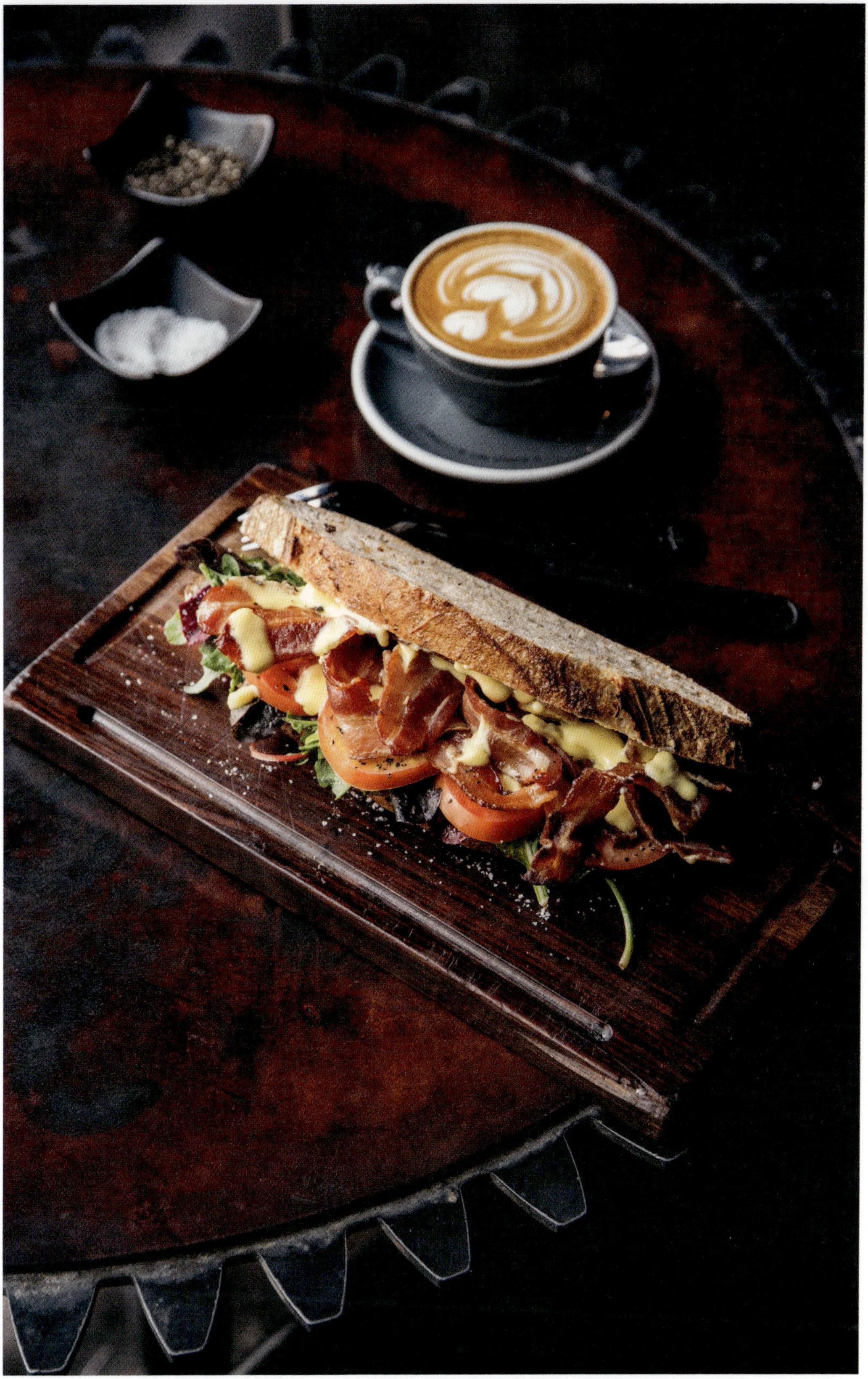

08 ARABIAN TEA HOUSE

Opposite Musalla Post Office, Al Fahidi St, Bur Dubai, Al Fahidi, Dubai, United Arab Emirates

TO VISIT BEFORE YOU DIE BECAUSE

This urban oasis in the centre of Dubai's old town offers a blend of history and culture as well as excellent coffee and local sweets.

Built in the 1890s by Persian merchants, the historic centre of Dubai encompasses the narrow alleyways around the old souk and Al Fahidi fort. A highlight of the area is this café opened in 1997 by Ali Al Rais to celebrate the local culture and food, and showcase 'what Emiratis eat at home'. Formerly known as the Basta Art Café, this Dubai favourite is located in an old mud and coral townhouse dating from the 1920s, with a shady courtyard and traditional wind towers. It's the ideal spot to enjoy a cup of Arabic coffee and an Emirati breakfast. The first, known as *gahwa*, is prepared with saffron and cardamom using coffee from Julius Meinl (a Viennese coffee roaster since 1862), while the second is a tray of sweet vermicelli, cheeses, beans, jams, chickpeas and black beans served with an assortment of bread. There's also a traditional seating area with majlis cushions and canopy where you can enjoy more coffee and plates of *lequaimat*, crispy golden Emirati dumplings drizzled with date syrup and sesame seeds.

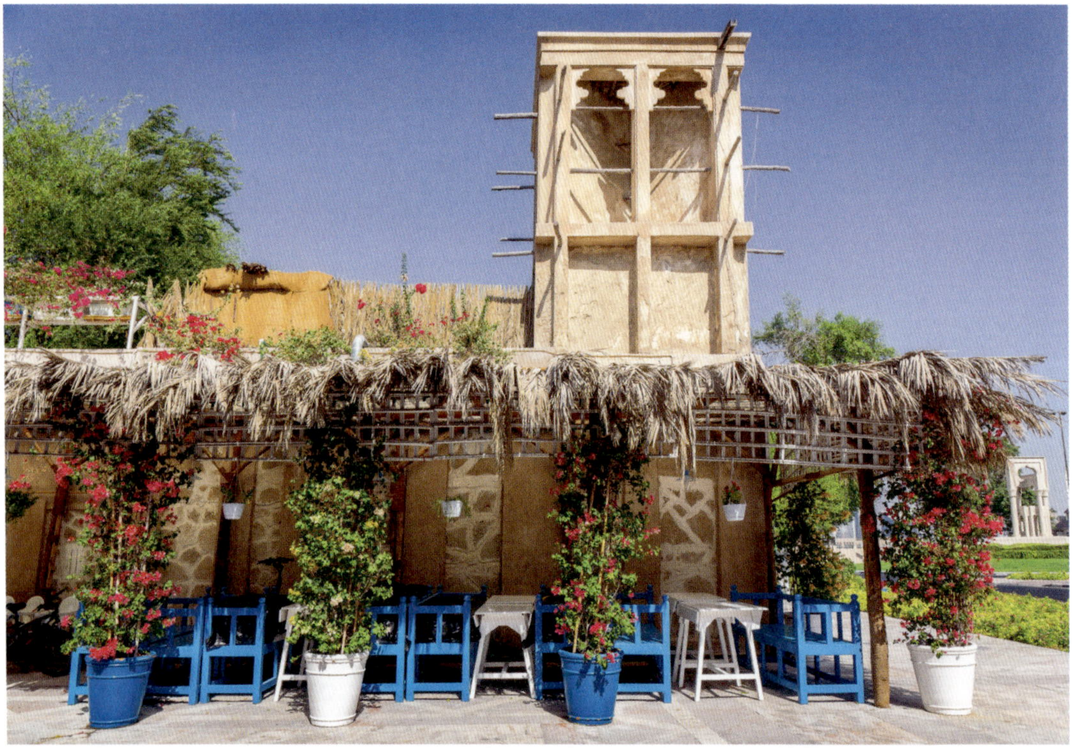

arabianteahouse.com

+971 4 353 5071

09 HISTORIC NIGHTS CAFÉ

Al Kabli Ln, Al-Balad, Jeddah 22236, Saudi Arabia

TO VISIT
BEFORE YOU DIE
BECAUSE

With its unique setting overlooking the old town of Jeddah, it's the most scenic place to sample the local Arabic coffee and hospitality.

Al-Balad, the historic centre of Jeddah, is famed for its traditional Hijazi townhouses, their typical wooden windows and balconies overlooking a maze of alleyways. The century-old layout of this UNESCO World Heritage Site means that it's actually quite difficult to find this establishment, also known as Layali Tarikhiya Café. Wander just south of the old city gate, an area home to a handful of quaint coffee shops and museum-houses open to visitors, and look out for a stone corner with wooden tables; an old cannon marks the café's entrance. Then head straight upstairs to the multilevel rooftop terrace for breathtaking views of the old city. Furnished with antiques, majlis sofas, old pots and local artefacts, it's the perfect spot to try a traditional Arabic coffee – spiced with cardamom, served in a traditional metal *dallah* pot, and accompanied by a bowl of sweet dates. Come for the sunset and enjoy your cup of coffee to the sound of the Maghrib prayer echoing from a neighbouring mosque. It's not open at lunchtime (too hot!) and is cash only.

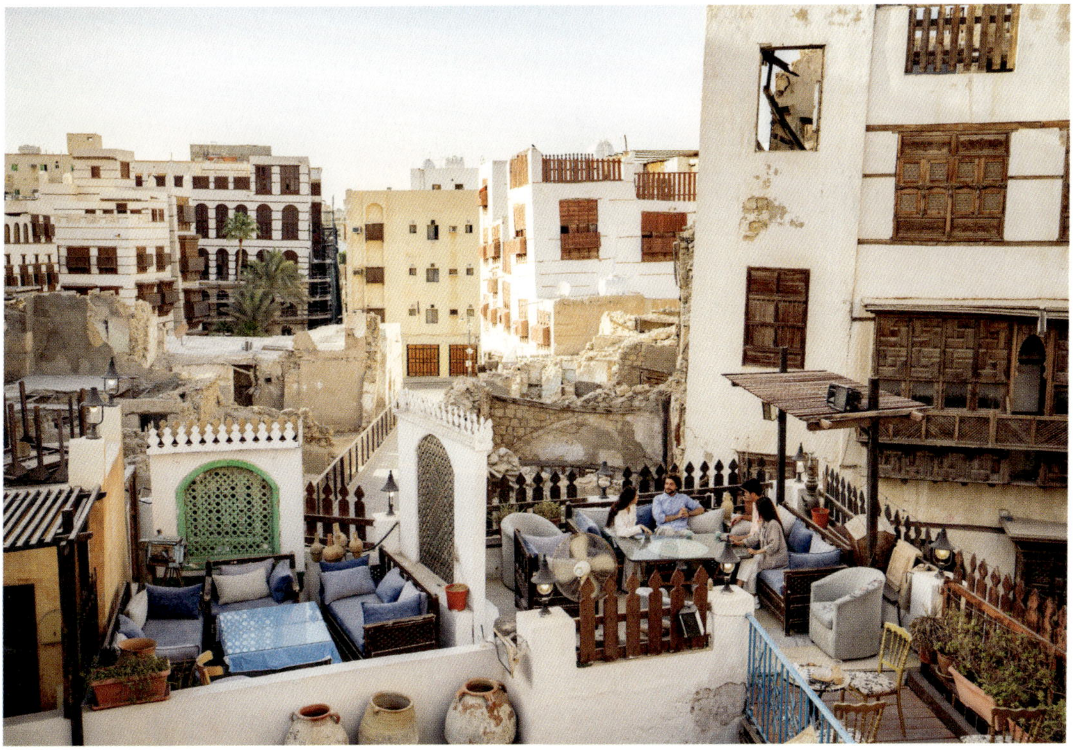

@layali_tarikhia

10 MEDD COFFEE AL FAYHA

Ivory Square, 7579 Abdullah Sulayman St, Al Fayha'a, Jeddah 22246, Saudi Arabia

TO VISIT BEFORE YOU DIE BECAUSE

World-class coffees and local flavours meet at this small roastery, the latest chapter in the country's long coffee history.

Coffee in Saudi Arabia is a source of national pride; the country's Khawlani coffee cultivation practices are recognised by UNESCO as an Intangible Cultural Heritage. It is also an ancestral symbol of hospitality and generosity, and the first thing you offer your guests to make them feel welcome. This long tradition continues at Medd Café & Roastery, founded in 2015 as Jeddah's first speciality coffee shop. Here customers are treated like old friends, and praise not only the friendly service but the Saudi-accented décor, the chilled atmosphere and of course the excellent coffee. Drinks include iced espressos, V60 pour-overs from Colombia to Java, as well as latte drinks infused with local spices, lavender or halva. To accompany this, try a thyme-flavoured croissant or a slice of Areeka cake (a unique creation involving dates, oats and a walnut crumble). And make sure to admire the rotating displays on the walls, created by a roster of local artists.

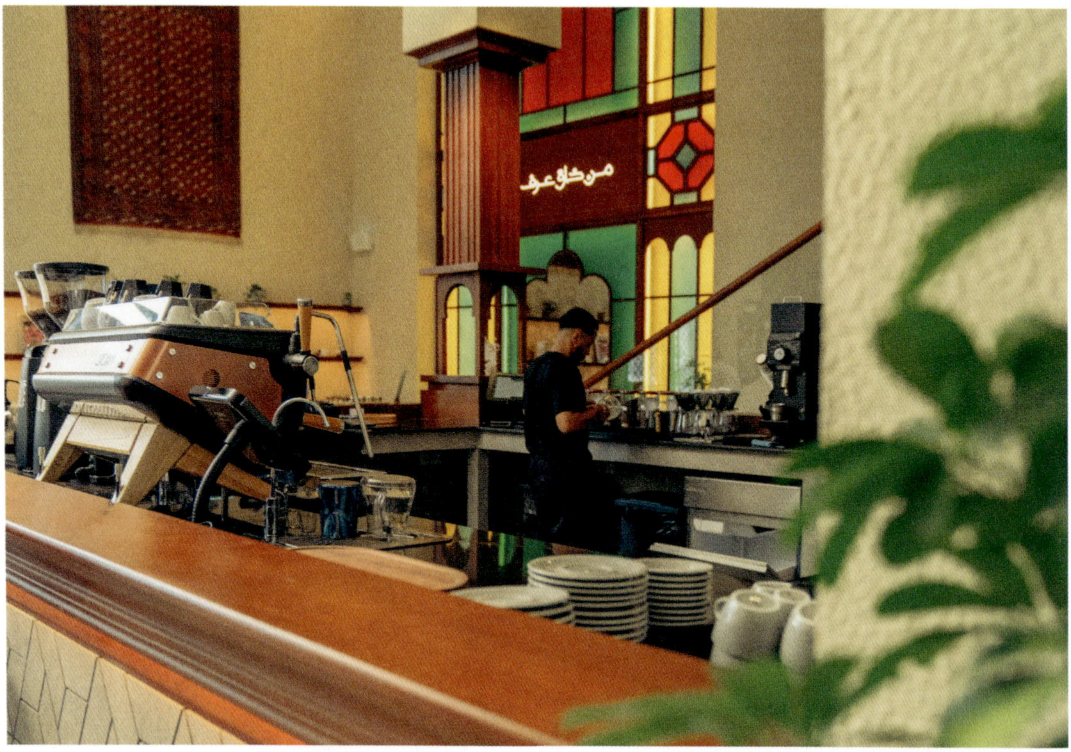

meddcoffee.com

+966 533 328 701

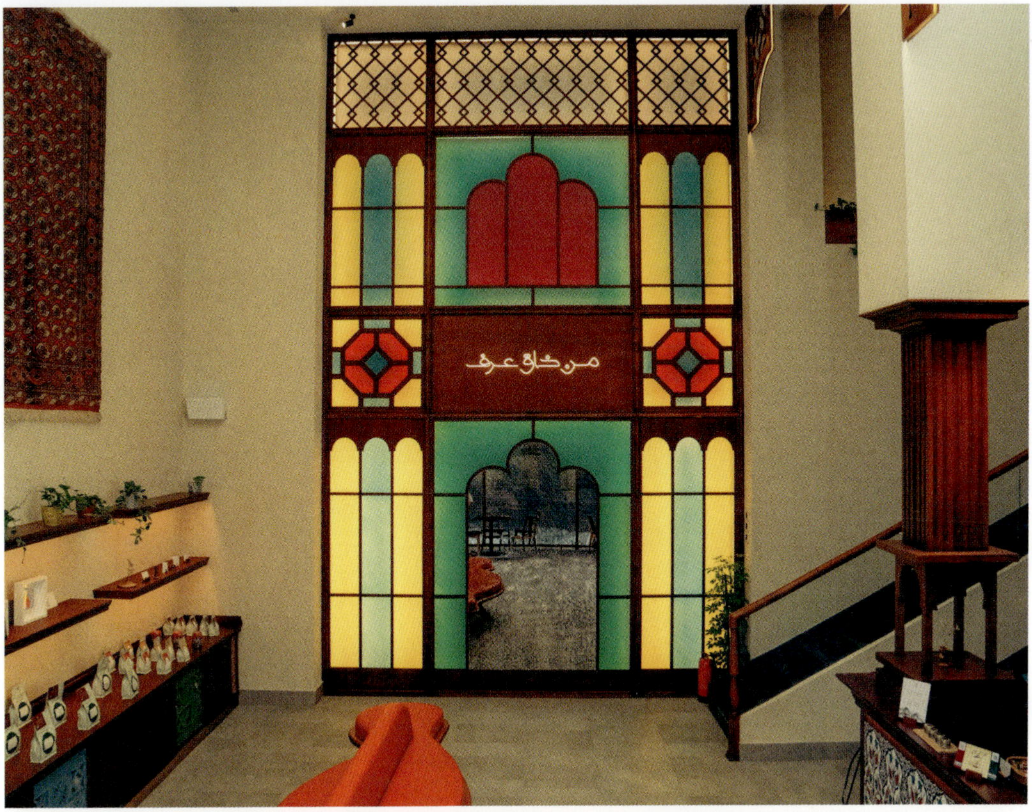
من ذاق عرف

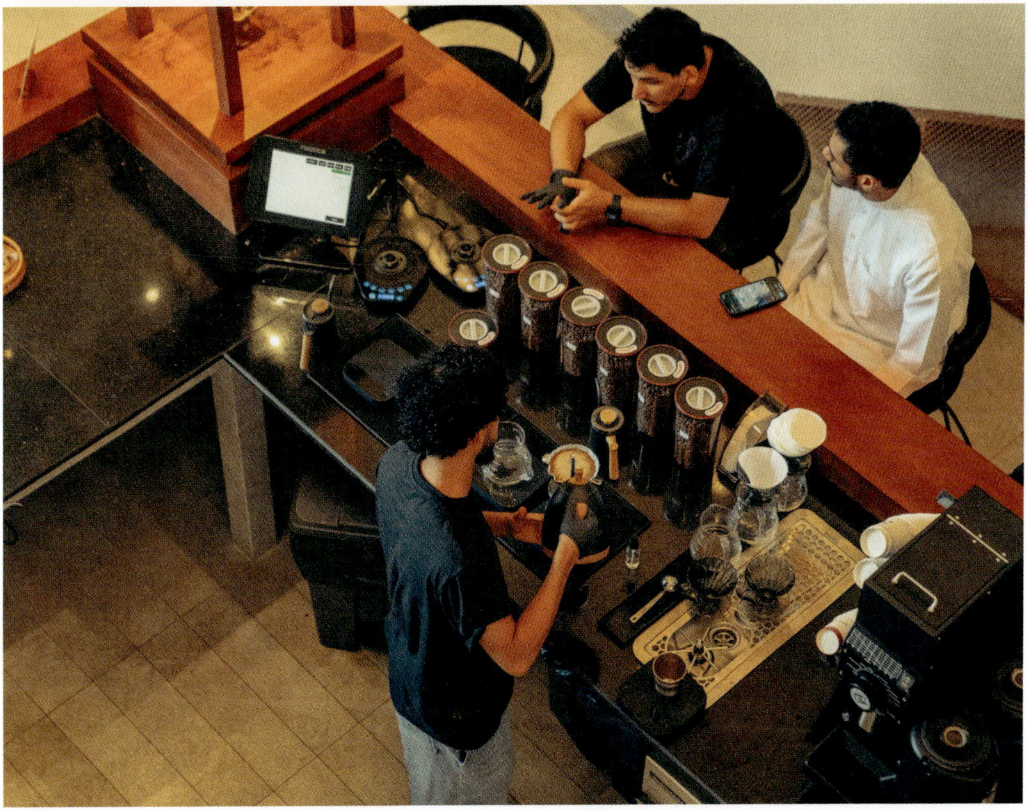

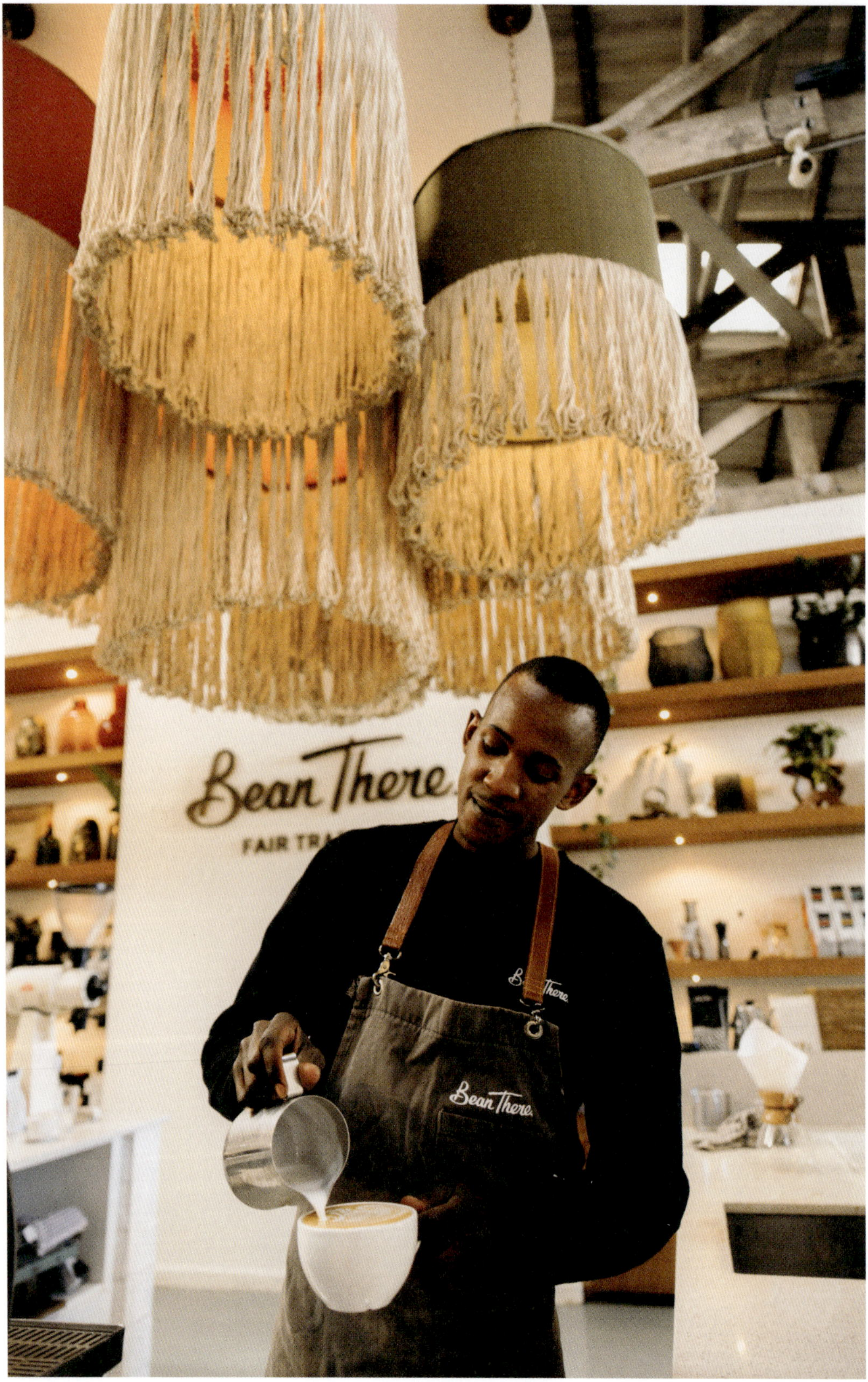
Bean There
Bean There
Bean There

11 BEAN THERE

44 Stanley Ave, Milpark, Johannesburg 2092, South Africa

TO VISIT BEFORE YOU DIE BECAUSE

Visit South Africa's first roaster of certified Fairtrade, organic African coffee for a guilt-free taste of the continent's best beans.

Bean There founder Jonathan Robinson recently celebrated climbing Kilimanjaro by enjoying a cup of his Tanzania Tarakea blend at the top, straight from the beans farmed on the slopes of the highest peak in Africa. That tells you a little something about the spirit of adventure and passion for African coffee that is at the heart of his company. At its cosy café in Milpark, you can taste the best arabica from Africa with a clear conscience: every bean here is directly and fairly traded. 'For too long coffee producers have been exploited and treated unfairly,' they say. 'Fair trade is not an obligation but an opportunity to actively support development, growth and social empowerment.' Which means regular trips to build close relationships with farmers from Rwanda to Uganda in search of the perfect coffee. A particular highlight is Olga's Reserve, which consists of micro-lots from all the coffee producing countries Bean There sources from. Named after Jonathan's coffee-loving grandmother, the highly perfumed exceptional micro-lot coffee is best enjoyed slowly... and with a piece of chocolate.

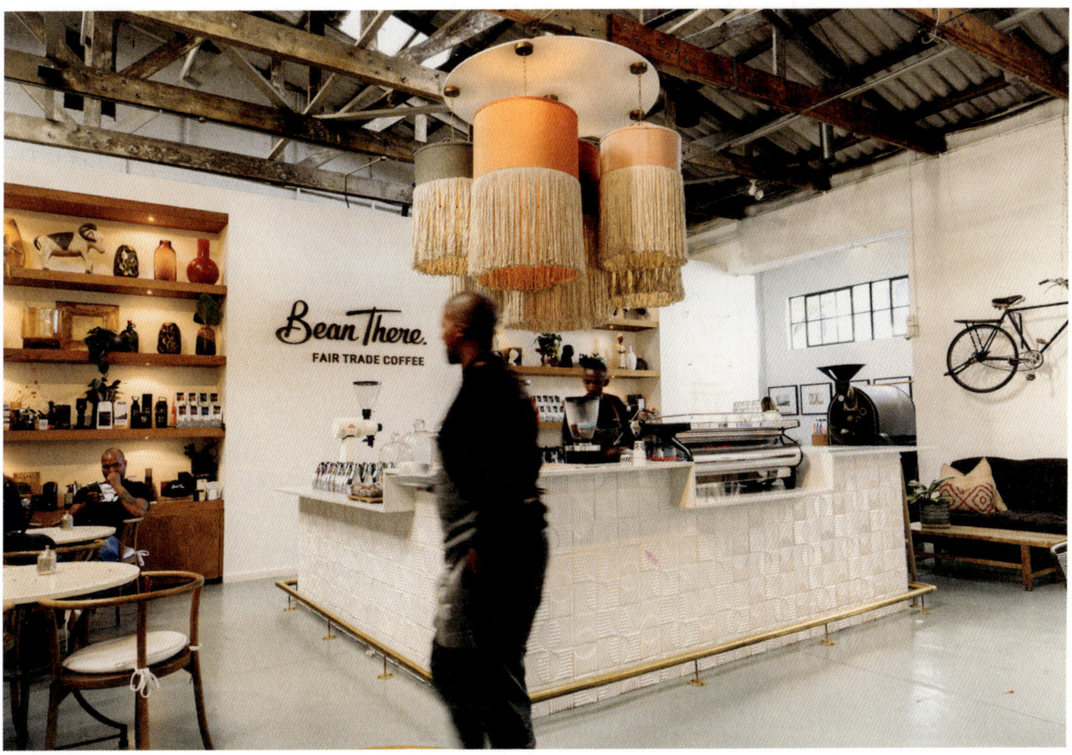

beanthere.co.za

+27 87 310 3100

12 FATHER COFFEE

19 Dartfield Rd, Kramerville, South Africa

TO VISIT BEFORE YOU DIE BECAUSE

These party-loving Joburg speciality coffee roasters focus on top coffee served with freshly baked pastries and plenty of good vibes.

Opened in 2013 by four friends who just wanted 'really good coffee in Jo'burg', Father is a speciality coffee roaster that 'sources, roasts and serves around sixty different coffees every year – each are unique exemplars of provenance, varietal and processing.' Its HQ is this Kramerville roastery, decked out like their other locations with herringbone wood panelling. Built inside an old foundry, this vast multi-use space also hosts Father's bakery, wine cellar, training rooms and tasting lab, where they host regular public cupping sessions that offer the chance to taste their full range of coffees in the same way coffee pros do – slurped straight from a spoon. On the menu are espresso-based drinks made using Father's Heirloom Blend; tasting flights featuring the micro-lot of the day served three ways (espresso, milk and filter); and special releases from outstanding producers such as Diego Bermudez. Plus, there's the obligatory delicious pastries, doughnuts and breakfast buns. The place is also a wine bar and hosts braaidays involving DJs and a BBQ made from a repurposed La Marzocco coffee machine.

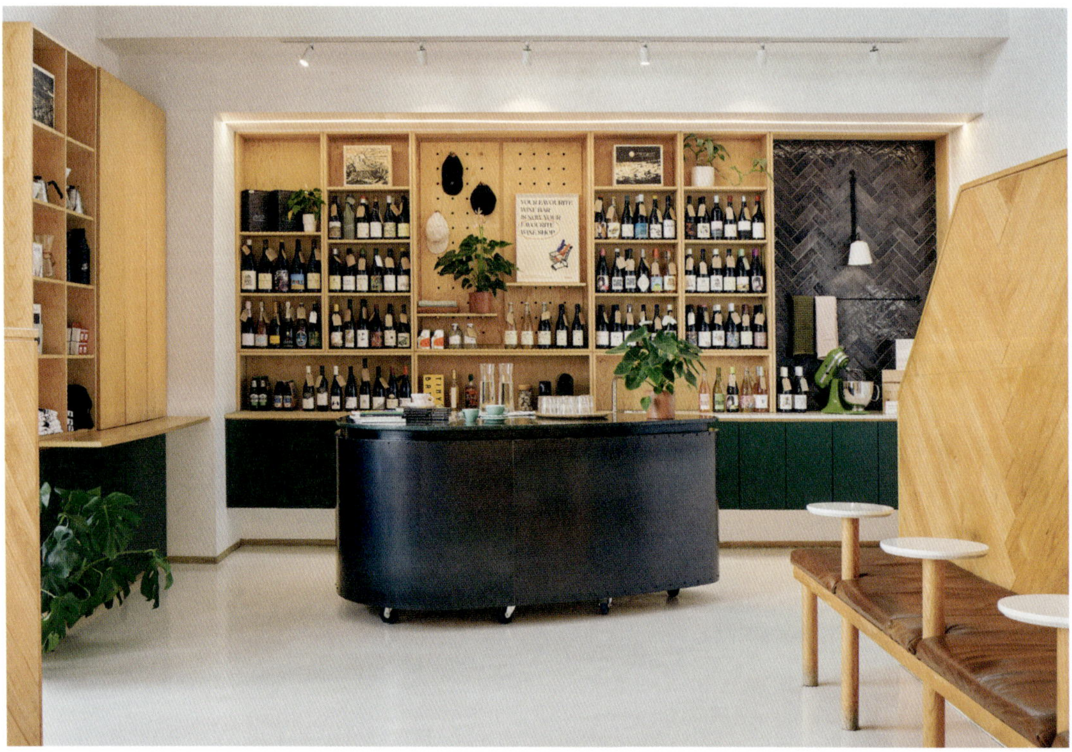

father.coffee

+27 83 228 1908

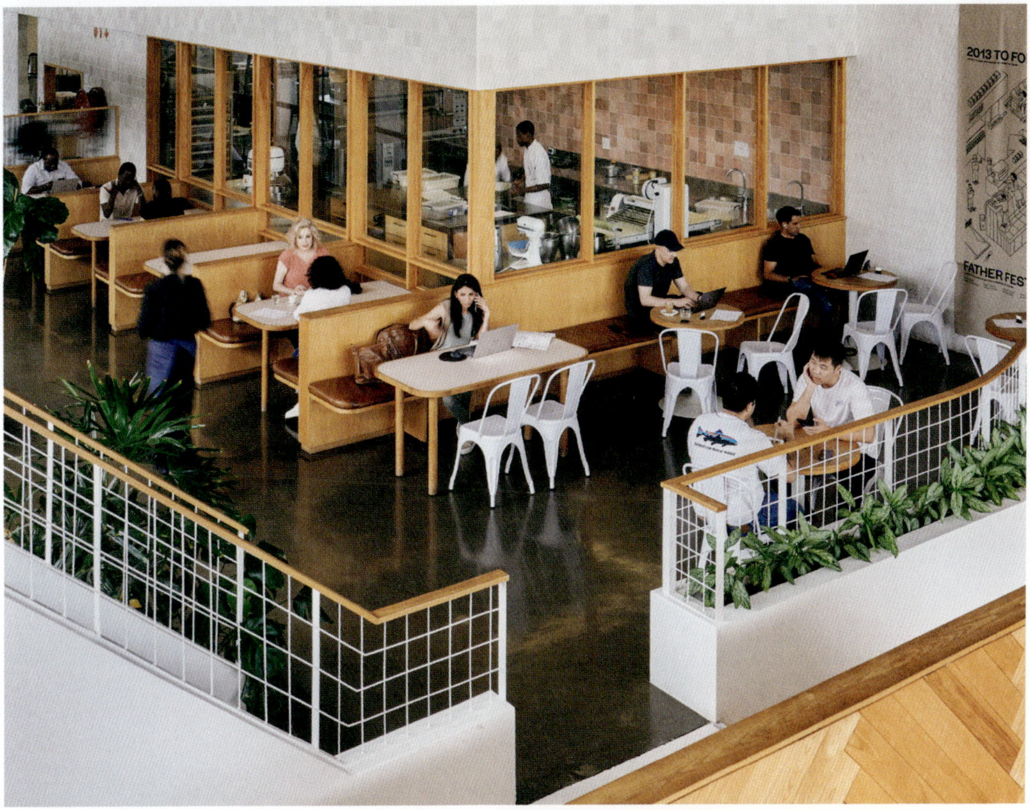

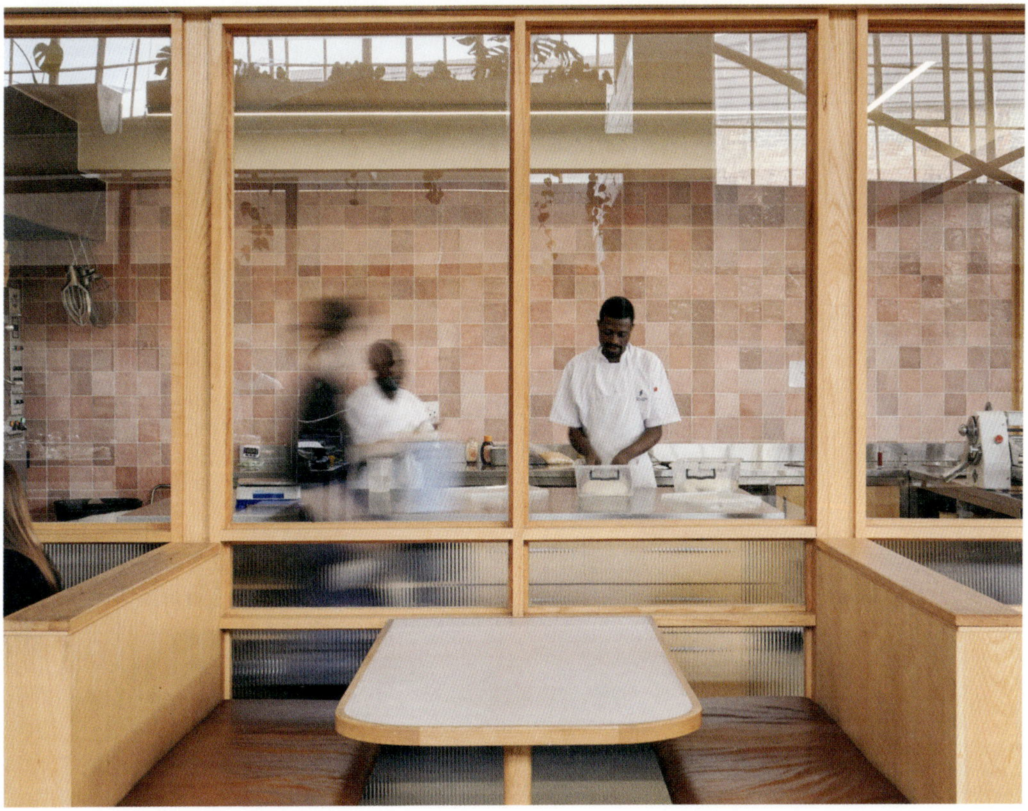

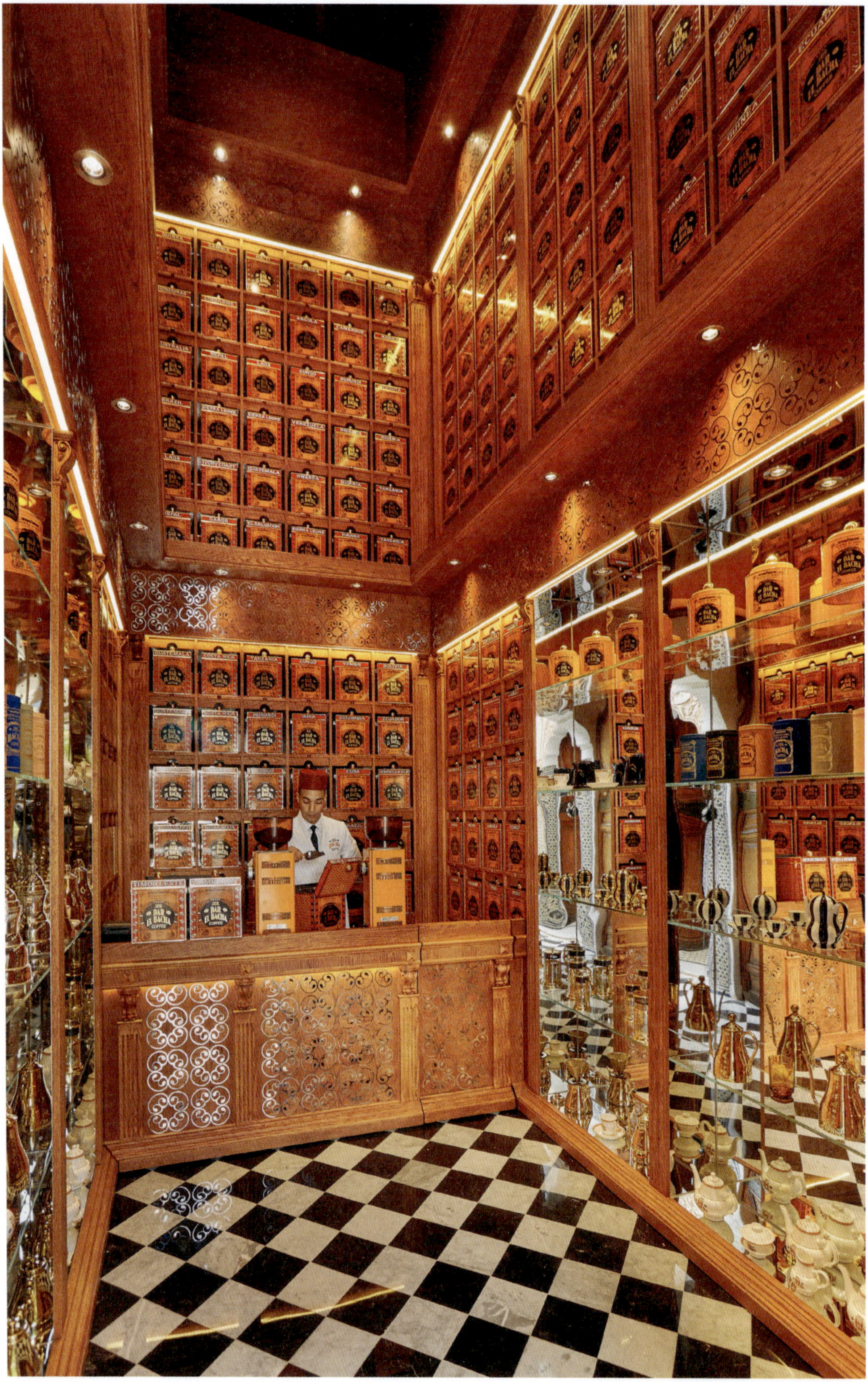
DAR
EL BACHA
COFFEE

13 BACHA COFFEE

Dar el Bacha, Rte Sidi Abdelaziz, Marrakech 40000, Morocco

TO VISIT
BEFORE YOU DIE
BECAUSE

Housed in a spectacular Moroccan palace next to the medina, this historic café offers a menu of over 200 different arabica coffees.

The former residence of the powerful Pasha of Marrakech, the Dar el Bacha museum is a wonderful example of Moroccan architecture, complete with bubbling fountains, ornate traditional salons and an orange tree-filled courtyard. In one of the riad's carefully restored patios you'll find Bacha Coffee, a historic coffee house opened in 1910 and visited by guests including Winston Churchill, Josephine Baker and Charlie Chaplin. It's a magical space with chequerboard floors, tall wooden shelves filled with colourful canisters, and sharply dressed, fez-wearing waiters whizzing around carrying hot coffee pots and sweet treats. These include opera cakes soaked in coffee syrup or a millefeuille flavoured with fennel and Grand Moka Matari coffee. The coffee menu focuses on 100% arabica speciality beans from thirty-five of the most reputable coffee-producing countries, and includes blends such as Marrakech Morning Coffee, with cinnamon and green almonds, and Moroccan Sahara Coffee with notes of coconut, honeyed nuts and hot chocolate. Come early to avoid long queues.

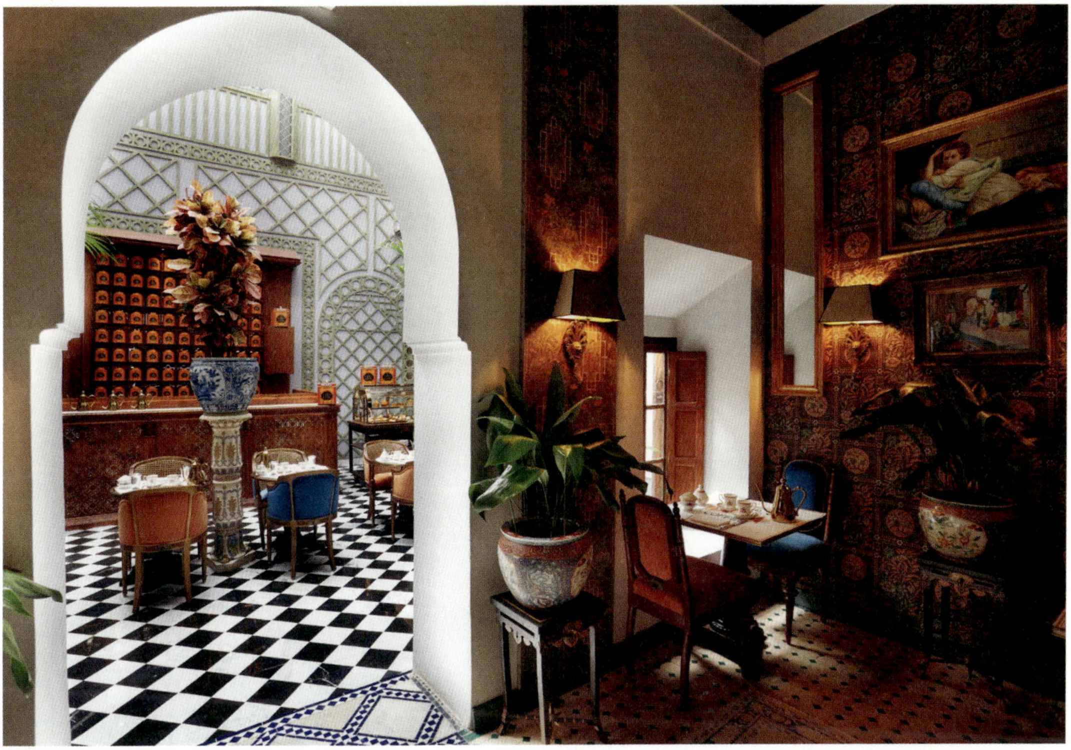

bachacoffee.com

+212 5243 81293

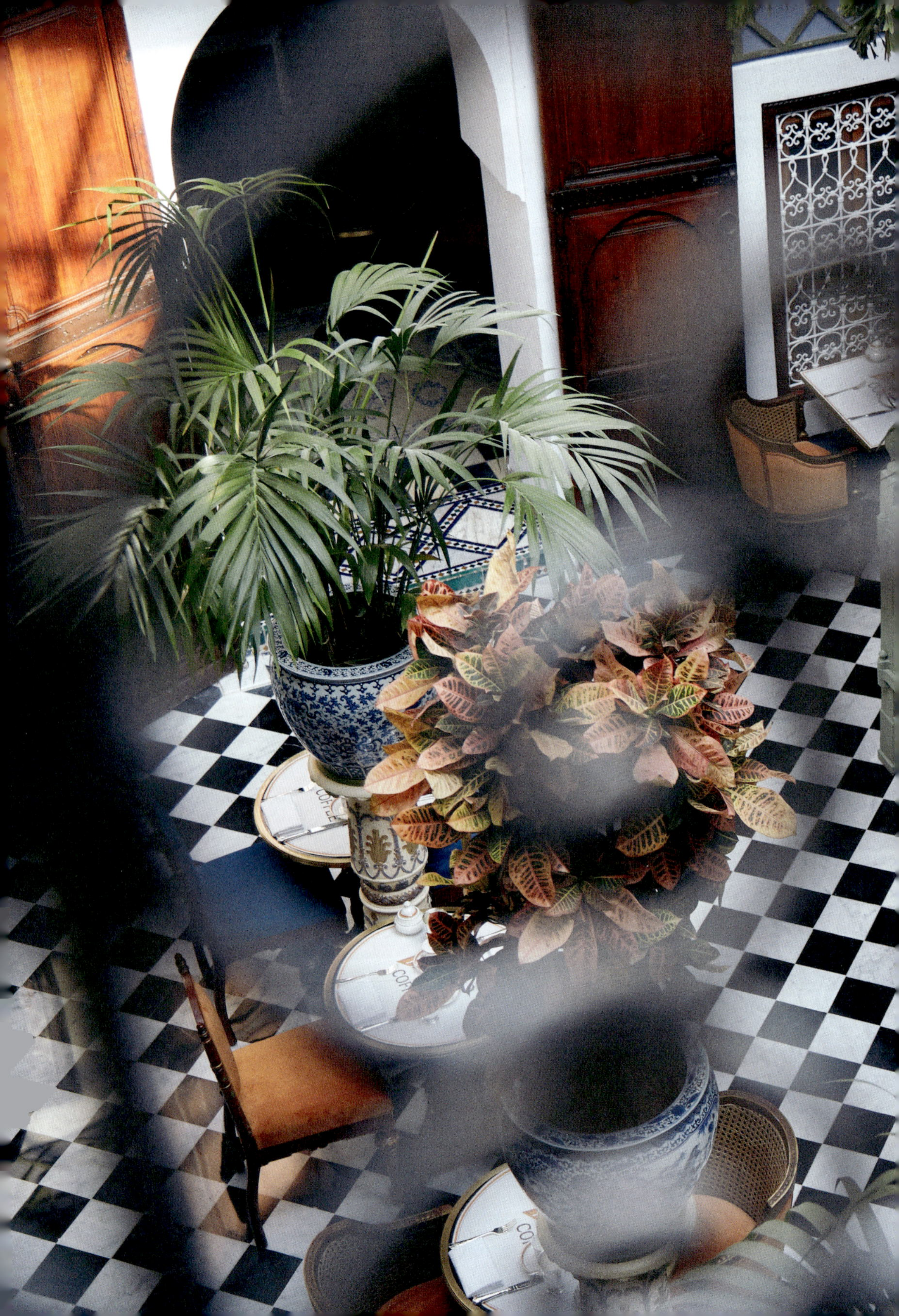

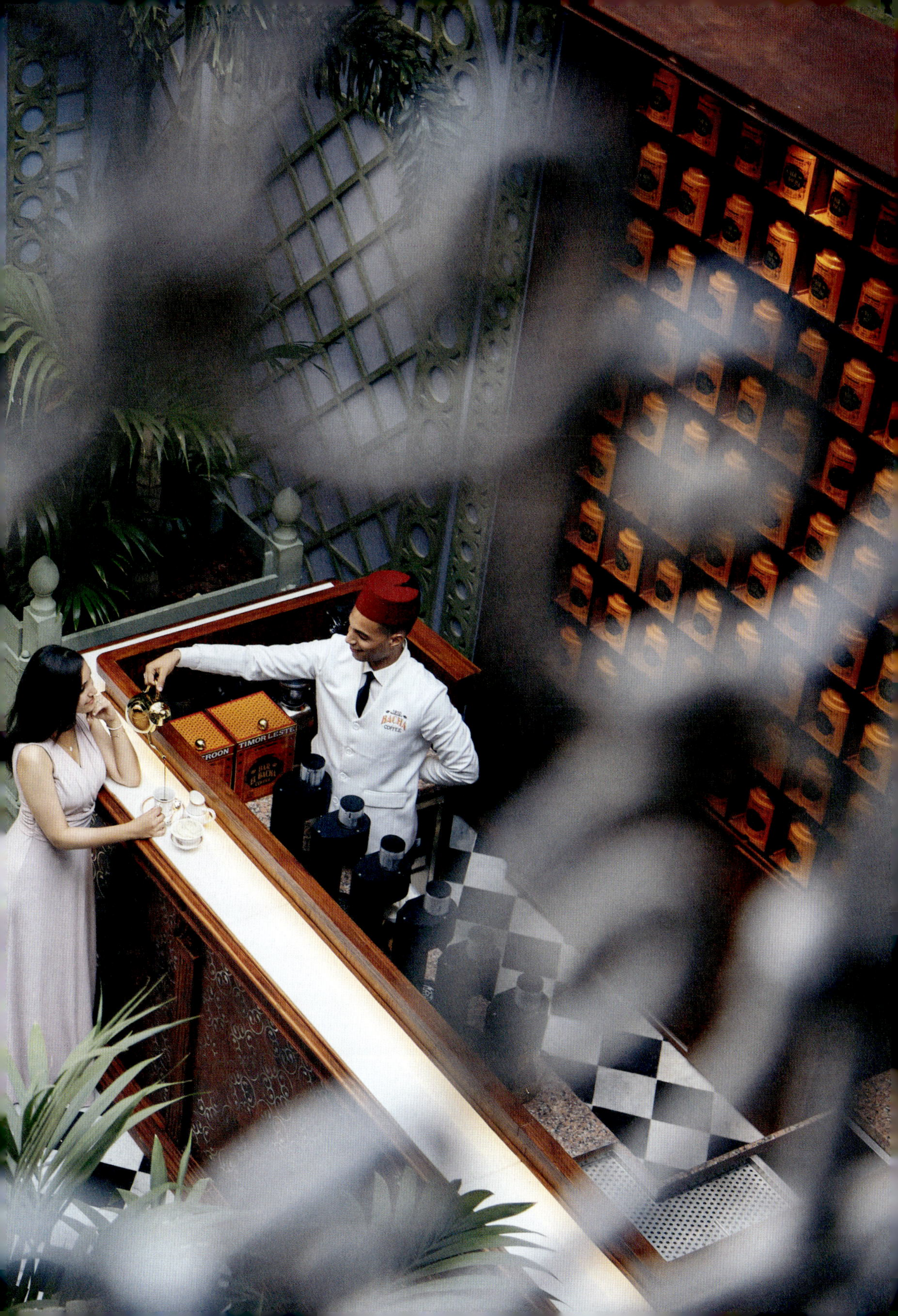

14 SPRING VALLEY COFFEE

Spring Valley Shopping Centre, Lower Kabete Road, Nairobi, Kenya

TO VISIT BEFORE YOU DIE BECAUSE

This cosy coffee shop roasts incredible green coffees in a Nairobi neighbourhood historically renowned for its coffee estates.

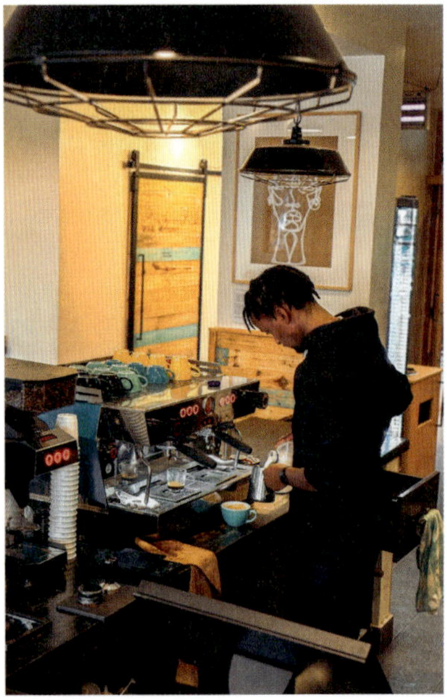

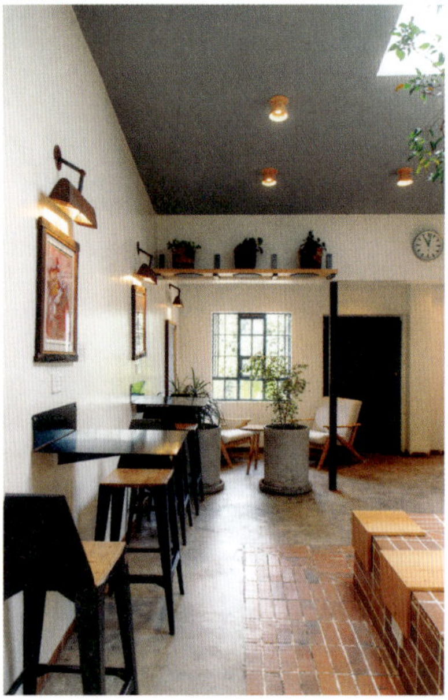

A residential area on the outskirts of Nairobi, Spring Valley was once home to some of the country's first coffee estates, established at the start of the 20th century. It is here that you will find the original location of Spring Valley Coffee, relaunched by Ritesh Doshi in 2018. When Ritesh bought the business, he inherited more than a location – he inherited a craft. Three long-standing roasters, Fred, Mohammed, and Godwin, remained with the company and continue working today from a roastery just a short walk away. The original café, recently refurbished, is a calm, light-filled space where design mirrors Kenya's coffee landscape: reclaimed timber pallets recall coffee trees; red-brick "seconds" from Kenya Clay Works echo fertile soils; and locally crafted metalwork nods to the washing equipment used in processing freshly harvested cherries. Sit under a gorgeous artwork by George Onkoba and try a coffee from the Endebess Estate on the slopes of Mount Elgon, or savour a cup of gourmet coffee, sourced from leading cooperatives in Kirinyaga, in the country's highlands. There are branches all over town, as well as one in London, UK, in the cute Camden Passage in Islington.

springvalleycoffee.com

+254 775 111 111

15 ARTISTA DE CAFÉ

5ta avenida sur no. 34B, Antigua Guatemala, Guatemala

TO VISIT BEFORE YOU DIE BECAUSE

This elegant contemporary refuge celebrates Guatemalan coffee with a fresh, honest perspective deeply respectful of its roots.

Tucked away on a quiet street in the old town of Antigua Guatemala, Artista de Café is an urban oasis filled with natural light and local crafts, where guests are encouraged to sit at one of the wooden tables or the bar to 'converse, ask questions, and explore' the richness of Guatemalan coffee culture. Founded in 2019 by María Andreé Negreros de Durán and Guillermo Durán, who wanted 'to dignify the coffee experience in a producing country, where exceptional beans are often exported and rarely enjoyed at home', the space is 'a gathering place for those who believe that coffee is a language capable of telling the story of a land, its people, and its vision for the future,' hope its owners. A variety of methods are used to brew beans from local producers including Santa Felisa, Herrarte, San Agustín and Vizcaya, while specials include an affogato and a couple of rum-based coffee creations. Beyond its daily menu, Artista de Café hosts cuppings and workshops.

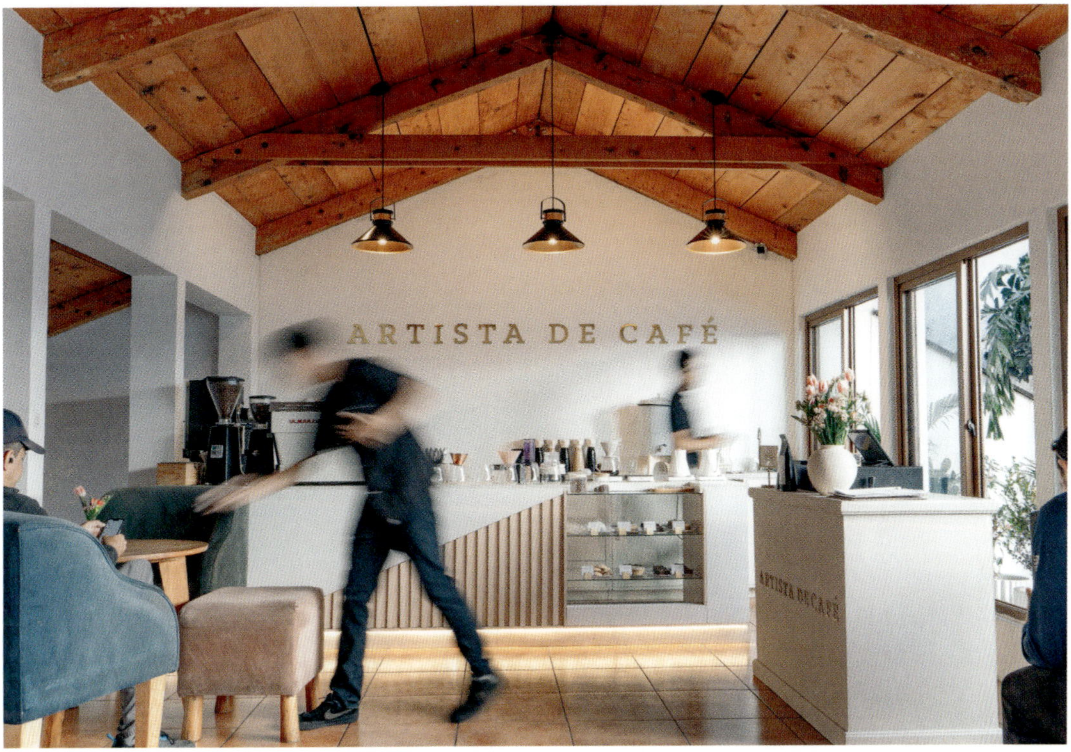

@artistadecafe +502 4795 6598

16 COLO COFFEE USAQUÉN

Cra. 6a #117-26, Usaquén, Bogotá, Cundinamarca, Colombia

TO VISIT BEFORE YOU DIE BECAUSE

Try exceptional local coffees at this colourful café opened by a local roaster committed to sustainability, quality and social impact.

Colo Coffee Roasters was founded in 2017 to serve better coffee to Colombians while helping coffee growers get their fair share. 'At our Usaquén café, guests are welcomed by a mural celebrating the fauna and flora of Colombian coffee farms, a visual tribute to the biodiversity that inspires every cup we serve,' explains Colo Coffee's Nathalia Neira. 'This location also houses our own roastery, which is powered by solar panels, a reflection of our commitment to operating sustainably.' On a mission to select, roast and serve the best Colombian coffees, the Colo team has embraced the farm-to-cup philosophy, working with producers to create three distinct coffee collections. Diversos celebrates Colombia's biodiversity and regional variety; Ancestros honours the legacy and ancestral knowledge of Colombian coffee growers; and Contemporáneos focuses on experimental lots with alternative fermentations and extended processes. Try the house's nitrogenated cold brew or choose your preferred grind and brewing method for a truly bespoke cup.

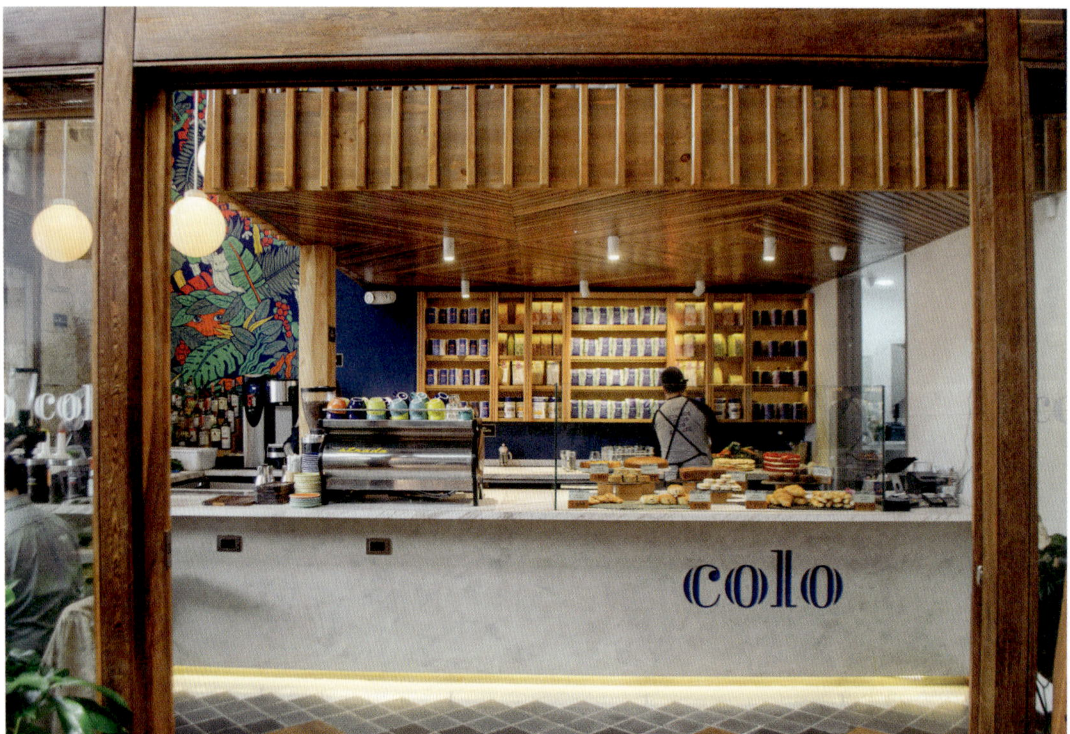

colo.com.co +57 323 231 5269

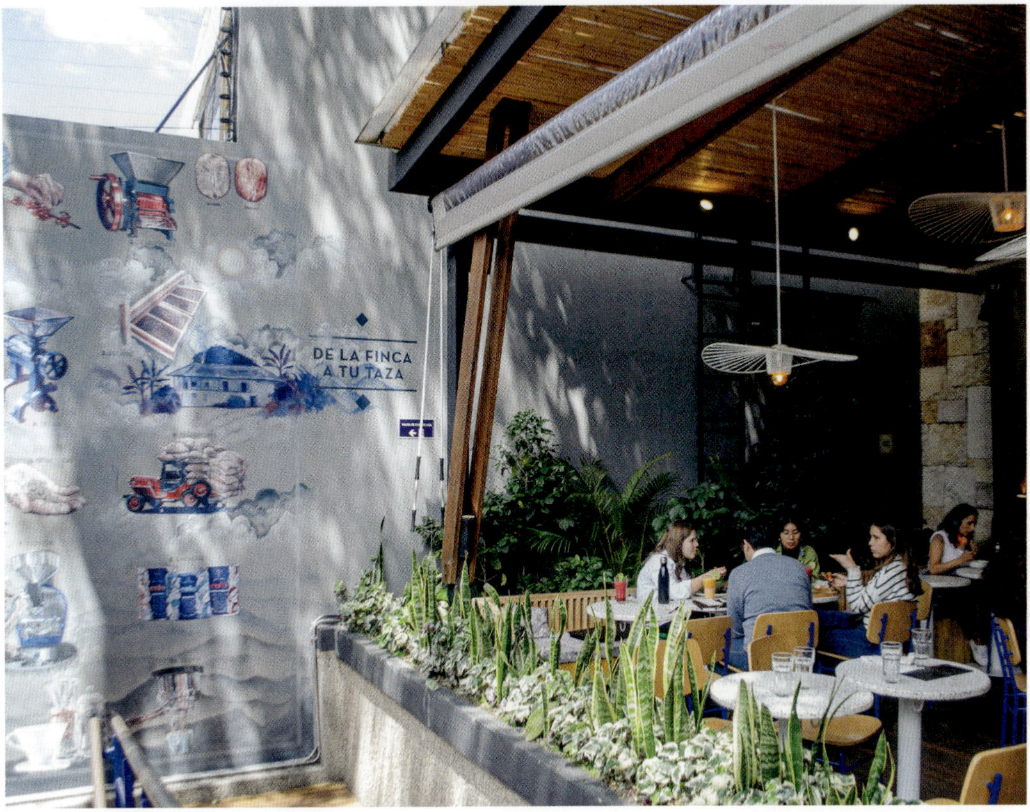
DE LA FINCA
A TU TAZA

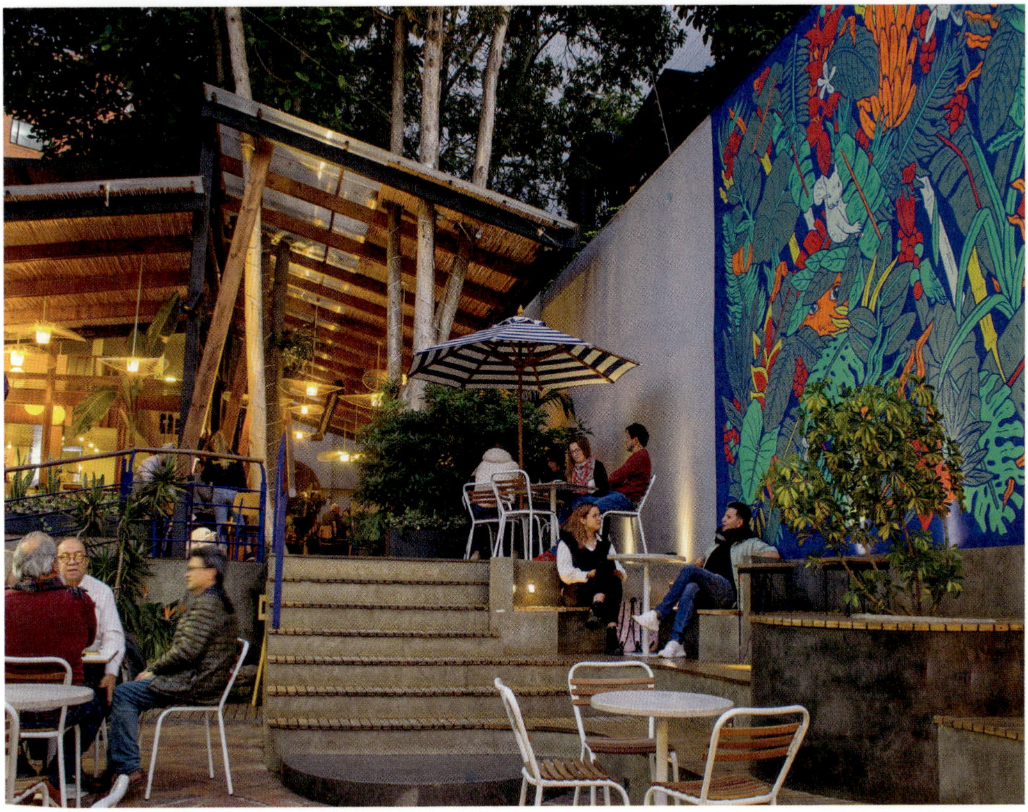

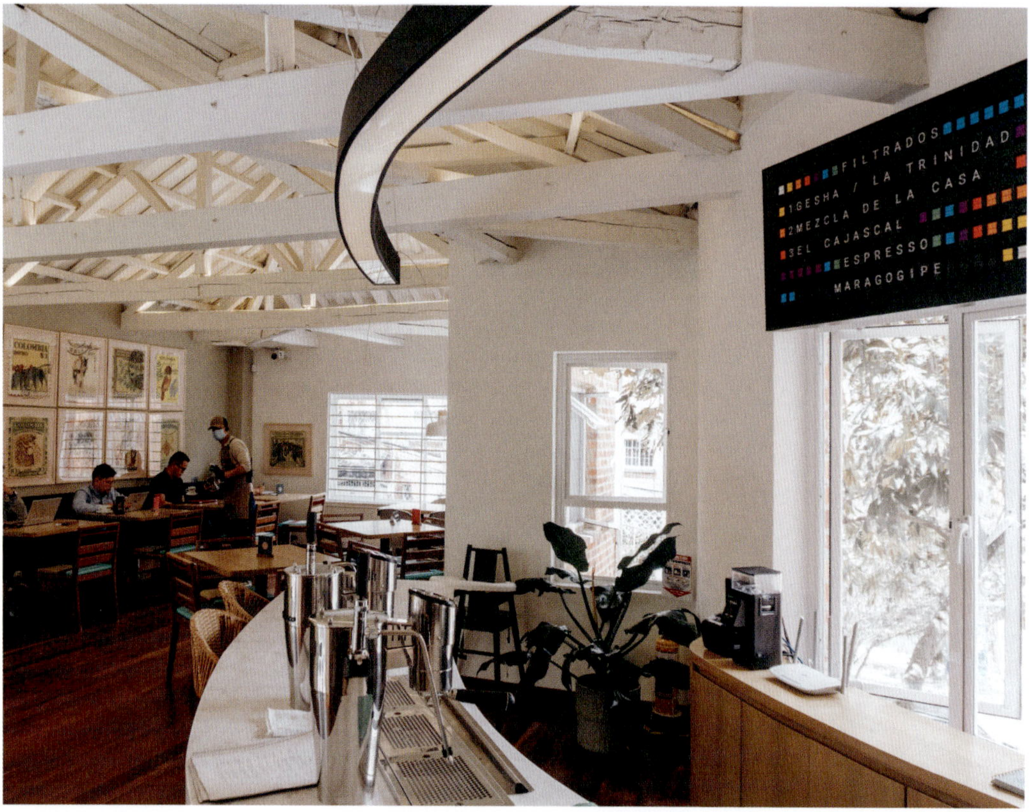
FILTRADOS
1GESHA / LA TRINIDAD
2MEZCLA DE LA CASA
3EL CAJASCAL
ESPRESSO
MARAGOGIPE

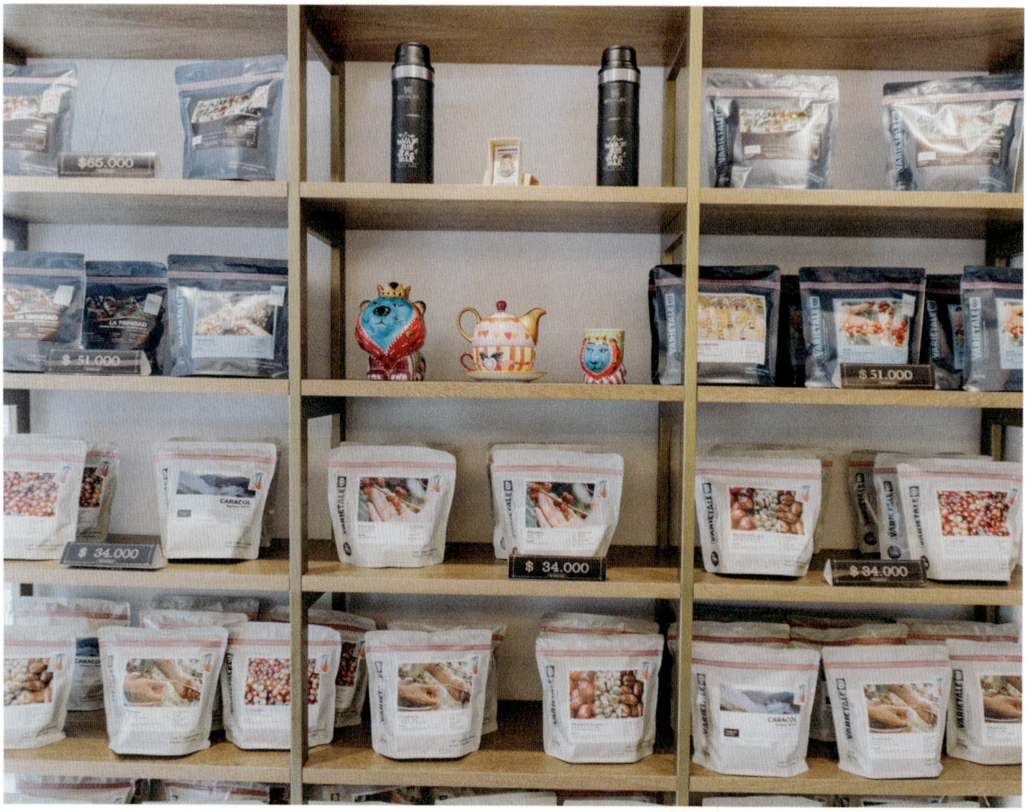
$65.000
$ 51.000
$ 51.000
CARACOL
$ 34.000
$ 34.000
$ 34.000
CARACOL
CARACOL

17 VARIETALE CHAPINERO

Cra. 4a #57-02, Bogotá, Colombia

TO VISIT
BEFORE YOU DIE
BECAUSE

Try Colombia's best speciality coffees or a classic tinto at this cute café and roastery in the capital's upscale Chapinero neighbourhood.

In Colombia, coffee is known as tinto, and the strong, dark brew is served everywhere you go, from street carts (some come with their own roasters and grinders) to shops and offices, where you're treated to a free cup while you wait. But if you still fancy more, and prefer lightly roasted speciality coffee, head to Varietale Chapinero. Located in an old villa, with plenty of cosy spaces, a large terrace and an in-house bakery, it offers a range of local Colombian beans, such as a limited-edition bourbon rosado, grown by Doris Gómez in Santa María, Huila, or a castillo grown just outside the city in Anolaima, Cundinamarca. As well as a slice of torta Maria Luisa (Colombia's Victoria sponge, with orange zest and dulce de leche), here you can order classic lattes and cappuccinos (made with two shots of espresso), discover a range of filter coffees brewed using one of nine methods, including Chemex and V60; or keep it traditional with a tinto campesino, an extremely popular black coffee flavoured with panela (a mix of brown sugar, cinnamon and cloves).

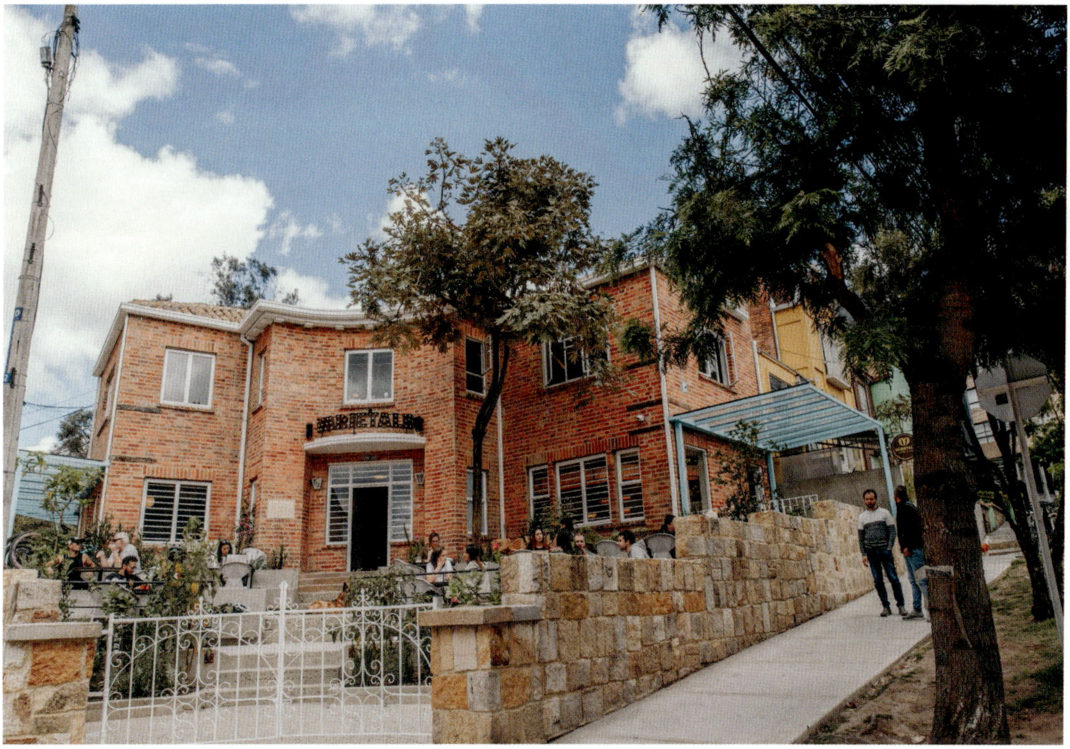

varietale.com

+57 324 255 0397

18 CAFÉ TORTONI

Av. de Mayo 825, C1084 Cdad. Autónoma de Buenos Aires, Argentina

TO VISIT BEFORE YOU DIE BECAUSE

Step into Argentina's historic coffee culture before enjoying some tango or a game of dominos in the oldest café in town.

Despite its name, Tortoni was first opened in 1858 by a French immigrant, Jean Touan, who was inspired by a famous Parisian café. It moved to its present location in the 1890s, and has been a city landmark ever since. Easily spotted thanks to its grand entrance by leading architect Alejandro Christophersen, the historic haunt welcomes pool and domino players. It is also home to a former hairdresser section turned into a library, and a slightly scary wax statue marking the great writer Jorge Luis Borges' favourite table. The basement, first opened to welcome the city's most influential club, La Peña, in the 1920s, now boasts a stage for jazz and tango artists. The most popular coffee in Argentina is the cortado, which you can order everywhere by simply making a C shape with your thumb and index finger to the waiter across the room. Try the cappuccino served with cinnamon, the iced coffee with dulce de leche, or complement your double espresso (café en jarrito) with a submarino – a bar of dark chocolate melted in hot milk that's especially popular in the winter.

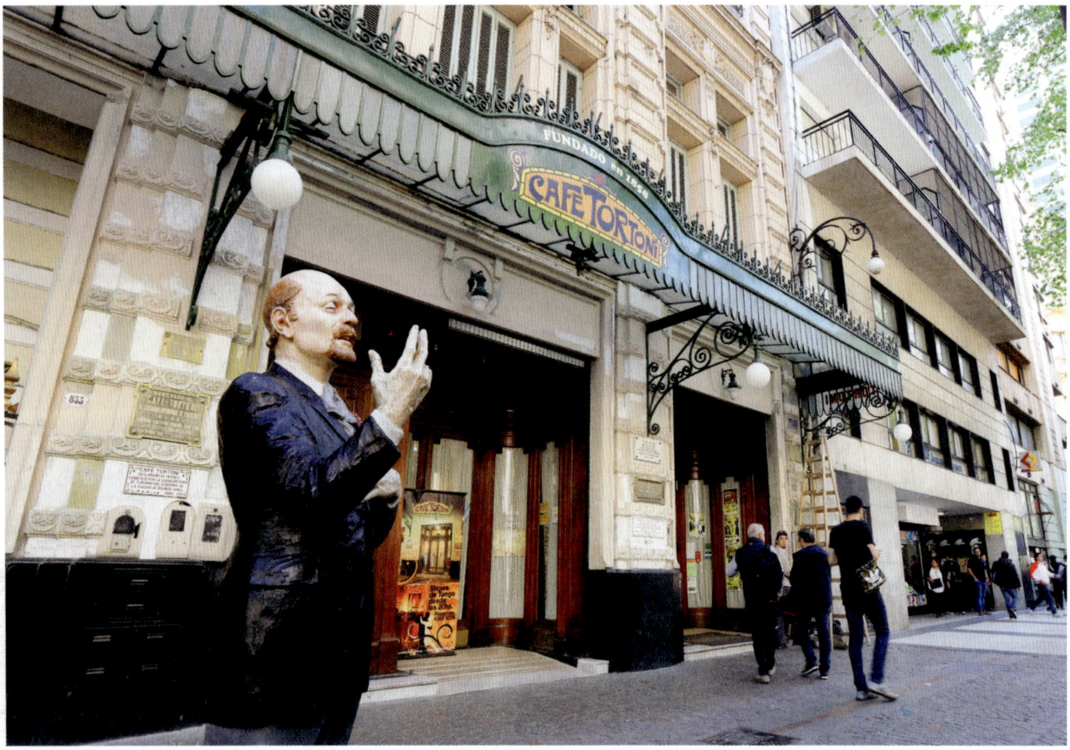

cafetortoni.com.ar +54 9 11 2392 6410

19 ROSSO

1402 9 Ave SE, Calgary, Alberta T2G 0T5, Canada

TO VISIT BEFORE YOU DIE BECAUSE

A slew of international awards and a B Corp Certification mean the beans at this family-run business are both ethically sourced and perfectly roasted.

Competitors at the World Barista Championship have 15 minutes on stage with an espresso machine to create an espresso, a milk beverage and a signature beverage for each of the four judges. And like any high-profile competition, these champions need the best coaches to lead them to victory. Which is exactly what Rosso's David Crosby and Cole Torode (a champion himself) do – and brilliantly so, having coached the World Barista Champion Roasters 2023 and 2024 (Mikael Jasin and Boram Um) as well as the Canadian Barista Champion 2024 Nelson Phu. All this to say that they take their coffee pretty seriously at Rosso. 'Our cups are acts of love, brewed to perfection for you,' writes co-owner Jessie Attrell. 'Embrace the ritual and savour the delight it brings to our lives.' Visit their homely Inglewood location to try a perfect cappuccino with next-level latte art from the friendly baristas. On the menu are great pastries, breakfast bagels and coffee blends such as the popular Homebody, a comforting medium roast that comes with its own Spotify playlist.

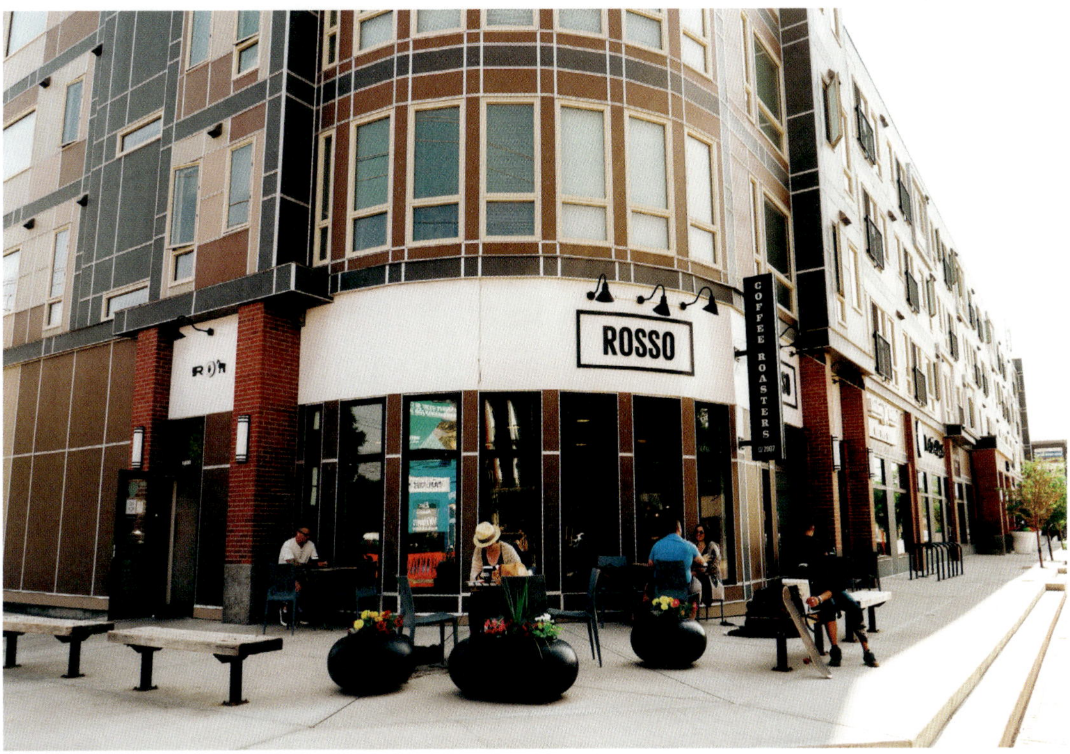

rossocoffeeroasters.com

+1 587 353 7677

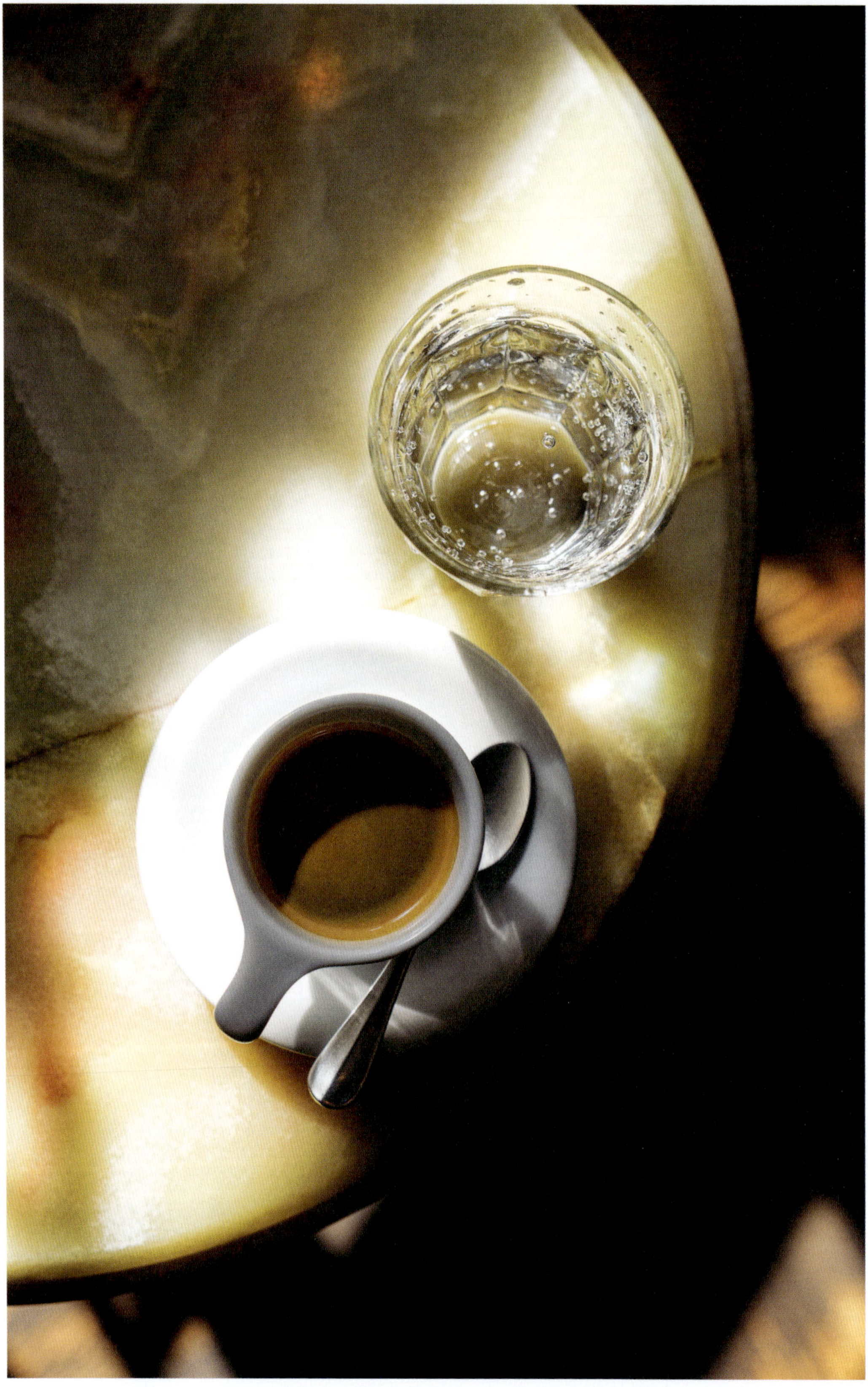

20 FOUR LETTER WORD

3022 W Diversey, Avondale, Chicago, Illinois 60647, United States

TO VISIT BEFORE YOU DIE BECAUSE

Pop in for a single-origin espresso or while away a weekend morning with a coffee and a second-hand book at this friendly café.

'We are known for our espresso shots, people come here for them to enjoy a little break and a chat,' says Ria Neri, who co-founded Four Letter Word with childhood friends Eylem Ozkaya and Shlumper, who is also an artist. United by 'a love for good coffee, good design and good people', they first opened a roastery and café in Turkey before setting up shop in their hometown of Chicago in 2018. Stock up on Ecuador La Papaya Anaerobic by Juan Peña, wrapped in beautiful, bold packaging, or pick a treat from the old Cadbury Chocolate glass display, which is filled with delicious cakes, sometimes produced by special guests. The next chapter in the friends' story will delight all book lovers. 'We recently acquired a warehouse next door, and upon opening it up realised it was filled with over 50,000 books,' says Ria. 'Since the café is so small, on weekends when we get busy, we open the space also known as Four Letter Books – people are able to sit here, enjoy their coffee, listen to music and read or purchase vintage books.' Sounds heavenly.

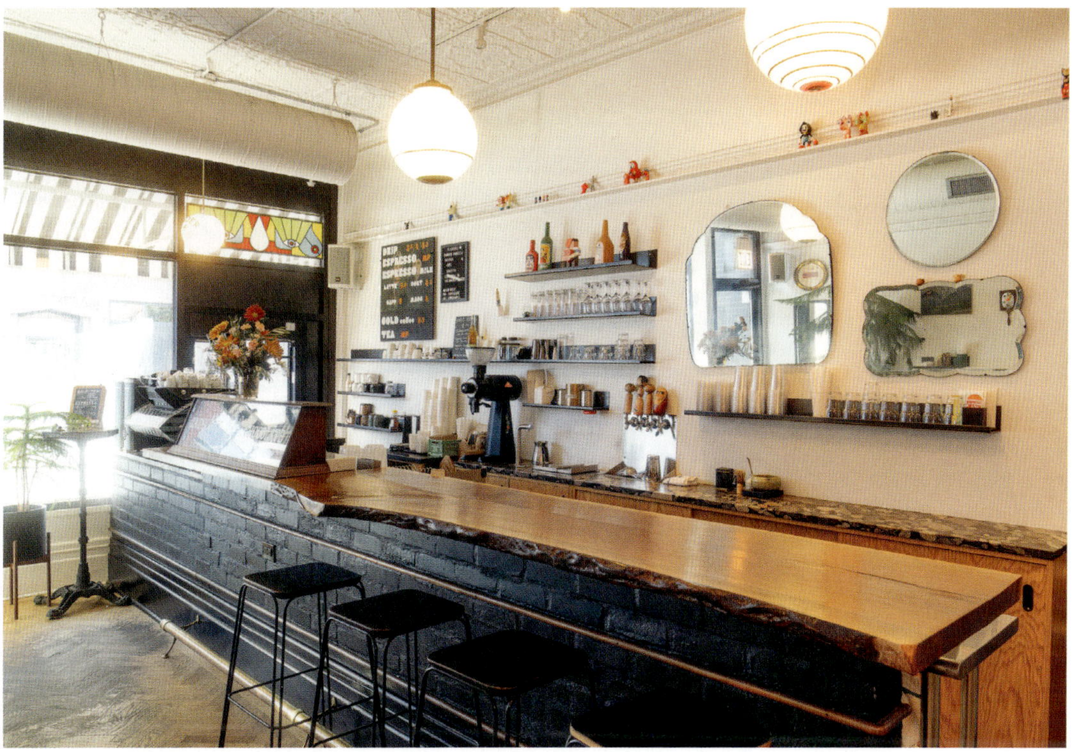

4lwcoffee.com

21 MILLI BY METRIC COFFEE

3110 N Kedzie Ave, Chicago, Illinois 60618, United States

TO VISIT BEFORE YOU DIE BECAUSE

Light, airy and serving delicious flaky pastries, the new HQ of Chicago speciality roaster Metric is pretty much the perfect neighbourhood spot.

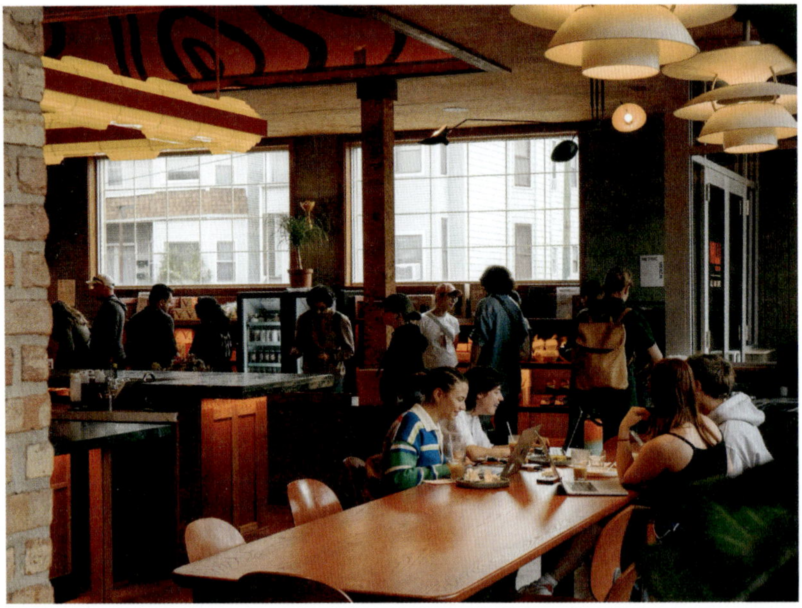

'When we dreamt up Milli, it wasn't just about coffee, wine or pastries. It was about creating a place where neighbours could meet, strangers could connect, and a community could take root around a shared table,' explain Xavier Alexander and Darko Arandjelovic, who started Metric Coffee in 2012. After years of work, they have just opened their flagship café, roastery and lab in an old antique warehouse in Avondale. Called Milli after the measure used to make coffee drinks, the light-filled space features marble counters, a 3D-printed lamp and colourful tabletops. It was an instant hit: 'People come for a cup, for a croissant, for a glass – and stay for one another. And that's the heartbeat of Milli: not just a café, but a hub where curiosity, care and connection live side by side,' says the pair. So sit back, relax, and pair your single-origin espresso – including the likes of Ethiopia Gerba Dogo Sodu Washed – with a perfectly laminated golden croissant or a slice of courgette cake flavoured with bergamot oil and white pepper – just two of the many delicious creations prepared by culinary director Kirstin Alexander and head baker Lou Turner.

milliallday.com metriccoffee.com +1 773 904 290

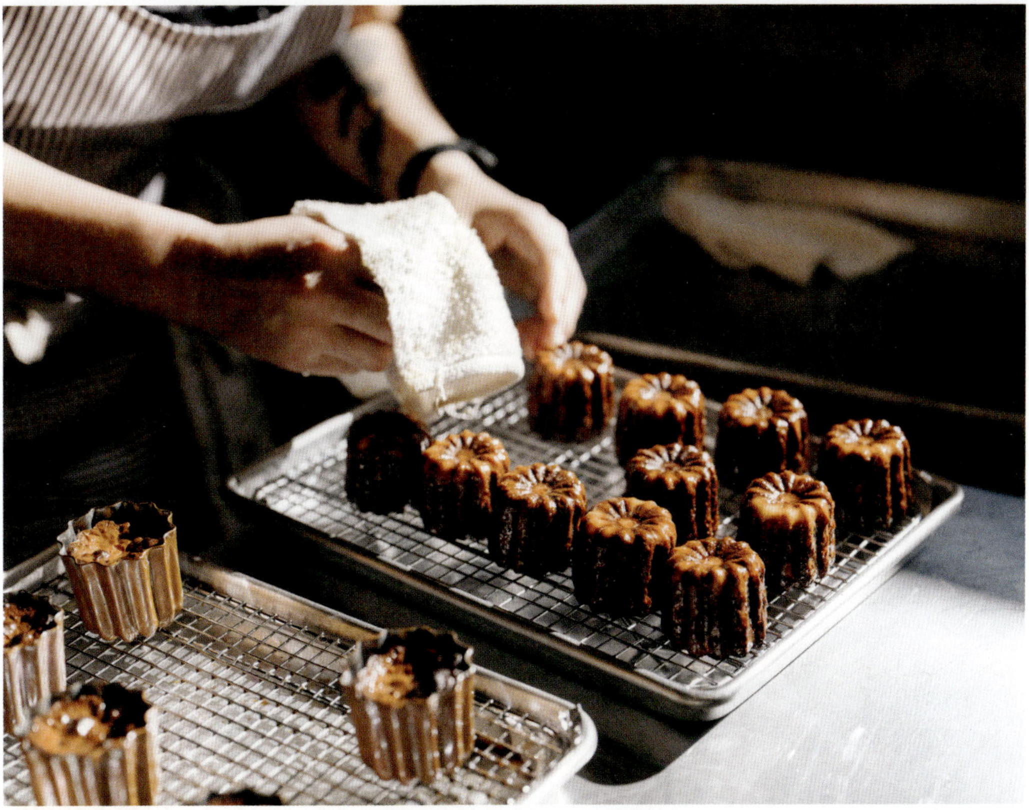

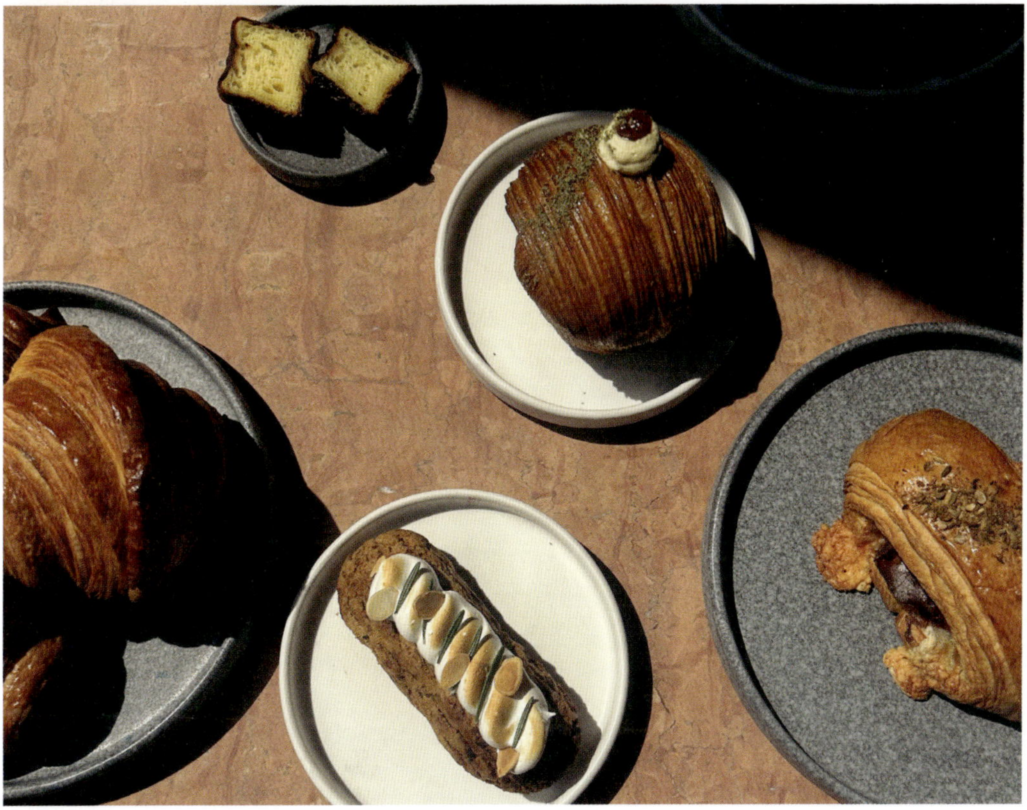

22 STARBUCKS RESERVE ROASTERY

646 Michigan Ave, Chicago, Illinois 60611, United States

TO VISIT BEFORE YOU DIE BECAUSE

The largest coffee house of the biggest coffee chain in the world wows visitors with a spectacular celebration of coffee, spread over four floors.

Born in Seattle in 1971, Starbucks took over the world with its cosy seating and oversized, sweet milky drinks – some of them even had a dash of coffee in them. Although it's having a tough time today (people now seem to prefer cheaper coffee or independent cafés), for many it's still the first point of entry into the coffee world thanks to its ubiquity – the chain has 38,587 coffee shops in over 80 countries. The biggest of them all is this 3,250 sq m behemoth on Chicago's Magnificent Mile. At its heart is a 17m cask offering views of freshly roasted coffee moving through tubes in all directions, from the ground-floor coffee bar, roastery and gift shop to the upstairs café, experiential bar and fourth-floor cocktail bar. Exclusive creations range from pumpkin-spiced drinks to a tiramisu latte and nitro almond milk mocha, while beans are sourced from West Java to the Galápagos. Enjoy an espresso martini flight with three different liqueurs on a winter's night, or head to the summer roof terrace for a Cold Brew Spiced Rum.

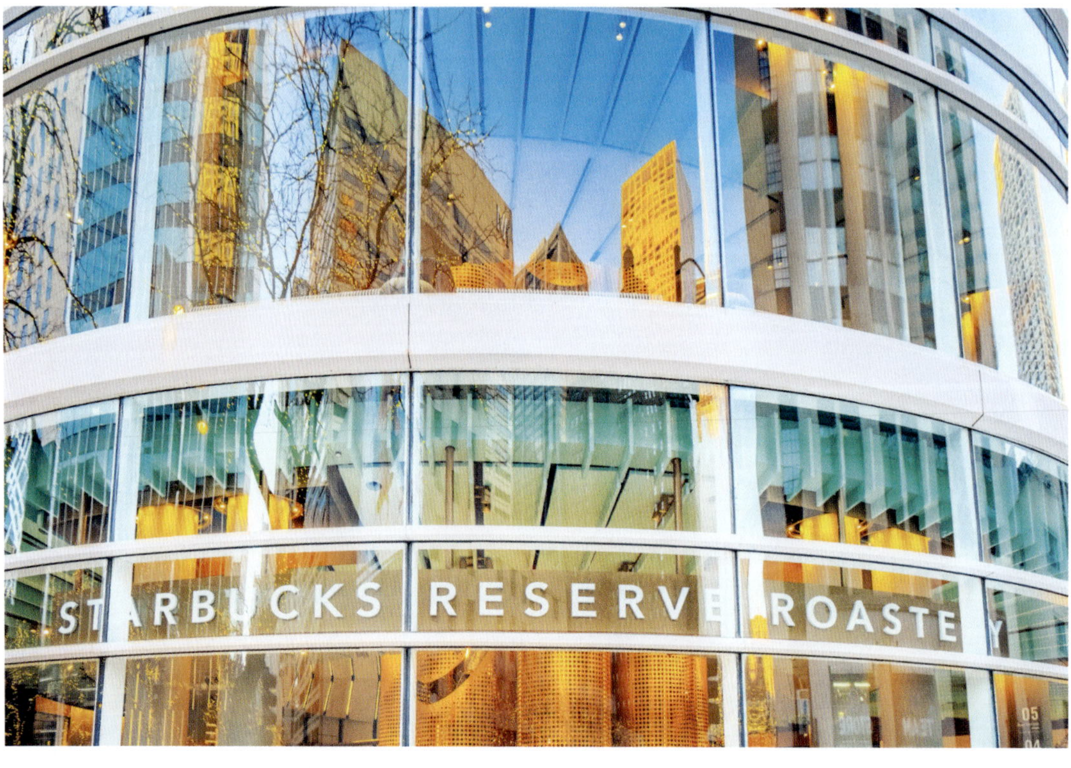

starbucksreserve.com

+1 312 283 7100

23 BLUE SPARROW COFFEE

3070 Blake St #180, Denver, Colorado 80205, United States

TO VISIT BEFORE YOU DIE BECAUSE

Bring your own cup and savour an iced coffee with a clear conscience at this beautifully designed neighbourhood café.

Founded in 2017 by Jeffrey Knott and Fiona Arnold, Blue Sparrow Coffee is the perfect example of how a small independent coffee shop can make a difference. Decorated with signature patterned floor tiles and a long blue banquette, its Blake Street café is not only a cosy, friendly space but also the first location of a growing company that cares about its impact on the world. It hires baristas trained through social enterprise Prodigy's apprentice programme; implemented a $15 minimum wage before it was mandatory, and openly shares annual insights into equity and sustainability. And all that on top of serving excellent coffee, of course. Featured roasters include Rosso (page 39), as well as US names from Arizona's Mythical Coffee to Washington's Elm Coffee Roasters. Make sure to try the house speciality, iced coffee. Varieties include Strava Gold nitro iced coffee on tap; Japanese iced coffee (brewed hot, then flash-chilled over ice to 'lock in' its delicate notes), or Made for Milk, an iced coffee created to 'stand up to a splash of milk without tasting sour'.

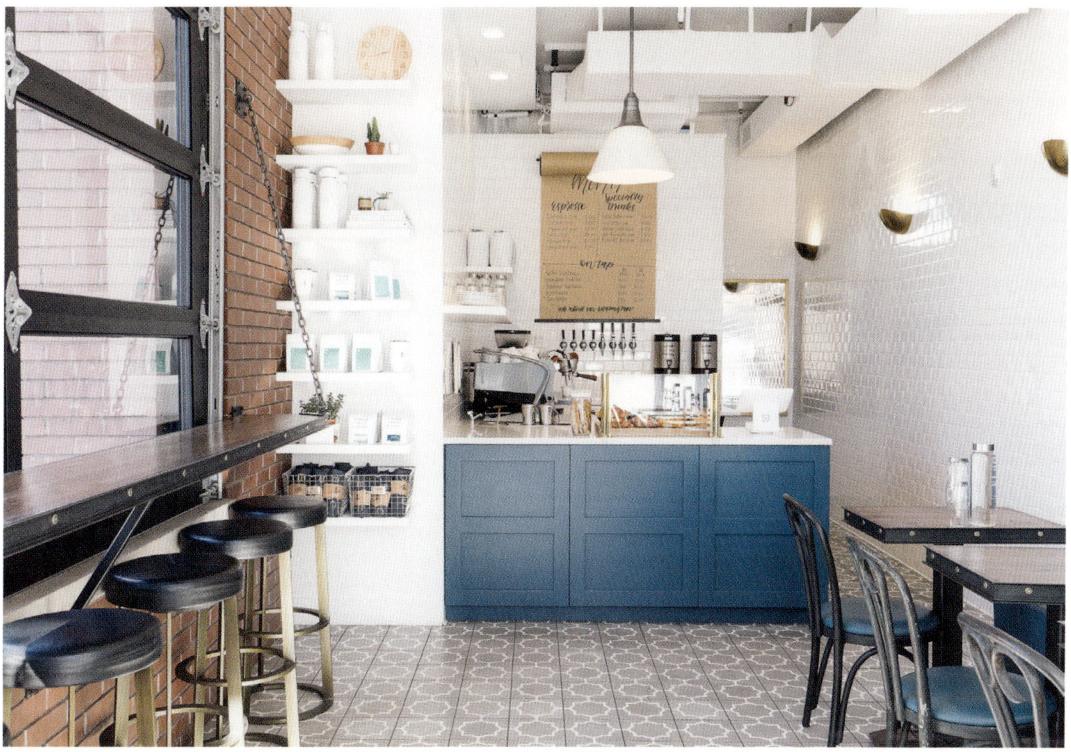

bluesparrowcoffee.com +1 303 800 2633

24 KONALANI COFFEE BAR

78-1136 Bishop Rd, Holualoa, Hawaii 96725, United States

TO VISIT
BEFORE YOU DIE
BECAUSE

Learn all about Kona coffee straight from the experts at this welcoming hilltop café on a beautiful Big Island coffee plantation.

Hawaii's stunning volcanic landscape is also a fertile ground for coffee growing. Cultivated in the Kona District since an American missionary brought in some arabica cuttings in the 1820s, Kona coffee is known for its smooth flavor with notes of chocolate, fruit, and nuts. To find out more about the area's ideal climate and history, tour the 16-hectare Heavenly Hawaiian farm in the hills of Holualoa in the heart of Kona. Founded by Dave and Trudy Bateman, Heavenly Hawaiian has been producing world-class coffee since 1994, and is home to the first ever farm-side coffee bar in Kona. Based on the dream of one of their team members in 2019, Konalani Coffee Bar is the place to hang out after a farm experience. Its menu spans pour-overs of geisha, the 2025 top-rated coffee in Paris, to Hawaiian endemic Mamaki tea with house-made pineapple syrup. Try a classic shaken specialty cold brew, the Kona Miel, with farm-raised honey and organic cinnamon. With panoramic views of the Pacific Ocean, Konalani is the perfect location for relaxing while sipping a classic Hawaiian coffee.

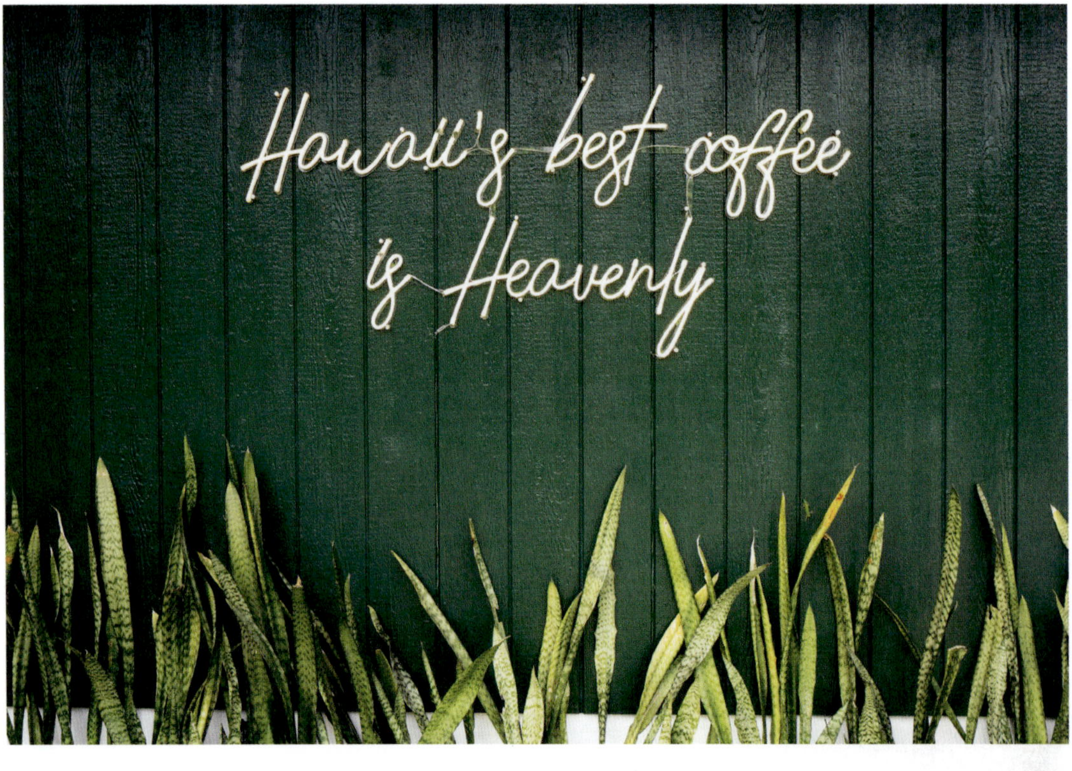

heavenlyhawaiian.com/konalani-coffee-bar

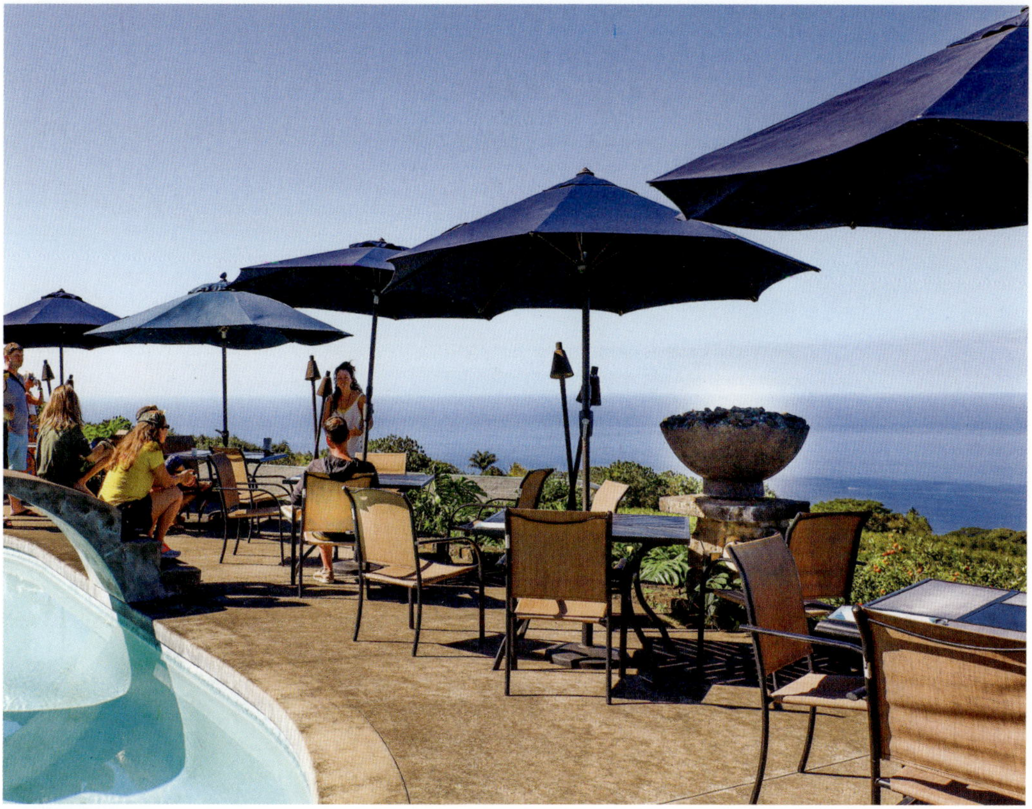

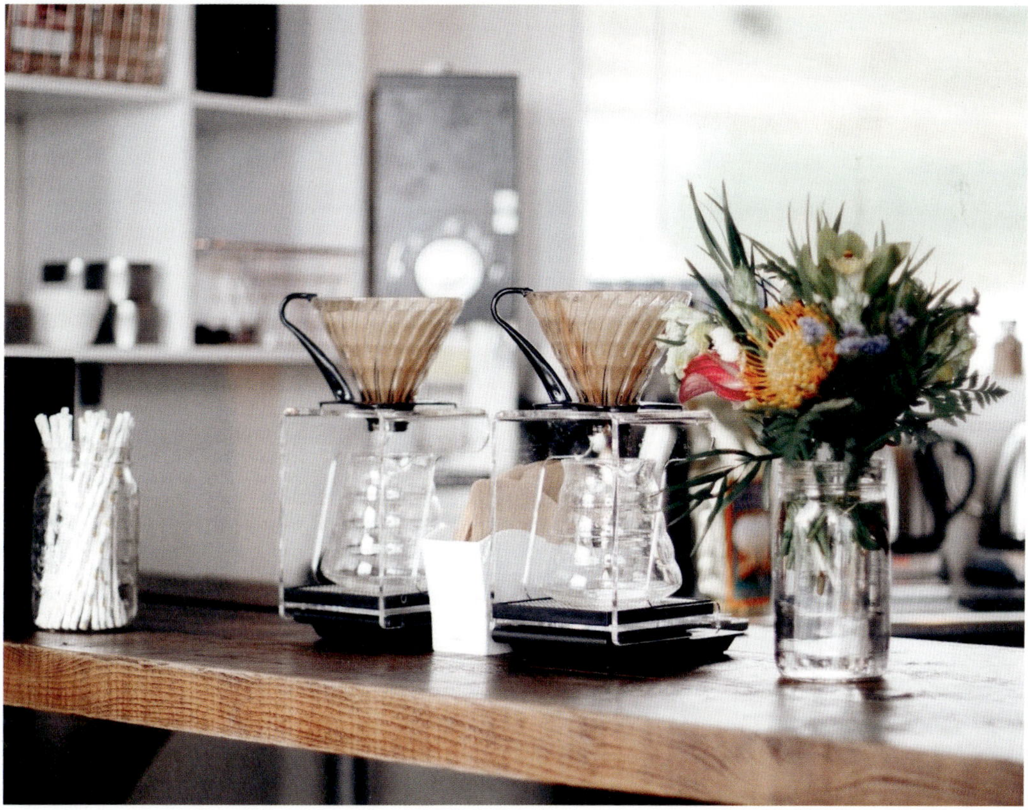

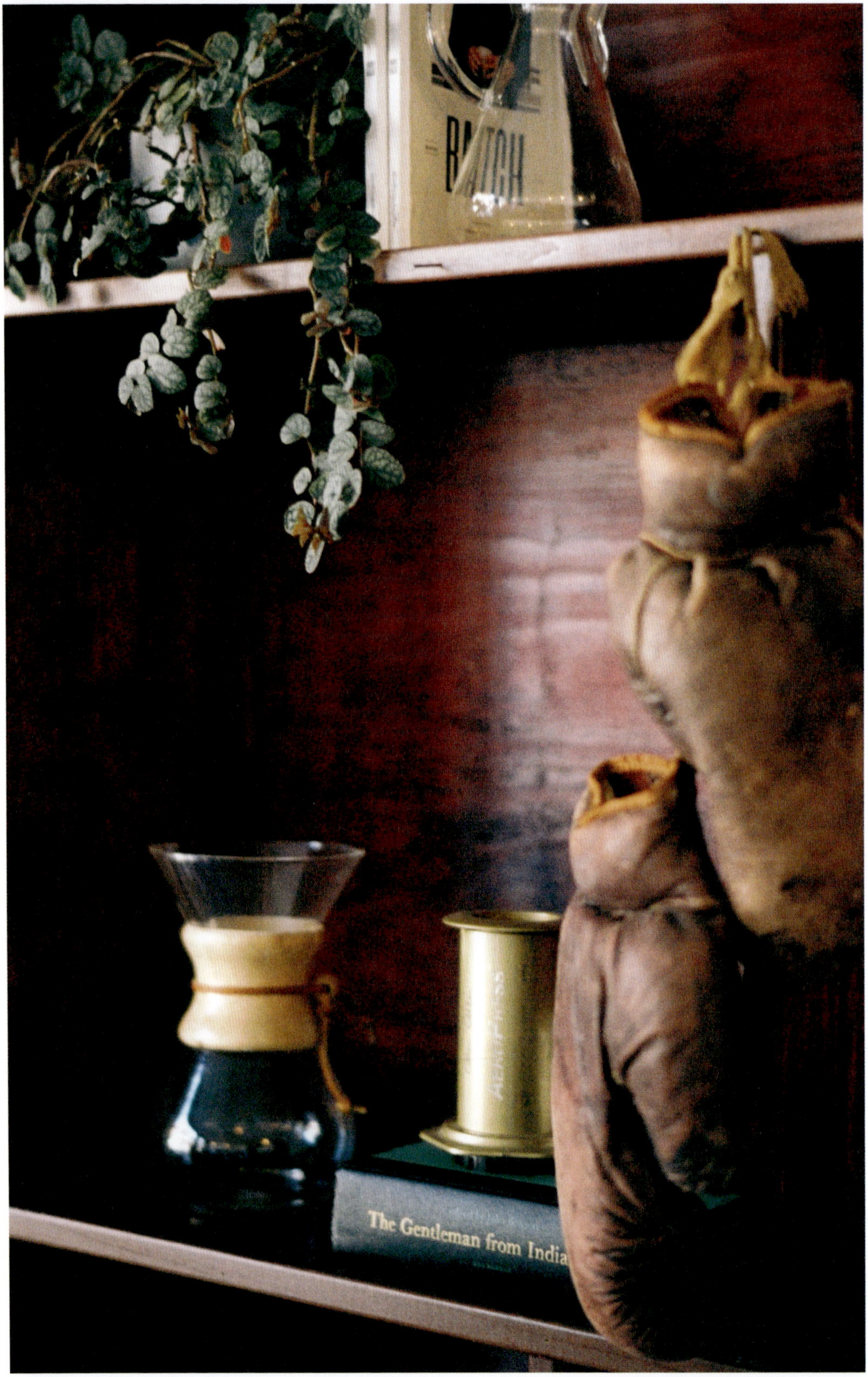
BATCH
The Gentleman from India

25 AMBERSON COFFEE & GROCER

401 S College Ave, Indianapolis, Indiana 46203, United States

TO VISIT BEFORE YOU DIE BECAUSE

Discover your next favourite drink at this award-winning café with an ever-changing menu of seasonal specials and beans from top roasters.

Founder Hugo Cano opened Amberson Coffee just as the pandemic was sending us all into lockdown, but this tricky start hasn't dampened his enthusiasm. Nearly five years later – and having made it into the US Brewer's Cup Top 10 in 2023 and 2024, and US Barista Top 10 in 2024 – he is still involved in the day-to-day running of the shop, often waking up at 4am to bake the day's pastries, and staying after closing time to train for competitions. This passion shines through everywhere you look at Amberson, a welcoming space in a converted 1930s petrol station. Come in on any given day and you'll be able to discover something new, whether it's a coffee from one of the roasters of the month – these have included the likes of Prodigal or Fritz (page 126) – or seasonal offerings such as the Barista Breakfast, a flat white and triple chocolate chip cookie combo, and the Midwestern Latte, an espresso with butter syrup and milk, topped with a salted bourbon caramel cold foam.

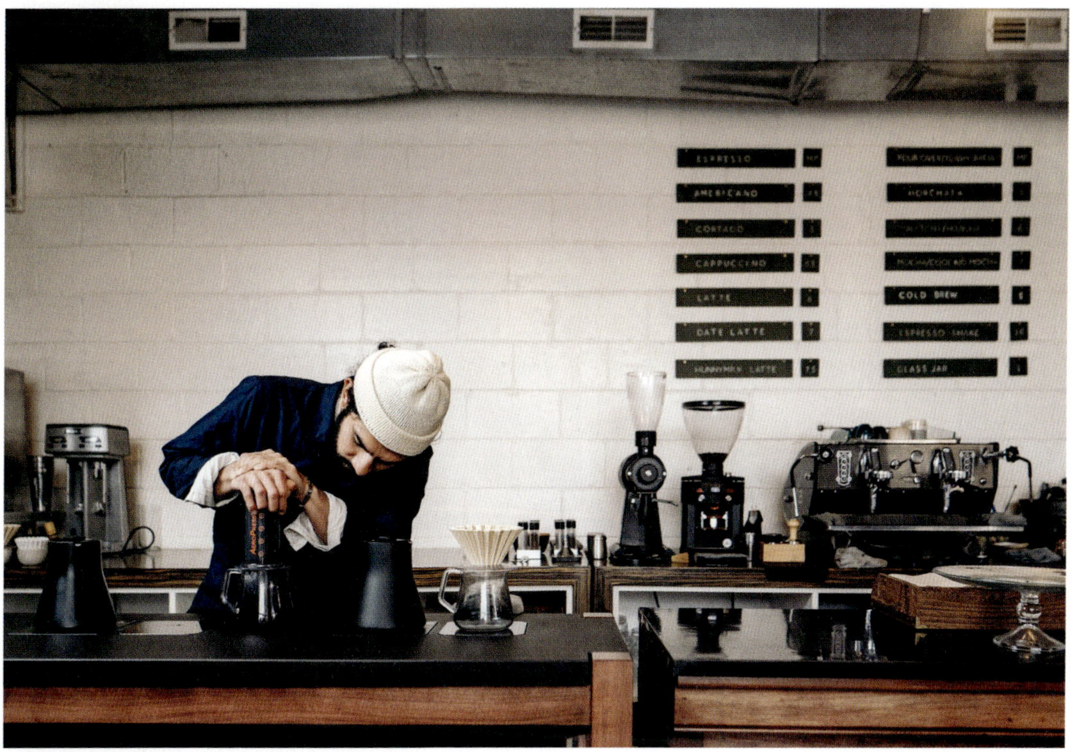

ambersoncoffee.com

26 CAFÉ BLUE

Main Road (B1), Irish Town, Jamaica

TO VISIT BEFORE YOU DIE BECAUSE

The journey along the narrow mountain road is worth it for a sip of Jamaica's famous Blue Mountain coffee and the panoramic views.

Up a winding and twisting road about a 30-minute drive from Kingston you'll find Jamaica's Blue Mountains, home to dense forests and small coffee farms. Renowned all around the world for its unique flavour – a harmonious blend of mild and sweet, with hints of chocolate and citrus – Blue Mountain coffee is as rare and expensive as the region is steep and hilly. Opened in 2005 by the Sharp family, also behind the renowned Clifton Mount Estate, Café Blue Irish Town comes with a wonderful terrace offering views of the lush landscape and fluttering hummingbirds. Sit on the balcony or at a large tree trunk table and enjoy home specialities including a cup of real Clifton Mount Estate coffee; a signature Blueccino with nutmeg, cinnamon and whipped cream; or Jamaica Blue Mountain coffee, slow-dripped and served over ice. There are also rum-based Blue Mountain Fog and Misty Blue cocktails, treats such as passion fruit cheesecake, and an all-day breakfast menu including smoked marlin wraps and jerk chicken sandwiches.

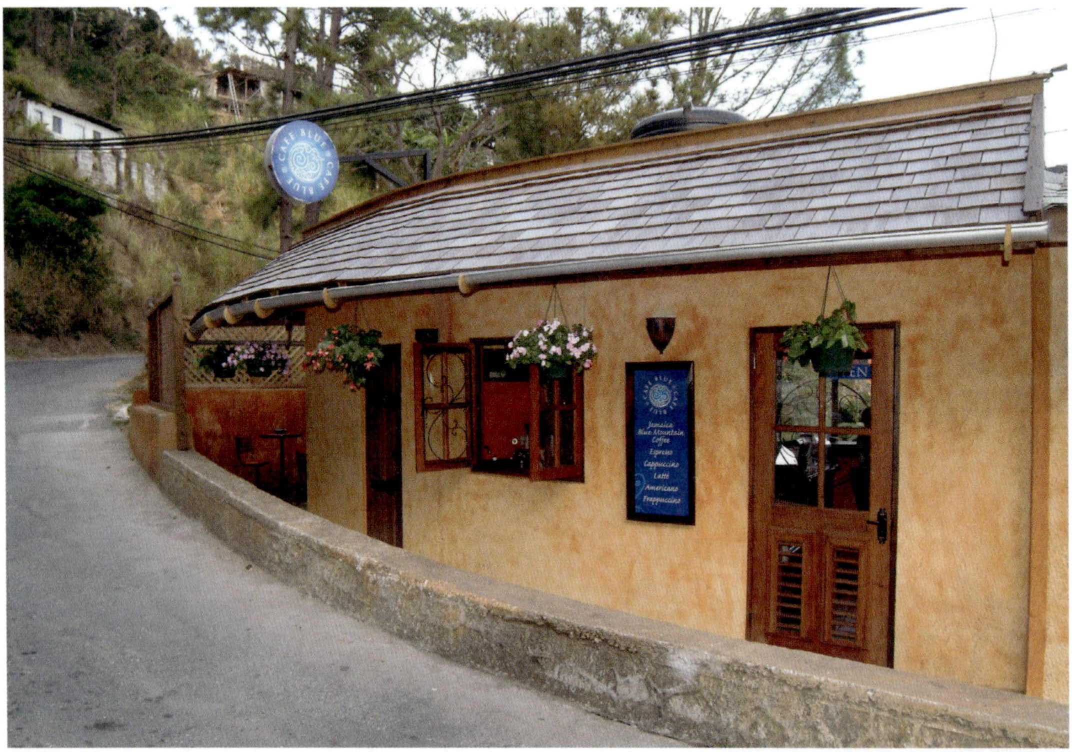

cafeblue.com +1 876 944 8918

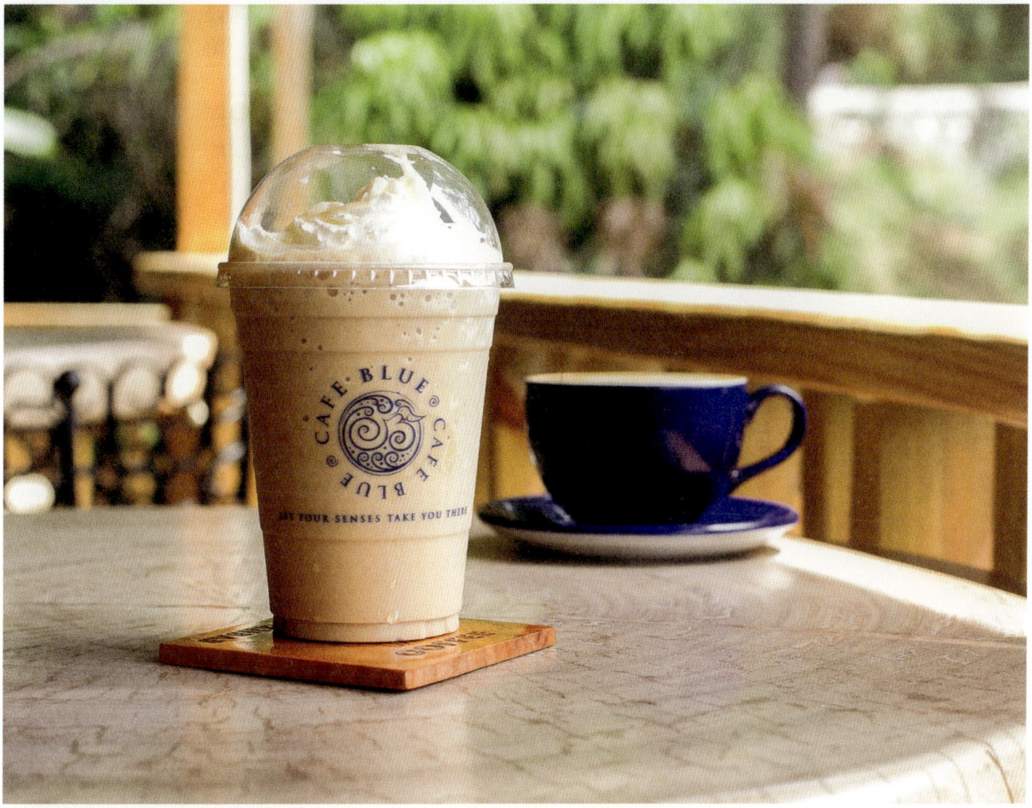
CAFE BLUE CAFE BLUE
YOUR SENSES TAKE YOU THERE

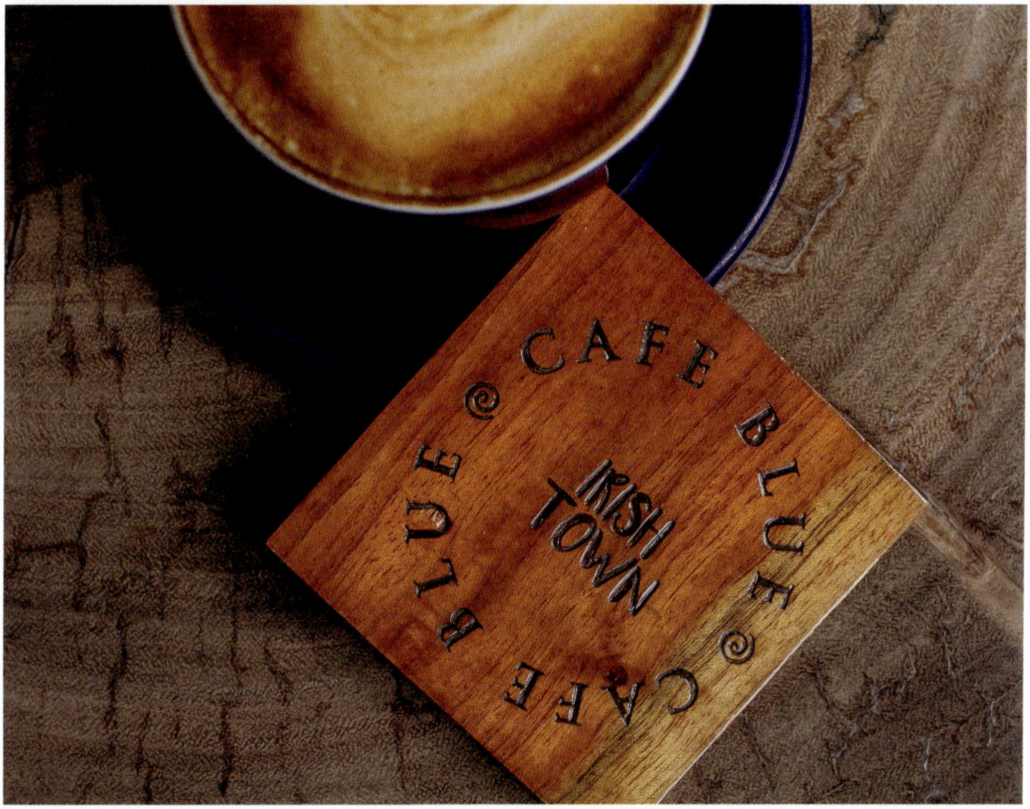
CAFE BLUE CAFE BLUE
IRISH TOWN

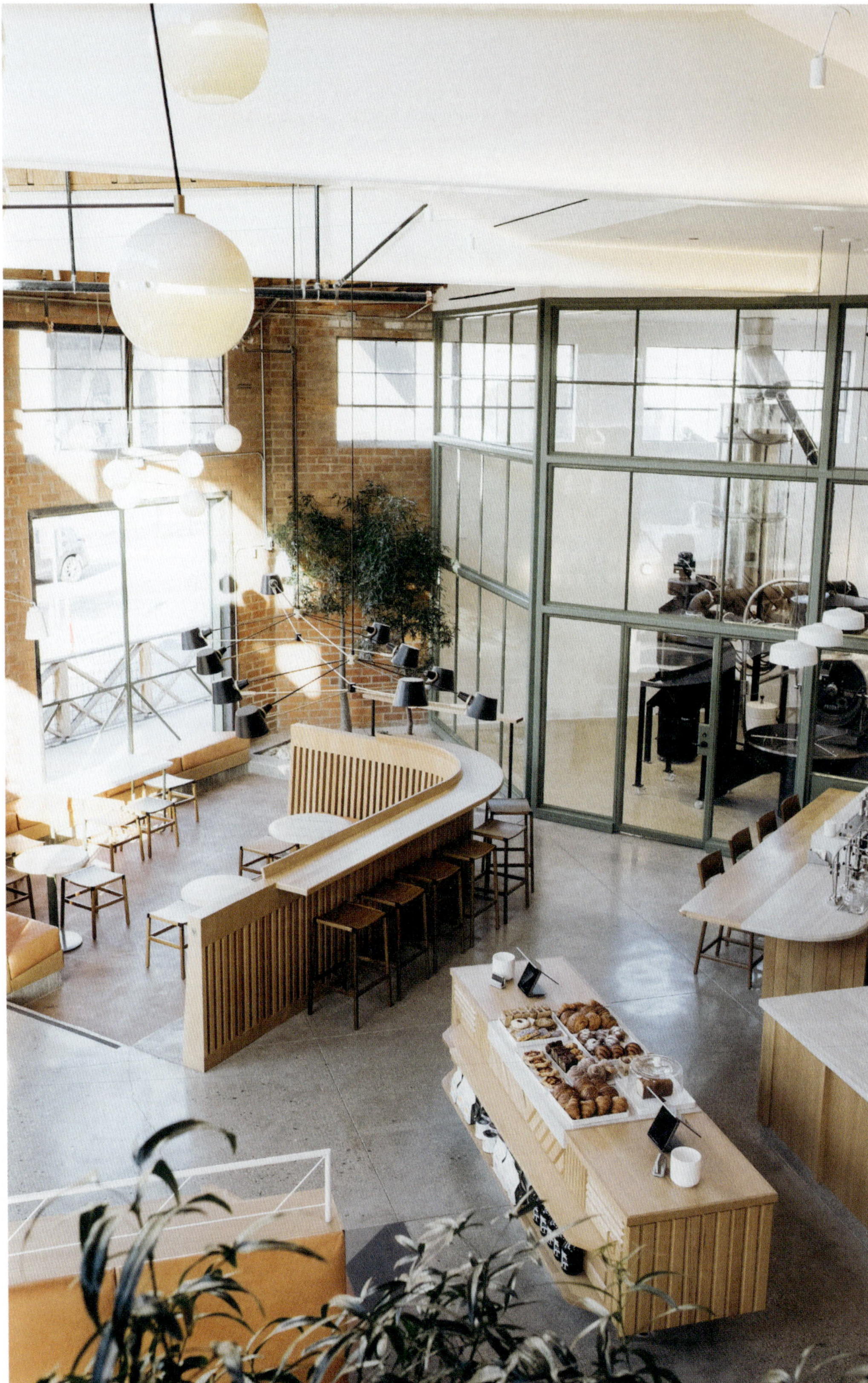

27 VERVE COFFEE ROASTERS

500 Mateo St #102, Los Angeles, California 90013, United States

TO VISIT BEFORE YOU DIE BECAUSE

Plan your next start-up at the LA HQ of this influential California coffee company, which delivers laid-back vibes and great coffee with flair.

Verve Coffee Roasters was established in 2007 when Ryan O'Donovan and Colby Barr started a small local venture along the rugged California coast and named it after their favourite jazz record label. Although the company, which has recently been awarded Roaster of the Year 2024, originally hails from Santa Cruz, we suggest you visit its flagship Los Angeles outpost, located in the city's Arts District. Featuring huge windows, a warm wooden interior, lush garden patio and macramé art, the 650 sq m double-height space is part café, part creative hub – on weekdays it is probably the coolest co-working space in town. The light and airy space (and the roastery on display behind a glass wall) reflects Verve's transparency on sourcing, evident in its Farmlevel Initiative, which is designed to improve the lives of smallholder farmers, help combat the impacts of climate change, and preserve heirloom coffee varieties. For the full LA experience, set up your laptop, sip on your signature Streetlevel espresso, and snack on a healthy avocado toast or acai bowl.

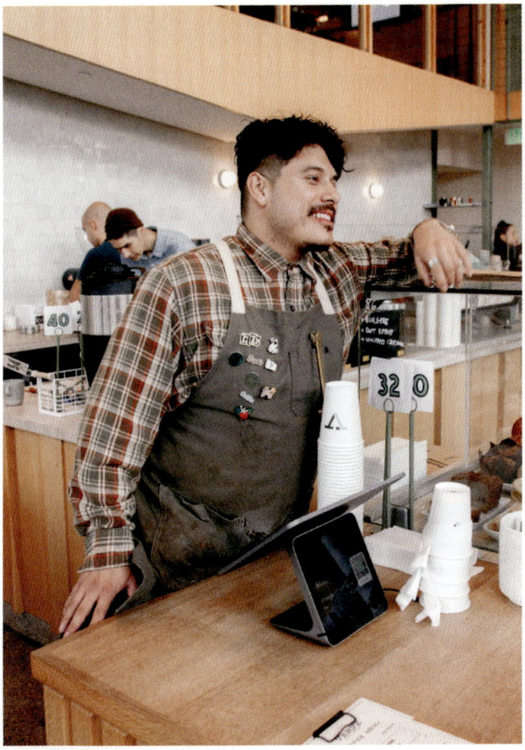

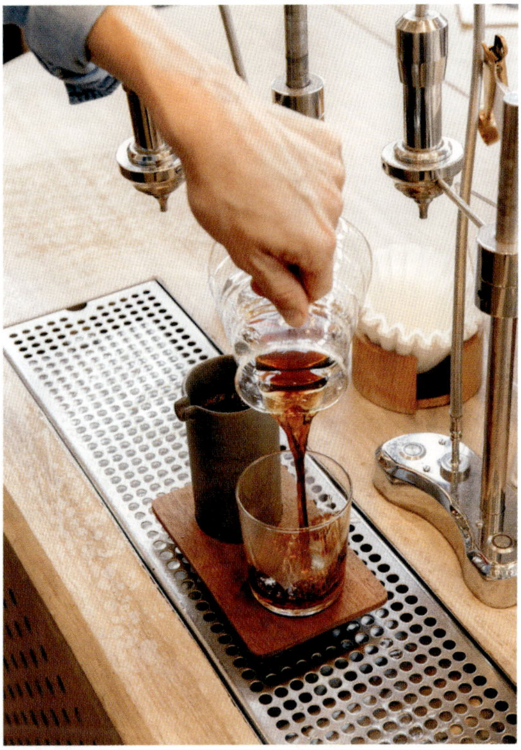

verveecoffee.com

+1 213 419 5077

28 EXPLORADORES DE CAFÉ

Santa Fé 596, Cuajimalpa, Mexico City, Mexico

TO VISIT BEFORE YOU DIE BECAUSE

Tired of the crowds in Mexico City's Roma district? Learn about the story behind each cup at this coffee oasis run by a team of true enthusiasts.

Mexico's café de olla, a blend of coffee, cinnamon and whole cane sugar traditionally served in a clay pot, is available on every street corner. But here at Exploradores de Café, you get to discover a different, lesser-known side to the Mexican love affair with coffee – one that even sees local farmers deliver their beans directly to the baristas. First opened in 2016 in an office building, Exploradores soon moved on from simply providing workers with their daily fix of caffeine. The team turned into roasters and seekers, travelling the country in search of the best beans and meeting the farmers. 'We slowly became not just baristas and roasters but ambassadors of coffee farmers and their entire communities,' they explain. Their new space is 'a place where you can experience the whole journey of the bean', try coffees from well-known farms such as Microbeneficio La Joya in Veracruz, or come for a tasting session. 'We have a specific cupping room where we give free classes on weekends. We believe cupping is the best way to hear the coffee's story.'

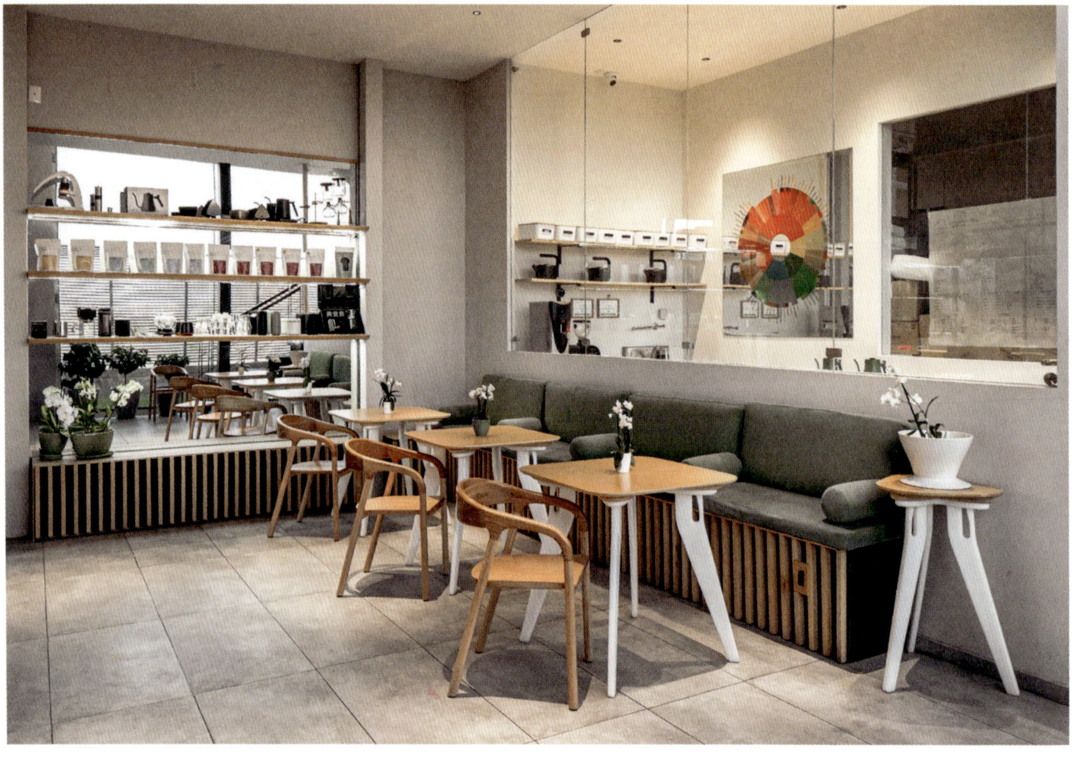

grupoexploradores.com

29 SUITE HABANA

2609 N Miami Ave, Miami, Florida 33127, United States

TO VISIT
BEFORE YOU DIE
BECAUSE

Cool down with a double-shot iced café con leche at this award-winning family-run café, the go-to spot for speciality Cuban coffee in Miami.

'Every roast, every cup, and every gathering around our coffee is a tribute to the culture that shaped us and the people we love,' say husband-and-wife team Manny Lopez and Nayelis Delisle, who opened Suite Habana in 2018. Their café is much more than a *ventanita* – the walk-up windows for ordering coffee and pastries that are central to Miami's vibrant Cuban community. Located in trendy Wynwood, it aims to recreate the atmosphere of a traditional Cuban *paladar*, a type of welcoming home restaurant. Here, you can have a nice chat over a *cafecito*. Comprising one single shot of espresso with half a teaspoon of brown sugar, it is made using a house blend of locally roasted Brazilian and Colombian beans with bold chocolate-and-tobacco notes that the couple spent years perfecting. Other highlights include a café con leche available hot or iced, *cafe bombón* ('condensed milk and coffee magic'), and treats including vegan banana bread and *canelés* filled with guava and cream cheese.

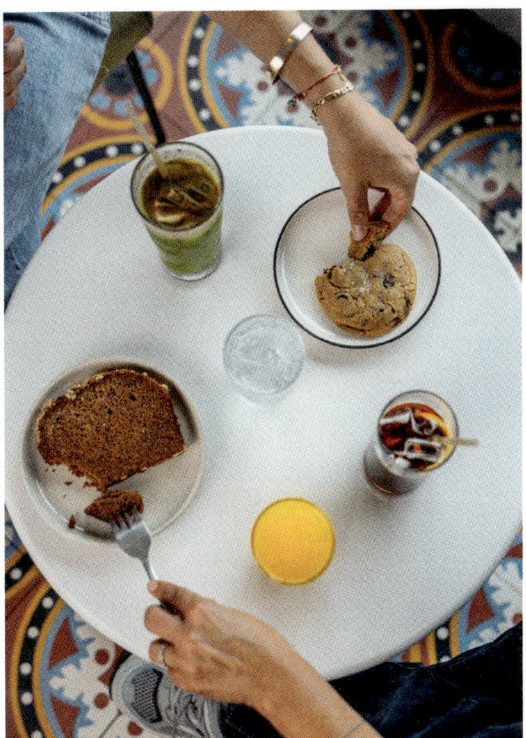

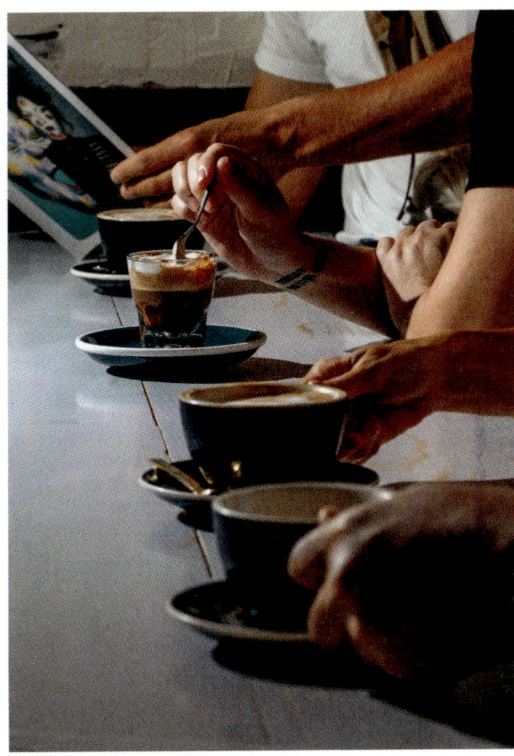

suitehabanacafe.com

30 KALI COFFEE ROASTERS

Av. Manuel Gómez Morín 900, Carrizalejo,
66254 San Pedro Garza García, Nuevo León, Mexico

TO VISIT
BEFORE YOU DIE
BECAUSE

This family-owned initiative turned a crisis into a profitable business and a force for good, transforming the lives of Mexican coffee growers.

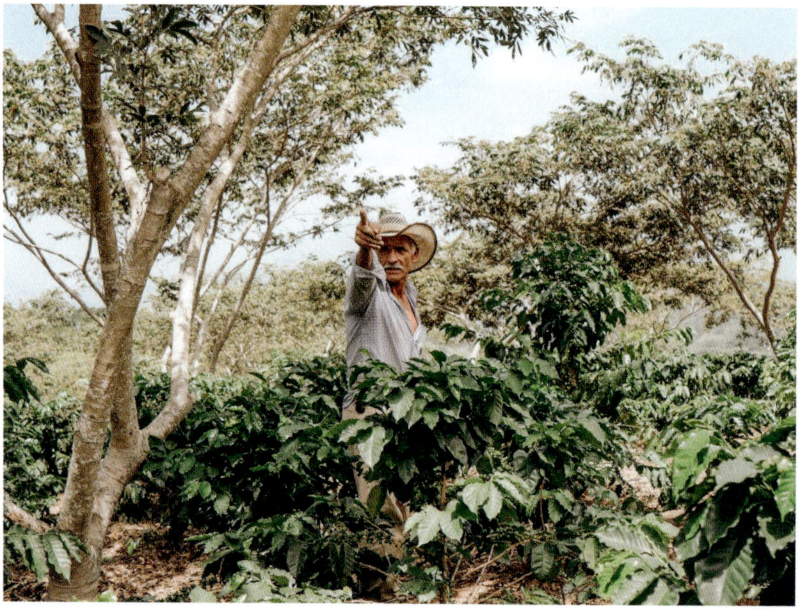

Kali Coffee Roasters didn't start off as a coffee shop, but as a response to an environmental, social and economic crisis that affected the entire coffee-growing area of Chiapas. The story goes back to 2014, when coffee leaf rust, a devastating fungus, destroyed over 95% of the coffee farms in the region, operated mainly by small producers of Tzeltal, Tzotzil and Chol origin. Local coffee experts and partners Maria Esther Saut and Pascual Castillo stepped in, giving away around 20 million coffee plants and endless support, and turning their own cattle ranch into a model coffee farm. Slowly but surely, they transformed the entire coffee chain, right up to the opening of eight cafés in Monterrey, including a flagship location in Vita Plaza. Designed by Mexican interdisciplinary studio Concéntrico, it comes clad in warm clay tiles that resemble coffee beans, a beautiful décor inspired by Chiapas' traditional construction techniques. Settle down with a *café del día* and a freshly baked cinnamon roll – available in classic, walnut, and Lotus options.

kalicoffee.com

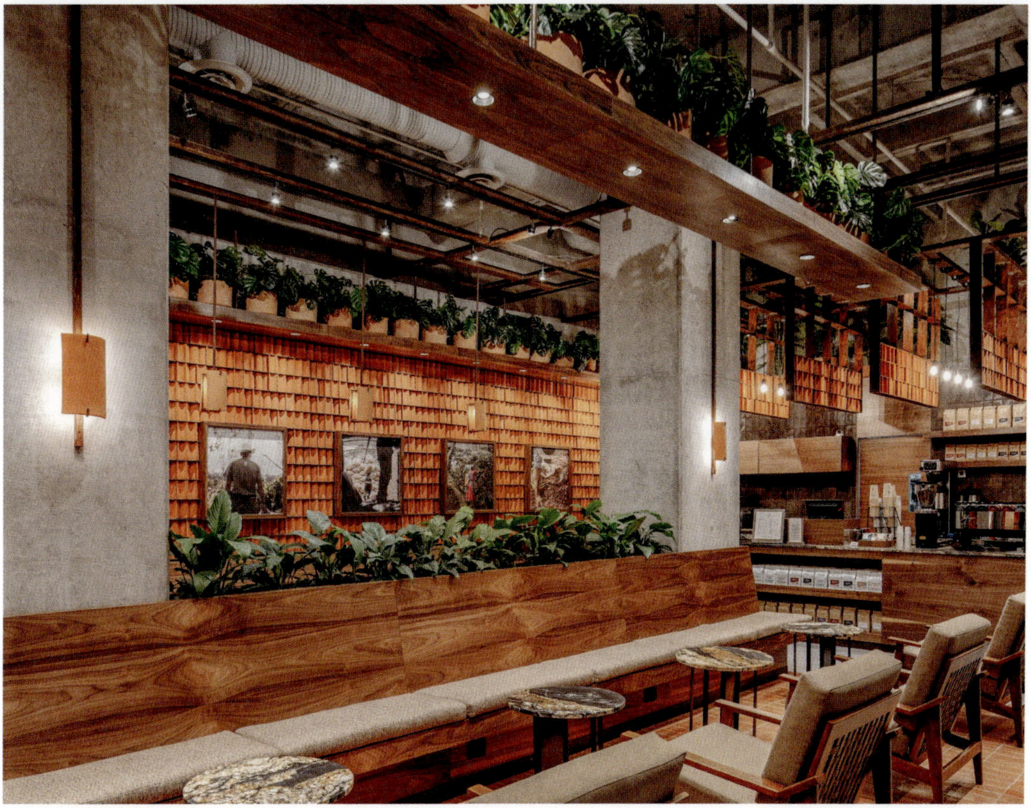

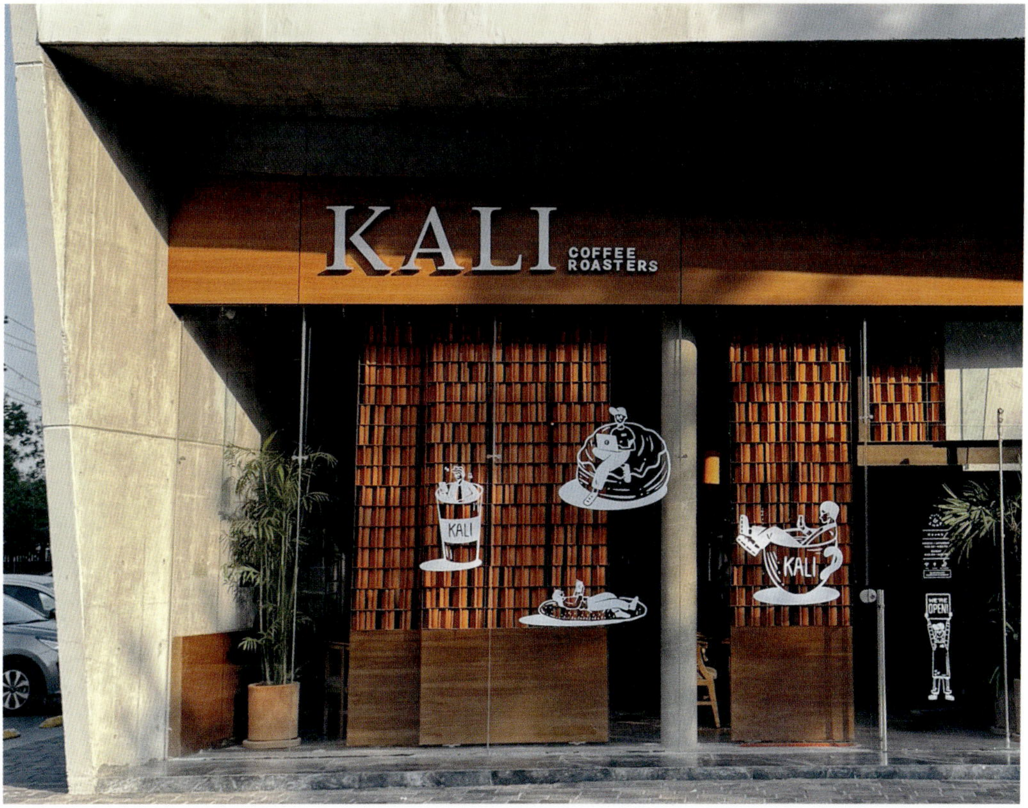
KALI
COFFEE
ROASTERS
KALI
KALI
WE'RE
OPEN!

31 CAFFETTIERA

2055 rue Stanley, Montreal, Quebec H3A1R7, Canada

TO VISIT
BEFORE YOU DIE
BECAUSE

This 1990s Italian-style stand-up bar serves only proper *caffè* – just follow the rules and you'll be fine.

This is one for the purists and for lovers of 1990s house music. You won't find any iced capps or French vanilla lattes here – as founder Andreas E. Vecchio makes clear, 'we serve only Italian coffee and do it right'. There's even a manifesto posted at the entrance, outlining a few non-negotiable principles, including: no sizes, no ice cubes, no café au lait, no Wi-Fi ('enjoy your beverage, look around, talk to a stranger') and also 'no tolerance for racism, sexism and ball-busting'. Don't worry, that doesn't mean no fun: you'll be bopping along to *La da dee la da da* in no time, relaxing and contemplating life with a proper coffee, maybe served with a spoon of Nutella. Designed by MRDK, the retro interiors feature a chequerboard inspired by Vans shoes and Rubik's Cube mirror frames. The coffee is equally impactful: 'Our coffee beans are roasted in Piacenza, Italy, and are 80% arabica, 20% robusta,' explains Andreas. 'We use 85mm grinder blades and brew the espresso with San Marco Piston machines.' Stay for a focaccia sandwich or an aperitivo with spritz.

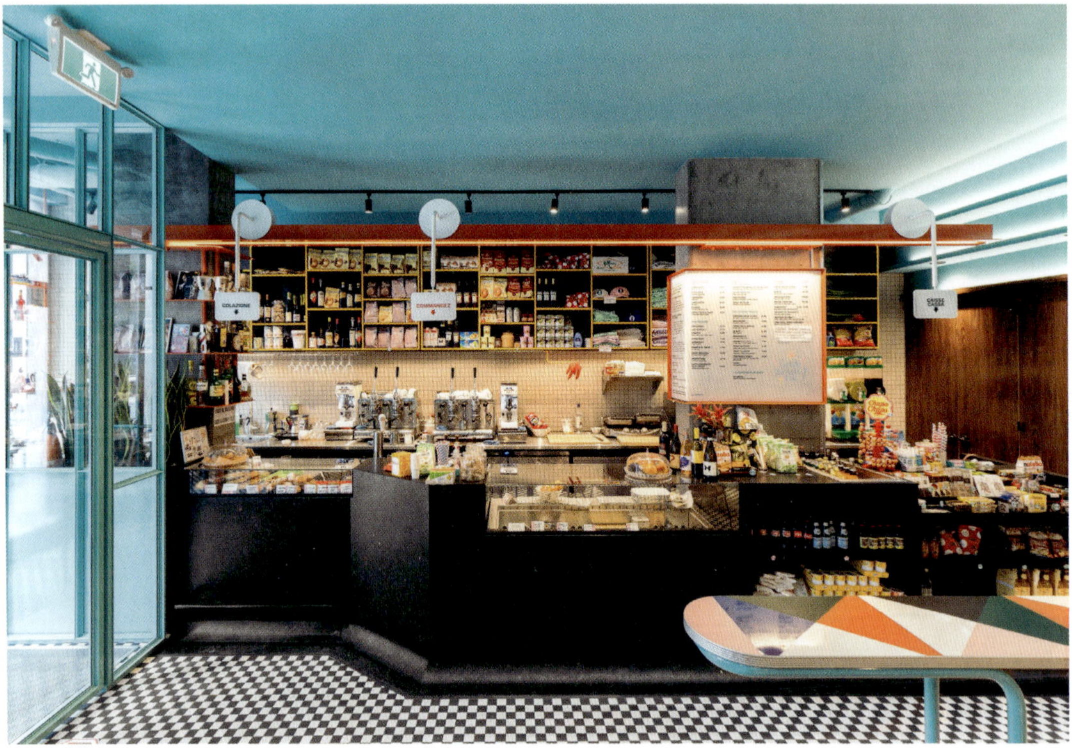

@caffettieracaffebar

+1 514 885 4419

32 CREMA COFFEE ROASTERS

226 Duke St, Nashville, Tennessee 37207, United States

TO VISIT
BEFORE YOU DIE
BECAUSE

Forget the country's ubiquitous drive-throughs and stop at the charming takeaway café of this Nashville zero-waste coffee roaster.

Crema Coffee Roasters was founded in 2008 by Rachel and Ben Lehman in downtown Nashville, but it's this location, a little takeaway café opened in 2019 in East Nashville's Talbot's Corner neighbourhood, that really stands out. Not only is it super cute, but it also offers the freshest coffee (the roastery is just at the back) and is run by one of the best and friendliest baristas in town, Mark Lemley. If you're in luck, you can grab one of the handful of seats inside; if not, the patio is the perfect spot for a morning coffee on a nice day. Choose from the full espresso menu or rotating seasonal speciality drinks including Crema's own take on the pumpkin latte, or try the very popular coffee soda (carbonated iced coffee with demerara sugar syrup, garnished with an orange peel) or a mocha with house-made Askinosie dark chocolate sauce. Pastries from Dozen Bakery complete the offering. Hungry for more? Crema Coffee Roasters are big on education; head downtown to try one of their coffee classes on mastering espressos, latte art or home-brew methods.

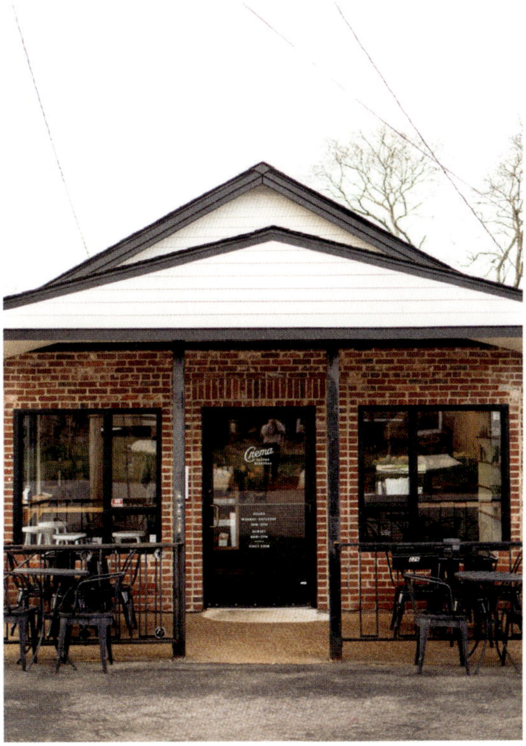

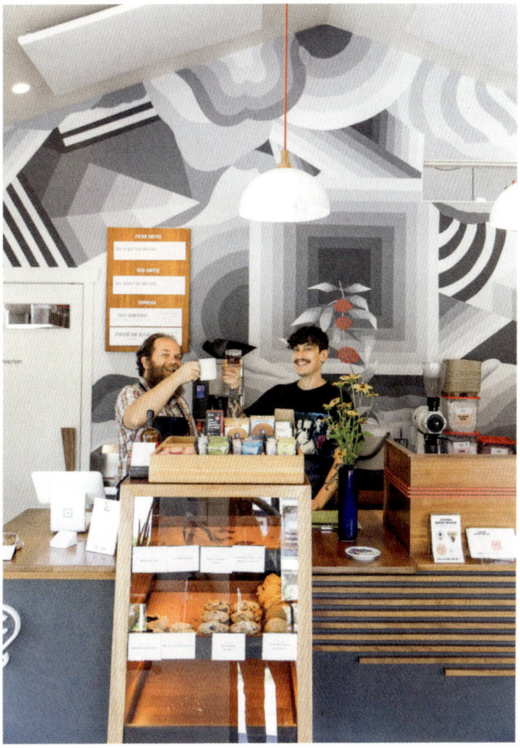

crema-coffee.com

+1 615 747 2001

33 CAFÉ DU MONDE

800 Decatur St, New Orleans, Louisiana 70116, United States

TO VISIT BEFORE YOU DIE BECAUSE

New Orleans' original French Market coffee stand has been selling square beignets and chicory-flavoured café au lait since 1862.

If you're heading to this New Orleans institution, perhaps don't wear a black top. For one, it won't match the city's vibrant colour palette, and two, there's every chance you'll spill icing sugar all over yourself while enjoying the house speciality, beignets, served with a generous dusting of the white powder. Ordered with a cup of chicory coffee, the fritters are the main attraction at Café du Monde. Established in 1862 in the French Market, and owned by the Fernandez family since the 1940s, the café has been open all year round ever since – apart from Christmas Day, and the occasional hurricane. Its roots lie in the French heritage of the Acadians who brought these specialities and many other customs with them when they took refuge in Louisiana in the late 18th century. Chicory (the root of the endive plant) was once used as a cheap coffee alternative and is still popular in France to this day. Café du Monde's blend is four-part dark roasted coffee and one-part chicory, and is traditionally served au lait, mixed half and half with hot milk.

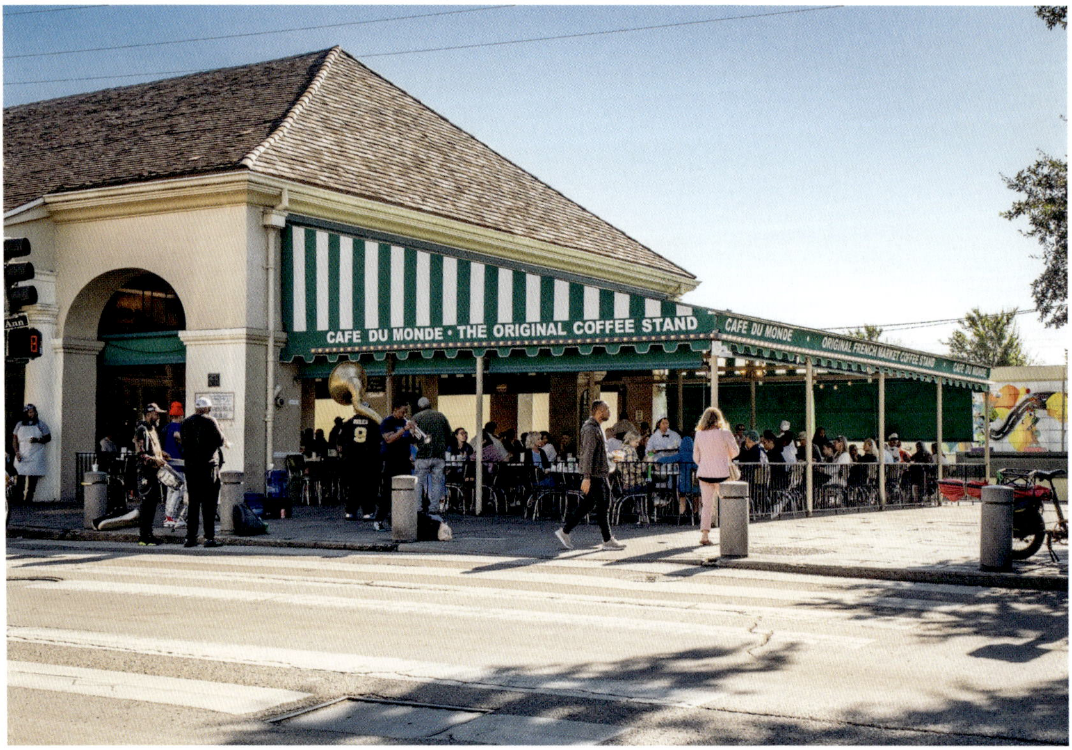

shop.cafedumonde.com

+1 504 587 0833

34 COFFEE PROJECT NEW YORK

239 E 5th St, New York, New York 10003, United States

TO VISIT BEFORE YOU DIE BECAUSE

Try seasonal specials and concept drinks such as the deconstructed latte at this East Village passion project, first opened in 2015.

Awarded *TimeOut New York*'s 'Most Loved Coffee Shop' on three separate occasions, Coffee Project New York has become a stalwart of the city's coffee scene. It was founded by Chi Sum Ngai and Kaleena Teoh, who quit their jobs to open this tiny, cosy place with exposed brick walls and marble-top tables. On a mission to improve the quality of life for every person in the coffee supply chain, from producers to consumers, they've created an expansive menu featuring award-winning farms, niche varieties, experimental processes and women producers. Warm and inviting, the East Village café is the ideal spot to try the house's famous deconstructed latte, a tray with a glass of sparkling water, espresso, milk and latte, plus a cookie. 'It is meant to guide new coffee tasters through the tasting process, using side-by-side flavour comparison to build tasting skills,' explains the team. And it's also delicious, of course. The company's HQ is actually in Long Island City, where they've opened a roastery and academy offering public tasting sessions, events and courses.

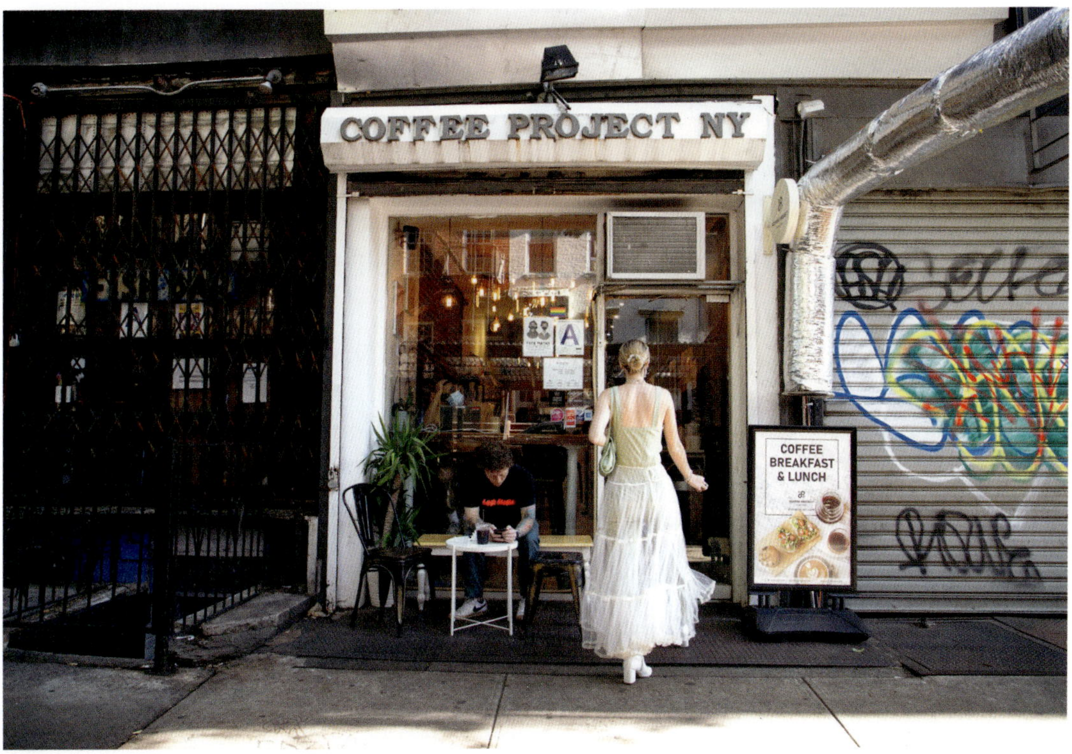

coffeeprojectny.com +1 212 228 7888

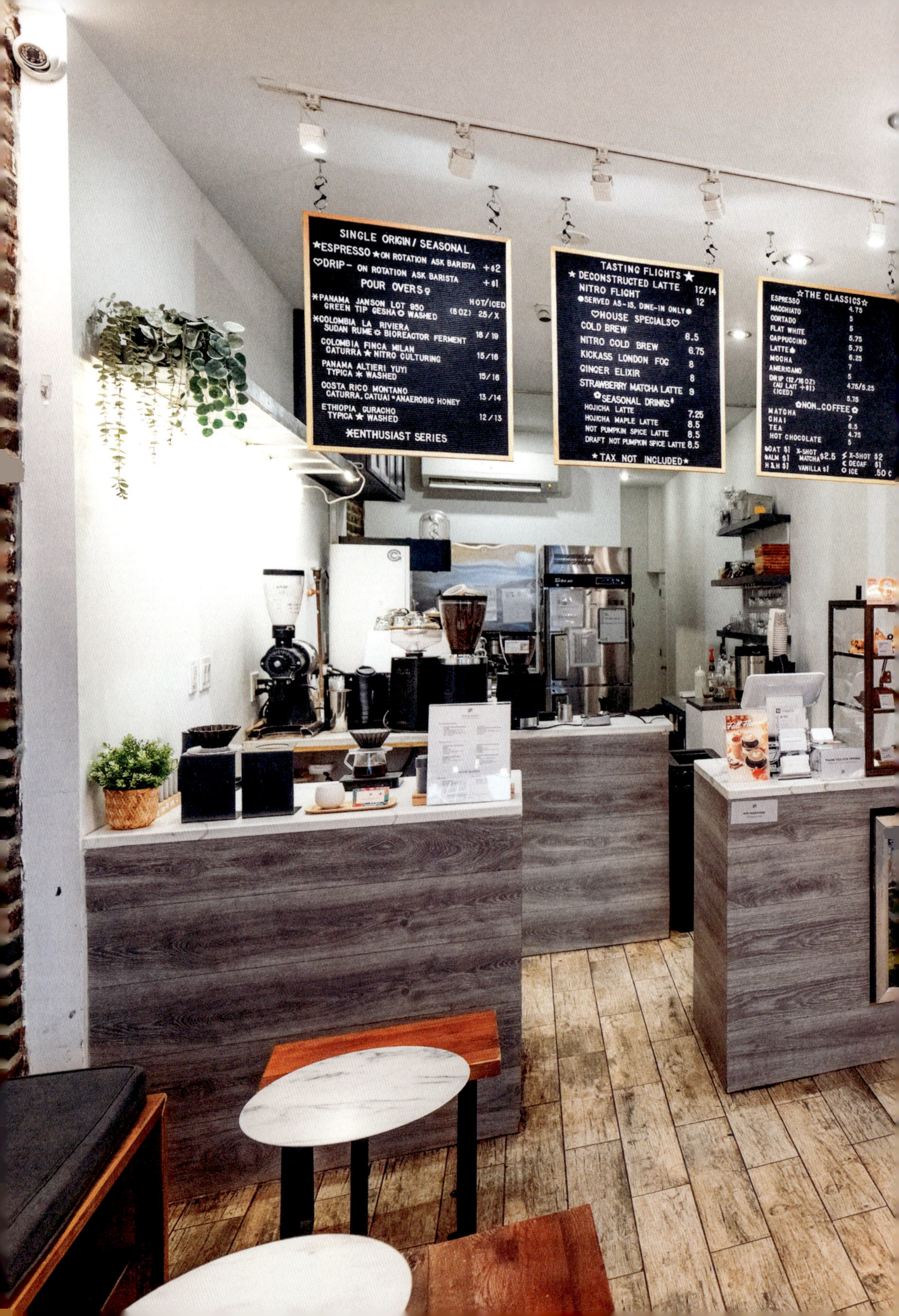
SINGLE ORIGIN/ SEASONAL
*ESPRESSO *ON ROTATION ASK BARISTA +$2
DRIP - ON ROTATION ASK BARISTA +$1
POUR OVERS
*PANAMA JANSON LOT 850 GREEN TIP GESHA WASHED HOT/ICED (8OZ) 25/X
*COLOMBIA LA RIVIERA SUDAN RUME BIOREACTOR FERMENT 18/19
COLOMBIA FINCA MILAN CATURRA * NITRO CULTURING 15/16
PANAMA ALTIERI YUYI TYPICA * WASHED 15/16
COSTA RICO MONTANO CATURRA, CATUAI * ANAEROBIC HONEY 13/14
ETHIOPIA GURACHO TYPICA * WASHED 12/13
*ENTHUSIAST SERIES
TASTING FLIGHTS
* DECONSTRUCTED LATTE 12/14
NITRO FLIGHT 12
SERVED AS-IS, DINE-IN ONLY
HOUSE SPECIALS
COLD BREW 8.5
NITRO COLD BREW 6.75
KICKASS LONDON FOG 8
GINGER ELIXIR 8
STRAWBERRY MATCHA LATTE 9
SEASONAL DRINKS
HOJICHA LATTE 7.25
HOJICHA MAPLE LATTE 8.5
NOT PUMPKIN SPICE LATTE 8.5
DRAFT NOT PUMPKIN SPICE LATTE 8.5
* TAX NOT INCLUDED *
THE CLASSICS
ESPRESSO 4.75
MACCHIATO 5
CORTADO 5
FLAT WHITE 5.75
CAPPUCCINO 5.75
LATTE 6.25
MOCHA 7
AMERICANO 5
DRIP (12/16 OZ) (AU LAIT +$1) 4.75/5.25
(ICED) 5.75
NON_COFFEE
MATCHA 7
CHAI 6.5
TEA 4.75
HOT CHOCOLATE 5
OAT $1 X-SHOT MATCHA $2.5 X-SHOT $2
ALM $1 DECAF $1
H&H $1 VANILLA $1 ICE .50¢

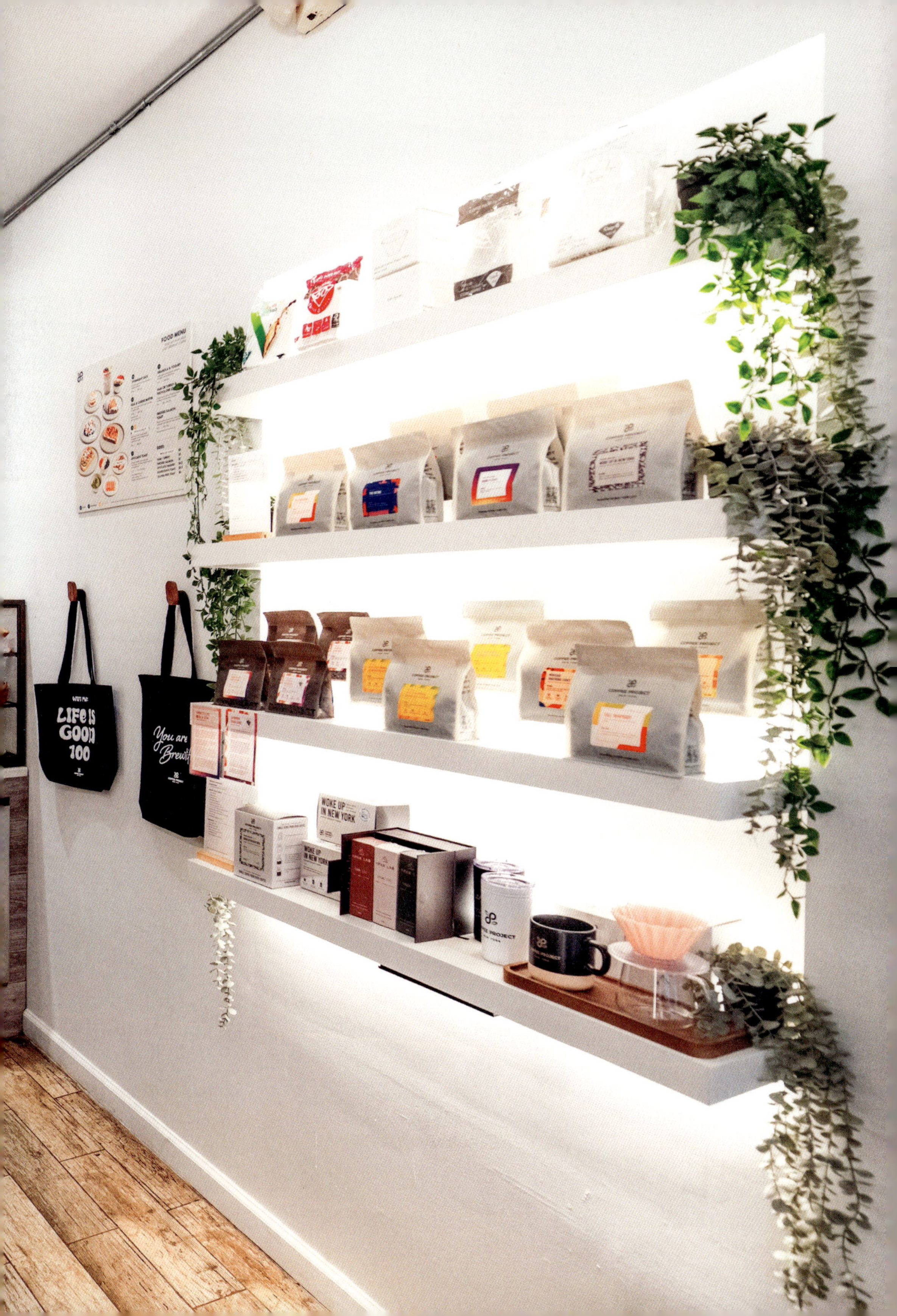
FOOD MENU
LIFE IS GOOD 100
WOKE UP IN NEW YORK

35 SUITED

45 John St, New York, New York 10038, United States

TO VISIT BEFORE YOU DIE BECAUSE

Wear your finest three-piece suit to enjoy tailor-made coffee and snacks at this unique café in New York's historic financial district.

Coffee expert Andrew Fazio and chef Wilson Johnson opened Suited in 2020 near Fulton Street as a tribute to their dads. Respectively an Italian-born tailor, and an artist and craftsman, both fathers are known for their one-of-a-kind creations and attention to all the finer details. That approach is key to Suited, an elevated café experience showcasing beans from the likes of Sey in Brooklyn, Prodigal in Colorado, Apollon's Gold in Tokyo (page 134) and SubText in Canada. The team 'prides itself on always having their hand on the pulse of this niche market', so you will be sure to get all the latest good stuff here. Your drink will be served in gorgeous cups by local ceramicist Yuko Nishikawa, or in a takeaway cup adorned with a single white tie logo – we told you they were perfectionists. Even better is the awesome service, and the fact that you can pair your *cawfee* with an egg sandwich or a maple doughnut. To keep everyone at the top of their game, Suited has also started hosting some events, including latte art competitions and barista throwdowns.

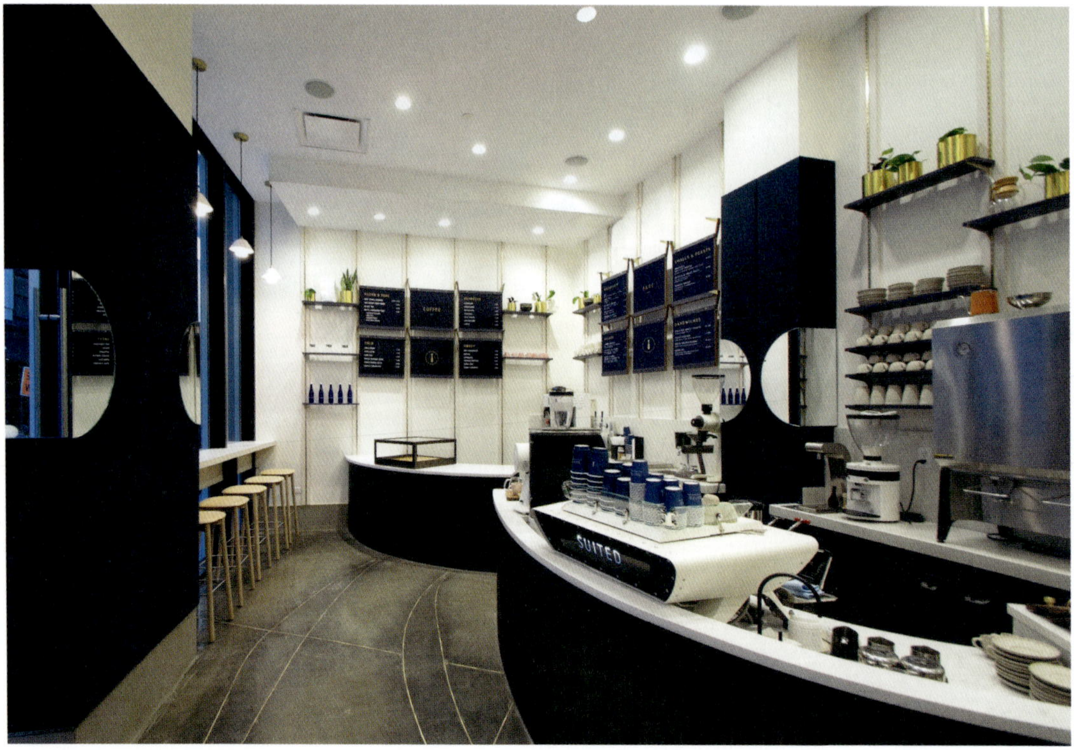

suitednyc.com

36 CASA SUCRE

Calle 8 y Ave. B, Calle 8a Oeste, Casco Viejo, Panama

TO VISIT BEFORE YOU DIE BECAUSE

Learn all about Panama's famed geisha coffee at this welcoming old-school café in the capital's historic Casco Viejo district.

Its name might be French for sugar, but this place is all about Panama and its amazing coffee. Opened in 2013 by Californian couple Rich and Alyce Sherman in a beautifully restored colonial building dating back to 1873 (when the French were trying to build the Panama Canal), Casa Sucre is a cosy spot with a relaxed vibe, ideal for sampling the country's best coffees. Come for breakfast and feast on a fruit platter and tamales, before savouring a cup of geisha, a rare coffee prized for its unique flavour profile of floral and sweet notes. The Shermans are keen to share their appreciation for the high-quality, locally sourced coffee, from growers including Café de la Luna, Finca Hartmann and Abu Geisha. 'The quality of our coffee makes our espresso shots, macchiato, latte, cappuccino and drip coffee a memorable experience,' says Rich. 'Try our Yama slow-drip ice coffee with our blend of geisha and pacamara coffee beans, and don't hesitate to ask our baristas for recommendations!'

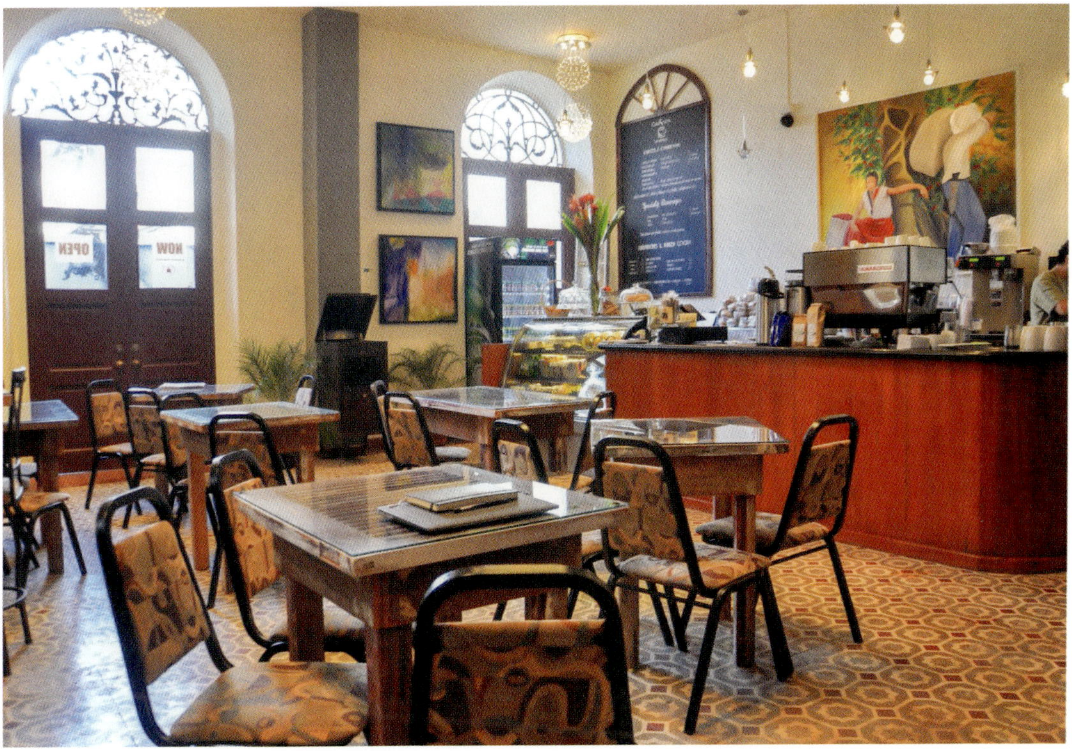

37 KEEPER COFFEE

4515 SE 41st Ave, Portland, Oregon 97202, United States

TO VISIT BEFORE YOU DIE BECAUSE

A home from home welcoming everyone with great service, homemade bakes and community vibes.

'Keeper Coffee is built on friendship, community and good coffee,' says founder Brittany Huff, who grew up in her family's delis in New York before taking a first job in coffee in Baltimore at age 14. 'We source incredible beans from Coava, a Portland roaster who is committed to long-term, sustainable partnerships with coffee producers. Everything made to eat comes from the Keeper kitchen (and hearts).' Expect vintage vibes, wonderful latte art (the bear design is a hit with the little ones), and delicious pastries and cakes made by the in-house baking team. There are seasonal specials such as a Christmassy peppermint mocha with house-made marshmallows, as well as inventive toppings – you can add the likes of coconut cream, pumpkin pie or tiramisu cold foam to your favourite coffee order. Keeper has recently launched its first coffee with Antonio Medina, from Guatemala. It boasts 'a rich and balanced profile with tasting notes of orange zest, graham cracker and baker's chocolate'. A second branch opened in Milwaukie in 2025.

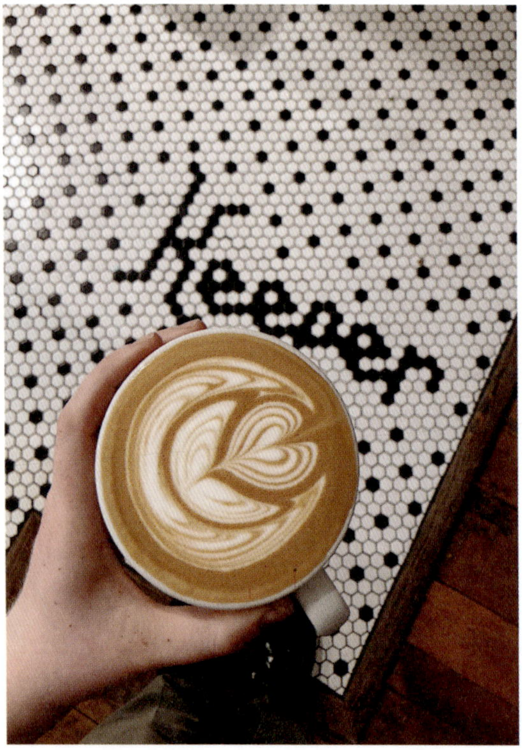

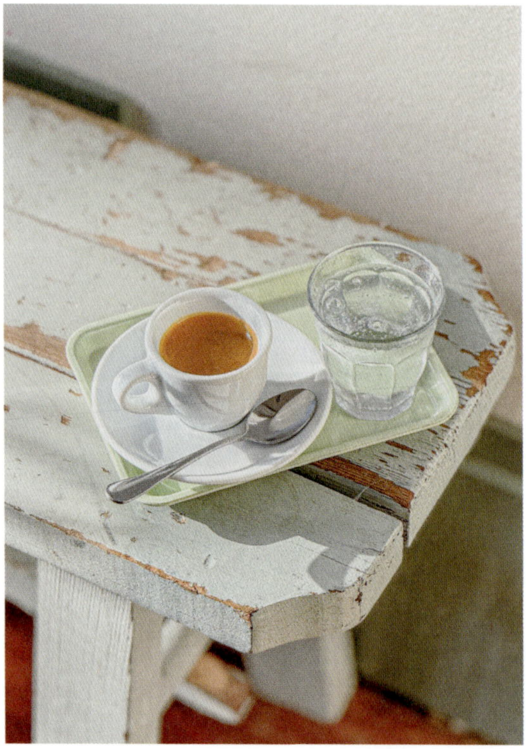

keepercoffee.com

+1 503 891 5828

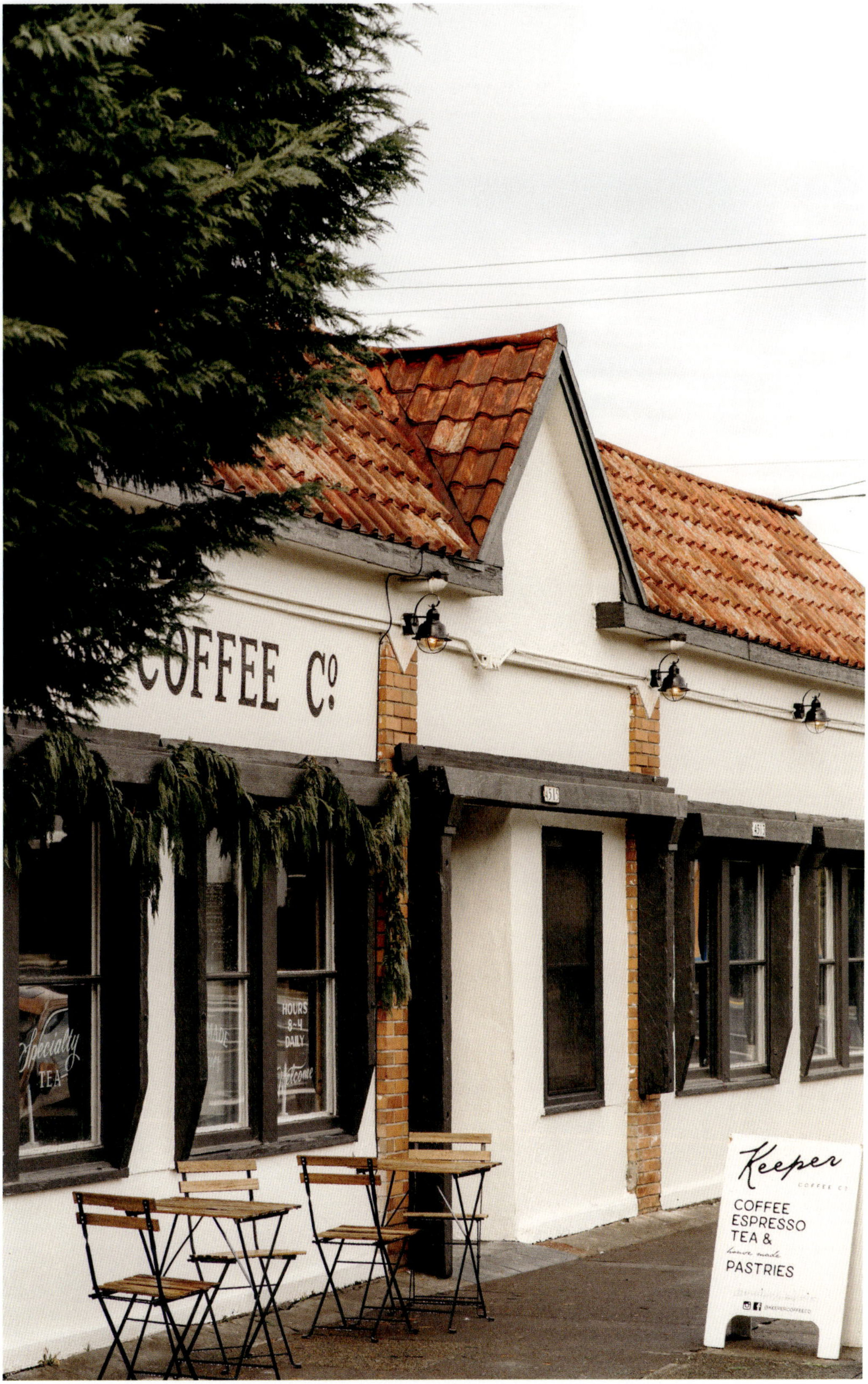
COFFEE C^o
HOURS
8-4
DAILY
Welcome
Specialty
TEA
Keeper
COFFEE CO
COFFEE
ESPRESSO
TEA &
house made
PASTRIES

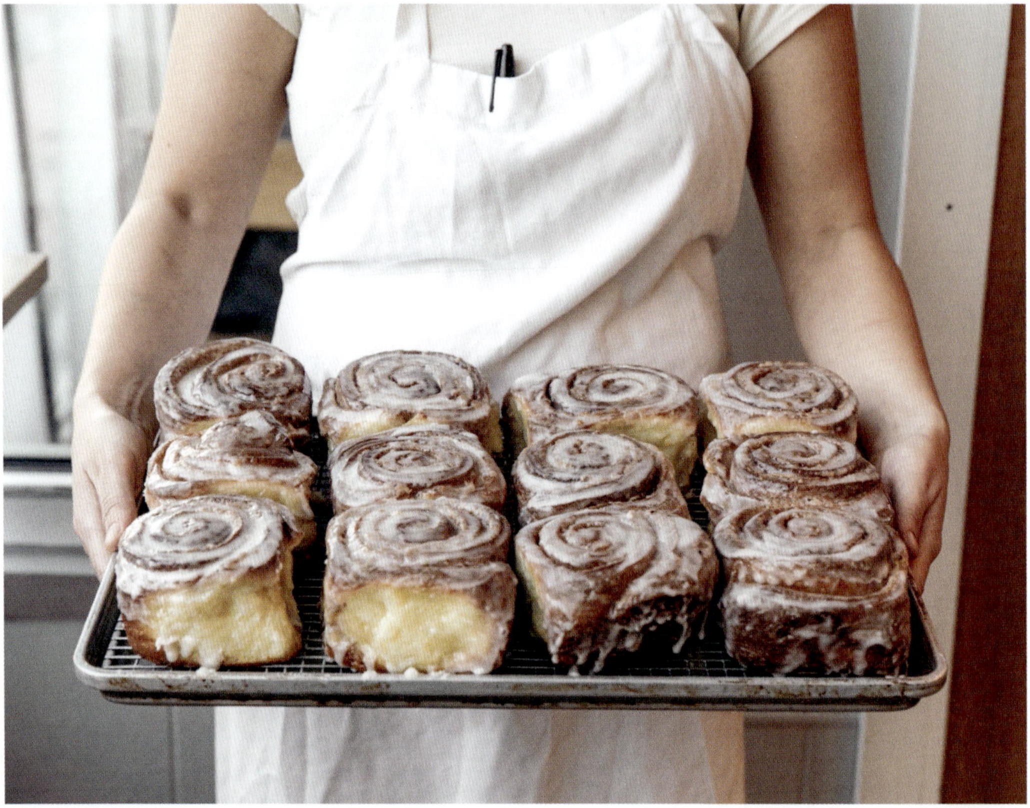

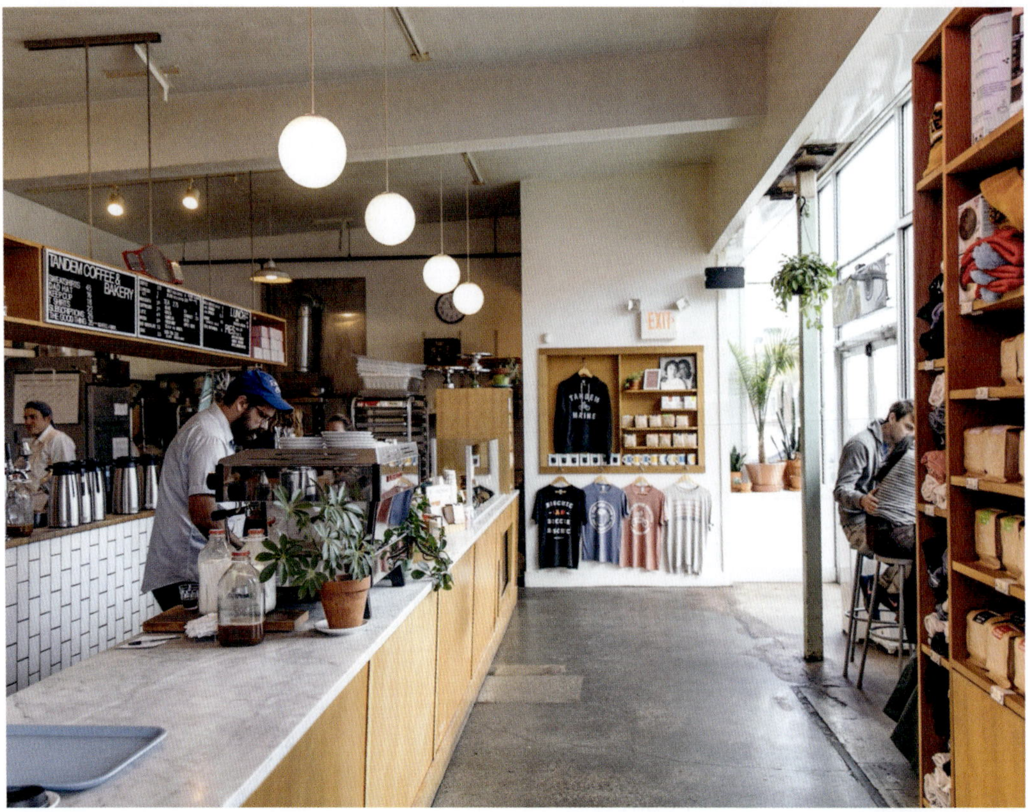
TANDEM COFFEE &
BAKERY
SWEATSHIRTS
DAD HAT
KEEPCUP
T-SHIRTS
SUBSCRIPTIONS
THE GOOD THING
LUNCH
PIES
EXIT
TANDEM
MAINE

38 TANDEM COFFEE + BAKERY

742 Congress St, Portland, Maine 04102, United States

TO VISIT BEFORE YOU DIE BECAUSE

As Tandem demonstrates, two is better than one, especially when that means a double whammy of outstanding coffee and cakes.

Let's be honest: for many of us, a cup of coffee is an excuse to eat a sweet treat. You pop in for a cappuccino, and then, inexplicably, end up with a lovely slice of apple pie on your table. Well, consider yourself warned: that sort of thing might well happen to you at Tandem Coffee + Bakery, the second location of a company launched in 2012 in Portland, Maine, by talented duo Will and Kathleen Pratt. Housed in a converted 1960s petrol station, it offers the best of both worlds – excellent coffee *and* cakes. The first category includes carefully sourced, immensely respected single-origin coffees and seasonal blends such as Time & Temperature (Guatemala and Ethiopia), while the second comes courtesy of long-time friend Briana Holt, a born baker and James Beard nominee. There's a perfect type of coffee to go with all her creations, which range from the classic (buttermilk biscuit or apple cider scone) to the adventurous (kimchi-cheddar scone) and the frankly decadent (raspberry-Campari custard pie). If it's too busy, try their East Bayside café and roastery.

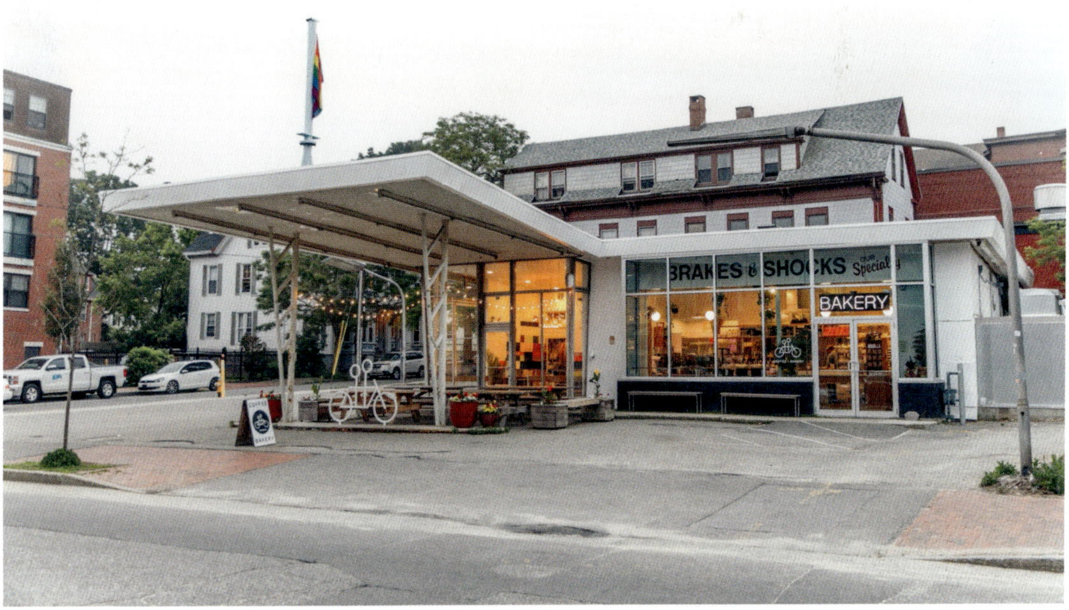

tandemcoffee.com

+1 207 760 4440

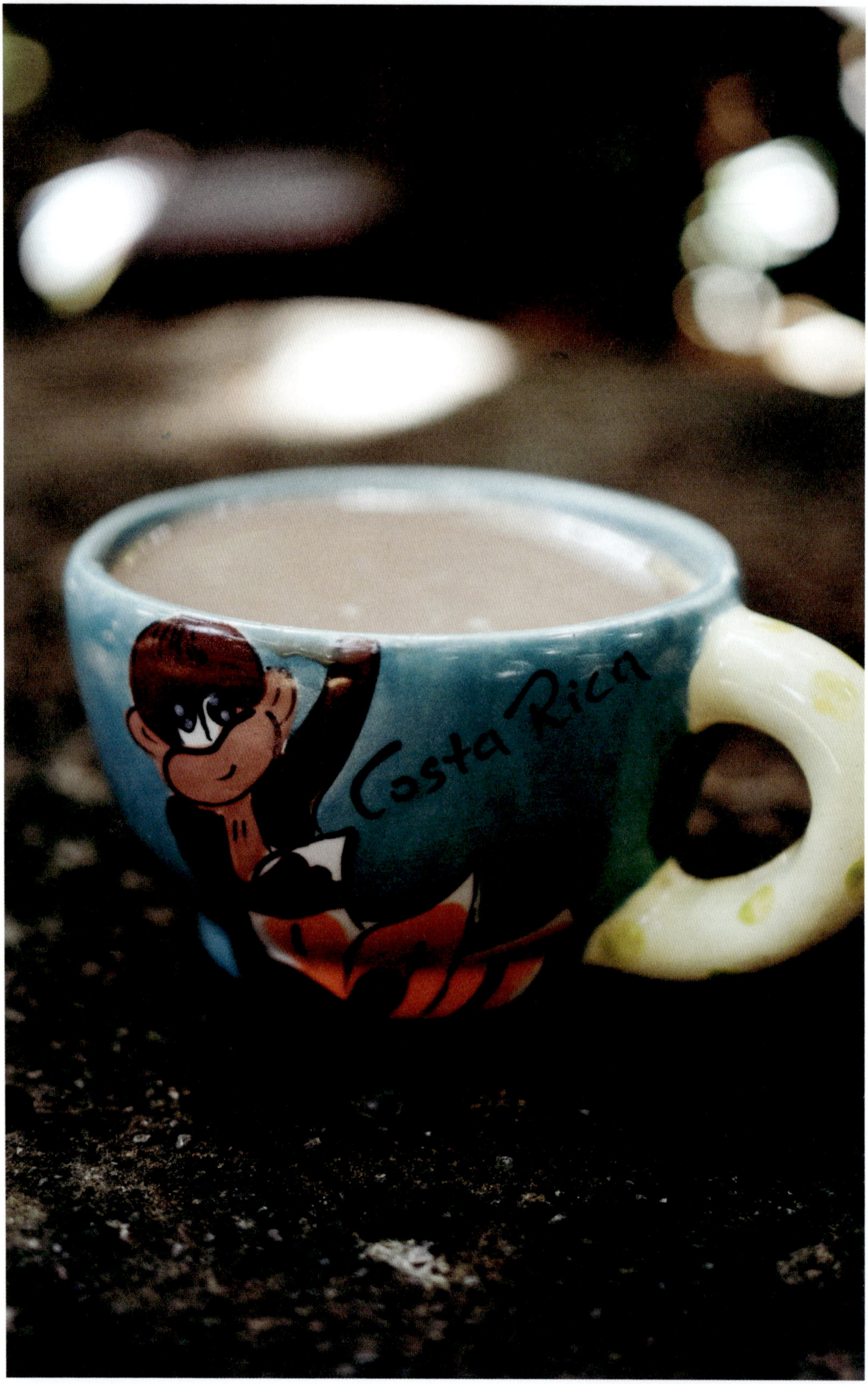
Costa Rica

39 CAFÉ RICO

Av. 69, Limón, Puerto Viejo de Talamanca, Costa Rica

TO VISIT
BEFORE YOU DIE
BECAUSE

Escape the hustle and bustle at this lush garden café serving award-winning breakfasts, second-hand books and carefully roasted local beans.

In Costa Rica, the phrase *pura vida* (pure life) is both a greeting and the national motto, symbolising the carefree, optimistic lifestyle of the Ticos. And nothing embodies this laid-back positivity more than this garden café surrounded by tropical vegetation. Here, green Costa Rican coffee beans are roasted in-house in small batches and served in handcrafted cups made by local artisans. 'Our Tarrazu beans are roasted at multiple temperatures to create a broad depth of flavour. This process brings out the best in every bean, highlighting subtle notes that range from nutty and chocolatey to bright and fruity,' says the team. 'Our iced coffees are chilled with cubes made from brewed espresso, so your drink stays bold and never diluted – a rare treat in Puerto Viejo!' Other highlights include huge breakfast plates such as the Ana Rosa, with crispy potatoes, ham, avocado and fried egg; the chance to browse the largest library and book exchange in town; and a clever laundry service that means you can relax with a coffee while your clothes are being cleaned.

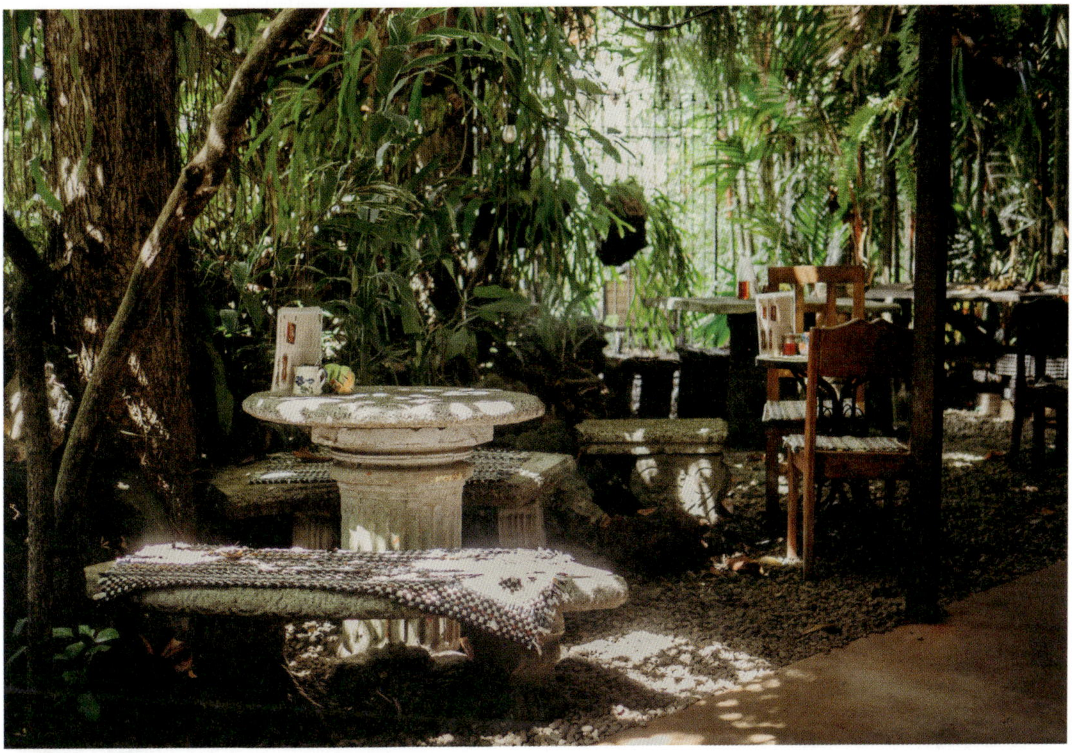

 cometocaferico.com +506 2750 0510

40 CAFÉ SAN ALBERTO TERRACE

Cra. 2, Buenavista, Quindío, Colombia

TO VISIT BEFORE YOU DIE BECAUSE

Discover 'the magic behind Colombia's most award-winning coffee' at this family-run coffee farm at the heart of the country's coffee axis.

Founded in Colombia's Quindío Valley in the 1970s, the San Alberto coffee plantation has kept growing ever since, garnering plenty of awards for its high-quality coffee along the way. Today it is managed by brothers Gustavo and Juan Pablo Villota, who were inspired by the elegant tasting rooms, hotels and restaurants opened by wineries all around the world, to launch their own café in 2009. A great idea, perfectly executed: the café offers jaw-dropping views of the valley, the small town of Buenavista and coffee farm, and is staffed by passionate baristas happy to share their knowledge of the house's coffee, praised for its luscious, sweet aromatic notes, reminiscent of caramel and mellow dark chocolate. After enjoying a farm tour, sit on the large terrace and enjoy beans brewed at the table (Chemex, Siphon, Coffee Press or Dripper) or an espresso made using the bar's Marzocco Linea. Other highlights include the ice mochaccino, carajillo (hot coffee with a shot of Amaretto), and the very unusual, ice-cold *fretta acervezada* – a mix of coffee and beer.

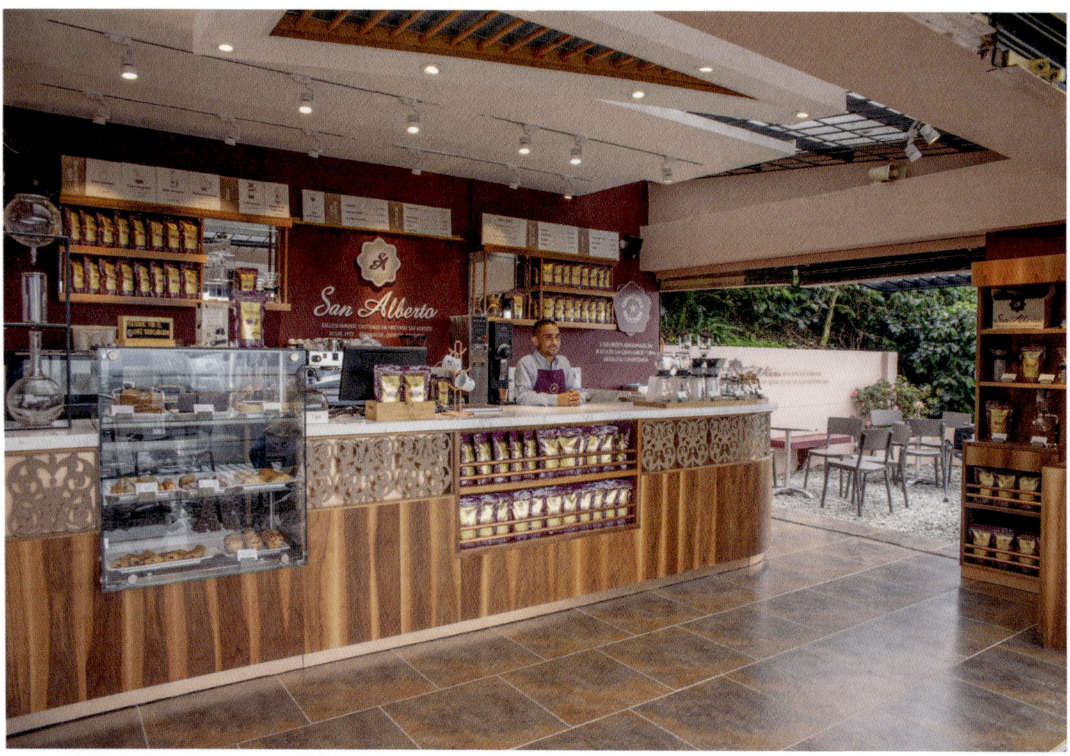

cafesanalbertoint.com +57 316 827 1421

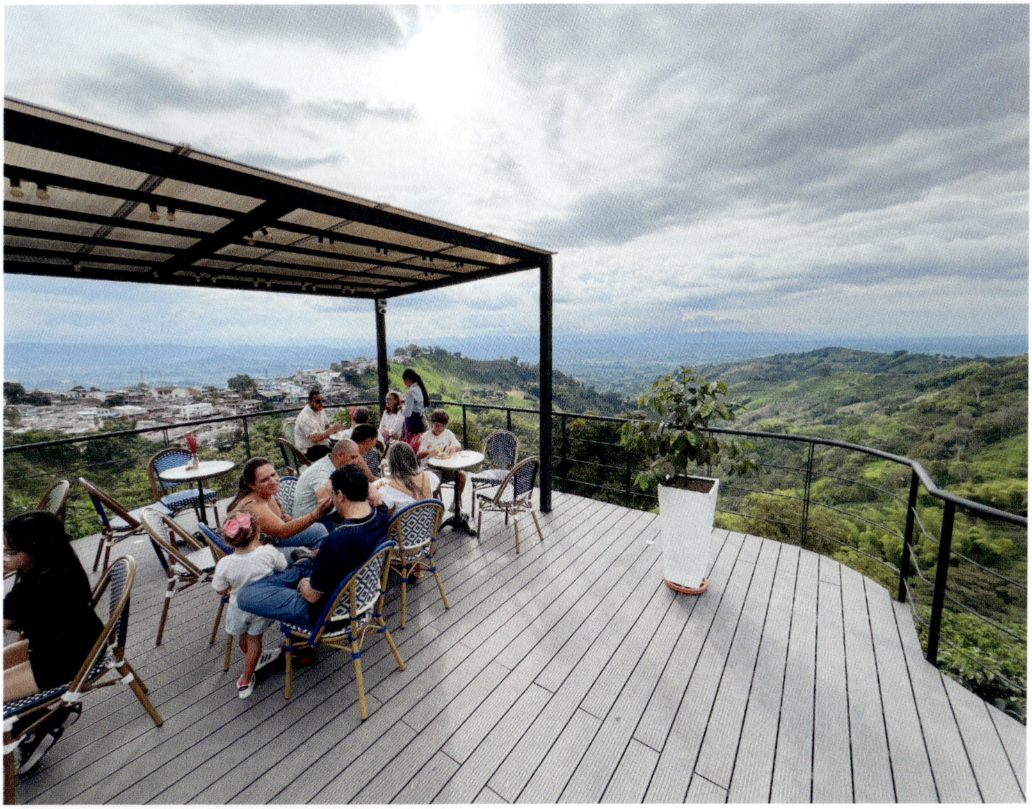

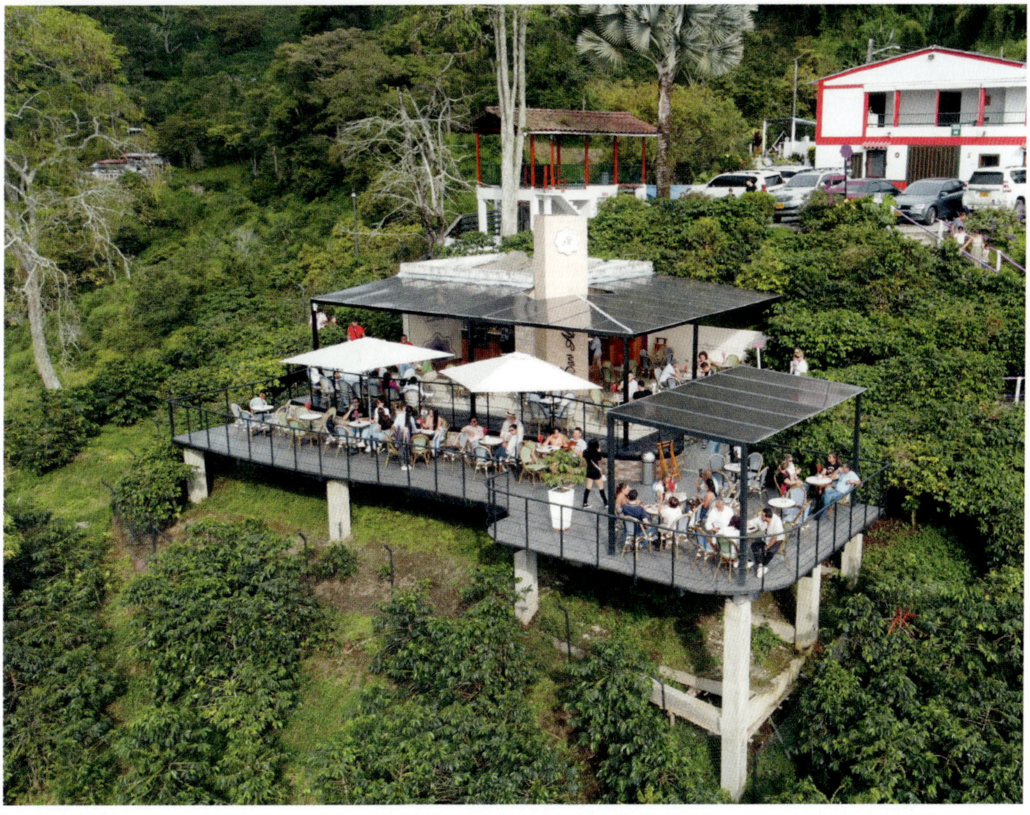

41 CONFEITARIA COLOMBO

R. Gonçalves Dias, 32, Centro, Rio de Janeiro, Rio de Janeiro 20050-030, Brazil

TO VISIT BEFORE YOU DIE BECAUSE

Enjoy a taste of Rio's glamorous past along with Portuguese and Brazilian pastries at this landmark coffee house.

While Brazil is the world's largest coffee producer, locals here mostly like to keep it simple and affordable with *cafezinho* – a small, strong black coffee enjoyed throughout the day. There is, however, a famous place in the old town of Rio where the precious brew becomes a special occasion: Confeitaria Colombo. At this historic coffee house, you can sit under a stained-glass skylight and enjoy a cup of Colombo cappuccino, made with beans sourced from the best plantations in Brazil, and served with whipped cream and cinnamon. Built in 1894 by two Portuguese immigrants inspired by European cafés and French Belle Époque style, and renovated in 1912 with art nouveau elements, the oval dining room is full of original features, from the patterned floor tiles and Belgian mirrors to the Brazilian rosewood furniture. Come hungry: it's famous for its pastel de nata (Portuguese custard tartlets), Brigadeiro (Brazilian chocolate truffles) and the house's speciality, a walnut tartlet sprinkled with cashew nuts and served with ice cream and caramel sauce.

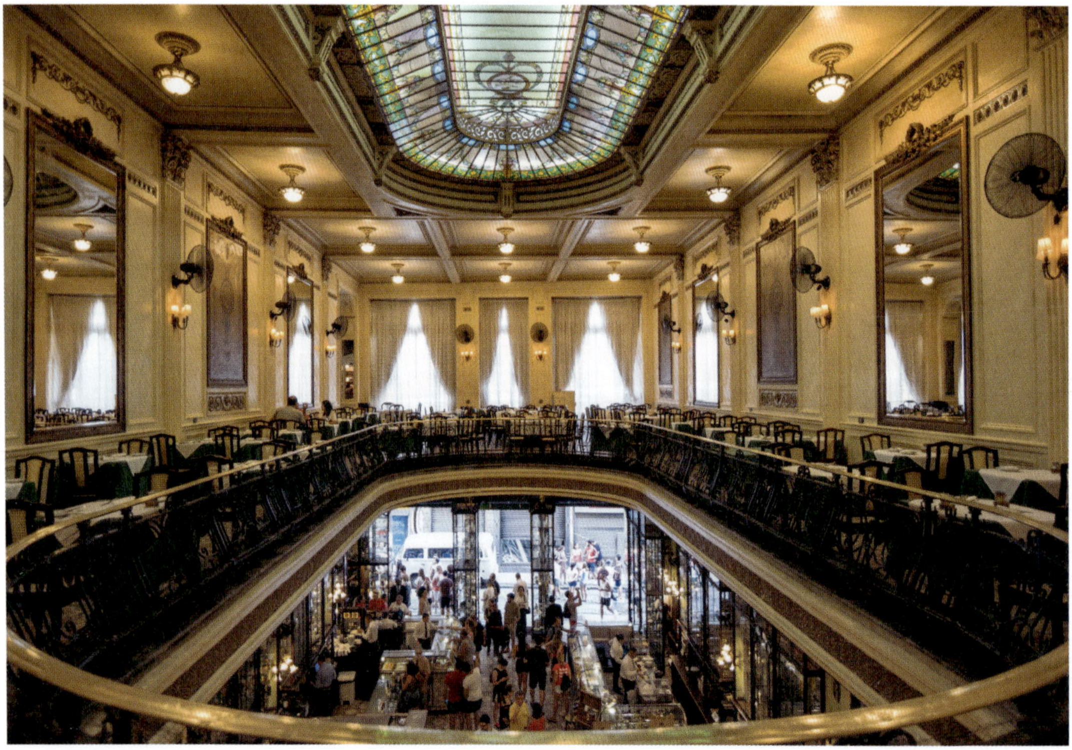

confeitariacolombo.com.br

42 ONYX COFFEE LAB

101 E Walnut Ave, Rogers, Arkansas 72756, United States

TO VISIT BEFORE YOU DIE BECAUSE

Visit the cosy HQ of a small coffee roaster gone big by 'seeking quality, truth and accountability in coffee'.

A small city in Arkansas, Rogers has one big claim to fame: it is the birthplace of retail giant Walmart. But to coffee lovers, it is better known as the hometown of Onyx Coffee Lab, from which delicious speciality beans are dispatched all around the country. Founded by Jon and Andrea Allen in 2012, the solar-powered roaster has become known for the quality of its coffees, including all-time favourite Geometry, an Ethiopian and Colombian blend – 'our answer for everything,' they say. Also remarkable is the focus on transparency – all the information on the coffees, including origin, roaster model, pricing and trade data, is available on its website. Located in a historic brick building in downtown Rogers, Onyx's HQ comprises the roastery, a barista training lab, and this beautifully designed café and bakery. Sample the Onyx Delight (espresso with honey, cinnamon, vanilla and milk), a pour-over including Kibingo Estate (Kenya) or Nestor Lasso (Colombia), or try a seasonal special such as a black sesame maple shaken espresso or a fig citrus nitro tonic.

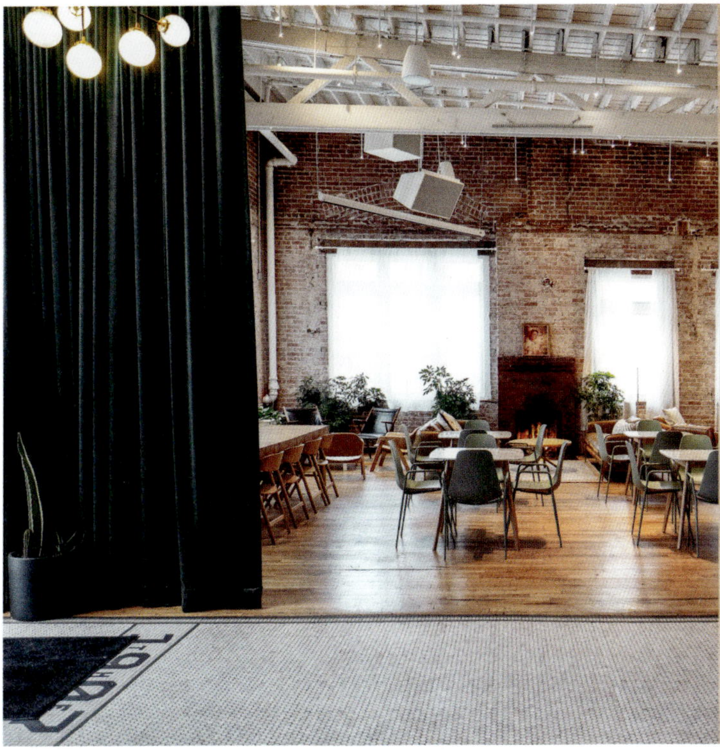

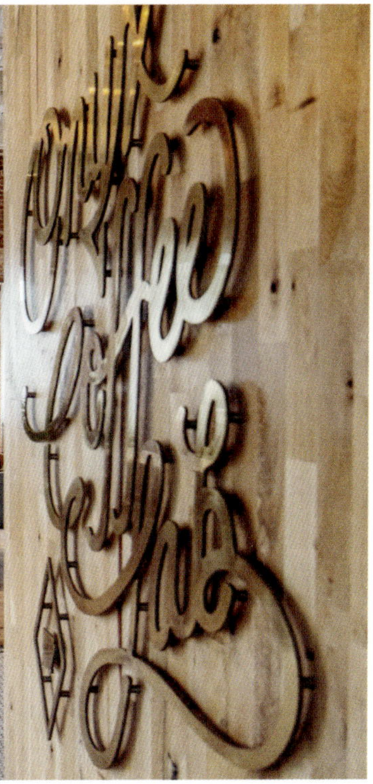

onyxcoffeelab.com

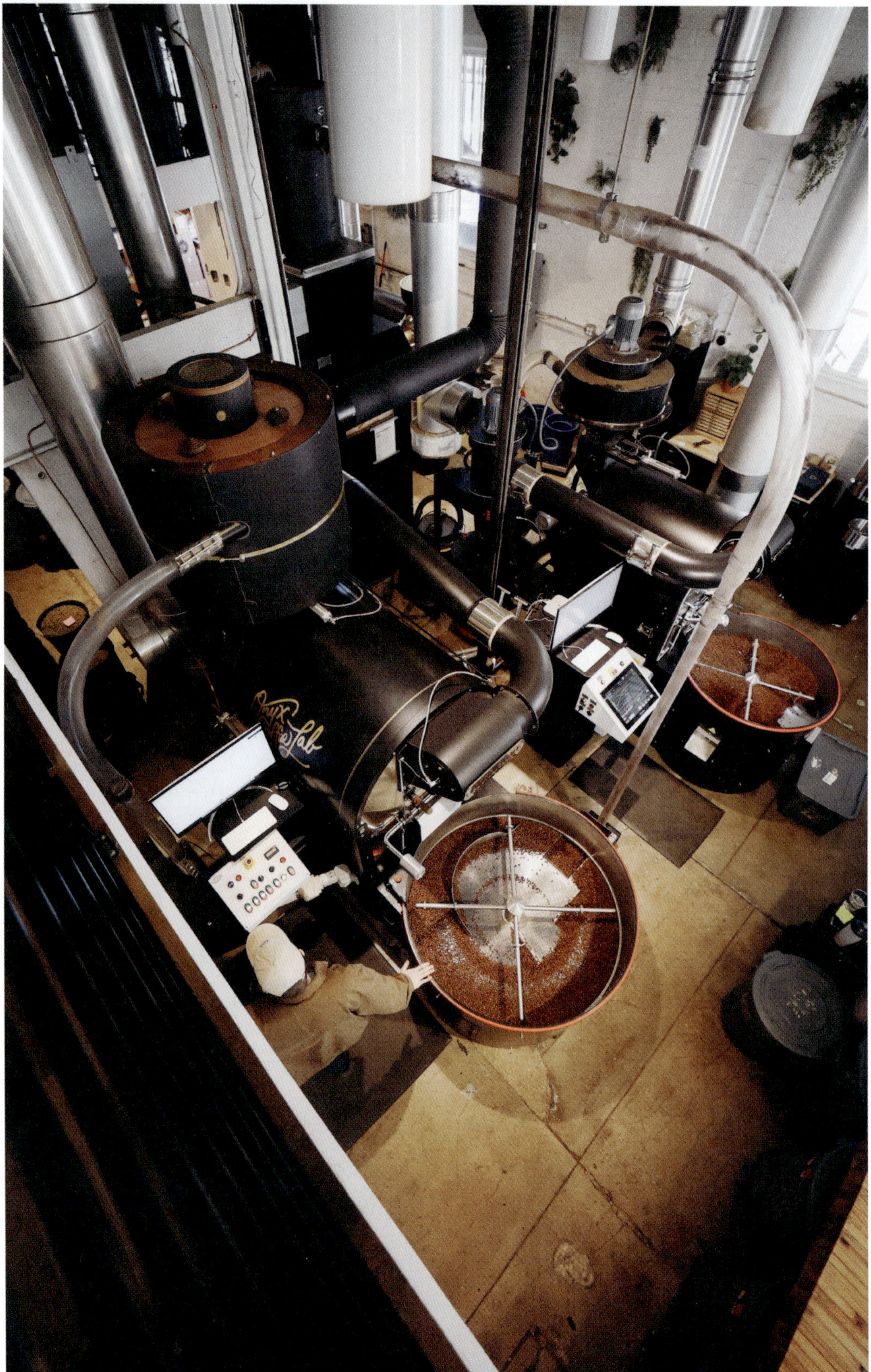

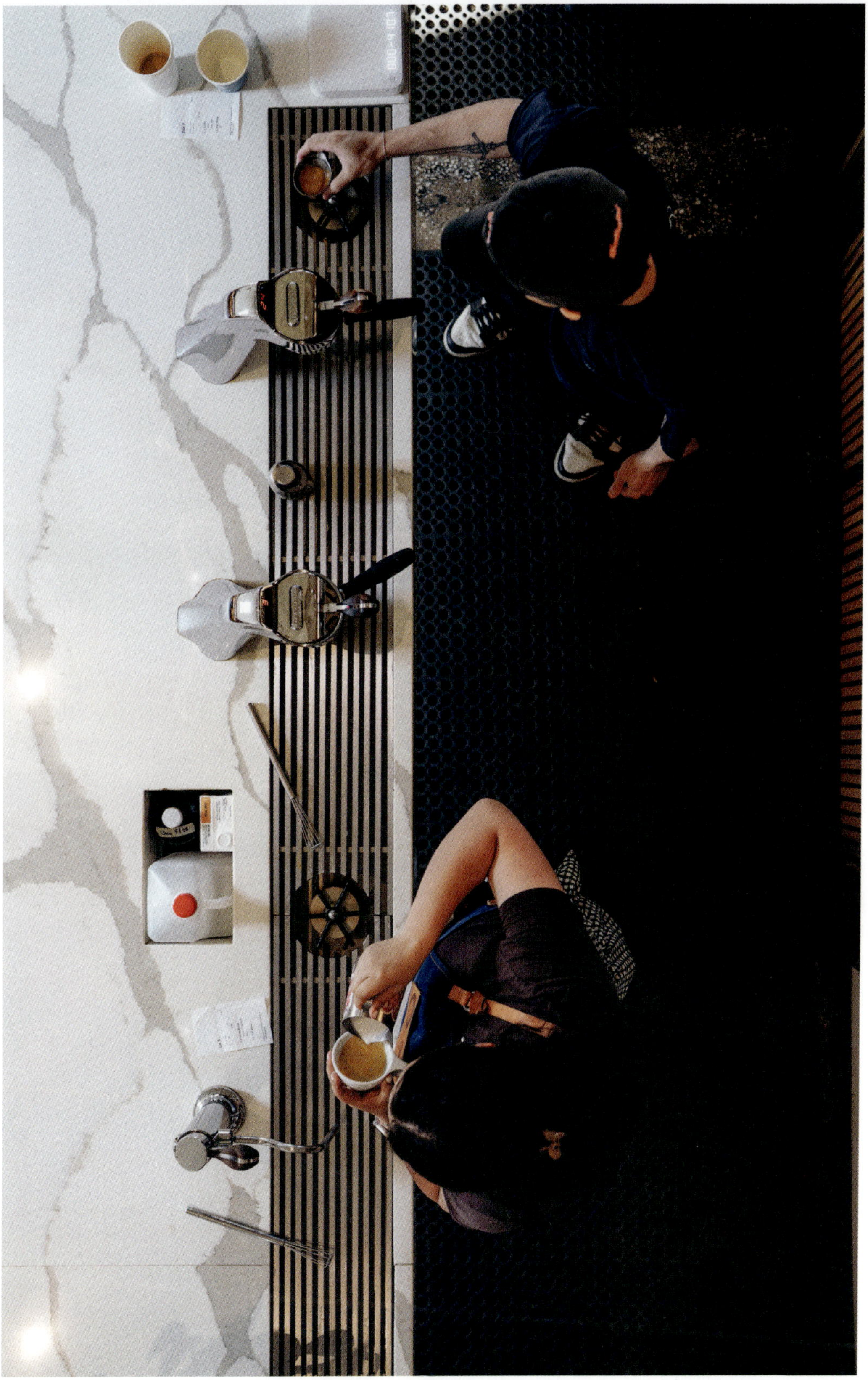

43 CAFFÈ TRIESTE

601 Vallejo St, San Francisco, California 94133, United States

TO VISIT
BEFORE YOU DIE
BECAUSE

A hub for poets and musicians opened in 1956, this is the first ever espresso coffee house established on the West Coast.

On a hilltop in San Francisco's Little Italy, North Beach, is a storied red-and-green coffee shop where Francis Ford Coppola wrote much of the screenplay for *The Godfather*, and Jack Kerouac, Allen Ginsberg and their beatnik friends were once regulars. Named in homage to the capital of northern Italy and its great coffee houses, Caffè Trieste was opened by Italian immigrant 'Papa Gianni' Giotta in 1956 and helped popularise the espresso in the region before starring in countless Hollywood films and shows. Its Saturday music sessions are the stuff of legend, with the entire family, including 'Mamma Ida', known to join the singalongs. But it is the drink that proved key to its success. 'No big deal,' Papa Gianni would say when asked about his coffee. 'Buy the best beans, roast them yourself, and brew each cup like it's for you.' Today you can enjoy a double espresso con panna and a couple of biscotti in what is still an atmospheric space with walls lined with fading photographs. As you'd expect, it's cash only.

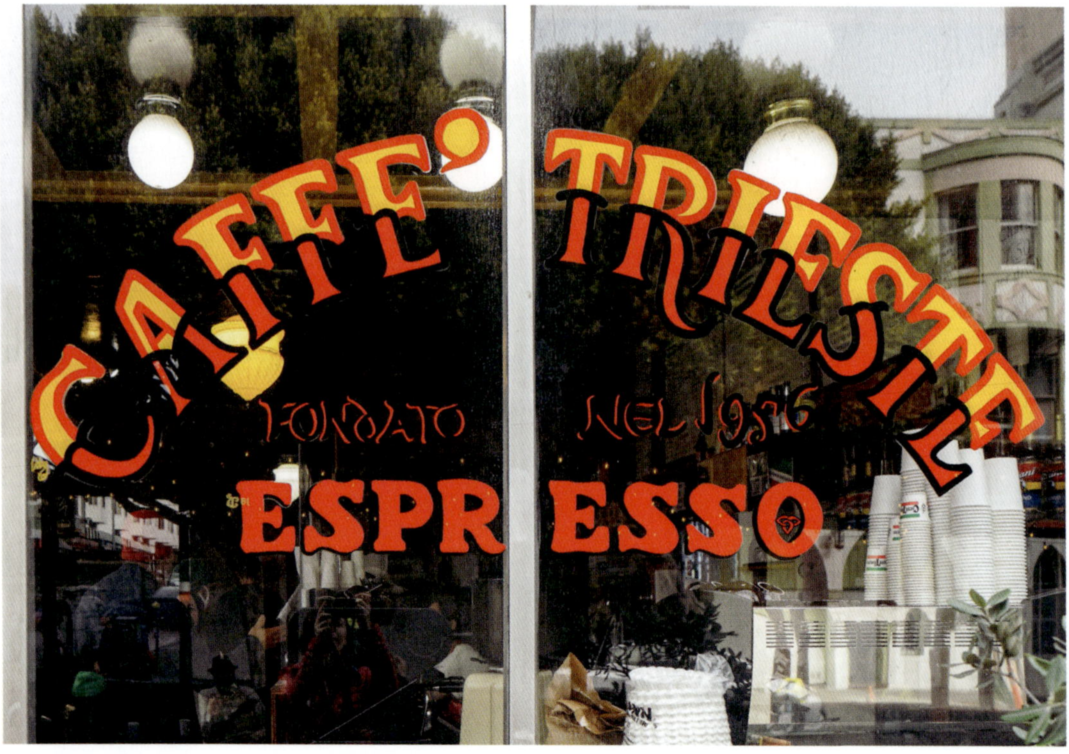

caffetrieste.com +1 415 392 6739

44 RITUAL COFFEE ROASTERS

1026 Valencia St, San Francisco, California 94110, United States

TO VISIT BEFORE YOU DIE BECAUSE

Soak up some San Francisco vibes at the flagship café of a local, fully independent and woman-owned coffee roasting company.

A shot of espresso can change your life. That's exactly what happened to Eileen Rinaldi at pioneering Seattle café Espresso Vivace (whose co-owner David Schomer is credited with introducing latte art to North America). After a cup of Vivace's dark elixir, she 'knew right then what she must do: open a shop, dedicated solely to coffee, in her favourite city'. And that's exactly what she did, founding Ritual in an old furniture shop in 2005. San Francisco was ready for it; by day 3, there was already a queue around the corner. With a relationship-based sourcing model since 2006, the little coffee shop and roastery has stayed on top of innovation and kept true to its core values of kindness, inclusivity and fun. Its Valencia café has pioneered V60 pour-overs, and 'caffeinated more than a few artists, writers and start-up entrepreneurs on their way to the next big thing'. The drinks menu includes seasonal or single-origin espressos showcasing blends such as Florescence and growers such as Burundi's Incuti, as well as specials such as Day Off in Kyoto, a hojicha and vanilla bean latte.

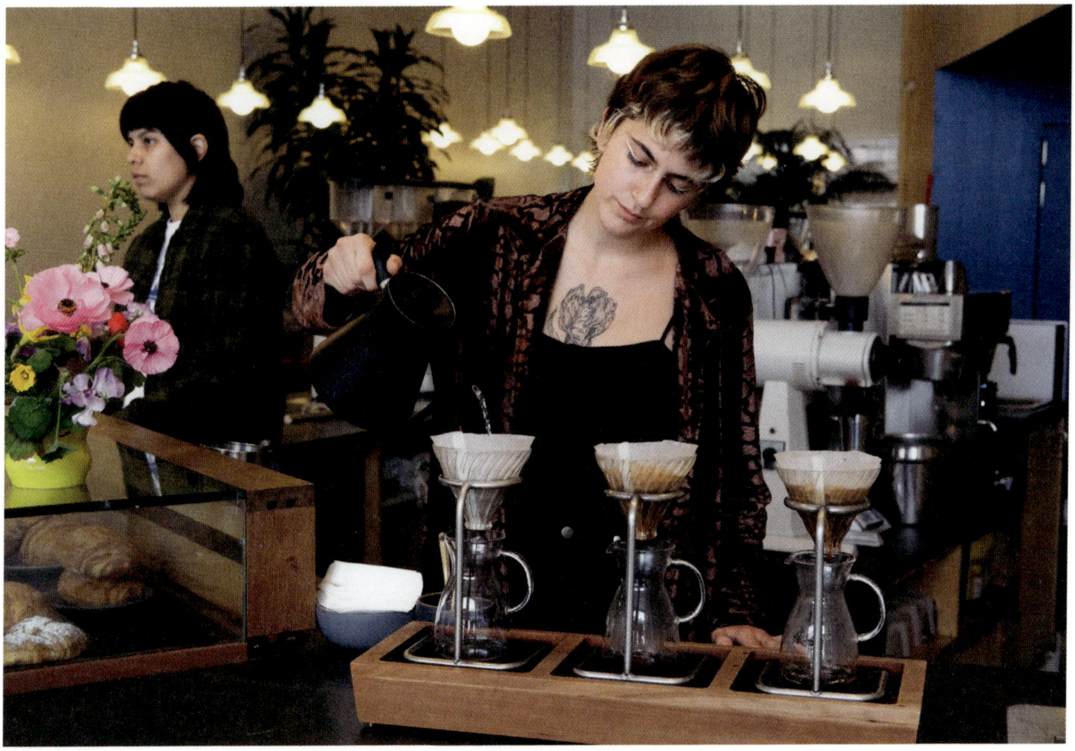

ritualcoffee.com @ritualcoffee +1 415 641 1011

45 CAFÉ LA MANCHA

Avenidas central y primera, C. 1, San José Province, San José, El Carmen, 10101, Costa Rica

TO VISIT BEFORE YOU DIE BECAUSE

Try a fresh cascara drink with a side of live jazz music and art exhibitions at this speciality coffee shop that is also a creative and cultural space.

San José's historic Steinvorth building, opened in the early 1900s by German immigrants as a commercial warehouse selling imported goods, is now a unique space home to half a dozen small businesses arranged around a large iron structure. When Alberto Font visited the landmark building in 2015 as part of his job as a photojournalist, it was love at first sight. Inspired, he decided to leave his photography career behind and dedicate himself to his long-time passion: speciality coffee. 'We roast coffee weekly and aim to create a warm community atmosphere where art, books and conversations blend with great coffee,' says Alberto. Working closely with small, family-run coffee producers from rural areas, the café is known for its signature cascara tea, 'a refreshing drink made from the coffee cherry husk with a hint of local lemon – a form of upcycling that adds value to a byproduct often discarded in coffee production'. There are many coffee flights to choose from, including one with filter coffee, espresso and a Henry Blend mocktail with cold brew and cascara.

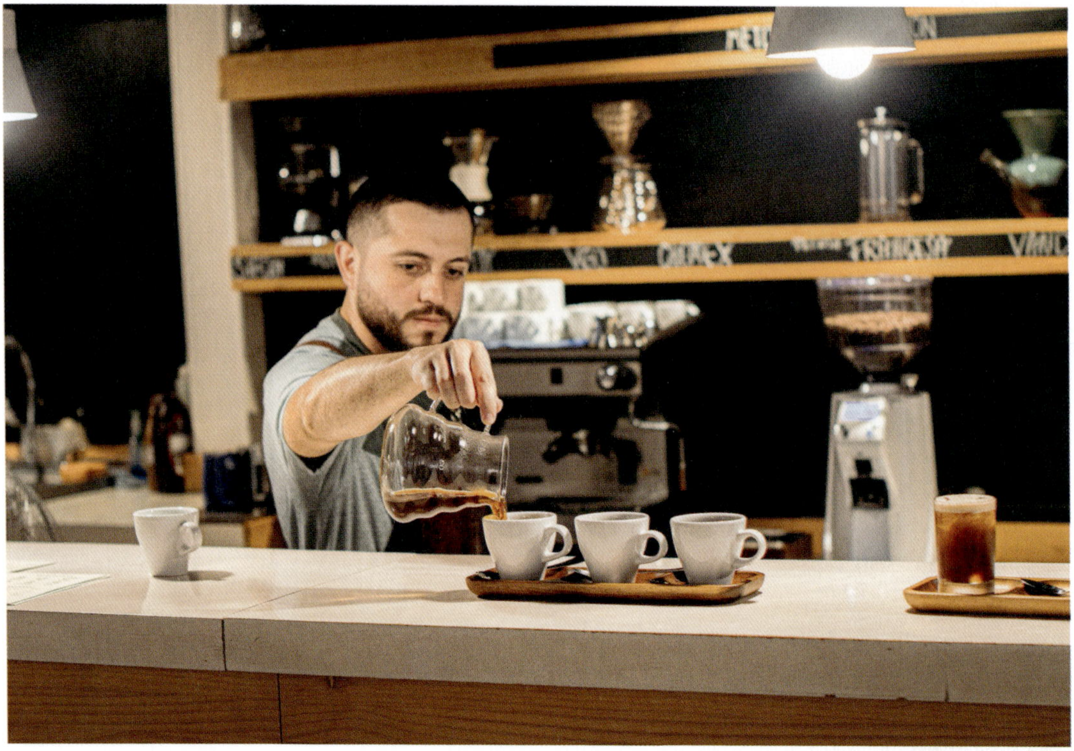

@cafe_lamancha +506 2221 5591

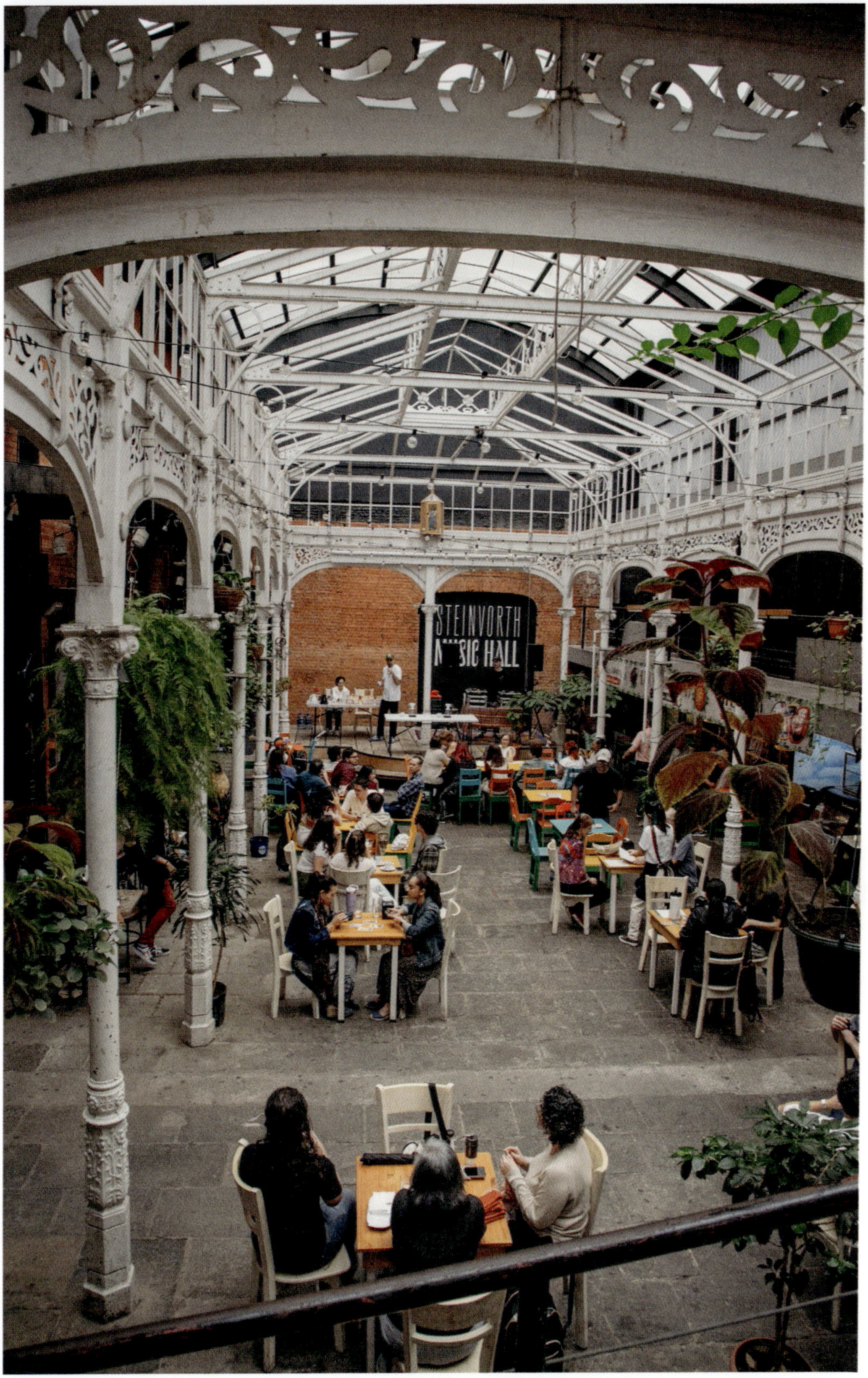
STEINVORTH
MUSIC HALL

46 UM CAFÉ

R. Julio Conceição, 553, São Paulo, Brazil

TO VISIT BEFORE YOU DIE BECAUSE

Enjoy some of the country's finest and rarest beans at this contemporary café, opened by a family of coffee lovers.

The Um family's association with coffee started in 2002 when patriarch Stefano Um acquired a coffee farm in the south of Minas Gerais. Focusing on quality and innovation, he soon transmitted his passion to his sons Boram (World Barista Champion 2023) and Garam (Brazilian Brewers Cup Champion 2023). Quite a journey for someone who immigrated from South Korea in the 1970s with his parents, and had no links to the coffee industry – just pure curiosity and drive. The Ums' Bom Retiro café is one of the few places in the city serving top-quality coffee (the best beans are usually exported, although this has started to change recently). Its menu includes 'nanolots' of rare and unique beans, including a Pink Bourbon with notes of jasmine, mandarin and wild honey, which you can pair with a full menu ranging from salads to cheesecake and orange brioche. The Ums also run a coffee academy, or you can find out more about Brazil's complicated history with coffee at the Museo del Café in the nearby town of Santos.

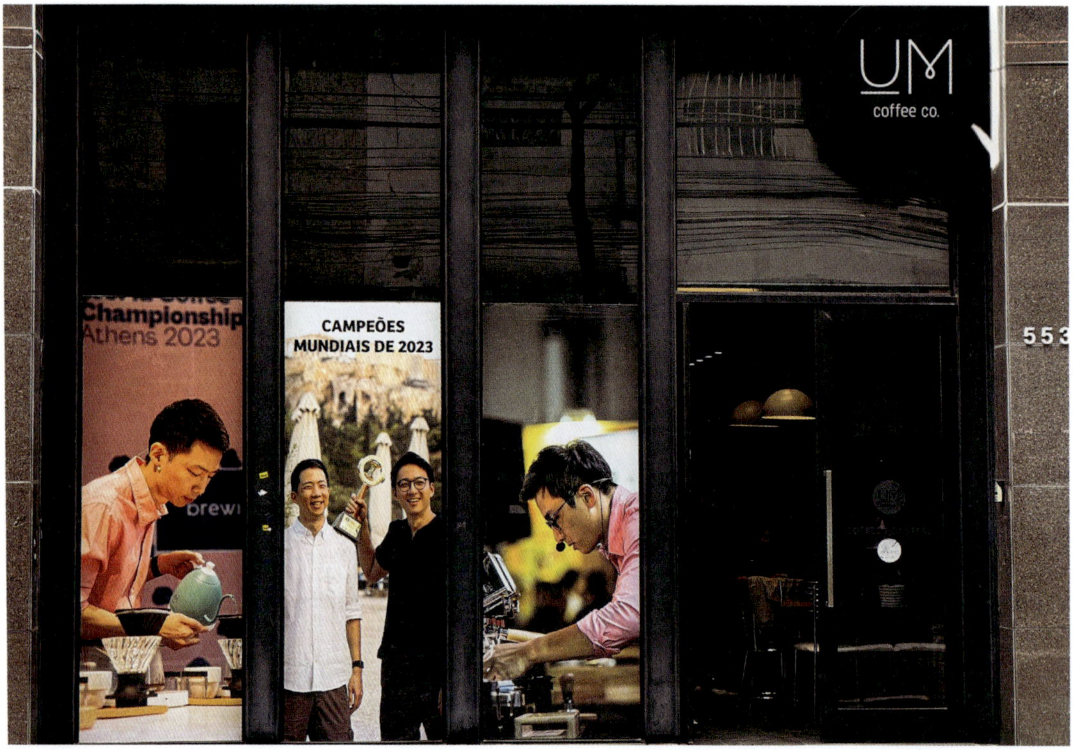

umcoffeeco.com.br

47 CAFÉ ALLEGRO

4214 University Way NE (entrance is in the alley), Seattle 98105, Washington, United States

TO VISIT BEFORE YOU DIE BECAUSE

Visit this Seattle classic, hidden in an alleyway, to better understand the city that sparked a new wave of espresso culture in the US.

Coffee is big in Seattle, where locals consume more coffee than in any other American city. They have plenty of independent cafés to choose from, including Café Allegro, the city's oldest espresso bar. Established in Seattle's University District in 1975, it is famous for its espresso blend and iconic poster wall, showcasing the neighbourhood's latest events. 'Our beans are imported from family farms around the world and roasted in small batches onsite at our café,' explains owner Chris Peterson, who started working there while a student in the 1980s. There's no better place to be on a rainy day than at one of Allegro's wooden tables, with an espresso and an almond croissant. Allegro's history is also inextricably linked to Seattle giant Starbucks, founded in Pike Place Market in 1971. The mermaid corporation pinched Allegro's master roaster Dave Olsen, while former CEO Howard Schultz once said that 'Café Allegro was a prototype for what Starbucks later became, although its style was more bohemian.' Well, to be honest, we much prefer the original. May it never change.

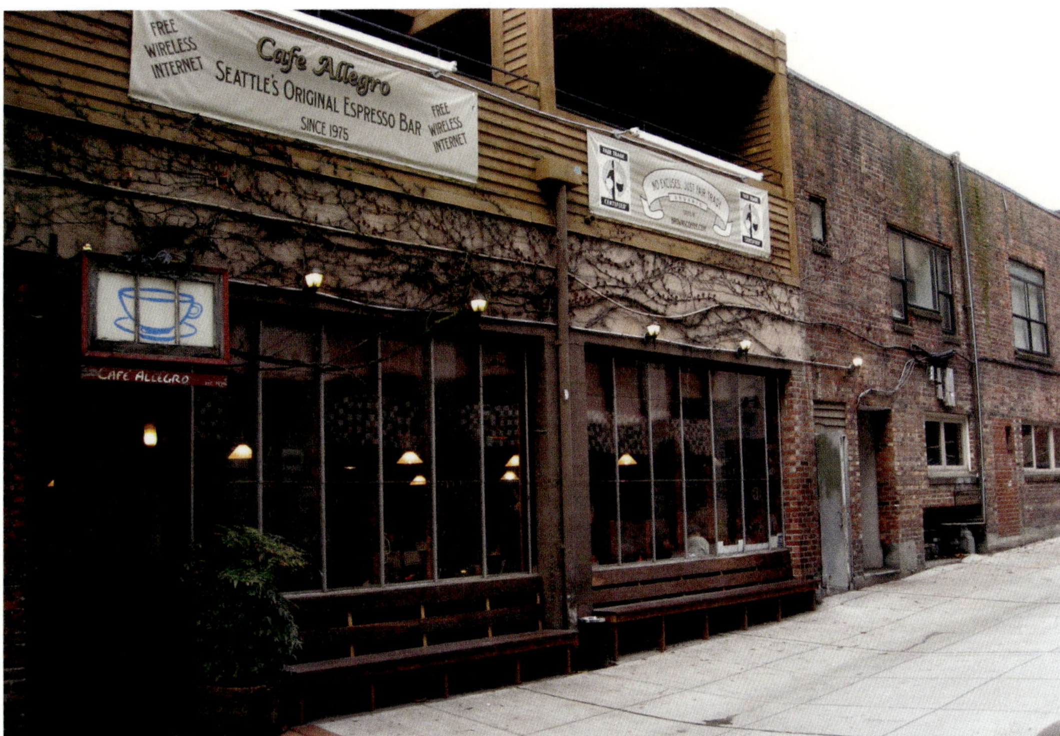

seattleallegro.com

48 PILOT COFFEE ROASTERS TASTING BAR

50 Wagstaff Dr, Toronto, Ontario M4L 3W9, Canada

TO VISIT BEFORE YOU DIE BECAUSE

Try an espresso flight at this state-of-the-art roastery and café on an industrial strip now home to great food businesses.

Pilot Coffee Roasters first started out as Te Aro, a café and micro-roastery opened by Jessie Holmes and Andy Wilkin, a then freshly minted Q Grader, in a small garage in Toronto's Leslieville neighbourhood. Taking its name from Andy's hometown in coffee-mad New Zealand, it quickly became a hub for speciality coffee enthusiasts. A few years later, they had a new name, new HQ and roastery on Wagstaff Drive, in a former warehouse in Toronto's East End transformed by local architects Williamson Williamson. The front of the industrial building was turned into a roastery tasting bar in 2013. The sleek space comes with a long U-shaped counter with Modbar espresso machines, views of shelves packed full with giant coffee bags and the Probat G60 roaster, and a cupping lab used for training, quality control and workshops. A rotating selection keeps things exciting, with favourites including Ana Sora, a coffee with strawberry notes from Ethiopia's Guji region.

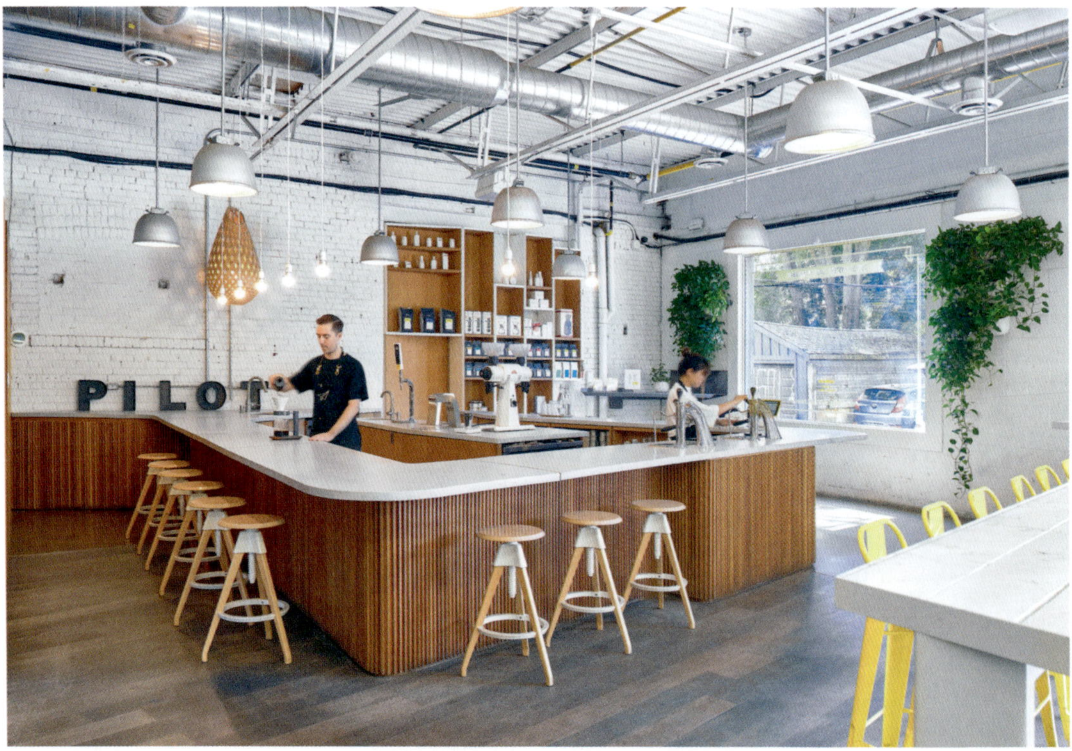

 pilotcoffeeroasters.com

49 REVOLVER

325 Cambie St, Vancouver, British Columbia V6B 2N4, Canada

TO VISIT BEFORE YOU DIE BECAUSE

The excellent team of baristas, immense choice of beans and roasters, and cool industrial vibes make this a must-go for coffee lovers.

Revolver is an award-winning coffee shop opened in 2011 by the Giannakos family in Vancouver's historic Gastown. 'Though the coffee making takes place in a building that is over 100 years old, the techniques and style are new,' says the team. 'We offer a wide range of coffee daily on our brewed-to-order coffee menu, which features classic and familiar flavours, as well as super experimental processing methods and flavours that are wildly exploratory.' Divided into two categories (fruits, florals, exotics; or cocoa, nuts, patisserie), the constantly rotating menu of coffee roasters from around the globe includes local favourites (Ex Animo, Monogram) and renowned American and European roasters such as Barcelona's Nomad (page 148). Particularly interesting are the espresso tasting flight, where you get to try a straight espresso and macchiato of two different espressos for a compare and contrast session. Snack on a tasty coffee cake or a jam cookie and check out the arty map on the wall – each brown nail marks a coffee-growing area.

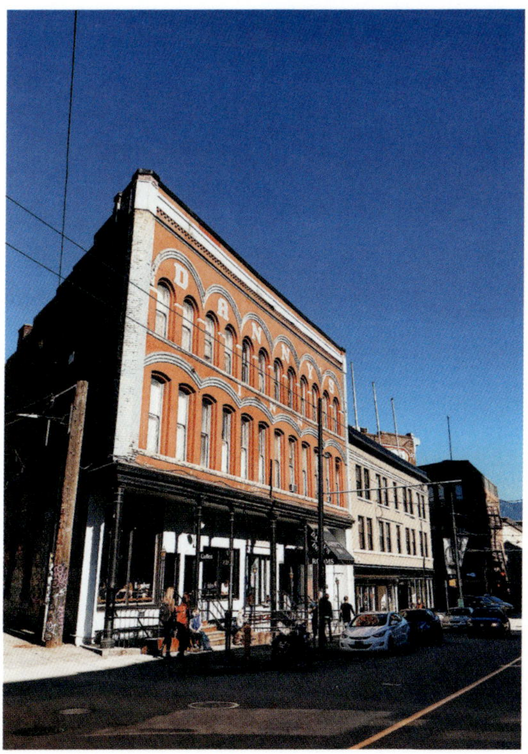

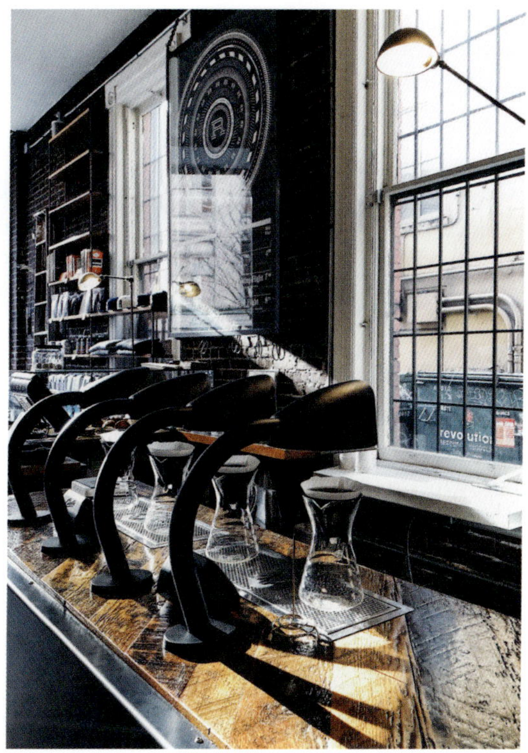

revolvercoffee.ca

50 JULIUS

Kabanbay Batyr St 83, Almaty 050000, Kazakhstan

TO VISIT BEFORE YOU DIE BECAUSE

This little 'coffee sanctuary' in the centre of Almaty offers a good dose of smart design to accompany your daily caffeine fix.

The starting point for the stylish concept behind this small speciality coffee shop just across from the national opera house was a La Marzocco coffee machine, purchased long before the project began. Design practice NAAW references its bright red colour in the café's front door, bold accents, outdoor seating and logo; the small space also features coffee-and-milk-coloured wood panelling, and a pale brick floor that turns into a bar counter. Sit on the cosy banquette, a Gubi chair or a sculptural 'Backenzahn' wooden stool and admire local artist Nurbol Nurakhmet's charcoal sketches before savouring an espresso or a V60. Beans come courtesy of Rockets Coffee or local roasters Massimo, and you might be able to choose between a Geisha La Indonesia from Colombia or a rare Busasa from Burundi. Summer specials include cold brew with pomegranate juice, while snacks range from thick focaccia sandwiches to homemade apple pies, soft poppy seed buns and delicate tartlets. NAAW is also behind Fika, another stylish Almaty café.

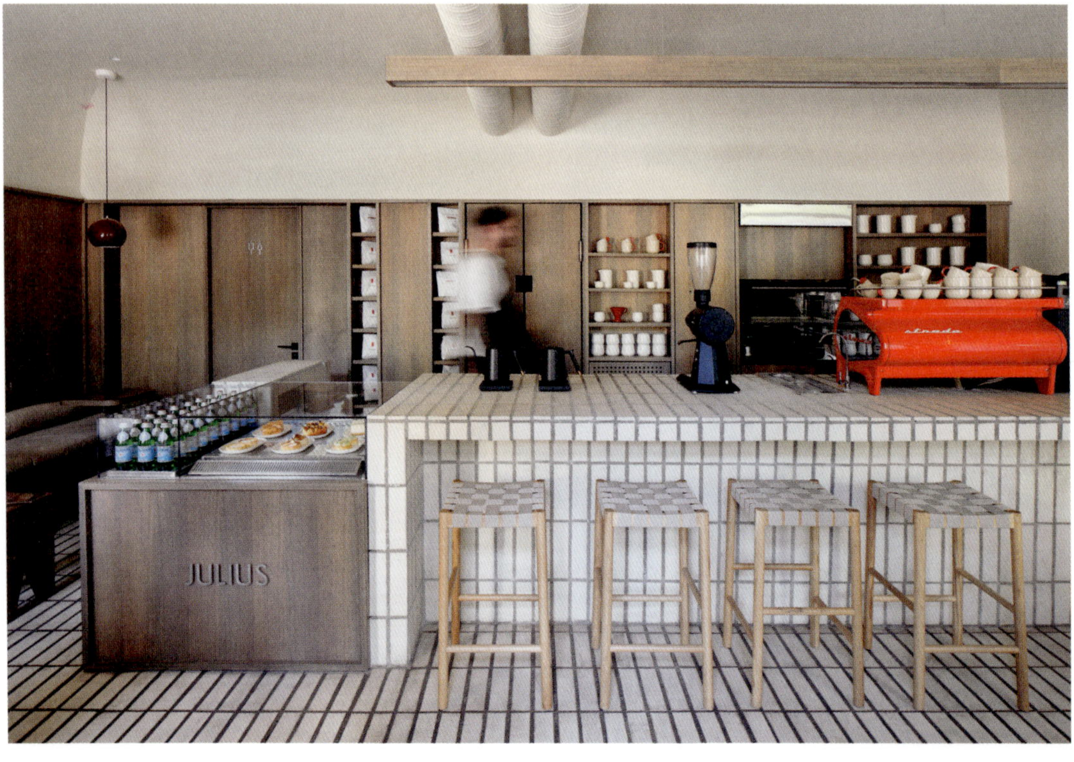

@julius.cafe +7 771 722 8447

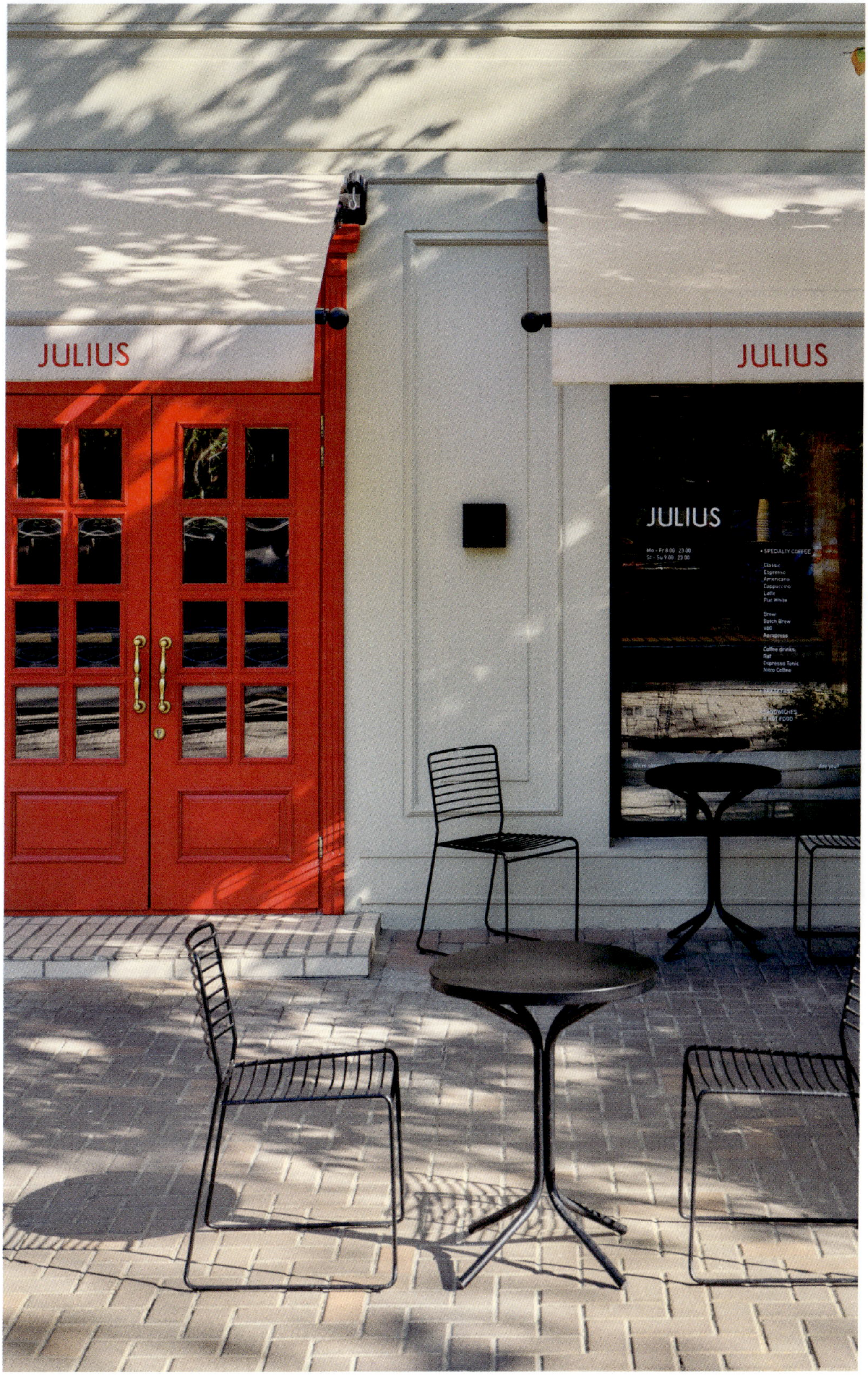
JULIUS
JULIUS
JULIUS
Mo - Fr 8.00 - 23.00
St - Su 9.00 - 23.00
• SPECIALTY COFFEE
Classic
Espresso
Americano
Cappuccino
Latte
Flat White
Brew
Batch Brew
V60
Aeropress
Coffee drinks
Raf
Espresso Tonic
Nitro Coffee
Are you?

51 KAWISARI COFFEE FARM SHOP & EATERY

Jl. Pantai Batu bolong, Canggu, Kec. Kuta Utara, Kabupaten Badung, Bali 80361, Indonesia

TO VISIT BEFORE YOU DIE BECAUSE

Try a Javanese coffee sweetened with coffee-flower honey or stock up on beans perfumed with lemon basil and ginger at this welcoming spot.

This farm shop and eatery is one of six cute cafés spread around Indonesia that are linked to Tugu Hotels' Kawisari Coffee Plantation, which sprawls over 850 hectares of lush emerald green slopes of Mount Kawi, in neighbouring Java. Located just a stone's throw away from Canggu Batu Bolong beach, this Balinese outpost comes with a little green takeaway kiosk frequented by local surfers; a lovely lounge with panels explaining the plantation's history (it's the oldest in Java); a beautiful terrace surrounded by greenery; and a deli section where you can stock up on coffee-flower honey and whisky-infused coffee. The coffee menu ranges from vanilla hazelnut and cinnamon coconut cream lattes to a coffee flight showcasing three different brews. The plantation produces arabica coffee (including arabica peaberry) as well as an award-winning robusta, a medium-dark roast with notes of Earl Grey and dark chocolate. Stay for lunch to try the beautifully presented Javanese specialities or seafood laksa, and finish with an espresso and Kawisari chocolate truffles.

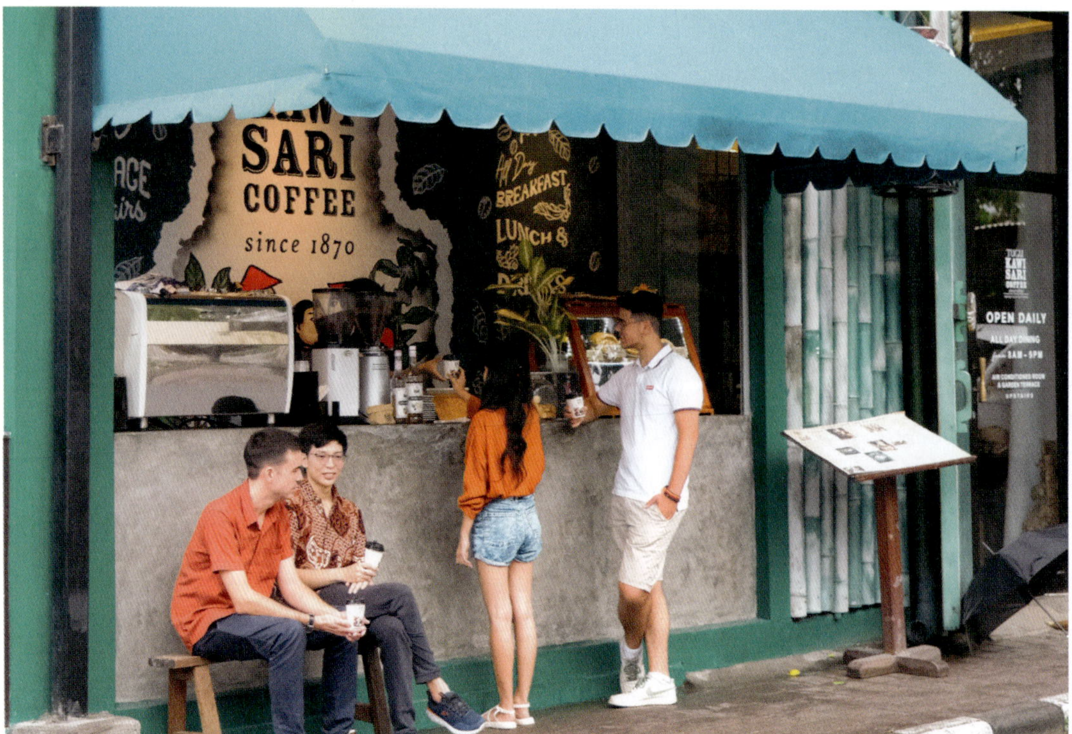

kawisaricoffee.com +62 81 1388 3553

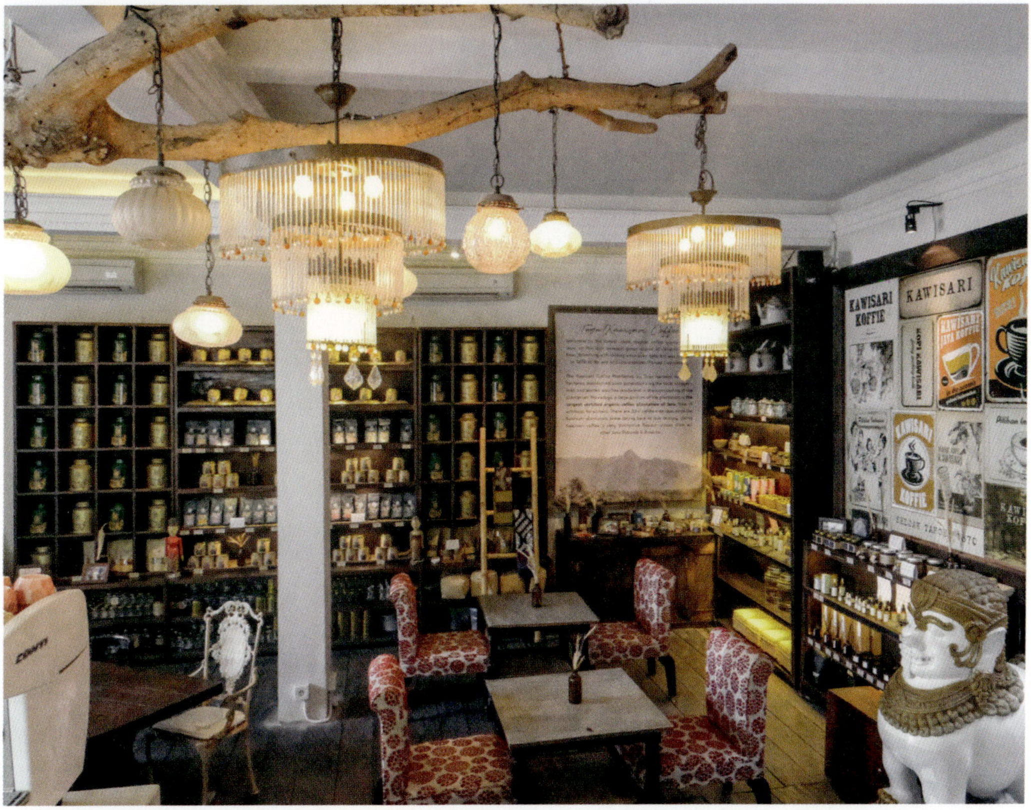
KAWISARI KOFFIE
KAWISARI

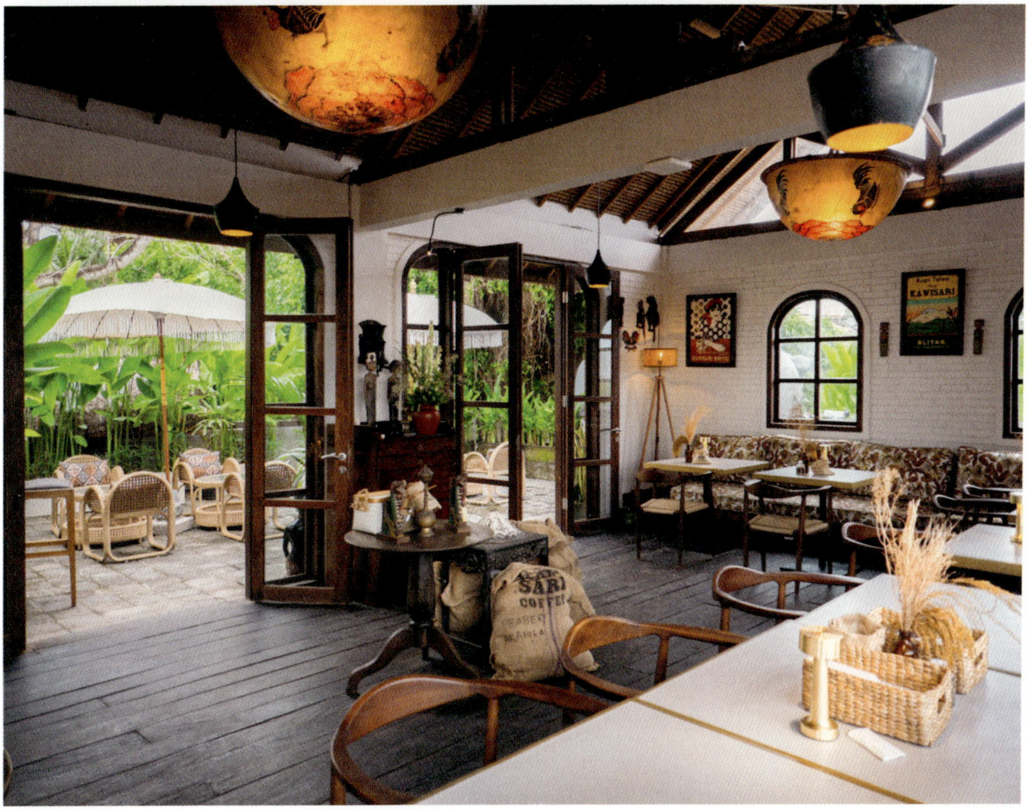
KAWISARI
BLITAR

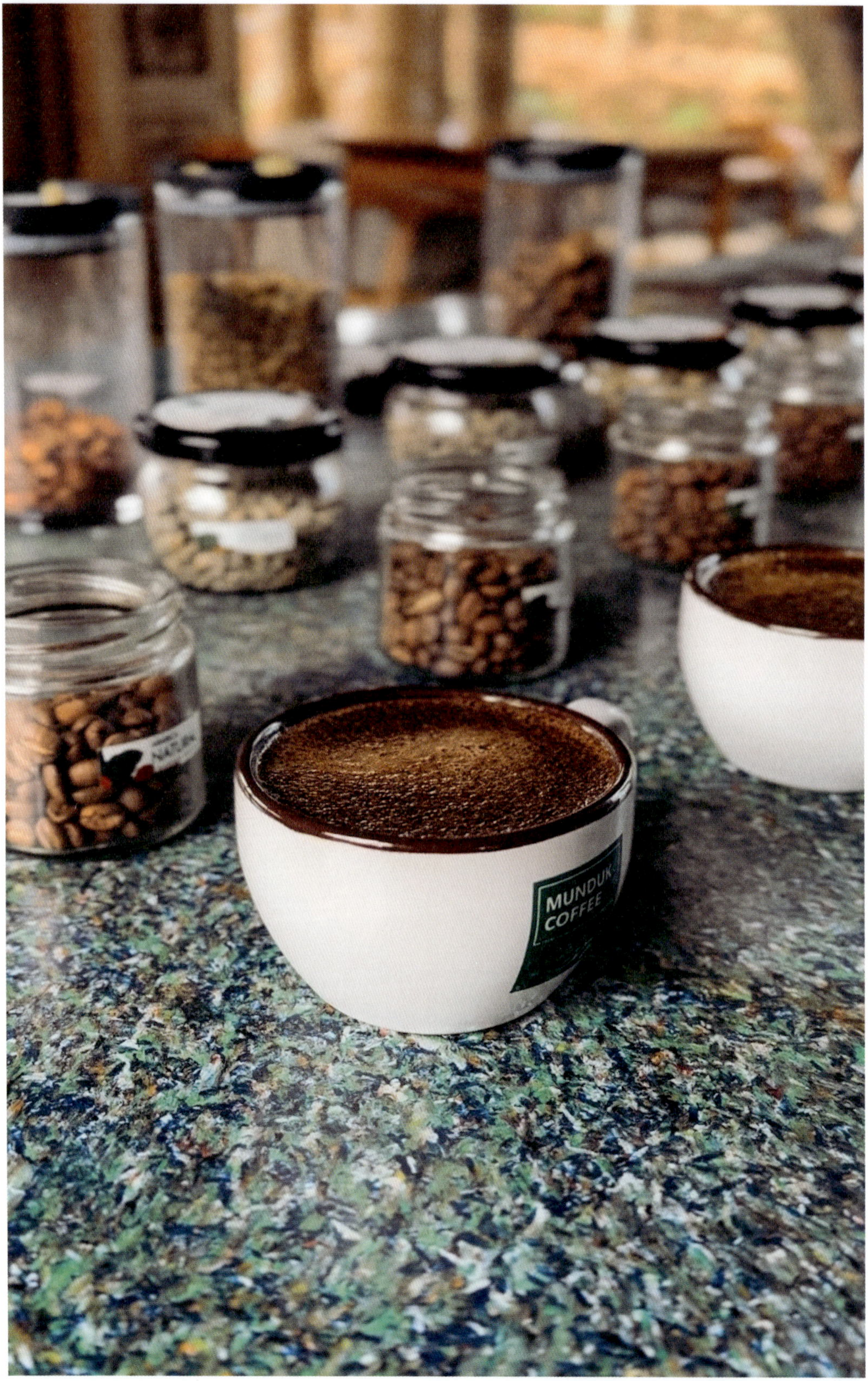
MUNDUK
COFFEE

52 MUNDUK MODING PLANTATION

Desa Gobleg, Buleleng, Bali 81152, Indonesia

TO VISIT BEFORE YOU DIE BECAUSE

Try a rare kopi luwak – the famous civet-digested coffee – or relax by the pool with a cup of freshly roasted local beans at this hilltop luxury resort.

Munduk Organic Coffee Plantation was established by a Balinese and European partnership with the goal of reviving high-quality coffee production in Bali's central hills region, known for its rich volcanic soil and highland climate. Today the farm and nature resort is open to visitors for immersive experiences including guided coffee plantation walks, roasting demonstrations and cupping sessions, 'all designed to deepen the connection between guests and the origin of their cup'. Here you can enjoy freshly brewed Munduk coffee in many different spots, including a terrace with firepit overlooking the misty jungle at sunrise; the tasting area in the roastery; and the bar next to the resort's infinity pool (the best spot for an espresso martini). As well as the plantation's organic arabica beans, used to prepare everything from cold brews to espressos and affogatos, the highlight of the coffee menu is the rare wild luwak coffee, crafted from beans that have undergone a unique journey through the digestive tract of the elusive Asian palm civet, or luwak.

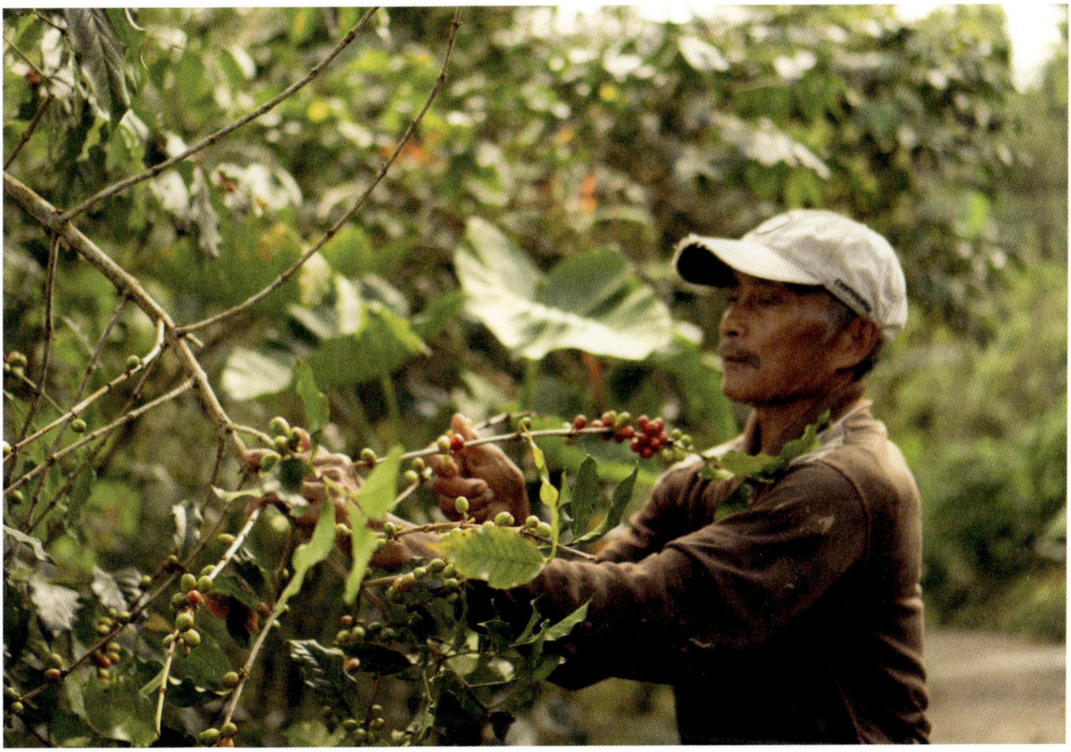

mundukmodingplantation.com +62 81 1381 0123

53 BALLAD

337 Charoen Nakorn Rd, Banglamphu Lang, Khlongsan, Bangkok 10600, Thailand

TO VISIT BEFORE YOU DIE BECAUSE

This stylish speciality coffee shop, 'where coffee and music speak', comes with its own resident 'cat manager' and shelves full of vinyls.

With its minimalist wooden furniture and sleek record shelves, this cosy corner café in Bangkok's busy Khlong San riverside district has been designed with an eye for detail. No wonder: it was founded by Dit Chaengsiricharoen, a former art director in the magazine industry. But make no mistake, the real boss here is called Bailiang, a Scottish Longhair cat who likes nothing more than to perch on your laptop. As well as cat cuddles, Ballad offers a beautifully curated soundtrack to your morning coffee, with a wide range of mostly classical and jazz LPs to choose from. Equally exhaustive is the choice of single-origin brews, including the likes of a Finca Tamana from Tim Wendelboe (page 190), Herbazu from Fritz Coffee (page 126) or a Santa Teresa from Prolog (page 162). Also worth trying is the Coffee Libre, a refreshing mix of craft cola, lime and coffee that is perfect on a hot day. There are baked treats, too: customers rave about the carrot cake and lemon tart. The same team is behind the equally cosy and extremely popular Walden Café, located just up the road on Somdet-Chaophraya.

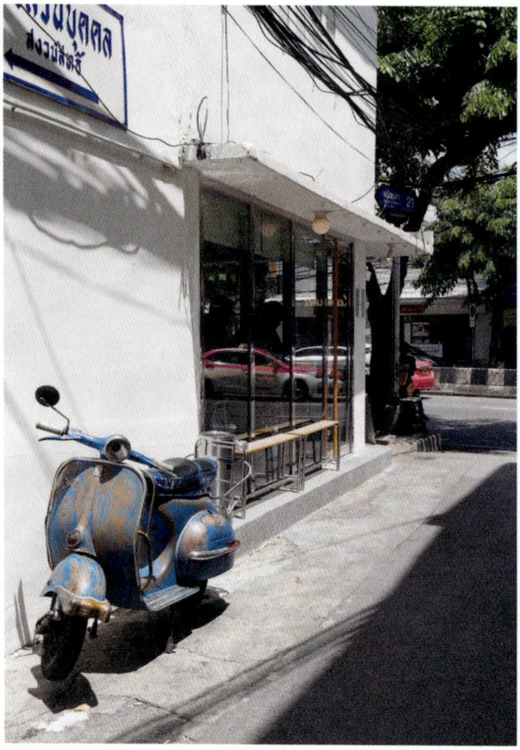

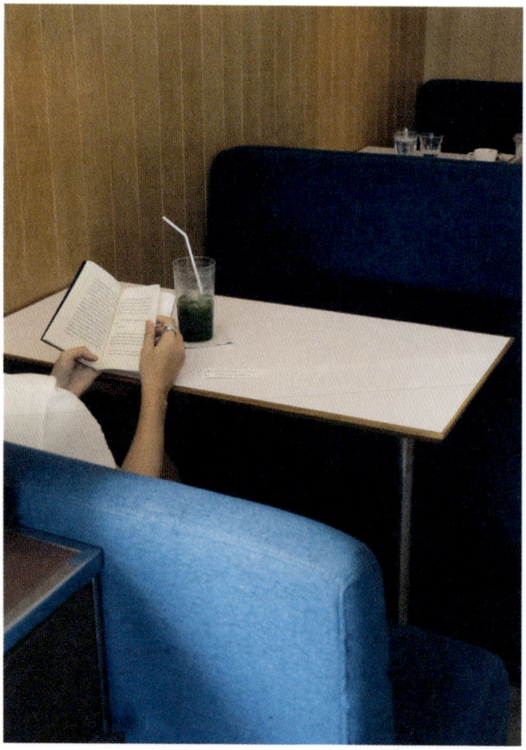

@ballad.coffeebar

+66 93 664 4615

54 CRAFTSMAN ROASTERY & BREW BAR

12 Soi Chan 43 Yaek 45, Khwaeng Bang Khlo,
Khet Bang Kho Laem, Bangkok 10120, Thailand

TO VISIT
BEFORE YOU DIE
BECAUSE

Located in a historic lathe factory, this café offers architecture with heritage, curated music, evocative scents, and coffee brewed with care.

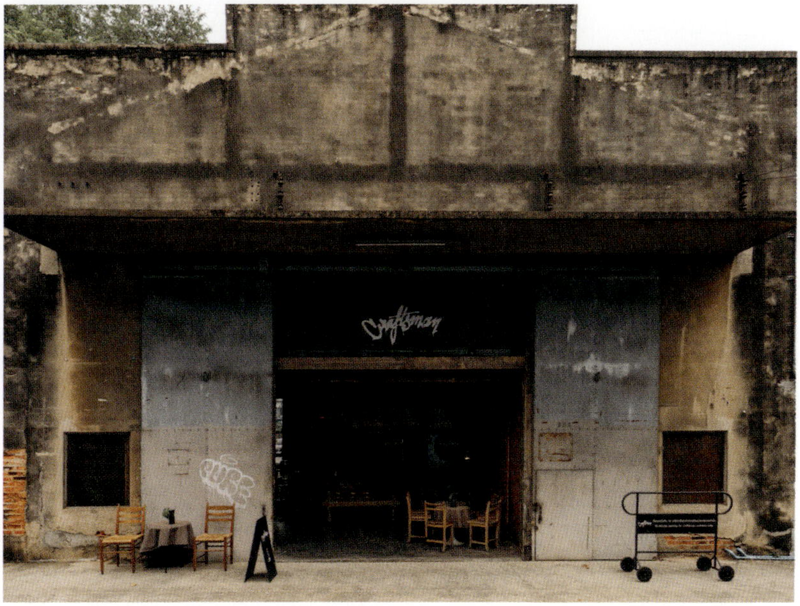

The story of Craftsman began in 2015 as a tiny three-table coffee corner inside Niiq, a Thai design furniture house. It takes its name from the former profession of its founder, Netnapa Narathasajan, a woodworker-turned-barista. 'The brand name reflects our philosophy: care, precision, and a respect for materials – whether wood or coffee beans,' she says. Today Craftsman has expanded into a full coffee house with two outposts: one in the old town, and this roastery and brew bar in Rama 3. Both are located in historic buildings, carefully restored by Niiq design director Rangsan Narathasajan with the help of architectural historians. 'This ensures that the charm and stories of each location remain intact,' says Netnapa. 'This sense of place, tied to history and craft, is central to our identity.' As for the beans themselves, they are sourced from organic-certified farms in Northern Thailand, blended with selected origins from around the world, and roasted in-house with six distinctive house blends. Seasonal specials include Samui Holiday, made with coconut blossom nectar and fresh coconut, and Amber Dirty, enriched with Thai tea mochi.

@craftsmanroastery

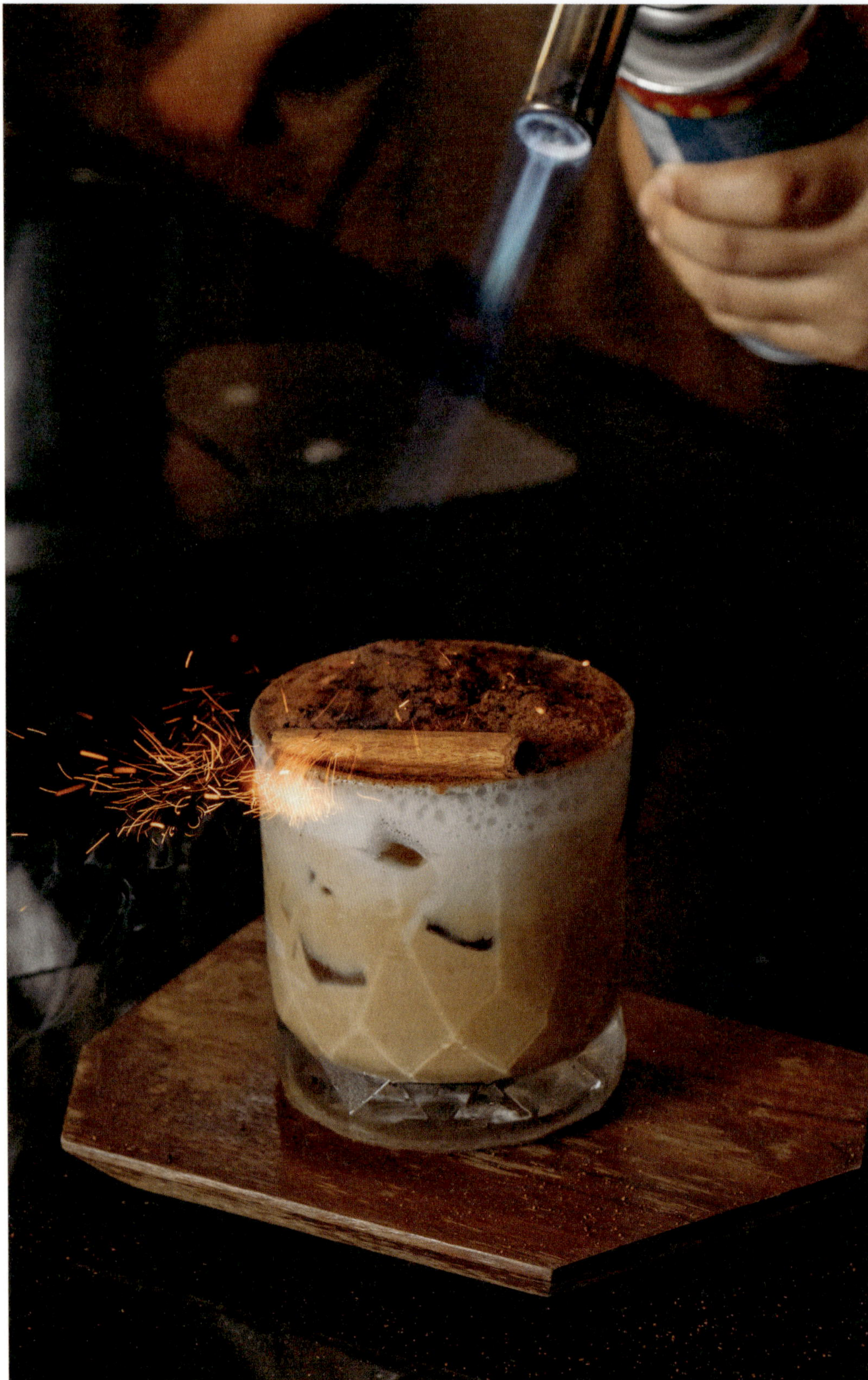

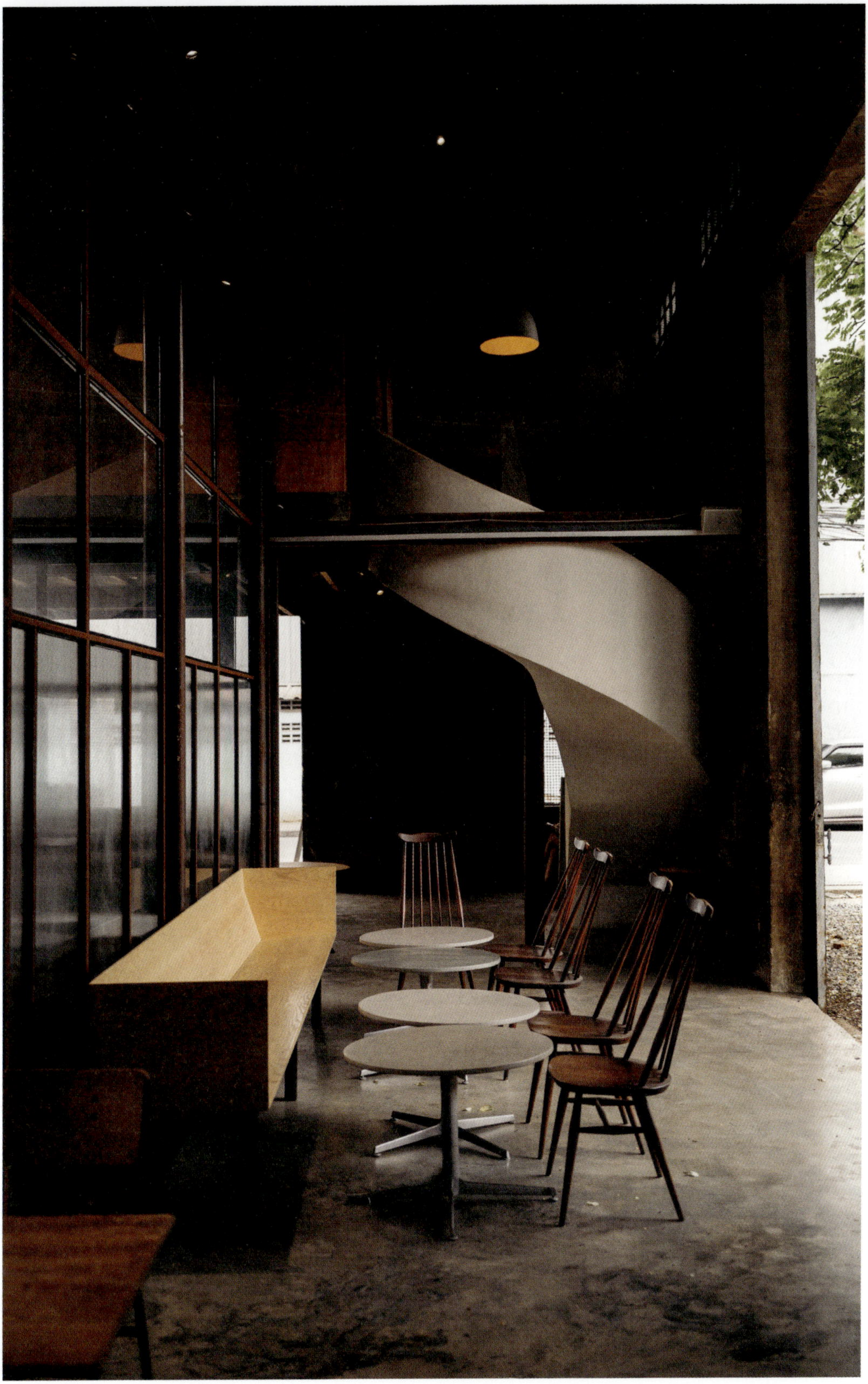

55 METAL HANDS WUDAOYING HUTONG

61 Wudaoying Hu Tong, Guozijian Dongcheng, Beijing, China, 100011

TO VISIT BEFORE YOU DIE BECAUSE

Try a dirty coffee at this charming café in one of Beijing's surviving historic alleyways, one of the country's first speciality coffee shops.

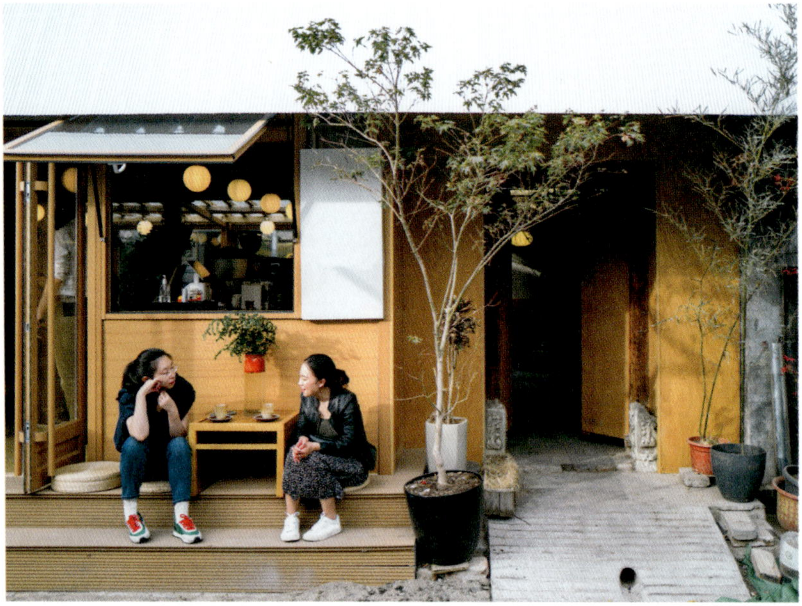

A short walk to the north of Beijing's Confucius and Lama Temples is a maze of traditional hutongs that has somehow survived the Chinese capital's relentless modernisation, narrowly avoiding destruction and replacement by a new giant highway interchange. It's a charming area home to many shops and eateries, including the first ever café of trendy Beijing coffee roasters Metal Hands, opened in 2016 by Jiangtao Ding. Named after the twin levers of an ancient coffee machine (still on the counter here), it now has dozens of outposts in Beijing, Hangzhou and Shanghai (all in different styles, all beautifully designed), and has collaborated with the likes of Louis Vuitton. The simple storefront on Wudaoying hides a deceptively spacious, light-filled café with a courtyard, where concrete walls and wooden furniture are paired with fresh flowers. The espresso-based menu includes dirty coffee, a Chinese favourite consisting of a double shot poured directly onto cold milk (great with the house cheesecake), while the four rotating single origins, available as V60 or cold brews, showcase top growers from around the world.

@metalhandscoffee.co

56 PHILOCOFFEA

Takiguchi Building 201, 2-2-13, Honcho, Funabashi-shi, Chiba 273-0005, Japan

TO VISIT BEFORE YOU DIE BECAUSE

This café was founded by Tetsu Kasuya, the inventor of the 4:6 Pour-Over Method, a simple yet super-effective signature brewing technique.

Philocoffea is a gourmet speciality coffee company founded by Tetsu Kasuya, who in 2016 became the first Asian to be crowned World Champion at the World Brewers Cup. The company's motto is 'Delivering a special coffee experience', so it is fitting that its locations range from a cute train station kiosk (its first shop) to a high-tech roastery/lab and this minimalist space hidden on the first floor of a building in Funabashi, just to the west of Tokyo. 'Our mission is to provide unforgettable coffee experiences resulting from the best beans and the optimal roasting and brewing methods for each coffee type,' explains Tetsu. Stock up on his favourite blend, Rudder, a mix of beans from Ethiopia, Colombia and Guatemala – 'its colourful sweetness will increase as it cools down' – or try unique seasonal creations such as a a cold brew made with ice and top-grade coffee; you can enjoy a cleaner and richer texture as it cools. Philocoffea has recently opened a flagship café in Toyko's Omotesando, bringing unforgettable speciality-coffee experience to the heart of the capital.

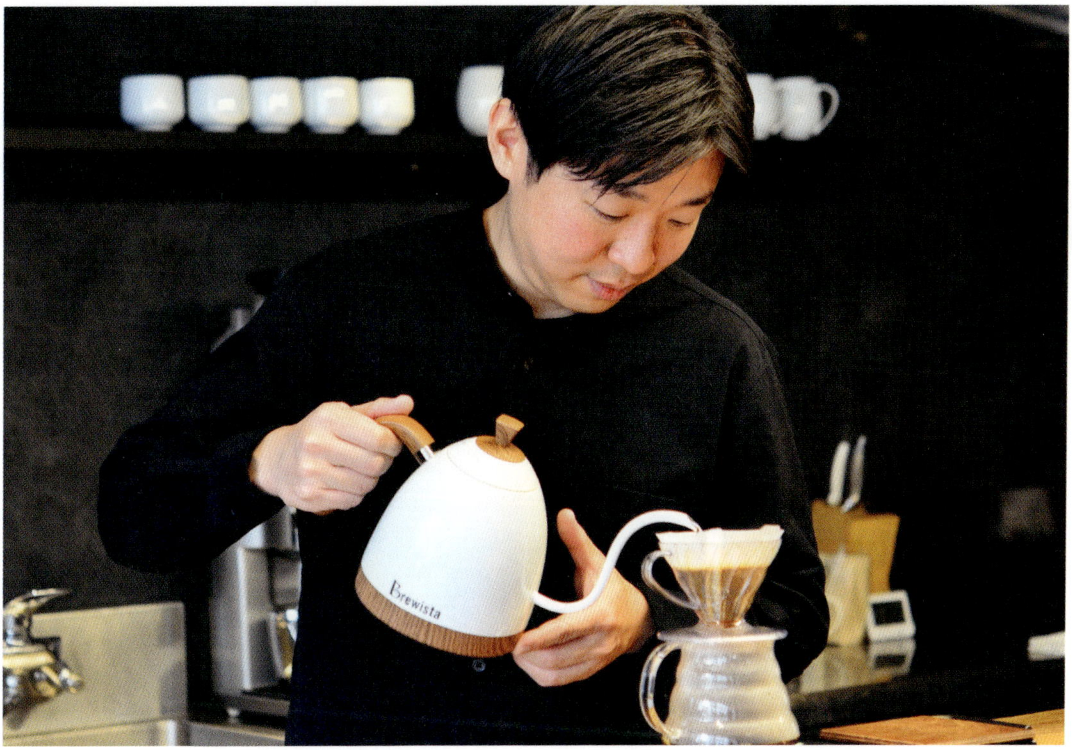

philocoffea.com +81 47 401 5950

57 ANH COFFEE ROASTERY

200 Pasteur, Xuan Hoa ward, Ho Chi Minh City 700000, Vietnam

TO VISIT BEFORE YOU DIE BECAUSE

Come for the stunning architecture and stay for the delicious coffees, including a Mr Special cold latte with fresh avocado.

Like so many cafés in this book, Anh Coffee started with a tiny booth and grew bigger and bigger, eventually opening this stunning coffee shop and roastery in Ho Chi Minh City's bustling Pasteur neighbourhood. The work of local architects Red5studio, the flowing red brick building is designed to evoke 'a sense of floating, as if drifting through a highland enveloped in misty clouds'. The bricks contrast beautifully with the trees shading the outdoor terrace, and the lush greenery found on the first-floor seating area, which is lit by a central skylight. The drinks menu offers everything from Italian-style coffee and hand-brewed pour-over to traditional Vietnamese Phin-filtered coffee. 'I want to treat coffee lovers with the most unique and high-quality things,' says founder Nguyen Thanh An, with a background as a high-end event organiser. 'The quality of Anh coffee cups must start from the selection of the best materials: we prioritise the most natural and high-quality ingredients to enhance their original, delicious flavours.'

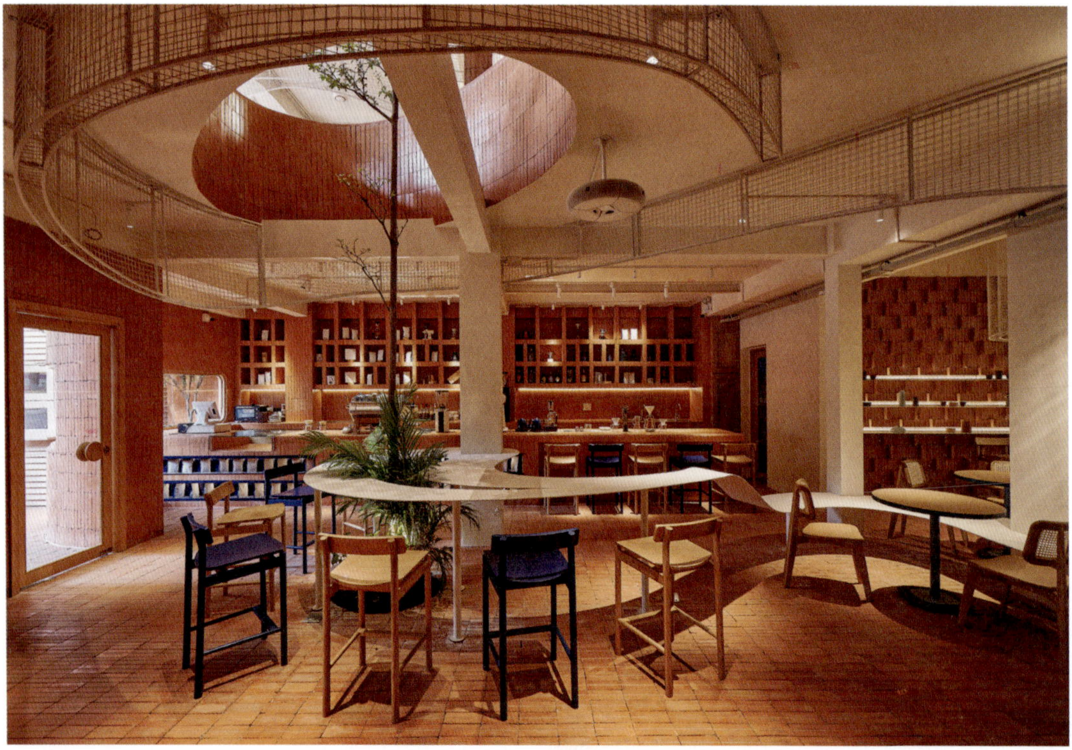

@anhcoffeeroastery +84 886 292 099

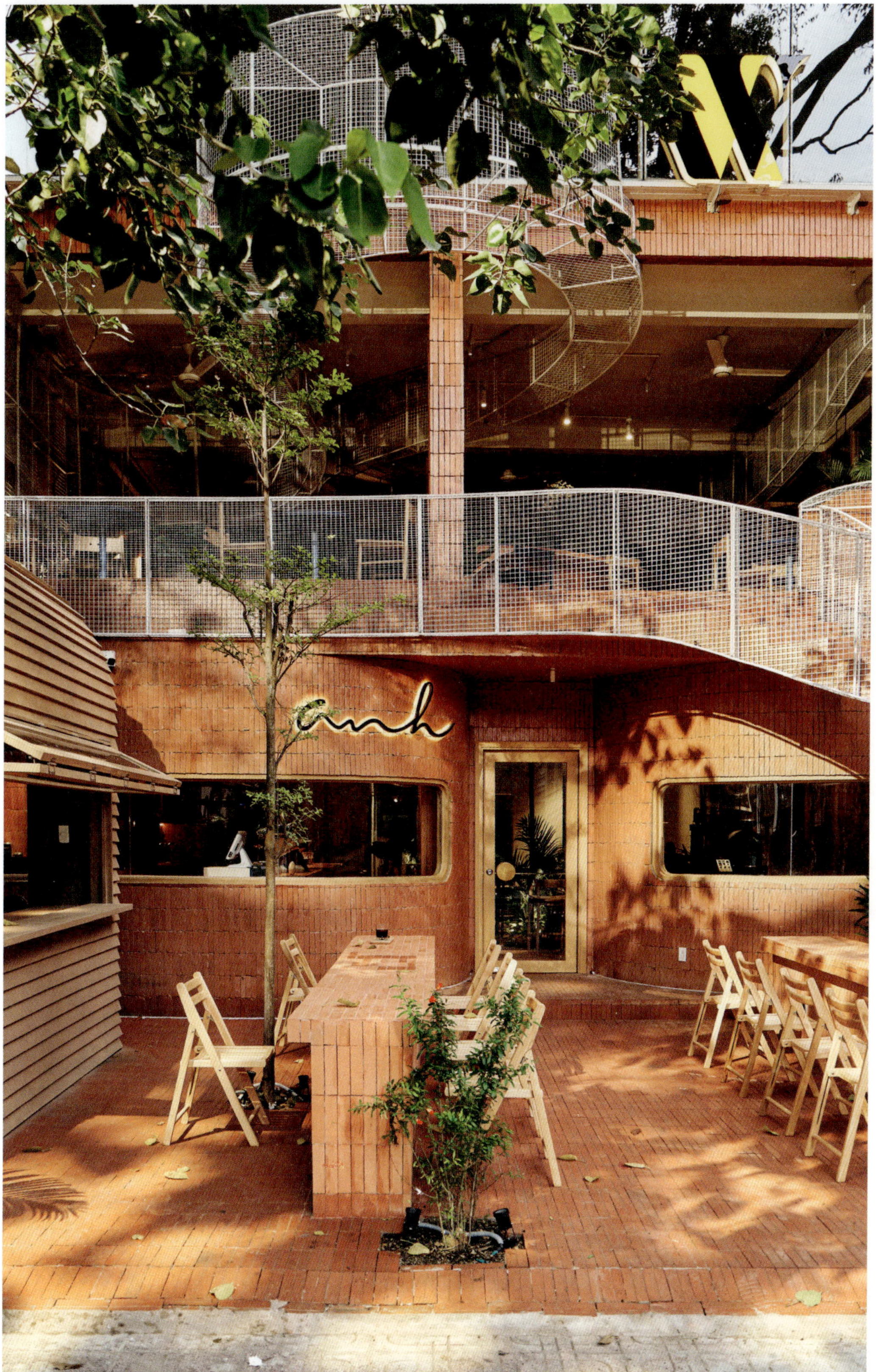
anh

58 CHART COFFEE

Shop 218, 2/F Central Market, Central, Hong Kong

TO VISIT BEFORE YOU DIE BECAUSE

Visit Hong Kong's iconic Central Market to fill up on local goodies, including lovely beans selected by a trio of passionate coffee experts.

A rare example of Bauhaus architecture, Hong Kong's recently restored Central Market is now home to over 250 stalls. Number 218, on the second floor, is Chart Coffee, where you'll spot a display case holding quite a lot of golden trophies. They belong to co-founder Wilson Chung, a talented barista who opened Chart Coffee with friends and Q Graders Jo Chan and Kenson Cheung. As you'd expect, the coffee is delicious. 'We brew top-notch coffee with beans proudly roasted in Hong Kong,' says the team. 'Here, we share single-origin coffee with the community at an affordable price.' Specials include Chart's signature fruity option, a vibrant washed Yirgacheffe that celebrates Ethiopia's floral terroir; and Nutty, a classic El Salvador Red Bourbon, medium-roasted to highlight a comforting nutty sweetness. There's a handful of stools to sit on, or you can head to the balcony to sip your espresso tonic (with cola and soda) while admiring the clean lines of the 1939 architectural landmark. Chart Coffee also serves classic milk tea, in a tribute to Hong Kong's cultural memory.

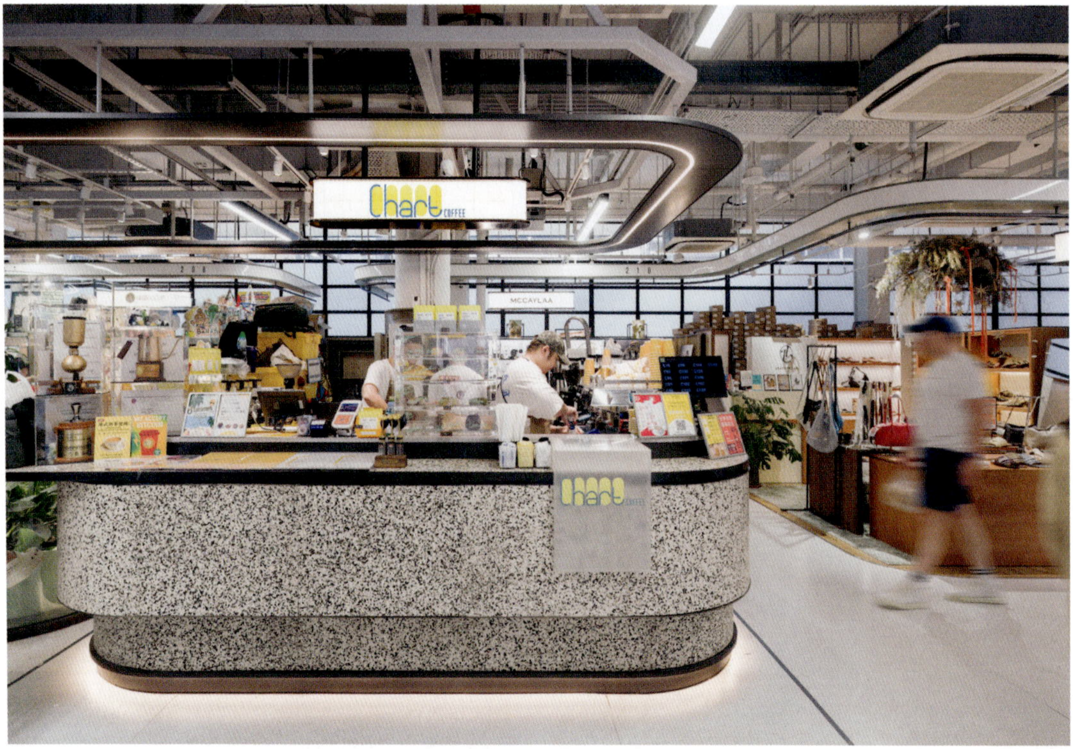

chart.coffee

59 HALFWAY COFFEE

4-6 Soy St, Mong Kok, Hong Kong

TO VISIT BEFORE YOU DIE BECAUSE

Sip a local honey latte in a vintage cup in this atmospheric coffee shop – a little bit of peace and quiet in one of Hong Kong's busiest neighbourhoods.

In a city known for its skyscrapers and constant transformation, it's so refreshing to see a bit of the old-school charm of Hong Kong in the neon signs, metal shutters and antique shops of the busy district of Mong Kok. This cultural heritage is also key to Halfway Coffee's seven coffee shops, whose owner Tommy Chui is a keen collector of old crockery, glasses and furniture. 'Preserving the past is a good way to connect with different kinds of people,' he says. 'People will come and share their stories, which makes a community more beautiful and long lasting.' Here on Soy Street, your coffee will be served in traditional vintage cups, or takeaway cups printed with the traditional Chinese pattern known as 'Boundless Longevity'. On the menu is a selection of coffees from Brazil, Columbia, Indonesia and Ethiopia, while signature drinks include a latte sweetened with Longan honey from Shatin Wing Wo Bee Farm. For even more sugar, try the lemon tart or brownie, served with fresh fruit.

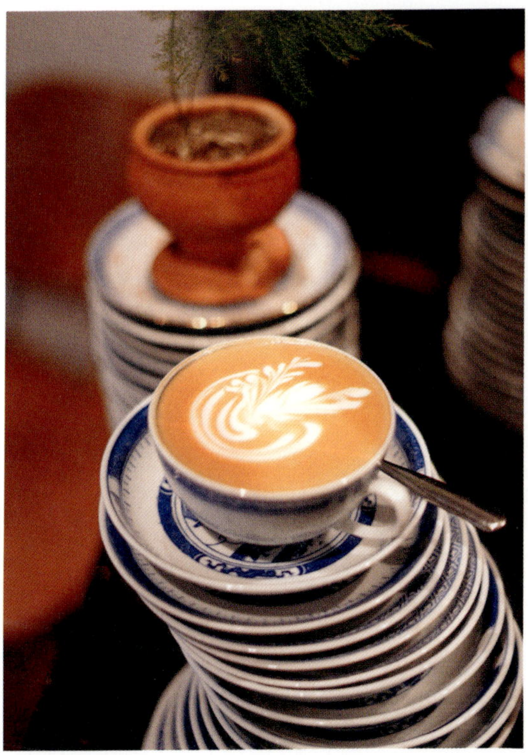

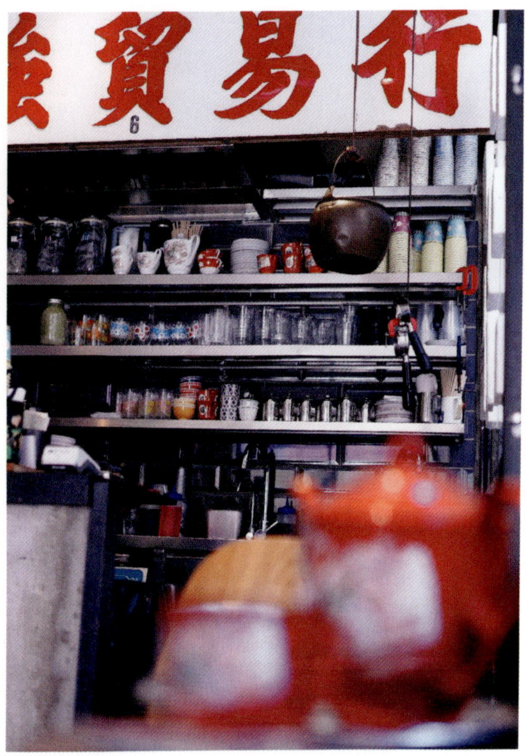

@halfwaycoffee

+852 9511 7197

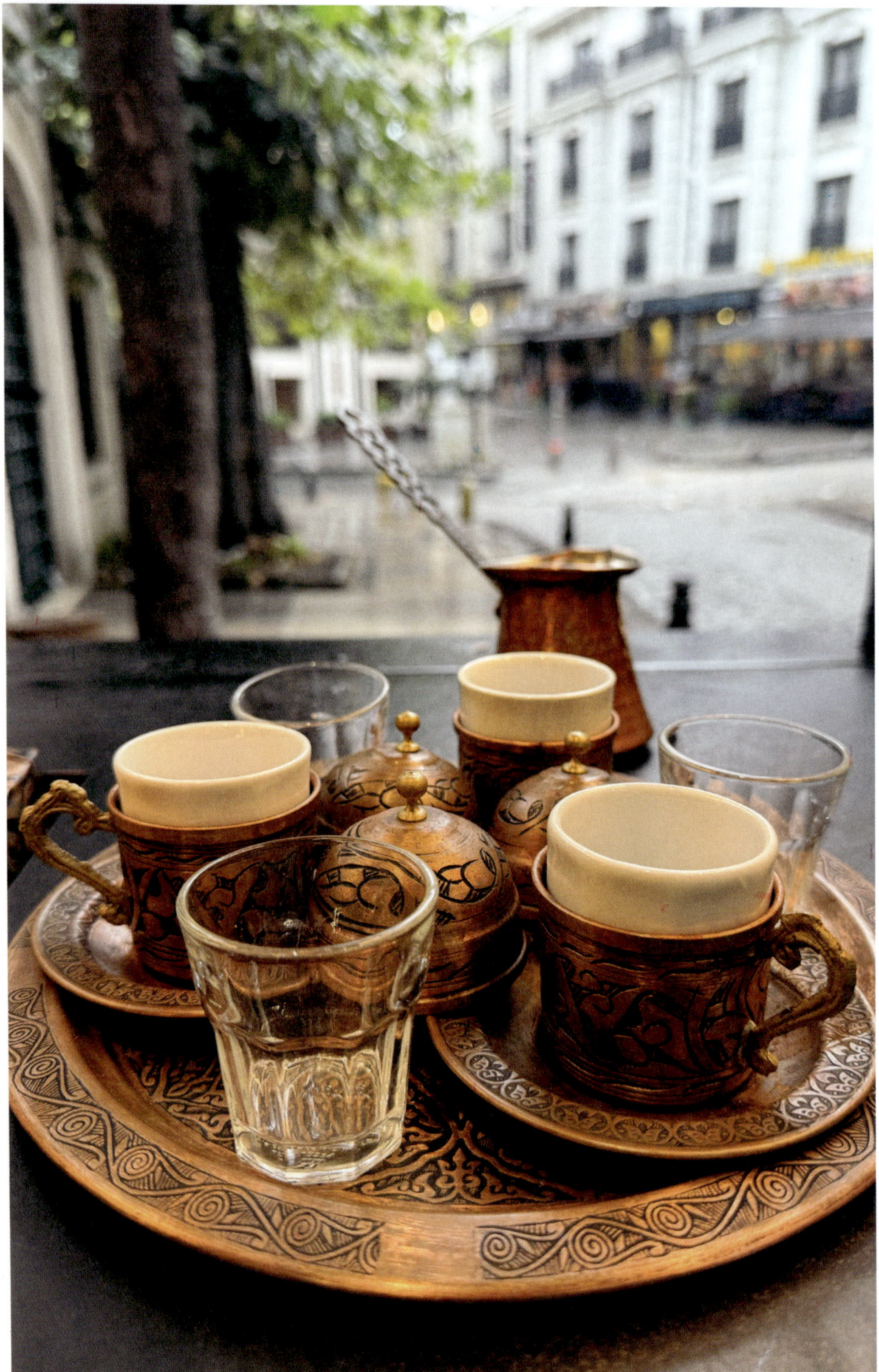

60 COFFEE NO 4

Alemdar, Molla Fenari Sk. No:4, 34110 Fatih/İstanbul, Turkey

TO VISIT BEFORE YOU DIE BECAUSE

Discover sand-brewed Turkish coffee and pistachio coffee at this small café in Istanbul's old town.

Perfectly located equidistant from Istanbul's Blue Mosque and Hagia Sofia in the capital's historic Fatih district, this small independent café is known for its traditional Turkish coffee brewed slowly in hot sand. The Ottoman-era technique, which makes the most of the slow, even heat of the sand, has roots in the nomadic tribes of the empire, and has seen a surge in popularity in the past few years. At No 4 the Ottoman coffee – including the other house signature, a delicious Turkish pistachio coffee – is served in traditional brass *cezve* pots on matching trays. You might want to try other local drinks, such as *salep*, a winter drink made from wild orchid tubers, milk and cinnamon, or stick with the long coffee menu. It includes all the espressos as well as a Special section featuring No 4 Dark coco (dark chocolate, coconut) and No 4 Nutoff (caramel, hazelnut). Try them on the small terrace in summer or inside by the woodburning stove in colder months.

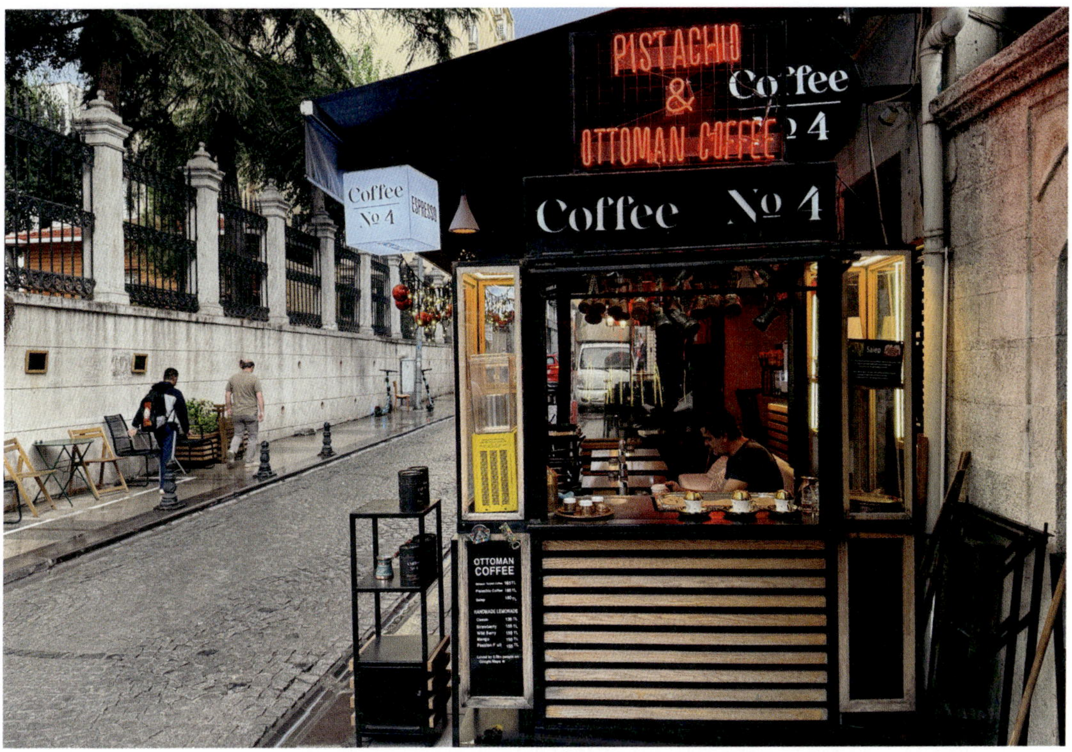

coffeeno4.com +90 552 805 4358

61 MANDABATMAZ

İstiklal Cad. Olivia Geçidi 1/A, 34430 Beyoğlu İstanbul, Istanbul, Turkey

TO VISIT BEFORE YOU DIE BECAUSE

Try a proper cup of extra strong, extra rich Turkish coffee at this landmark coffee shop in one of Beyoğlu's historic alleyways.

In Turkish, breakfast is known simply as *kahvaltı*, 'before coffee', and to be fair much of the rest of the day is spent having coffee one way or another – here it accompanies everything from office gossip to the afternoon snack and cigarette break, and can even be used for fortune telling if you're so inclined. That's because traditional Turkish coffee is a thick nectar made of extremely finely ground beans (finer than espresso), which form about a centimetre of grind at the bottom of the cup. And a great place to enjoy it is Mandabatmaz, an Istanbul classic, run for years as a hole in the wall by coffee master Cemil Filik. Since he passed away in 2019, the café has expanded with an interior seating area, but the best place to enjoy a coffee and perhaps a slice of cake is still a rickety stool in the little alleyway, decorated with colourful murals. The name of the shop – literally 'the buffalo will not sink' – refers to the thickness of the foam on top of the coffee here, which has become legendary.

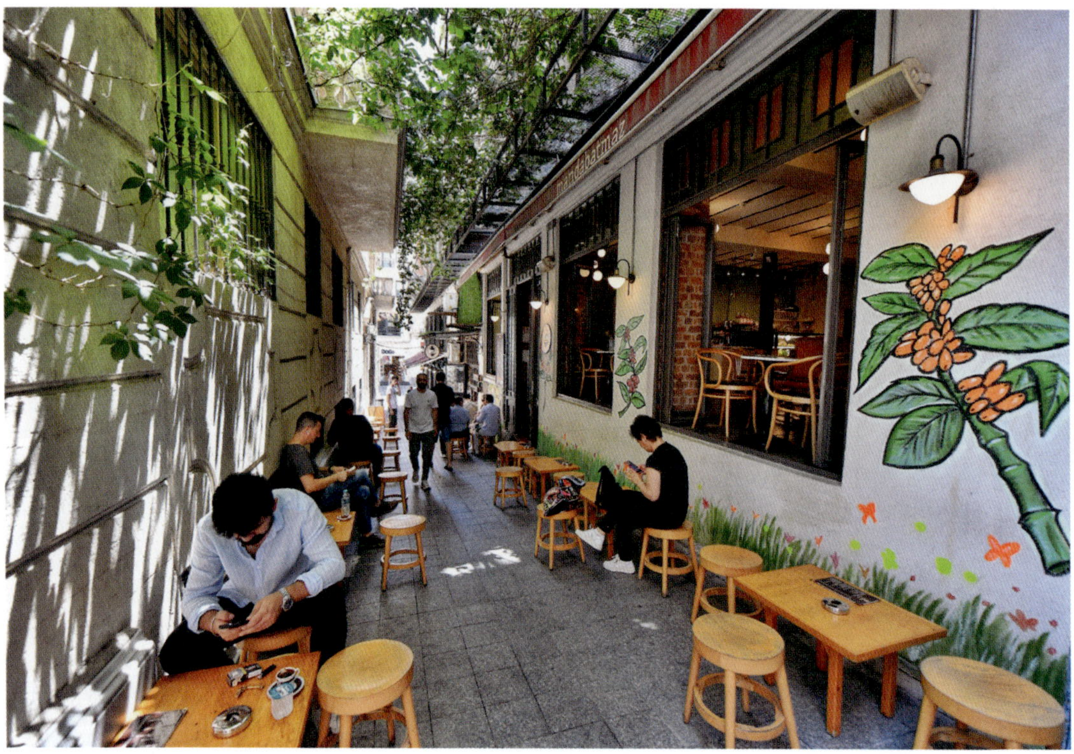

mandabatmaz.com.tr @mandabatmazkahvesi

62 MONTAG MODA

Caferağa, Bademaltı Sk. No:22/A, 34710 Kadıköy/İstanbul, Turkey

TO VISIT BEFORE YOU DIE BECAUSE

There are no blue Mondays at this espresso bar in Istanbul's trendy Moda, known for its great flat white and cortado.

'The idea of Montag was born in my mind as a place where nice people would come together and share unforgettable memories. Good coffee was absolutely crucial because it has the capacity to bring all these nice people together. But in time, coffee on its own turned into an obsession for me,' says founder Burak Bener. The self-described coffee nerd founded Montag in 2015 in Kadıköy, then just a few years later launched another branch in Bomonti and this espresso bar in Moda. As one of the few pioneering coffee roasters that introduced speciality coffee to Turkey, Montag is known for its skilled baristas and expertly roasted coffees. Loyal customers enjoy its peaceful ambience and carefully curated espresso menu, which includes two seasonal single-origin coffees as well as the house's Luna espresso blend, made with Brazilian beans. The roast level is medium to dark, making it a classic and approachable option for everyone. But it's not just about espressos: other brew methods are available too, including V60 pour-overs and Delter press.

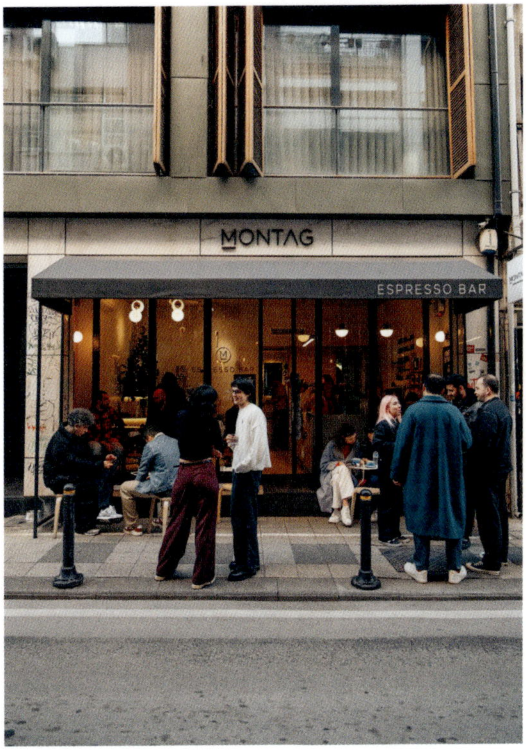

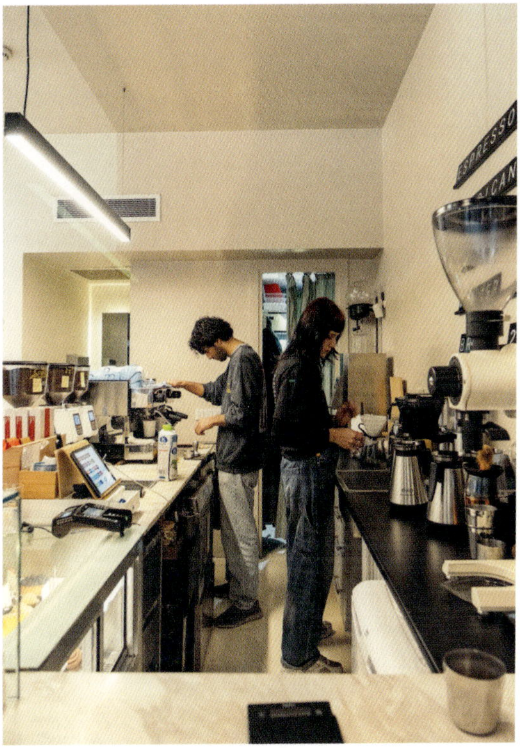

montagcoffee.com

+90 850 582 0747

63 COMMON GROUNDS TERRA

Surabaya St No.8, RT.1/RW.5, Menteng, Central Jakarta City, Jakarta 10310, Indonesia

TO VISIT BEFORE YOU DIE BECAUSE

Home to Indonesia's barista, brewers cup and latte art champions, this ace coffee shop comes with its own tennis court.

Common Grounds was co-founded by Yoshua Tanu, Aston Utan and Daryanto Witarsa in Jakarta in 2014, at a time when locals were turning away from *kopi susu* (milk coffee) to explore the world of coffee. On a mission to make Indonesian coffee great again, the three experts have won many trophies and awards, working with the country's best baristas, including Mikael Jasin, winner of the 2024 World Barista Championship. It seems their competitive streak extends to the tennis court: among their 16 cafés in the capital is this stunning coffee house and tennis club in Menteng, right across from the city's antique market. Inspired by Palm Springs and its iconic country clubs, with warm terracotta tones recalling the Roland Garros clay, Terra is the only place you can sample Common Grounds' Major Tom blend of Colombia Aji Bourbon and Indonesia Aceh Pantan Musara. Follow up with a session on the court and a tasty lunch, or book ahead for a 2-hour experience in the upstairs Trophy Room, where the country's top baristas will prepare rare beans for you.

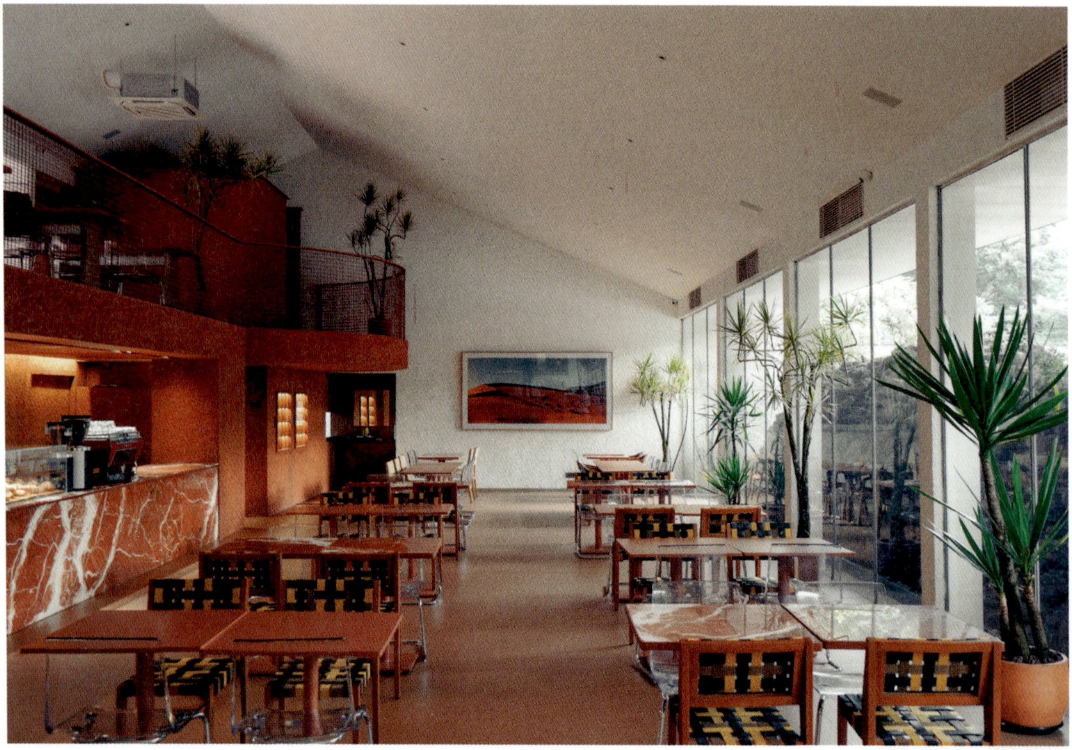

commongrounds.co.id

+62 81 9222 7700

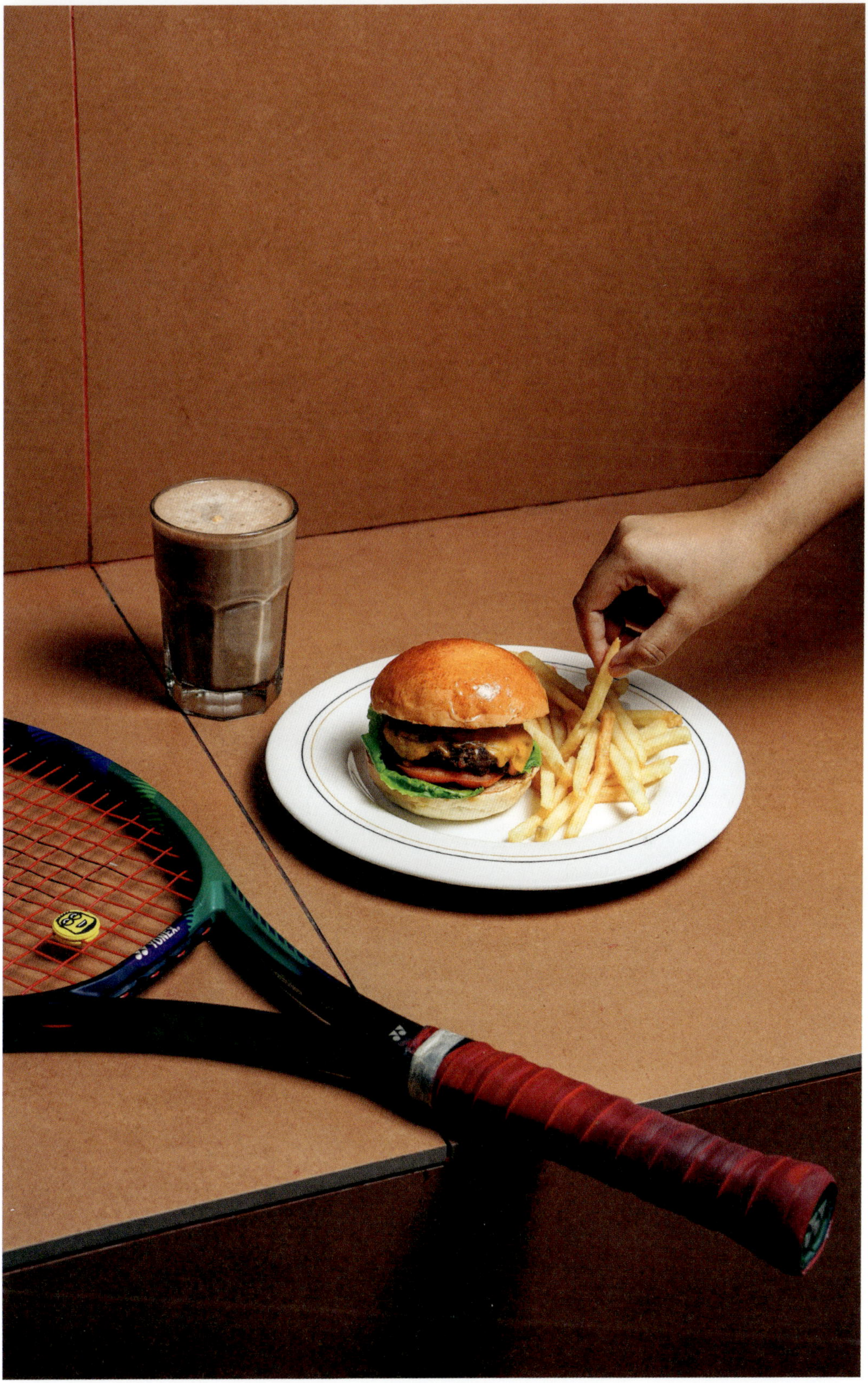
YONEX

64 ROAST8RY

157 29 Thanon Mittraphap, Nai Muang, Mueang Khon Kaen, Khon Kaen 40000, Thailand

TO VISIT BEFORE YOU DIE BECAUSE

Award-winning barista Arnon Thitiprasert serves 'high-end coffee brewed with passion' and delicate latte art at his strikingly contemporary café.

Thai barista Arnon Thitiprasert spent four years perfecting his coffee-making skills in Sydney before winning the World Latte Art Championship in 2017 and becoming World Barista Semi-finalist in 2024. Arnon's speciality is using a dry foam technique to draw rabbits, deer, foxes and unicorns by merging more traditional shapes like rosettas and tulips. But his talents don't stop at coffee making and latte art – Thitiprasert has also co-designed this amazing space in Khon Kaen, with the help of his friend Thicha at Syrah Design Studio. On the menu are experimental coffees, unique mixes such as Black & Yellow (dark coffee and mango), and the signature espresso champagne (grape, strawberry chardonnay and botanical sparkling water) and Satan latte (a mellow coffee with exquisite latte art). Events include everything from special geisha cupping sessions to daytime 'coffee music' DJ sets. You can also visit Roast8ry's flagship store in Chiang Mai; a Bangkok branch is due to open soon.

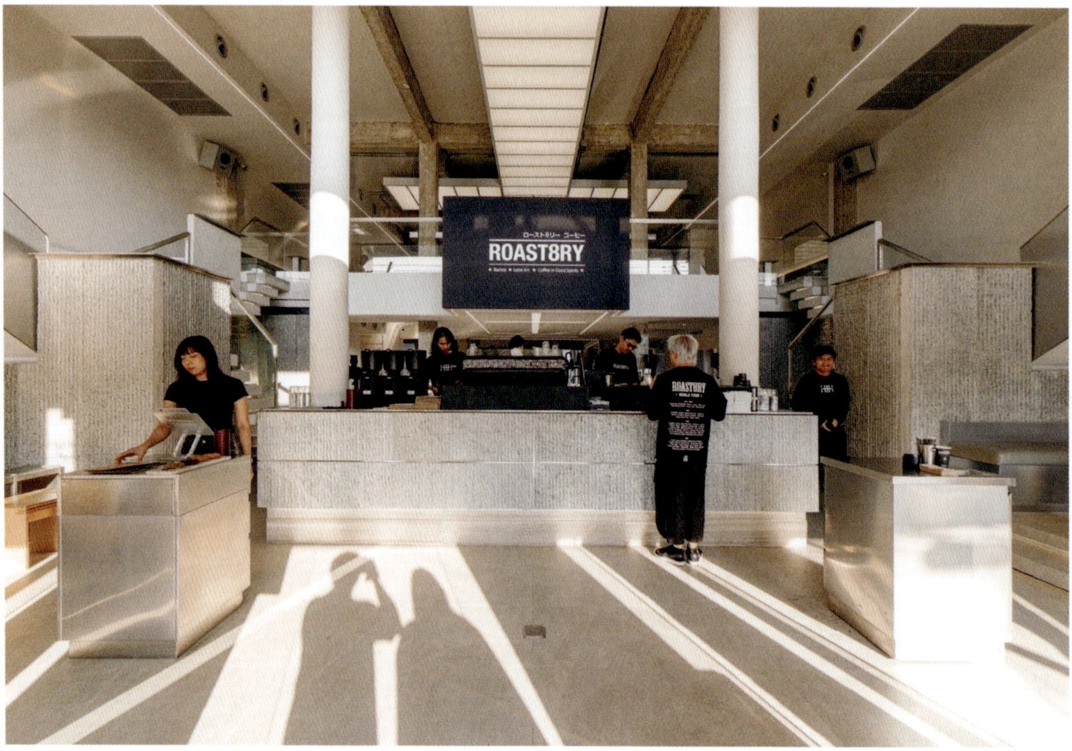

@roast8ry_khonkaen

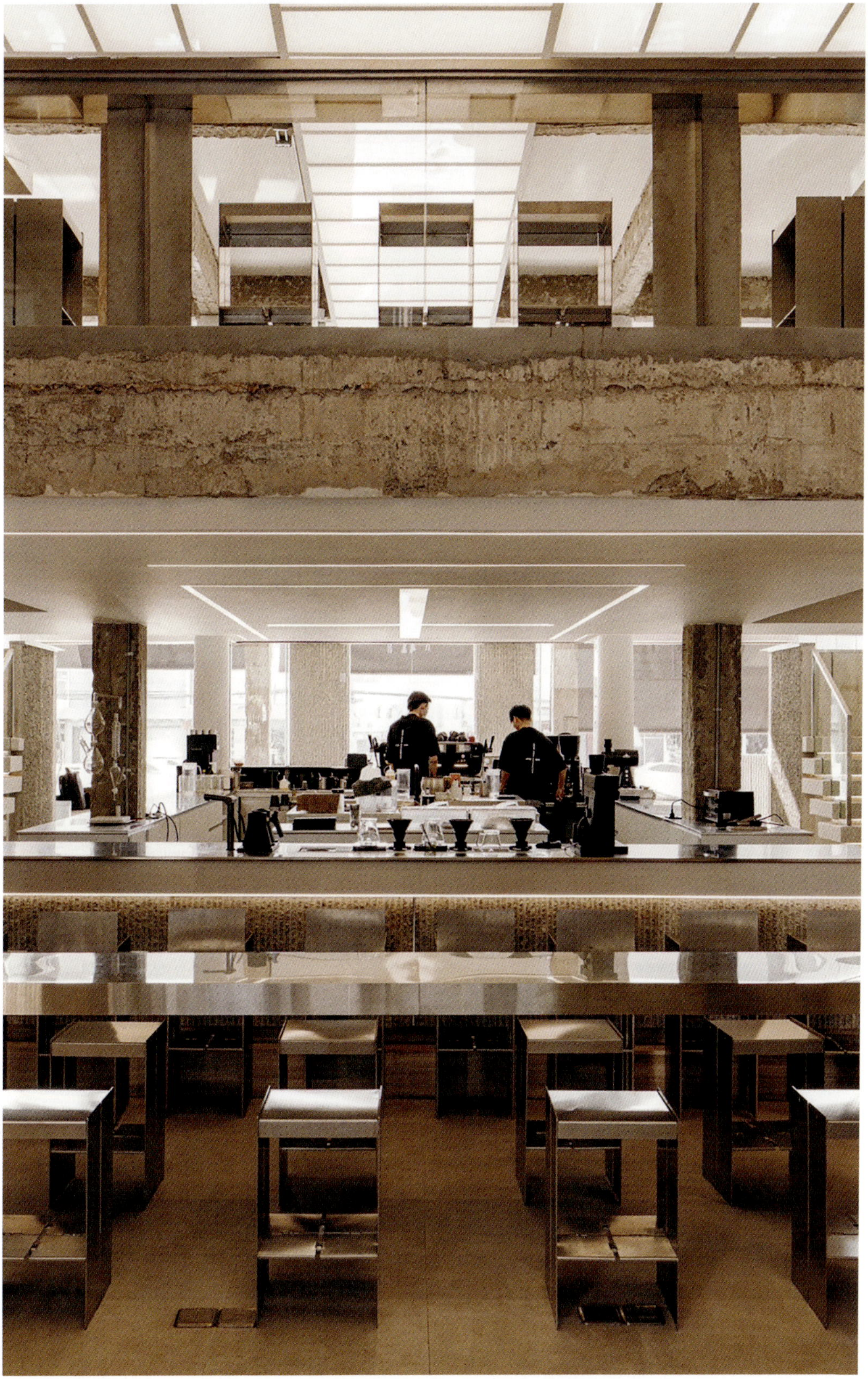

65 COLLEGE STREET COFFEE HOUSE

15 Bankim Chatterjee St, College Street, Kolkata, West Bengal 700073, India

TO VISIT BEFORE YOU DIE BECAUSE

With past patrons including freedom fighters and great poets, this Kolkata institution founded in 1942 serves coffee with a dash of nostalgia.

There are nearly 400 Indian Coffee Houses in the country; the most famous by a mile being this landmark establishment near the University of Kolkata and Presidency College. Once operated by the Indian Coffee Board and threatened with closure, the coffee houses were saved by the workers, encouraged by communist leader A.K. Gopalan. Today they are still run by a series of cooperatives – and India is still one of the world's leading coffee producers. Located in the 1876 Albert Hall, the College Street Coffee House was once a meeting place for students, professors, poets, artists and politicians – the perfect spot for *adda* (hanging out). Today its grand dining hall, with Formica tables and mismatched chairs, is full of friends and family chatting under the buzz of the ceiling fans. Don't expect fast service from the waiters, dressed in white from head to toe, but instead take some time to soak up the atmosphere over a cup of special hot coffee and a plate of onion pakora.

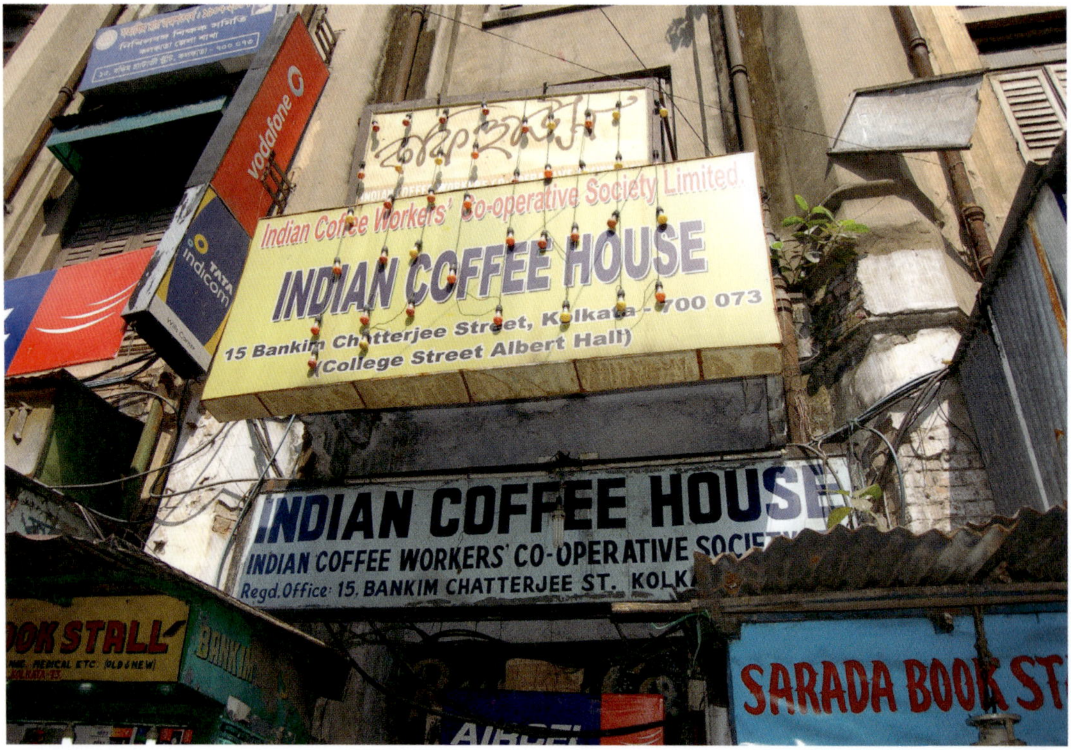

66 AFLOAT

2-15, Second Floor, Jalan Jalil Perkasa 13, Arked Esplanad, 57000 Kuala Lumpur, Malaysia

TO VISIT BEFORE YOU DIE BECAUSE

Levitate above the grind of daily life at this zen café where every cup reminds you 'to pause, to be present, and to simply stay afloat'.

Afloat is a minimalist roastery and café founded in 2022 by Loo Choy Leng and Jimmy Leong. The dark walls and long black counter pull you into a light-filled space opening onto a balcony lined with stools and offering views of the surrounding trees. 'Afloat is a micro-roastery born from a simple belief – that great coffee should be both exceptional in quality and comforting in experience,' explain the couple. 'Every cup we serve begins with intention: from mindful relationships at the farm level to precise roasting and brewing guided by daily calibration. Yet beyond the cup, Afloat is about more than coffee. It's a moment of calm amidst movement, a space where warmth and comfort quietly unfold.' In their pursuit of clarity and simplicity, the pair present their coffee curated in four distinctive categories – Macro, Micro, Unique, and Rare Find, 'each telling a story of craftsmanship, terroir and time'. Their signature is the Rare Find filter coffee that features seasonal competition series, and the cold Irish coffee that almost tastes like tiramisu.

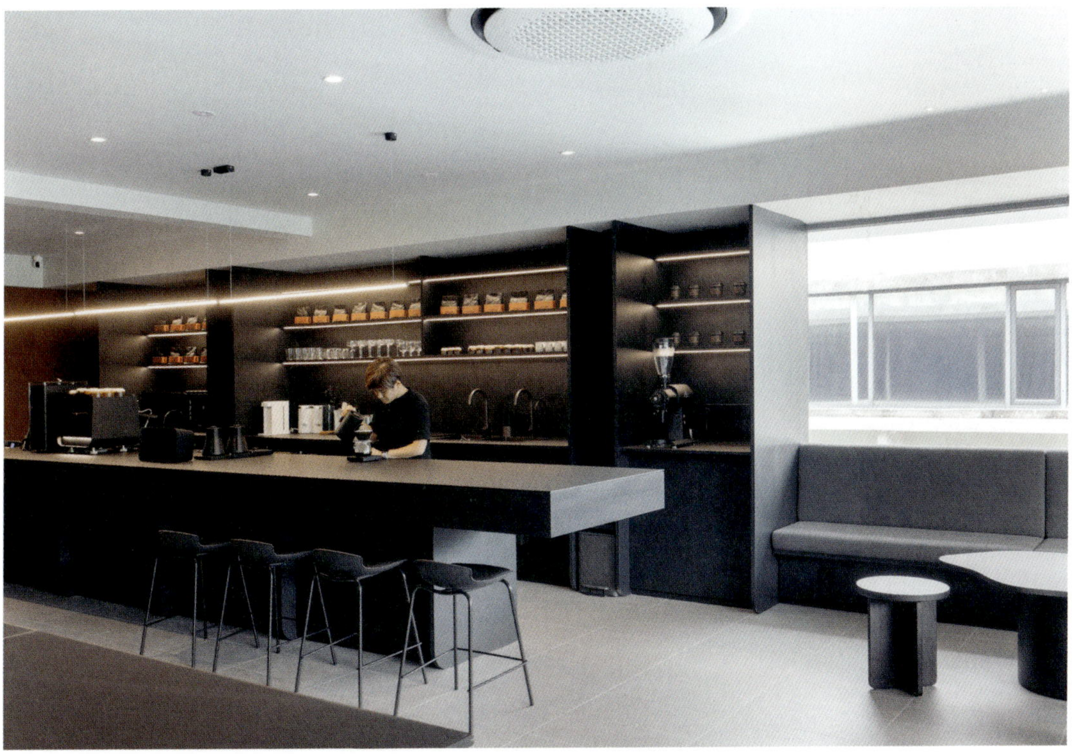

@afloatcoffeeroaster +60 19 727 1699

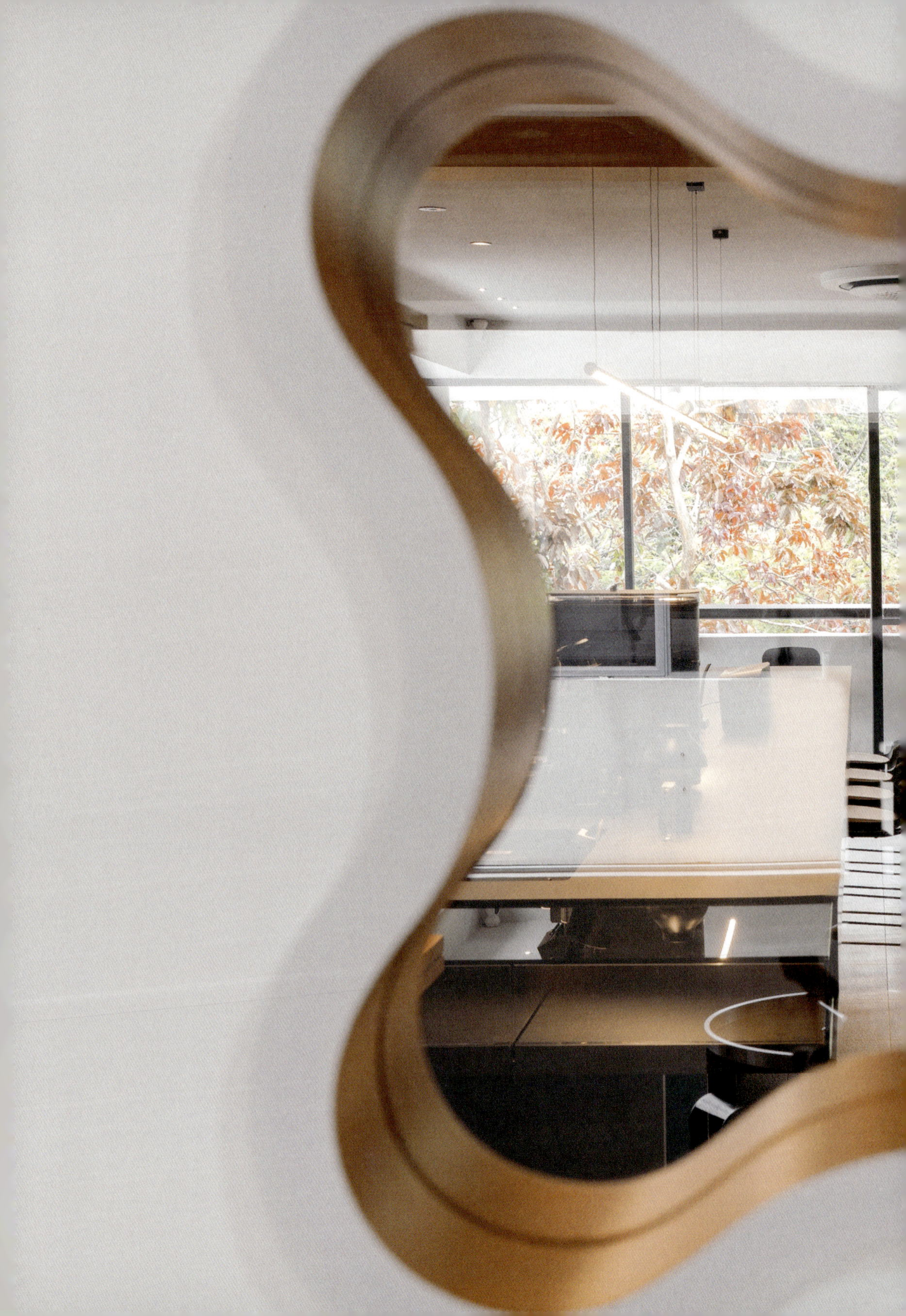

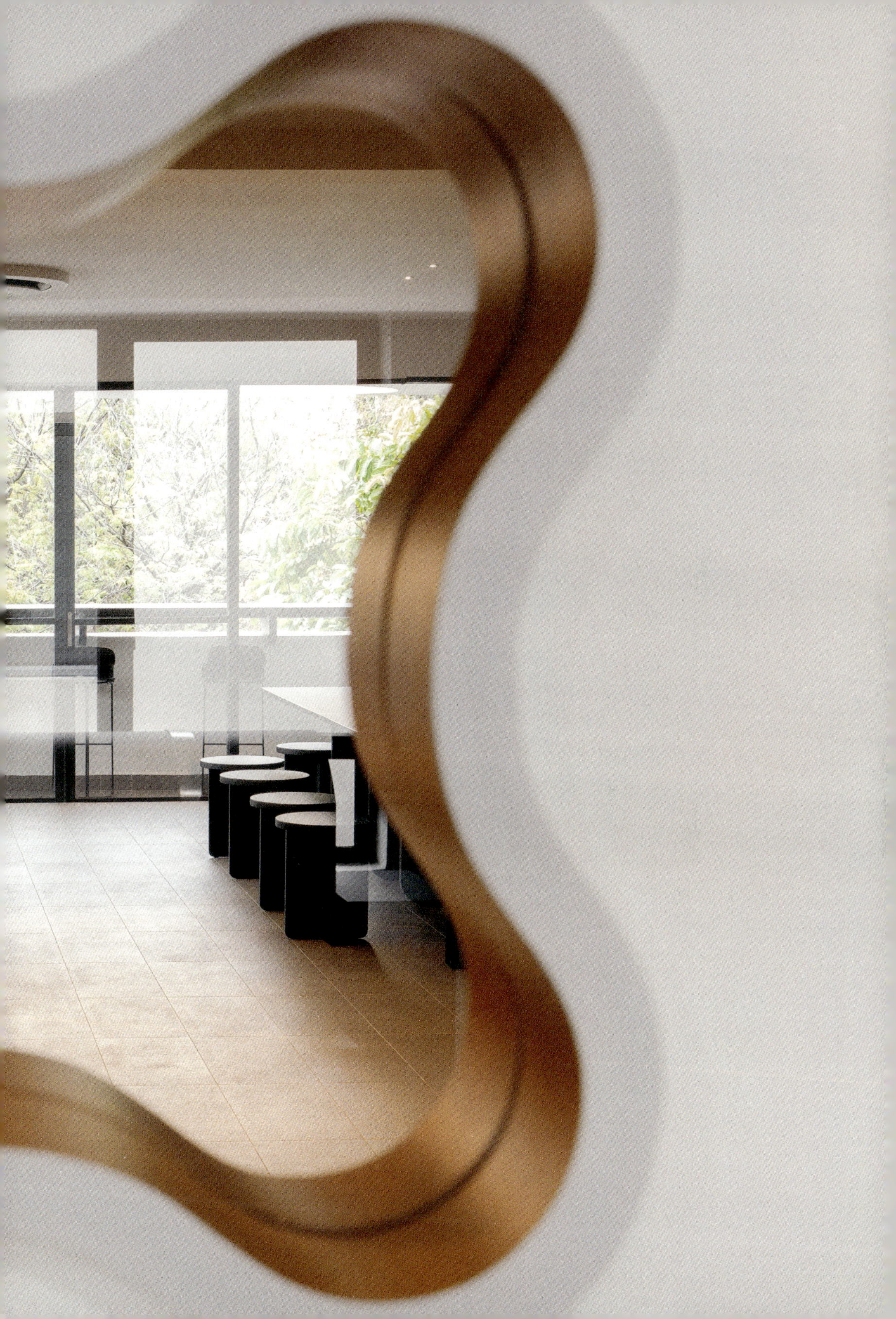

67 INODA COFFEE HOUSE

140 Doyucho, Nakagyo Ward, Kyoto 604-8118, Japan

TO VISIT BEFORE YOU DIE BECAUSE

Start the day with milky, sweet coffee and a hearty breakfast in one of the oldest Japanese-style cafés in Kyoto.

Kyoto is famous for its retro *kissaten*, European-style cafés that flourished in the 1920s as quieter, more elegant spaces to enjoy a cup of coffee. Although their name means 'tea-drinking shop', *kissaten* such as Inoda are primarily known for their coffee and breakfast. So much so that the saying goes: 'Kyoto mornings start with Inoda', referring both to the house's Pearl of Arabia dark-roast blend, designed to be enjoyed with lots of milk and sugar, and its Kyoto breakfast (croissant, scrambled eggs, ham and salad). Founded in the 1940s, when Shichiro Inoda discovered 15 bags of coffee beans in his warehouse after he returned from the war, Inoda is a true time warp. The traditional interiors are complemented by a little museum, a modern extension with huge windows, and a leafy garden where you can sit at tables with gingham tablecloths and have a plate of 'Italian spaghetti' – a recipe unchanged since the 1960s. And don't forget to try the signature pudding; this Japanese take on the crème caramel is a classic item in retro cafés.

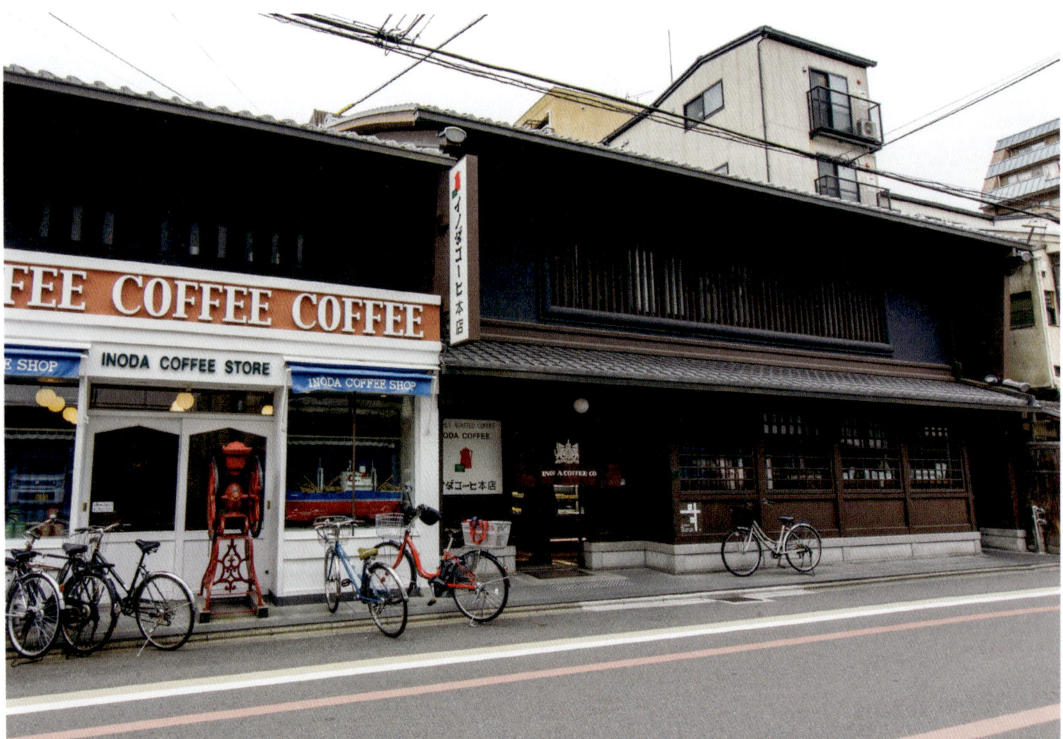

inoda-coffee.co.jp +81 75 221 0507

68 WEEKENDERS COFFEE TOMINOKOJI

560 Honeyanocho, Nakagyo-ku, Kyoto 604-8064, Japan

TO VISIT
BEFORE YOU DIE
BECAUSE

This charming, discreet café in a quiet corner of Kyoto celebrates the art of good coffee with a unique brand of thoughtful craftsmanship.

Masahiro and Ayumi Kaneko first met over a cup of espresso at a French café, and their story has been linked to the magic beans ever since. In 2005 they opened a traditional café with a food menu, but soon got frustrated by the quality of the coffee available in Japan at the time. In 2011, after an enlightening cupping session with Tim Wendelboe (page 190), they took matters into their own hands, turning their business into a speciality coffee roaster – despite neither of them having any experience with roasting. Now able to control their raw material, they spent years tirelessly connecting with top growers, perfecting their roasts and welcoming their customers with warmth. The result speaks for itself: their low-key stand-up bar, opened in 2016 in a traditional wooden townhouse, has become a cult destination for coffee fans. The lack of seating is intentional: it's designed to make people pay more attention to the coffee's light roast, and to the people you are enjoying it with.

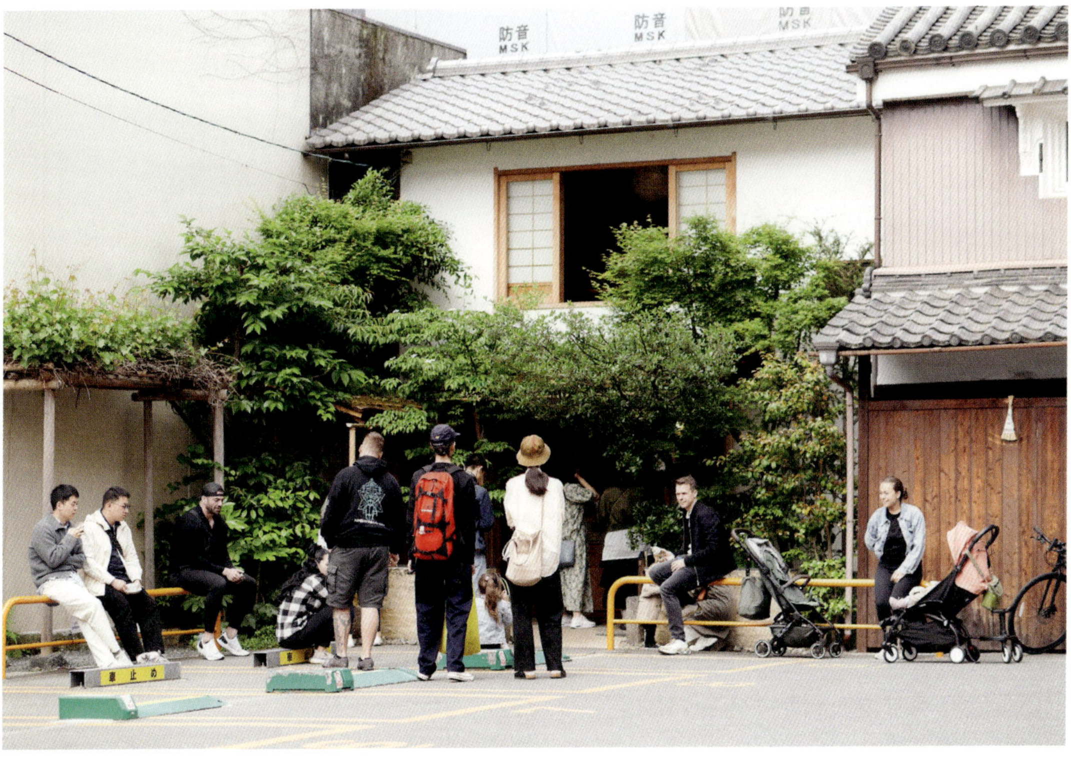

weekenderscoffee.com +81 75 746 2206

69 MARY LODGE BY SUBKO COFFEE

21A Chapel Rd, Ranwar, Bandra West, Mumbai, Maharashtra 400050, India

TO VISIT BEFORE YOU DIE BECAUSE

The original outpost of a homegrown coffee and chocolate specialists is a series of quaint atmospheric spaces filled with surprises.

The upscale Mumbai suburb of Bandra West is home to a maze of alleyways, filled with old shops, new boutiques and colourful street art. It is here, in a Portuguese bungalow dating from the 1920s, that Subko Coffee was founded in 2020 by Rahul Reddy, with a goal to place Indian speciality coffee on the global map. A short form of 'subcontinent', its name also means 'for everyone' in many Hindustani registers – and to be fair, the recently renovated building certainly offers something for everyone. There's a Coffee room, Chocolate room and Wheat room, as well as a Type room celebrating the work of the graphic design arm of Subko, and a Cacao Cellar displaying its complete range of craft chocolates. Not to mention an attic space with Japanese-style elevated floor seating, a corner dedicated to old-school 8bit games, and an audio/visual experience room. Sit at one of the communal tables to enjoy a mango French toast, washed down with a Salawara Estate Yeast Aerobic or a Strawberry cascara (made with the dried fruit of the coffee cherry).

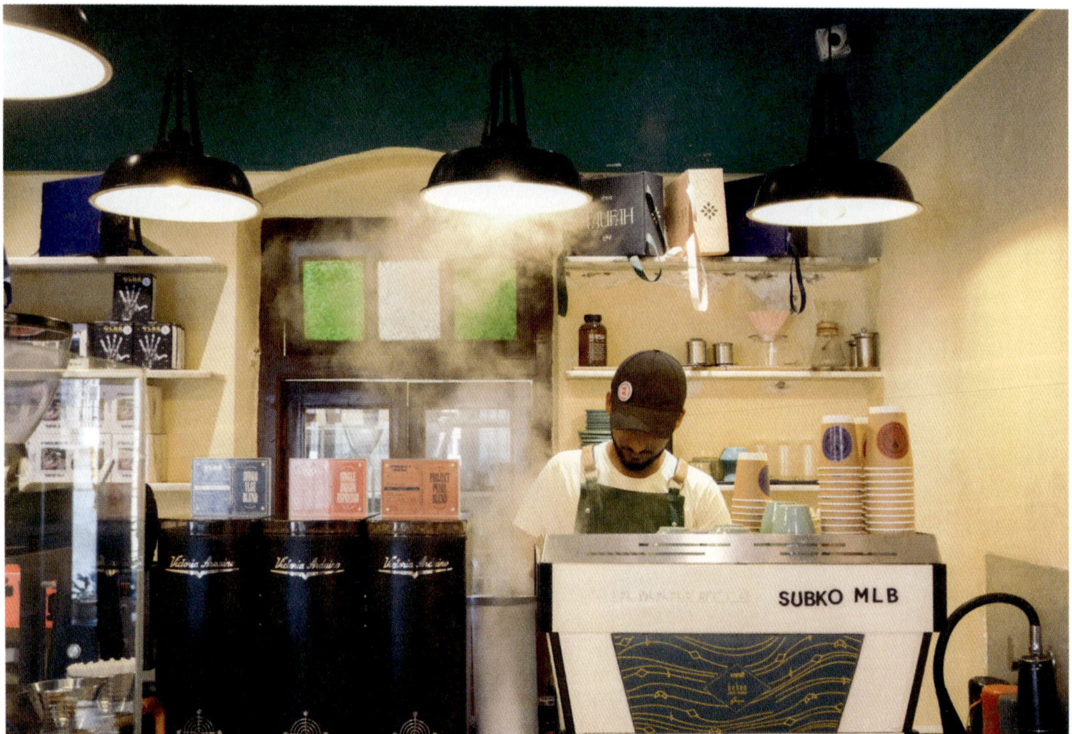

subko.coffee +91 85 9174 5691

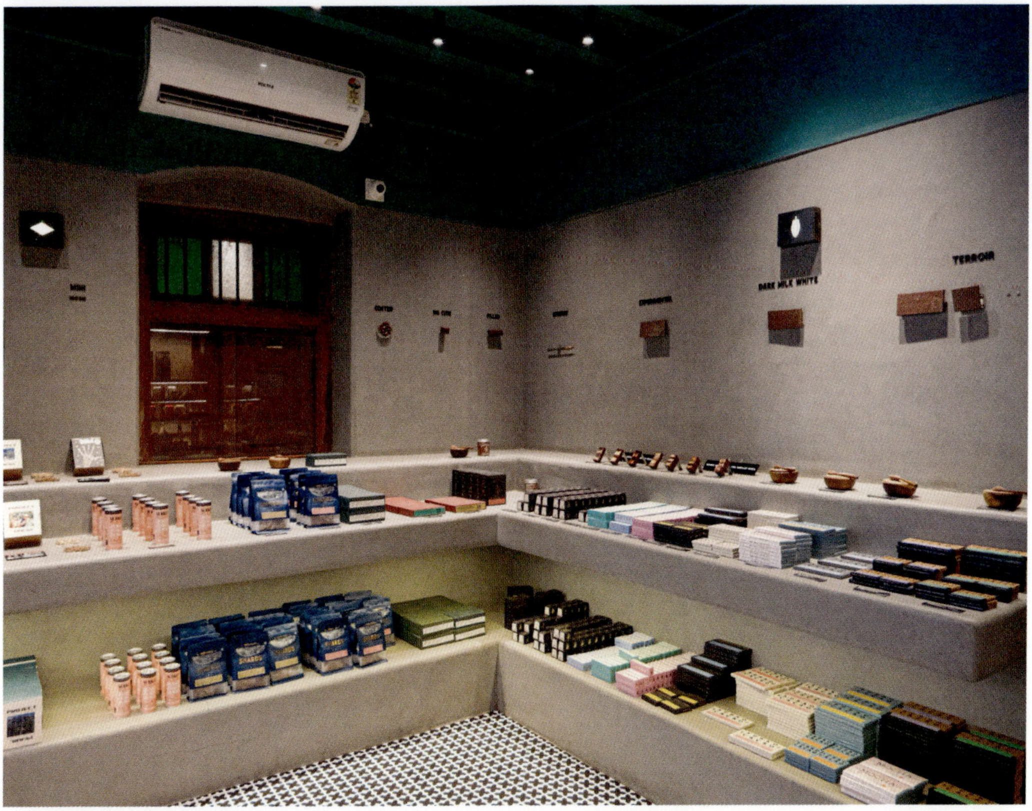
DARK MILK WHITE
TERROIR

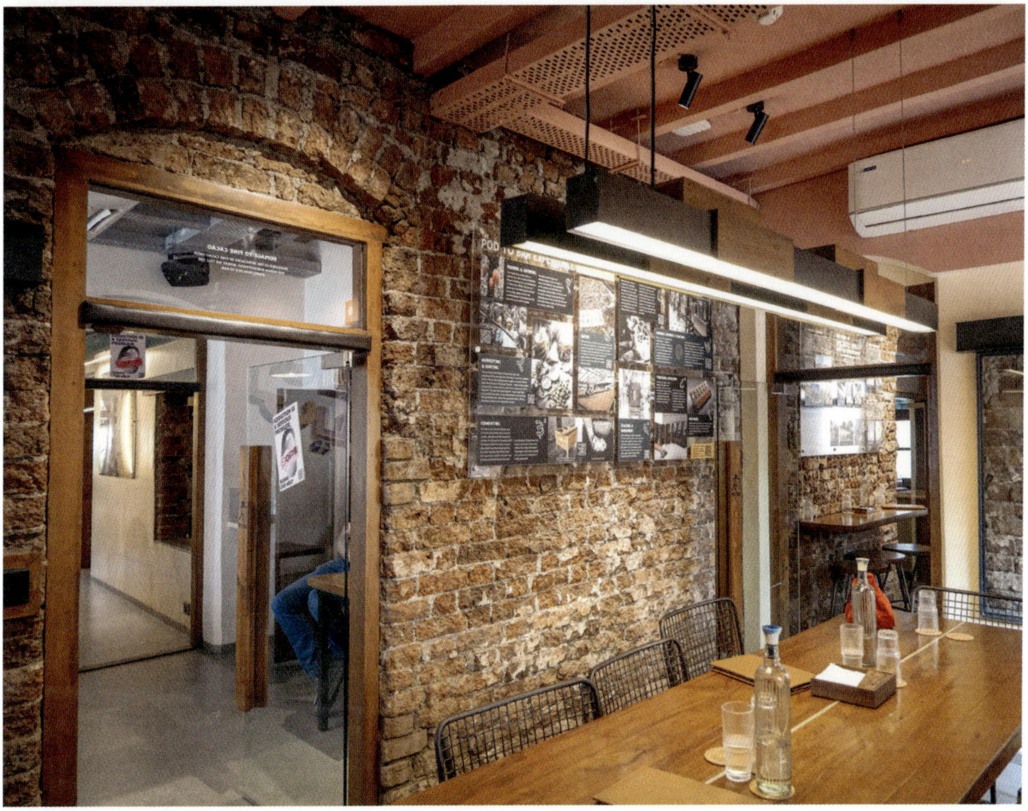

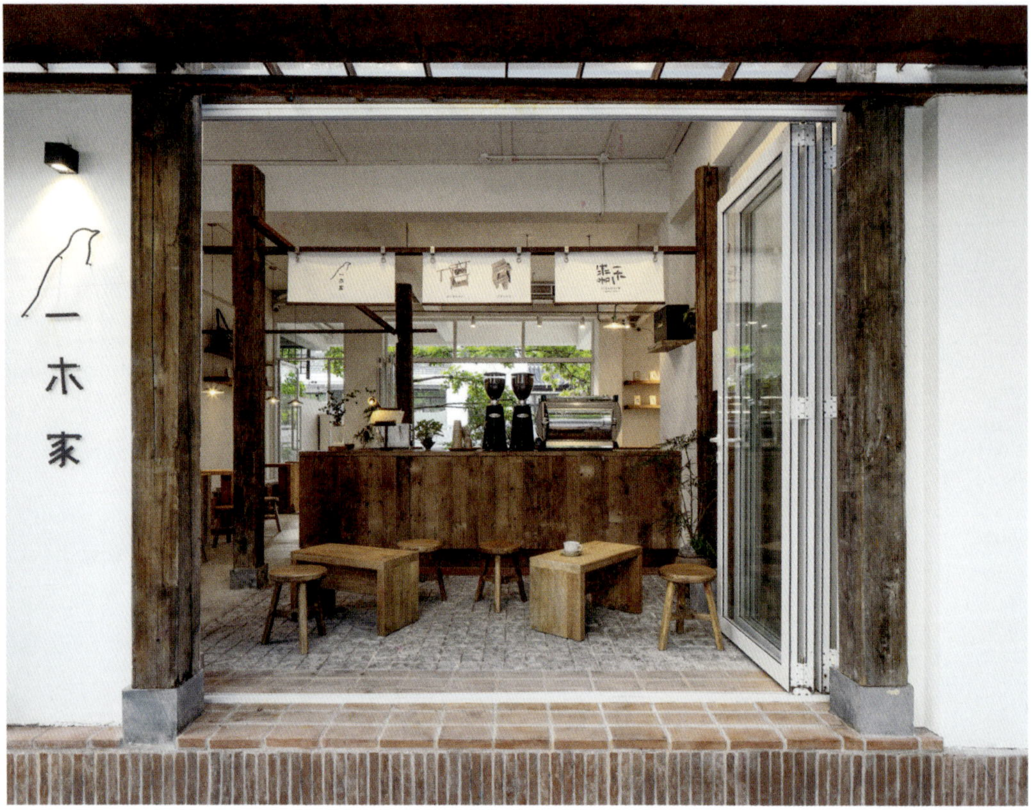
一木家

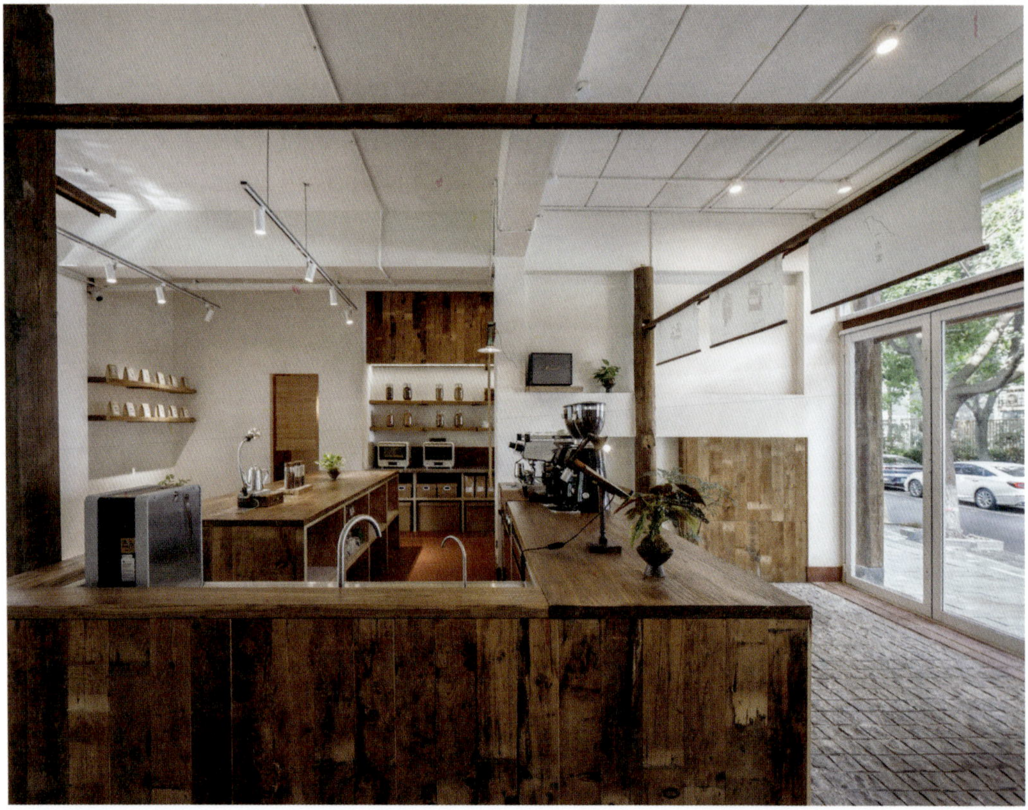

70 CAFÉ CHEZ W

105 Xin Fu He, Qin Huai Qu, Nan Jing Shi, Jiang Su Sheng, China, 210004

TO VISIT
BEFORE YOU DIE
BECAUSE

This beautiful café designed by Atelier TUO is a peaceful haven on the banks of the Qinhuai River serving great coffee and homemade cakes.

Café Chez W was first established in 2017 on Shanghai's Xiangshan Road, where its cosy interiors are signposted by the outline of a bird painted on the façade. The logo, by local studio Overice, refers to the story of the owner, Wei Yimu, a former engineer who flew back to his nest after studying in Paris. Since 2023, a second perch has opened for the black bird: this gorgeous café in nearby Nanjing. Designed by Atelier TUO, it's a contemporary take on traditional Chinese architecture celebrating the beauty of wood. A series of old cedar columns, raised on granite blocks, divide and balance the minimalist space, furnished with lauan wood furniture, hemlock decorative side panels and elm countertops. Paving stones bring an outdoor feel to the interior space, which opens onto a wooden riverside balcony. At the centre of it all is the bar, serving up everything from espresso to Turkish and Viennese coffee. Homemade cakes include freshly baked scones and matcha cookies.

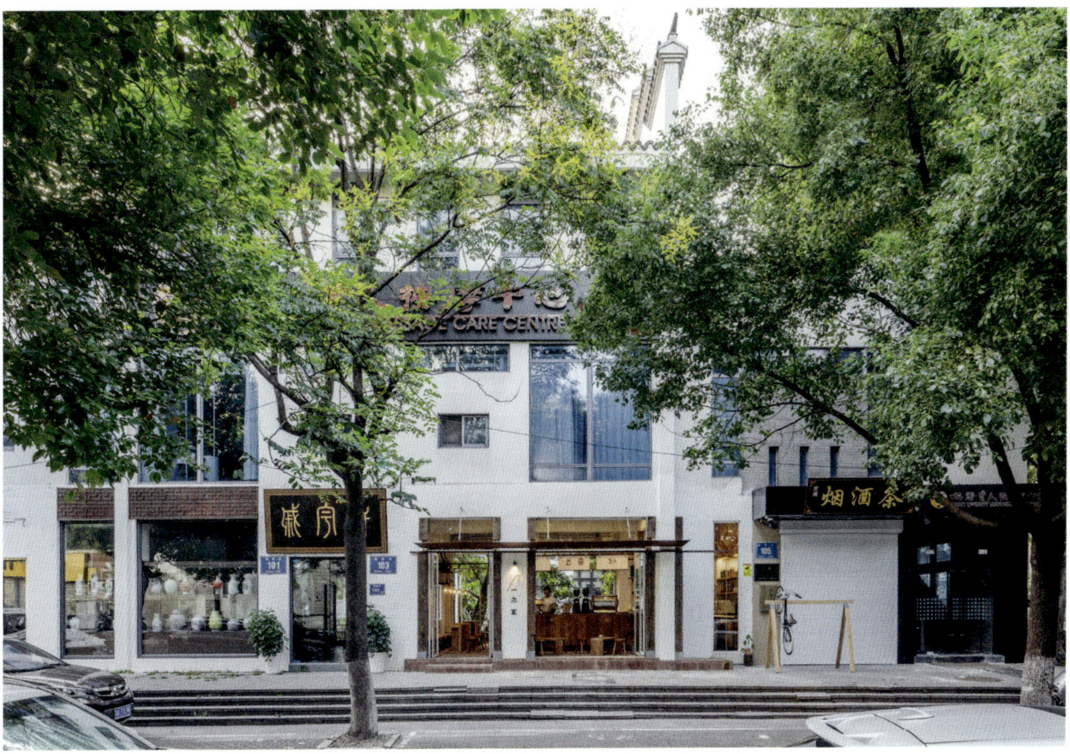

@cafechezw

71 LILO COFFEE KISSA

Kaneko Building 2F 2-7-25 Shinsaibashisuji Chuo Ward Osaka, Japan

TO VISIT BEFORE YOU DIE BECAUSE

Try a great variety of coffees and coffee-infused treats in this charming historic *kissaten* reinterpreted for the 21st century.

LiLo Coffee Roasters was founded in 2014 in Osaka, Japan. Their first outpost (in the same building where founder Kyohei Hotta had his hair salon) proved instantly popular, thanks to its selection of over twenty distinctive coffees at all times. Key to their success is the team's focus on 'enjoyment', 'diversity' and 'live in love', an approach that shines through the attitude of the friendly and passionate baristas. A modern interpretation of the traditional Japanese coffee house, their second café is housed in a *kissaten* previously under the same management for nearly fifty years. Perfectly preserved, the first-floor wood-panelled space offers peace and quiet away from the city street. Here, you can 'experience the depth of coffee through brewing methods like siphon and pour-over, where each cup brings out a different expression depending on the beans and equipment'. Try the best-selling coffee jelly or a decadent tiramisu made with LiLo's signature blend, or spend the evening sipping on coffee mocktails.

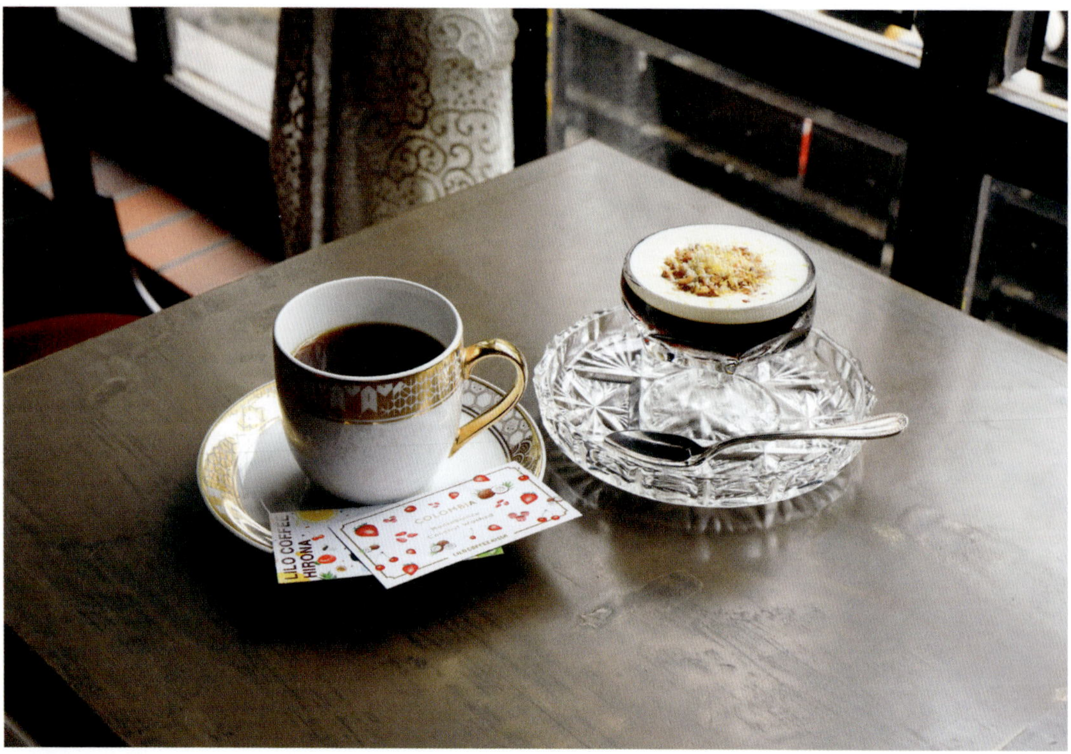

coffee.liloinveve.com +81 66 226 8682

72 EL UNION COFFEE

Great Northwest, Urbiztondo, San Juan, La Union, Philippines

TO VISIT
BEFORE YOU DIE
BECAUSE

Try ethically sourced Filipino coffees at this beachside café, known for its chilled vibes, music sessions and cool packaging.

'Happy people make world-class products,' say Amy and Kiddo Cosio, the founders of this cute café and roastery located a stone's throw from the surfer paradise that is San Juan beach. Always considering the humans behind every bean, they roast high-quality local coffees such as the Tuba Washed from Benguet, sourced in collaboration with long-time partner Kapi Tako. As for Future Fruit, an Excelsa coffee with notes of cherry produced by Jojo Esumadia, it is 'a continuation of the global south's journey with non-arabica coffees. We in the tropics have long loved our lowland varieties, and always will,' they say. As well as the usual cold brews and espressos, the menu showcases very local drinks, including a toasted rice coffee soda (a sweet, fizzy espresso drink made with house soda and the same rice tea used in El Union's classic rice horchata), Dulce kape (a Filipino-Spanish latte) and the Dirty Champorado, which is made by adding espresso to horchata and Malagos 100% Davao Single Origin chocolate. Feeling peckish? Try a cheese toastie with sriracha.

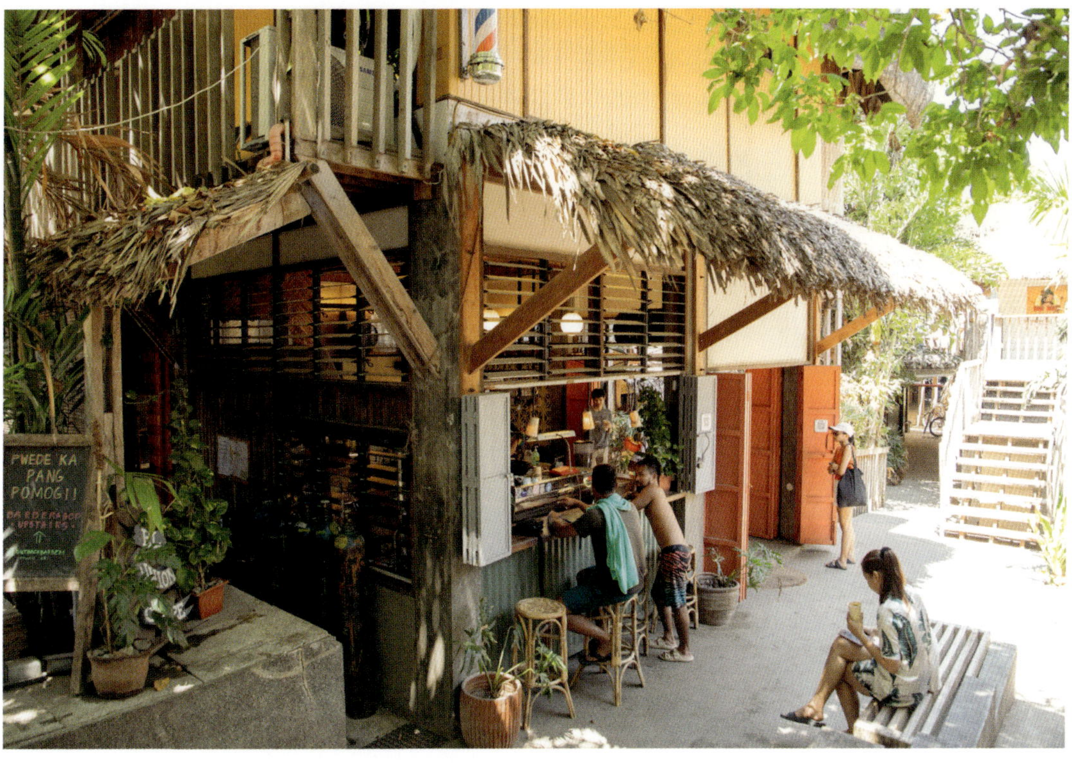

@elunion; elunioncoffee.com

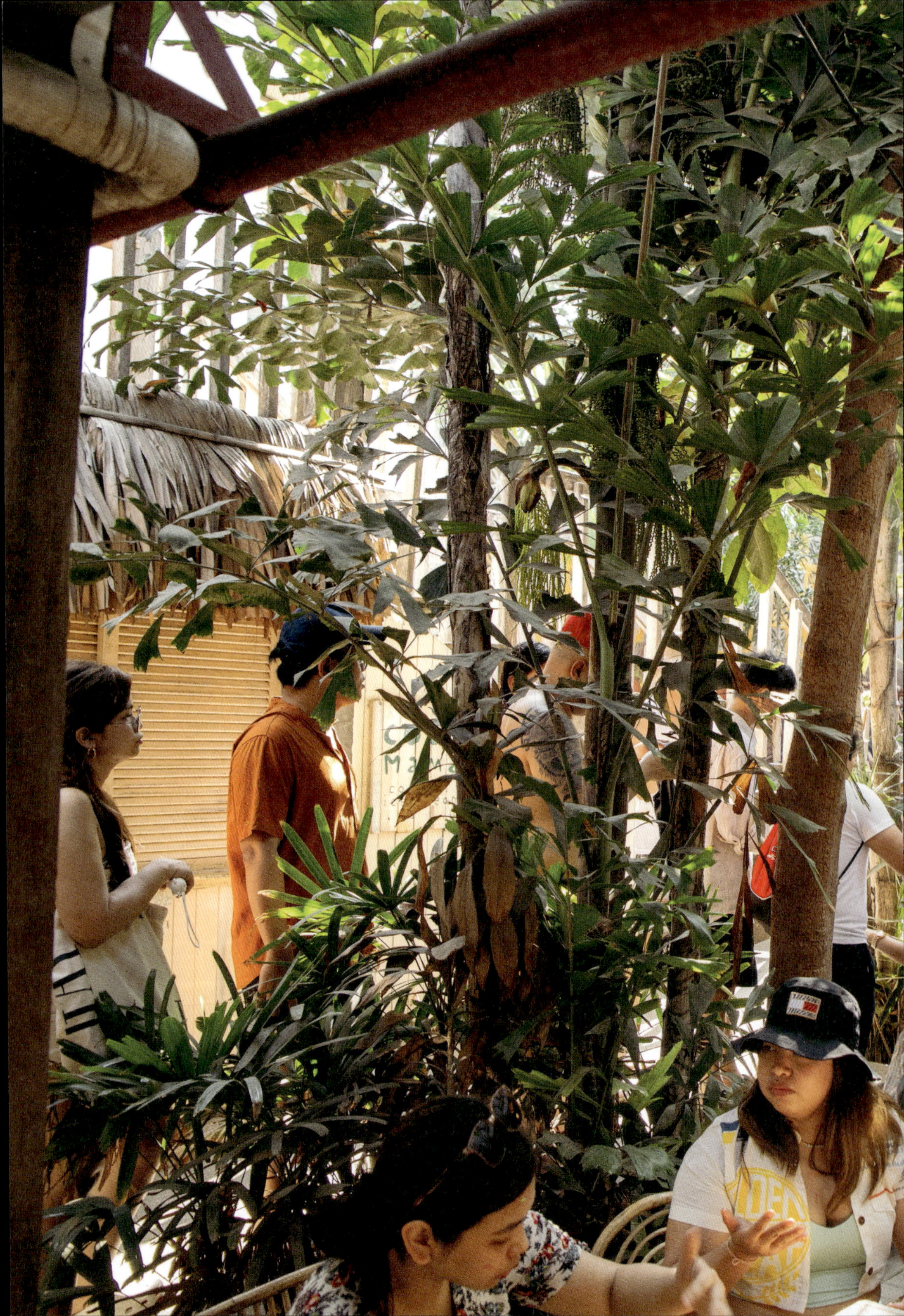

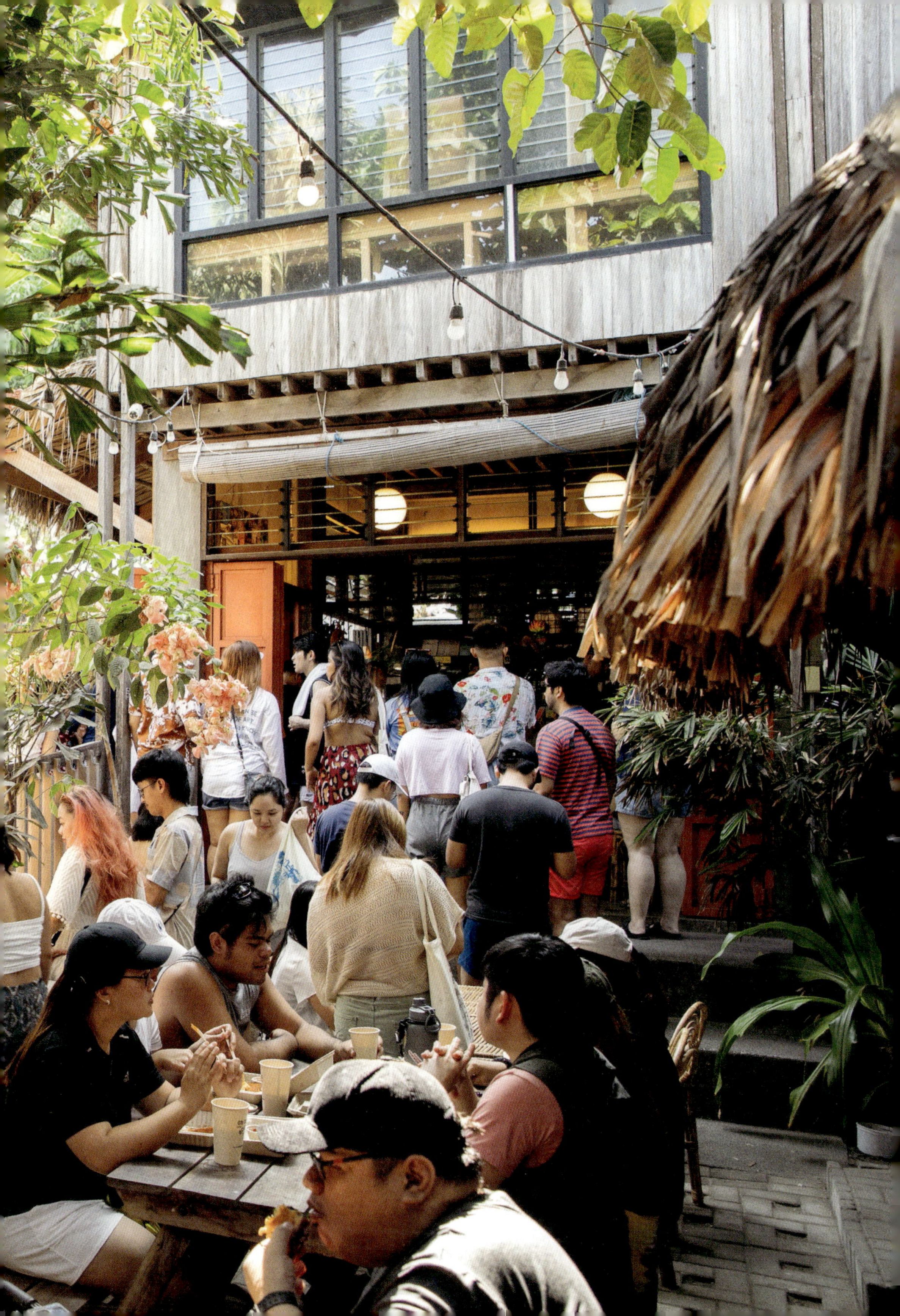

73 COFFEE NAP ROASTERS YEONMAN

70 Seongmisan-ro 27-gil, Mapo-gu, Seoul, South Korea

TO VISIT BEFORE YOU DIE BECAUSE

Try incredible, ethically sourced coffee in an unbelievable interior at this peaceful café loved by locals and tourists alike.

Coffee is both a stimulant and the excuse for slowing things down and taking a break. And, as its name indicates, it is this second use that independent South Korean coffee brand Coffee Nap Roasters are keen to support. Its cafés are places 'where you can enjoy a cup of coffee and spend some time relaxing,' but don't expect comfy sofas at their Yeonman branch, an altogether more conceptual space with an undulating brick floor. Studio Maoom's award-winning design for this tiny corner café in an alleyway removes the need for tables and chairs by building a hill out of 7,000 bricks, 'to create space and scenery within the café'. You can sit on the hill (there are some wooden benches and outdoor stools too) and enjoy the brick landscape, letting your imagination roam as the sun flows into the unique interiors. The ethical and sustainable coffee shop offers three house blends named 317, 218 and 420, the numbers representing the total number of farmers working in the various countries where the beans are grown.

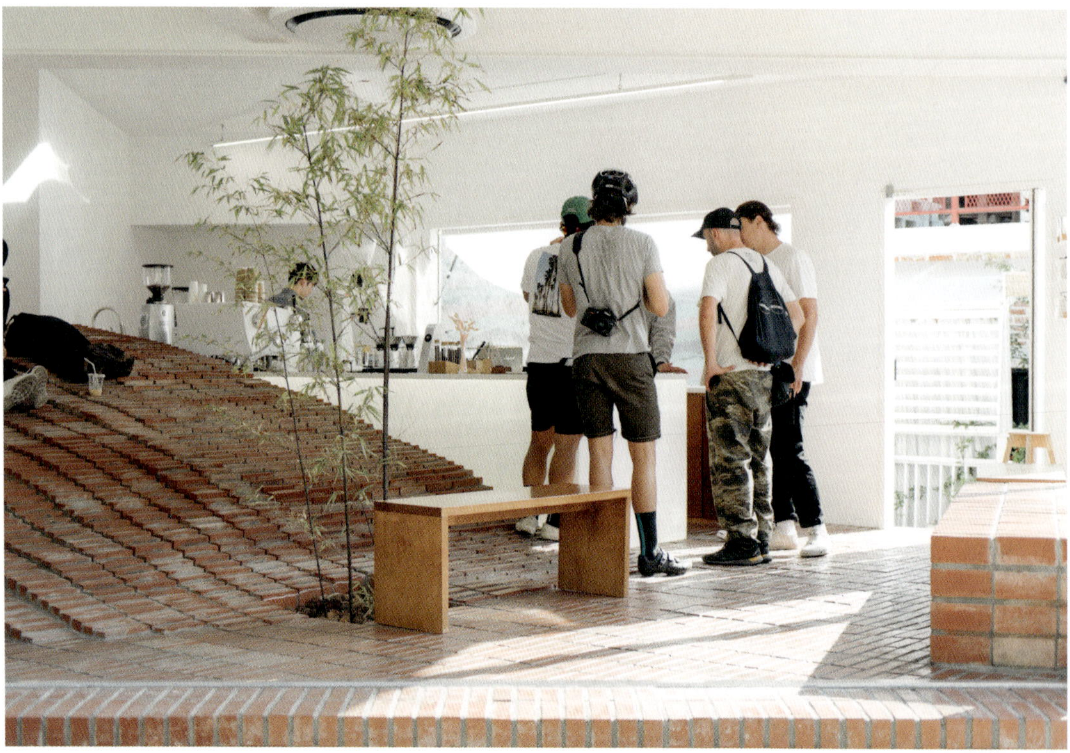

coffeenaproasters.com +82 2 332 4131

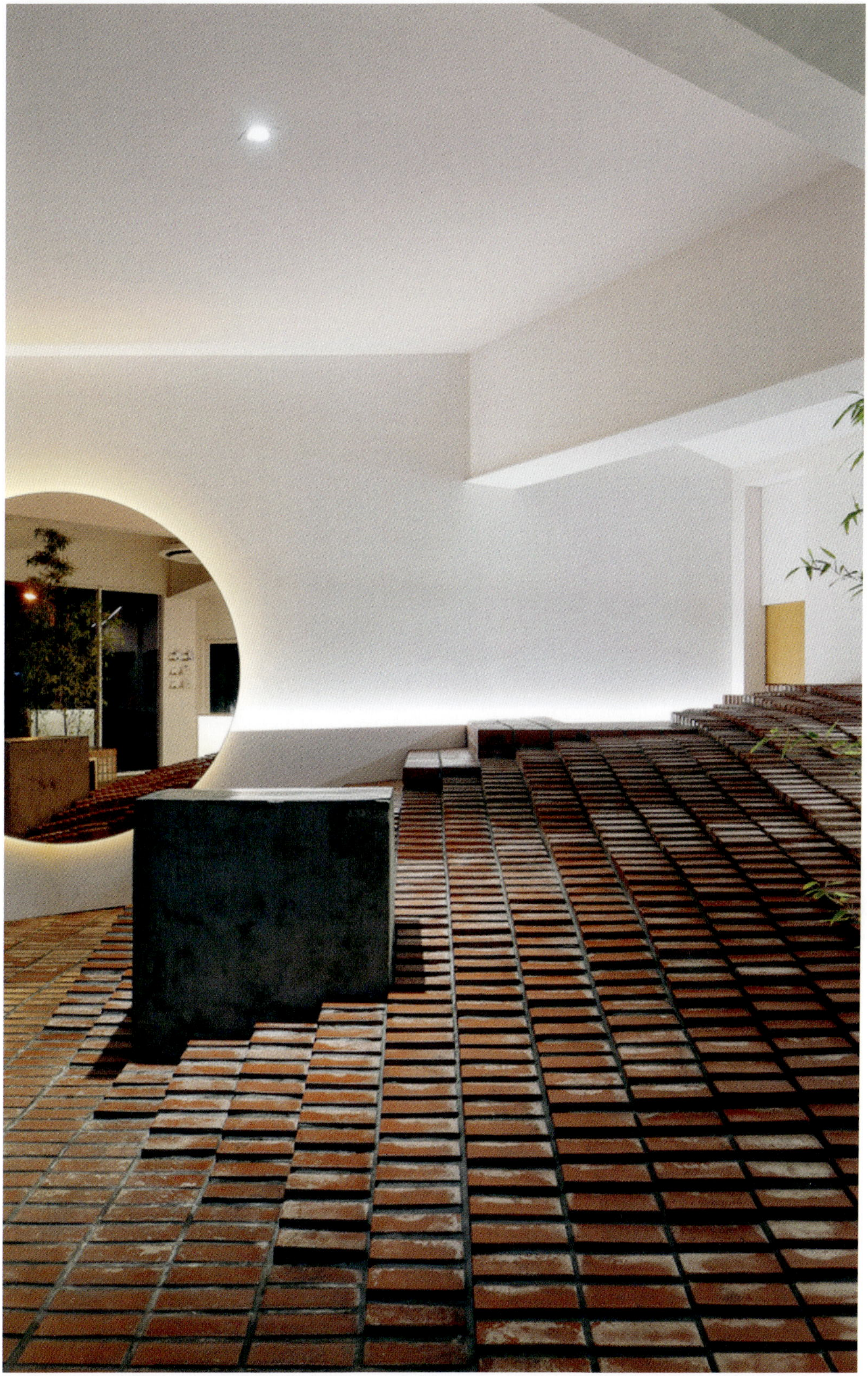

74 FRITZ DOHWA

17 Saechang-ro 2-gil, Mapo-gu, Seoul, South Korea

TO VISIT BEFORE YOU DIE BECAUSE

Try the original outpost of cult South Korean roasters Fritz, easily recognisable with is vintage-style, coffee-drinking seal mascot.

South Koreans are among the world's biggest coffee drinkers, with consumption levels more than double the global average. The black gold that once fuelled the country's post-war construction boom and today's long working hours is now an integral part of local culture. Founded in 2014 by a group of six friends (including a roaster, green bean buyer, baker and award-winning baristas) to create 'the best coffee experience in Seoul', Fritz Coffee has pioneered a sustainable, direct-trade and design-led approach to coffee in the capital. The company's first Seoul location in Dohwa is particularly worth a visit. Located in a renovated *hanok* with a peaceful courtyard and rooftop terrace, it's an atmospheric spot in a residential area with a jumble of tiny houses and towers. House blends include the sweet and perfectly balanced Everything Good and bittersweet Old Dog, while single origins range from Santa Teresa Geisha Washed to La Lucuma Marshell Natural. Enjoy an iced Americano (South Korea's favourite coffee) with the chef's special, a yellow peach Danish pastry.

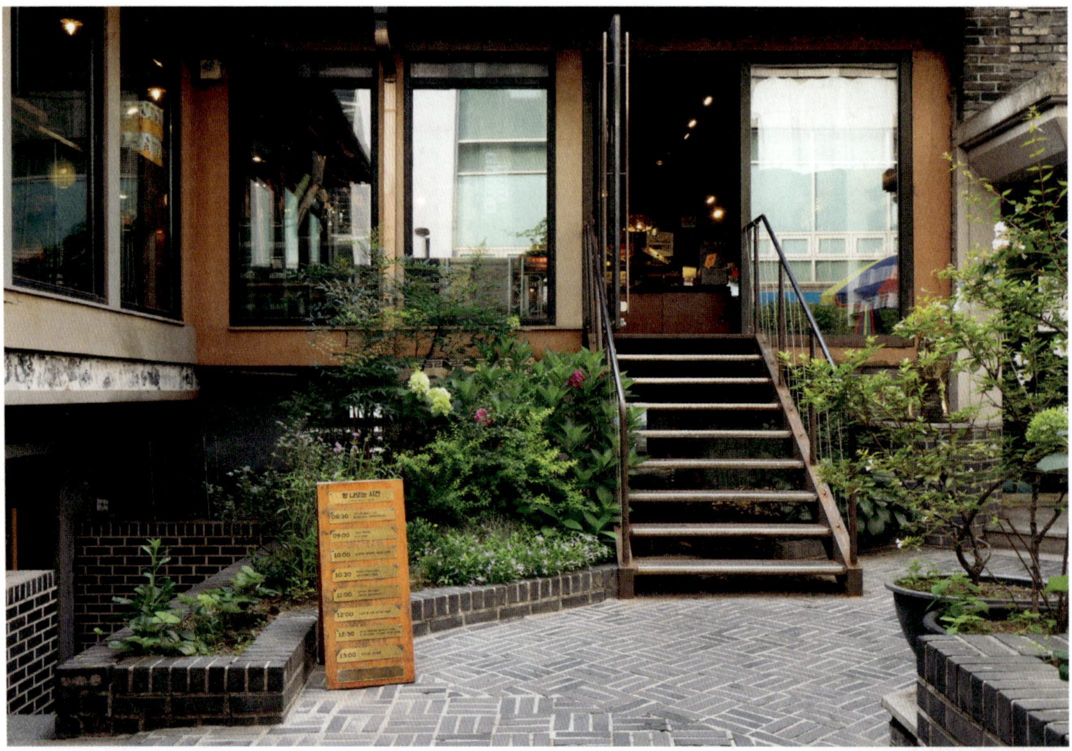

en.fritz.co.kr

+82 2 3275 2045

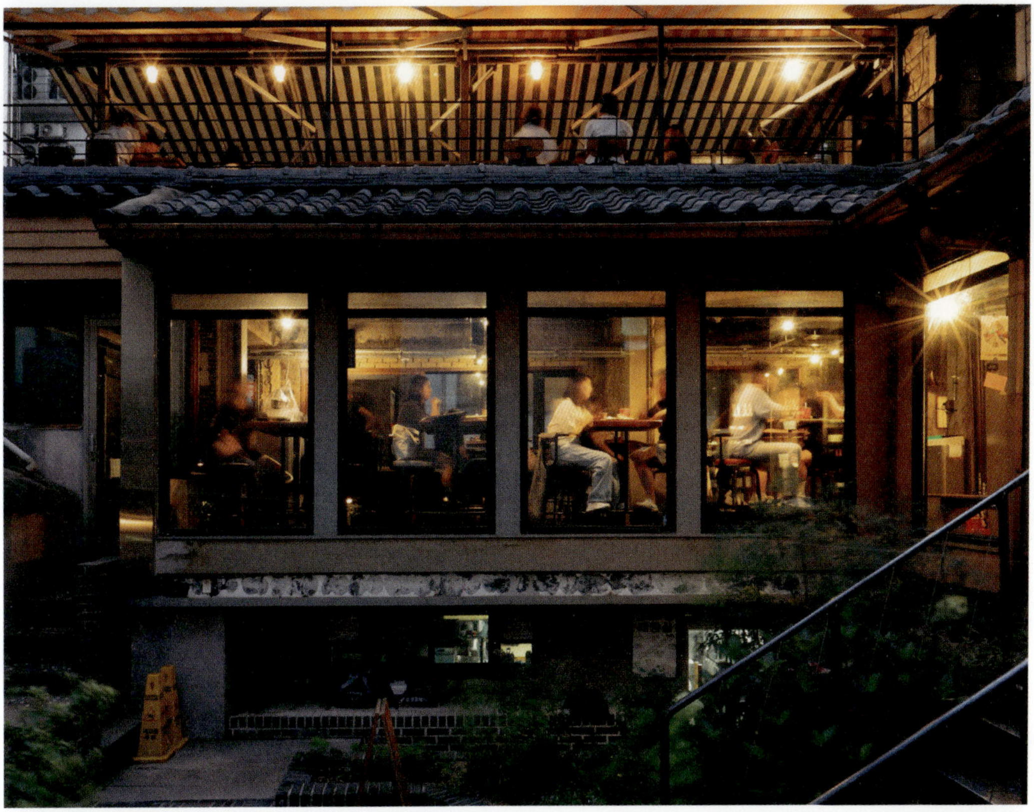

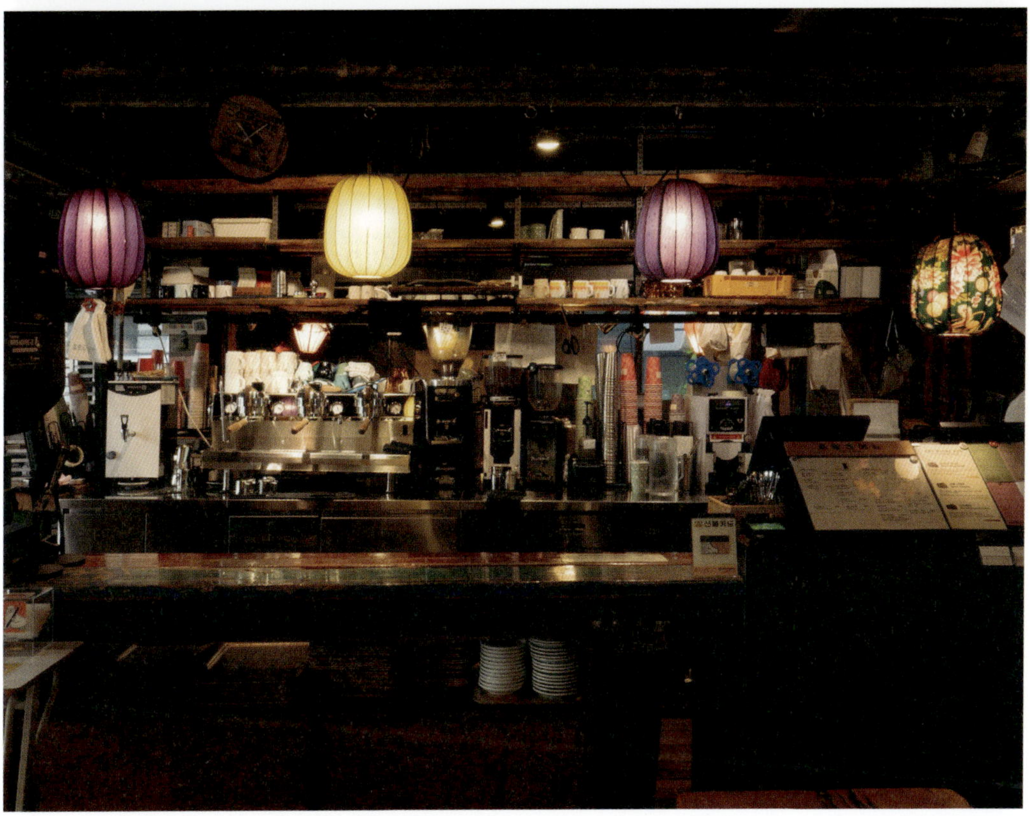

75 MANNER NORTH BUND

Baiyulan Plaza, 588 Dongchangzhi Rd, Hongkou, Shanghai, China, 200086

TO VISIT BEFORE YOU DIE BECAUSE

Contemplate how much China has changed in the last decades with a Yunnan coffee latte and skyline views at Shanghai's answer to Starbucks.

There's been a true coffee boom in Shanghai since the pandemic. Perhaps because the Chinese lockdown was so strict, locals are making up for lost time, meeting up and relaxing in one of thousands of cafés in the metropolis. And it is literally thousands – there are currently about 10,000 cafés in the city. This number includes the second biggest Starbucks in the world and the 500 – and growing – coffee shops of 'boutique' chain Manner. Founded in Shanghai in 2015 by a former vet, Hán Yùlóng, as a humble roadside stall, it's now popular across the country for its classic coffees and minimalist interiors. With prices a third lower than Western chains, it helped transform Chinese people's perception of coffee, which used to be considered a high-end beverage (a notch above Coke). Here on Shanghai's North Bund, sample Manner's famously creamy latte while admiring panoramic views of the river, Pearl Tower and a forest of skyscrapers. Most beans come from Yunnan, while flavoured lattes cater to both local (osmanthus-infused) and Western (caramel cinnamon) tastes.

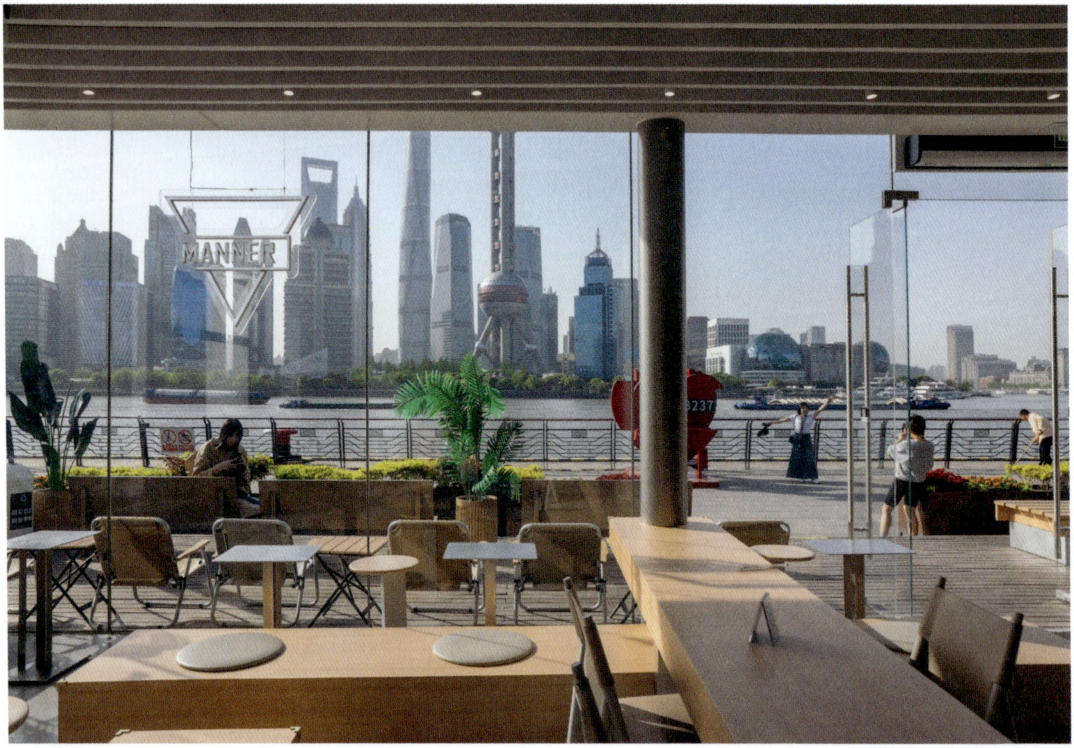

@manner_coffee

76 NYLON

4 Everton Park #01-40, Singapore 080004

TO VISIT BEFORE YOU DIE BECAUSE

Just a short stroll from Tanjong Pagar hawker market, this renowned coffee bar and roastery is the perfect stop for a post-prandial espresso.

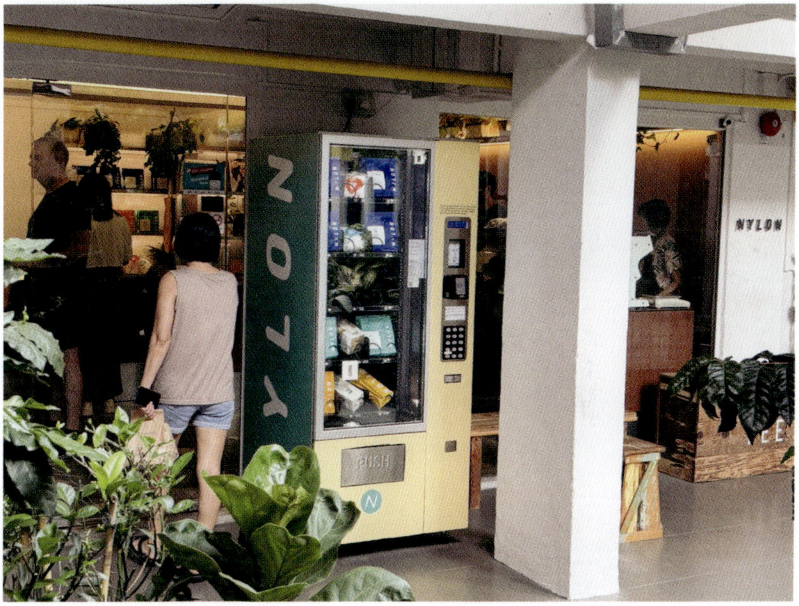

Singaporean duo Jia Min and Dennis got hooked on speciality coffee while working in the banking and IT industry in New York and London. And it is these two cities that have given its name to Nylon, founded in 2012 with the aim of telling the unique stories of each of their carefully selected coffees. Countless sourcing trips, establishing relationships with producers and 'focusing on behind-the-scenes work' have led the husband-and-wife team to earn their place as one of Singapore's finest roasters. 'We run a coffee bar adjacent to our roastery so that anyone can drop by to enjoy a cup or grab a bag of our beans,' they say. 'There's plenty of greenery in and out of the space to provide calm and tranquillity as you enjoy every sip from the cup. Feel free to chat with our team or even fellow customers – we pride ourselves on having a very friendly community who frequents our space.' Stock up on their seasonal coffee beans from different origins for brewing filters or espresso. Expect some queues on weekends, but nonetheless the team will do their best to provide a warm hospitality.

nylon.coffee +65 6220 2330

77 YA KUN FAR EAST SQUARE

18 China St, #01-01, Singapore 049560

TO VISIT BEFORE YOU DIE BECAUSE

Try a traditional coffee, roasted in margarine and sugar, along with crispy kaya toast at this Singapore institution.

Just like chocolate con churros or tea with scones, coffee is often part of a traditional gourmet duo that stands the test of time. Here in Singapore, *kopi* seems to be inseparable from its accompanying snacks, the *kaya* (coconut jam) toast and soft-boiled eggs. A popular place to taste this is at this colourful café near Singapore's Raffles Place station. Founded as a coffee stall by a hardworking Chinese immigrant from Hainan in the 1920s, Ya Kun was later dubbed 'The Most Courteous Stall in Lau Pa Sat' and moved into this old yellow shophouse on Far East Square in the late 1990s. A century later it still attracts the crowds with its breakfast of champions. *Kopi* is made from robusta coffee beans roasted in margarine and sugar, and served with condensed milk. There are many, many versions, including Kopi-O (black coffee with sugar), Kopi C (black coffee with sugar and evaporated milk) and the famous Malaysian pulled coffee, Kopi Tarik, a sweet coffee with a frothy top and condensed milk, made by pouring coffee between two cups.

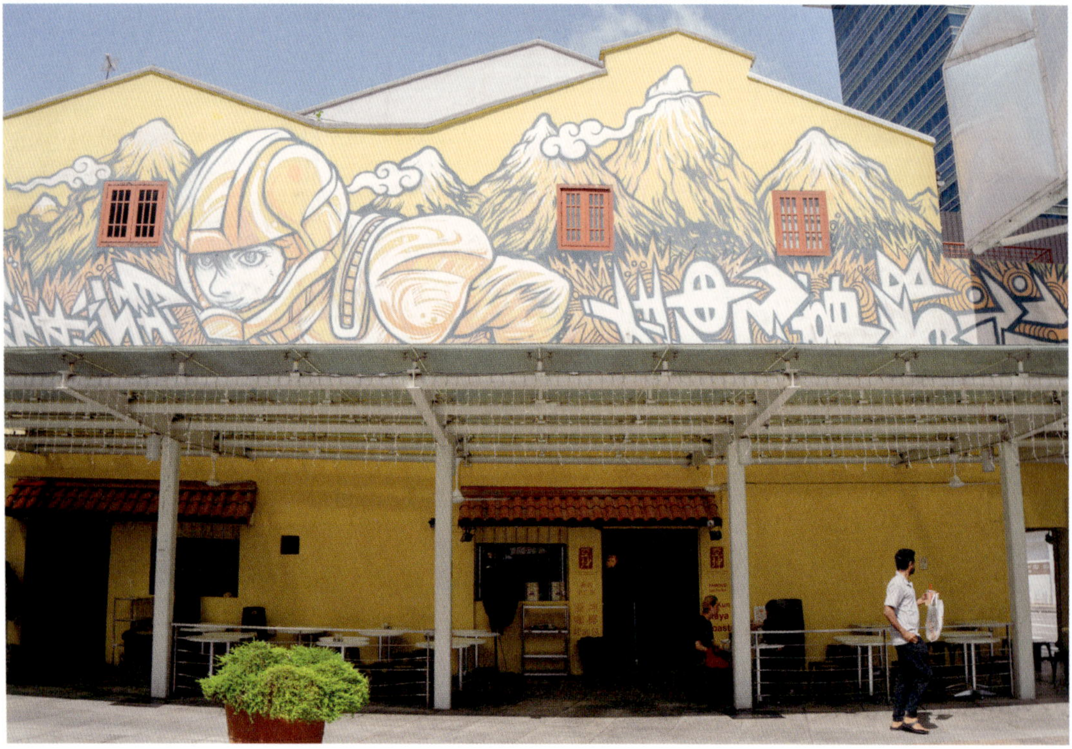

yakun.com +65 6438 3638

78 SIMPLE KAFFA HUASHAN

No. 27, Section 2, Zhongxiao E Rd, Zhongzheng District, Taipei City, Taiwan 100

TO VISIT BEFORE YOU DIE BECAUSE

Fine coffees are treated like fine wines at this elegant Taiwanese tasting bar specialising in luxury beans.

'We've always believed that coffee should be both simple and profound,' say Simple Kaffa founders Chee Lu and Berg Wu, who began with small experiments before opening their first café in 2011. 'What started as a dream soon became a space where people who love coffee could gather, and along the way we were honoured with three consecutive national barista championships and, in 2016, the World Barista Championship.' Their flagship café is housed in a restored heritage building near Huashan Creative Park and features an oval coffee bar, carefully chosen artworks and exposed brick walls. 'Every choice – from the materials we used to the bar's low design that brings baristas and guests closer together – reflects our belief that coffee is about connection as much as flavour,' says the pair. The ground-floor space offers an approachable and diverse all-day menu, while the upstairs special bar focuses on competition-style selections and auction coffees, including extremely expensive treats such as Elida Estate's Best of Panama (2024).

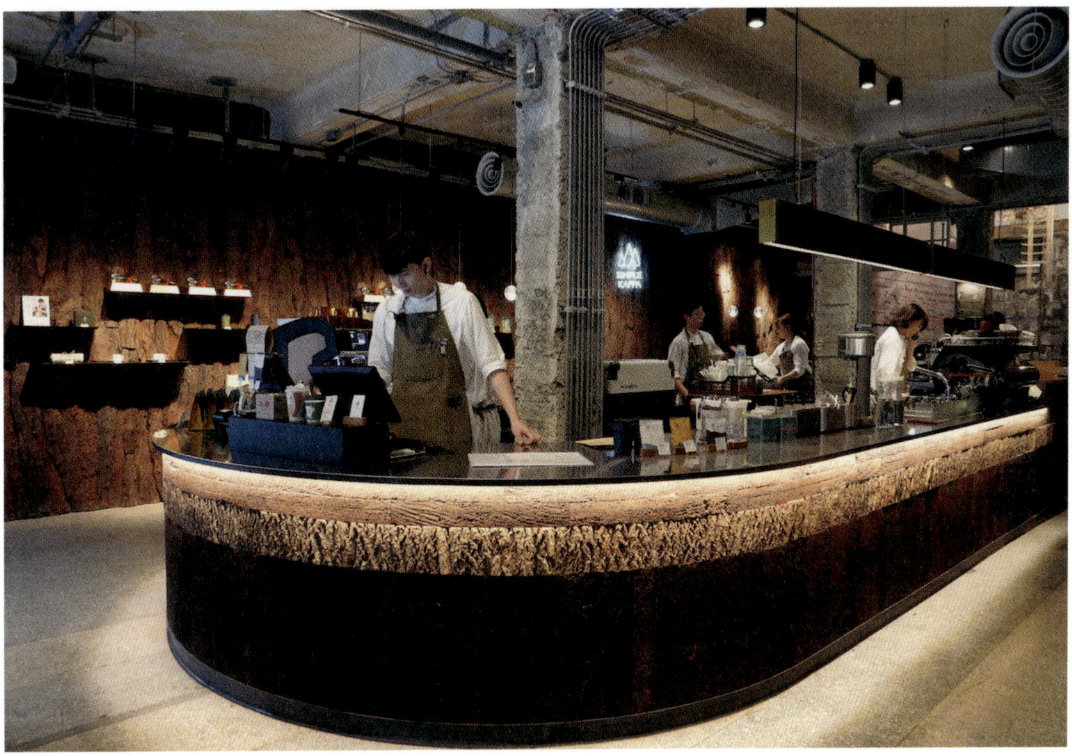

simplekaffa.com

+886 2 3322 1888

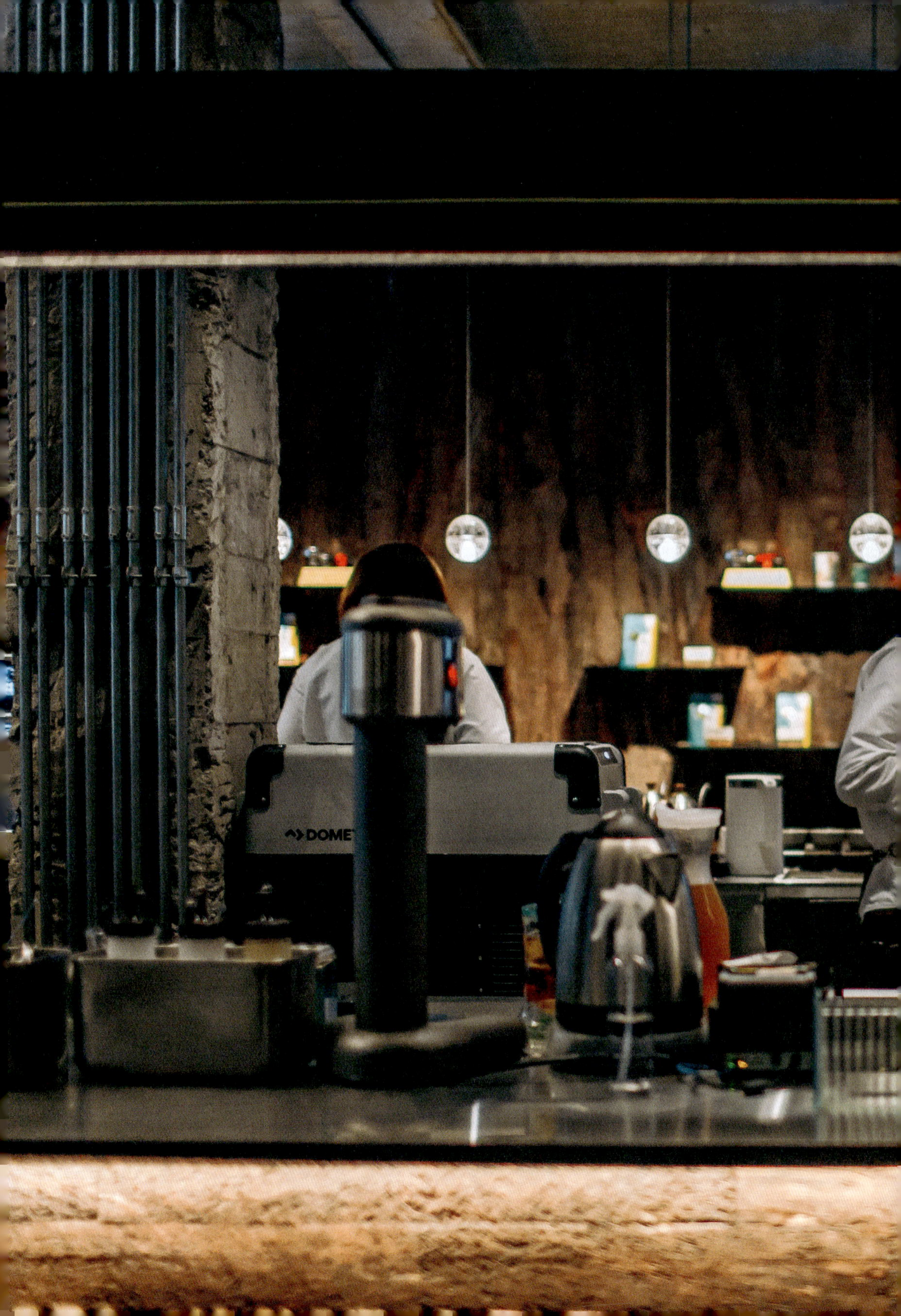

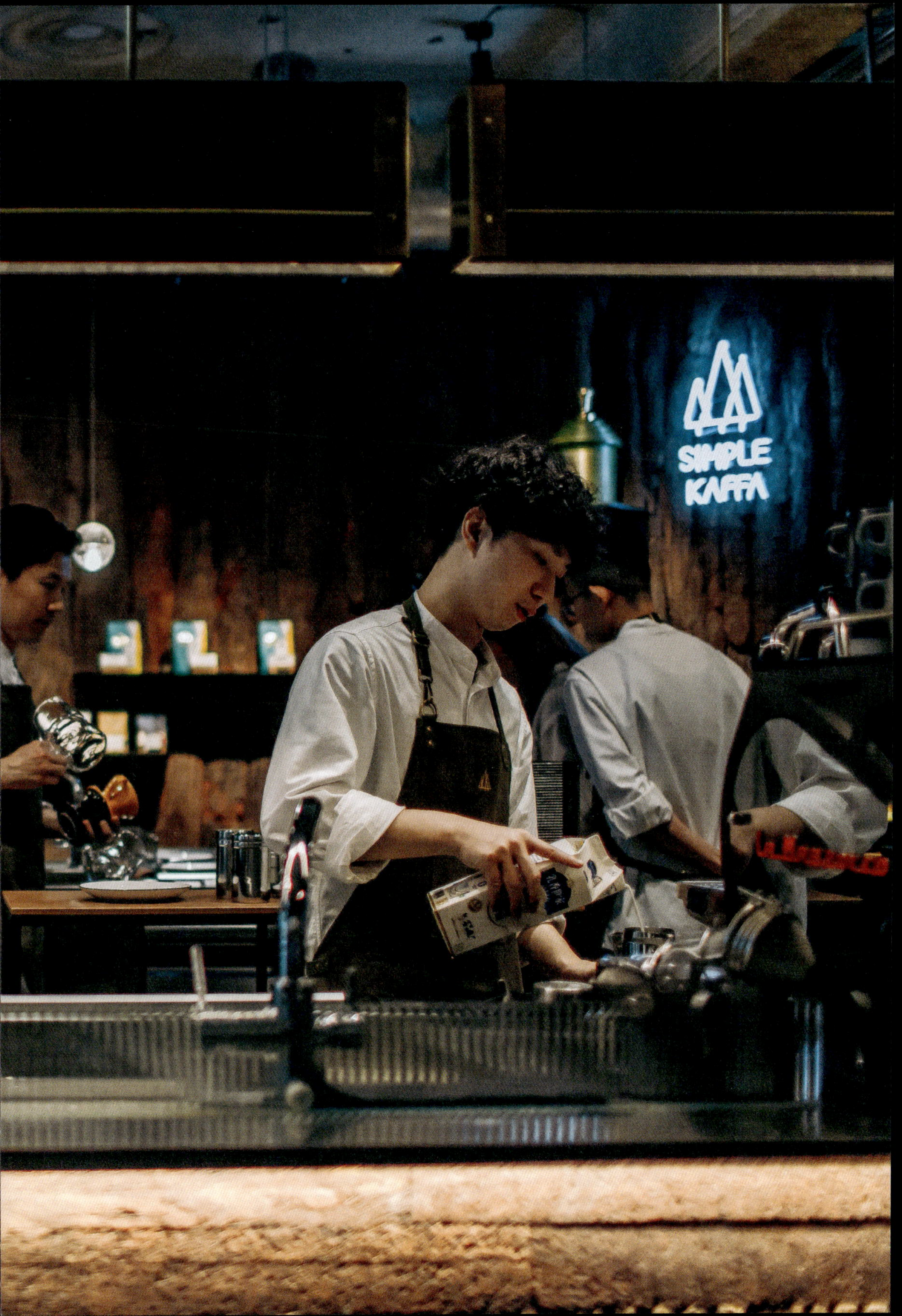
SIMPLE
KAFFA

79 APOLLON'S GOLD

1 Chome-14-13 Kudankita, Chiyoda City, Tokyo 102-0073, Japan

TO VISIT BEFORE YOU DIE BECAUSE

Coffee nerds will be in heaven in this new espresso bar from a roaster specialising in ultralight-roast premium coffees from renowned farmers.

Blend Japan's passion for coffee with the country's reverence for craftsmanship, and you get artisan roasters such as Apollon's Gold, founded by Yoshitatsu Arano in 2017. Always in search of the perfect coffee, the team works with top producers including Pepe Jijon in Ecuador and Hacienda El Obraje in Colombia. Its original café and roastery in Akasaka has been joined in 2025 by this new espresso bar in Kitanomaru, an easy stroll from the Imperial Palace, Edo Castle and surrounding parks. 'At the espresso bar, we offer customised shot profiles for each origin and type of beverage, including both milk beverages and single espresso,' explains Yoshitatsu. 'We offer around fifteen to twenty espresso options – the full line-up of the roastery – as well as three to five milk beverage options.' Coffee is served in Avensi coffee-enhancing glassware while the bar – or shall we say lab – is equipped with a DE 'pressure profiling' espresso machine, three coffee grinders, and state-of-the-art brewing stands, filters and drippers.

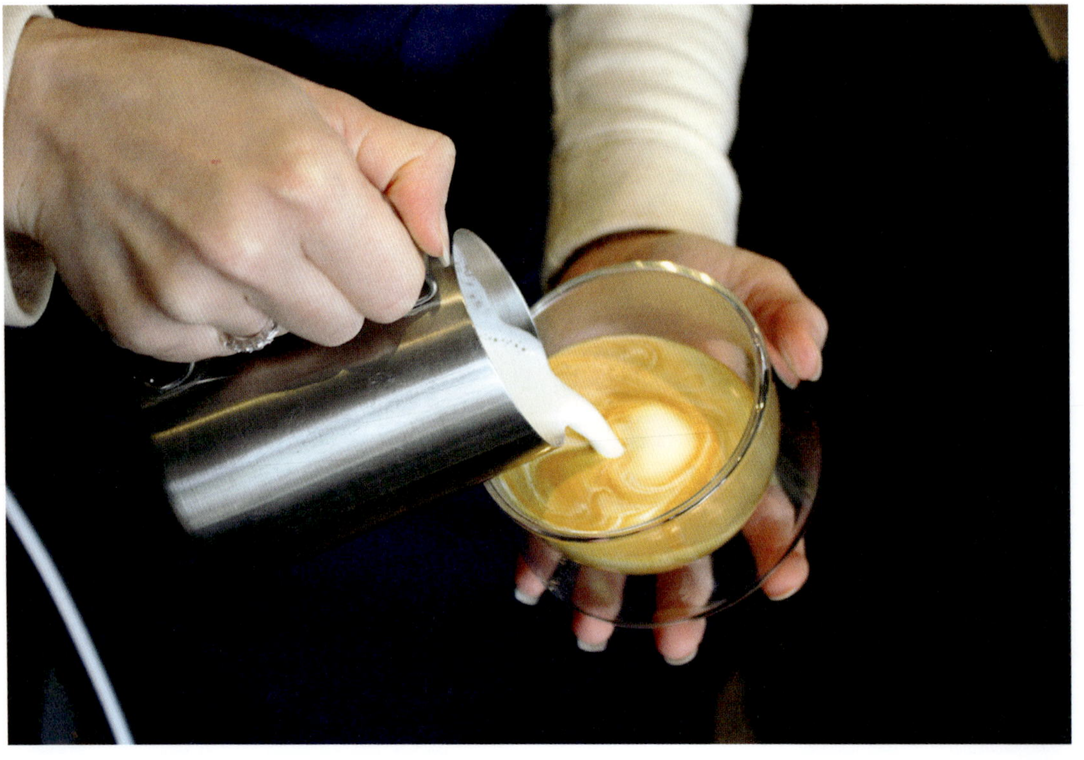

shop.apollons-gold.com +81 36 874 3815

80 KOFFEE MAMEYA KAKERU

2 Chome-16-14 Hirano, Koto City, Tokyo 135-0023, Japan

TO VISIT BEFORE YOU DIE BECAUSE

This coffee spin on the traditional omakase tasting menu combines a minimalist setting, interesting beans, unique pairings and guest collaborators.

After Eiichi Kunitomo travelled to Italy and discovered its vibrant coffee culture and chatty baristas, he decided to bring this back to Japan in the form of a warmer, more interactive take on *omotenashi*, the Japanese spirit of heartfelt hospitality. Eiichi opened a series of coffee shops – all instant hits – before starting Koffee Mameya in 2017. Far from a conventional café, it offers a reservation-only 'extraordinary coffee experience', which you can discover for yourself at three different branches, including Kakeru in Tokyo's Kiyosumi-Shirakawa district. Sit at the large counter, and let the barista take you on a wonderful coffee journey. 'It's as if you came to a restaurant to enjoy the chef's carefully selected ingredients and techniques,' explains Eiichi. There are various set menus to choose from, with drinks ranging from a cascara mocktail to milk brew and tea with coffee flower, and pairings with delicious small bites. Special sessions with leading guest patissiers, chefs and baristas such as Boram Um, Matt Winton and Hide Izaki are held regularly.

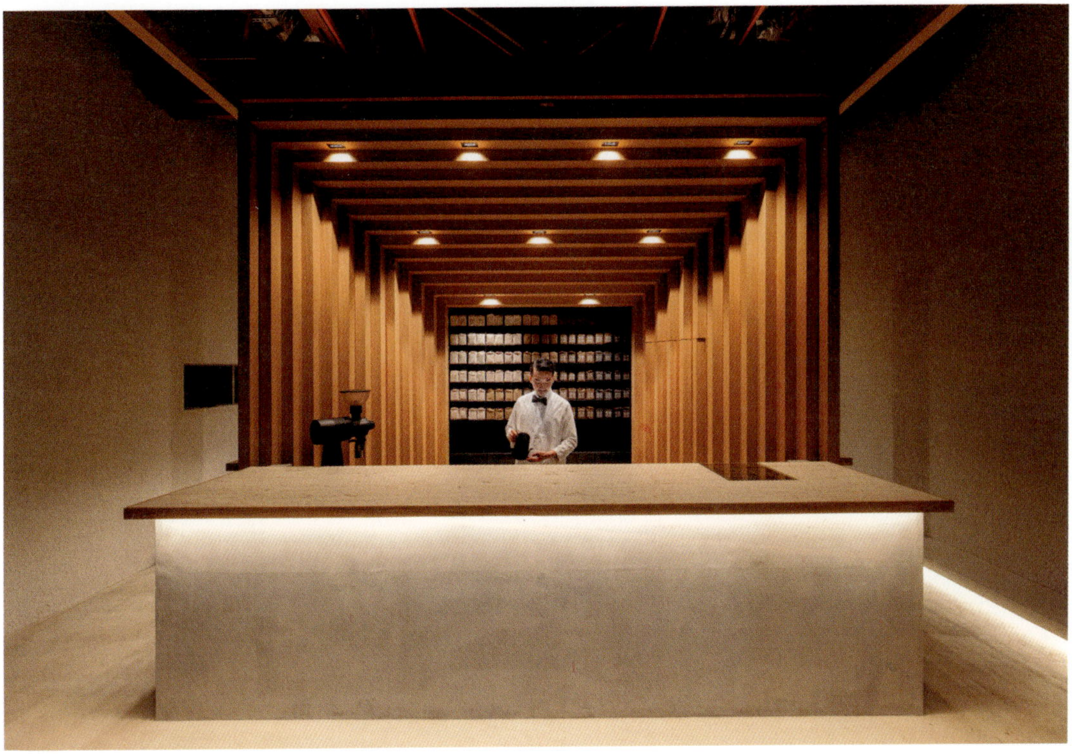

koffee-mameya.com

+81 50 1807 6375

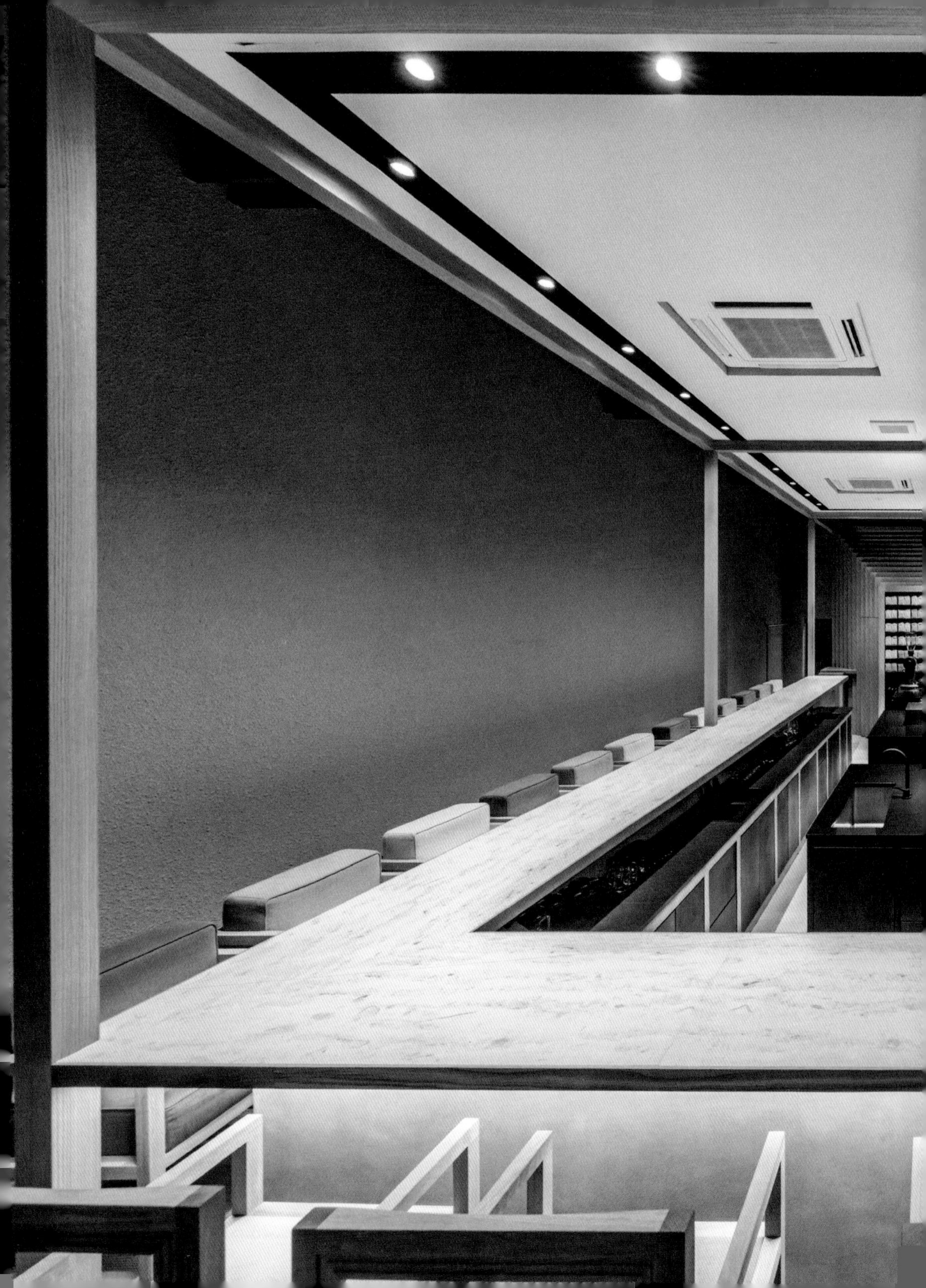

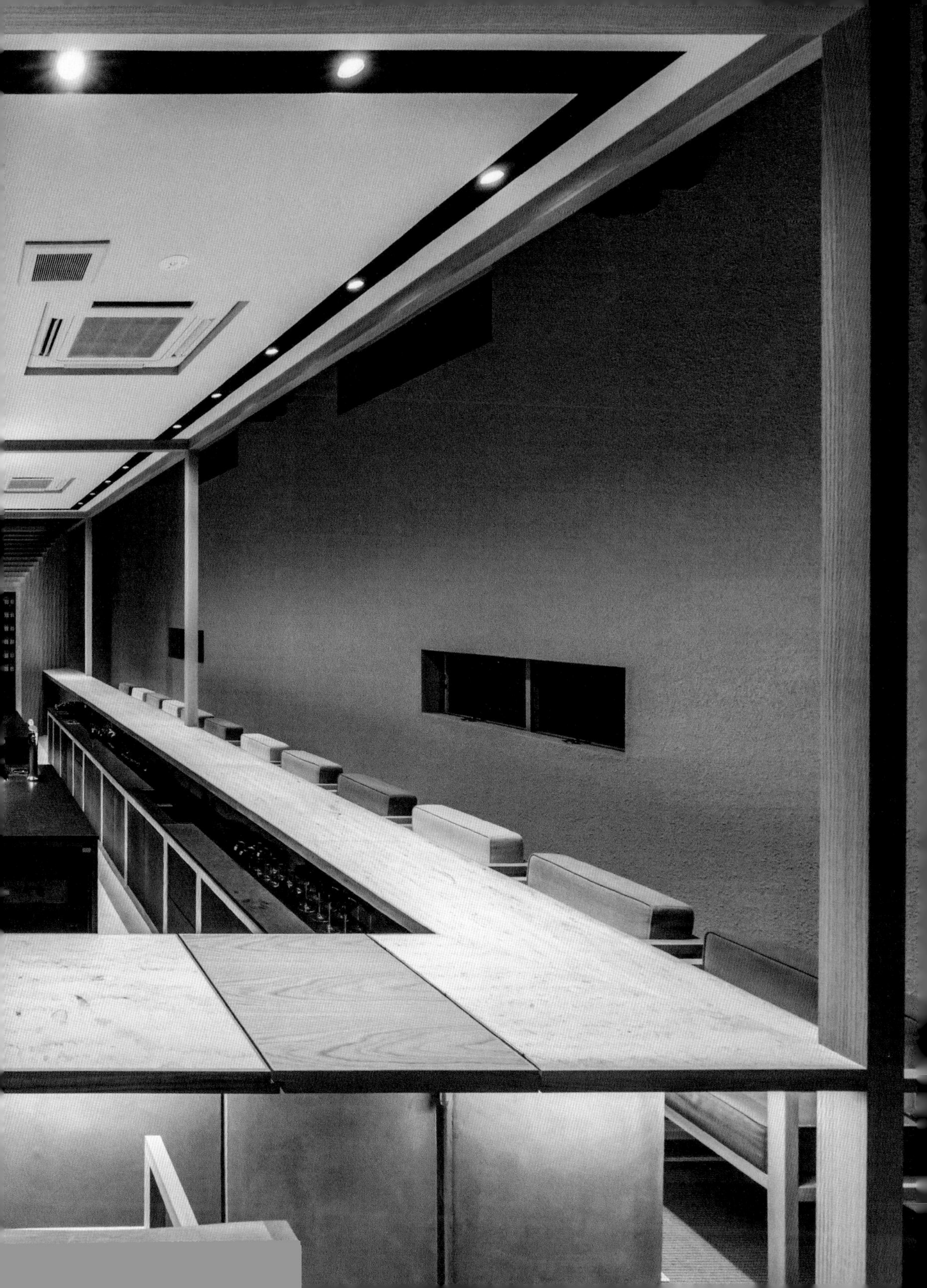

81 ONIBUS COFFEE NAKAMEGURO EKIMAE

2 Chome-14-1 Kamimeguro, Meguro City, Tokyo 153-0051, Japan

TO VISIT BEFORE YOU DIE BECAUSE

Join the community of coffee lovers who gather at this lovely station café in a wooden townhouse overlooking the Toyoko Line tracks.

Inspired by the artisanal coffee culture he experienced in Australia, Atsushi Sakao founded Onibus Coffee in 2012 to create a community hub 'enriching communities and everyday life through coffee'. Today it has shops across Japan and Asia, including this beautiful branch known as Nakameguro Ekimae, opened in 2016 just south of Shibuya. '*Ekimae* means "in front of the station",' explains chief sustainability officer Mai Yamada. 'While it welcomes many visitors from abroad, it's also deeply rooted in the local community. This sense of openness – where locals and travellers naturally blend – is one of our defining qualities, alongside our commitment to coffee quality.' The thoughtfully sourced speciality coffee menu features both hand-drip and espresso variants, while treats include fresh banana bread. It's a small café but there is a cosy upstairs room that is perfect for trainspotters, and lots of greenery around, including a vine-covered pergola. If full, you could also try Onibus's hip sister brand About Life Coffee Brewers, which has two locations in Shibuya.

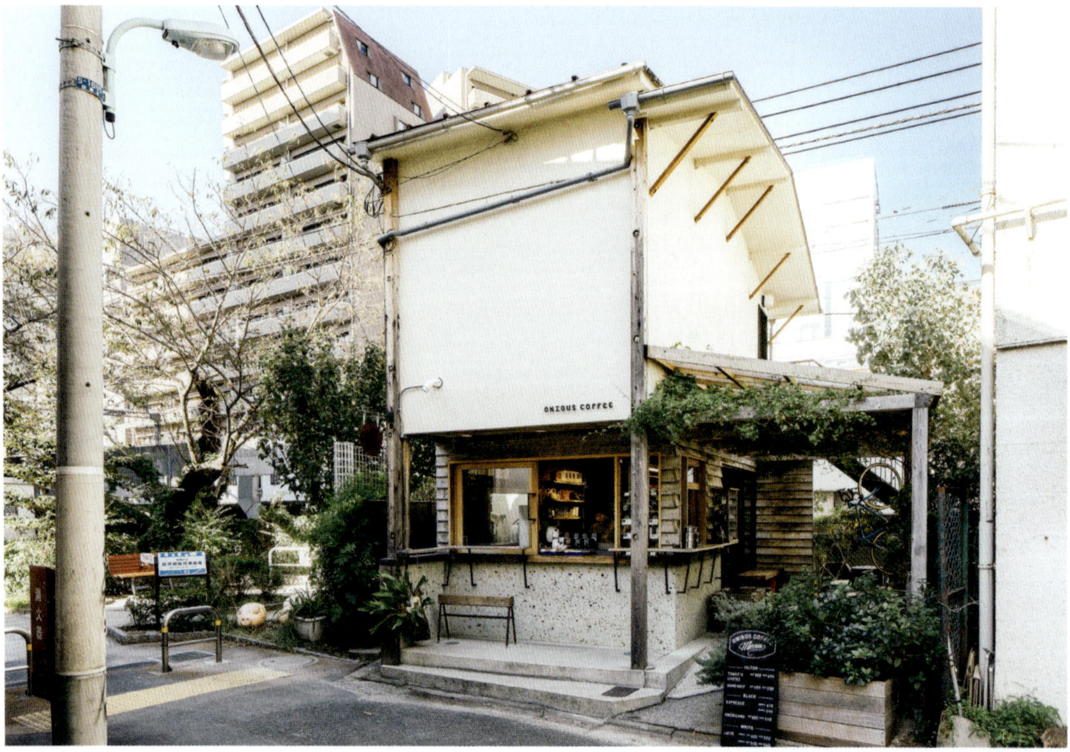

onibuscoffee.com +81 36 412 8683

82 LA CABRA

Graven 20, 8000 Aarhus C, Denmark

TO VISIT BEFORE YOU DIE BECAUSE

A star among roasters, this beautifully designed café has inspired many with its daily changing menu of seasonal coffees and baked goods.

It's easy to spot La Cabra's first café, opened in a pretty townhouse in Aarhus' picturesque Latin Quarter in 2012: there's usually quite a crowd and a few pushchairs out front, where patrons can perch on long benches to enjoy their coffee along with a cheese roll or cardamom bun. But it's actually quite difficult to describe how influential it is, especially when you know that founder Esben Piper opened it aged 24, while still at university. His passion for coffee spurred him on to open his own place, and a baker friend helped him discover his love for fresh sourdough. Combine the two, add a dose of cosy Danish design, with parquet floors and gorgeous tableware made by K.H. Würtz, and you get La Cabra – 'the goat', a name inspired by a Picasso sketch. 'Part of the advantage of growing in a small town is the lack of external influence, allowing us to forge an honest and novel approach to coffee,' says Piper of his success. From small town Aarhus to the rest of the world: La Cabra now has outposts in Copenhagen, New York and even Bangkok and Oman.

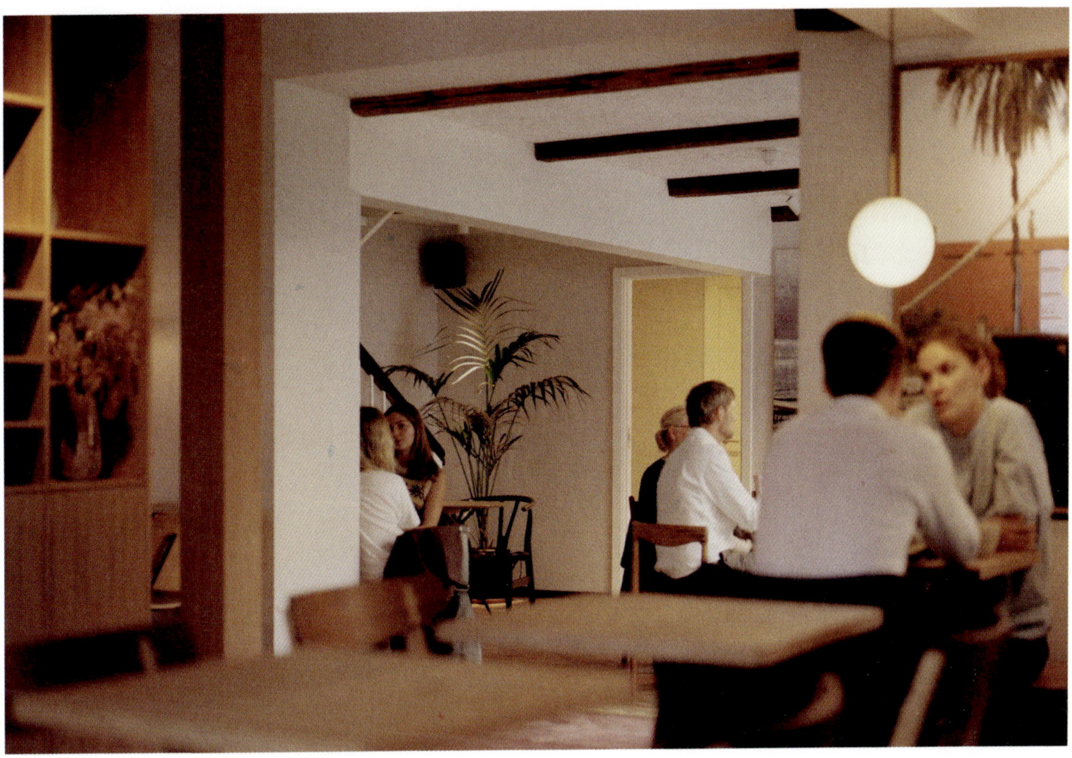

lacabra.com

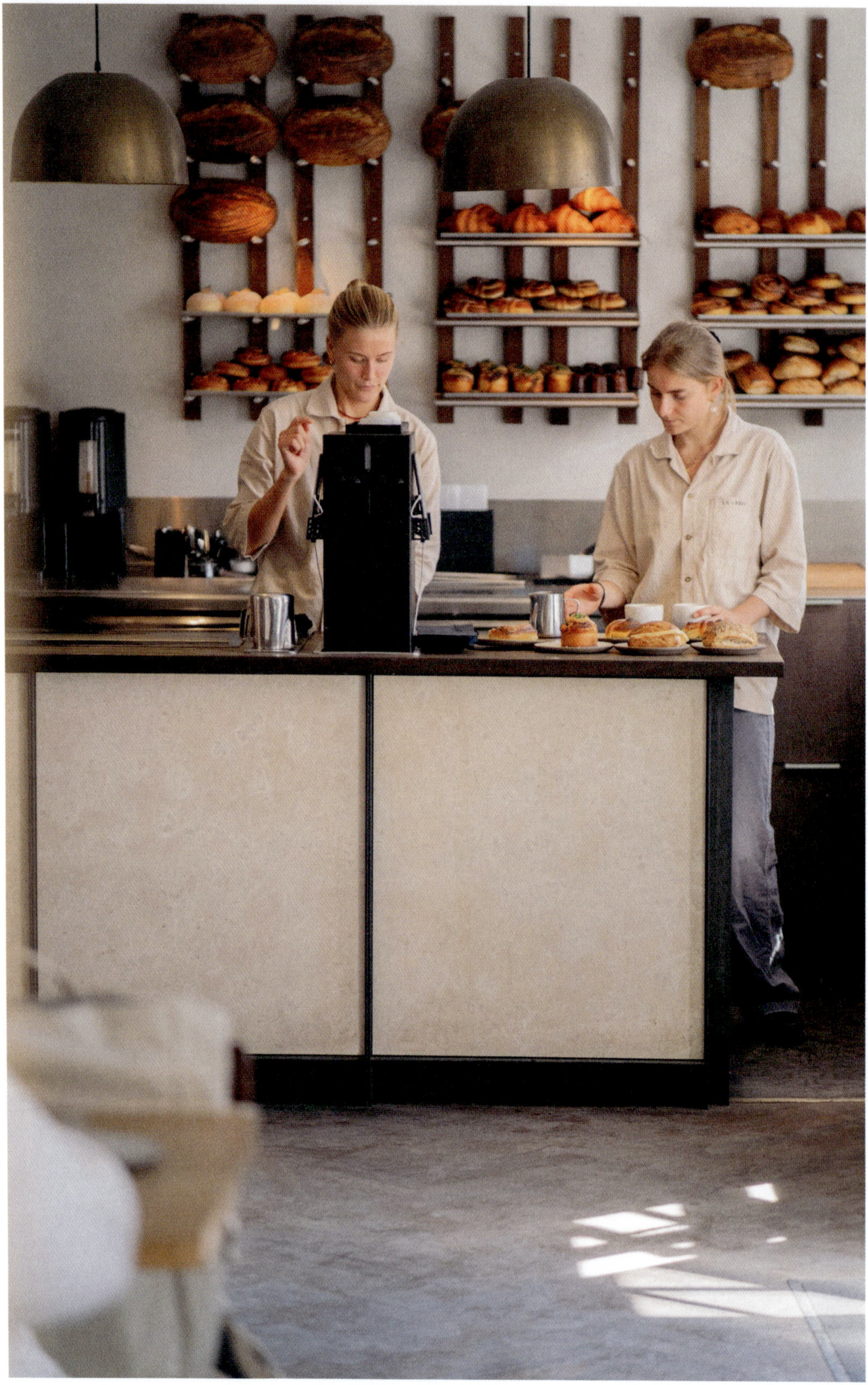

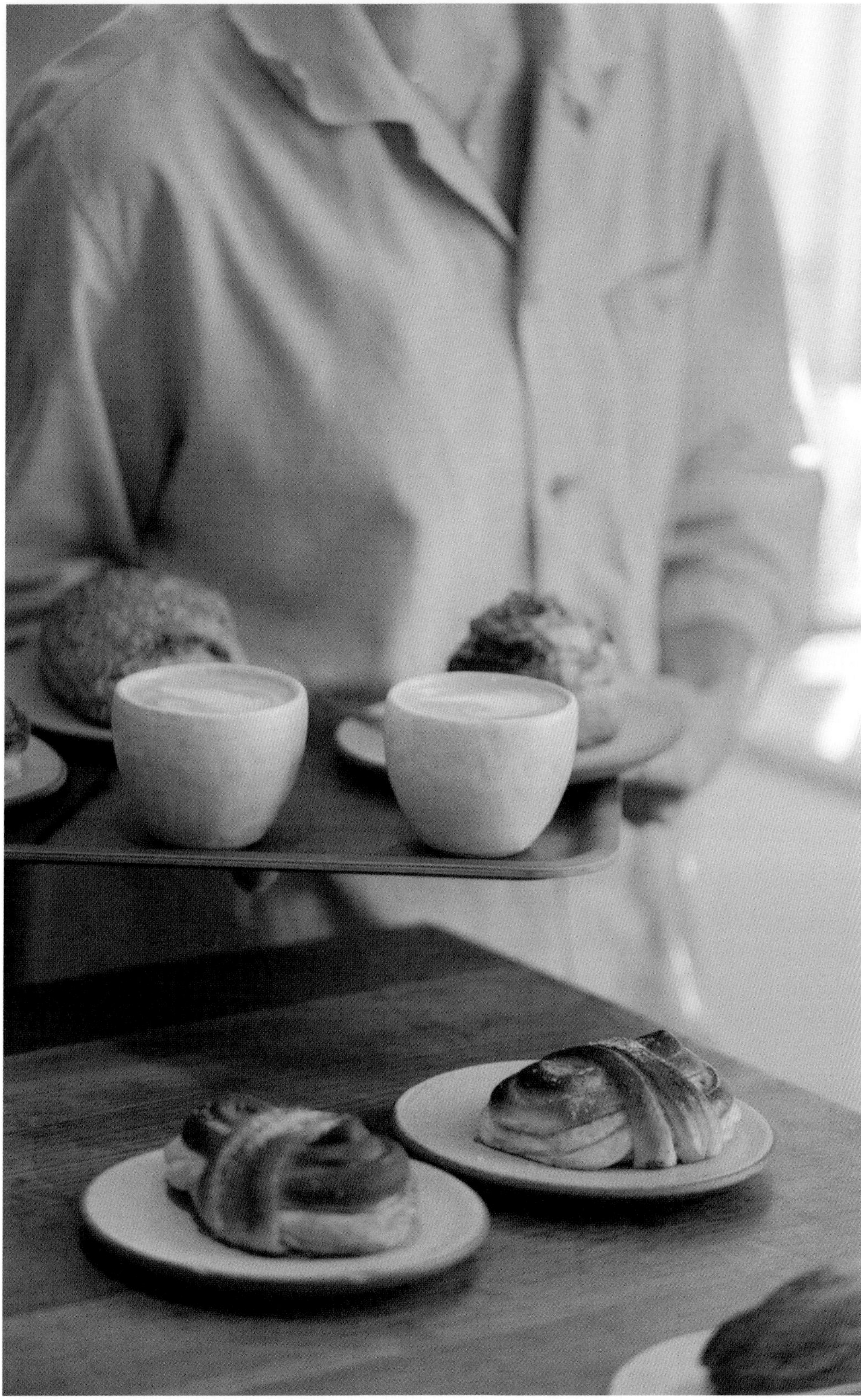

83 STILLER'S COFFEE

Klostergade 32, E, 8000 Aarhus C, Denmark

TO VISIT
BEFORE YOU DIE
BECAUSE

Enjoy exceptionally good coffee selected by a true coffee maestro, in a simple space tucked away in a historic courtyard.

'With my 40 years of ju-jitsu experience, I have tried to achieve a level of awareness and consistency in my practice. I have applied the same approach to developing my skills as a master barista,' explains Søren Stiller Markussen, eight-time Danish barista champion and the founder of this fantastic brew bar in Aarhus' old town. Opened in 2012, it is a great spot to sample some of the 55 different coffees he selects every year, working with coffee growers such as Costa Rica's Volcan Azul and El Salvador's Finca Santa Petrona. Espressos are served in cups specially designed by Studio Aarhus, while brewing methods include siphon, Hario, December or origami drippers. But as Stiller adds, 'great coffee is about more than precision – it's about emotion, storytelling, and the pursuit of balance,' so feel free to ask him or his team all about the beans and their origin. Not a coffee nerd, just a coffee lover? In this case you can sit outside and relax with a perfectly made iced coffee, paired with some great cookies or chocolate.

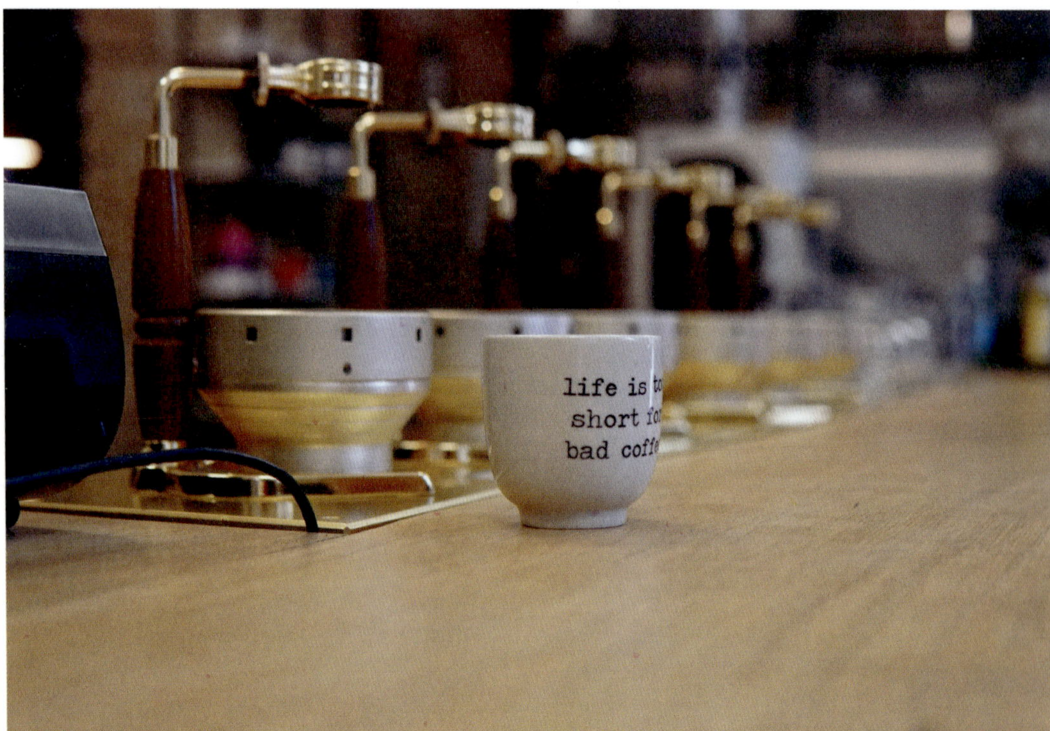

stillerscoffee.dk

84 FRIEDHATS FUKU CAFÉ

Bos en Lommerweg 136 HS, 1055 ED Amsterdam, Netherlands

TO VISIT BEFORE YOU DIE BECAUSE

Try a world-class espresso at the sunshine-yellow bar of this popular café in Amsterdam's Bo-Lo.

Fuku means 'happiness' or 'good fortune' in Japanese, and it's exactly what this bustling little café brings to the lucky people of Amsterdam. It was set up by Lex Wenneker and Dylan Sedgwick a few years after they founded the much-admired micro-roastery, Friedhats. 'We used to work in a café together, and after we had our roastery on track we kind of missed just being behind the bar, making coffee and talking to people,' explains Lex. Inspired by the Japanese way of focusing on one thing, and doing that really well, their café has both relaxed vibes and excellent coffee for all budgets. 'Some people just order a cappuccino and sit down without thinking too much about what they're drinking. But the coffee you drink at our café is pretty high level,' he says. Next level in fact – the 15–20 coffees on the menu are the type to be served at the World Barista Championship finals (where Lex won second place in 2018). Plus, you can stock up on colourful Friedhats coffee bottles from a retro vending machine in the hall.

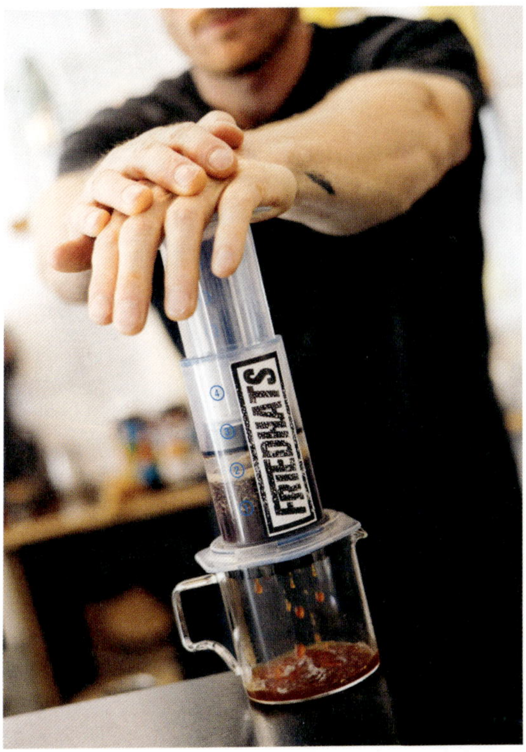

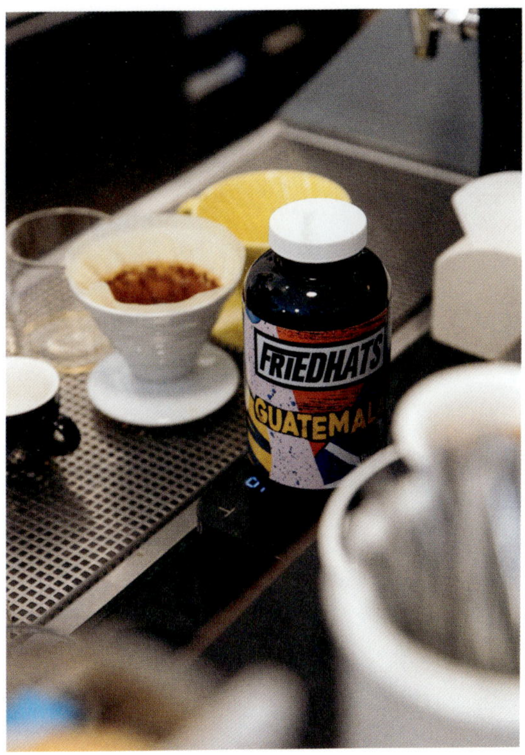

friedhats.com @friedhatsfukucafe

85 WHITE TURTLE COFFEE HOUSE

Stournari 43, Kaniggos 33, Athina 106 82, Greece

TO VISIT BEFORE YOU DIE BECAUSE

Enjoy Greek hospitality and excellent drinks at this welcoming café in Athens' alternative Exarcheia neighbourhood.

The opening of a cool new coffee shop is often the telltale sign that a neighbourhood is on the up. And that's just the case with White Turtle, which surfaced in Athens' Exarcheia at a time when the neighbourhood was considered a difficult area. 'Many business owners avoided investing there, fearing that the location might drive customers away,' says founder Stelios, who saw things differently and believed that 'there were also many people living and working there who deserved support'. It was the right decision: White Turtle has become a great community hub, where 'the goal is not only to serve speciality coffee but also to offer a "speciality" experience in its entirety and make a visit memorable to everyone' – and where the single-origin espressos, cold brews and iced flat whites are paired with freshly made sandwiches and pistachio rolls. For the full Exarcheia experience, combine with a visit to the National Archaeological Museum, where you can enjoy a frappé in a leafy courtyard, and to Exarcheion Square for its bohemian *kafeneons* and street art.

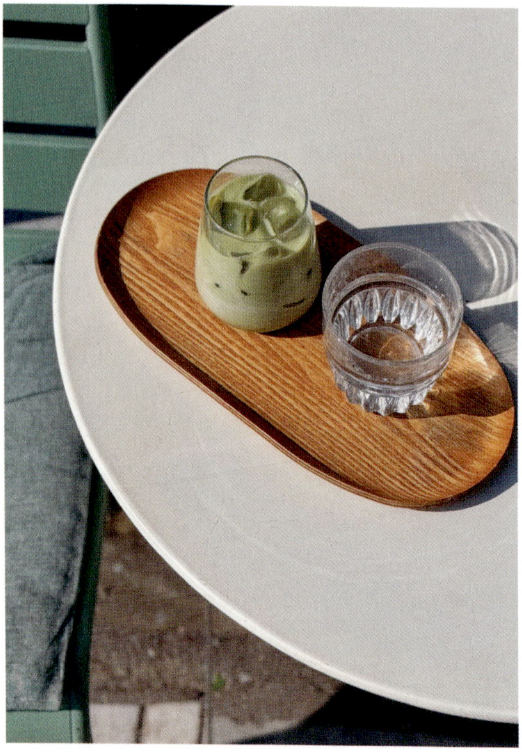

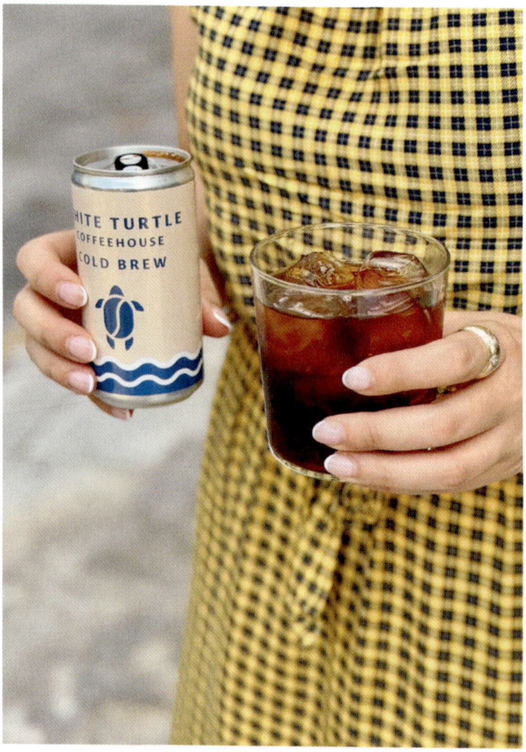

@whiteturtlecoffeehouse

+30 21 0330 0030

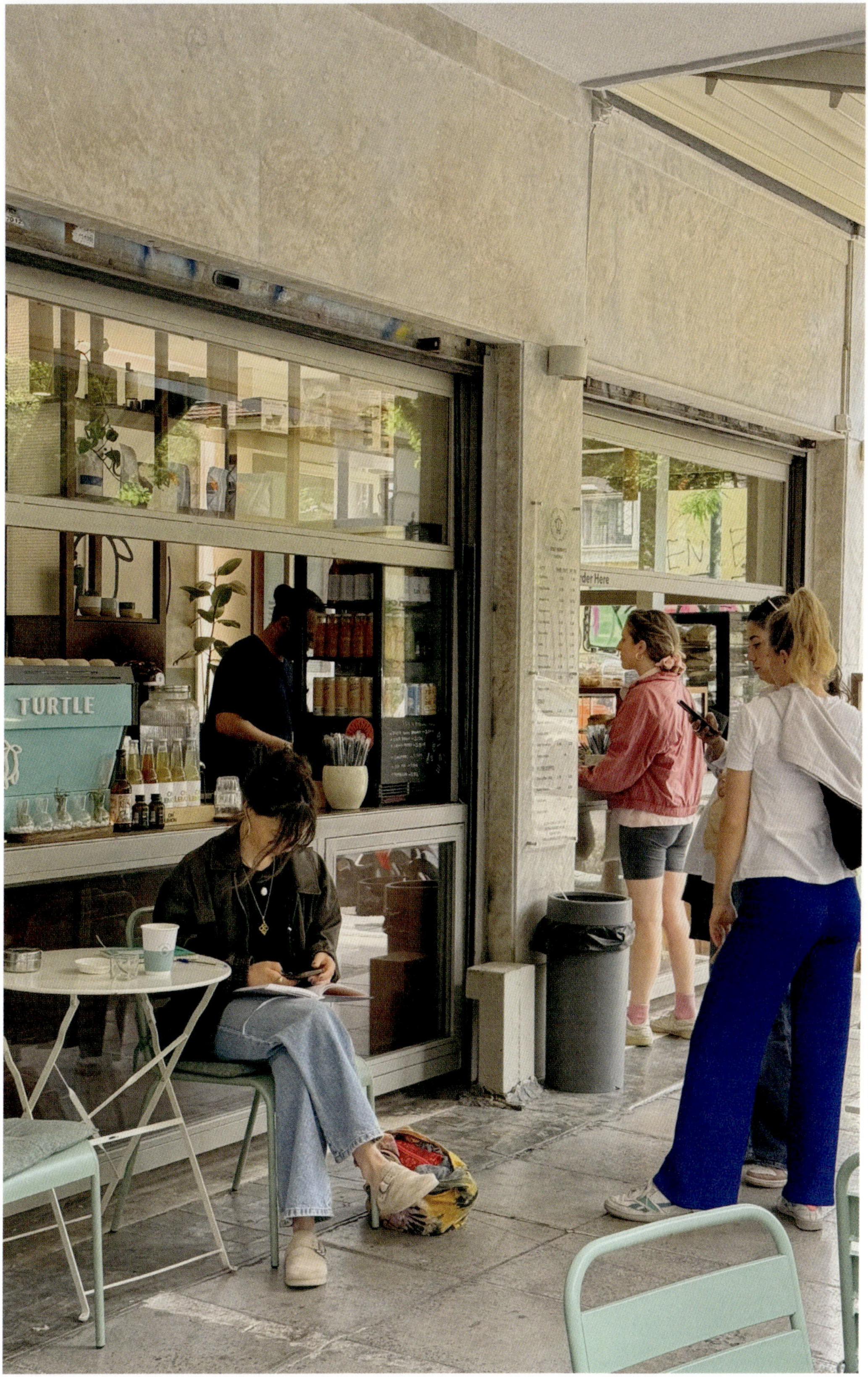
TURTLE
Order Here

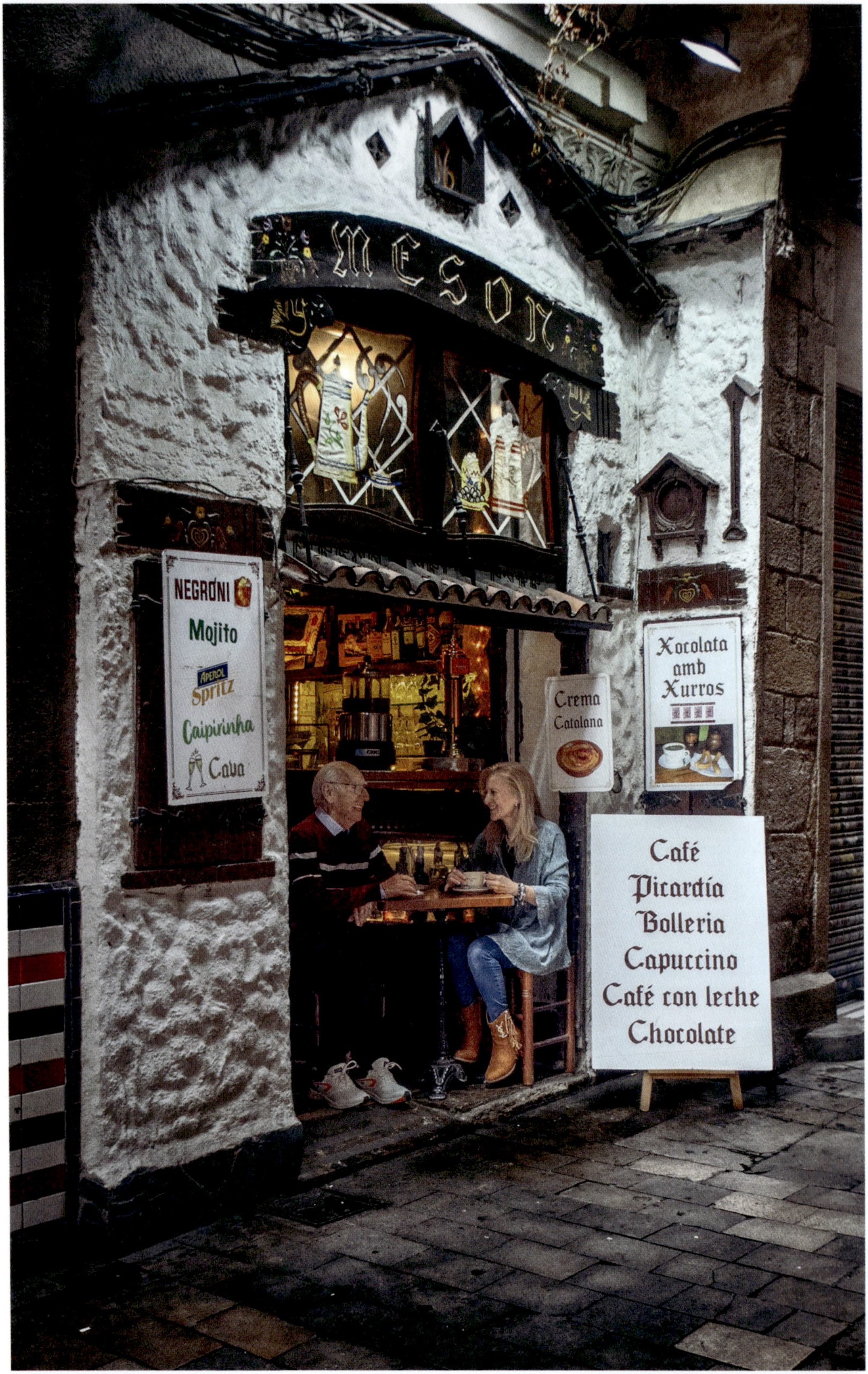

MESON
NEGRONI
Mojito
APEROL
Spritz
Caipirinha
Cava
Crema
Catalana
Xocolata
amb
Xurros
Café
Picardía
Bolleria
Capuccino
Café con leche
Chocolate

86 MESON DEL CAFÉ 1909

Carrer de la Llibreteria, 16, Ciutat Vella, 08002 Barcelona, Spain

TO VISIT
BEFORE YOU DIE
BECAUSE

You can't get more atmospheric than this century-old café in Barcelona's Gothic quarter, full of history and original features.

Blink and you'll miss it: this tiny white, house-shaped café really looks like a magical apparition in between the tourist shops of the Gothic quarter. The family-run establishment has been serving customers since 1909; its cute façade decorated with dark wooden shutters and stained-glass windows with coffee pots hides a long wooden room that was last renovated in the 1930s. Behind the counter you might find Montserrat, daughter of the late Antonio Peligros, custodian of the café from the 1950s to 2013. Don't miss the antique steam-powered coffee machine, decorated with golden palm trees, on display above the bar. Wonder at the tavern's vintage lamps and floral decorations before ordering one of the house specialities, which include the Picardia, made with coffee, condensed milk and whisky. The menu also features simple, homemade tapas and *crema calatana*, as well as churros and hot chocolate. Come for a breakfast of cortado and *pa amb tomàquet*, then return for a beer and some live music in the evenings.

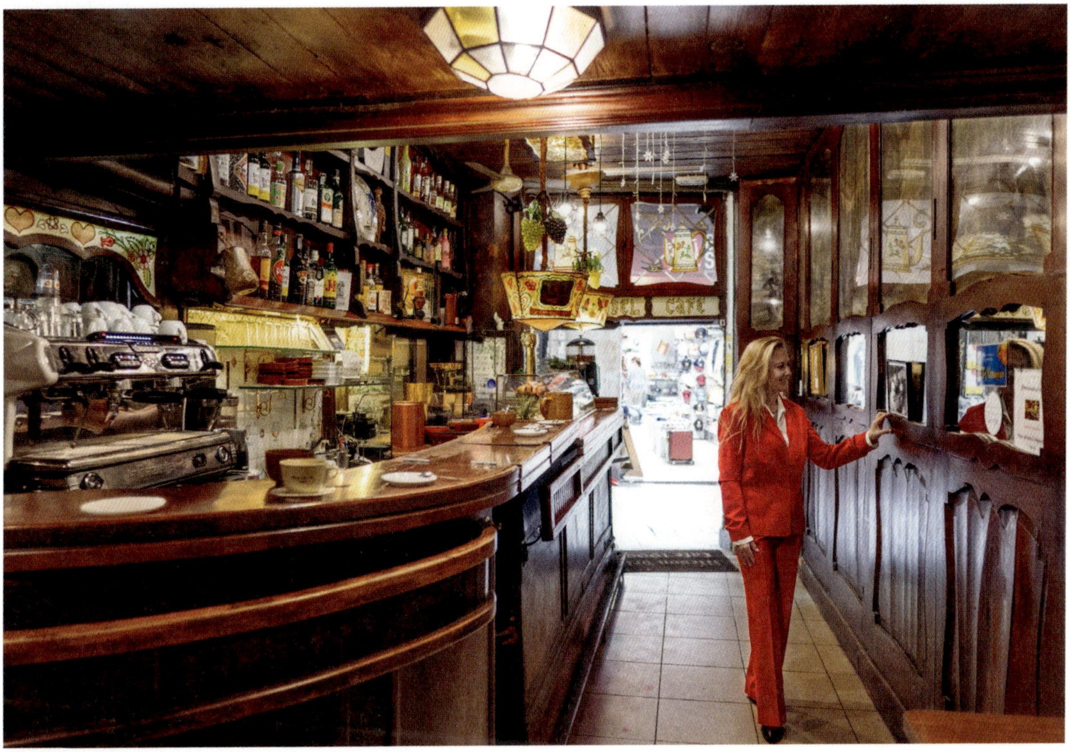

@mesondelcafe1909 +34 933 15 07 54

87 NOMAD FRUTAS SELECTAS

Carrer de Pujades, 95, Sant Martí, 08005 Barcelona, Spain

TO VISIT BEFORE YOU DIE BECAUSE

The elegant café of leading Spanish roastery Nomad serves top-quality coffees and freshly made treats from its sister bakery Pa de Kilo.

The story of this Barcelona roaster started in 2011 in London, where Jordi Mestre decided to use the skills he had picked up working at the capital's best cafés to start his own coffee cart and travel from market to market. Mestre went on to win Spain's National Barista Championship twice, before selling his beloved cart to set up shop in his hometown of Barcelona, joining forces with Fran González and becoming one of the industry's most respected roasters. Transformed by Jordi Veciana and Sky Maunsell, Nomad's Poblenou location, Frutas Selectas, is a warm space inspired by traditional cafés. Dark-stained wood walls and a shiny zinc counter provide the elegant backdrop for a menu including beans from growers such as the Primavera family from Guatemala or Korongo in Tanzania. Try a *tallat* (Catalan for cortado), seasonal specials such as coffee sangria, or a cold brew latte from Burundi, with notes of tangerine and grilled pineapple. Nomad has a handful of other locations, including a coffee academy.

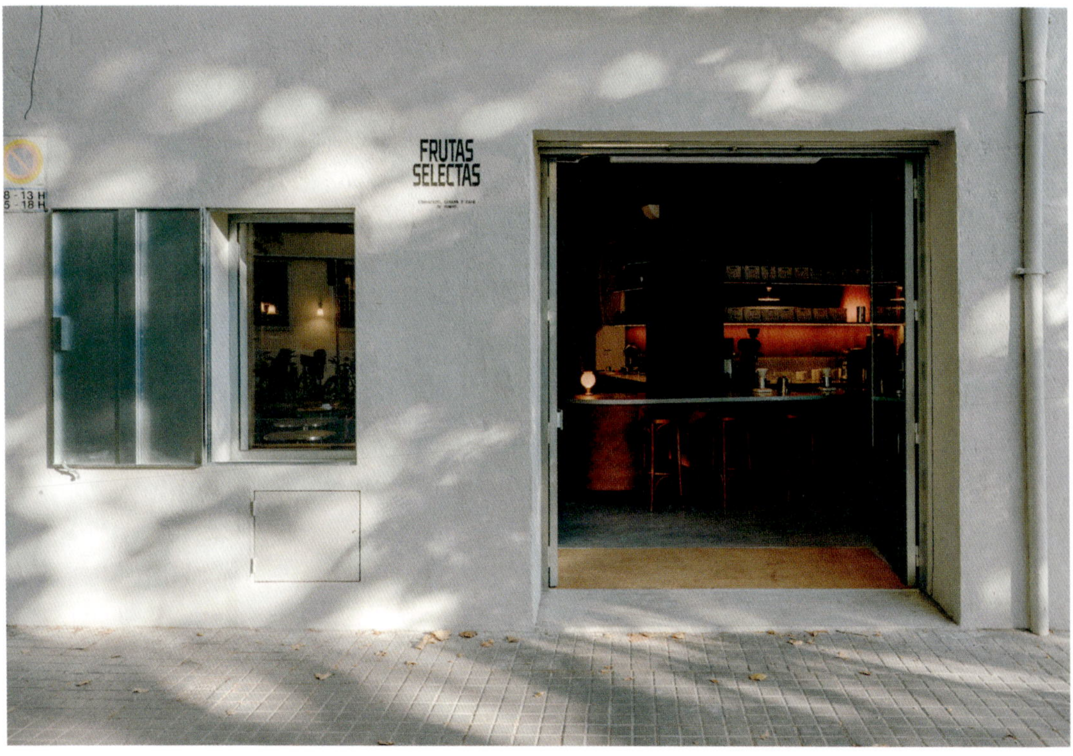

nomadcoffee.es +34 628 56 62 35

88 ROAST CLUB

Carrer de València, 190, L'Eixample, 08011 Barcelona, Spain

TO VISIT BEFORE YOU DIE BECAUSE

Everyone is welcome at this bright café, where the focus is on not just roasting speciality coffee but also 'making every customer's day better'.

Just like the best beans come from all around the world, the team at this cute breakfast spot in Eixample is an international crew of coffee lovers: founder Iker Zagos, who travelled from Australia to New York via the Balearic Islands, is joined by barista John, from Northern Ireland; chefs Mariana and Juanito from Venezuela and Argentina, and waiters Gabriel and Camila from El Salvador and Argentina. This coffee family will welcome you with some fine drinks – and the competition is strong in Barcelona, one of the world's coffee hotspots. On the menu are two filter and two espressos options; the first espresso blend of 2025, for example, was Blooming Delight, a clean, sweet blend of washed heirloom from the Anfilloo Highlands of Ethiopia, and a natural bourbon from the Simbi Washing Station in Rwanda. 'We recommend you pair our speciality coffee with our artisanal croissants, chocolate muffins and fruit tarts,' says Iker. Stay for brunch or take a break with a 'bikini', the local ham and cheese toastie, served here with a smoked porchetta, kimchi mayo twist.

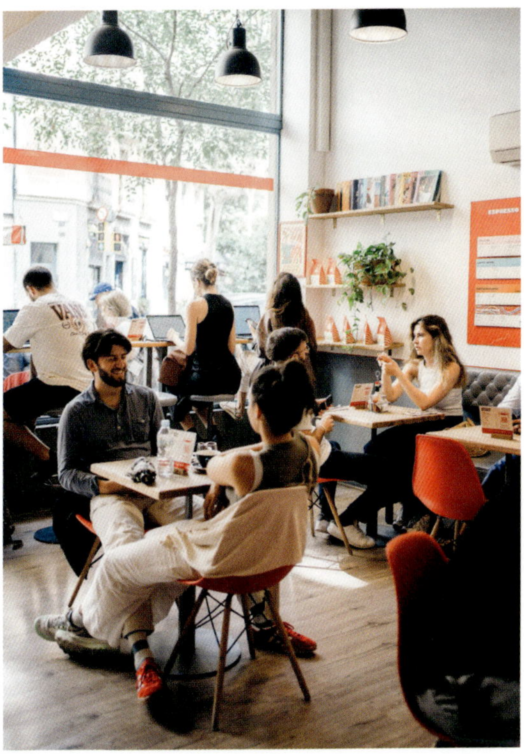

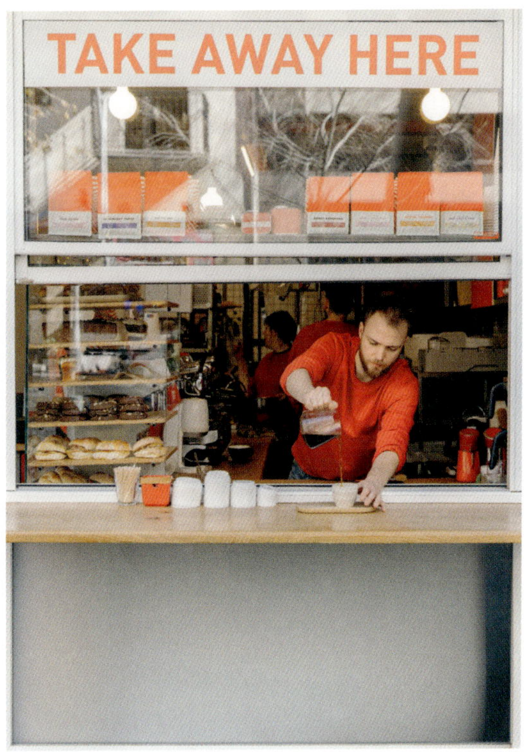

roastclub.coffee

+34 935 18 77 11

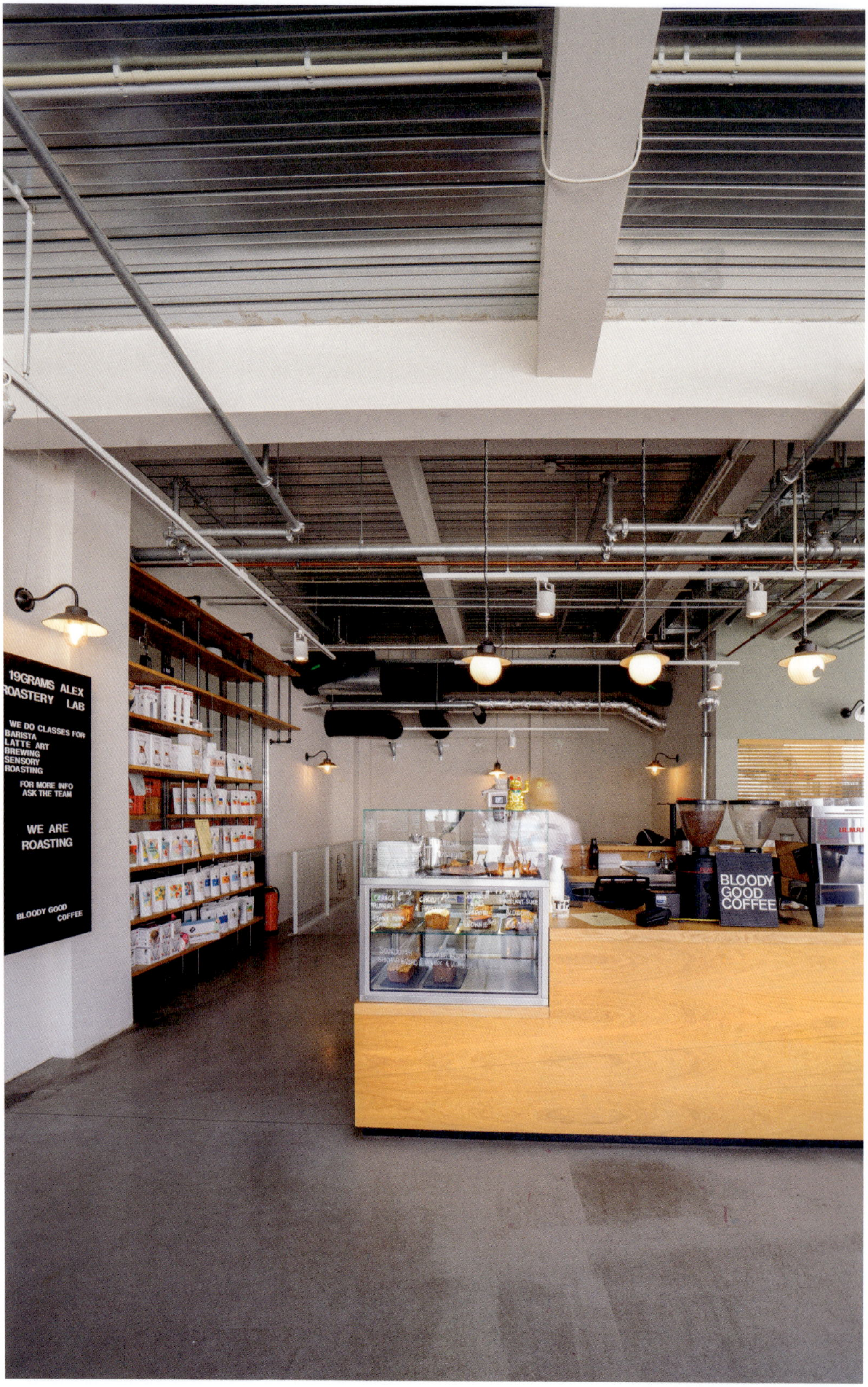
19GRAMS ALEX
ROASTERY LAB
WE DO CLASSES FOR:
BARISTA
LATTE ART
BREWING
SENSORY
ROASTING
FOR MORE INFO
ASK THE TEAM
WE ARE
ROASTING
BLOODY GOOD
COFFEE
BLOODY
GOOD
COFFEE

89 19GRAMS ALEX

Karl-Liebknecht-Str. 13, 10178 Berlin-Mitte, Germany

TO VISIT
BEFORE YOU DIE
BECAUSE

This pioneering German speciality coffee roaster started by three friends after a trip to Costa Rica in 2002 is still at the top of its game.

In the shadow of Berlin's TV Tower (known locally as 'Alex'), you'll find a sign saying 'Bloody Good Coffee'. No false advertising here – it is indeed showing you the way to one of the capital's top roasters, 19Grams. But we could quibble with the name itself, which was inspired by the dose for double espresso used when it first opened as Tres Cabezas. Today it's 17g, but don't worry, it still packs a punch. As for the slogan, it wasn't dreamt up during long meetings with brand managers; it's just something that an Australian employee came up with, when bored on a cold and rainy day without any customers. There's no shortage of coffee drinkers here now: the café is extremely popular rain or shine. You can not only smell and taste the coffee, but also follow its production through big glass windows framing the roastery and lab. Try a Wild At Heart (perfect espresso), grab one of their bestselling advent calendars, and brunch on a signature breakfast sandwich or an apple strudel 'snake'.

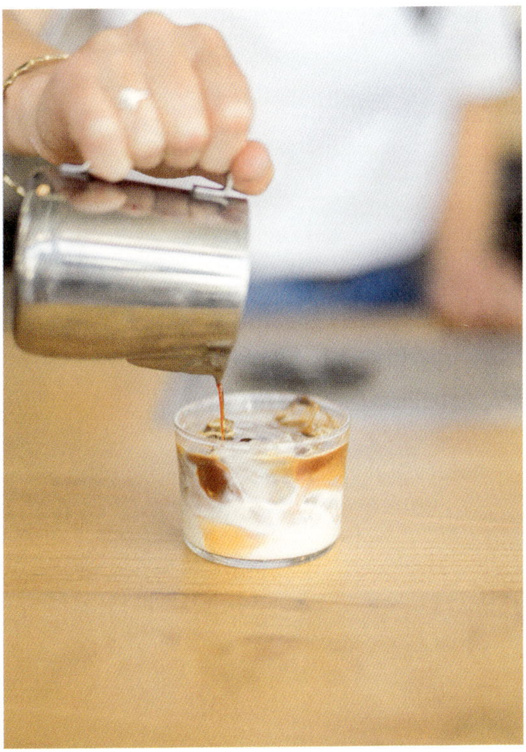

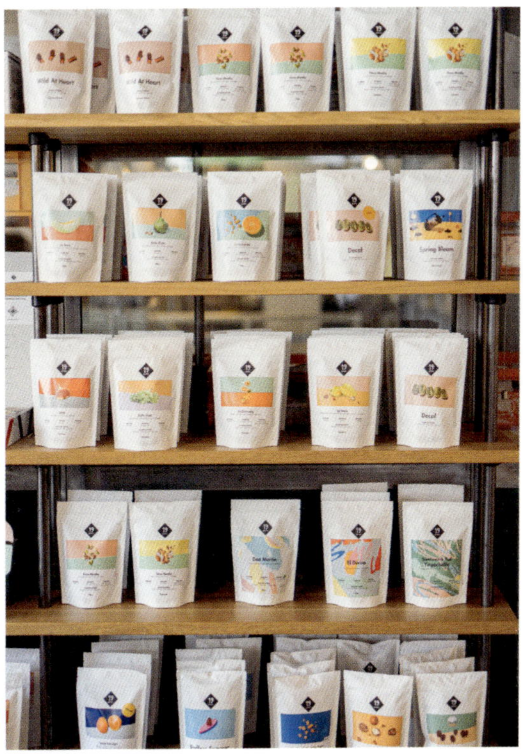

19grams.coffee

+30 16 639 599

90 FIVE ELEPHANT KREUZBERG

Reichenberger Str 101, 10999 Berlin, Germany

TO VISIT BEFORE YOU DIE BECAUSE

This cosy café is known for its unwavering quality, community engagement, dedication to sustainability – and fantastic cheesecake.

Five Elephant's first café opened in 2010, on a quiet, dead-end street in Kreuzberg, as Berlin's speciality coffee scene was still forming. 'We roasted our own coffee in the back, baked our cakes from scratch, and built everything ourselves, including a handmade drip bar using Hario V60s and welded copper pipes,' recall the founders, Sophie and Kris Schackman. 'It was honest, simple and hands-on. Filter coffee wasn't just a nod to nostalgia, but how we chose to highlight origin, process and varietal. For us, it was the most compelling way to share what coffee could be.' Refurbished recently by Sunst Studio, the cosy café now features a dedicated corner for hand brews, and a custom aluminium and granite bar where you can savour a slice of the bestselling Philadelphia cheesecake, a family recipe. Five Elephant has evolved into a global wholesaler and retailer of some of the world's best coffees, including special lots such as a Colombia Maranatha Geisha. The café is part of a community of small local businesses and friends including Bagel Bro, Atelier Dough and Senegambia – all also worth a visit.

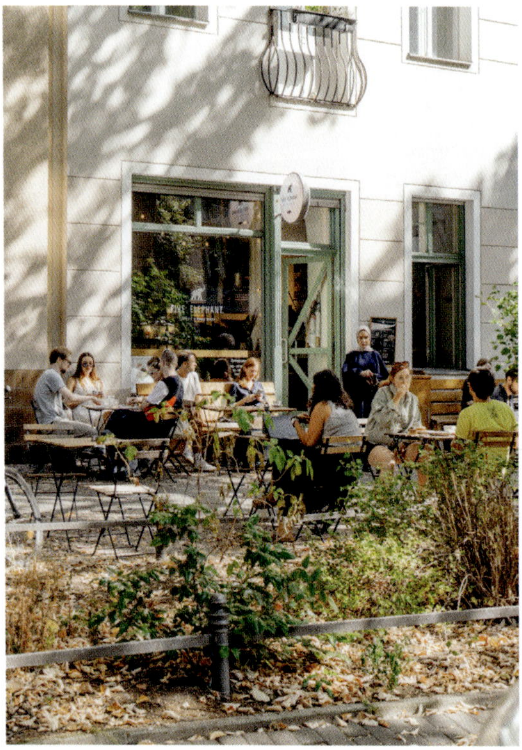

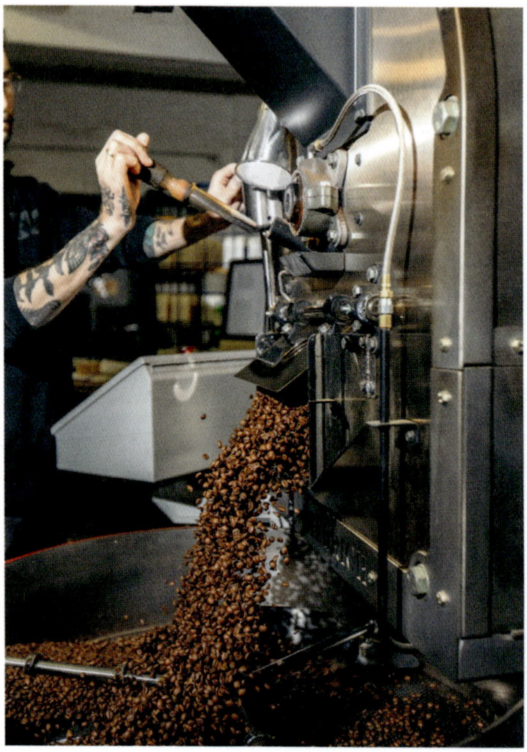

fiveelephant.com

91 MOK

Rue Antoine Dansaert 196, 1000 Brussels, Belgium

TO VISIT BEFORE YOU DIE BECAUSE

From top single origins to zero-waste blends, from peaceful atmosphere to sunny terrace, this small café has it all.

Founded in 2012 by two-times Belgian Cup Tasters Champion Jens Crabbé, MOK has two branches: the original one in Leuven, and this canal-side café in Brussels' fashionable Dansaert neighbourhood. 'MOK is about purity, integrity and quality, working year on year with the same farmers to build strong partnerships,' writes Jens. 'We are passionate about working highly seasonally and always have full traceability. We focus on growers who understand that quality comes from hard work and sustainable practices, so we are never driven by price.' He currently roasts on a Probat UG22 with Cropster, serving up hand brews, filter, espresso and also homemade fermented soft drinks and freshly baked treats (many gluten- or dairy-free) such as carrot cake and *canelés*. On a nice day you can sit on the terrace and enjoy a special such as geisha from Panama's Hacienda La Esmeralda in the sunshine or a nitro cascara coffee served straight from the Naiko tap. There are also intriguing vegetarian dishes like *okonomiyaki* with stracciatella cheese and grilled chicory.

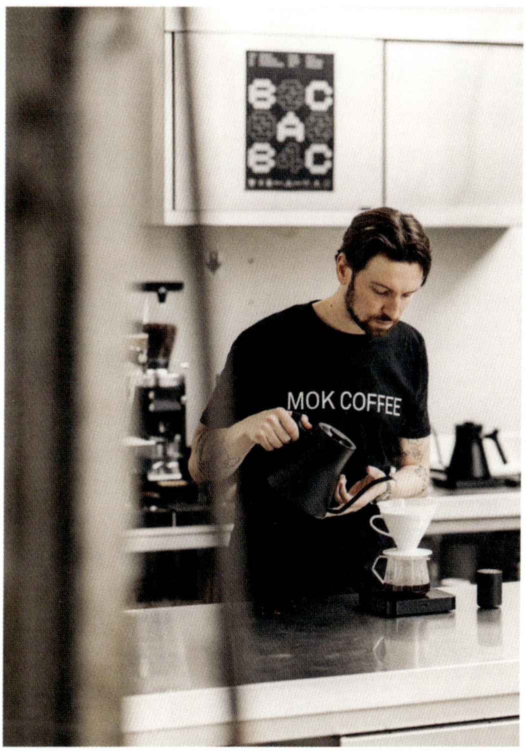

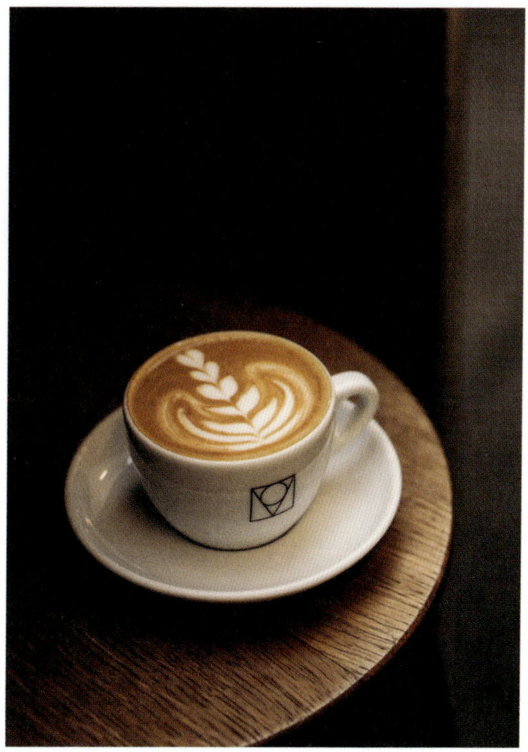

mokcoffee.be

+32 472 05 82 24

92 BOBXBVB

Șoseaua Nicolae Titulescu 4-8, Bucharest, Romania

TO VISIT BEFORE YOU DIE BECAUSE

This eye-catching café is the unlikely meeting point for speciality coffee lovers, students, and traders from the Bucharest Stock Exchange.

Located on the ground floor of the new headquarters of the Bucharest Stock Exchange, this innovative café was created in partnership between the exchange and BOB Coffee, the coffee chain founded by Alexandru Niculae, World Coffee Roasting Champion 2016. This space 'where energy, ideas and great coffee come together' was designed by Corvin Cristian and Alia Al-Jabbari, who took their cues from the circle, a core element of BOB's identity and an abstraction of the coffee bean. Aluminium cylinders and lab-like finishes are paired with bright red details – who would have thought a fire extinguisher would make such a cool decorative item? The menu features signature drinks such as Blue Chip brew and Uptick Cold brew latte: 'Each beverage tells a story and adds another layer of experience that completes the identity of this one-of-a-kind coffee shop,' concludes Alexandru. Make sure to also visit BOB's other locations, including its first café on Charles de Gaulle Square, and its latest opening, a garden oasis and bookshop on Gradina Verona.

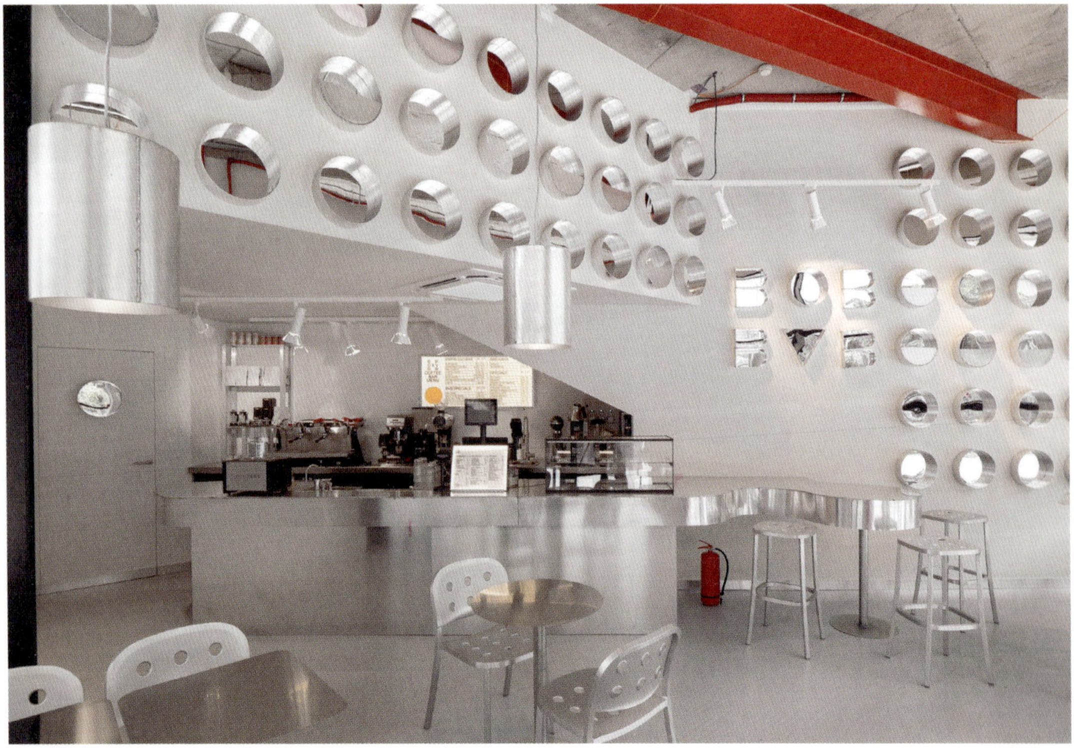

bob.coffee/en

+40 748 880 038

93 NEW YORK CAFÉ

Erzsébet krt. 9-11, Budapest, 1073 Hungary

TO VISIT BEFORE YOU DIE BECAUSE

Match your drink to the gilded surroundings of this classic grand café and tourist hotspot with a 24-carat gold New York cappuccino.

This is certainly not a hidden gem but one of the world's most famous cafés, a flashy Italian Renaissance-style salon opened in 1894 in the Anantara New York Palace Budapest Hotel. When you look at its grand chandeliers, ceiling frescoes and velvet-topped balustrades, it's hard to imagine that the vast room was only restored to its full glory in 2006. After years of disrepair, and the indignity of being used to house a sports shop, the grand café is back in the swing of things, with regular sets by the Lugosi Salon Gipsy Band and a pianist bringing the storied place to life. At the turn of the century, the New York Café was popular with writers and editors (the most influential newspapers were edited here, in the upstairs gallery), but today it's tourists who fill up the space. Although there is a full food menu, it is best to come for a cup of Hungarian coffee, served with Tokaji cuvée honey and whipped cream, and a slice of traditional poppy seed meringue cake.

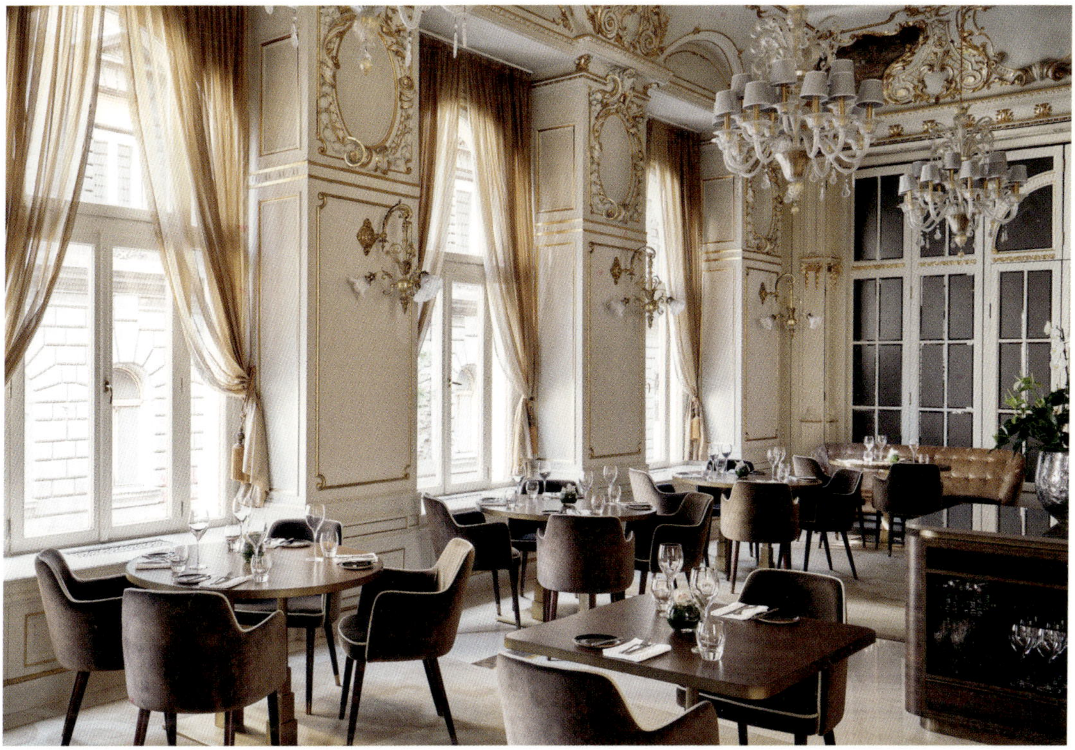

newyorkcafe.hu

+36 1 886 6167

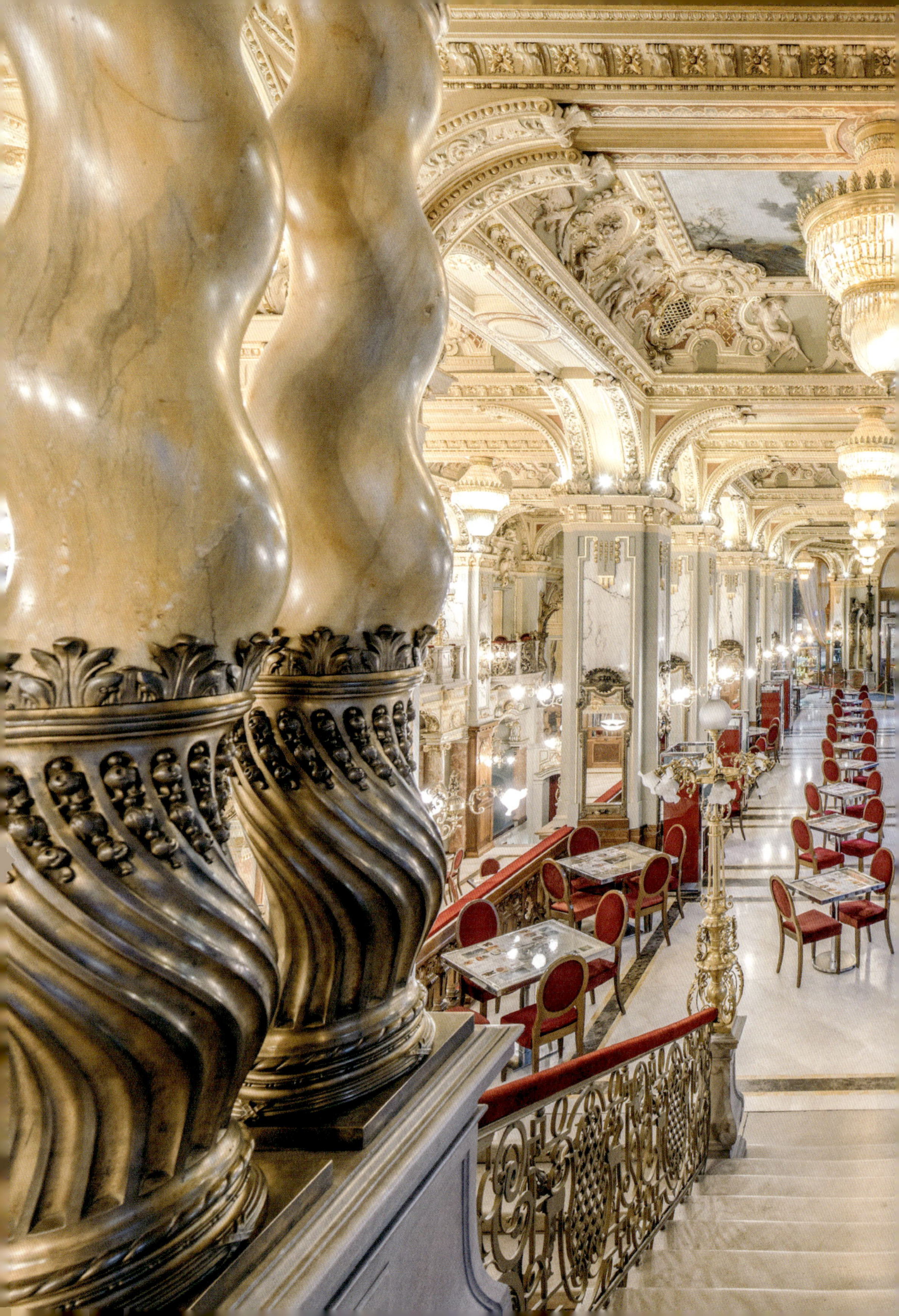

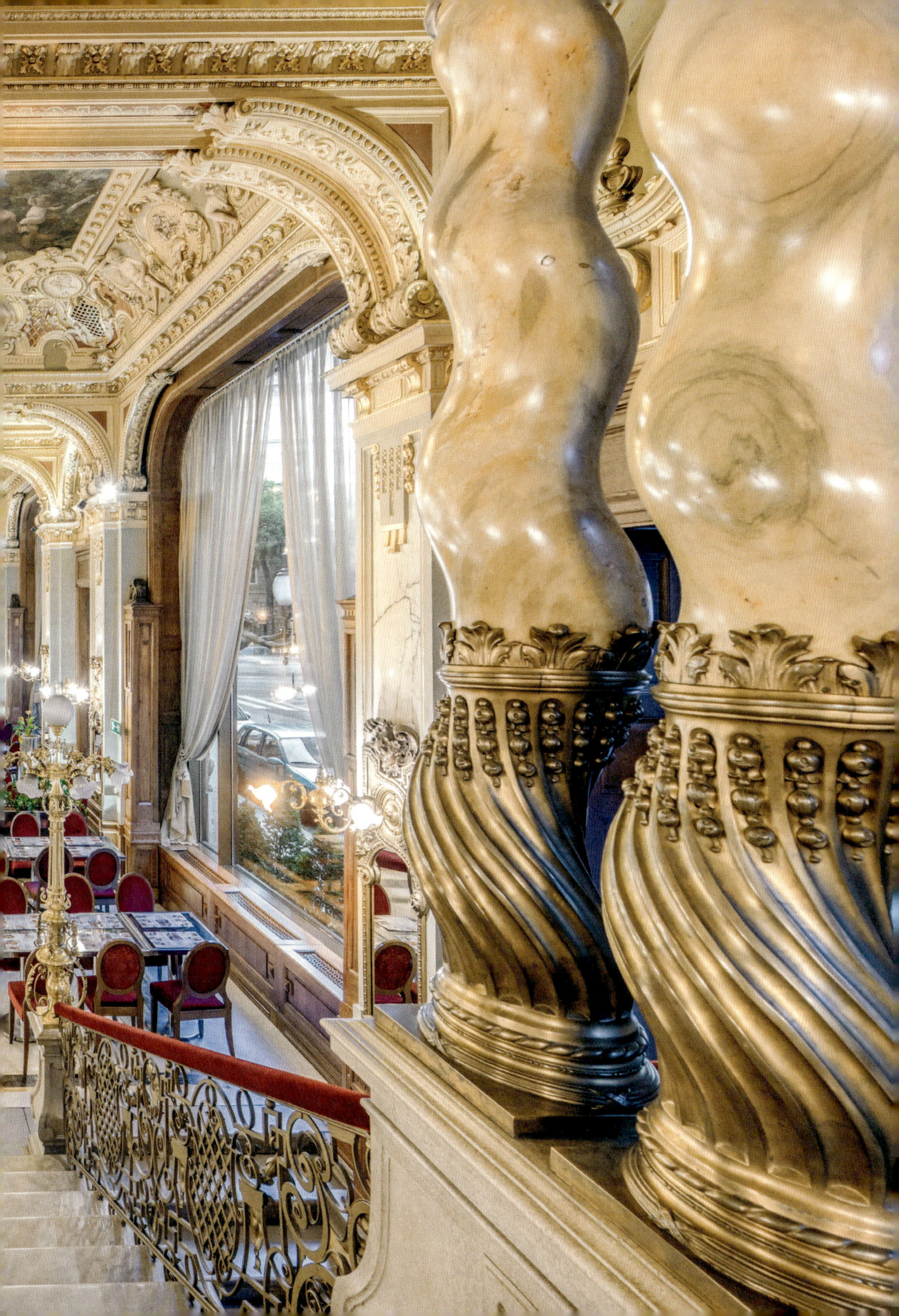

94 KROSS

28 Meletiou Metaksaki Str, Chania, Crete PC 73134, Greece

TO VISIT BEFORE YOU DIE BECAUSE

Grab an iced drip Kyoto style and a tasty homemade cake and let the world go by on the patio of this beautifully renovated townhouse.

Opened by three friends on Tsouderon Street in Chania, Kross is an award-winning roastery with several branches around town. 'Our daily interaction with the community is inspired by the traditional connections of the *kafeneia* (village coffeehouses) in small towns,' explains the team. 'We believe that we are here to make an impact on our surrounding community and make life just that little bit more beautiful.' And that's just what they did with this late-1800s neoclassical building, which they completely restored into a peaceful, three-level space with top floor working area, a basement studio space and a courtyard filled with olive trees. 'We feature small lots of coffee from all around the world and have an array of them based on seasonality,' they continue. 'Kit-wise we have quite a treat: a three-group La Marzocco Strada X, three La Marzocco Swan grinders and an EK43 by Mahlkönig.' Kross also has a roastery and training lab, housed in a beautiful former petrol station in Chania's Profitis Ilias, and a branch in Athens' Pangrati neighbourhood.

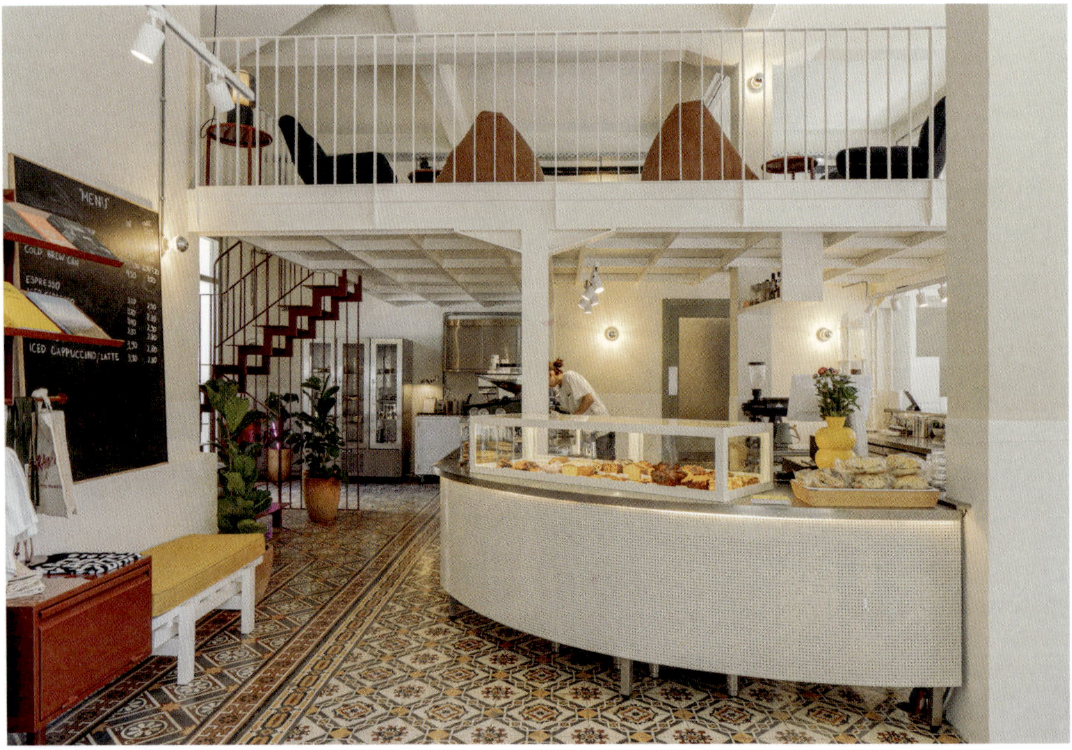

krosscoffeeroasters.com +30 28 2109 8524

95 LOKAL

Sønder Boulevard 59, 1720 Copenhagen, Denmark

TO VISIT BEFORE YOU DIE BECAUSE

Stop by for 'a hot coffee and a look at some beautiful things' at this elegant café/gallery in Copenhagen's vibrant Vesterbro.

Lokal's two large windows on Sønder Boulevard frame a heavenly scene of beautifully designed furniture and objects, as elegant and cosy as you'd expect to find in the design capital that is Copenhagen. But Lokal is not just an interiors shop: as well as its perfectly curated collection of homewares, it is also a delightful coffee shop serving the best beans around, from the likes of Prolog (page 162) or Nomad (page 148). It was opened by Anders Forup, founder of vintage gallery Dansk Form, 'based on an idea that quality, aesthetics and design go hand in hand'. Designed by Alice Chan and created by Vermland, it is a small but open space. 'This means that there is a lot less to separate us and it's much easier to connect. It doesn't take long to become a local at Lokal,' says manager Christian Jakobsen. 'We strive for an atmosphere that is reminiscent of being in your best friend's kitchen.' Perch on a wooden stool with a cappuccino to ponder your next purchase – a cheese roll or cardamom bun from Copenhagen Bakery, or perhaps a beautiful ceramic vase?

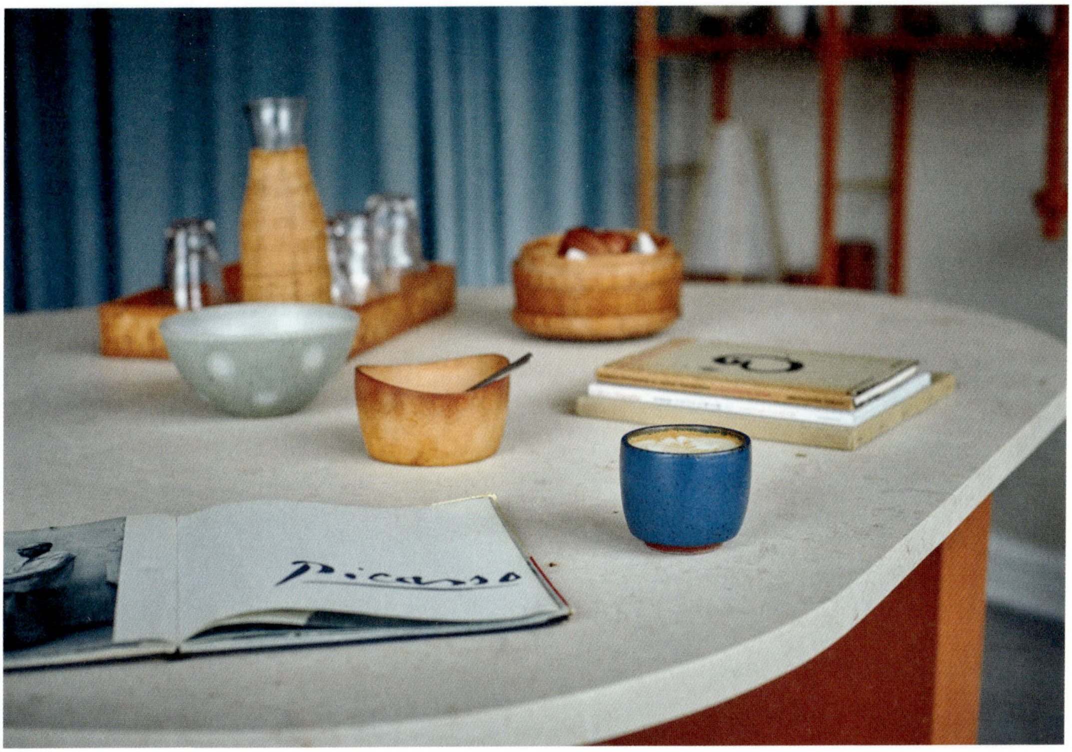

@lokalcph

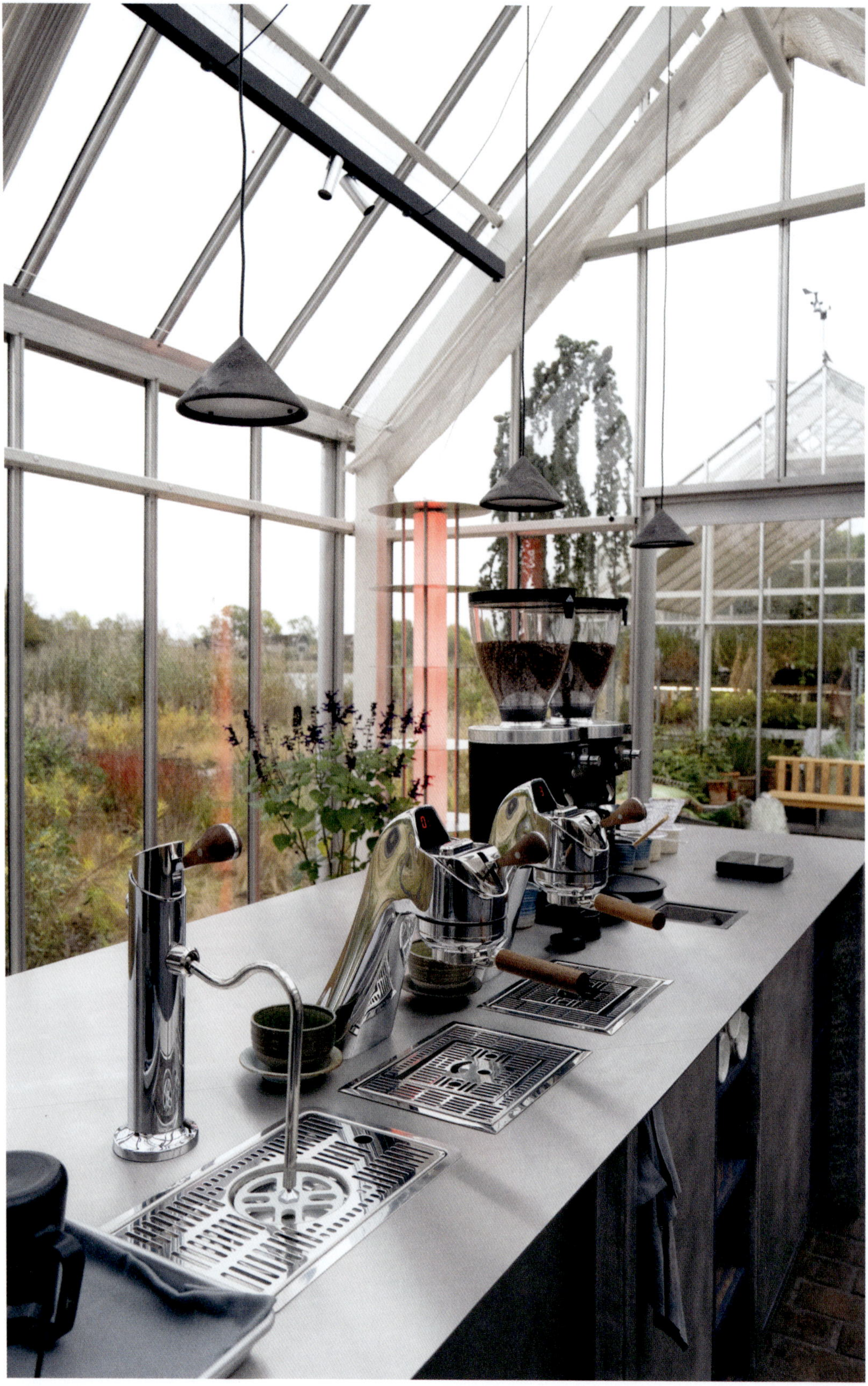

96 NOMA PROJECTS FLAVOR SHOP

Refshalevej 96, 1432 Copenhagen, Denmark

TO VISIT BEFORE YOU DIE BECAUSE

Enjoy a pour-over coffee and a taste of Noma's wonderful world of flavours at this welcoming greenhouse lab-café mixing craft and technology.

Copenhagen's three-Michelin-starred Noma, perhaps the most famous restaurant in the world, is operated by a talented bunch of innovators and flavour tinkerers. Unsurprisingly, they've been interested in coffee for a while, collaborating with Tim Wendelboe (page 190) and also starting their own in-house roasting operation. Now the team, including Noma's head of coffee Carolyne Lane, has just transformed the entrance to the restaurant into an exciting – and much more accessible – Flavor Shop showcasing their latest experiments. Designed by OEO Studio, it's a greenhouse-like space with hanging plants, as well as views of the garden, lake and the restaurant itself. But don't expect a traditional café; it's more like a laboratory where you can browse through a full pantry, including the new Noma Kaffe's range, ten years in the making. The inventive programme features beans from growers such as Colombia's La Perla del Otún, and six baristas to prepare them. Have your coffee in the garden, or stock up on the beautifully packaged goods, which make great gifts if you manage to not eat them yourself.

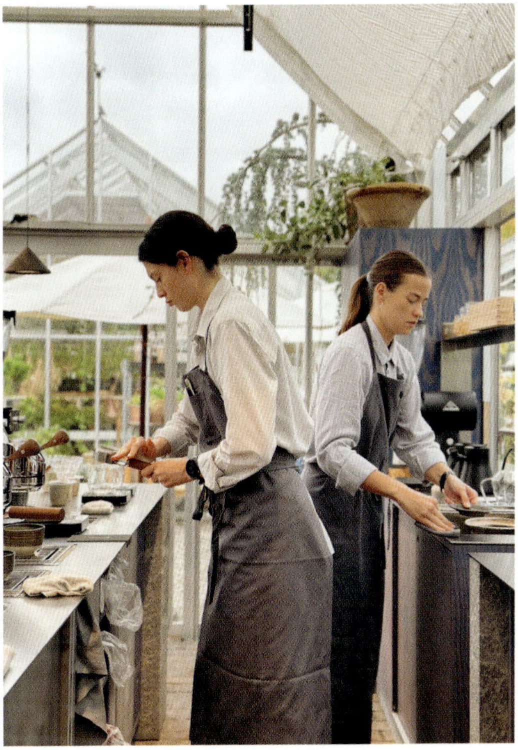

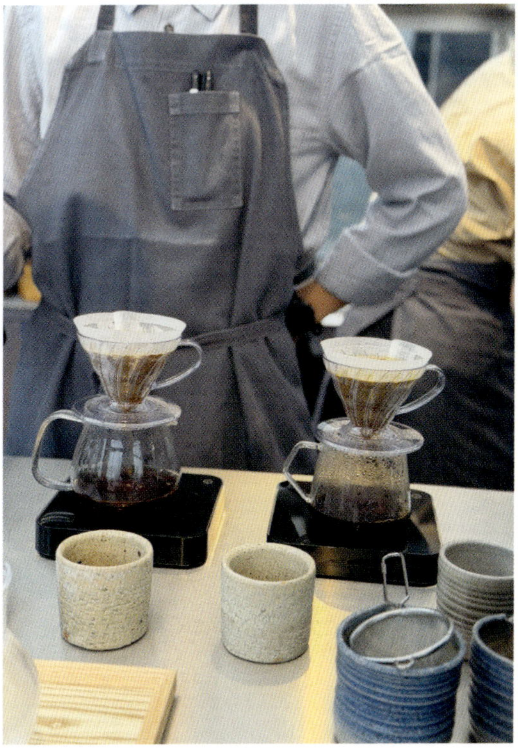

nomaprojects.com

97 PROLOG

Marguerite Vibys Pl 8, 2000 Frederiksberg, Denmark

TO VISIT BEFORE YOU DIE BECAUSE

Top coffee, flaky pastries, great music and good vibes are on the menu at this cosy neighbourhood café by one of the city's most revered roasters.

'We love coffee, the plant, the seed, the people, the roasting, the flavours, the sounds, the drink served, and the people composing the coffee shop communities,' says the team at Prolog, a celebrated roastery founded in 2016 by Sebastian Quistorff and Jonas Gehl. This passion shines through at Prolog's four locations in town, including this Frederiksberg gem, just a short bike ride away from the old town. The peaceful corner café is located right next to the roastery, itself a striking, small brick building (you can peek inside on roasting days). It's the only coffee shop in Denmark with a manual La Marzocco Leva, which 'gives our baristas a lot of control and room to play'. There might be a jazz record playing on the vintage stereo system, and the counter is packed with cardamom buns, cakes and pastries from Juno the Bakery. 'If you prefer oat milk in your pour-over, no one will judge you,' Sebastian once explained. 'Our focus is on making you feel at ease, rather than delivering lectures on what we believe is right.'

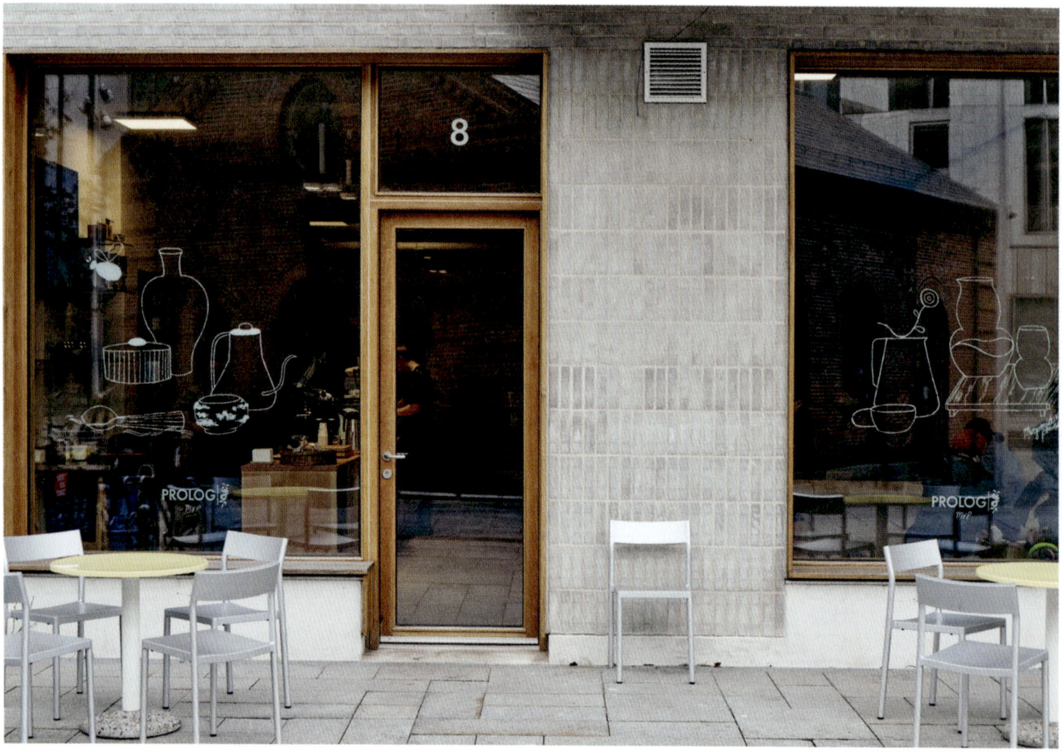

prologcoffee.com

98 VICE COFFEE

54 Middle Abbey St, North City, Dublin 1, D01 E2X4, Ireland

TO VISIT BEFORE YOU DIE BECAUSE

One of the city's best multi-roaster coffee bars, Vice specialises in award-winning Irish coffees and scrumptious toasties.

Wigwam is a night-time bar with DJ sets, karaoke, drag and ping pong contests. But during the day, it is home to an equally exciting programme courtesy of Vice Coffee, a multi-roaster bar that often hosts coffee competitions, tastings and events. Set up by third-wave coffee pioneer Tom Stafford in 2013, it offers a menu of international (Square Mile, Friedhats) and Irish roasters (3fe, Imbibe, Calendar) as well as great Irish coffees – the hot cocktail created in the 1940s by Joe Sheridan at the Foynes Airbase to warm up transatlantic passengers. Try a Plain Jaine (espresso, Kilbeggan whiskey), Luxurious Linda (cold brew, Teeling Stout Cask, Poitín) or Fancy Frankie (espresso, Teeling Small Batch) and soak up the good vibes with a cheesy toastie. It seems that coffee-in-music-venues is a thing in Dublin: four-time Irish Barista Champion Colin Harmon of 3fe, whose flagship café you can visit on Grand Canal Street, set up his first coffee stall in 2009 in the lobby of Dublin's Twisted Pepper nightclub and is now known as one of the country's top roasters. We predict the same success for Vice Coffee.

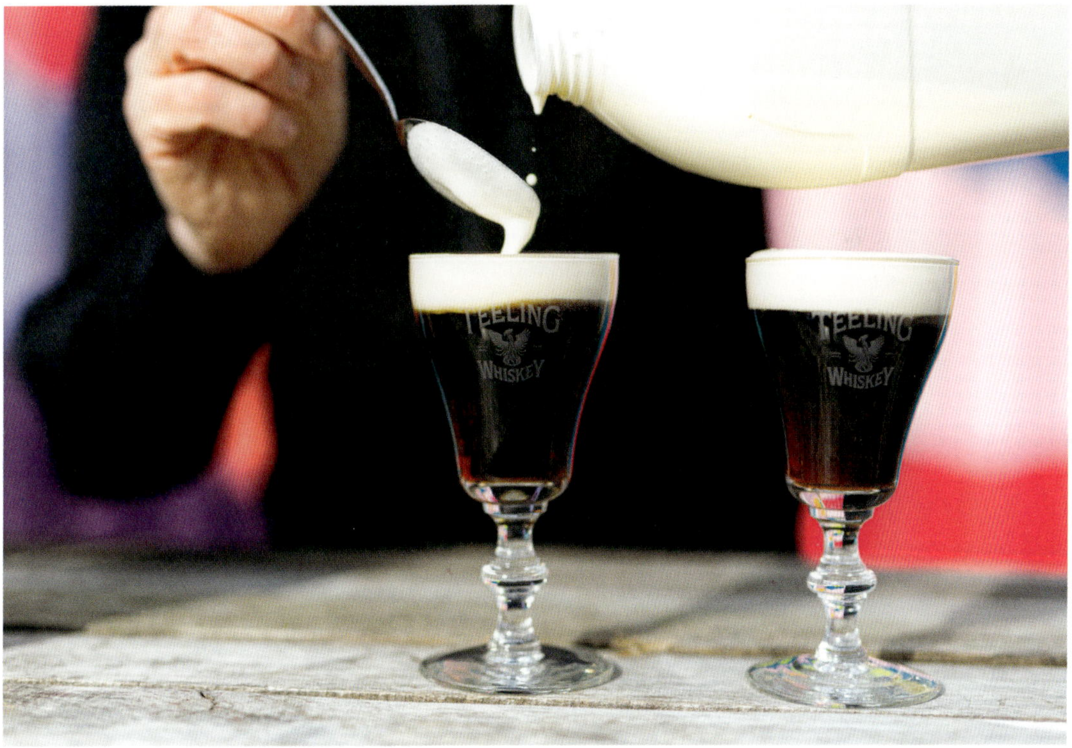

vicecoffeeinc.com

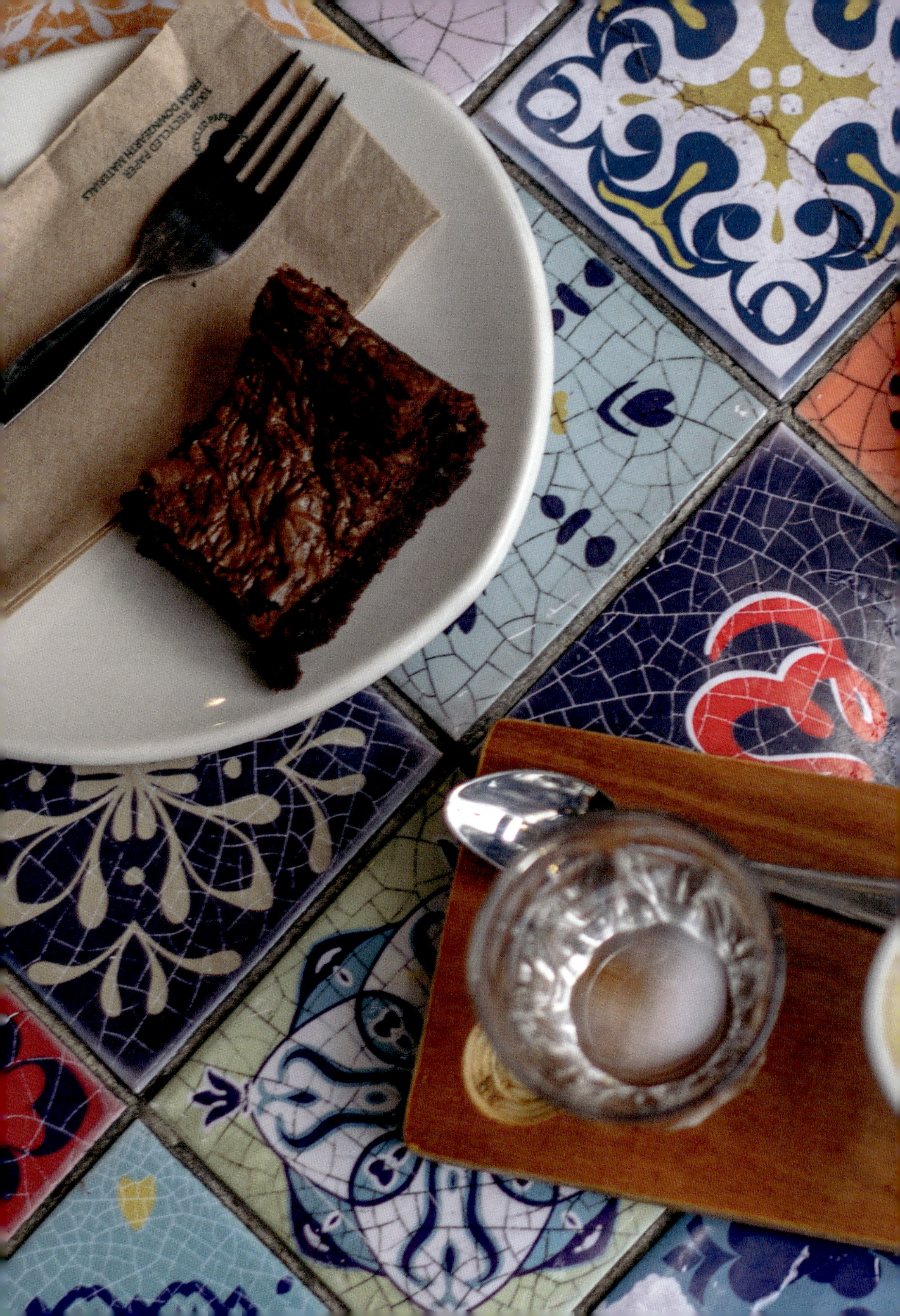

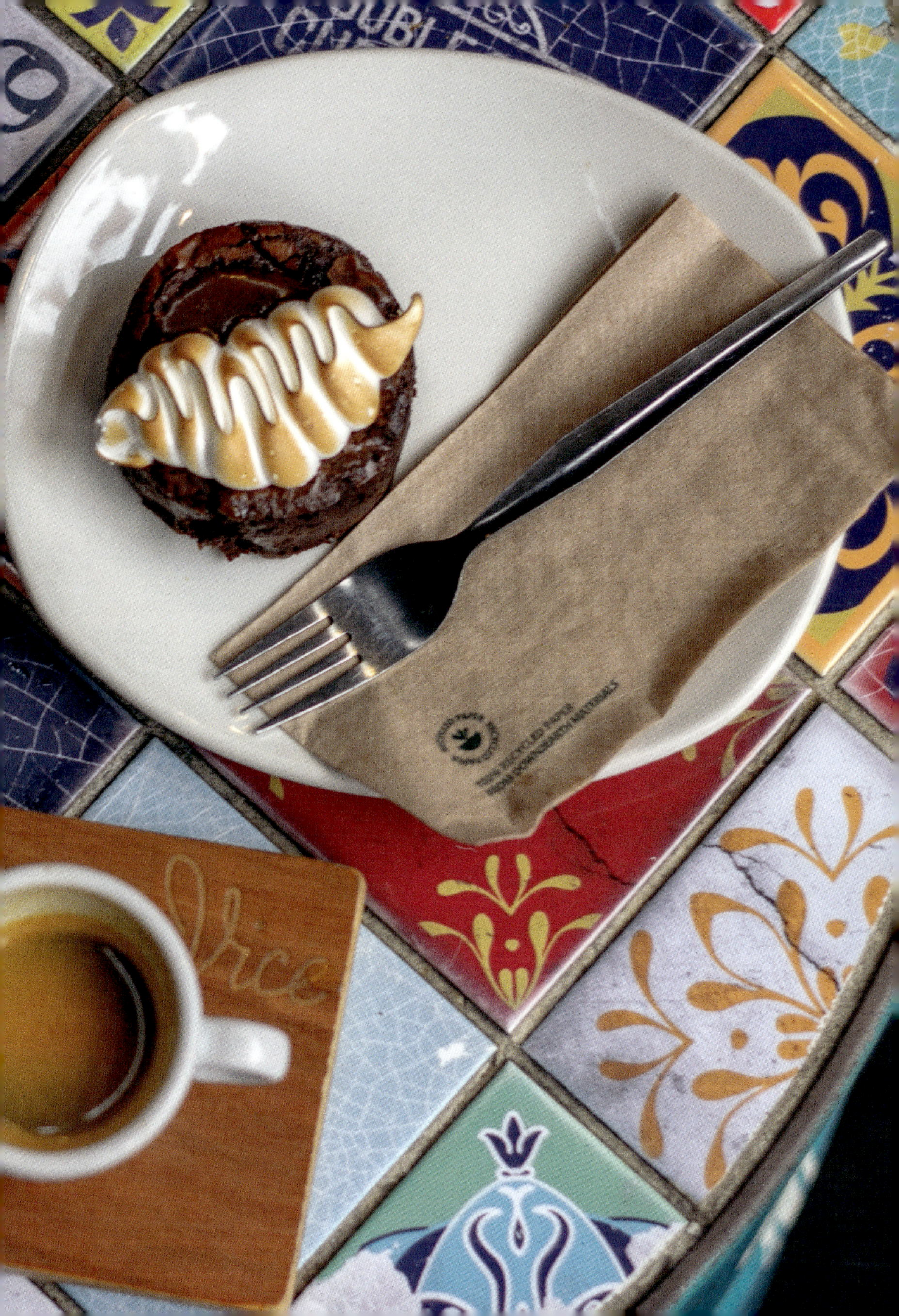

99 DITTA ARTIGIANALE

Piazza Ferrucci 1R, Florence, Italy

TO VISIT BEFORE YOU DIE BECAUSE

This café opened by a local champion barista is just a short stroll away from the Piazzale Michelangelo viewpoint and the banks of the Arno.

A coffee in Italy is traditionally downed at the bar during a quick morning break, but this beautiful café, designed to make people feel at home, invites you to take your time. Offering a caffeinated take on the country's famous slow food movement, it's part of the Ditta Artigianale third-wave roastery set up in 2013 by Francesco Sanapo, multiple award-winning barista champion and Italian Cup Tasters winner. Located in a former pub just next to the Arno River, the café and bakery aims to 'create an environment that combines artisanal products with a focus on the quality of the time spent there'. There's a lovely shaded terrace for summer mornings, while menu highlights include the Coffeemisù – tiramisu in a cup, topped with a biscotto – as well as freshly made pastries and bread. Visiting on a hot day? Cool down with a *shakerato*, the Italian iced coffee made by shaking ice, espresso and sugar together. And if you're serious about coffee, book a tasting session with a barista at Ditta Artigianale on via Carducci.

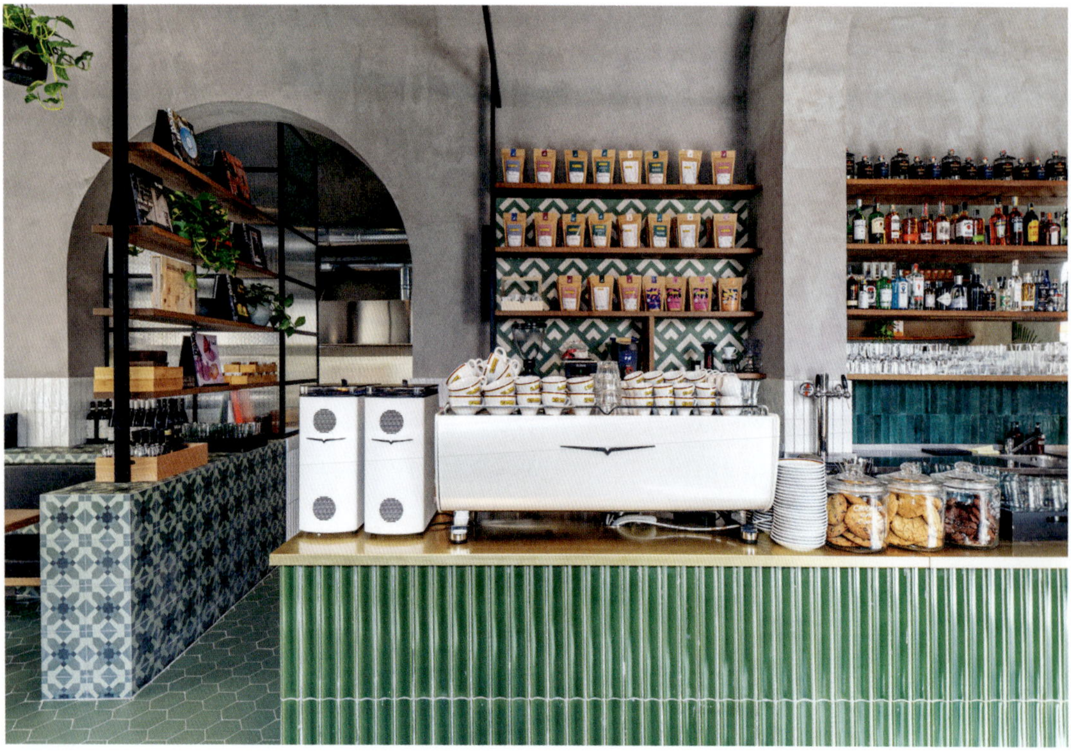

dittaartigianale.com +39 055 045 7163

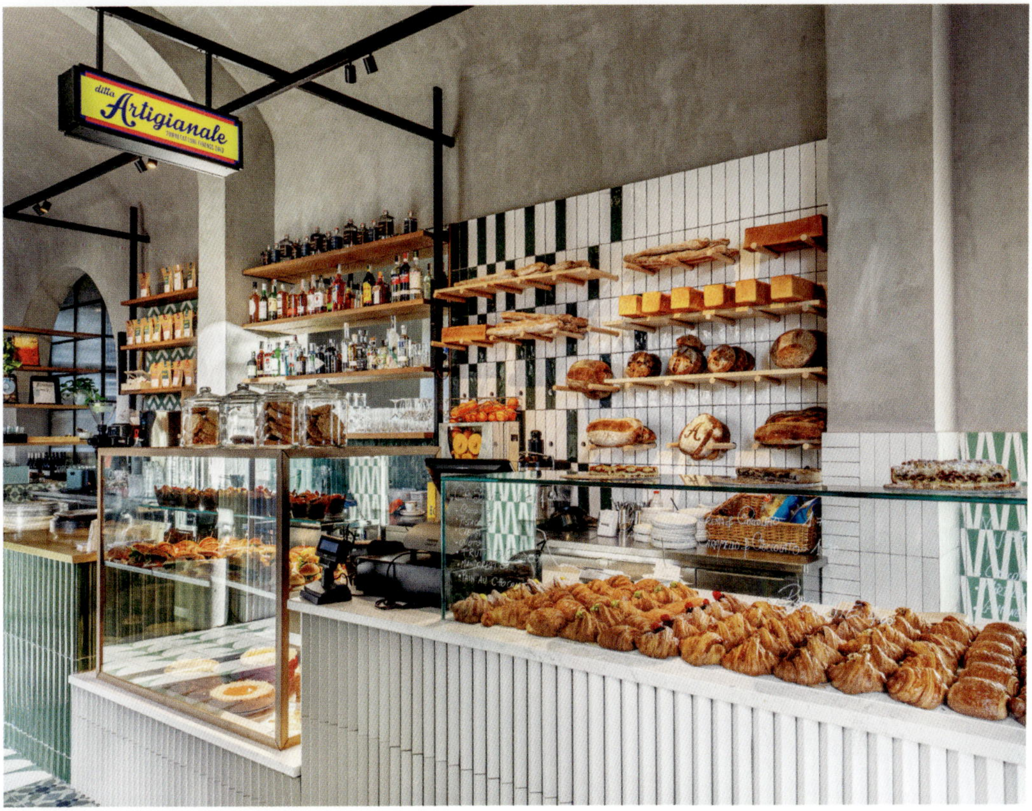
ditta
Artigianale

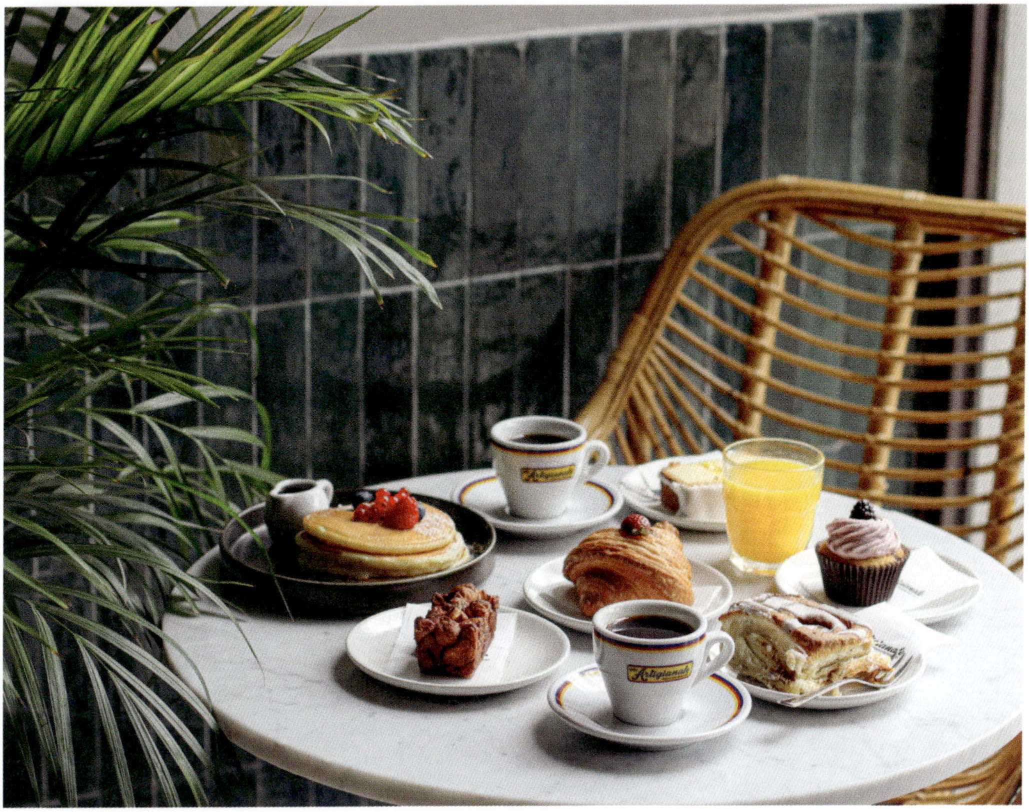
Artigianale

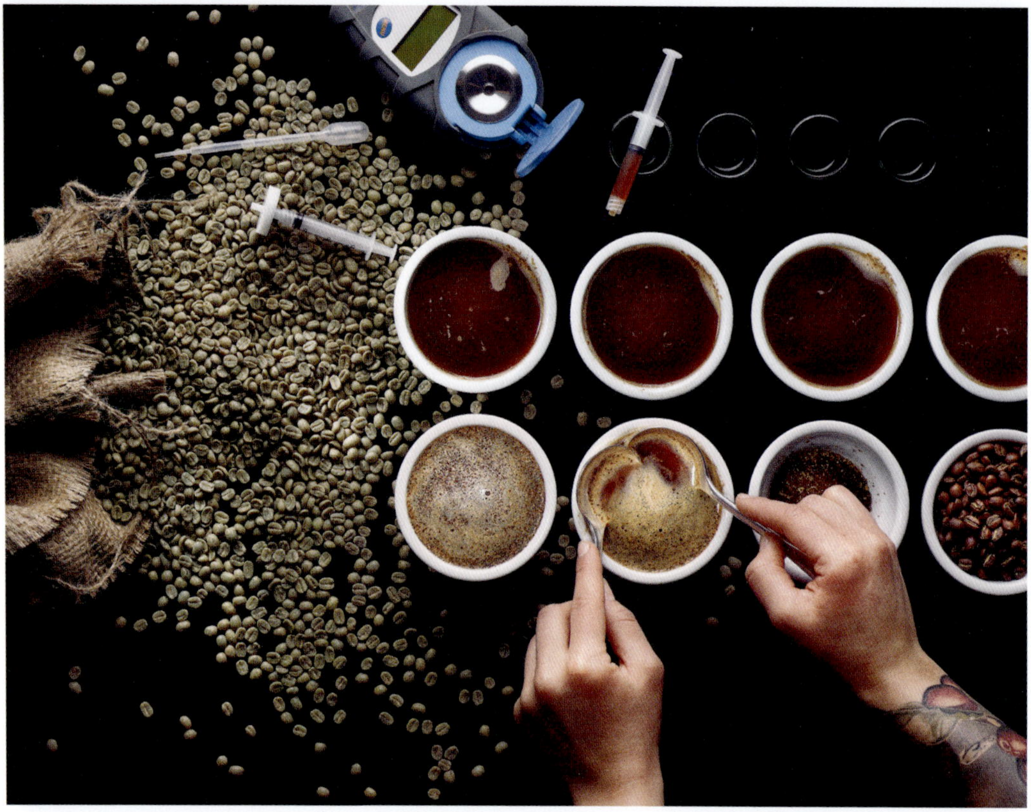

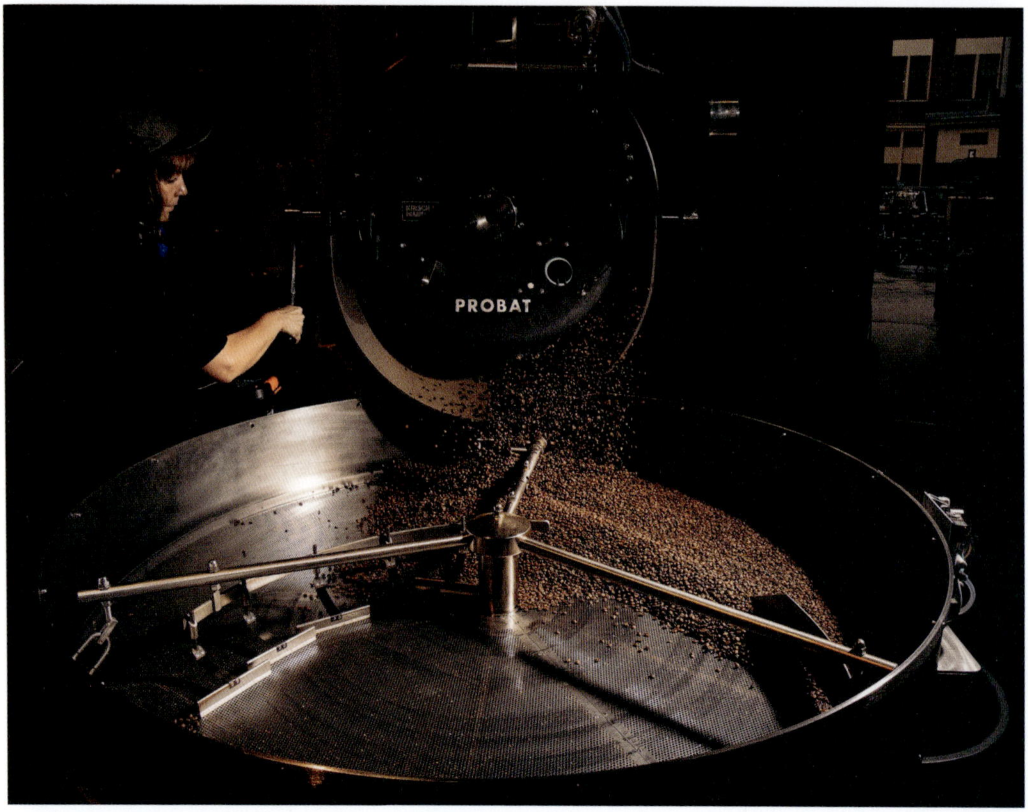
PROBAT

100 KAFFA ROASTERY

Pursimiehenkatu 29, 00150 Helsinki, Finland

TO VISIT
BEFORE YOU DIE
BECAUSE

Try a seasonal special such as an espresso tonic with elderflower or Tabasco-spiked coffee at this roastery in Helsinki's arty Punavuori.

Finland has the world's highest coffee consumption, with the average Finn drinking just over four cups of *kahvi* a day. There's a specific word for every coffee occasion, whether it's a mid-morning break (*aamupäiväkahvi*), nightcap (*yökahvi*), or served with cake (*kakkukahvi*). However, until very recently, all these cups were mostly enjoyed at home or the office rather than in a café. Thankfully we know a great spot to enjoy a *pullakahvi* (coffee with cardamom roll): Kaffa Roastery, opened in 2007 by Svante Hampf and his friends. Their first roaster was a popcorn machine, and they almost set fire to the place, but we're glad to say they've grown leaps and bounds since, even recently harnessing the power of AI to create a coffee blend. Their basement café is a perfect winter refuge, where you can hunker down with an almond croissant and a coffee made from a great choice of beans, using the brewing method of your choice or the Synesso espresso machine.

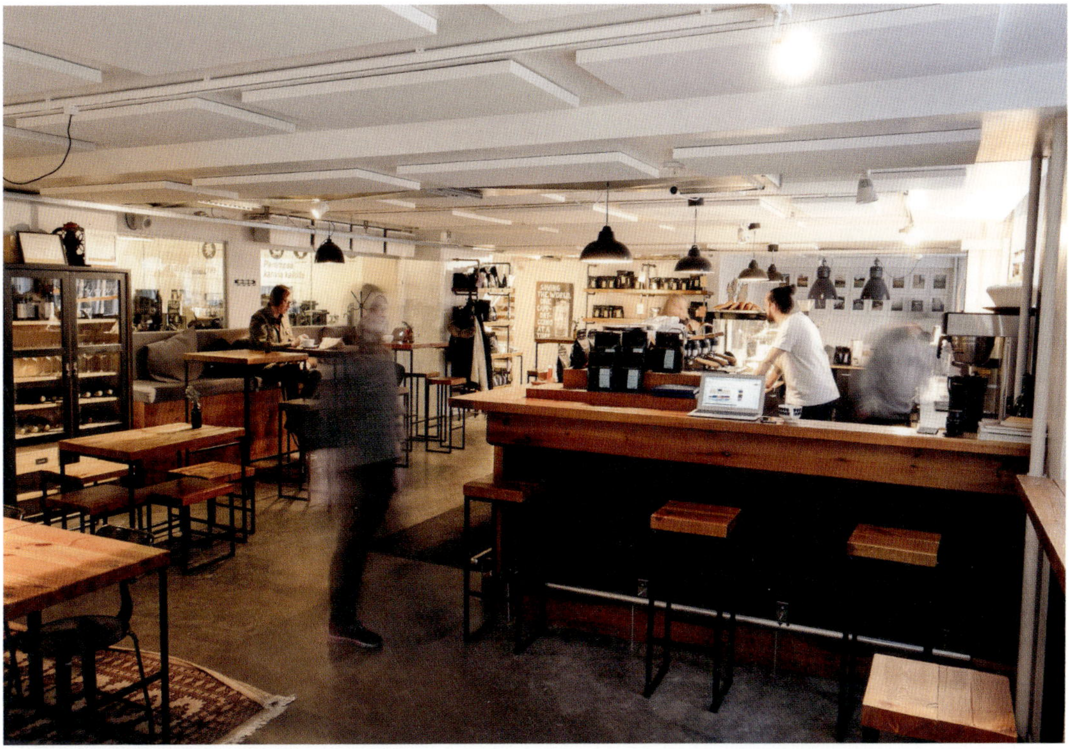

kaffaroastery.fi

+358 50 306 5499

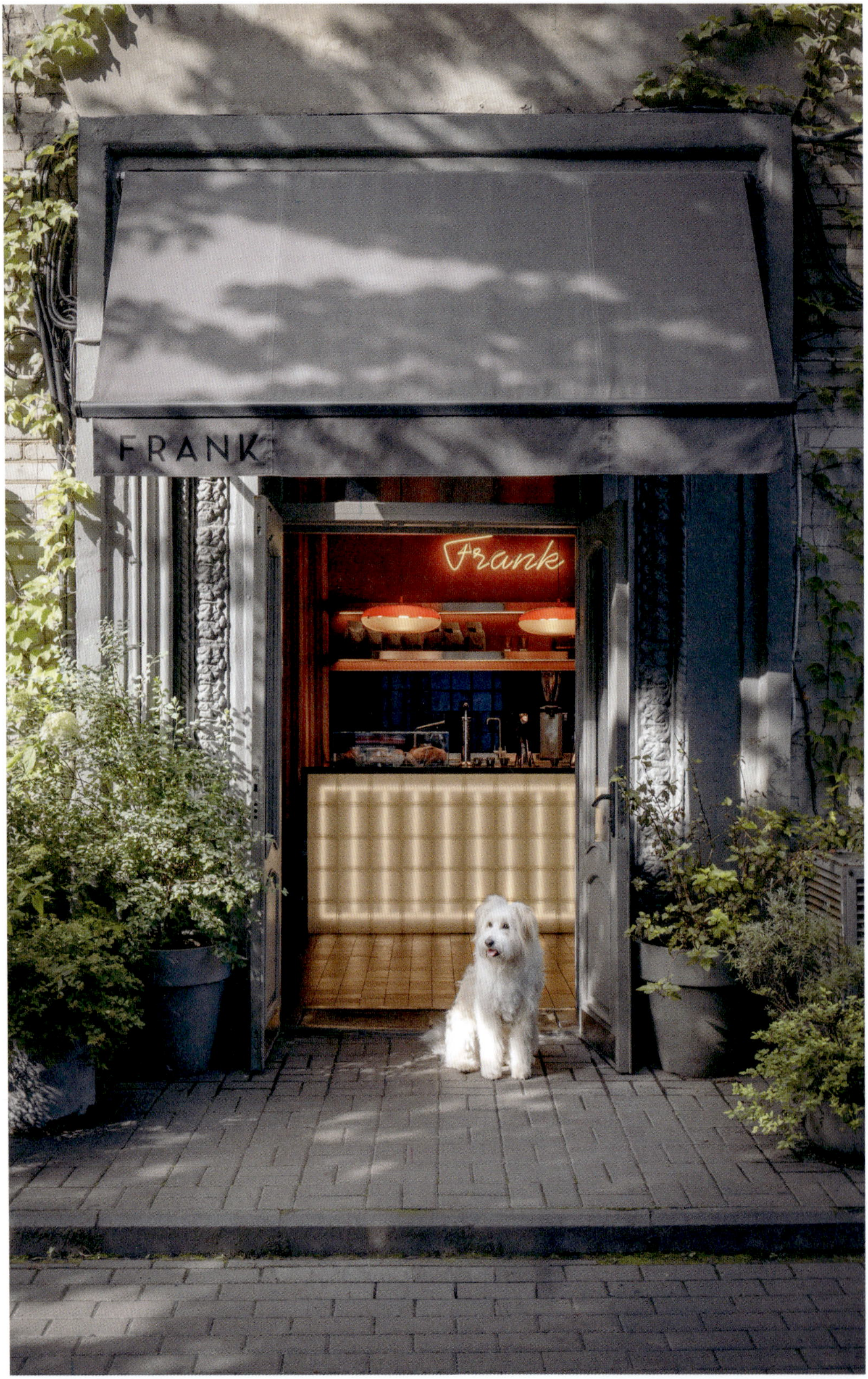
FRANK
Frank

101 FRANK

Yevgena Gutsala Ln, 3, Kyiv, Ukraine, 01011

TO VISIT BEFORE YOU DIE BECAUSE

This café represents the power of daily rituals, careful design and love for coffee that can help us through the worst of times.

When life takes a turn for the worse, it's often the little things like a cup of coffee and a treat that help you get through the storm. Resuming normal life is a form of resistance, and perhaps nowhere else is this more poignant than in Kyiv, where cafés continue to serve customers under challenging conditions. One such is Frank, a small coffee shop recently redesigned by Yana Molodykh for owner Evgeny Kopyl. She's carefully updated the 19 sq m café into a perfect Milanese-inspired haven – a change 'subtle enough not to scare off regular customers, because there is nothing sweeter in our rapidly changing and stressful life than holding on to traditions and rituals,' she says. The glass block counter is still there, while new 'Luna' pendant lights by Gio Ponti make the stainless-steel details and red walls glow. 'We have a classic coffee menu that has remained practically unchanged since the opening nine years ago,' says Evgeny. 'We brew beans from our friends and, in our opinion, the best Ukrainian roaster, Cafeboutique, and sell pastries from our own bakery, pâte.'

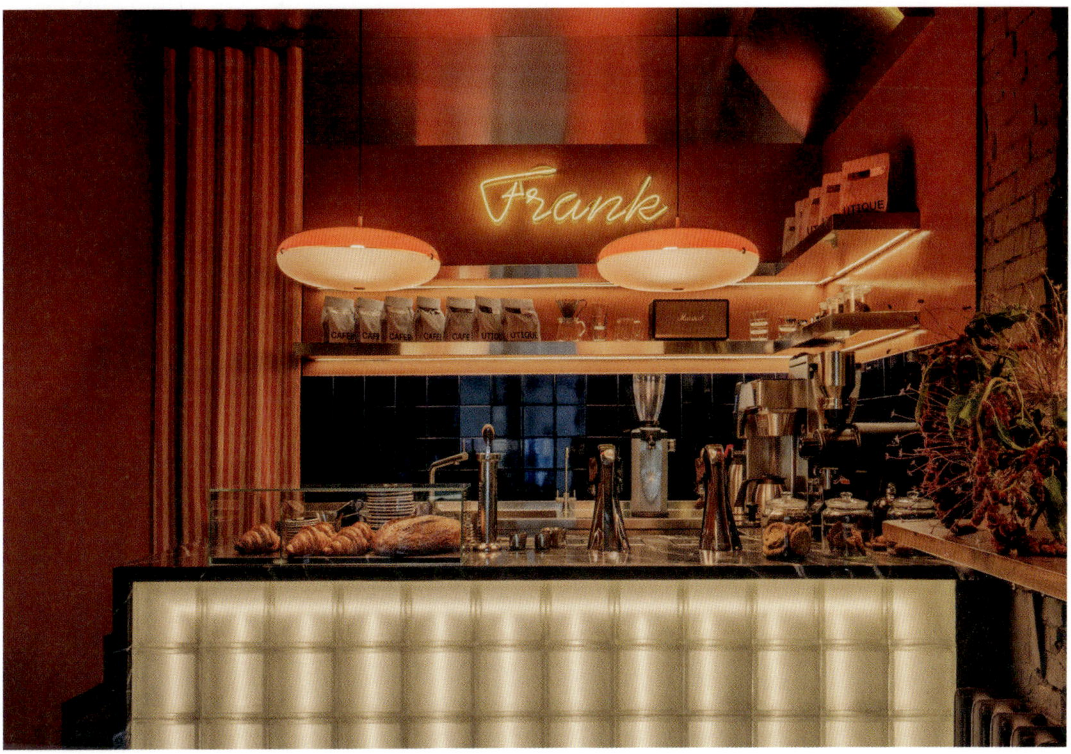

frank.menu

+380 95 041 4176

102 MADMUM

Tiensestraat 38, 3000 Leuven, Belgium

TO VISIT BEFORE YOU DIE BECAUSE

There's nothing better than spending a leisurely morning watching city life go by from a café terrace in a bustling European town.

Found on thousands of historic, pedestrian streets from Madrid to Krakow, the café terrace is truly a thing of beauty. But we do tend to take it for granted in Europe, so next time we get a sunny morning, please take a moment to head to your local café and enjoy it to the full. A fine example of the 'small town but big vibes' strain of coffee houses is Madmum in Leuven. Its first address, opened in 2018 on the city's bustling Tiensestraat, comes with the perfect café terrace to spy on shoppers and eavesdrop on local university students. It was founded by head barista Pieter Claes, with the simple goal of 'bringing people together around the best coffee there is, in a place where they feel at home'. A fourth-generation coffee roaster and Belgian Coffee Cupping Champion, Pieter continues his family's roasting tradition dating back to 1935. He chose the café's name as a tribute to his mum, Maddy. You are sure to be in good hands here, so order a flat white with whipped cream and a slice of choco-caramel cake, and breathe.

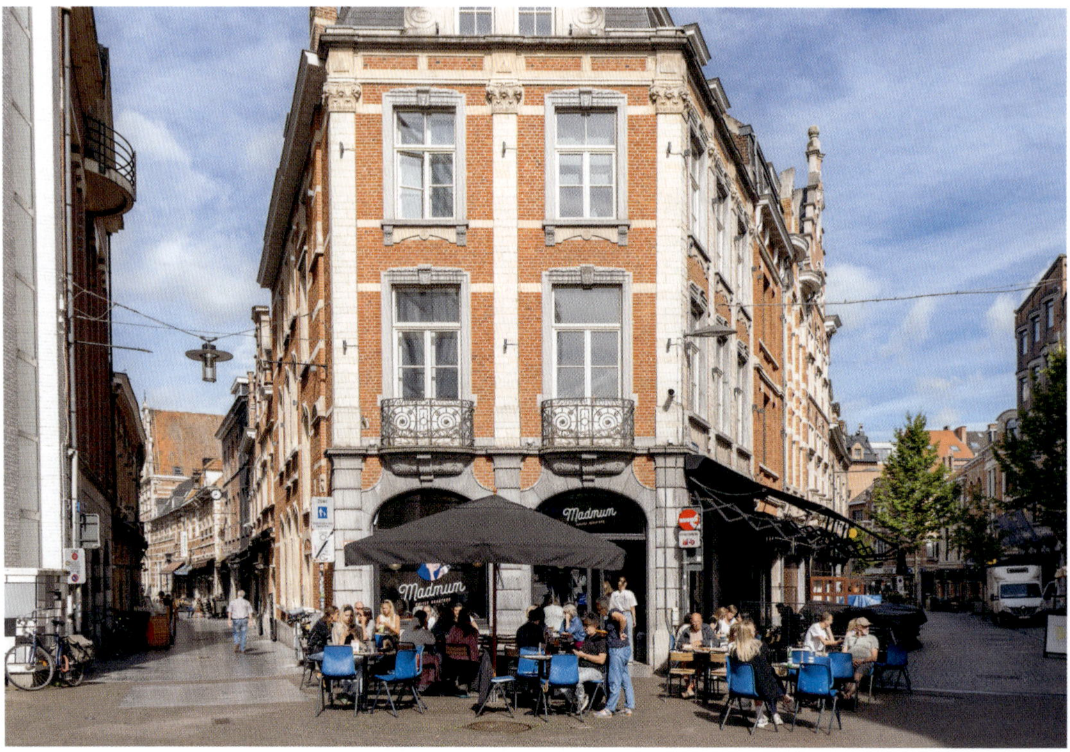

madmumcoffee.be

103 CAFÉ A BRASILEIRA

R. Garrett 120 122, 1200-205 Lisbon, Portugal

TO VISIT BEFORE YOU DIE BECAUSE

Time-travel back to the early 20th century with a *bica* espresso at this historic art deco café in Lisbon's old quarter.

A Portuguese merchant who travelled to Brazil in the 1870s and married the daughter of a large coffee producer in Minas Gerais, Adriano Telles was perfectly connected to open shops selling Brazilian beans on his return to Portugal. Settling down in Lisbon, he started by offering a free cup of coffee to any customers buying other goods he imported from Brazil, and soon turned his shop into a popular café. Redesigned in 1922 by Manuel Norte Júnior in the art deco style, it boasts a green and gold entrance, and elegant interiors with mirrored walls and wooden booths. Among the regulars at the time were artists and writers such as the poet Fernando Pessoa, who was apparently a fan of the café's steak Brasileira, served with coffee sauce (there's a bronze statue of him next to the terrace). Although it is a tourist hotspot, Café A Brasileira is still well worth a visit: it is after all the birthplace of the *bica* – the Portuguese espresso, made with a slightly lighter, smoother roast than the Italian version, and served with sugar. Enjoy with a freshly baked *pastel de nata* (custard tart), of course.

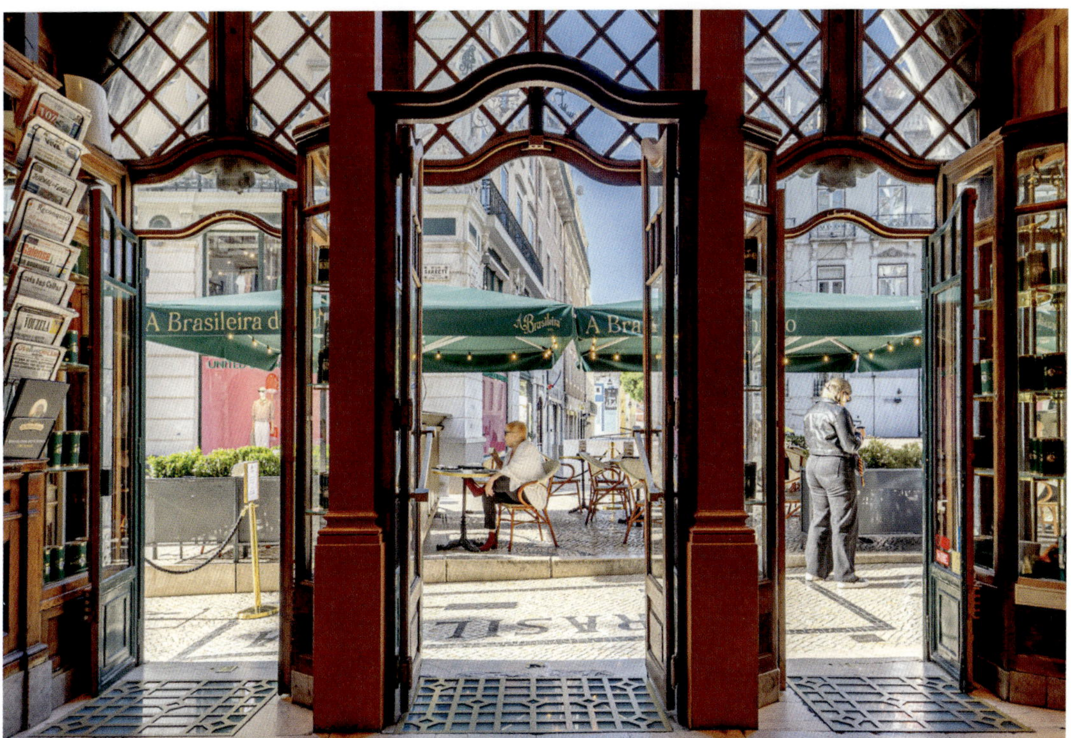

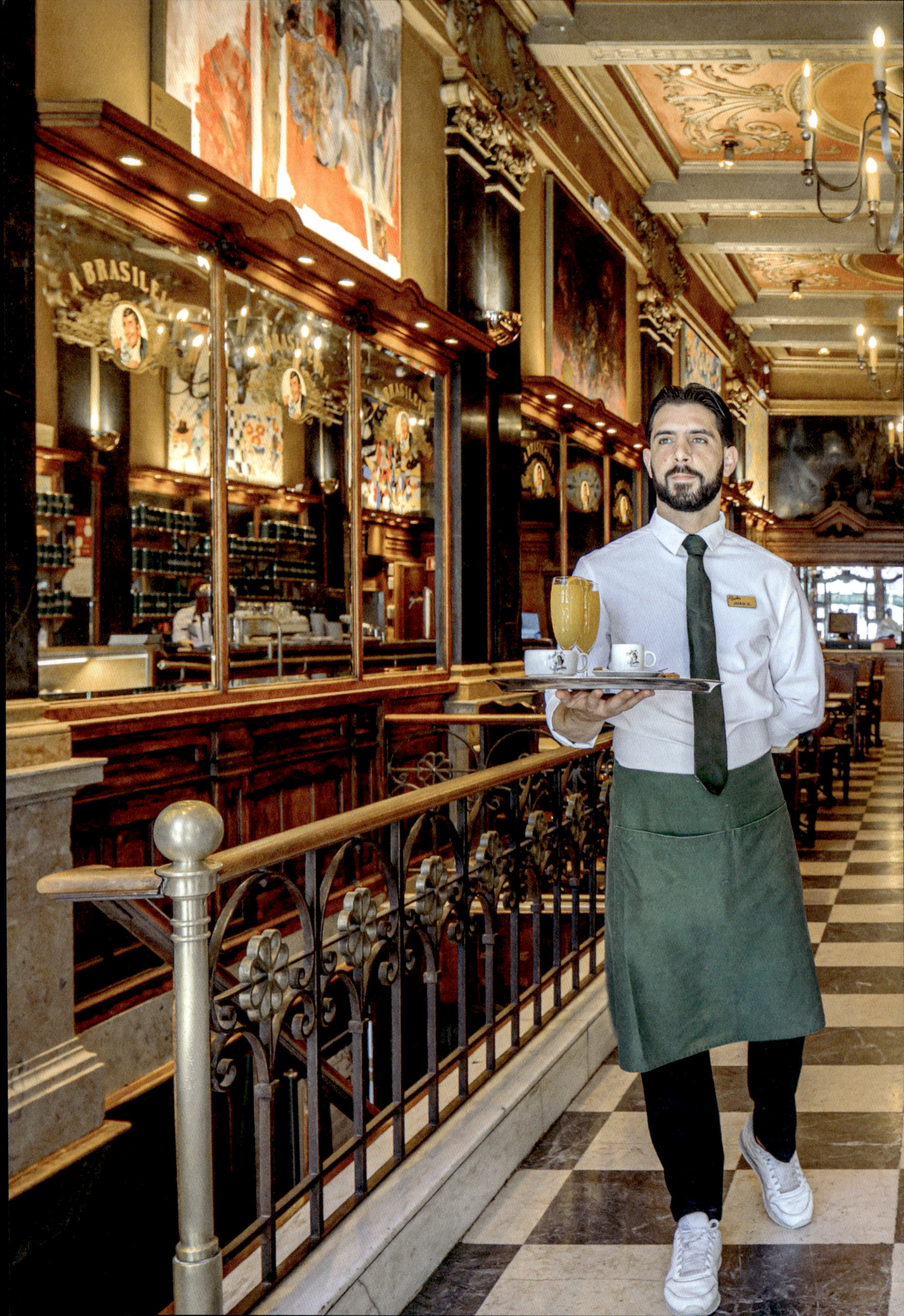
A BRASILEI

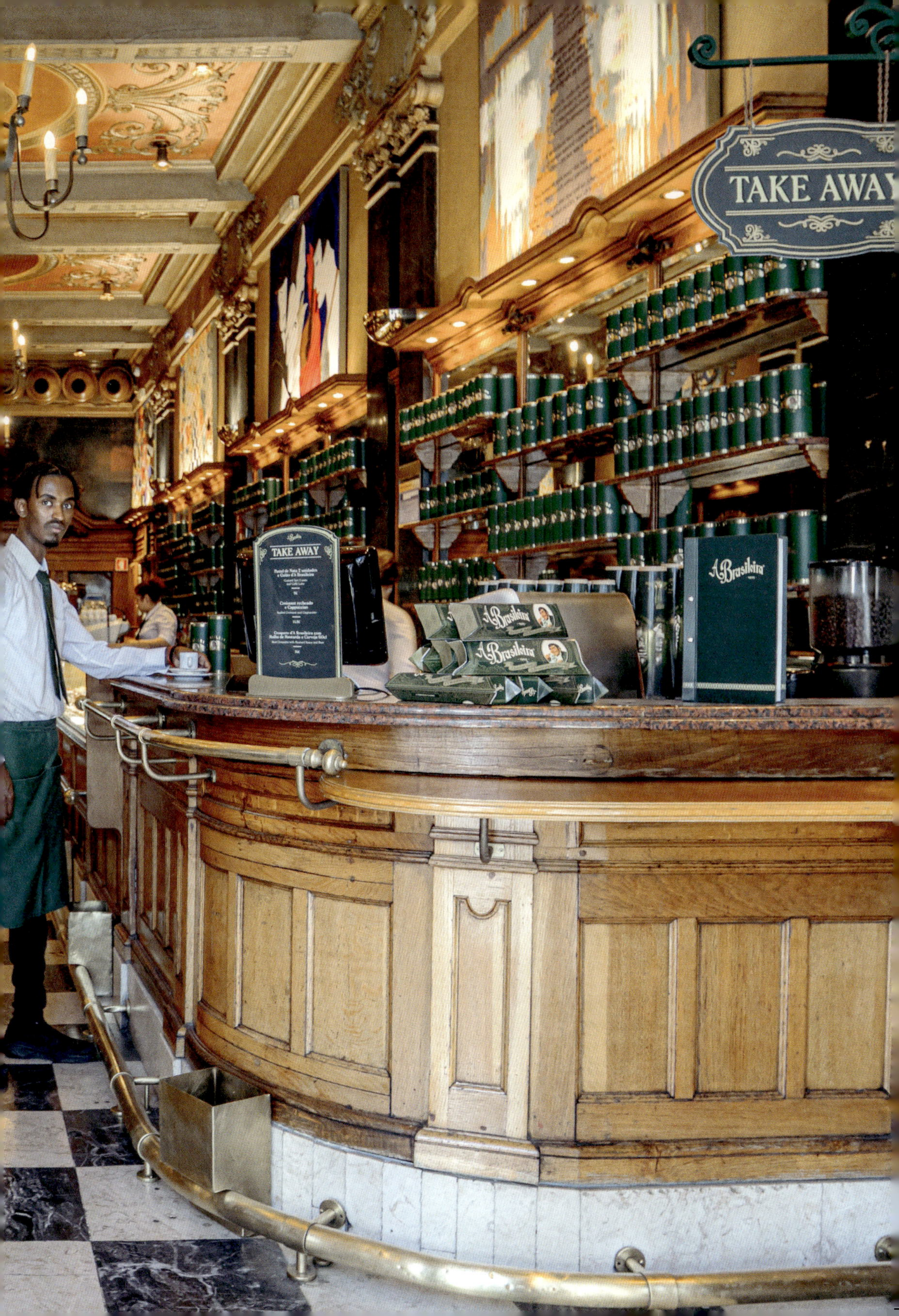
TAKE AWAY
TAKE AWAY
A Brasileira
A Brasileira
A Brasileira

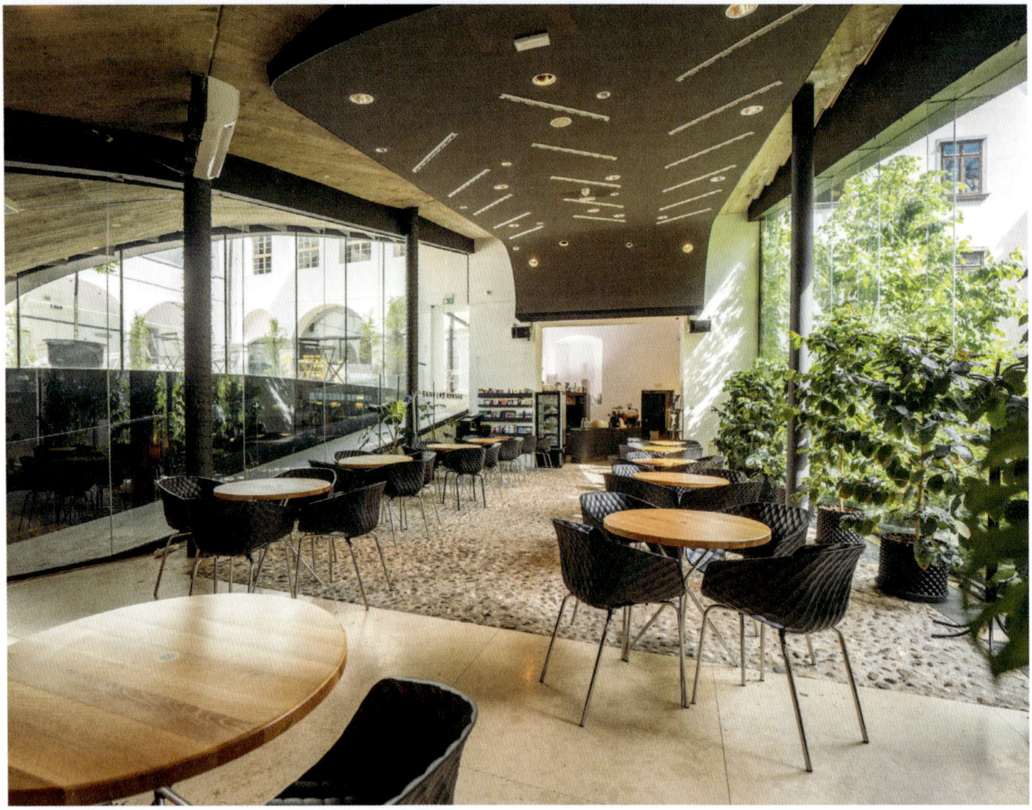

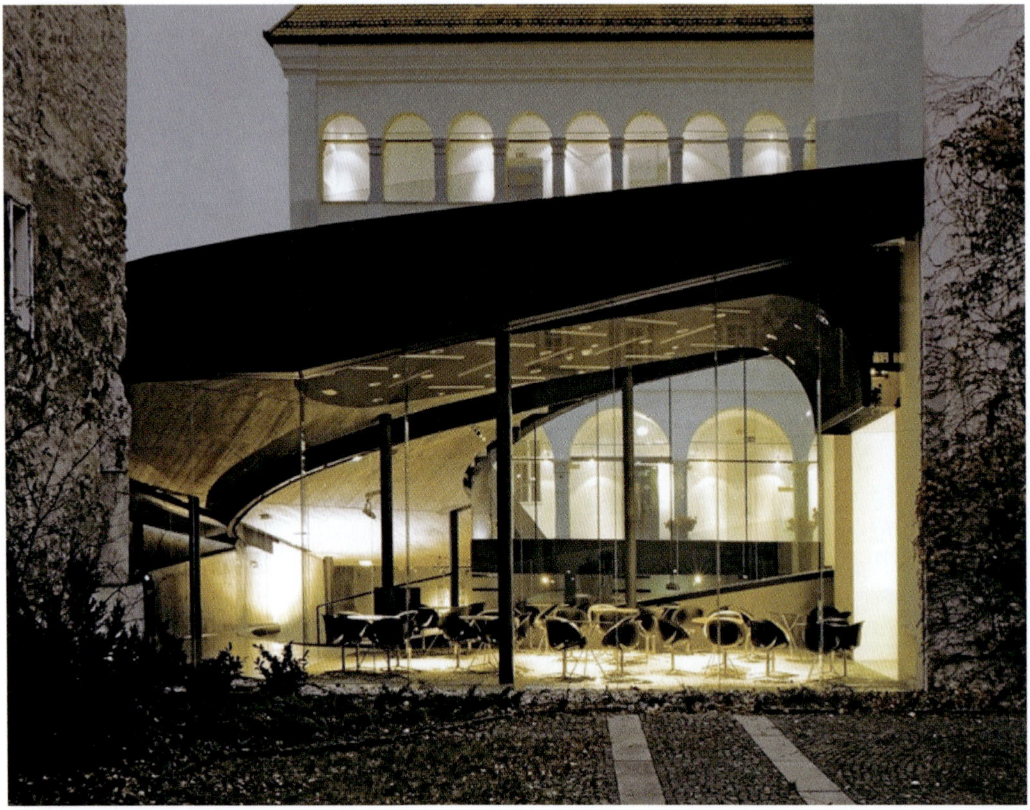

104 STOW

Gosposka ulica 15, 1000 Ljubljana, Slovenia

TO VISIT BEFORE YOU DIE BECAUSE

More than just a museum café, this is the light and airy flagship of Slovenia's leading speciality coffee roastery.

There are plenty of treasures to be found behind the late baroque façade of Ljubljana's Auersperg Palace, now home to the City Museum of Ljubljana, but most interesting to us is of course the café, housed in a beautiful sweeping concrete extension with floor-to-ceiling glass walls (you don't need a ticket to the museum to access it). Boasting views of the historic courtyard and real coffee plants inside, this peaceful spot is home to speciality coffee roasters Stow, founded in the Slovenian capital in 2016 by Aleš Turšič. Try a cascara tea from Panama's Carmen Estate (notes of fruit punch, berries and sweet lemon), or a signature Negroni+ with cold brew, as well as a range of coffees from Colombia to Malaysia. Ask the friendly team of baristas for advice, choose your brewing method, and pair your drink with a slice of warm banana bread or fruit pie. Stow also has another coffee shop at Cukrarna Gallery, in an old sugar factory, as well as a coffee academy.

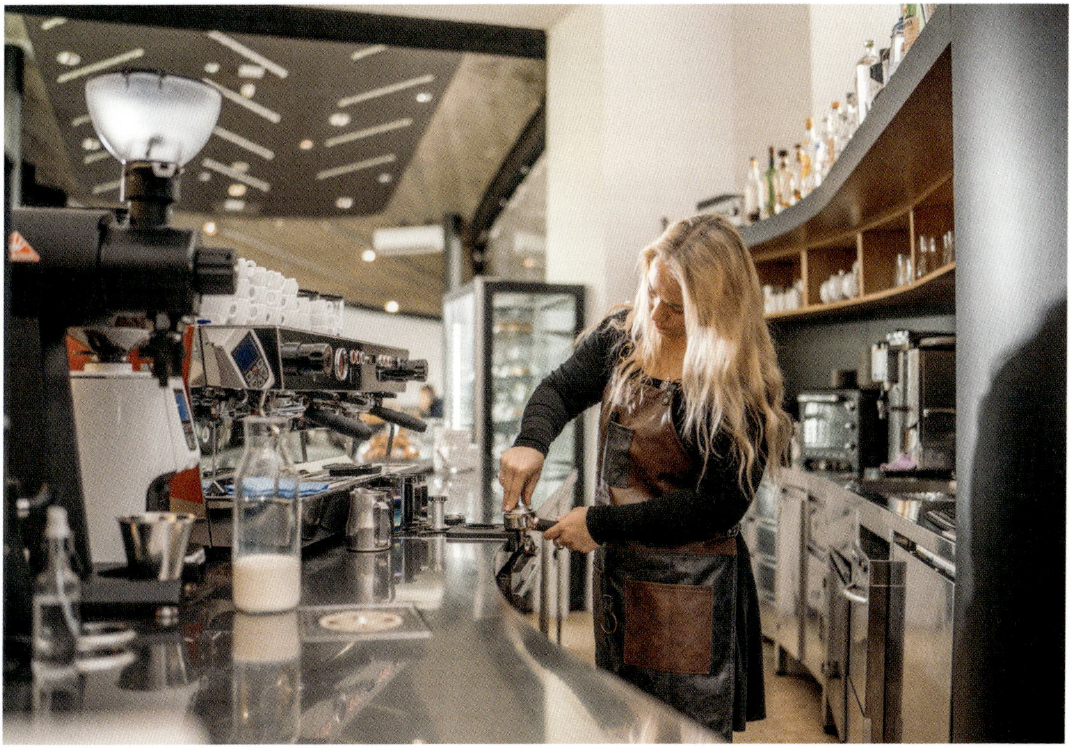

stow.si/en +386 40 318 135

105 BAR ITALIA

21 Frith St, Soho, London W1D 4RN, UK

TO VISIT BEFORE YOU DIE BECAUSE

This legendary Soho café is open from 7am to 4am, taking you from morning cappuccinos to late-night espresso martinis.

Bar Italia was founded by Lou and Caterina Polledri in 1949 in Soho, when the area was home to a flourishing Italian community. Bar Italia was the social hub it needed, with waiters stopping for a chat between shifts, and friends catching up after difficult times (many, including Lou, had spent part of the war interned in a camp on the Isle of Man). Known for its cappuccino and warm welcome, the family-owned business has thankfully been left largely intact. Patrons – including celebrities such as Kylie Minogue and Francis Ford Coppola – can continue to admire the original red and white Formica bar, Gaggia machine (still going strong after 50 years) and the polished terrazzo floor laid out by Uncle Torini. If you're after a quiet coffee break, don't visit when the Azzurri (the Italian football team) are playing, as thousands of supporters meet here, at the broken clock, under the giant poster of boxer Rocky Marciano. Just around the corner on Old Compton Street is another Soho classic, the 1887 Algerian Coffee Stores.

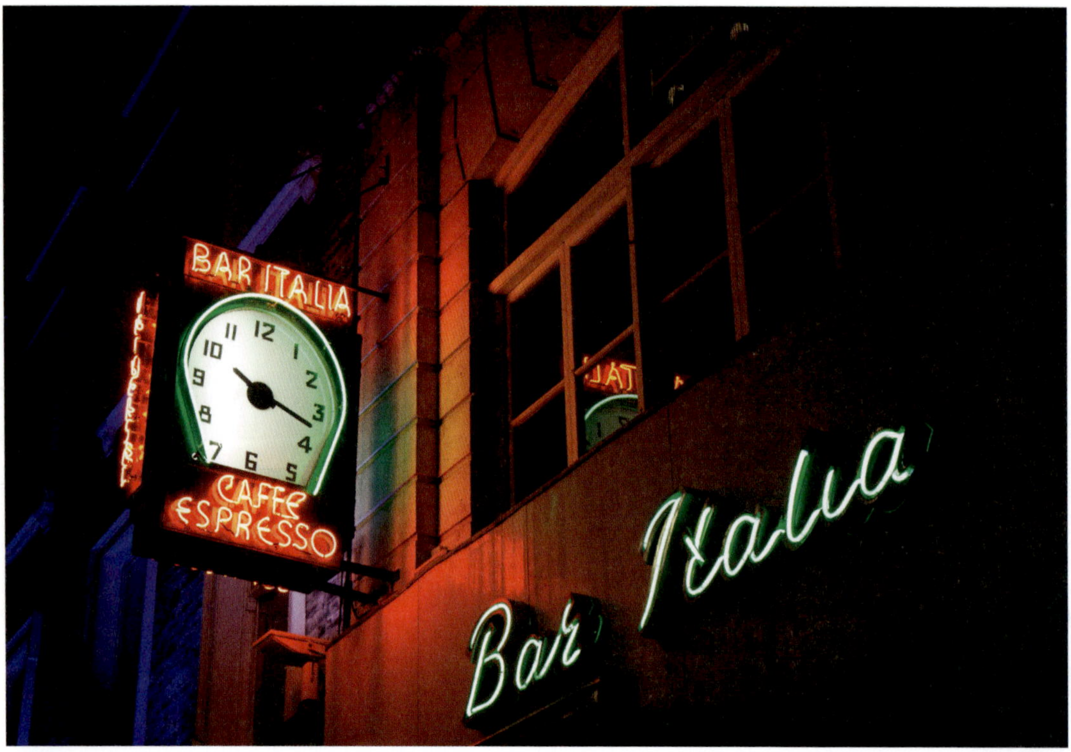

baritaliasoho.co.uk +44 20 7734 4737

106 MONMOUTH COFFEE ROASTERS

27 Monmouth St, London WC2H 9EU, UK

TO VISIT
BEFORE YOU DIE
BECAUSE

The small but mighty Covent Garden café of pioneering London roasters Monmouth has become a classic that never disappoints.

We could fill this entire book with London coffee shops a few times over – there are over 3,500 cafés in the capital today, about the same number of coffee houses there were in England during the coffee boom of the 17th century. But one in particular shines brighter than others: the Monmouth Coffee Company, which first began roasting in 1978 in the basement of its Covent Garden shop. The company's groundbreaking focus on sustainable trade and interesting coffee varieties quickly set a new benchmark. The roastery outgrew the original location years ago; it is now housed in a row of arches in Bermondsey, a space with Loring roasters filled with carefully selected single-origin arabica beans. But the Covent Garden café is still going strong, and you'll spot it easily among the cute boutiques of Seven Dials, thanks to the queue forming every morning just outside the dark shopfront. You'll have to be quick to grab a seat, and bring your own takeaway cup if you don't want to rent or buy one of theirs, as there are no disposable cups here.

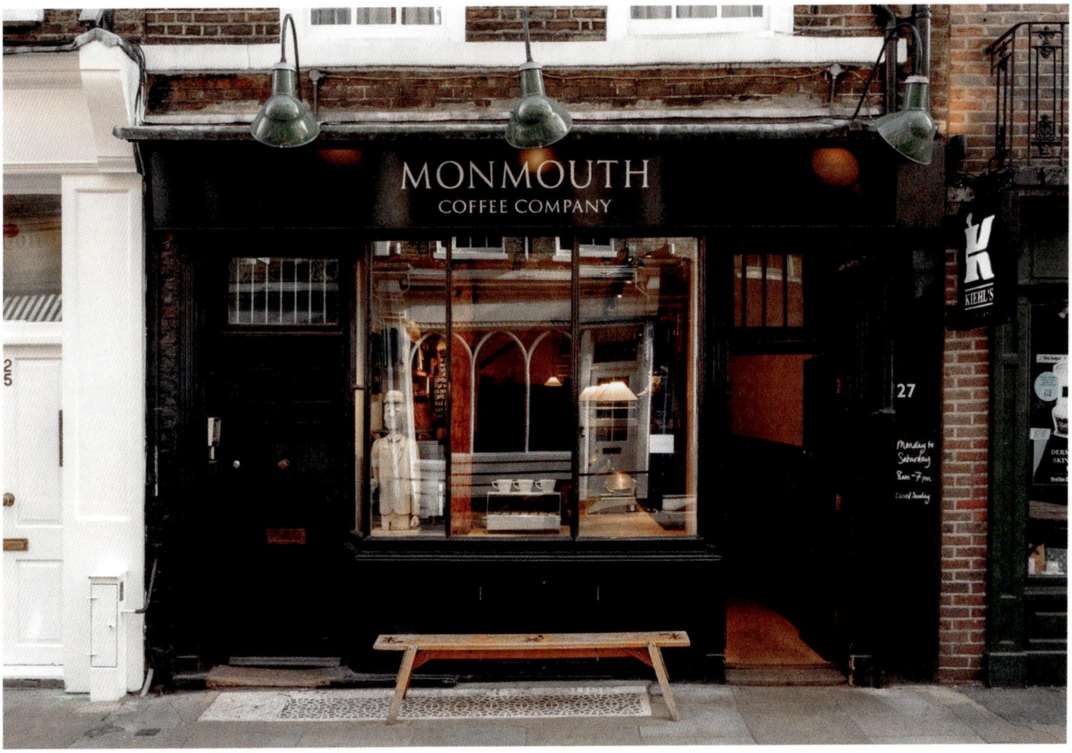

monmouthcoffee.co.uk +44 20 7232 3010

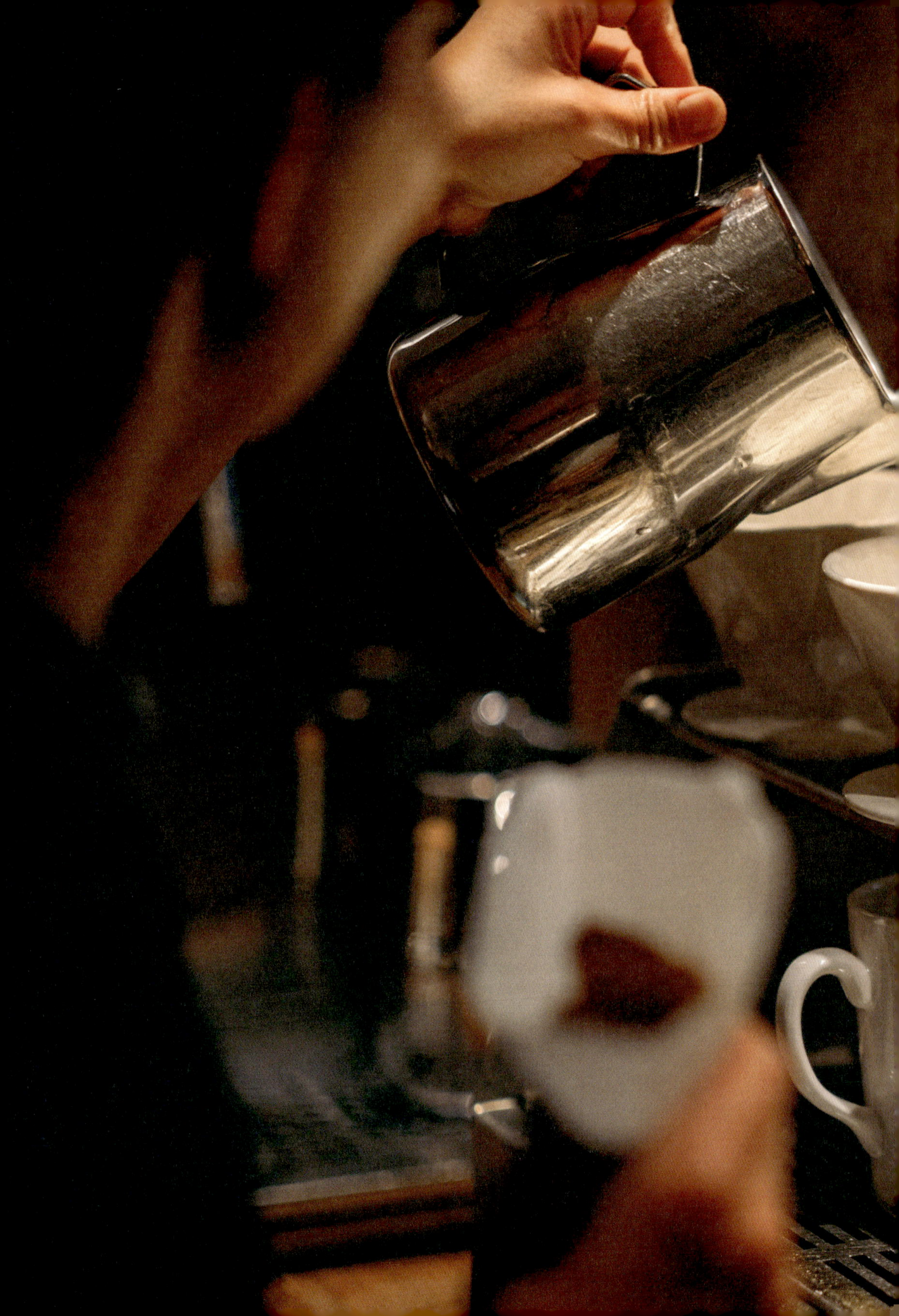

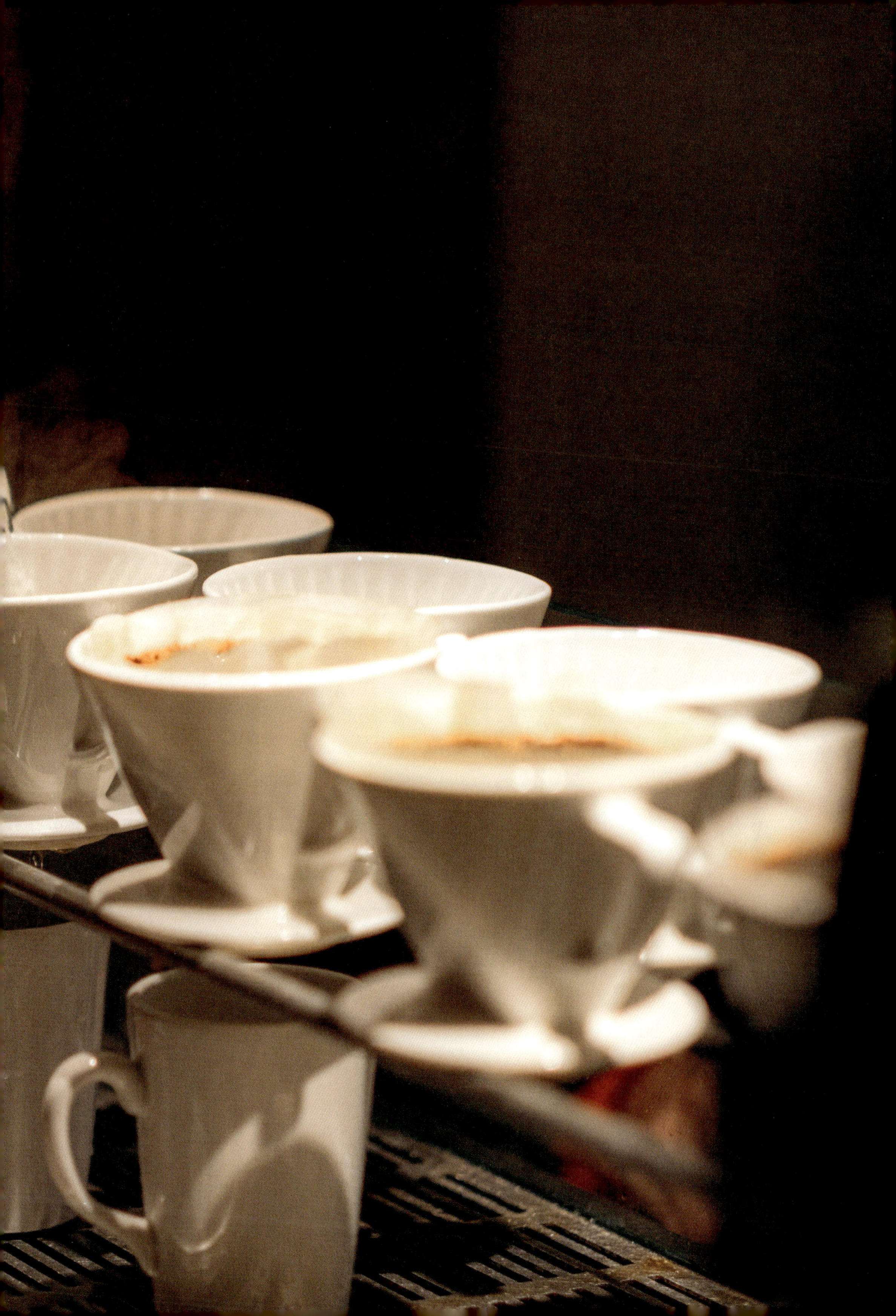

107 QIMA

21-22 New Row, London WC2N 4LE, UK

TO VISIT BEFORE YOU DIE BECAUSE

The UK's first true tree-to-cup café, offering ethically sourced, exceptional coffees alongside world-class pastries in the heart of Covent Garden.

From environmental to social issues, there is much to improve in the world of coffee. And one way to do this is to control every step of the way, from plant, to process, to pour. That's exactly what British Yemeni entrepreneur Faris Sheibani is doing with Qima, initially founded in 2016 as an ethical sourcing business focused on supporting smallholder farmers in Yemen, the birthplace of coffee culture. Its beautiful Covent Garden location, opened in 2025, serves 'coffee that is not only rare and delicious but deeply meaningful', with over 10% of profits pledged to the Qima Foundation. Sample some of the rarest coffee around, from rediscovered Yemenia beans grown on ancient terraced hillsides and served in traditional *ibrik* pots, to exotic Sidras and Wush Wush from the Andes, in a beautiful space designed by DLSM Studio. Signature drinks like the Qishr Latte and Cascara Fizz celebrate the full coffee fruit, while treats include za'atar-spiced viennoiseries and a showstopping coffee-cup-shaped dessert made with espresso toffee, coffee and dark chocolate mousse, and chocolate lid.

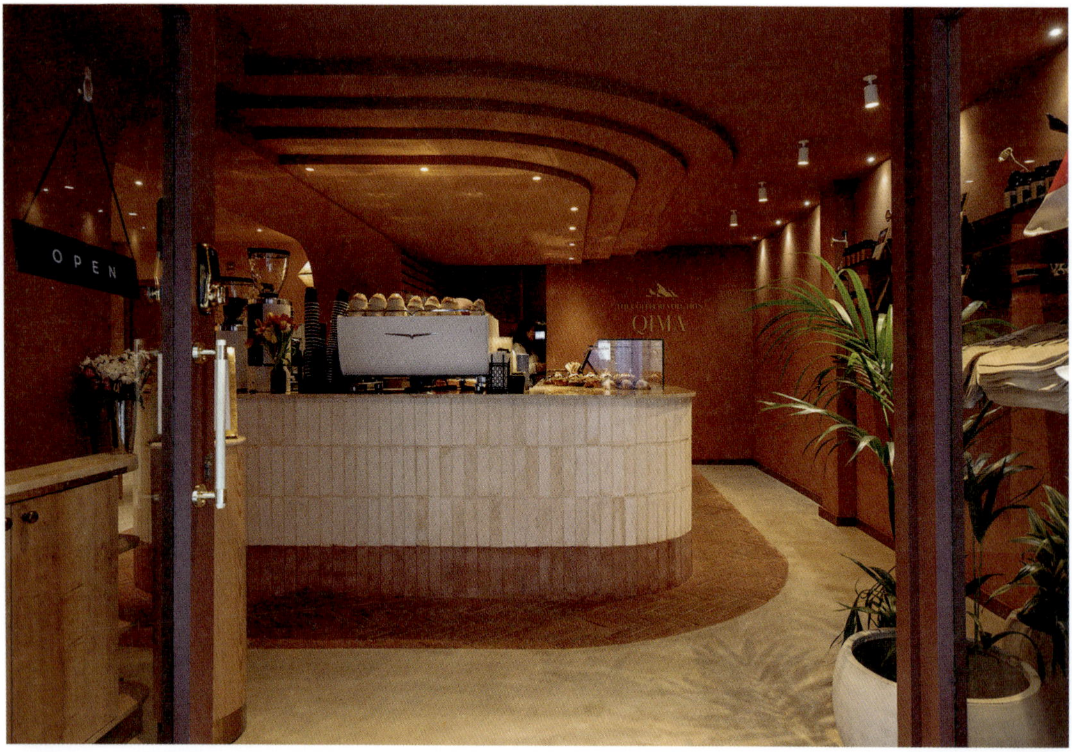

qimacafe.com

+44 20 7209 8200

108 REDEMPTION COFFEE ROASTERS

96-98 Islington High St, London N1 8EG, UK

TO VISIT BEFORE YOU DIE BECAUSE

Enjoy a superb coffee while making a positive social impact at this Islington café boasting a décor full of surprises.

This café in London's Angel neighbourhood might look like your standard big city coffee shop from the outside, but it's so much more than that. Firstly, and most importantly, it's one of the 12 outposts of a B Corp Certified chain first founded by Max Dubiel (also behind Black Sheep Coffee) and Ted Rosner in 2015 with a mission of reducing reoffending through coffee. Redemption trains prison leavers and people at risk of offending with the skills they need to gain secure and meaningful employment. There are about a hundred participants currently in employment in their coffee shops; the reoffending rate is 0% (compared to a national average of 38%). The company's Angel outpost also comes with a couple of eye-catching bonuses: a secret garden at the back of the historic Georgian townhouse, and an all-white basement grotto filled with strange statues and objects, installed by the former landlord in the 1960s. You can also sit on a bench at the front with a chocolate sea salt cookie and cup of Valientes from Colombia.

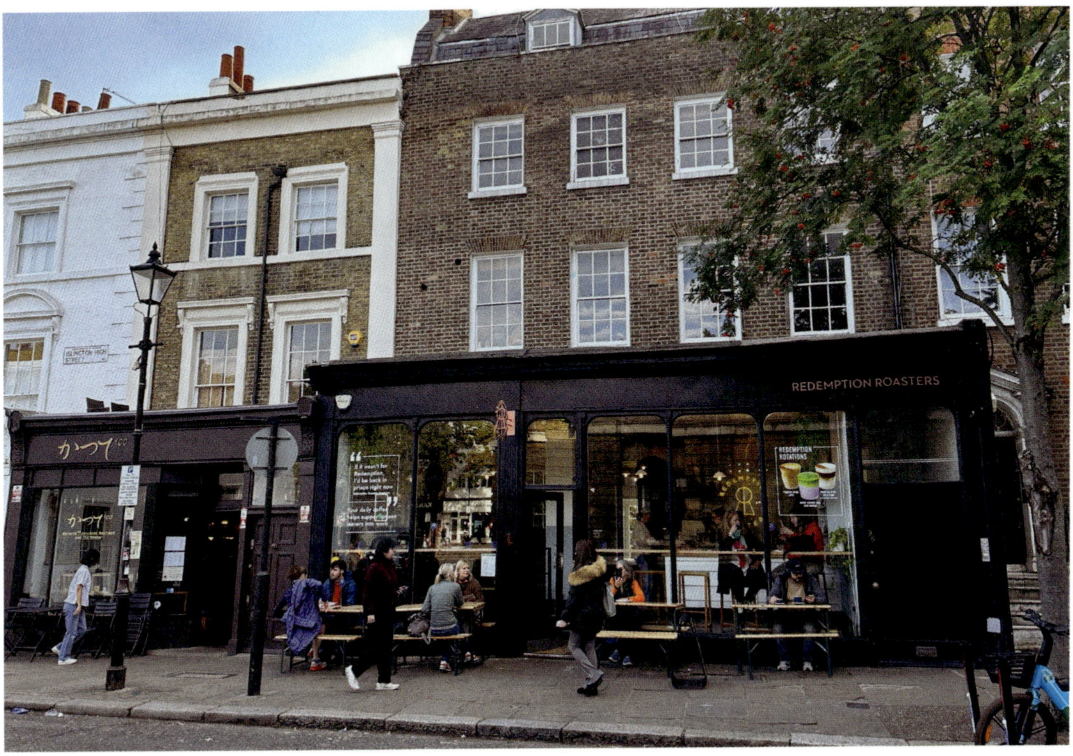

redemptionroasters.com

109 HOLA COFFEE

Calle de Lagasca, 42, Salamanca, 28001 Madrid, Spain

TO VISIT BEFORE YOU DIE BECAUSE

Vibrant details, quality cups and top coffee are on the menu at this welcoming spot, which helped popularise third-wave coffee in Madrid.

Every detail counts in a minimalist space, and so it is at Hola's Lagasca café, where the pared-back décor provides the backdrop for bold pops of colours, including the roastery's vibrant coffee bags and handmade tableware. Indicated only by a tiny sign with Hola's happy coffee cup logo, the small space was opened by two friends, the leading barista and roaster Pablo Caballero and Nolo Botana. They started Hola Coffee in 2016, quickly becoming a reference in speciality coffee, and now have a podcast, and a coffee academy and roastery in the Carabanchel neighbourhood. Key to their success is not only the simplicity of the space but also the focus on inclusivity ('speciality coffee should not be elitist') and enjoyment. That's made clear by the adorable canary yellow takeaway cups with smiley faces, and the friendly service. Lagasca is their second location; if you're lucky you might be able to sit inside by the Modbar espresso machine, and enjoy a Lucero blend or blueberry lavender cold brew.

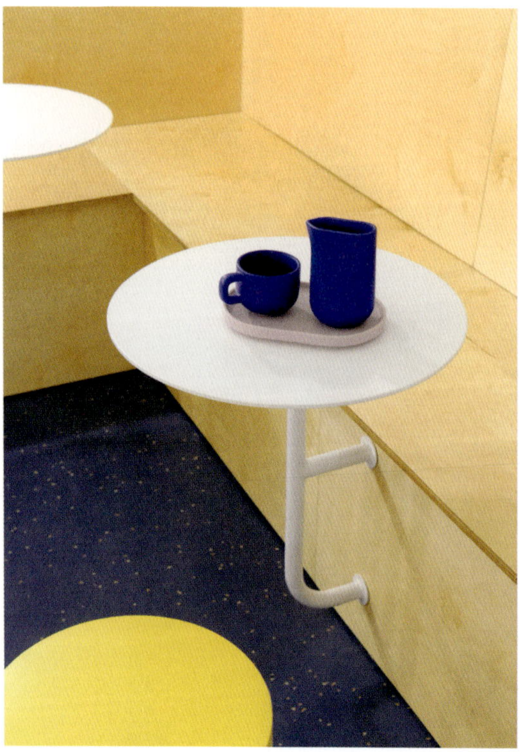

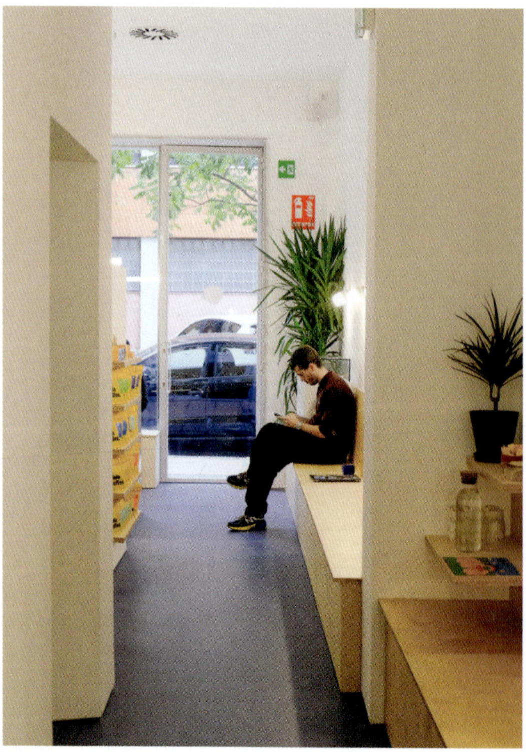

hola.coffee

+34 915 55 97 15

110 CAFEZAL COFFEE HUB

Viale Premuda, 14, 20129 Milan, Italy

TO VISIT
BEFORE YOU DIE
BECAUSE

The Best Cafeteria d'Italia 2024–2025 bridges the gap between Italian coffee culture and the speciality coffee movement.

Milan's tram- and tree-lined Viale Premuda might not be in most guidebooks, but it is in fact a key location in the history of coffee making. It is here that in the 1930s, Achille Gaggia invented the first steam-free, high-pressure coffee machine for his family's *caffè*. Happily, the birthplace of modern espresso is now home to Cafezal Coffee Hub, where you'll find another Italian design classic: a top-of-the-range Black Eagle coffee machine by Victoria Arduino. Founded by Italian-Brazilian Carlos Bitencourt in 2018, the speciality micro-roastery 'invites customers to explore and personalise their coffee experience' with a menu blending 'international brewing methods with Italian coffee rituals'. Having spent time on the ground in Brazil building relationships with farms and producers, the team is committed to serving 'coffee that's not only exceptional in taste, but also transparent in its story'. Come for a brunch paired with a Cappuccino Garibaldi, or an aperitivo with Cafezal martini with coffee liqueur or cold brew Negroni. Cafezal has five other locations in the city.

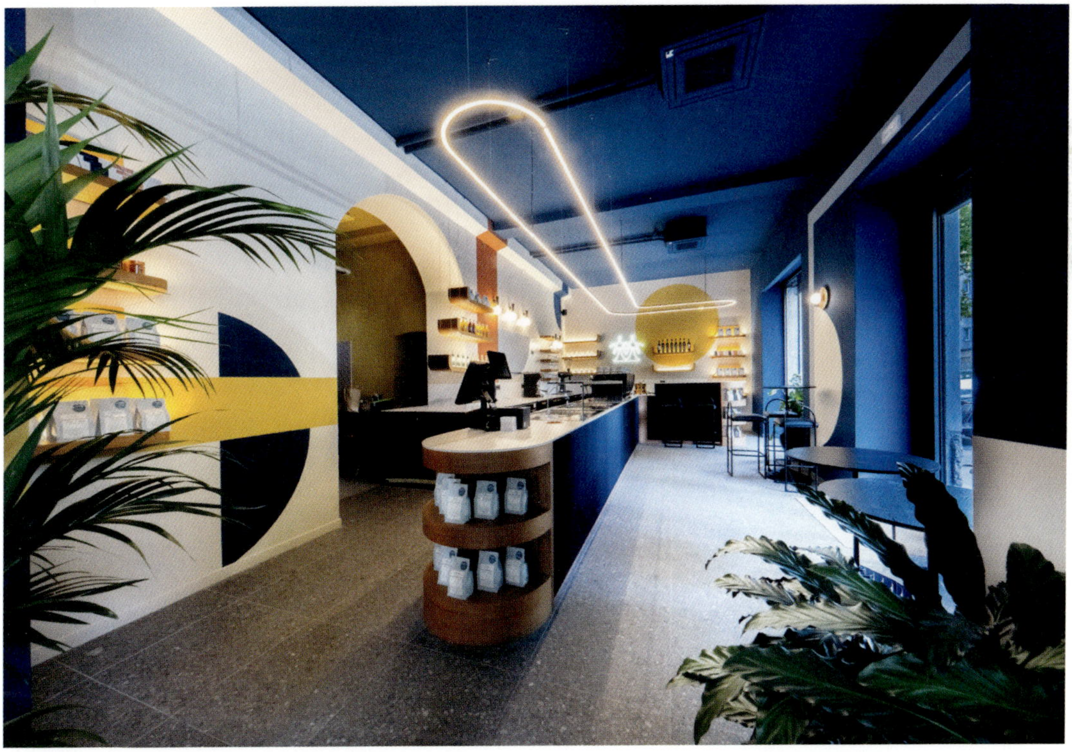

cafezal.it +39 023 657 9282

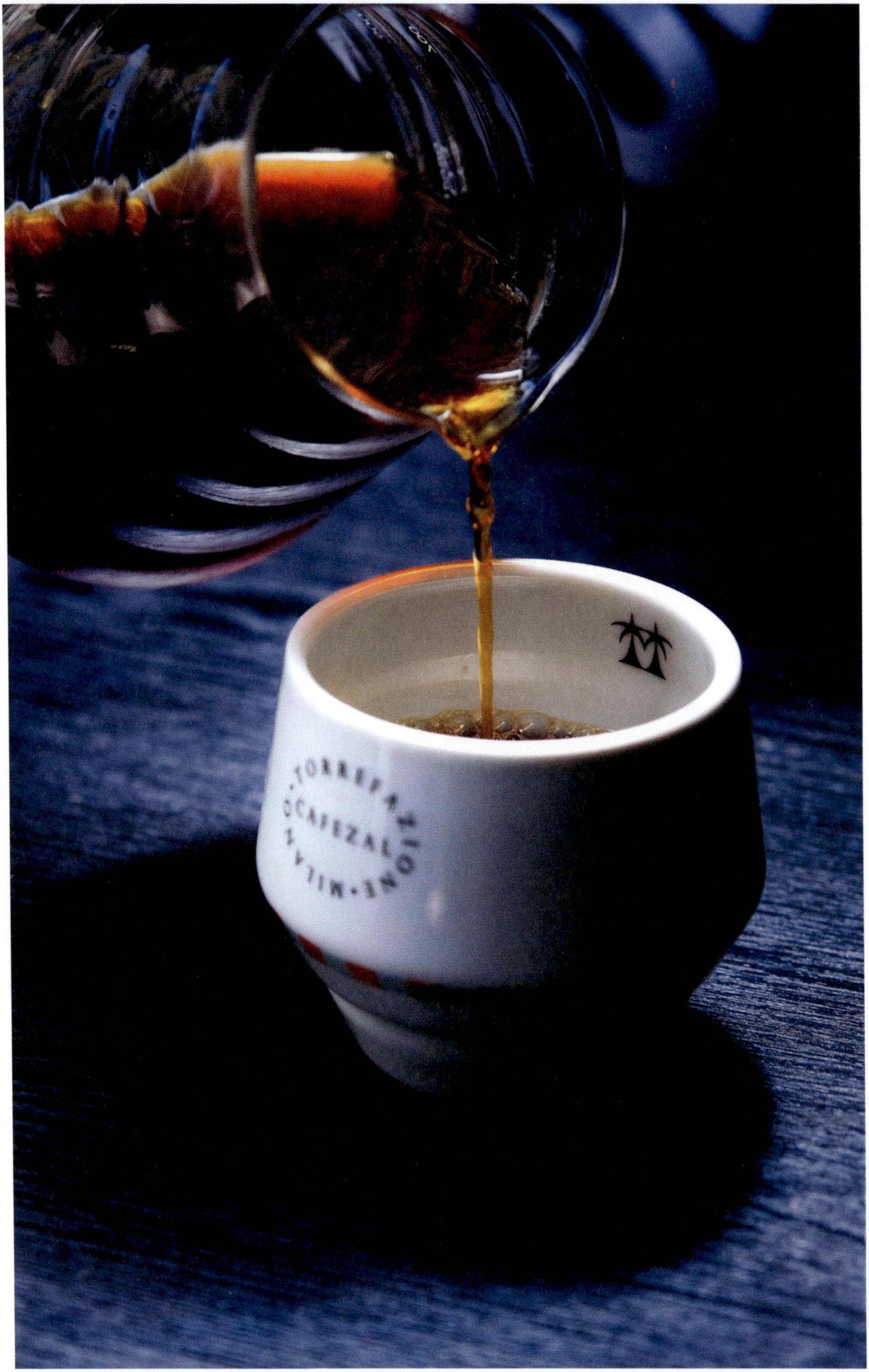
TORREFAZIONE · MILANO
CAFEZAL

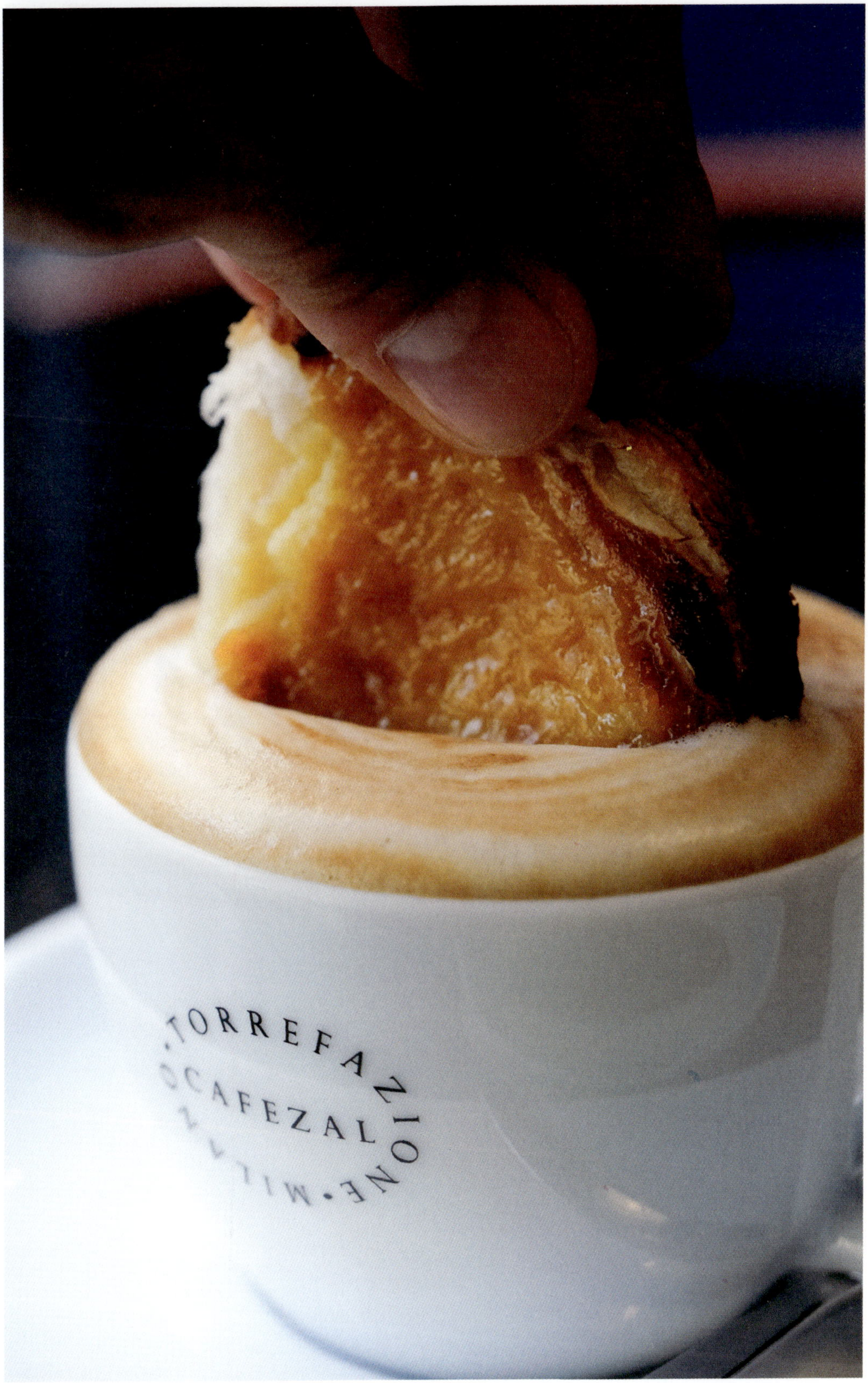
TORREFAZIONE
CAFEZAL

111 GRAN CAFFÈ GAMBRINUS

Via Chiaia, 1, 80132 Naples, Italy

TO VISIT BEFORE YOU DIE BECAUSE

This Belle Époque salon, art gallery and historical landmark is the place to savour a bold Napoli espresso and *sfogliatella* pastry.

'I have the simplest tastes. I am always satisfied with the best,' once said Oscar Wilde. No wonder that the great playwright became a regular at Naples' most prestigious café during his last years in exile. Located near the Teatro di San Carlo, Gambrinus was once a meeting place for actors and musicians, but also leading intellectuals such as Gabriele D'Annunzio, Filippo Tommaso Marinetti and Guy de Maupassant. Revived and beautifully restored by the Sergio family in the 1970s, its elegant art nouveau interiors still welcome the great and good – including Pope Francis, who came here to have breakfast in 2015. Admire the original frescoes and landscape paintings while enjoying a coffee gelato, syrup-soaked baba and a cup of dark-roast liquid gold. While you're in Naples, make sure to join one of the best local traditions: the *caffè sospeso*, or suspended coffee, which started in the city's working-class cafés. Pay for two cups of coffee but only drink one, leaving the second as a gift for a stranger in need to claim later.

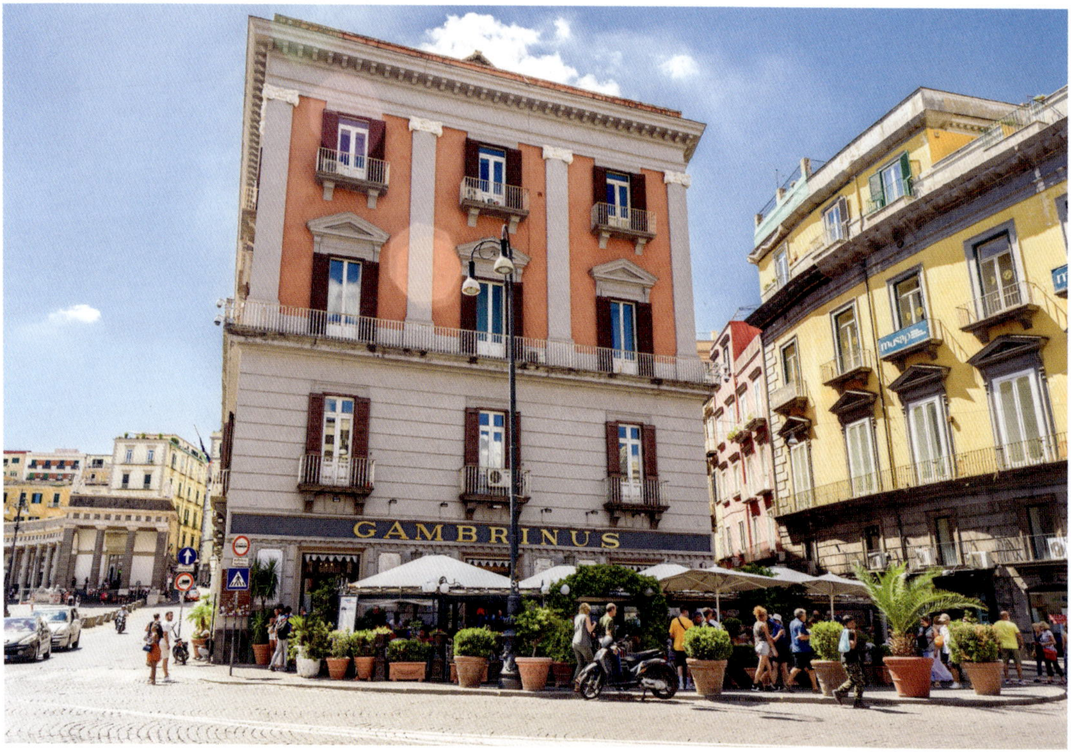

grancaffegambrinus.com +39 081 417 582

112 FUGLEN

Universitetsgata 2, 0164 Oslo, Norway

TO VISIT BEFORE YOU DIE BECAUSE

Try a lightly roasted, Nordic-style coffee of the day served with vintage vibes, Norwegian waffles and a dash of Japanese culture.

Kaffeefuglen first opened in 1963, and although it gained a new name and a facelift in 2012, key elements of the original coffee house have been preserved, including the bar and wallpaper. They've been paired with Scandinavian mid-century pieces or bespoke designs (many are available to buy), giving the café a unique look that is proving popular around Asia, with new branches of Fuglen opening from Tokyo to Jakarta. The original Fuglen Oslo offers single-origin, direct-trade coffee by day, and cocktails by night. 'Our coffee is lightly roasted, the Nordic way,' says the team. 'It's a process that enhances the unique flavour characteristics of the coffee. Light roasts present brightness and a light, silky body, and you can expect to taste flavours like honey, fruits and flowers.' Founder Einar Kleppe Holthe has worked to build cultural bridges between Norway and Asia, which means specials might include tasty fish-shaped *taiyaki* waffles. There is a great programme of events, including monthly coffee tastings and Ethiopian food pop-ups.

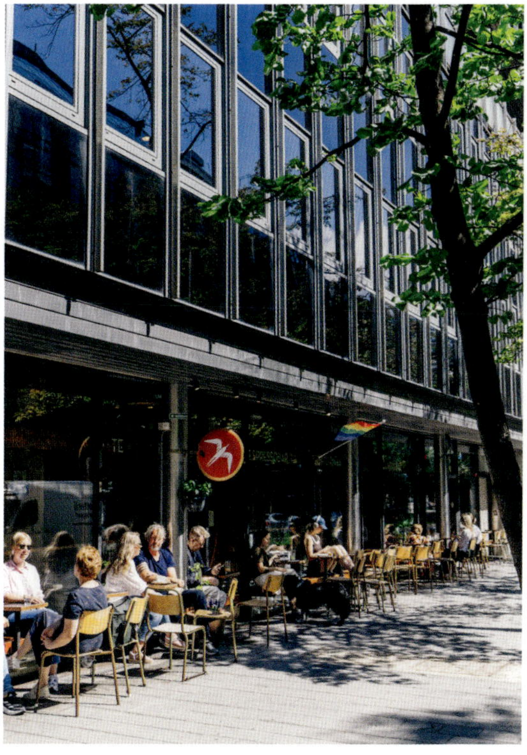

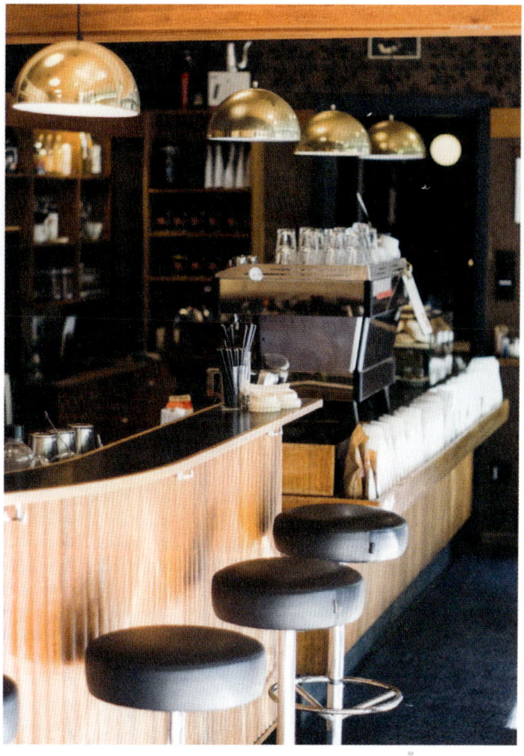

fuglen.no

+47 22 20 08 80

113 TIM WENDELBOE ESPRESSO BAR

Grüners gate 1, 0552, Oslo, Norway

TO VISIT
BEFORE YOU DIE
BECAUSE

Try light-roasted, freshly brewed black coffee at the only café of one of the best roasteries in the world.

'We like to think of our espresso bar as a coffee showroom where people can be inspired to try something new, or see the world of coffee in a different light,' says World Barista Champion Tim Wendelboe, who opened this corner café in 2007. 'We try to challenge our customers' habits, and help them explore what coffee can be, not what they think it should be.' A former hair salon located on a quiet side street, the bar features an unusual stone façade, exposed brick walls and a wooden bar. The cosy space offers a seasonal menu of coffees brewed to order and a small range of espresso-based drinks with or without milk. There is nothing else but coffee here, an approach that means the staff can focus their energy on the beans themselves, and how to be more creative with them. And don't expect a chain of coffee shops from Tim – he's happiest working with a small team, perfecting the art of coffee making, and growing his own coffee on his own farm in Colombia, Finca el Suelo.

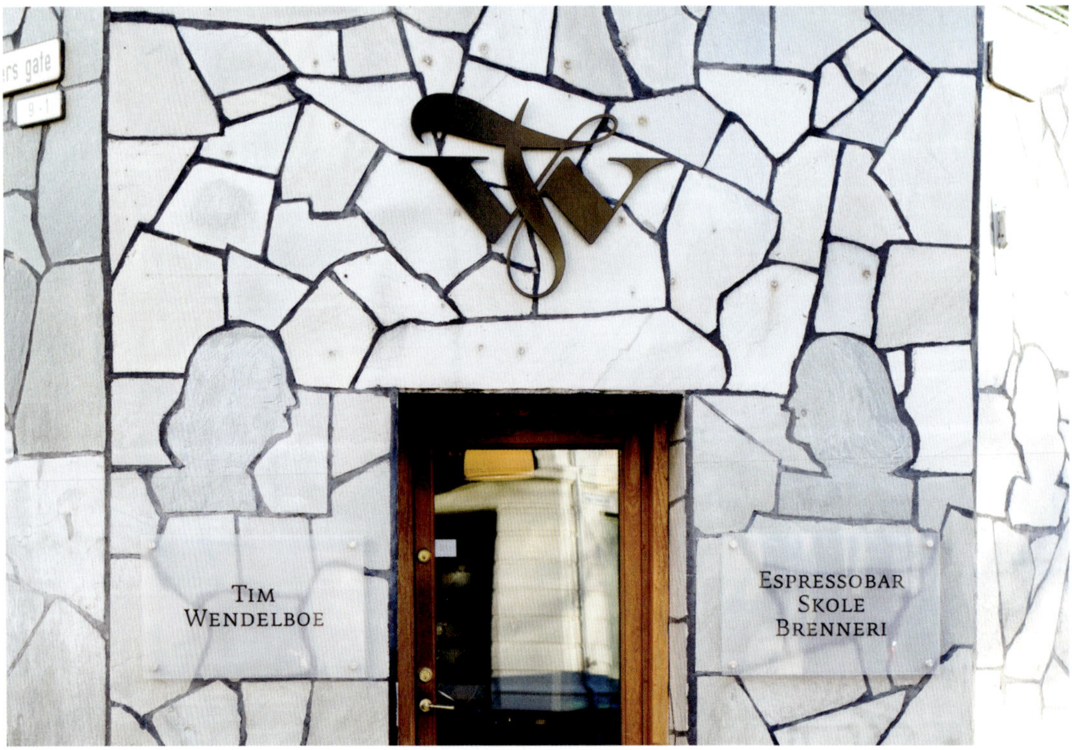

 timwendelboe.no

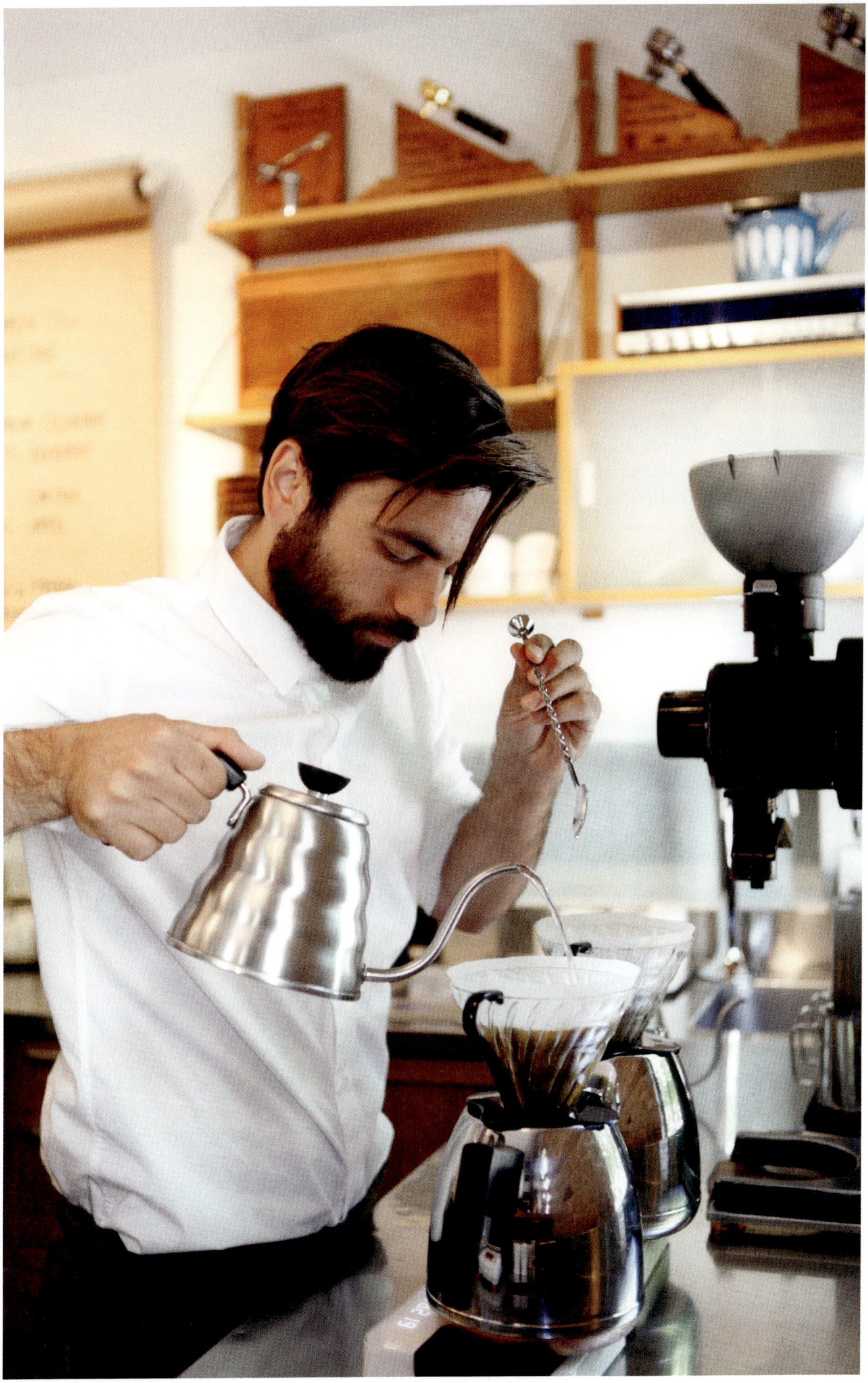

114 CAFÉ NUANCES

51 rue des Francs-Bourgeois, 75004, Paris, France

TO VISIT BEFORE YOU DIE BECAUSE

More art installation than coffee shop, this futuristic space in the Marais is a temple to contemporary coffee culture.

A spaceship has landed on the ground floor of a 1950s building in Paris' fashionable Marais district: the latest outpost of speciality roasters Café Nuances, founded in 2021 by brothers Charles and Raphaël Corrot. Designed by Harry Nuriev of Crosby Studios, the space features a glowing light wall in the company's signature orange, as well as sculptural metal furniture. Evoking French artist César's compressed car parts totems, the stools and bar counter represent a 'crushed geometry of used coffee cups', and glow under the orange light. But it's not just style over substance: Nuances offers six bean varieties – from Brazil, Ethiopia, Peru, Tanzania, El Salvador and Mexico – from early morning to late afternoon. Home specialities include a Rose latte and coconut mocha (their Kyoto-sourced Rose matcha is also very popular). Pair your coffee with a freshly baked croissant, and if the metal stools don't appeal, try a bench on the charming Square Charles-Victor Langlois next door. Nuances has three other locations in Paris, all equally eye-catching.

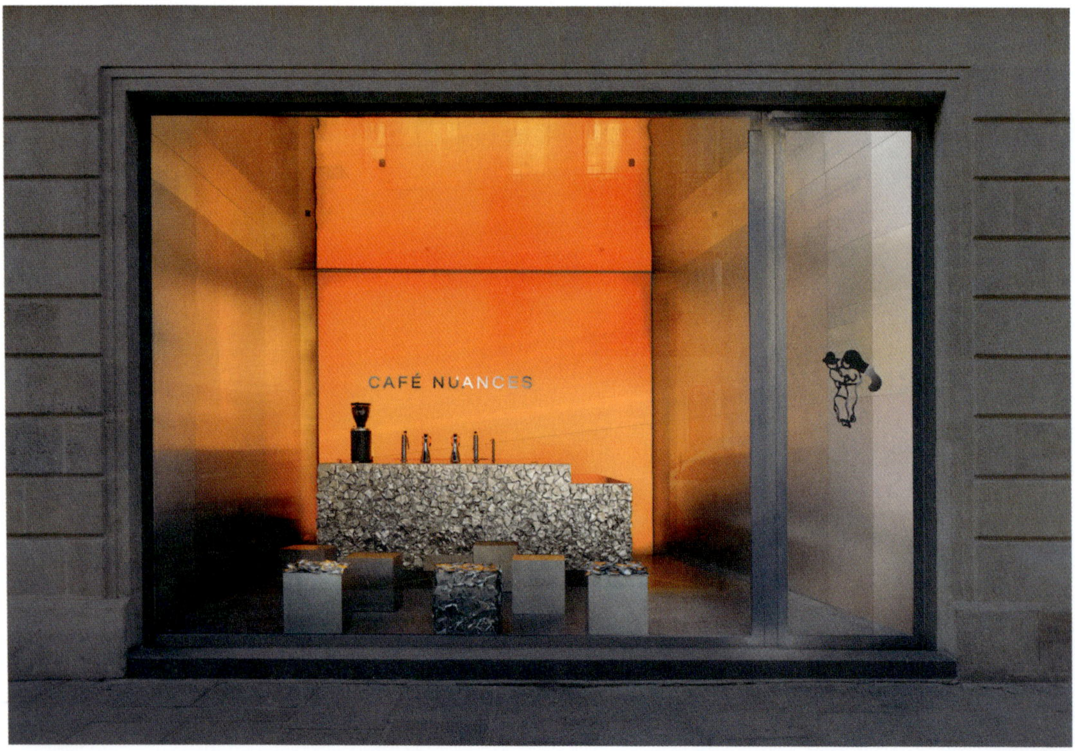

cafenuances.com

115 LE PROCOPE

13 rue de l'Ancienne Comédie, 75006 Paris, France

TO VISIT
BEFORE YOU DIE
BECAUSE

Follow in the footsteps of Voltaire, Rousseau, Diderot and Benjamin Franklin at this legendary café in the heart of Saint-Germain-des-Prés.

Paris is known as the city of love, but really, it should be the city of cafés. With its perfectly lined-up rattan chairs and full brasserie menu, the Parisian café is as iconic as the Eiffel Tower. And the oldest of them all is Le Procope, opened in 1689 opposite the Comédie Francaise by Italian immigrant François Procope. It was the first restaurant in the capital to democratise coffee by offering table service in a porcelain cup, and became a favourite meeting place for countless authors, actors and musicians, who were often joined by fortune tellers using coffee grounds for their prediction. Today the brasserie is home to a Salon de Café, which you can visit in the afternoons only. On the menu are Ethiopian Grand Cru prepared in a French press and coffee-based cocktails such as Amore di Caffè, with organic Massaya espresso, as well as a chocolate-coffee tartlet created by pastry chef Christelle Brua. Don't miss the profiteroles, which have been served here since opening day, with Le Procope's other great speciality, ice cream.

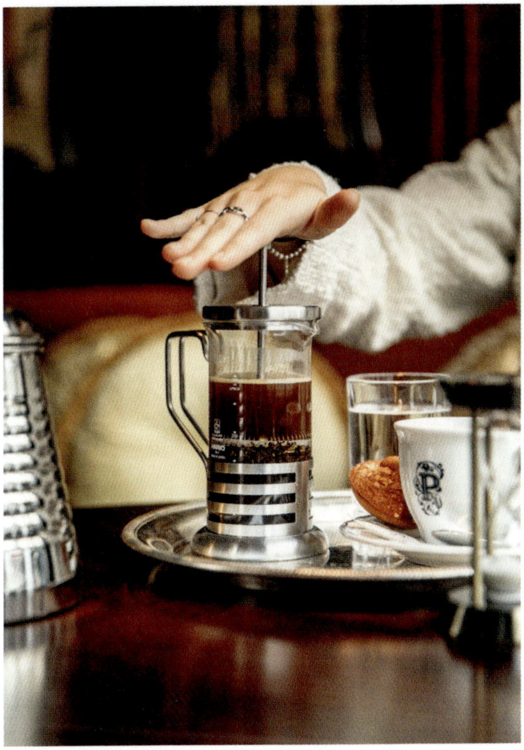

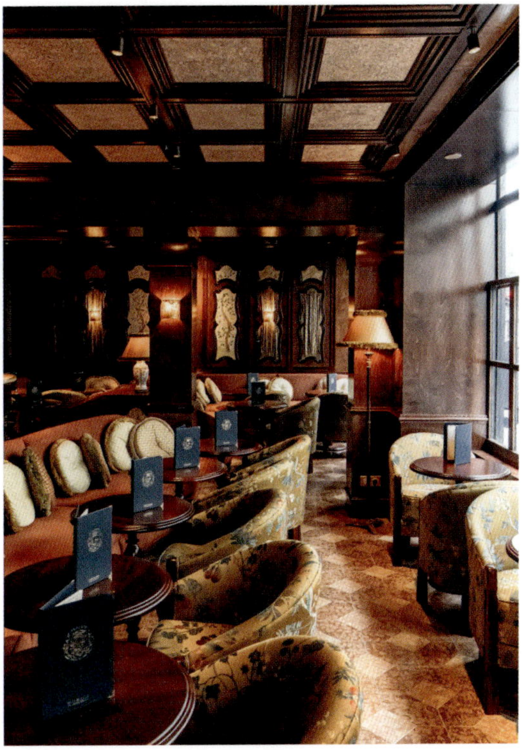

procope.com

+33 1 40 46 79 00

116 SUBSTANCE CAFÉ

30 rue Dussoubs, 75002 Paris, France

TO VISIT BEFORE YOU DIE BECAUSE

Enjoy a personalised coffee experience at this truly unique reservation-only tasting bar in Paris' speciality coffee triangle.

Don't expect any pastries, takeaways cups, music or even sugar at this experiential and experimental café, opened by husband-and-wife team Joachim and Alexandrine Morceau in 2019. 'The aim is to focus on what we think is essential – the terroir – hence our name Substance,' explains Alexandrine. 'Our menu comprises various versions of the coffee of the day, as well as a list of grand crus.' The friendly pair only welcomes about twenty-five customers every day around their U-shaped counter, taking the time to share their knowledge and provide perfectly tailored suggestions. It's a relaxed, peaceful spot where you can taste competition-level coffees including Panama Geishas, but also learn from a true coffee aficionado: Joachim will tell you the story behind every bean, and many say he has served them the best coffee they've ever had. Substance is located in an area known for its amazing speciality coffee shops; take some time to explore the surrounding streets between Les Halles and Bonne Nouvelle and you'll be sure to make some further discoveries.

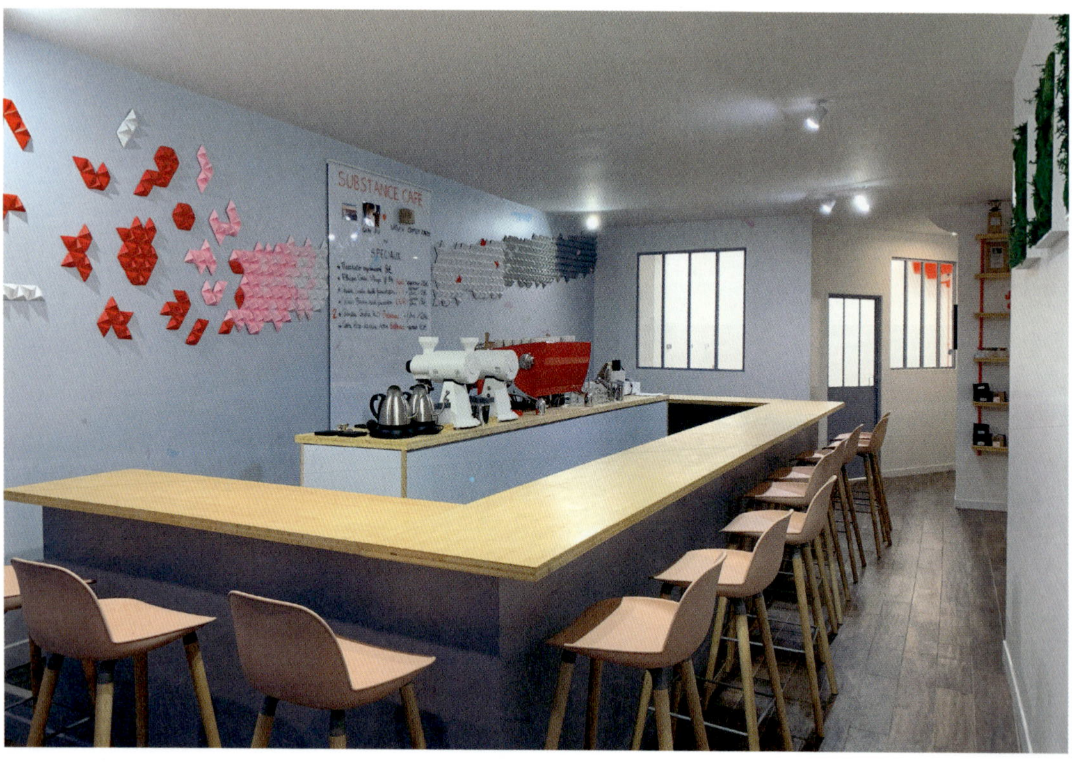

substancecafe.com @substancecafe

117 MAJESTIC CAFÉ

R. de Santa Catarina 112, 4000-442 Porto, Portugal

TO VISIT
BEFORE YOU DIE
BECAUSE

Stop for a *cimbalino* at this historic café, one of the most beautiful examples of art nouveau in Porto.

From Combi Coffee Roasters to Von&Vonnie, Porto is now home to many great micro-roasteries and independent cafés. Before them, there were the cafés of Baixa, intellectual hubs that fuelled the great Liberal revolution in the 1820s, kickstarting a golden age for Porto's café culture. The city's landmark Majestic Café opened in 1922 on the pedestrian Santa Catarina street, with a striking art nouveau frontage featuring floral elements, curved windows, and two little cherubs holding a stone garland above the entrance. This garland motif appears inside on everything from the wooden mirror frames to the embossed leather chairs and plasterwork (and there is real greenery at the back, on the terrace). The interiors were restored to their former glory in the 1990s, and the magical setting surely inspired J.K. Rowling, who is said to have spent many hours here writing the first Harry Potter book. If it's too crowded, head to the equally inspiring Café Guarany for a French toast with egg custard and a milky *galão*.

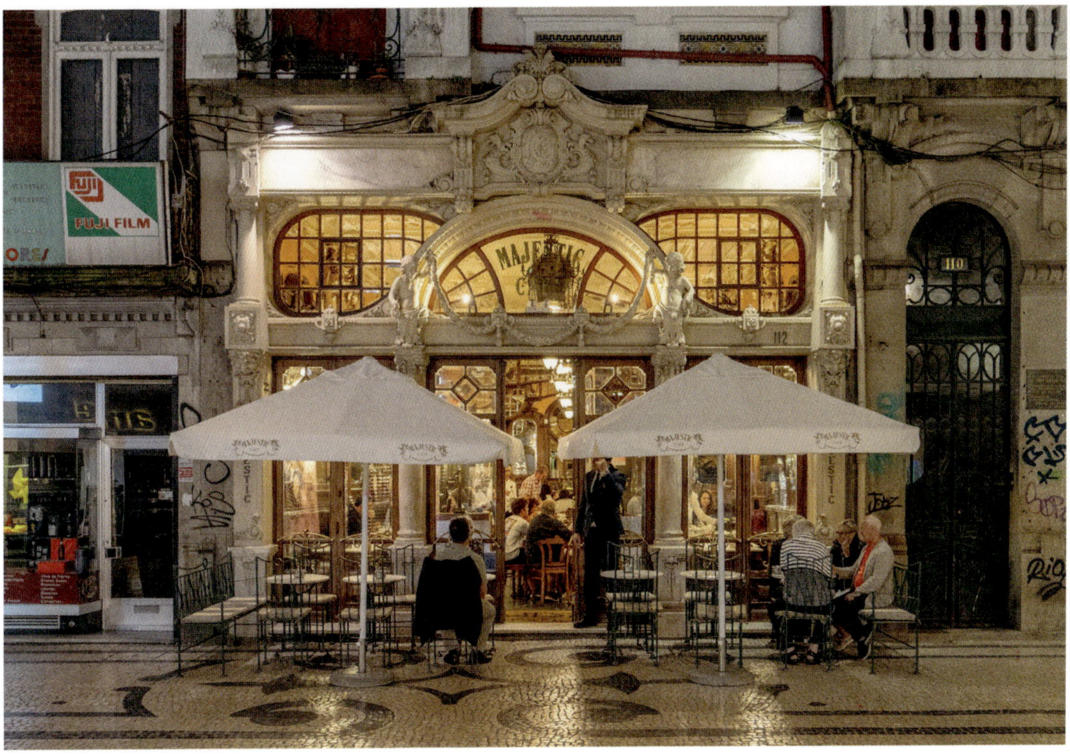

cafemajestic.com

+351 22 200 3887

118 GRAND CAFE ORIENT

Ovocný trh 19, 110 00 Staré Město, Czechia

TO VISIT BEFORE YOU DIE BECAUSE

Discover Czechia's unique contribution to Cubism at this striking café next to a museum dedicated to the avant-garde movement.

Design and architecture fans will love a coffee break at this unique café, located on the first floor of the House of the Black Madonna in the old town of Prague. Designed by architect Josef Gočár, who was only 31 at the time, it is an iconic work of Czech Cubism with green-and-white stripy upholstery, chevron wallpaper and original chandeliers. It's hard to believe it closed down only ten years after its opening when Cubism went out of fashion, and was only recently restored to its former glory. The service can be a bit hit and miss, but that will give you time to admire every angle of the interiors, from the zigzagging golden coat hooks to the glass cabinet. Try a *turek* (Turkish coffee, the most common coffee here) or a Viennese coffee (topped with whipped cream) as well as the geometric house specialities, including a square *věneček* (custard-filled choux pastry) and chequerboard Punčový cake. And for another first-floor Prague classic, try Café Louvre on Národní, once frequented by Franz Kafka, Karel Čapek and Albert Einstein.

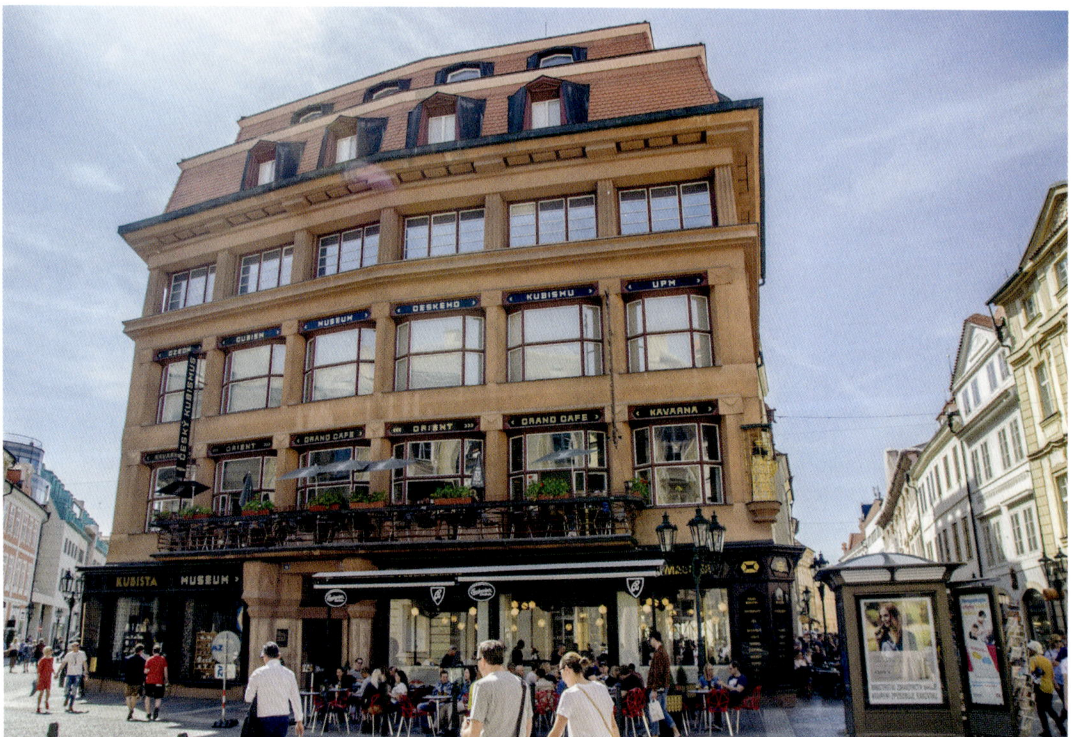

grandcafeorient.cz +420 224 224 240

119 MŮJ SÁLEK KÁVY

Křižíkova 386/105, 186 00 Praha 8-Karlín, Czechia

TO VISIT BEFORE YOU DIE BECAUSE

Join the locals for carefully sourced drinks, tasty brunches and freshly baked cakes at Doubleshot's cosy café in hip Karlín.

A former industrial district turned trendy foodie and nightlife hub, Karlín, just to the east of Prague's old town, is well worth a visit. Especially as it is home to one of the best cafés in town, 'My Cup of Coffee'. It is one of four locations opened by popular Prague coffee company Doubleshot, who have been roasting speciality coffee since 2010. They source over 90% of their beans directly from producers they know personally and visit regularly, which means you are guaranteed that the drinks will be top-notch. Matching the colourful packaging of coffee such as Era, their signature single-origin espresso (Costa Rica Don Oscar), or Flirt, a basic filter blend, the bright décor features bold murals, plants and wonderful glass lighting. Try the tasting flight or the signature Irish coffee. There's a full brunch menu as well as really good desserts, from chocolate roulade with hazelnut to lime cake with strawberries and *laskonky* meringue 'sandwiches' (made by the in-house bakery). Plus, there's a barista centre next door offering public cuppings and events.

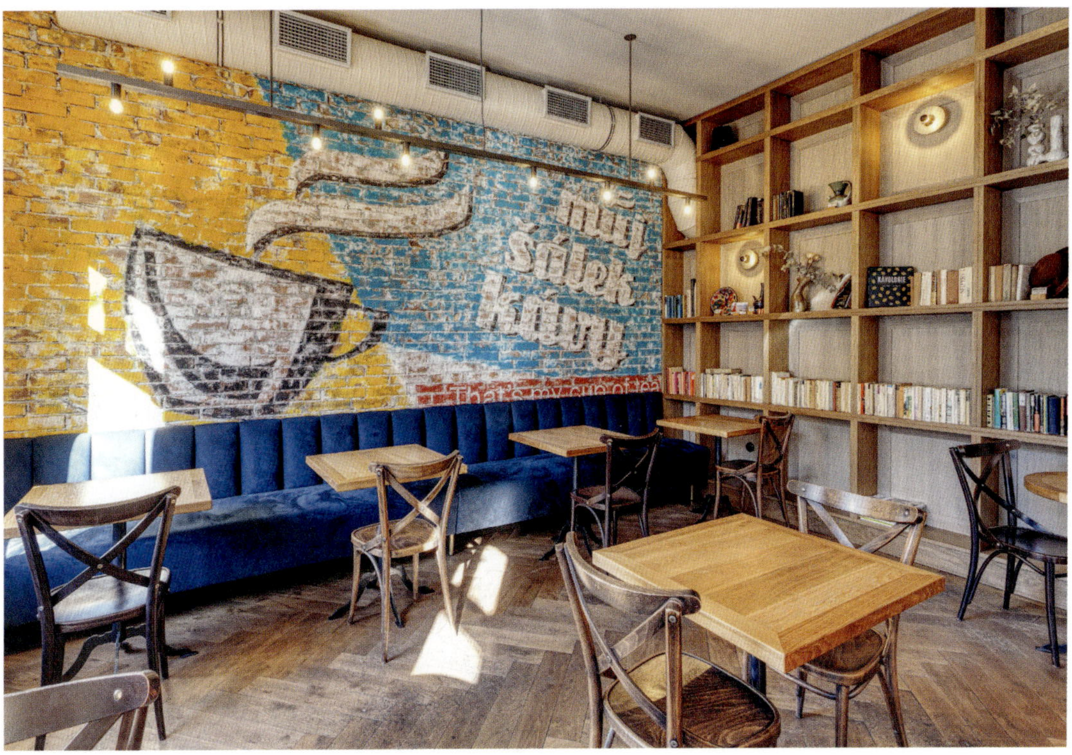

mujsalekkavy.cz +420 725 556 944

120 CAFFÈ GRECO

Via dei Condotti, 86, 00187 Rome, Italy

TO VISIT BEFORE YOU DIE BECAUSE

Doubling up as an art gallery and museum, the oldest coffee house in Rome is too spectacular to be closed for long.

Despite having survived countless upheavals in the past 250 years, this historic café near Rome's Spanish Steps was closed at the time of writing, due to a long legal battle between its owners and managers. But it is unimaginable that such a landmark and protected historic monument would ever close permanently. This classic stop on the Grand Tour, opened in 1760 by Nicola di Madalena, has welcomed everyone from Casanova, Lord Byron and Goethe to Charles Baudelaire and Mark Twain. They came for fresh news and gossip, and stayed for coffee, conversations and parties. Later, the likes of Pasolini and Sophia Loren had coffee here, in the richly decorated rooms featuring paintings and sculptures, many given away by the artist-customers themselves. Fingers crossed the Greco has reopened by the time you read this, and you can once again sit down at a marble table and enjoy the gilded décor and classic artworks over a cappuccino. If not, then take this entry as an homage to all the great cafés lost to time.

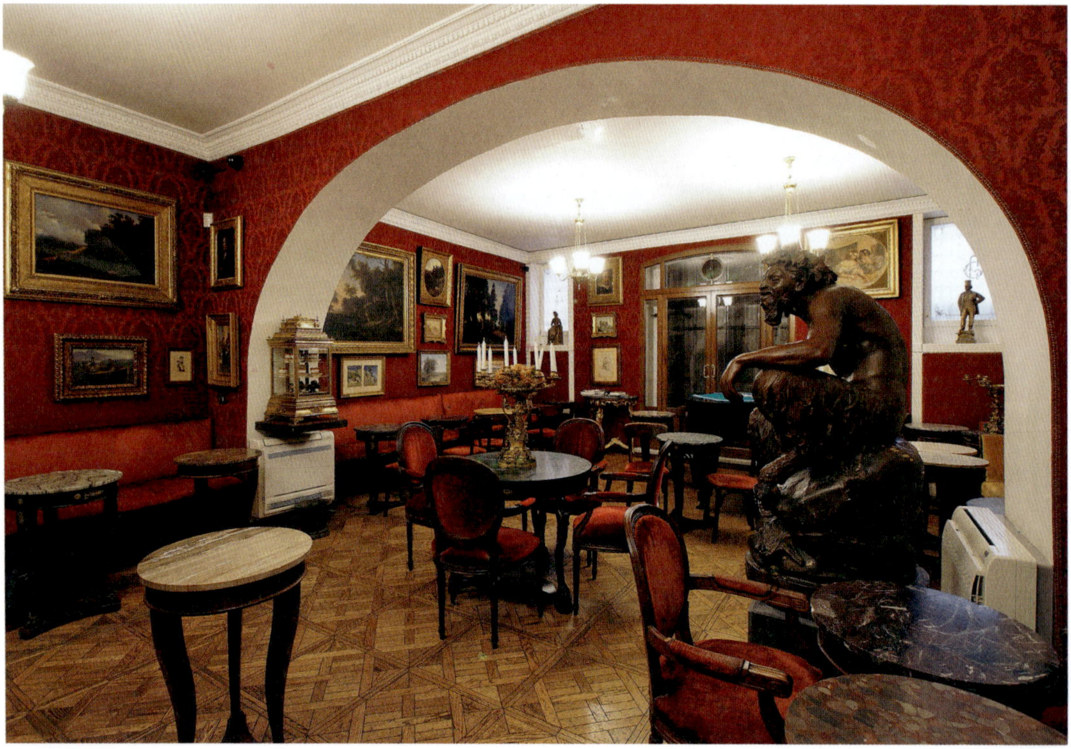

121 FARO

Via Piave, 55, 00187 Rome, Italy

TO VISIT
BEFORE YOU DIE
BECAUSE

A short stroll from Villa Borghese you'll find Rome's first true speciality coffee bar, still buzzing nearly a decade after it first opened.

Founded in 2016 near Piazza Fiume, Faro was among the first to bring the speciality coffee format to Italy. 'In the beginning, it was very difficult to explain to Italians, who believe themselves to be the homeland of coffee, that the true story of coffee was something entirely different, and that we were inviting them to try it without sugar,' explains the team at Faro. 'In Italy, and especially in Rome at the time, it was almost a pioneering mission, and Faro was our icebreaker, slowly attracting its own audience.' And a very successful mission it was, winning them *BarGiornale*'s Best Bar in Italy in 2020. Serving only beans from its own roastery, Aliena Coffee Roasters, the café offers two different filter coffees every day, a cold brew, and double-shot espresso-based drinks made with coffees from Colombia's Finca El Jardin and Ethiopia's Keramo. To accompany this there is a full brunch menu featuring homemade bread, as well as classic Roman *maritozzi* (brioche buns filled with whipped cream) and *focaccetta*. The group has recently opened a restaurant and bakery called Luna.

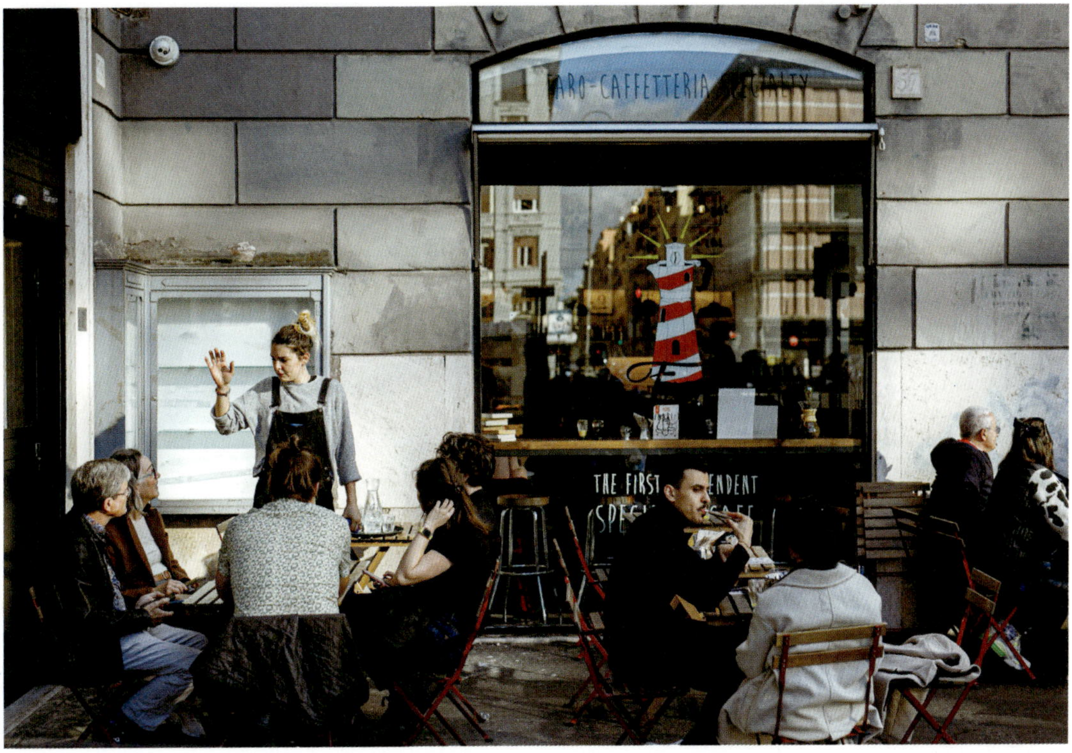

farorome.com

+39 064 281 5714

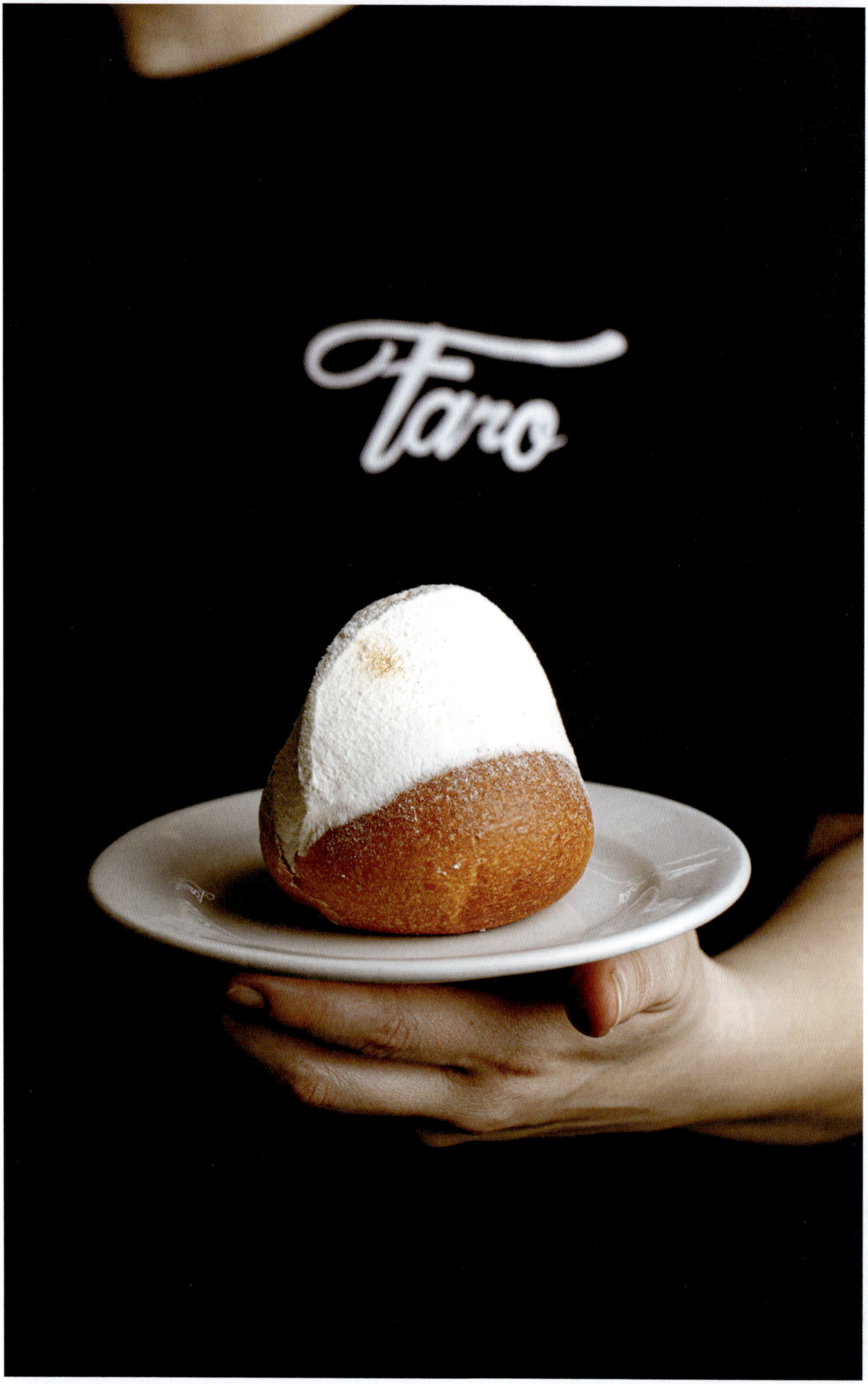
Faro

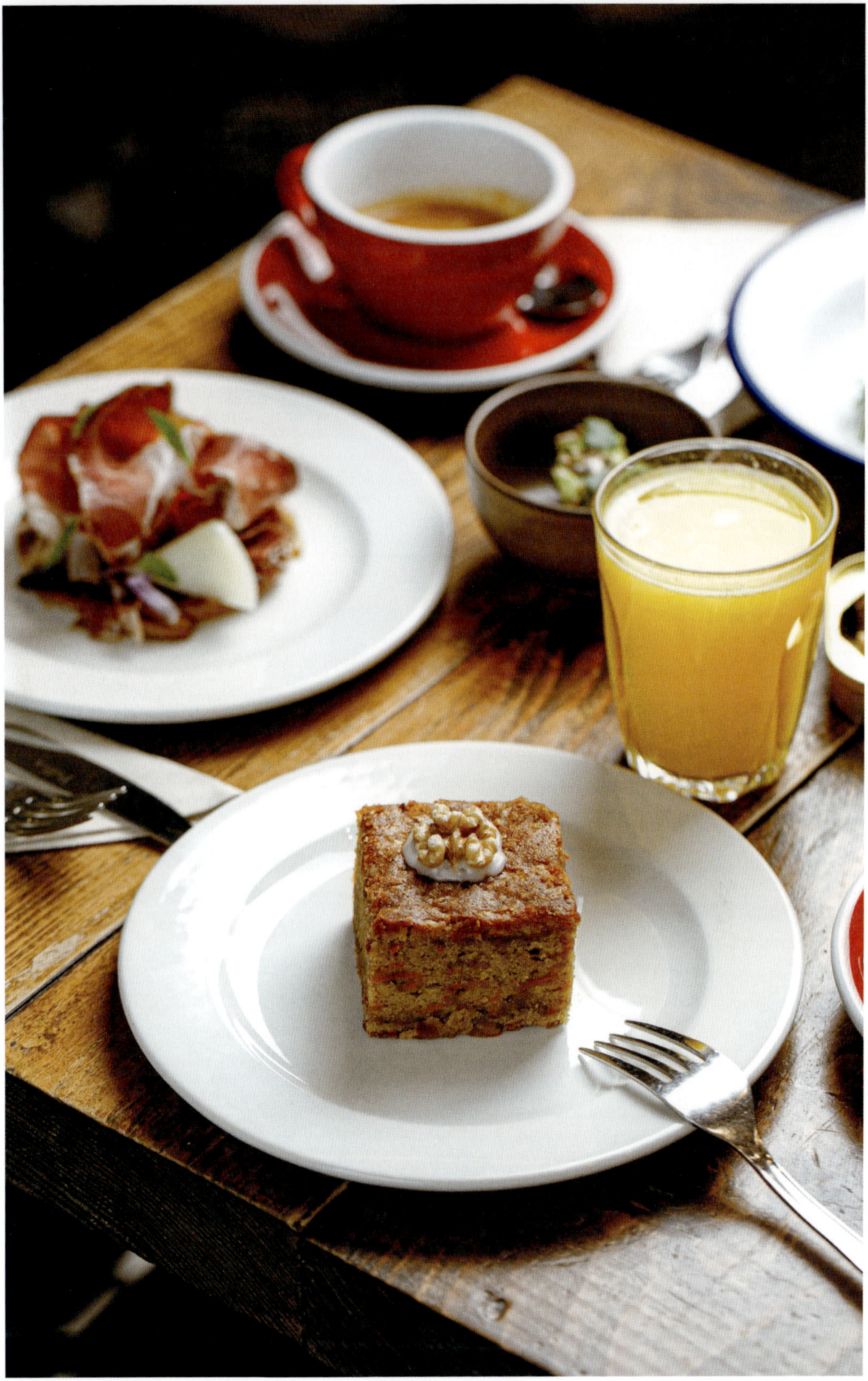

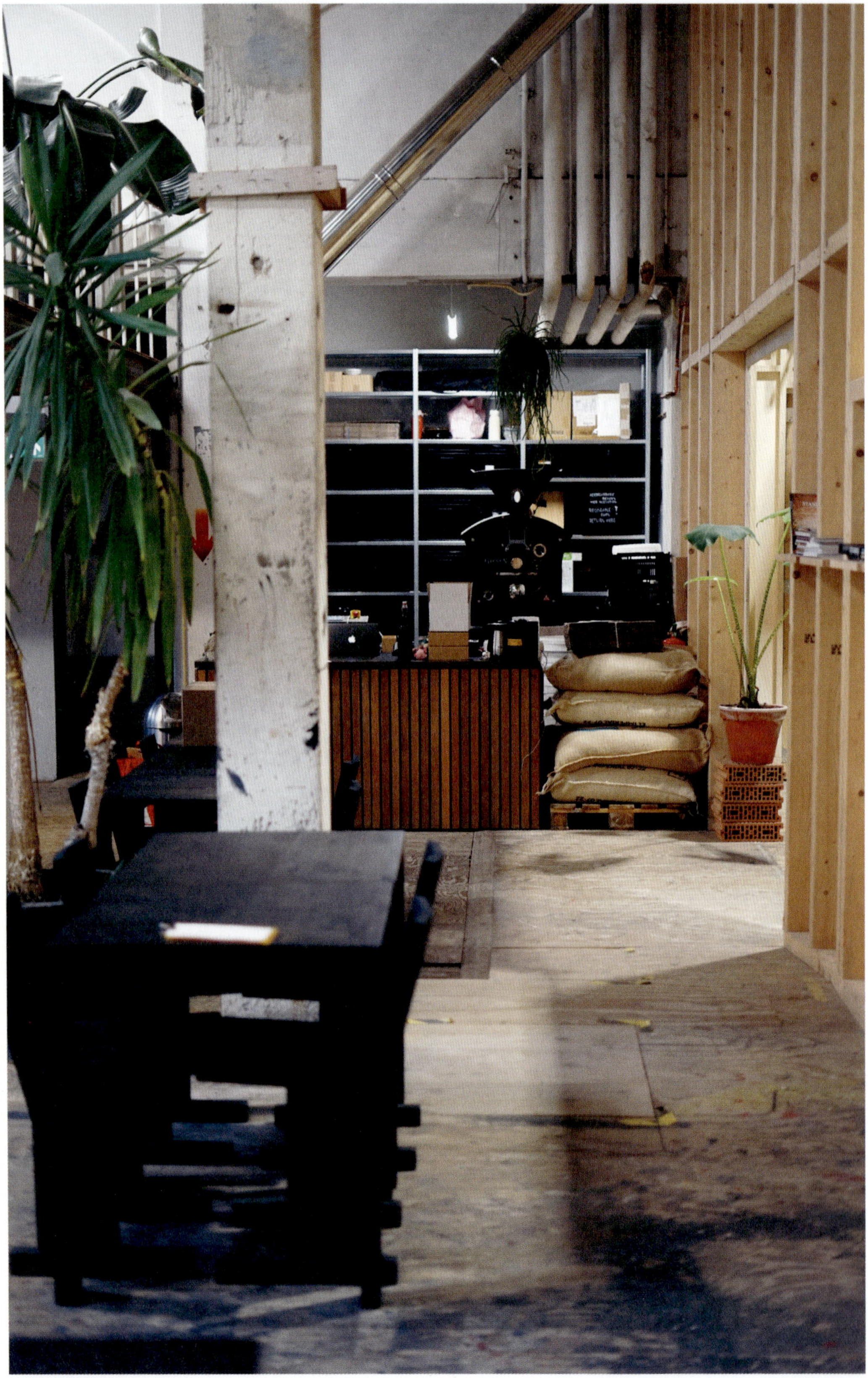

122 SCHOT COFFEE ROASTERS

Diepeveen Gebouw – De Huidenclub, Pelgrimsstraat 5c, 3029BH Rotterdam, Netherlands

TO VISIT BEFORE YOU DIE BECAUSE

This cool coffee hub, located off the beaten track in a landmark industrial building in West Rotterdam, is certainly worth the trek.

With a name like this, was there any doubt that John Schot would end up serving fine espressos in style from his roastery on the outskirts of Rotterdam? The former coffee trader set up shop in 2011, after realising he couldn't get good coffee in his local area. He found the ideal location in the Diepeveen building, a beautiful 1929 warehouse designed in the Cubist expressionist style with a 30m-high tower used as an advertising column. The local landmark was turned into a cultural hub by Atelier Tomas Dirrix in 2022, and today the smell of John's premium beans, roasted in a W15 Giesen, wafts over the centre's gallery, workshop and bookshop. It's a beautiful space in which to enjoy two types of espressos, hand brews and competition-range coffees. 'Our focus is on washed, honey and natural coffees – we're looking for layered, complex and clean coffees that show the characteristics of the region and variety,' explains John. Pair your drink with a carrot cake and a browse of the temporary exhibition.

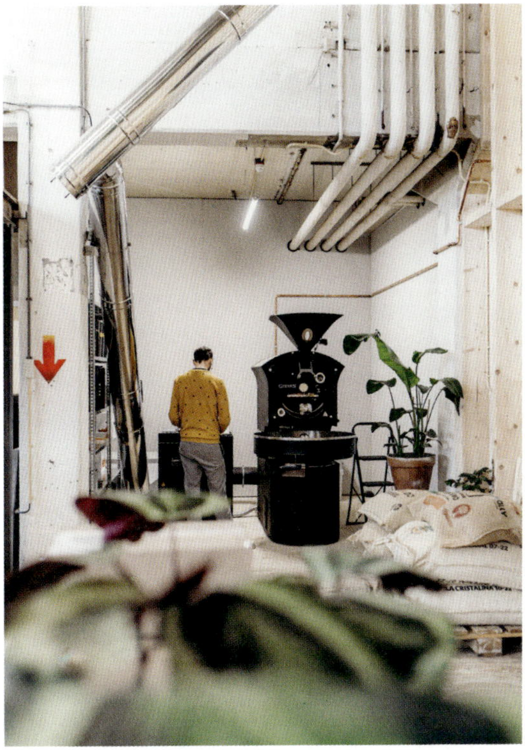

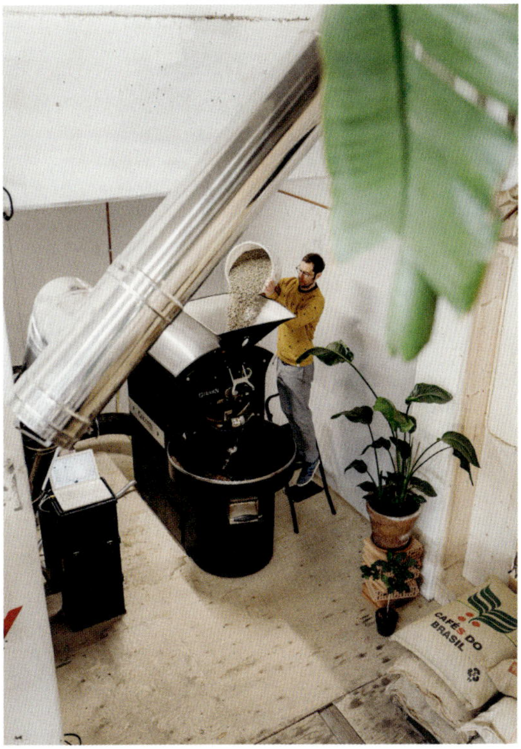

schotcoffeeroasters.nl

+31 6 39 74 25 38

123 CAFÉ TOMASELLI

Alter Markt 9, 5020 Salzburg, Austria

TO VISIT BEFORE YOU DIE BECAUSE

Treat yourself to delicious coffee and cake on the charming terrace of the oldest coffee house in Austria.

The origins of this coffee house can be traced back to 1700, but it really took off in the 1850s, under the management of confectioner Carl Tomaselli, whose father Giuseppe, a tenor, moved to Salzburg from Milan to work with the Mozart family. Its café, coffee kiosk and ladies' parlour became a favourite of Salzburg's middle classes, and the wood-panelled salon buzzing with waiters in dinner jackets hasn't changed much since. Coffee is served on a small silver tray, with a glass of water and sugar, and involves a special Tomaselli blend roasted by Viennese roast master Julius Meinl. Specialities include mélange, a mocha with milk and whipped cream; Häferlkaffee, a big cup of coffee with whipped cream and milk foam; and Tomaselliums Kaffee, a strong mocha with Mozart liqueur. As soon as you've been served your cup of choice, you'll be attended by a Kuchendame in her white apron, carrying a tray laden with sweet treats. There are 40 to choose from, including strudel and Sachertorte, but also strawberry tartlets and walnut-filled *kipferls*.

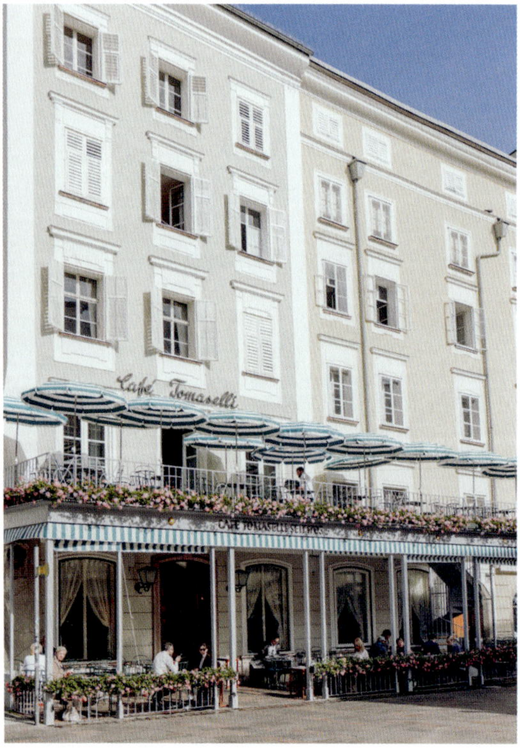

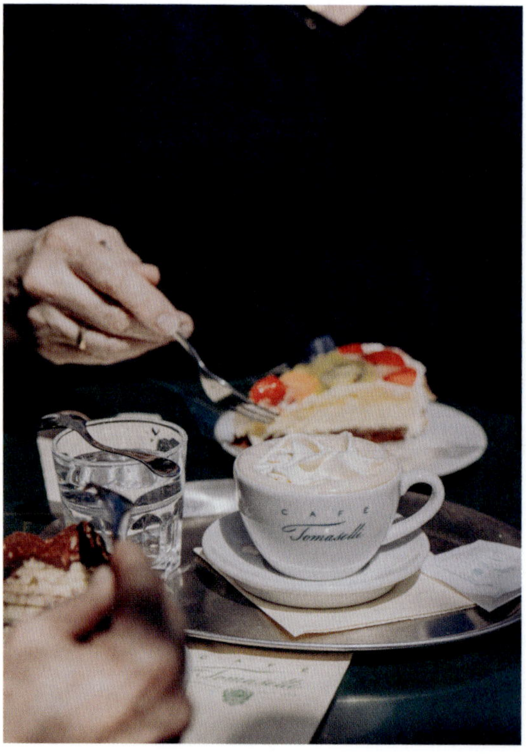

tomaselli.at/en

+43 662 844 4880

124 THE DUDE SPECIALTY COFFEE

Apostle Guslarot 16, Skopje 1000, North Macedonia

TO VISIT BEFORE YOU DIE BECAUSE

You should feel right at home at this welcoming bohemian café, a pioneer of North Macedonia's speciality coffee scene tucked away on a side street.

Housed in a beautifully restored old Skopje apartment, The Dude Specialty Coffee 'offers a space where history and modern speciality coffee culture meet'. It feels like stepping into someone's cosy living room, with comfy sofas and dark painted walls creating a warm, welcoming atmosphere. The café first opened its doors in the middle of the Covid pandemic, a time when most places were closing. 'This bold step turned it into a symbol of resilience, showing that even in the hardest times, something beautiful and meaningful can be created,' says founder Mirche Chashule. 'Speciality is at the heart of everything. Beans are sourced from small, carefully chosen farms around the world, roasted and prepared with precision to bring out their natural complexity. Whether it's a bright, fruity filter coffee, a velvety espresso or a refreshing cold coffee, each cup tells its own story.' Sit in the courtyard garden with one of the resident cats and enjoy a brownie and single-origin espresso, served in a vintage cup and saucer.

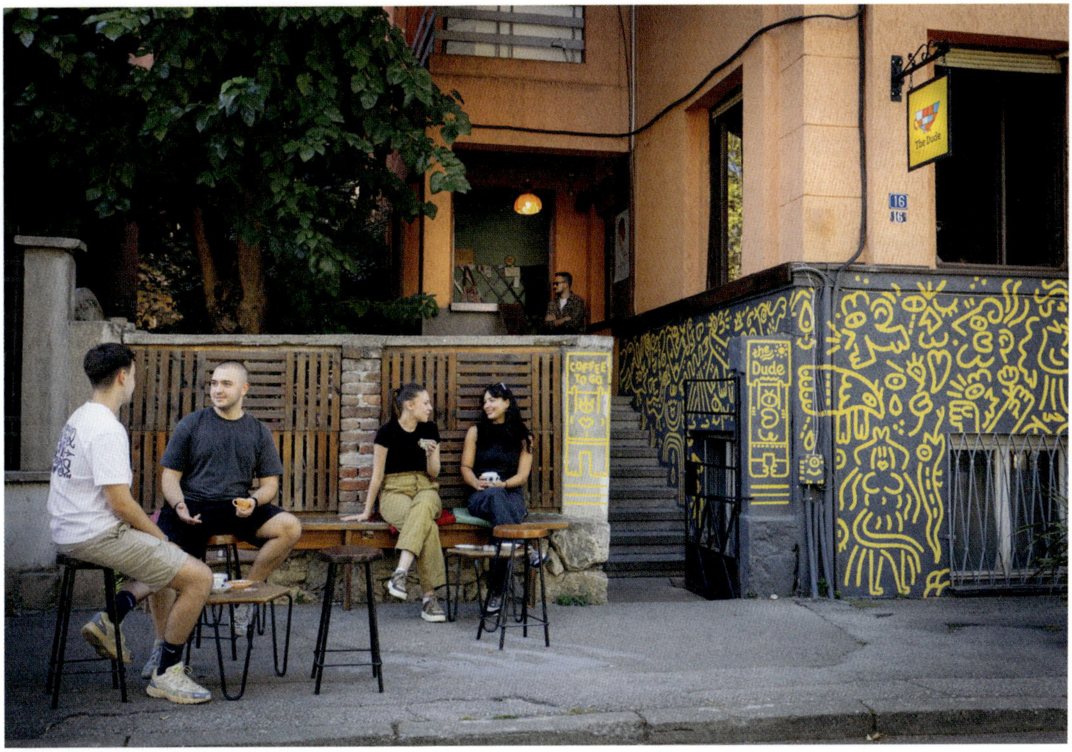

thedude.mk +389 70 200 021

125 KAVA2

Ul. Ante Starčevića 2/1, 21000, Split, Croatia

TO VISIT BEFORE YOU DIE BECAUSE

Hospitality is at the core of this beautifully designed courtyard café, loved by locals and tourists alike.

'Travelling the world shooting weddings, we fell in love with speciality coffee,' explain Kava founders Ivana and Marko, who started off with a tiny space in Hvar and now also run a shop and roastery in Split. 'Somehow coffee took over our hearts, not only for the sake of enjoying hot or cold brews prepared in meticulous ways, but more importantly for the warmth and happiness around people who enjoy them.' There's a real community feel at their Split coffee house, located a short walk to the north of the old town. The interior is very small but it does come with a gorgeous courtyard with lemon trees, the perfect spot for a cold brew tonic on a summer's day. Specials include caramel latte served hot or cold and V60 filter coffee, with coffees including Panama Geisha and Burundi Gihere Ngozi, and snacks ranging from focaccia sandwiches to chocolate chip cookies. Kava's first shop, located in a picturesque stone alley on the island of Hvar, is also well worth a visit (it's open during the summer months only).

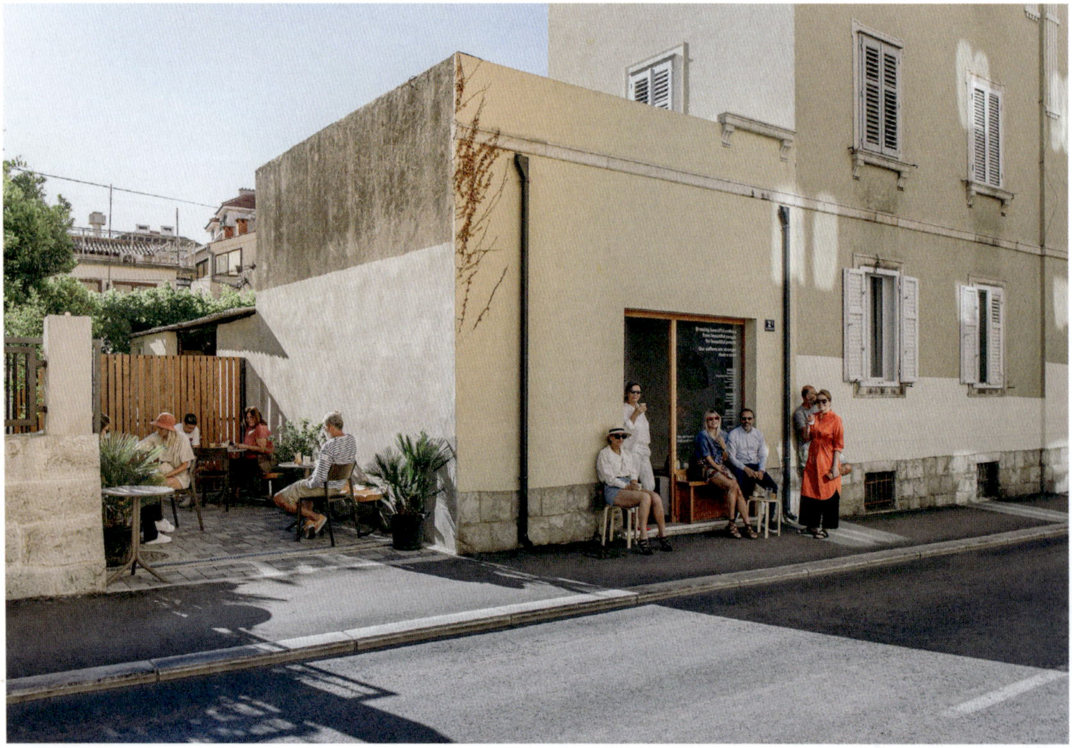

kava.family

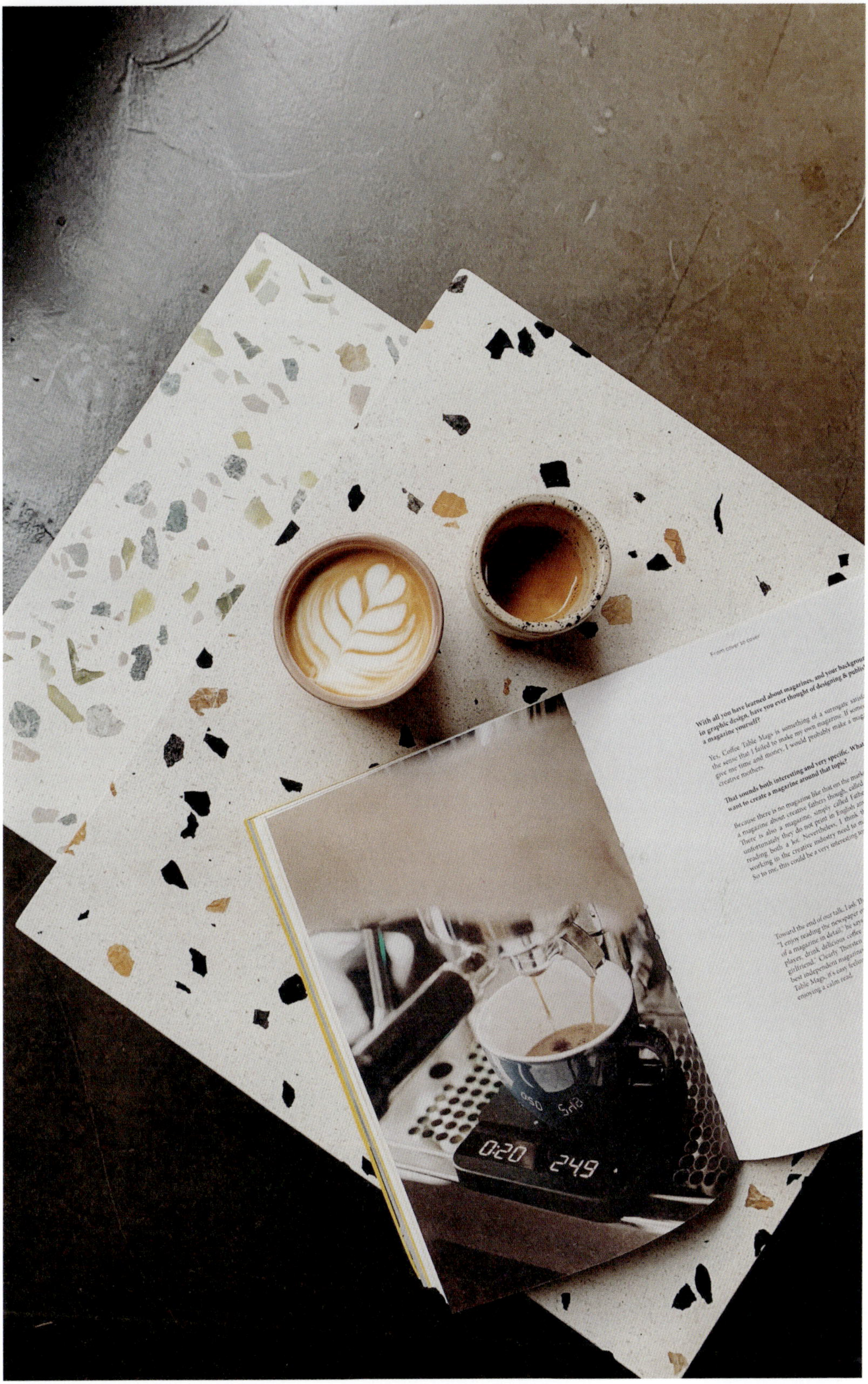

126 DROP COFFEE

Wollmar Yxkullsgatan 10, 118 50 Stockholm, Sweden

TO VISIT BEFORE YOU DIE BECAUSE

Try an ever-changing line-up of sustainably sourced single-origin coffees at this renowned café with exceptional service.

A hip café in Stockholm's Södermalm, Drop is co-owned by Joanna Alm, a three-time Swedish Coffee Roasting Champion, and her husband, founder of Hasbean and co-owner of 3fe, Stephen Leighton. Joanna learnt the ropes working at a café in Oslo selling beans from Tim Wendelboe (page 190), making a life-changing discovery in a geisha from La Milagrosa, Panama, and then starting at Drop as a barista in 2010. Having upgraded from the initial small roaster on site to a 25kg Diedrich roaster in a dedicated facility to the north of the city, the duo only buys from farms they have visited, working alongside a small, skilled team of roasters and baristas to offer single-origin coffees only. 'Transparency is central to our mission, with FOB prices disclosed and annual sustainability reports published,' say the team. 'All coffees are roasted in small batches of 8–16kg, ensuring freshness, zero waste, and a focus on each bean's unique origin and flavour profile.' Uniquely, you can also buy Drop's coffee jute sacks, used to carry the raw beans from coffee farms worldwide to the Swedish roastery.

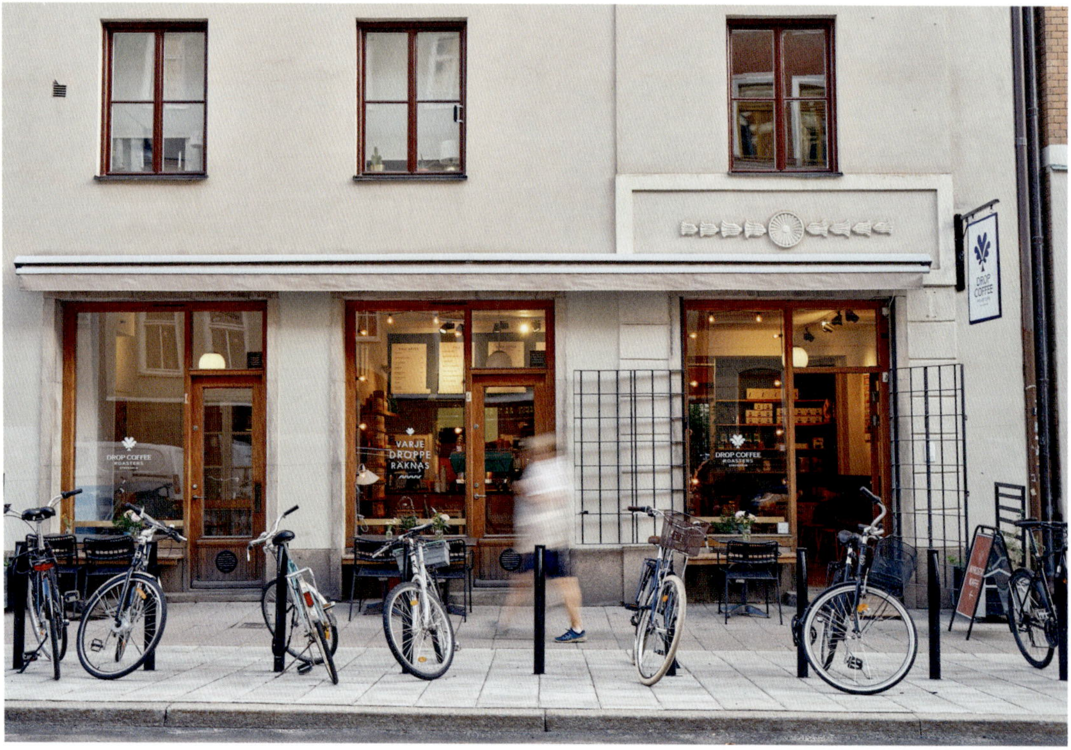

dropcoffee.com +46 70 777 9488

127 KOMET CAFÉ

Kungsholmsgatan 10, 112 27 Stockholm, Sweden

TO VISIT
BEFORE YOU DIE
BECAUSE

Enjoy Sweden's renowned coffee-and-cake tradition at this fantastic artisan bakery café offering delicious buns and a cosy atmosphere.

Sweden's most beloved ritual is the *fika* break, a cornerstone of daily life involving great conversation, a sweet treat and, of course, coffee (the name comes from the old Swedish word for the drink, *kaffi*). And one of the best places to pause, connect and recharge over a cup of coffee is Komet, opened by Nicolas Viry and Marie Rossi in 2021. A talented French baker, Nicolas prepares some fine pains au chocolat, but fear not, all the Swedish classics are also present, from tasty *kanelbullar* (cinnamon buns) to fluffy *semla* brioches (filled with whipped cream and almond paste, sometimes infused with coffee). Everything is made using organic, local ingredients, while the coffee comes courtesy of Swedish companies including Stockholm Roast, Standout Coffee and Swerl. There's also a food menu featuring salads, sandwiches and soups. Try a pistachio roll with cold brew on the small terrace, or warm up with the filter coffee of the day and a grilled cheese croissant. The cherry on top? The café's mascot, Léon the dog, who 'runs quality control for cuddles and crumb cleanup'.

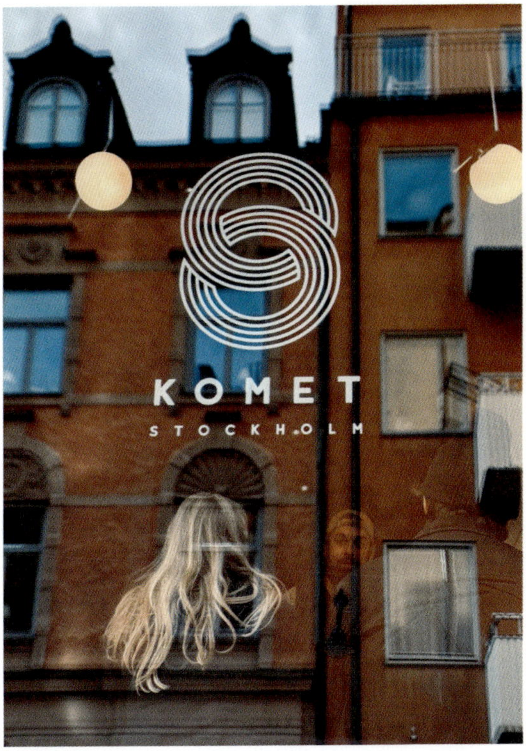

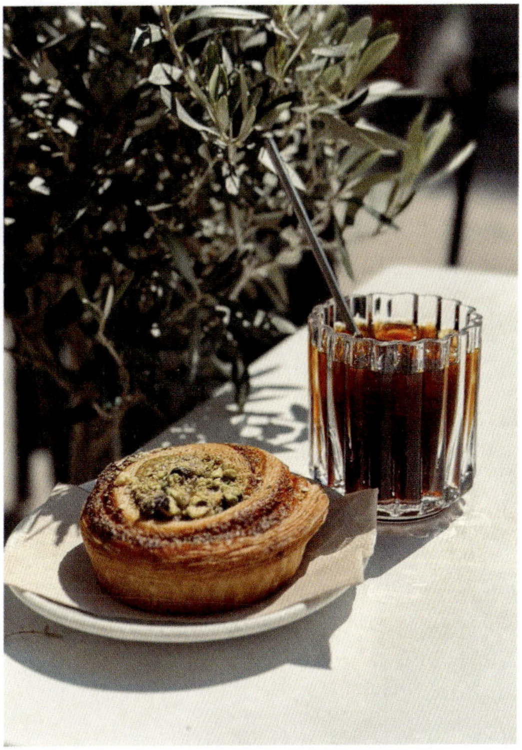

kometstockholm.com

+46 73 530 9955

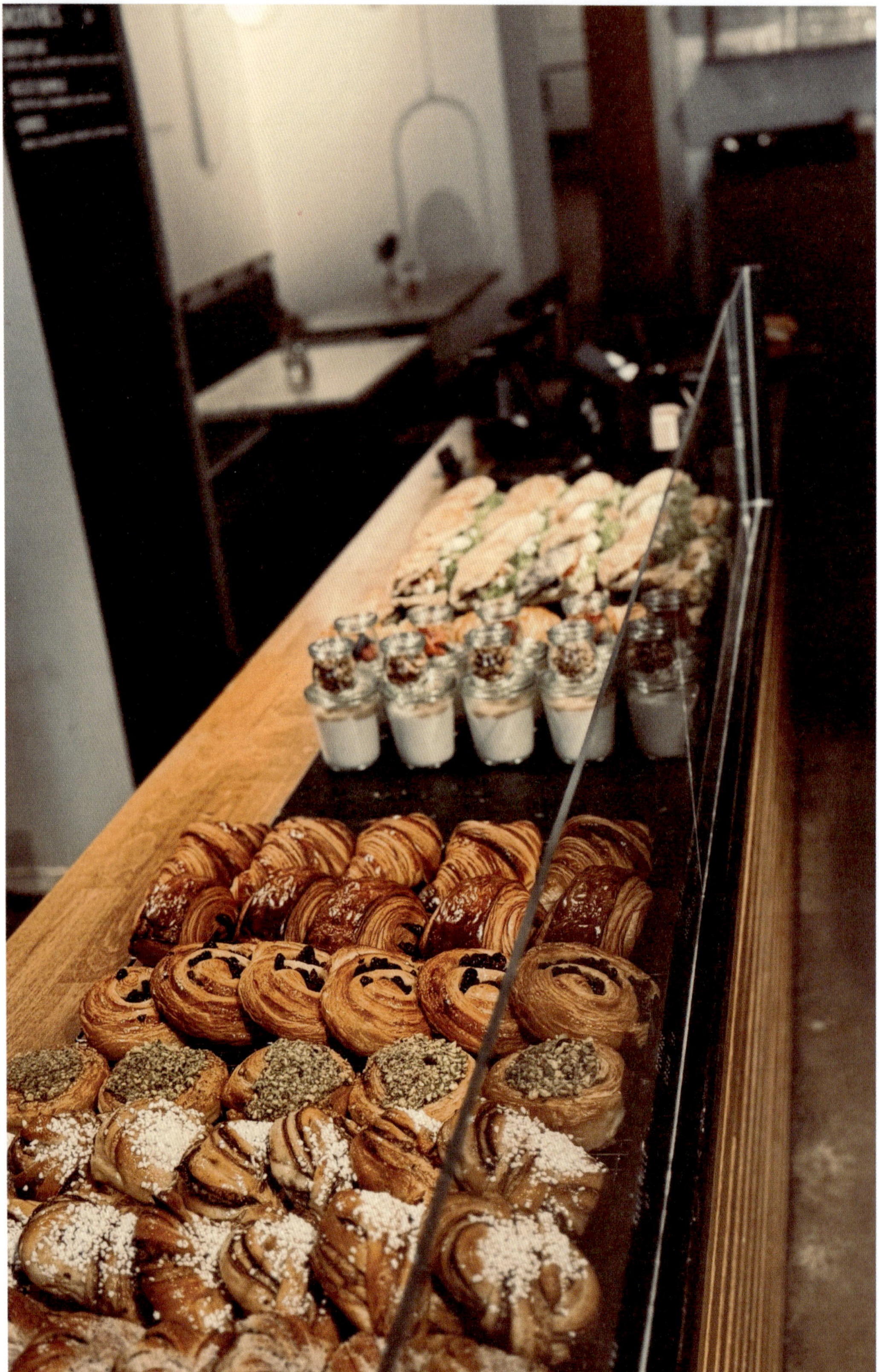

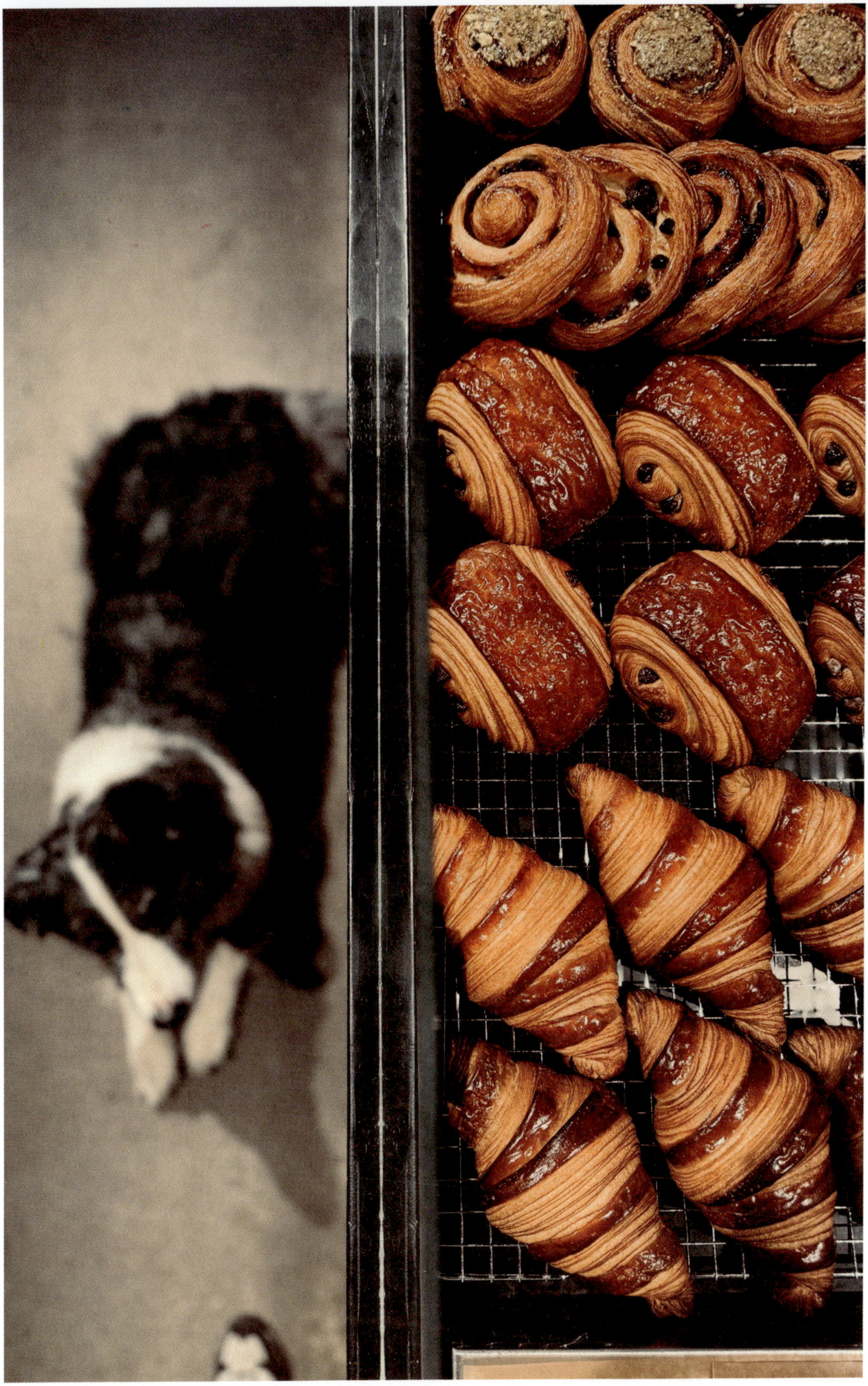

128 KOKOMO COFFEE ROASTERS

Ankru tn 10, 11713 Tallinn, Estonia

TO VISIT BEFORE YOU DIE BECAUSE

Try carefully prepared speciality coffees at this welcoming, family-owned micro-roastery that has just celebrated its 10th anniversary.

Starting in 2013 with a series of pop-up cafés and festival stalls in Estonia, Kokomo has gone from strength to strength, moving into this wonderful old rubber factory on Tallinn's Kopli peninsula in 2019. Just a 15-minute tram ride from the city centre, Põhjala Factory is 'a cultural hub, a community of bright minds, a place where old meets new, a place that allows you to slow down,' explain founders Mari and Roland. 'You'll be greeted by the smell of the sea and freshly roasted coffee from Kokomo.' The pair roasts their coffee in small batches, with delicate care, to ensure every cup is fresh, full of flavour and of the highest quality. To enjoy your Kenya Zawadi Peaberry, you can either sit in the main lounge, with tall windows and antique rugs; the sunny courtyard, with plant pots and street art; or the stylish black glasshouse. Snacks include yogurt bowls, toasties and freshly baked pastries, and we love the colourful, retro-looking stamps on the simple coffee bags, designed in collaboration with British illustrator Ryan Chapman.

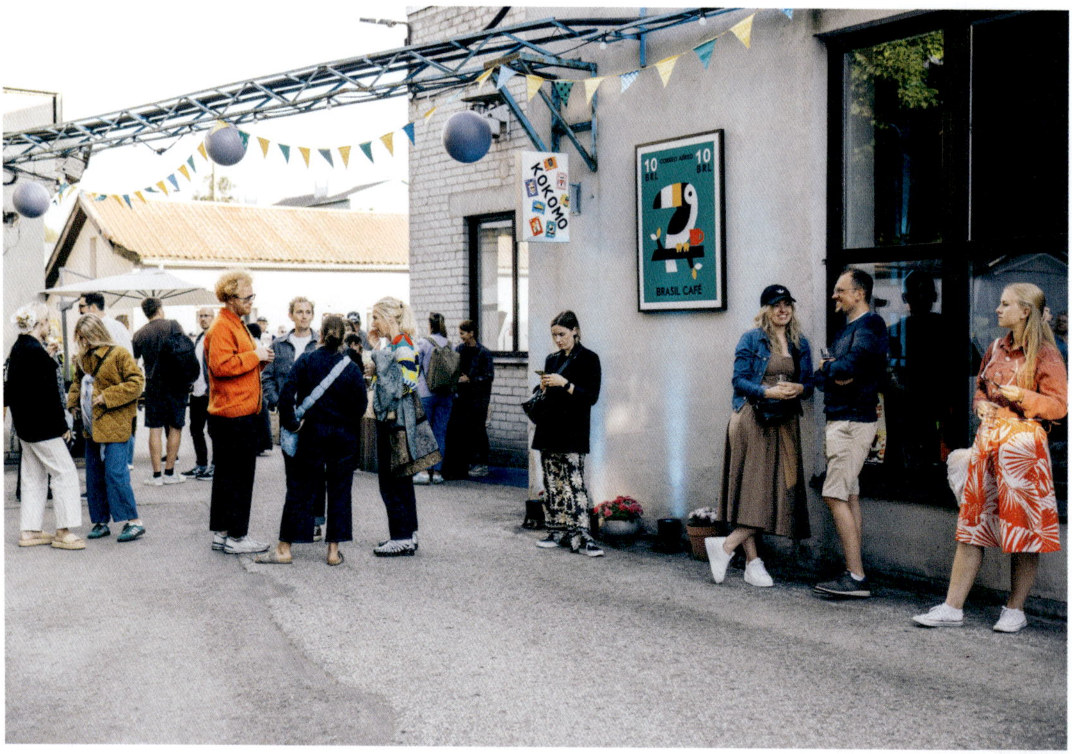

kokomo.ee +372 5624 0970

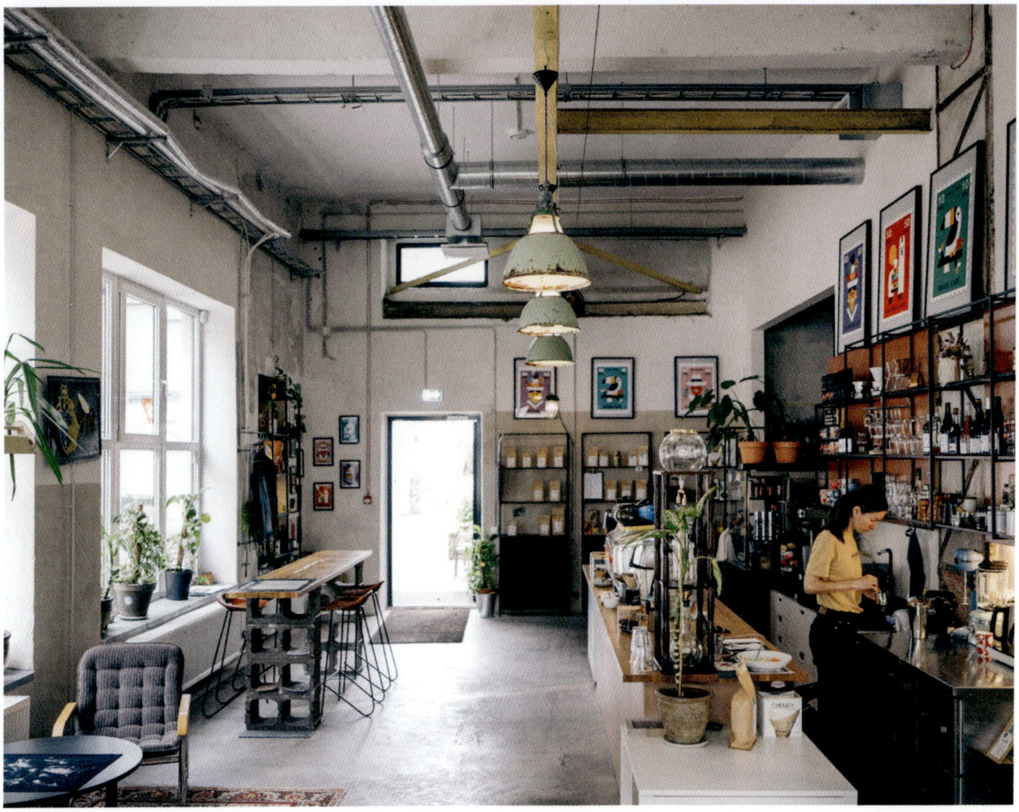

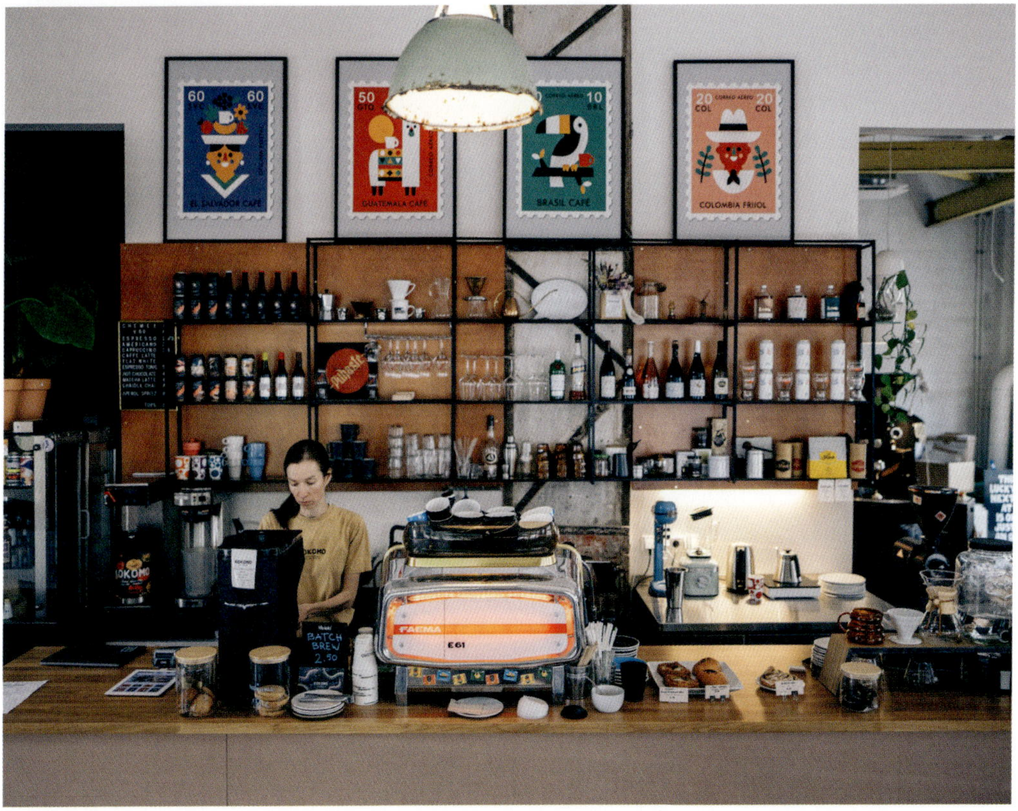
EL SALVADOR CAFÉ
GUATEMALA CAFÉ
BRASIL CAFÉ
COLOMBIA FRIJOL
BATCH BREW 2,50
FAEMA
E61

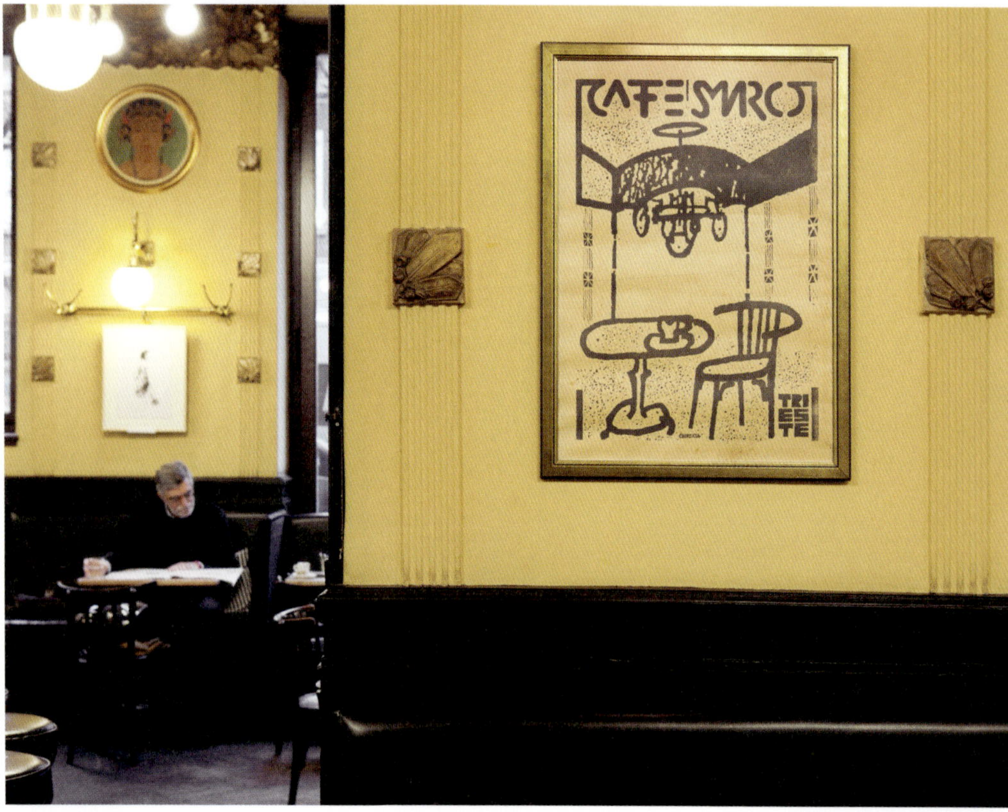
TRIESTE

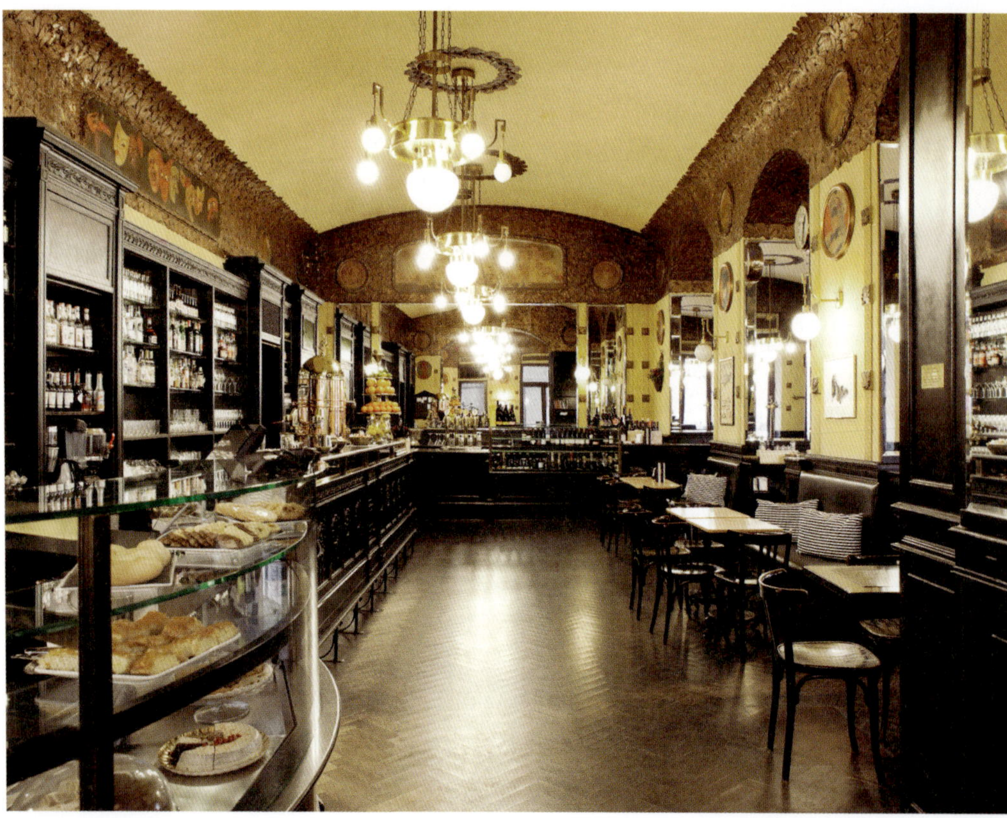

129 ANTICO CAFFÈ SAN MARCO

Via Cesare Battisti, 18, 34125 Trieste, Italy

TO VISIT BEFORE YOU DIE BECAUSE

Known for its distinctive Viennese Secession-style interior and literary clientele, this elegant café is Trieste's top cultural destination.

Trieste is known as the 'world capital of coffee', with coffee consumption here double that of the rest of Italy, and about one café for every 300 inhabitants. The most famous establishment is Caffè San Marco, a historic literary haunt that nearly didn't make it through the First World War. In 1915, only a year after it was opened by Croatian entrepreneur Marco Lovrinivich, a great admirer of Venice, the café was set on fire by anti-Italian groups (Trieste was part of the Austro-Hungarian Empire at the time) and nearly destroyed. Thankfully, its wonderful décor was carefully restored, and you can still admire its wraparound friezes featuring bronze-coloured coffee leaves, brass chandeliers and Verona red marble tables – just like James Joyce and Italo Svevo before you. Settle down with a slice of the signature 1914 cake (made with in-house coffee vermouth) and the local favourite, *capo in bi* (macchiato coffee served in a glass). The café is also a bookshop and cultural venue, and is lively all day long.

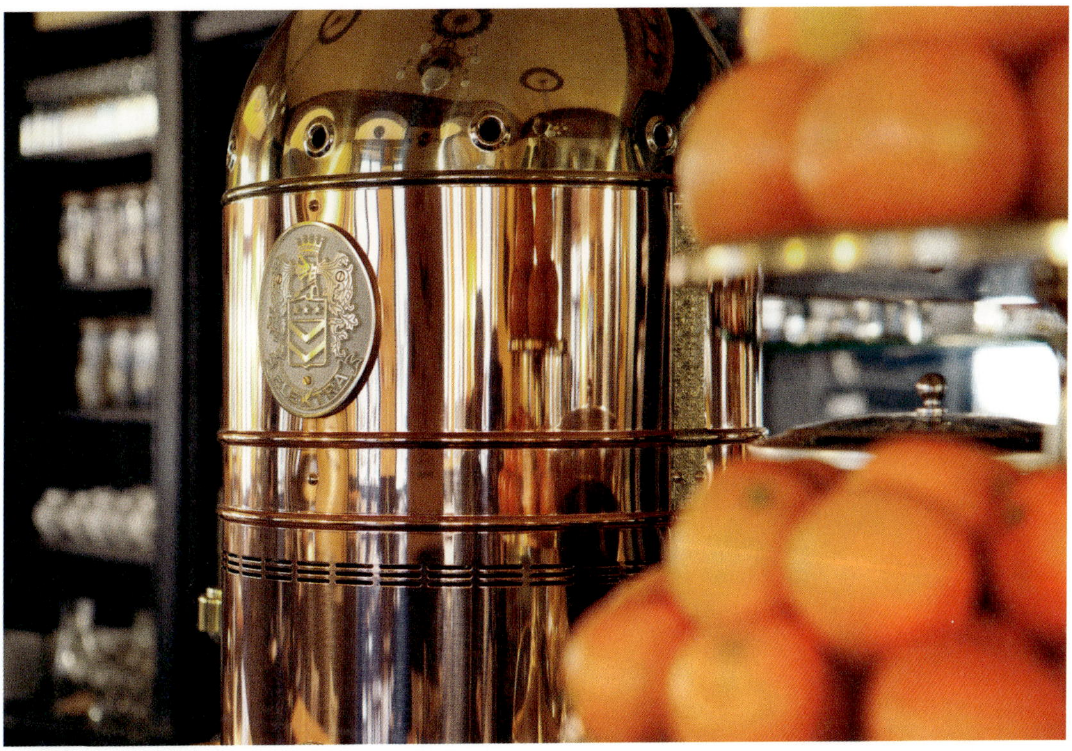

caffesanmarco.com +39 040 203 5357

130 CAFFÈ AL BICERIN

Piazza della Consolata, 5, 10122 Turin, Italy

TO VISIT
BEFORE YOU DIE
BECAUSE

Try Turin's famous *bicerin* at this historic café, which for years was one of the few places in town where women could be seen on their own.

Is there a more delicious trio than coffee, chocolate and cream? Probably not, and it seems that the people of Turin agree, since the city's speciality is the *bicerin*, a drink combining the three flavours to perfection. You'll find it, as well as house specialities such as cold dark chocolate and zabaglione, at this landmark coffee house in the old town of Turin. Al Bicerin counts Cavour, Nietzsche, Dumas and Puccini among its famous customers, and was a favourite of Umberto Eco, who used it as a setting in one of his novels. It's only a small room with wood-panelled walls and a marble bar and tables, but it boasts a large terrace on which to enjoy the house signature coffee and chocolate torta. It's definitely the real deal: its late owner, Maritè Costa, spent years researching local sweets and original recipes, to celebrate Piedmont's culinary traditions and ingredients. Make sure to grab a bag of coffee grains coated in chocolate and other goodies from the shop next door.

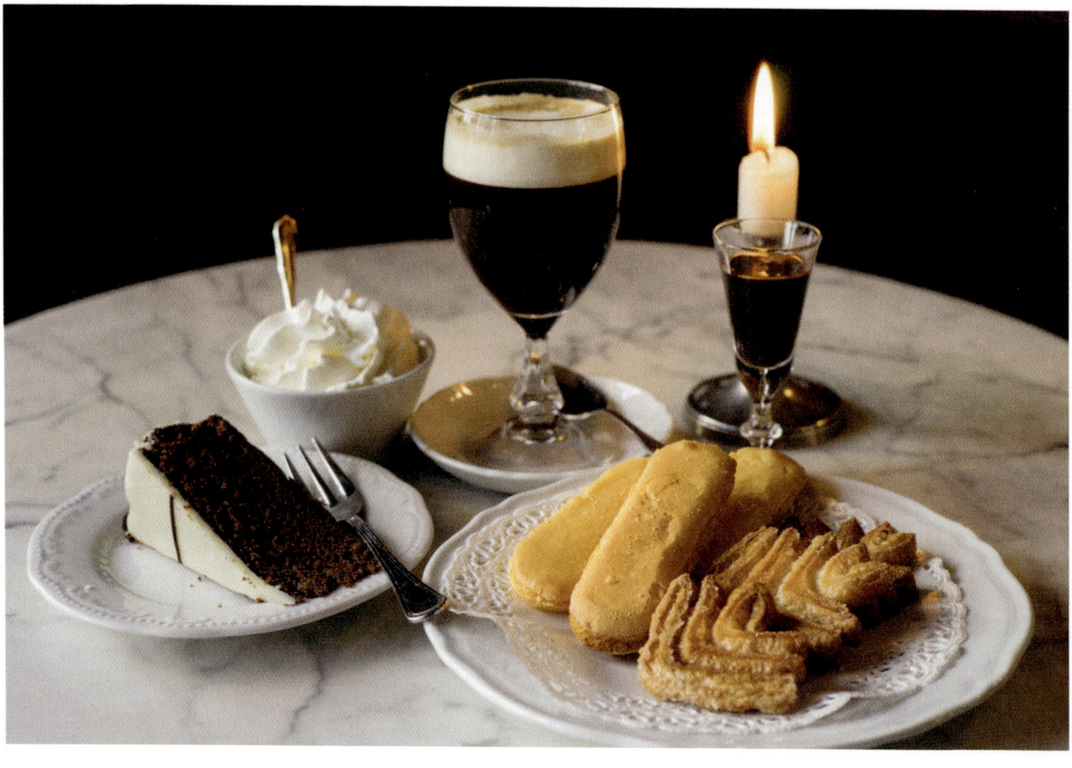

bicerin.it

+39 011 436 9325

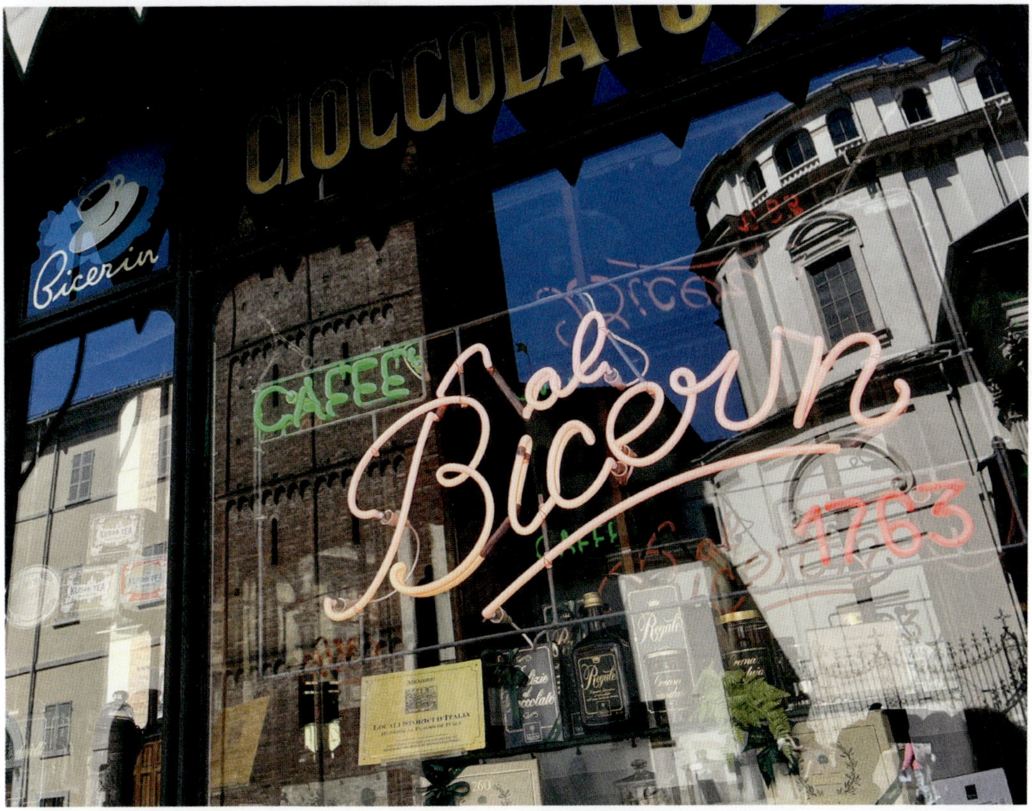
CIOCCOLATO
Bicerin
CAFFE'
al Bicerin
1763
LOCALI STORICI D'ITALIA

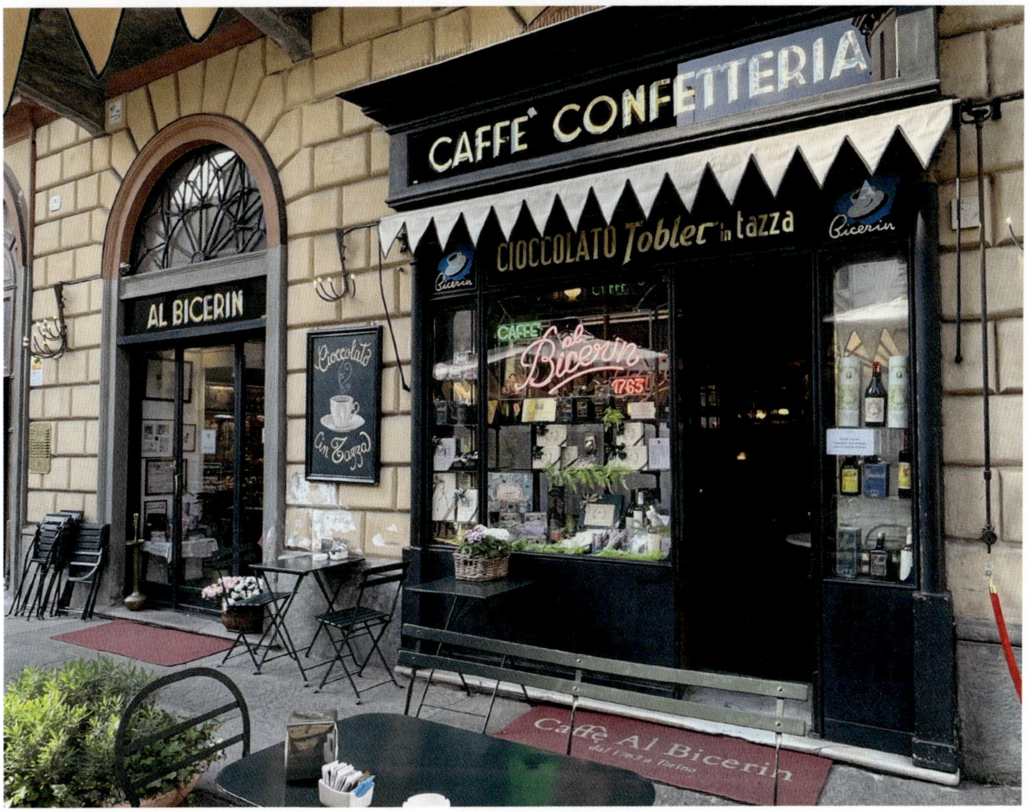
CAFFE' CONFETTERIA
CIOCCOLATO Tobler in tazza
Bicerin
AL BICERIN
Cioccolato in Tazza
CAFFE'
al Bicerin
1763
Caffè Al Bicerin
dal 1763 a Torino

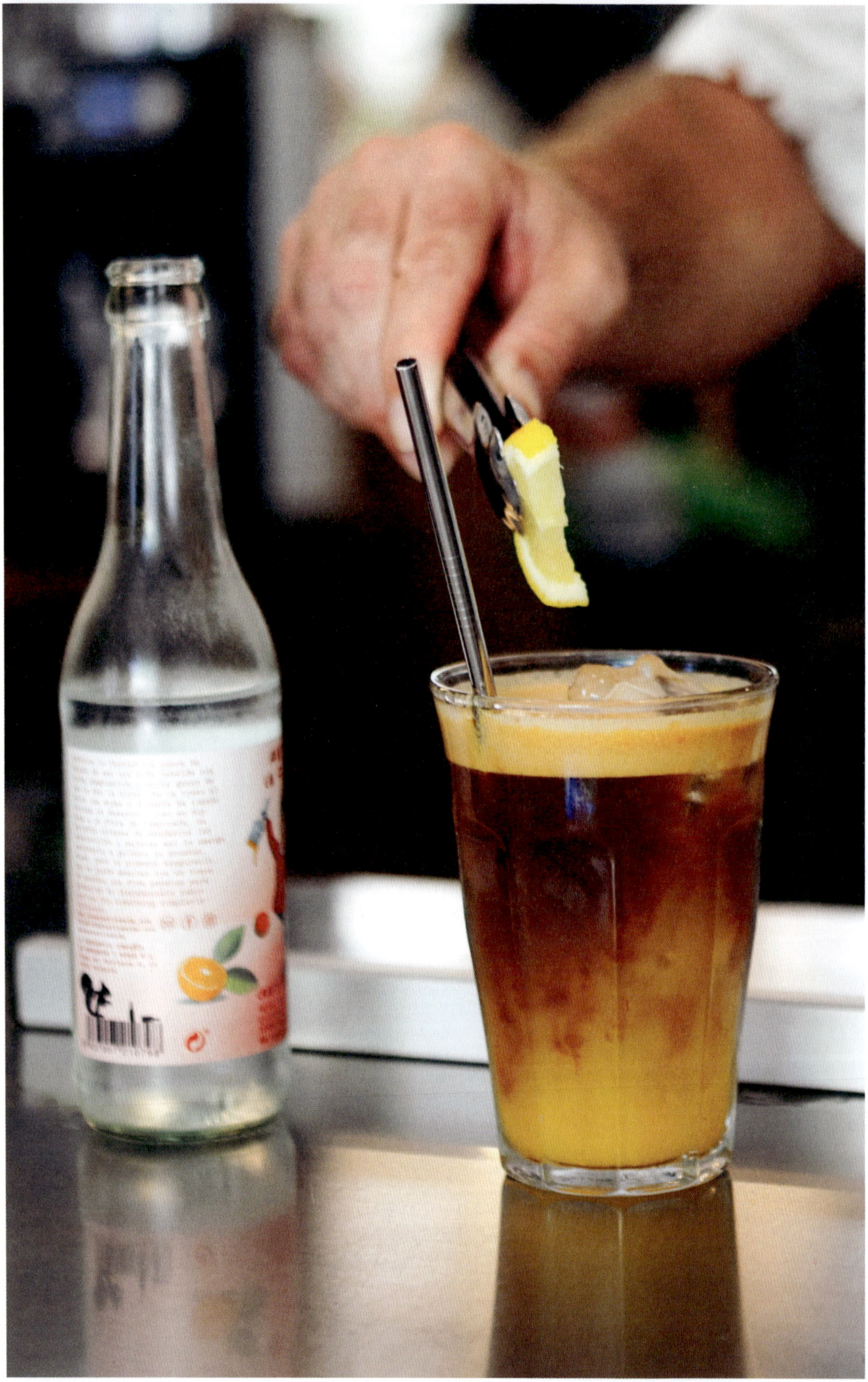

131 TALLAT COFFEE ROASTERS

C/ de la Barraca, 25, Poblats Marítims, 46011 València, Valencia, Spain

TO VISIT BEFORE YOU DIE BECAUSE

Combine a trip to the beach with a break at this awesome neighbourhood café, which focuses on 'making good coffee for real people, every day'.

Valencia's old fishing district of El Cabanyal is full of beautiful little town-houses, lined up next to the city's long sandy beach. It's here, in a century-old building, that Tallat was set up in 2019 by Lorenzo, a Milanese and former Londoner keen to create a community of like-minded people. 'I've chosen this neighbourhood not only for the beauty of the colourful houses or the proximity to the beach, but for the feeling of living in a small village where everybody still knows and greets each other,' says Lorenzo, who wanted to combine the Spanish habit of socialising around a coffee with the use of freshly roasted high-quality coffees. 'Our name is from the Valencian word for cortado, pronounced "tie-yat", a very popular milky drink in Spain, in a tribute to the city that welcomed us.' Lorenzo's signature drinks are based on Valencia's famous oranges and orxata: 'The first is a mix of orange juice, tonic water and espresso; the latter is the Dirty Orxata – cold brew mixed with orxata.'

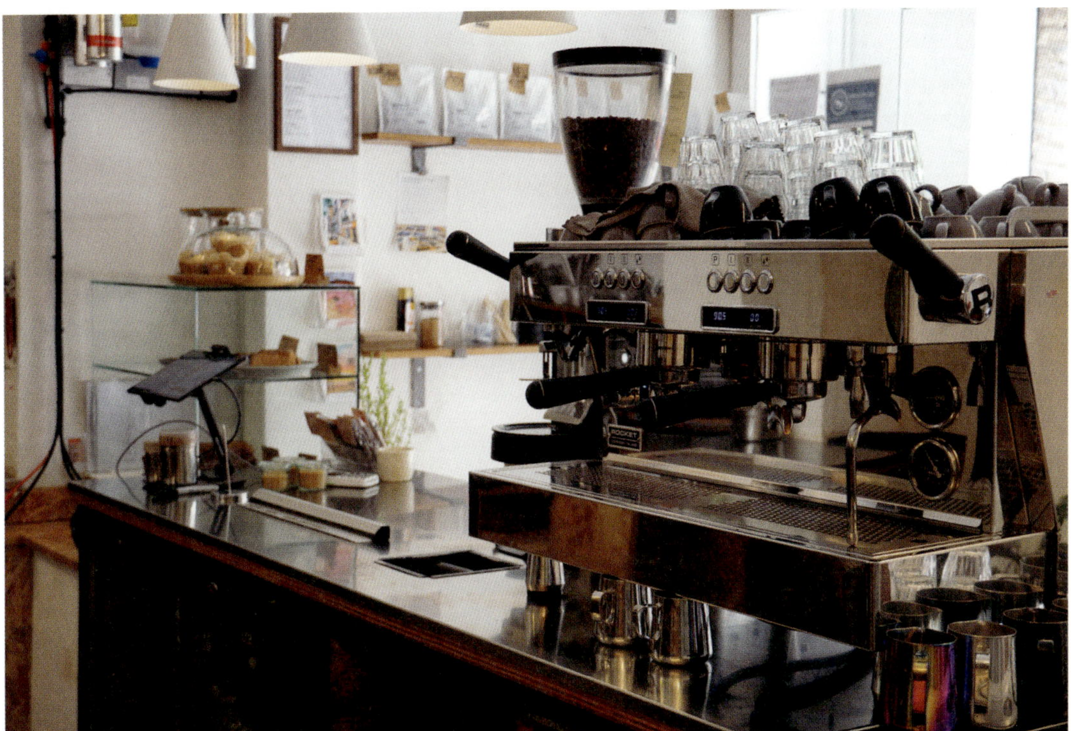

tallat.coffee +34 960 83 64 46

132 CAFFÈ FLORIAN

Piazza San Marco, 57, 30124 Venice, Italy

TO VISIT BEFORE YOU DIE BECAUSE

At over 300 years old, this grande dame of coffee houses, on Venice's iconic St Mark's Square, offers a postcard-perfect experience.

This historic café opened on St Mark's Square in 1720 under the name Alla Venezia Trionfante ('Triumphant Venice') but in a few short months, Venetians began calling it Florian after the name of its founder, Floriano Francesconi. For the past few centuries, many a local has exclaimed 'Andemo da Florian!' ('Let's meet at Florian's'), although that would usually mean having a quick espresso while standing at the bar, as is the traditional Italian way, rather than paying extra for a seat. From the two simple rooms of its beginning, the café has evolved into a fascinating series of richly decorated rooms, including the Senate Room, the Chinese Room and the Liberty Room. You might even come across a temporary contemporary art installation, in a nod to the café being the birthplace of the Venice Biennale. Note that in the summer, there is an extra music charge for most of the sitting areas, as live music is provided by an in-house orchestra. Try the Seasons' Room or Room of Ilustrious Men if you prefer a slightly smaller bill and somewhat quieter experience with your espresso or affogato.

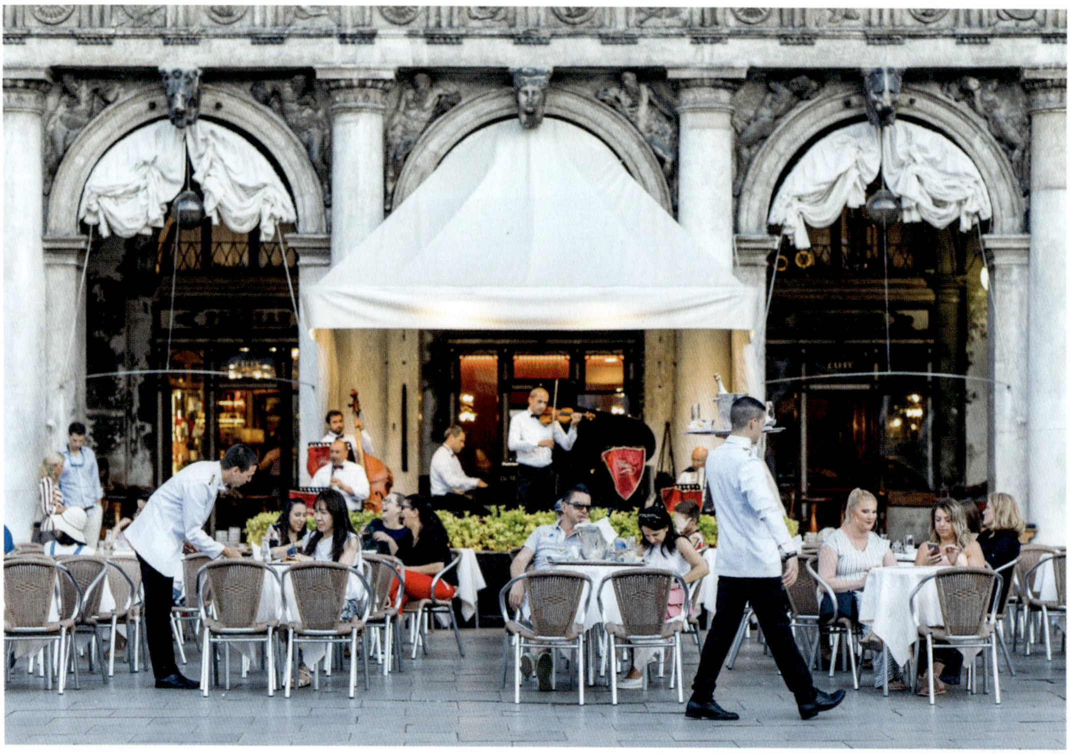

caffeflorian.com +39 041 520 5641

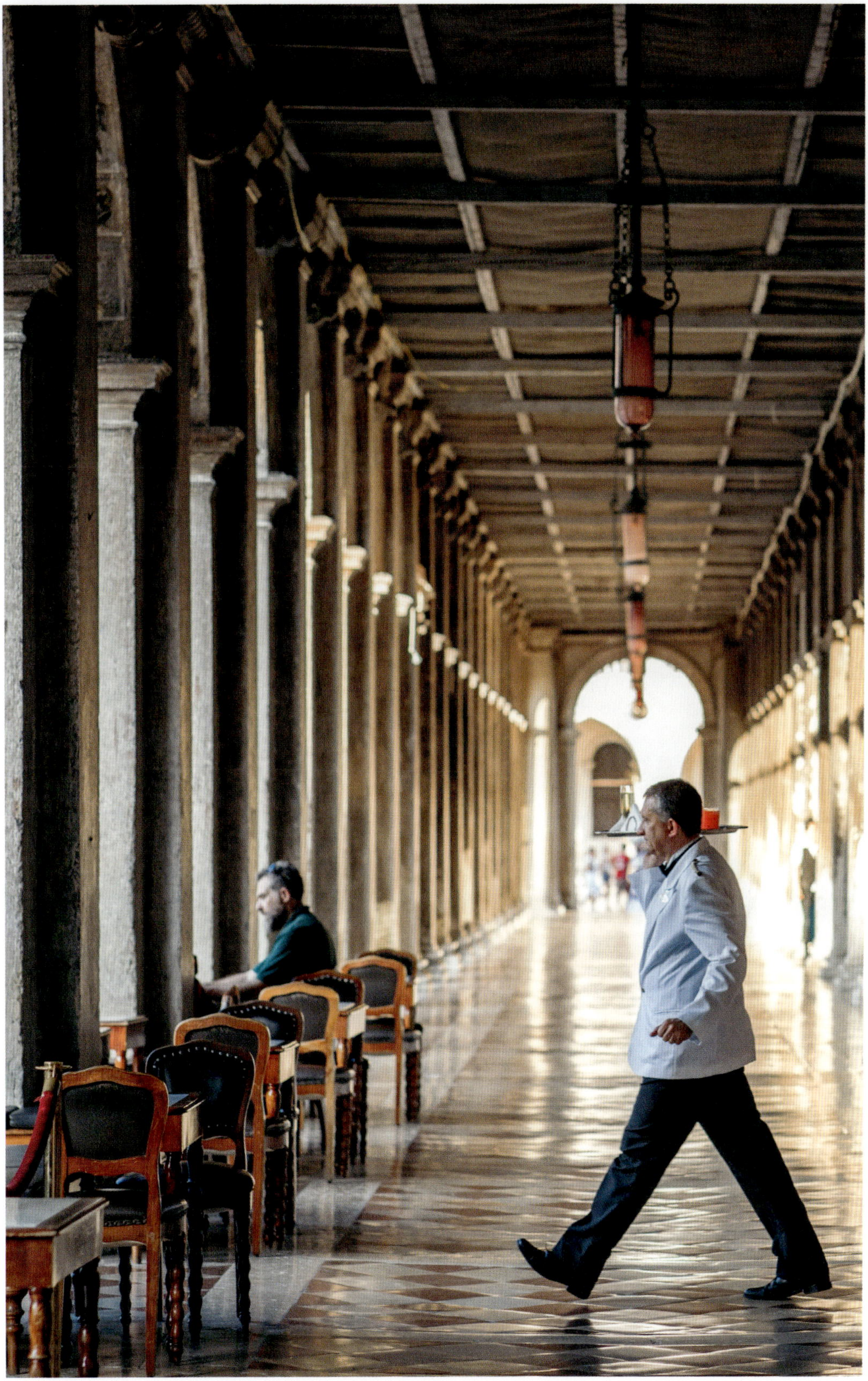

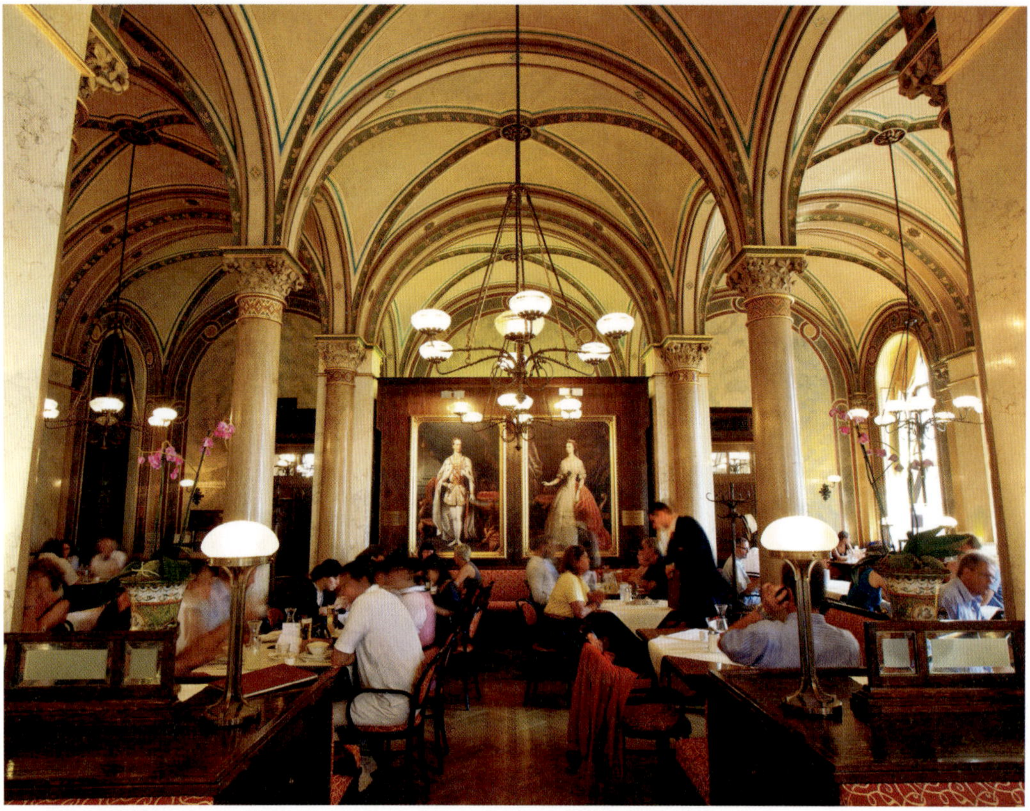

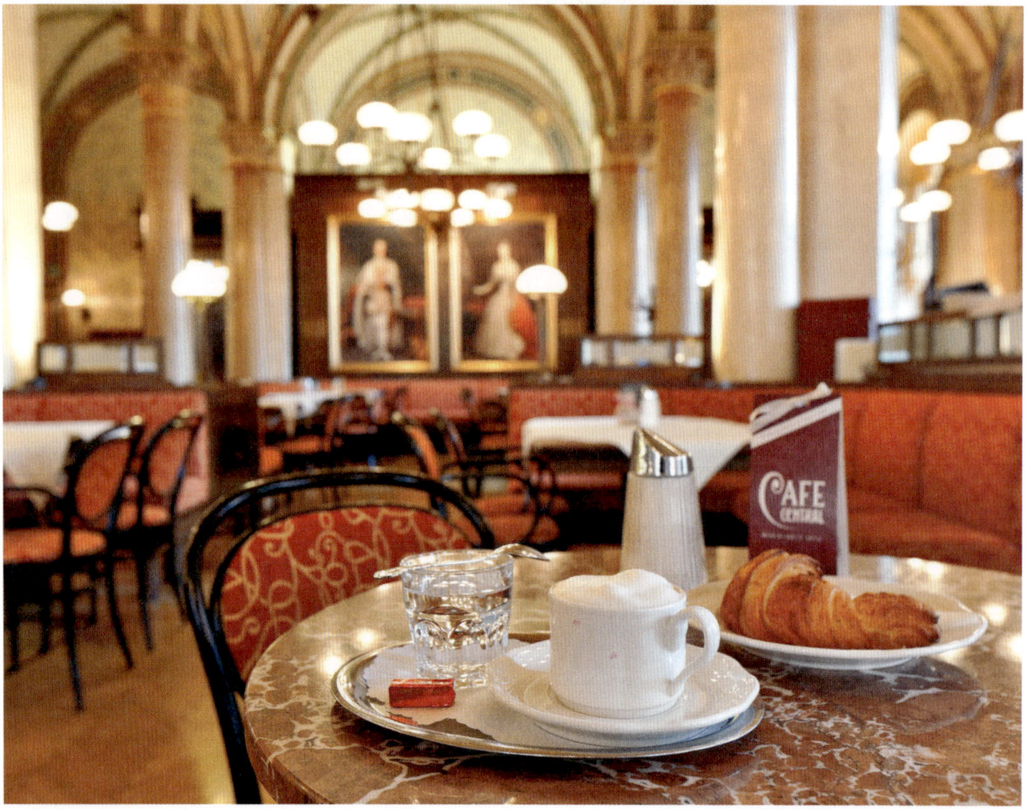
CAFE
CENTRAL

133 CAFÉ CENTRAL

Ecke Herrengasse/Strauchgasse, 1010 Vienna, Austria

TO VISIT
BEFORE YOU DIE
BECAUSE

First opened in 1876, this spectacular Viennese café offers classic coffees, wonderful cakes, and the chance to step back in time to Vienna's golden age.

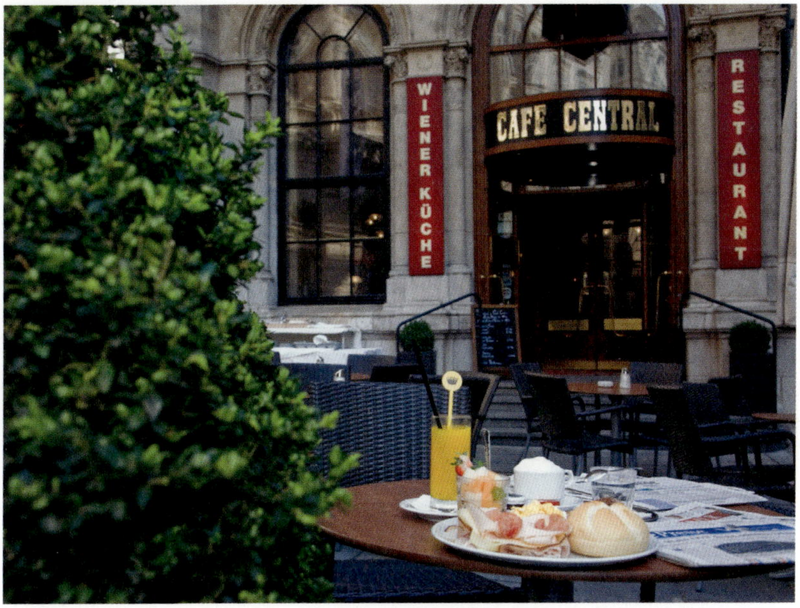

With their marble tables, Thonet chairs, newspapers on sticks and heated discussions, Vienna's cafés were quintessential meeting points, disseminating fresh ideas and theories for the price of a cup of coffee. Now a UNESCO-listed Intangible Cultural Heritage, the capital's cafés were described as 'the best place to keep up with everything new' by the Austrian writer Stefan Zweig, a regular at Café Central along with Freud, Trotsky, and all the century's great dictators (it turns out some ideas were in fact really not worth sharing...). Located on the corner of Vienna's imposing Palais Ferstel, the iconic café boasts stunning vaulted ceilings and polished marble columns. Intellectuals, chess masters and tarot players have long gone, but you can still get a great Wiener mélange (one espresso shot, steamed milk and a milk foam topping, served in a large cup) and a flaky croissant – or if you're in need of a boost, a double espresso with apricot liqueur and whipped cream, accompanied by *Kaiserschmarrn* pancakes, strudel or Sachertorte. Come early to avoid the queue (and if it's too long, try the nearby Café Landtmann, another classic, and come back later).

cafecentral.wien +43 153 337 6361

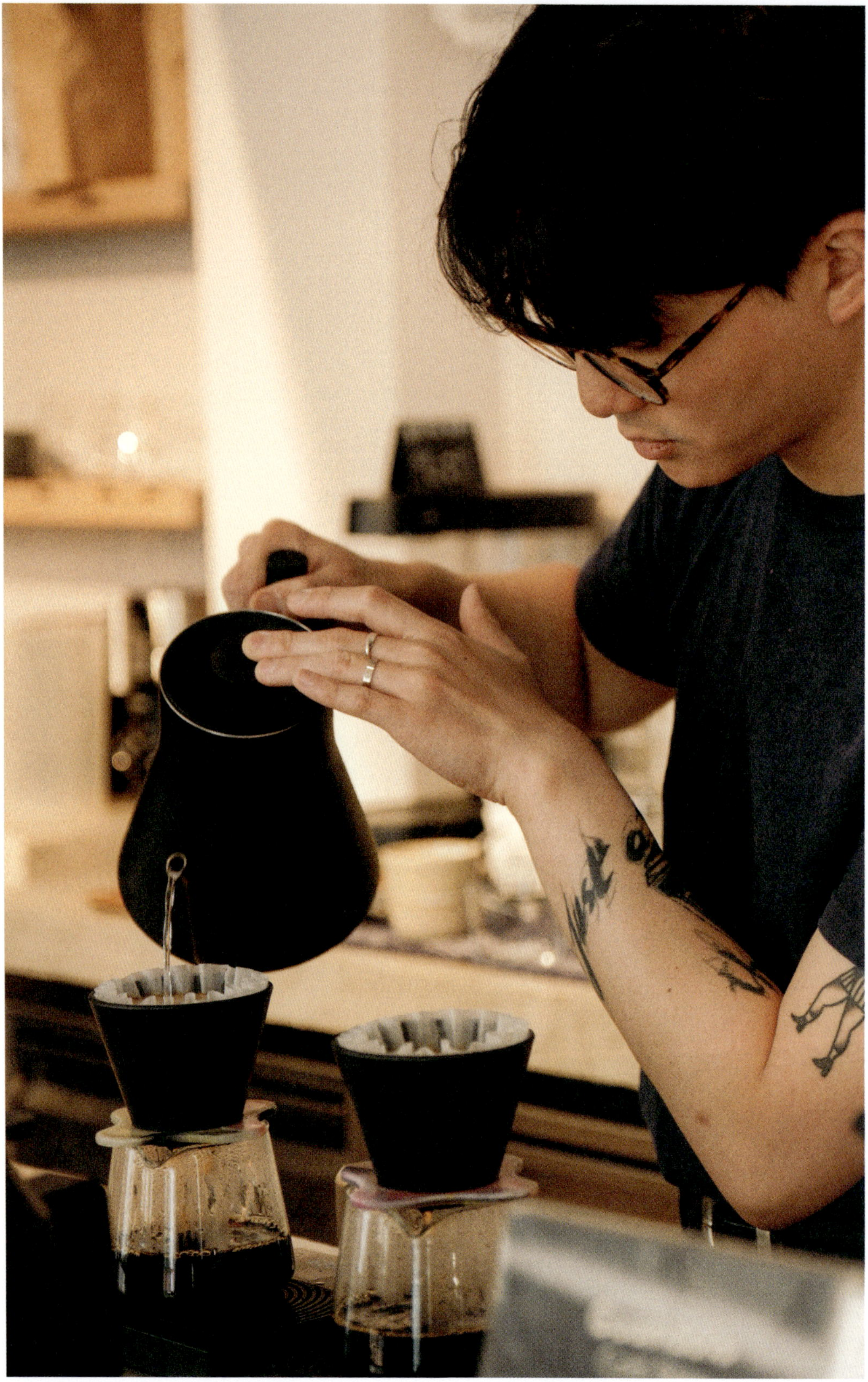

134 JONAS REINDL COFFEE ROASTERS

Westbahnstrasse 13, 1070 Vienna, Austria

TO VISIT BEFORE YOU DIE BECAUSE

Enjoy a fine espresso at this young roastery, on a mission to update the city's coffee traditions by serving amazing coffee without the snobbism.

As well as its historic cafés, Vienna is home to a new generation of coffee houses, including speciality coffee company Jonas Reindl Coffee Roasters. Founder Philip Feyer opened its first café in 2014, in Schottentor, a historical landmark and a transport hub known as Jonas' Pan by the locals. A roastery followed a few years later, securing the quality and direct trade of every delicious cup. 'We aim to be an institution in our own niche of high-quality, light roast brews, valuing new ideas and creativity, while keeping Vienna's café culture and its timelessness somewhere in the corner of our eye,' explains the team. Designed by Philip with cosiness and timelessness in mind, using vintage pieces and natural materials, the flagship café and roastery serves a signature espresso named Misty Mountain, sourced from Finca Los Alpes in Nicaragua, as well as a rotating line-up ranging from co-fermented wild cards to clean geisha. The brand's coffee bags come adorned with public domain artworks made by artists with a connection to Vienna and Austria.

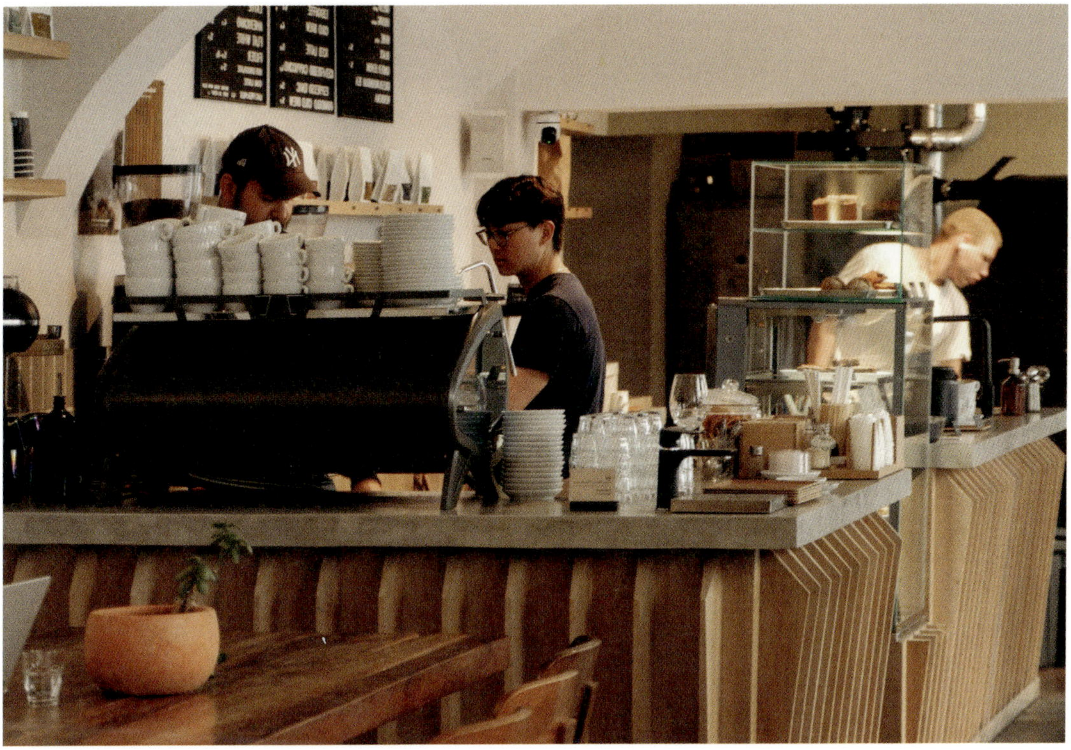

jonasreindl.at

135 SKOOL BEANS CAFÉ

Klettsvegur, 870 Vík, Iceland

TO VISIT BEFORE YOU DIE BECAUSE

Iceland's smallest micro-roaster and first speciality coffee bus is nestled under the mountains of the Katla UNESCO geopark.

The small coastal village of Vík in southern Iceland is known for its black-sand beaches, volcanos, dramatic landscape... and, more unexpectedly, this cute little café housed in an old American school bus. Skool Beans Coffee was opened by Holly Keyser, a British glacier guide who was inspired by her time in Melbourne. She saved the bright yellow bus (left over from a US military base that was closed down in the early 2000s) from the scrap heap, and set out to work with the help of her family, and the cuddles of her ginger cat, Sir Jeffarious. After a slow start during the pandemic, customers including Iceland's president and Brad Pitt (although they were too busy to serve him...) have been queuing up for the high-quality coffees, excellent chai-spresso, and Glam Slam Shablam, a super special – and expensive – hot chocolate topped with gold leaf and edible flowers. Skool Beans is closed in the deep winter months (December to March), when the snow engulfs the bus.

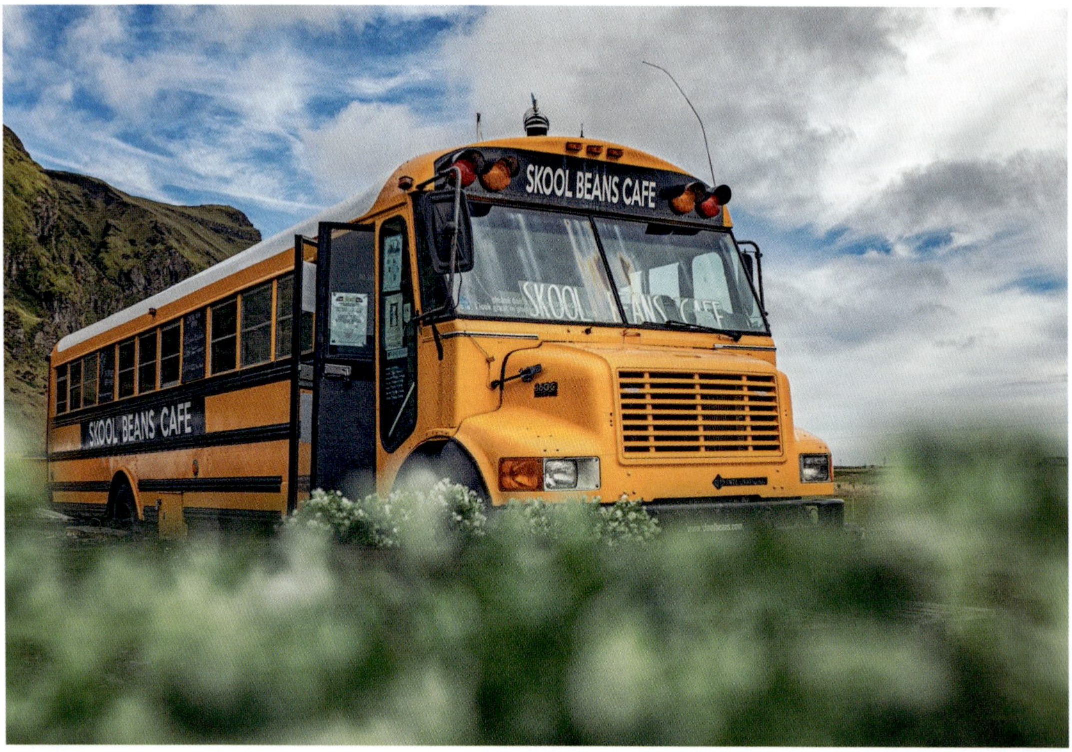

skoolbeans.com +354 830 0079

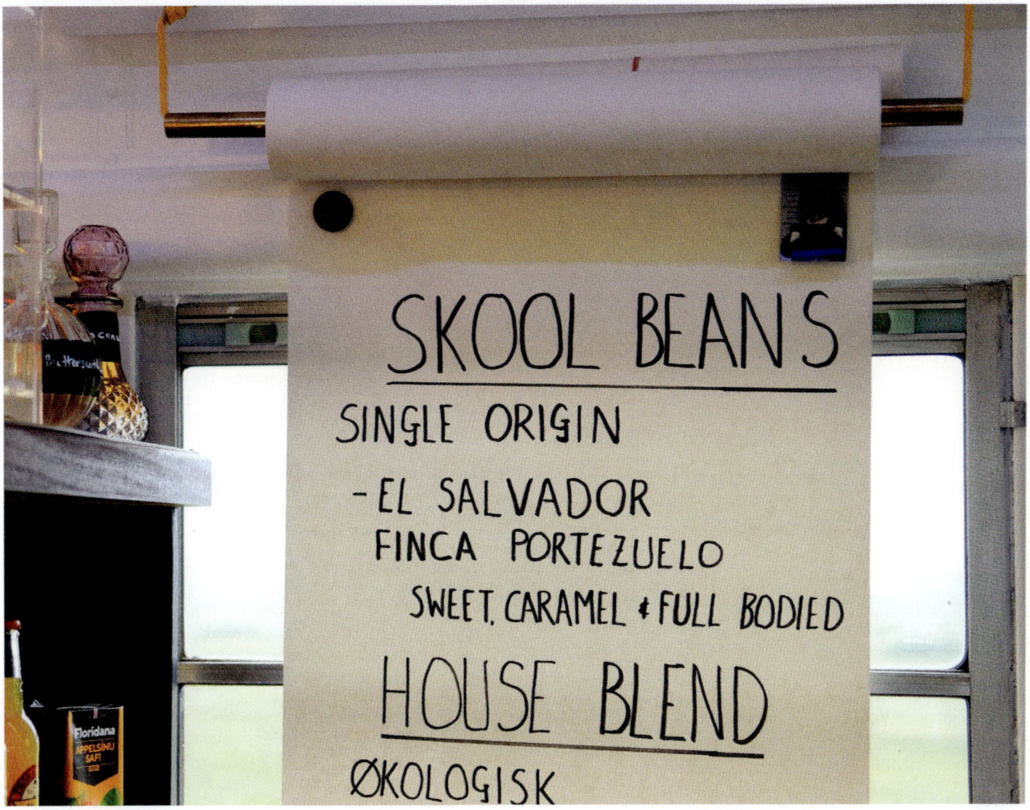
SKOOL BEANS
SINGLE ORIGIN
-EL SALVADOR
FINCA PORTEZUELO
SWEET, CARAMEL & FULL BODIED
HOUSE BLEND
ØKOLOGISK
Floridana
APPELSINU
SAFI

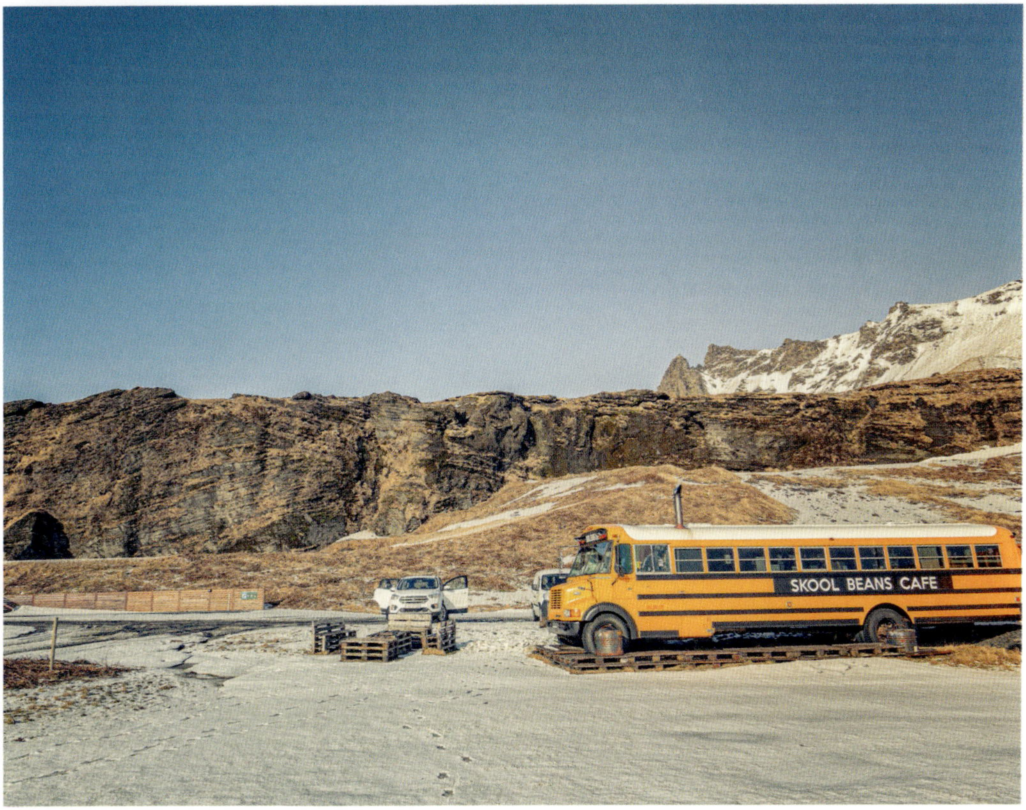
SKOOL BEANS CAFE

136 CROOKED NOSE & COFFEE STORIES

V. Kudirkos g. 6, Vilnius, 03105, Lithuania

TO VISIT BEFORE YOU DIE BECAUSE

This friendly micro-roaster and coffee school specialises in the 'rarest coffees for the most curious noses'.

Emanuelis and Inga first started out in the coffee world by opening a slow café, where they experimented with a signature coffee maker created from wood and linen filters. Passionate and super knowledgeable, they then decided to pivot to a coffee school, sharing their love for the mighty bean in a beautiful minimalist home created by Inga, an interior designer by trade. A coffee school, roastery and concept coffee shop under one roof, the space is used for events, so although you cannot order a cup of coffee here, you can join one of the many tasting sessions and workshops. Recent weekend sessions have focused on making a good espresso, using the iconic La Marzocco Linea Mini Machine, and a coffee and food pairing masterclass. Or else, simply come to stock up on great coffee. 'During the week we are open as a shop where you can come, choose, discuss all coffee topics and buy our freshly roasted beans or some other curated products,' explains Emanuelis, who is the author of an excellent new book, *Let There Be Coffee*.

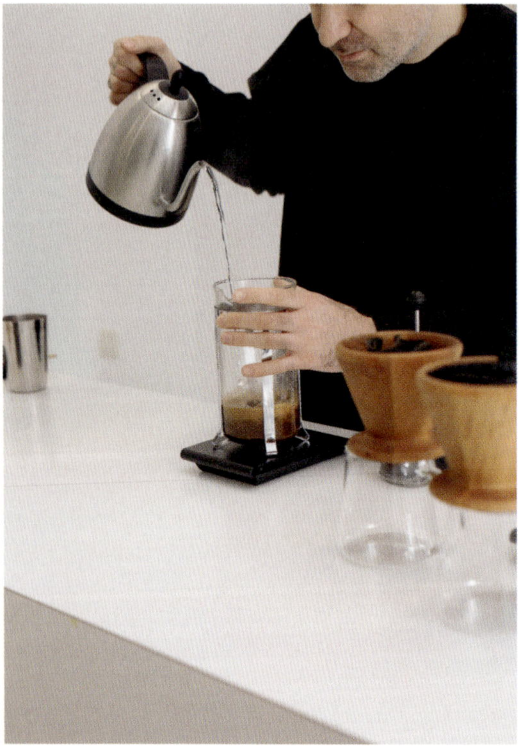

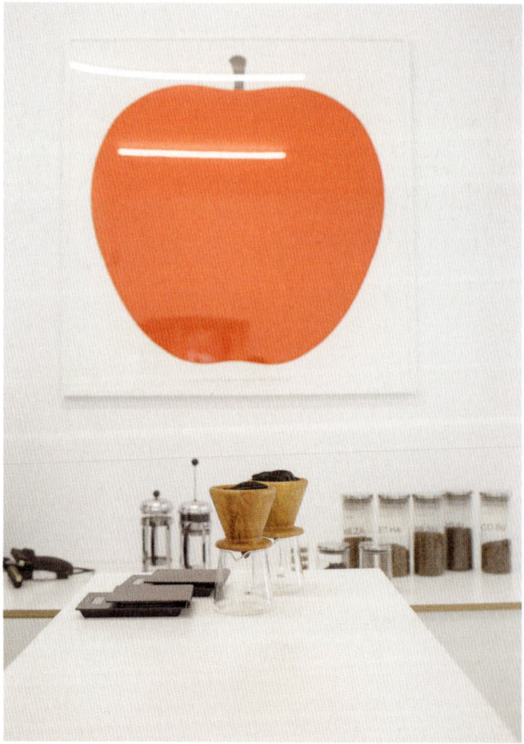

crooked-nose.com

+370 6708 1803

137 LUTA

Ul. Radoslava Lopašića 14, 10000, Zagreb, Croatia

TO VISIT BEFORE YOU DIE BECAUSE

In just three years, this neighbourhood multi-roaster has become a magnet for those in search of rare beans, a fun atmosphere and sports buddies.

Since opening in 2022, Luta has quickly become a favourite among Zagreb's coffee fans thanks to an ever-changing selection featuring coffee from the likes of La Cabra (page 139), Prolog (page 162) and Friedhats (page 143). Brothers Matej and Danijel Losić, together with Neven Kamenski, opened the café 'out of love, more as a hobby', but spent months perfecting their concept and built the entire place, from the bar to the terrace, by themselves. Luta generally offers three options for espresso: a basic one with a classic flavour profile; a fresher, citrusy option; and a more experimental one (anaerobic, fermented) served as a double espresso. The menu and the interiors are constantly being updated; whether it's a new roaster from the other side of the world, or a fresh coat of paint, it keeps things lively and creative. The trio – all endurance sports fans who have lived in Canada and the US – have also started a running club, and their café is a hub for cycling and running enthusiasts.

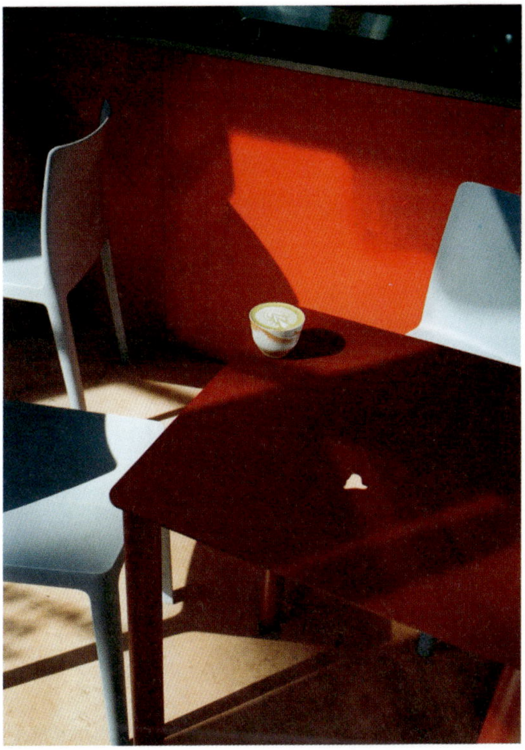

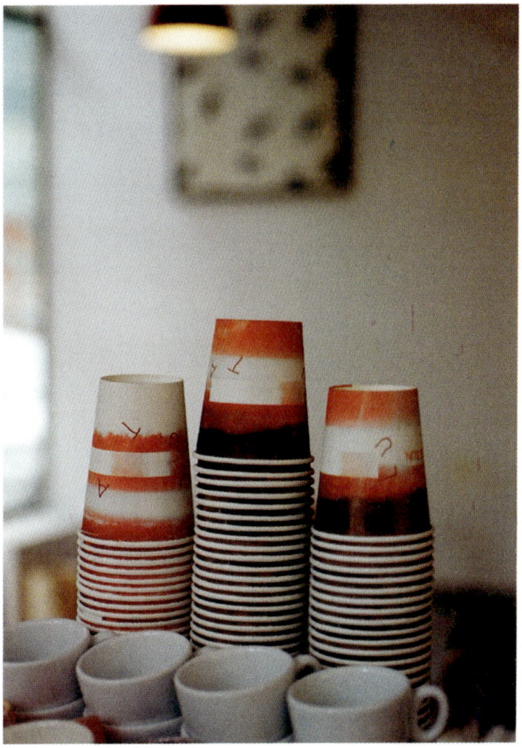

@luta.coffee

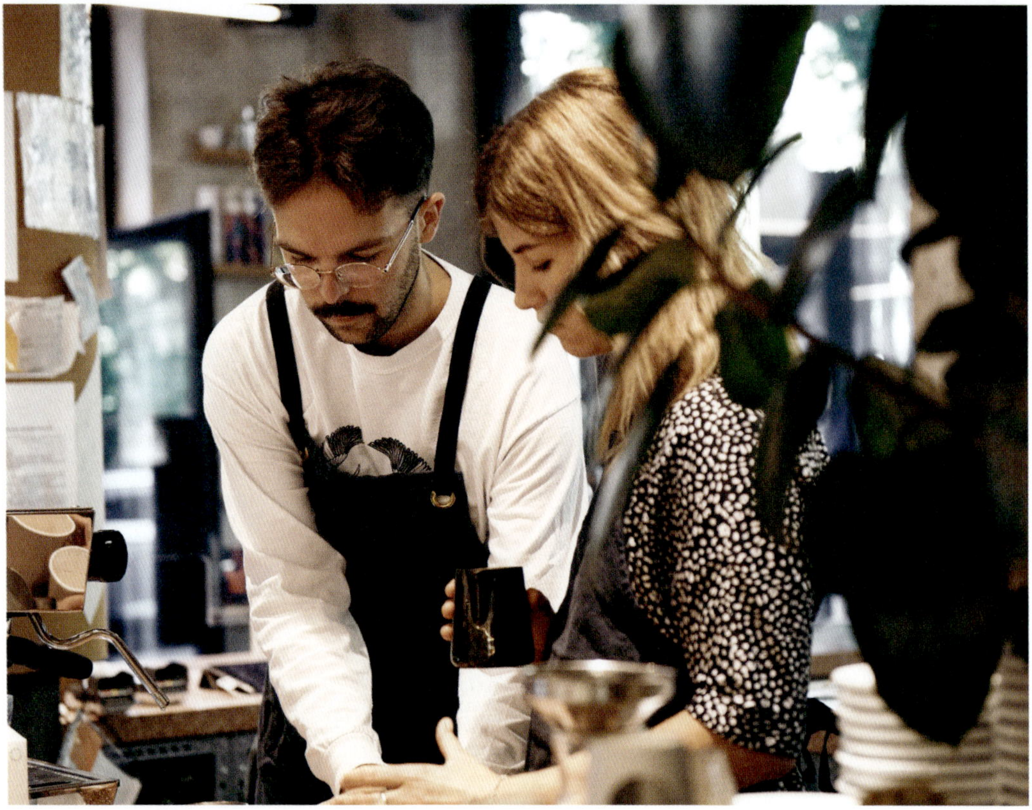

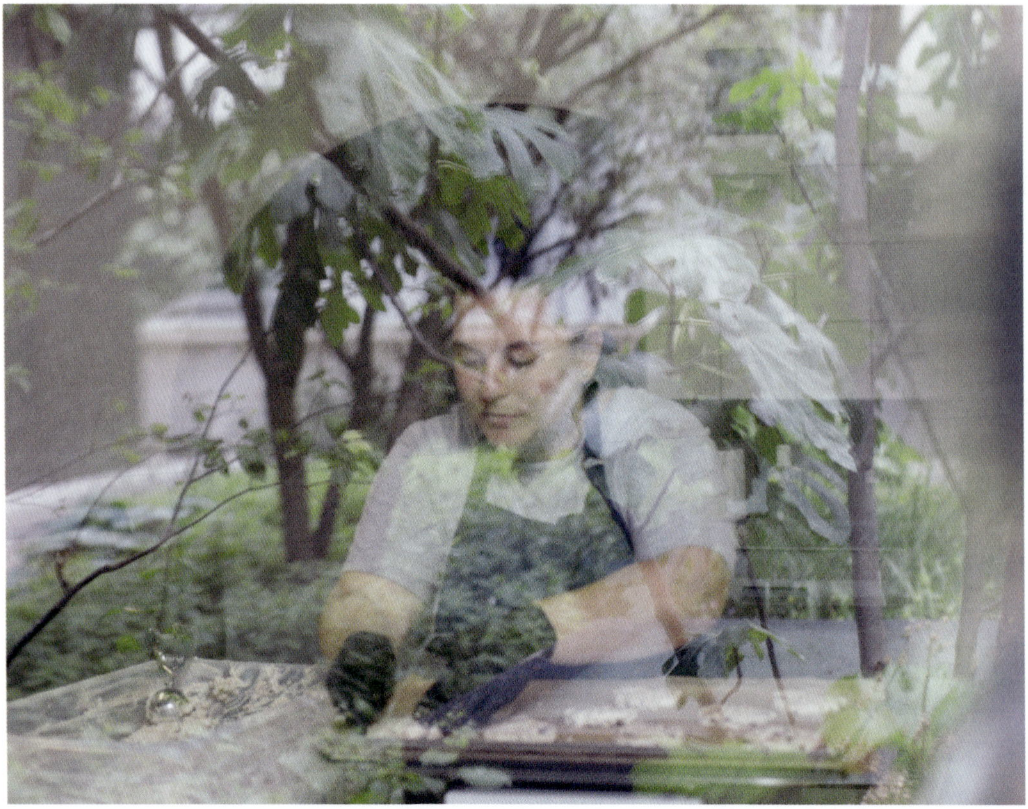

138 MIRÓ

Brauerstrasse 58, 8004 Zurich, Switzerland

TO VISIT BEFORE YOU DIE BECAUSE

Switzerland's Roaster of the Year 2025 has gone from coffee truck to coffee shop in just over a decade.

Boutique roastery Miró Manufactura de Café was founded in 2013 by Dani and David Sanchez after Dani got hooked on speciality coffee in Australia. Inspired by their Spanish roots and Melbourne's coffee scene, they started with a coffee cart and 5kg Probat roaster in a small garage in the suburbs of Zurich. They now have two shops and this flagship café, all serving only seasonal, direct-trade coffee of the highest quality. Its minimalist interiors are complemented by a courtyard terrace and temporary art exhibitions, while the design and architectural elements are the result of a competition with the local students at the ETH Zurich university. The espresso-based drinks are joined by three types of filter coffee and a range of cold brew and iced coffees. There are croissants, banana bread and chocolate brioches, as well as a full brunch menu of French toast and breakfast burritos at the weekend. Miró also offers workshops and masterclasses to help 'today's coffee lovers become future espresso baristas, filter nerds and latte artists'.

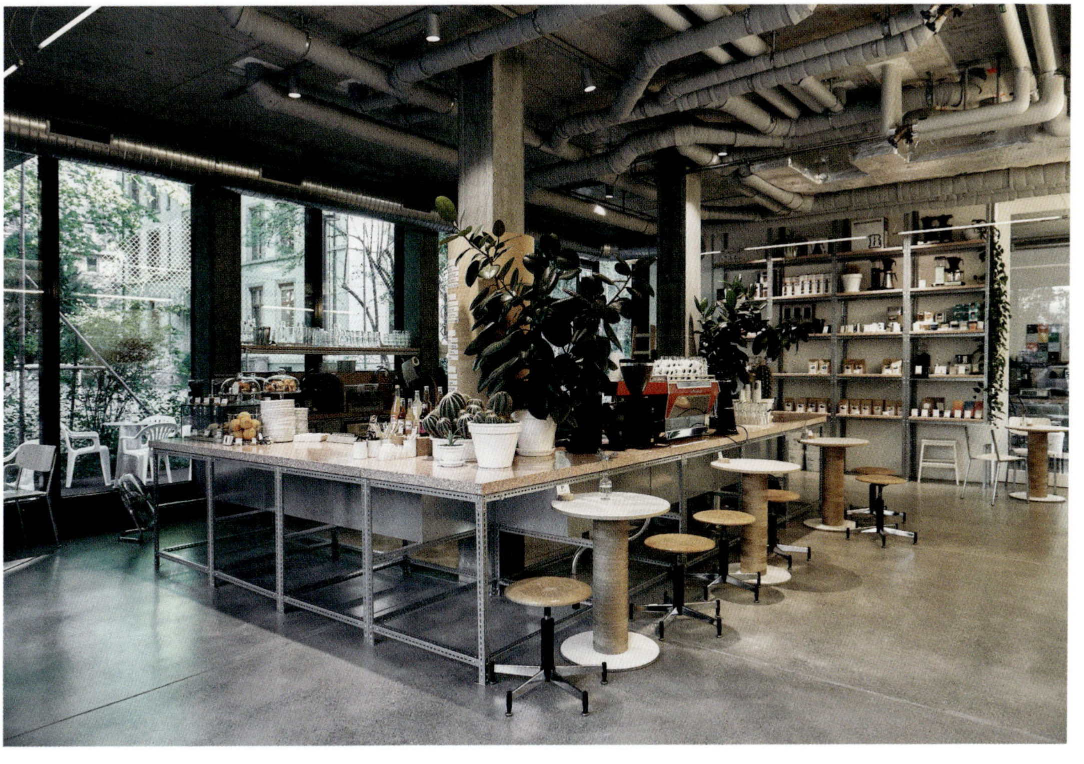

mirocoffee.co

+41 43 548 35 37

139 D.O.S.E ON HIGH

5 High St, Auckland Central, Auckland 1010, New Zealand

TO VISIT BEFORE YOU DIE BECAUSE

This dark and intimate espresso bar concocts creative fruit-infused coffees and cocktails designed to make you feel good.

Stepping into D.O.S.E ON HIGH is like diving into a cup of smooth espresso: the minimalist space has black walls, a long black counter and an all-black coffee machine. Yet instead of bringing you down, it's an invigorating, joyful place; its name refers to both the addictive qualities of good coffee, and to happy hormones – dopamine, oxytocin, serotonin and endorphin. The (black-capped) dealers behind this espresso bar are Reinaldo Tanudjaja and Connie Chung, who have shaken and stirred their love for Japanese-style cocktail bars to create this unique space, making the most of Reinaldo's barista training and bartending expertise. They are known for not only their excellent espressos but also their fruit-infused seasonal creations, such as a nashi pear and kiwi-infused cold brew topped with honey miso foam and freeze-dried manuka honey, or a grapefruit and thyme coffee milk punch. Simpler pleasures include a near-perfect flat white with Jersey milk from the Lewis Road Creamery and bite-sized *canelés*. Whatever you decide to go for, you're sure to leave on a high.

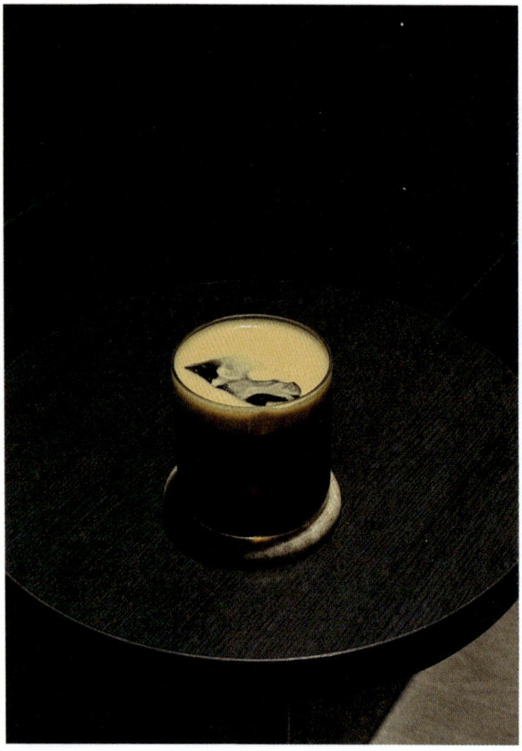

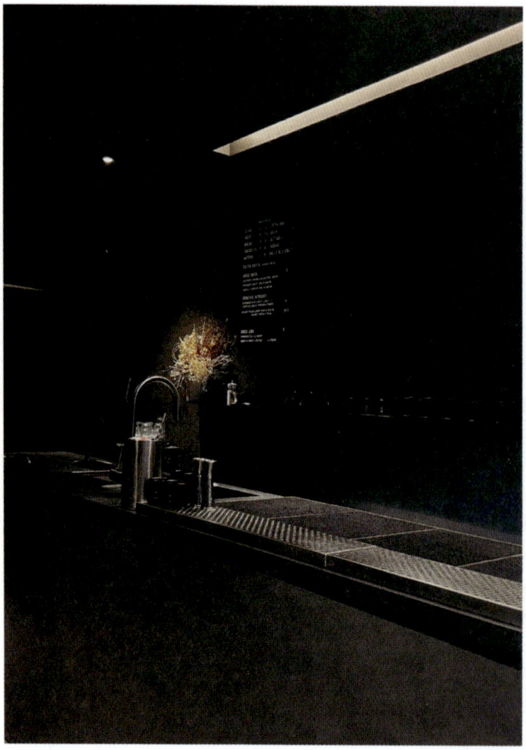

@d.o.s.eonhigh

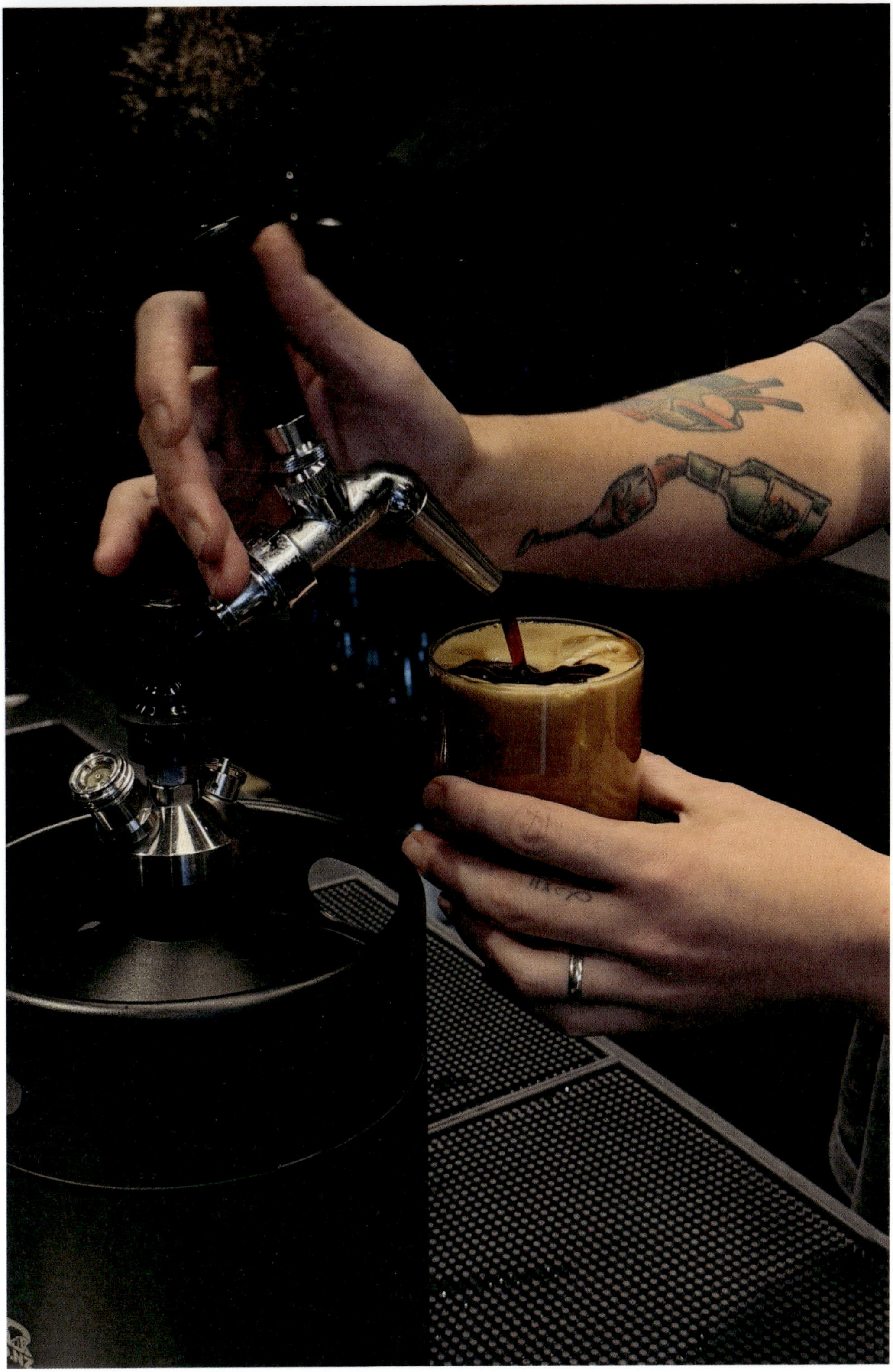

140 ESPRESSO STUDIO BY FUSHOKEN

6/82 Cashel St, Christchurch 8011, New Zealand

TO VISIT BEFORE YOU DIE BECAUSE

An award-winning barista calls the shots at this small but mighty takeaway-only coffee shop in Christchurch's CBD.

Two shots are not simply enough for this Riverside Market stalwart, which has been serving its 'triple shot standard' coffee to loyal CBD workers since 2019. This bolder, stronger coffee experience is the work of Fumi Takai, a Tokyo native who never says no to a long black, and started coffee making as a hobby before opening his own little coffee stall. He's won Barista of the Year at the Canterbury Hospitality Awards for three consecutive years, so expect a small queue during the morning rush. 'Our beans come from local roasters the Lyttelton Coffee Company,' says Fumi. 'I love their Ethiopia Single Origin as it has a great fruity flavour, and we use it for black coffee.' Bestselling items on the short menus include classic long black coffee and flat white, ever-popular matcha lattes, and brownies from Badass Brownies, another local supplier. A strong coffee and brownie, followed by a walk along the river to the botanic gardens – sounds like the perfect morning treat.

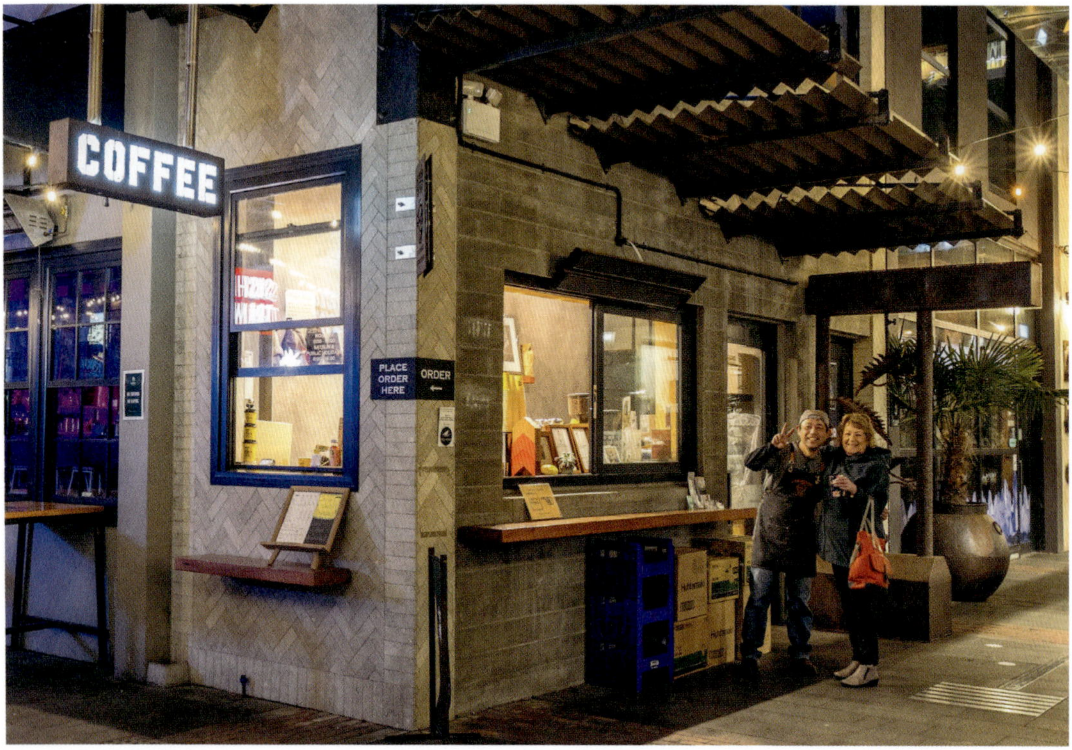

@espressostudiobyfushoken

141 SKYBURY CAFE & ROASTERY

136 Ivicevic Rd, Paddy's Green, Queensland 4880, Australia

TO VISIT BEFORE YOU DIE BECAUSE

Gain an insight into the craft of Australian coffee and sample award-winning coffee liqueurs at this delightful plantation café with treetop views.

Australia is home to many coffee plantations, and the oldest of all can be found in the Atherton Tablelands near Cairns, a region that offers the perfect conditions for coffee growing. It is here that for over twenty years the family-owned plantation Skybury has been producing its bourbon coffee, known for its dark chocolate aroma, buttery mouthfeel and nutty taste with hints of caramel and citrus. First opened in 2006, the café and roastery was born out of a vision 'to share our favourite family gathering spot, a place where we would toast the end of a rewarding day tending the coffee plantation,' says general manager Candy MacLaughlin. 'It began as a dream to let others experience that same sense of connection to the land.' Take in the lush scenery and try the house roast, along with a whole range of homemade goodies (including a delicious affogato and Skybury Espresso Liqueur), as well as dishes showcasing the farm's other speciality, the papaya. Visit in October to see Skybury's 90,000 coffee trees in bloom.

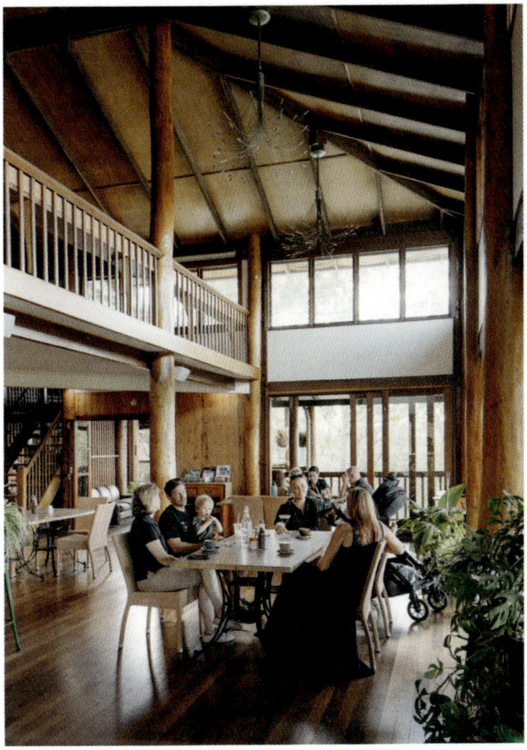

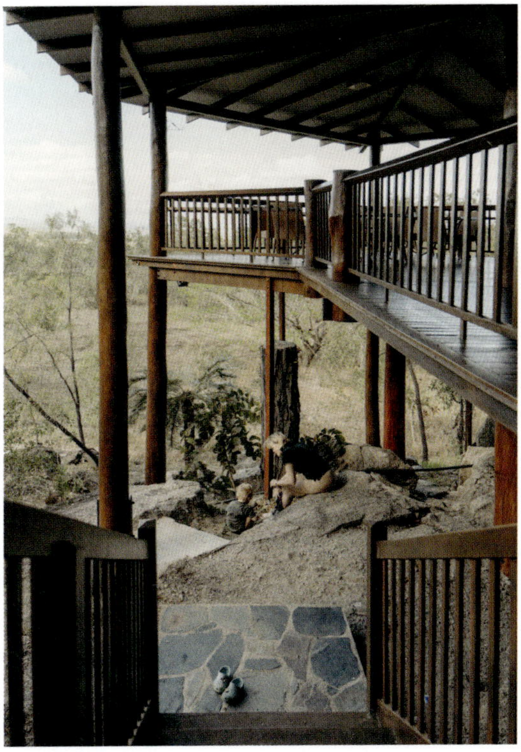

skybury.com.au

142 AUNTY PEG'S

200 Wellington St, Collingwood, Victoria 3066, Australia

TO VISIT BEFORE YOU DIE BECAUSE

The roastery tasting bar of Melbourne institution Proud Mary offers 'a unique and pure coffee experience' for black coffee lovers.

Founded by husband and wife Nolan and Shari Hirte in 2009, Proud Mary won a Golden Bean Award for its Ghost Rider blend only a few years later. Just a short walk from its original café in Collingwood is Aunty Peg's, a tasting bar and roastery opened in 2014 in an old carpet factory. Designed as a gateway to the world of Proud Mary Coffee Roasters, it serves exclusively black coffee and offers tasting flights, regular cuppings and tasting events. Named after Nolan's nana, a matriarch known for her boundless hospitality and legendary baking, the café is designed for customers to 'learn the art of brewing with expert baristas, stock up on premium beans, and find top-notch coffee equipment'. Staff favourites include Geisha Town, while the deluxe pour-over menu includes papayo from Colombia and arara from Brazil. Showcased coffees can range from a snap chill from Kenya and Ethiopia to an espresso from the Elida Estate, Panama and a bourbon from Café Garmas, Peru.

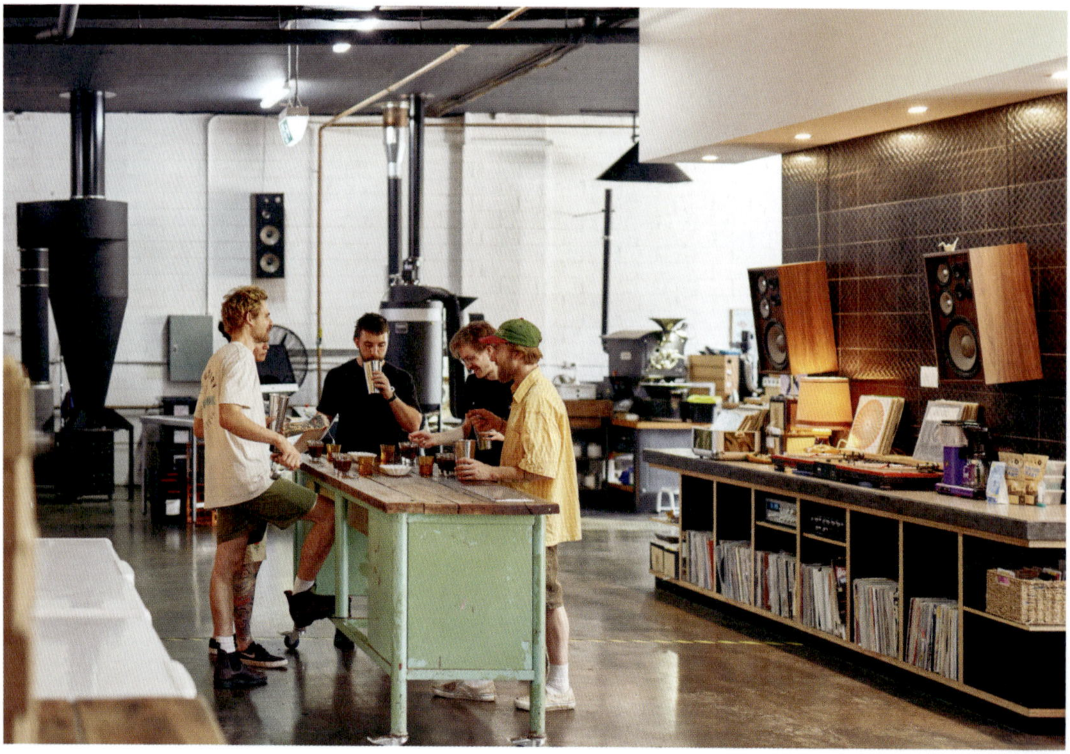

proudmarycoffee.com.au

143 MANTA RAY

12 Beech St, Nunawading, Victoria 3131, Australia

TO VISIT BEFORE YOU DIE BECAUSE

This award-winning roastery turns the art of coffee into a cinematic spectacle, in a beautifully designed warehouse on the outskirts of Melbourne.

A former mechanics workshop in the suburb of Nunawading is the unlikely location for this stunning café. Manta Ray is a dream come true for founder Gao Chuan, also known as Vincent, who spent years learning the art of coffee roasting at Melbourne's renowned Code Black. With its polished concrete floor, dark furniture, bonsai and Chinese scholar's rock, it's a great spot for a meditative cup of coffee, observing the working roastery. 'We care about transparency and want anyone curious about our coffee to be able to peer in and see how we operate,' says Vincent from behind his Kees Van Der Westen Slim Jim – the Rolls-Royce of espresso machines. 'Feel free to ask any of our staff about our beans or the fancy gear that we have on the bar, including recipes or advice for brewing at home.' The espresso bar serves an Outsider Blend and Seasonal Blend; the brew bar offers a rotating roster of single-origin filters; and the attention to detail extends to a range of sweet and savoury treats.

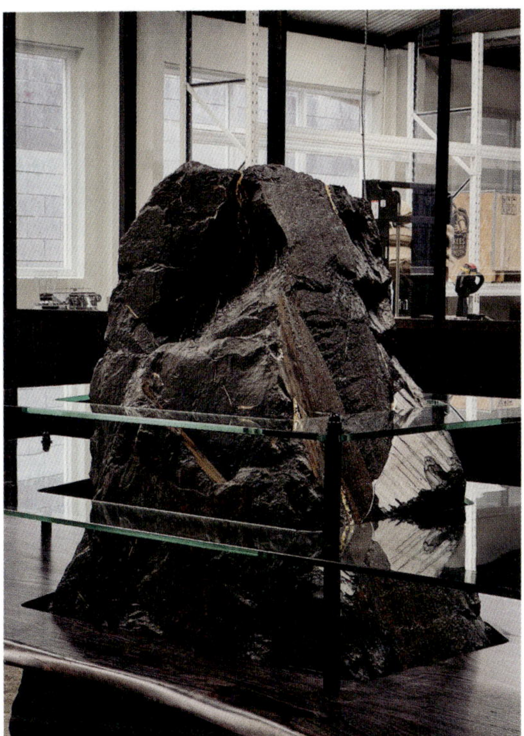

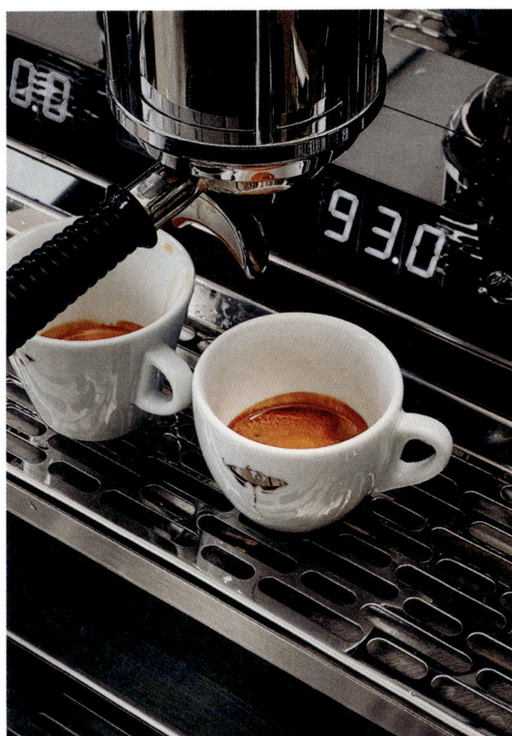

mantaraycoffee.com.au

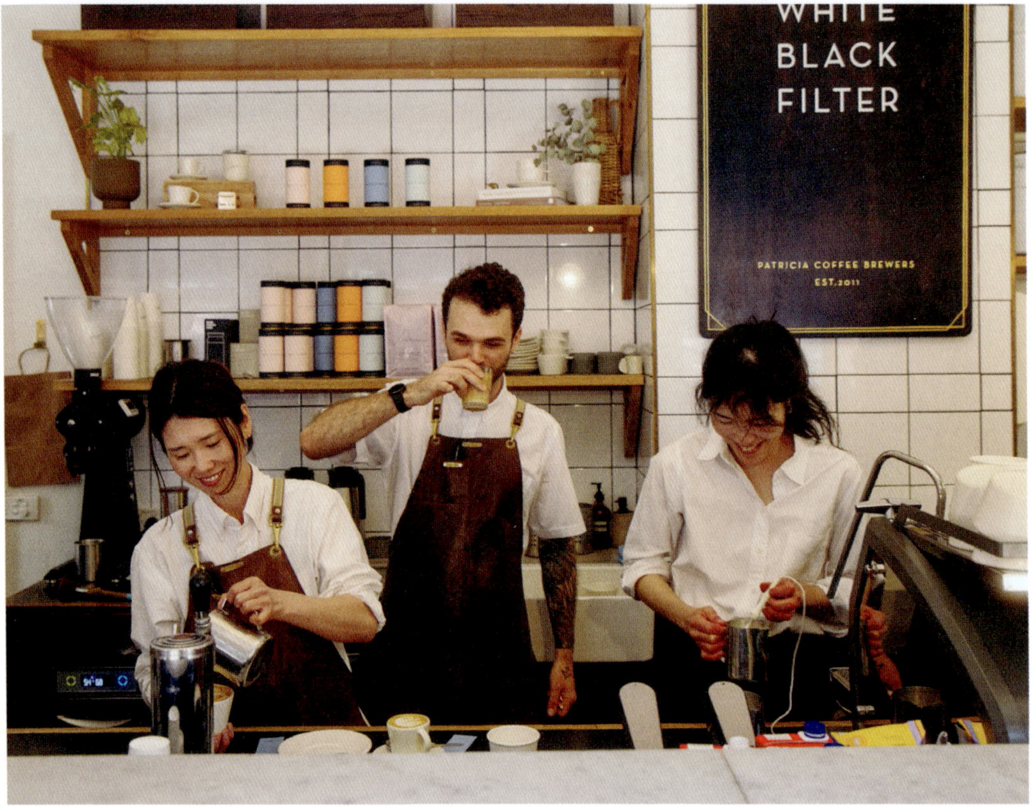
WHITE
BLACK
FILTER
PATRICIA COFFEE BREWERS
EST. 2011

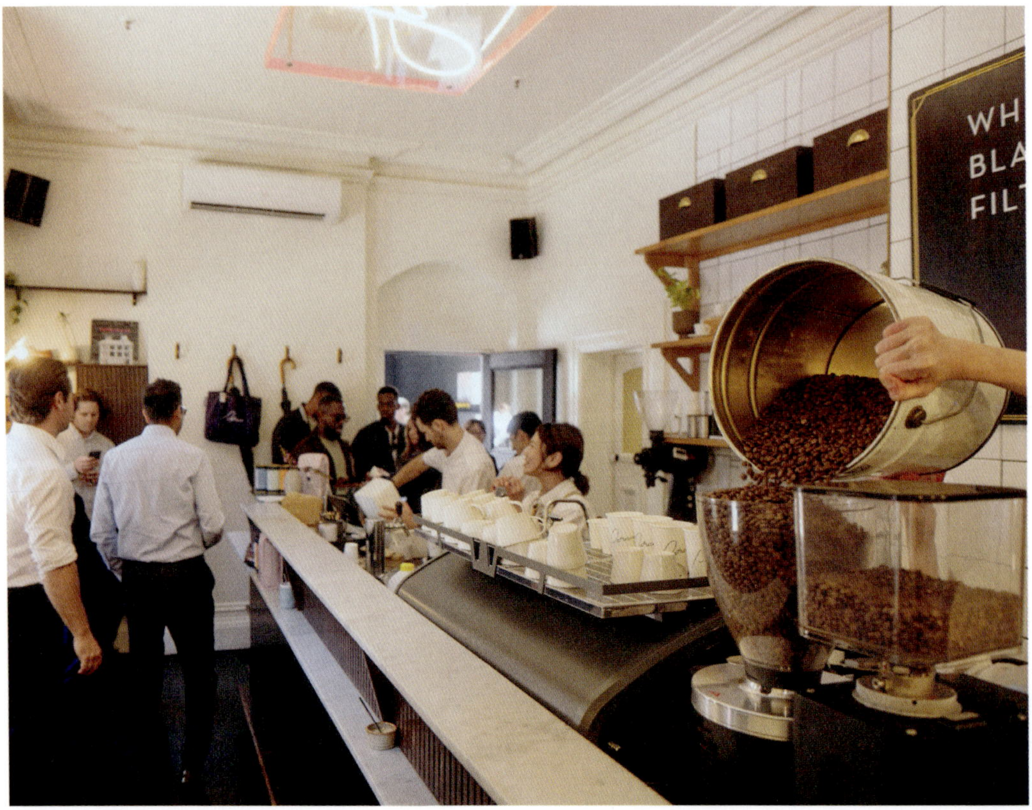

144 PATRICIA COFFEE BREWERS

Rear of 493-495 Little Bourke St, Melbourne, Victoria 3000, Australia

TO VISIT BEFORE YOU DIE BECAUSE

Hidden away in a little alleyway in Melbourne's CBD, this standing room-only café is much loved for its atmosphere and friendly service.

A coffee-drinking crowd hanging around and chatting on the street, some perched on simple plastic crates, will help you find this tiny café with a big reputation. Founded in 2011 by best friends Bowen Holden and Pip Heath, and named after their respective grandmothers, Patricia Coffee Brewers started out by showcasing coffee from local roasters such as Seven Seeds, before roasting their own beans at Fieldwork. In 2024, Patricia moved to their own roastery and started roasting all of their coffee on a Loring S15 Falcon. They now offer a full menu of their own espresso and filter coffees, which are available behind the bar, online and through their coffee subscription Accompanying these are a range of treats from favourite Melbourne bakeries including Mörk and Sucette. Although it gets very busy, everything runs smoothly and efficiently thanks to the amazing team of welcoming baristas. 'The utmost care is taken to be present and connected with anyone who has gone out of their way to visit us,' say the founders. 'We sincerely hope that if you come and see us, you can tell.'

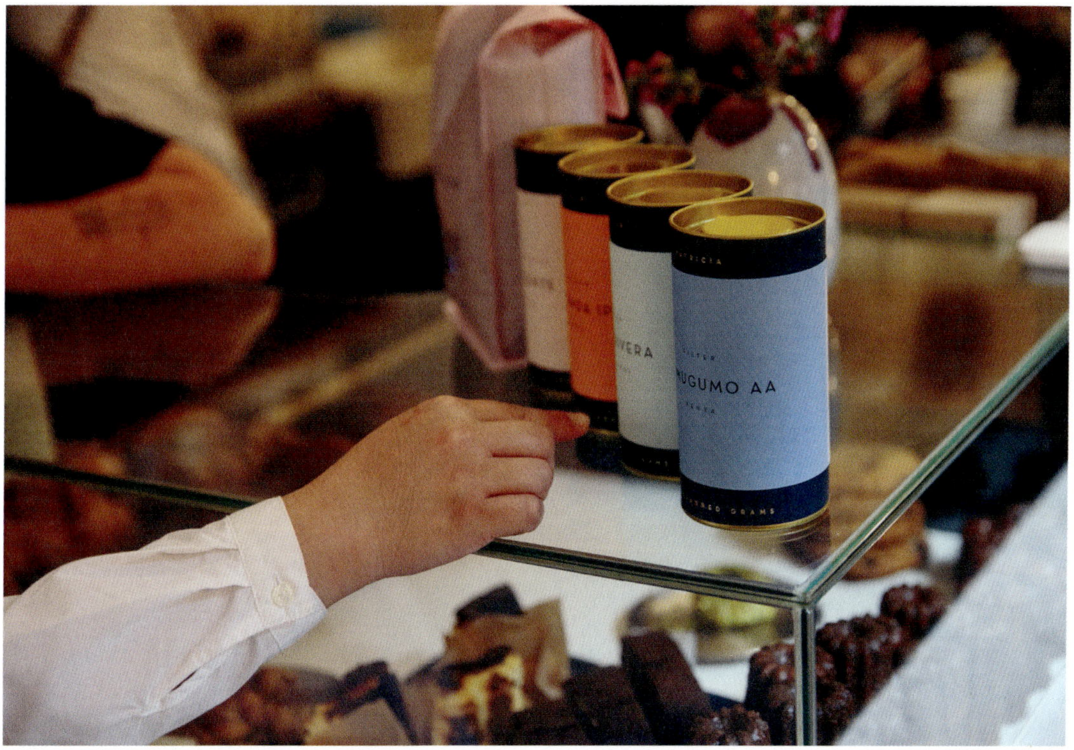

patriciacoffee.com.au

145 COMMUNITY COFFEE SUBIACO

292a Barker Rd, Subiaco, Western Australia 6008, Australia

TO VISIT BEFORE YOU DIE BECAUSE

This urban hideaway in a converted warehouse is dedicated to meticulously roasted beans and a friendly, community-centric vibe.

'Community Coffee Co began as a discreet espresso bar and roastery tucked away behind a shopping centre car park,' explains co-owner Michael Roach. 'More than just a coffee shop, it's a local institution built on quality, ambience and a love for all things hospitality. As our name indicates, we are all about the community spirit, creating a casual setting for everyone to enjoy, dogs and family alike, in a place that is local and authentic.' The chilled vibes come with a great coffee menu: the roasters are renowned for their in-house offering, sold all around Australia under the name Loot Coffee. They include Sunrise, roasted especially for milk-based coffee, using a regional lot such as the Mantiqueira mountains of Brazil, and Werka, 'a bright, juicy and floral' coffee from Ethiopia's West Arsi region. Also popular are the huge sandwiches (the egg sando with chilli sauce is a favourite), the freshly baked treats and Greek specials such as spanakopita.

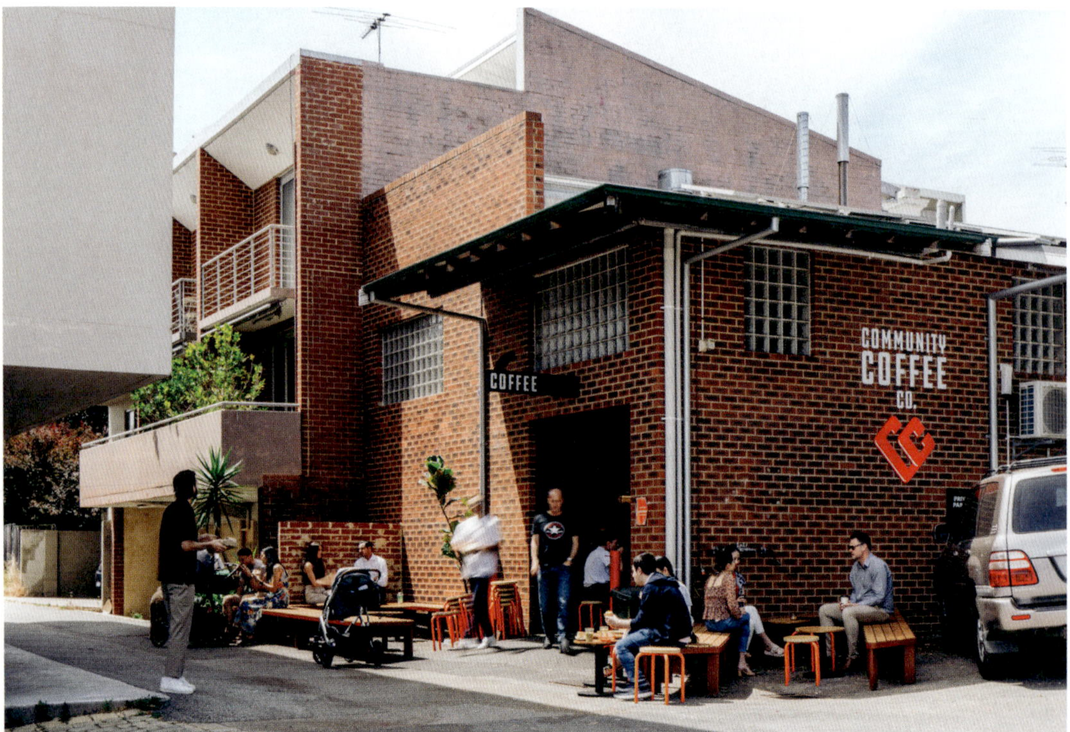

communitycoffee.com.au

146 GENOVESE COFFEE HOUSE

1/3 Lawrence St, Alexandria, New South Wales 2015, Australia

TO VISIT BEFORE YOU DIE BECAUSE

Sample Italian-style espressos and hospitality at this stylish family business, set in a former industrial building in Sydney's Alexandria.

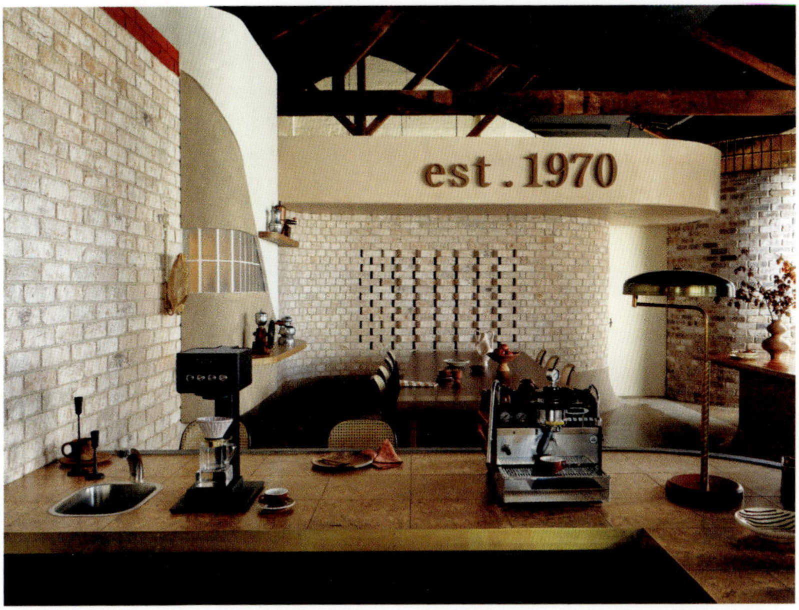

The Italian and Greek immigrants who settled in Australia after the Second World War were instrumental in turning the country into a coffee-loving, flat-white-slurping paradise. Among them was Alfio Genovese, who established his family-owned coffee brand in 1970 after deciding to roast coffee that resembled the true Italian style that he knew and loved. Fifty-five years on, his grandson Adam established the Genovese Coffee House to bring the brand's iconic Melbourne vibe to a new Sydney audience. Referencing 1970s style and the site's industrial heritage, the 300 sq m space in Alexandria was beautifully renovated in 2021 by Alexander &CO. It features reclaimed brickwork, a warm terracotta palette, and an indoor awning inspired by Italian shop fronts. Its Italian roots are clear in the menu, which includes a 'house-baked focaccia that has now achieved, as our customers say, "cult status", and chef Kate's Nonna's biscotti, which sell out daily,' says Adam. 'Another Italian tradition we have brought to Australia is our "caffè al banco" – a standing espresso bar where you can enjoy a quick espresso or macchiato for $2, just like back home.'

genovesecoffeehouse.com.au

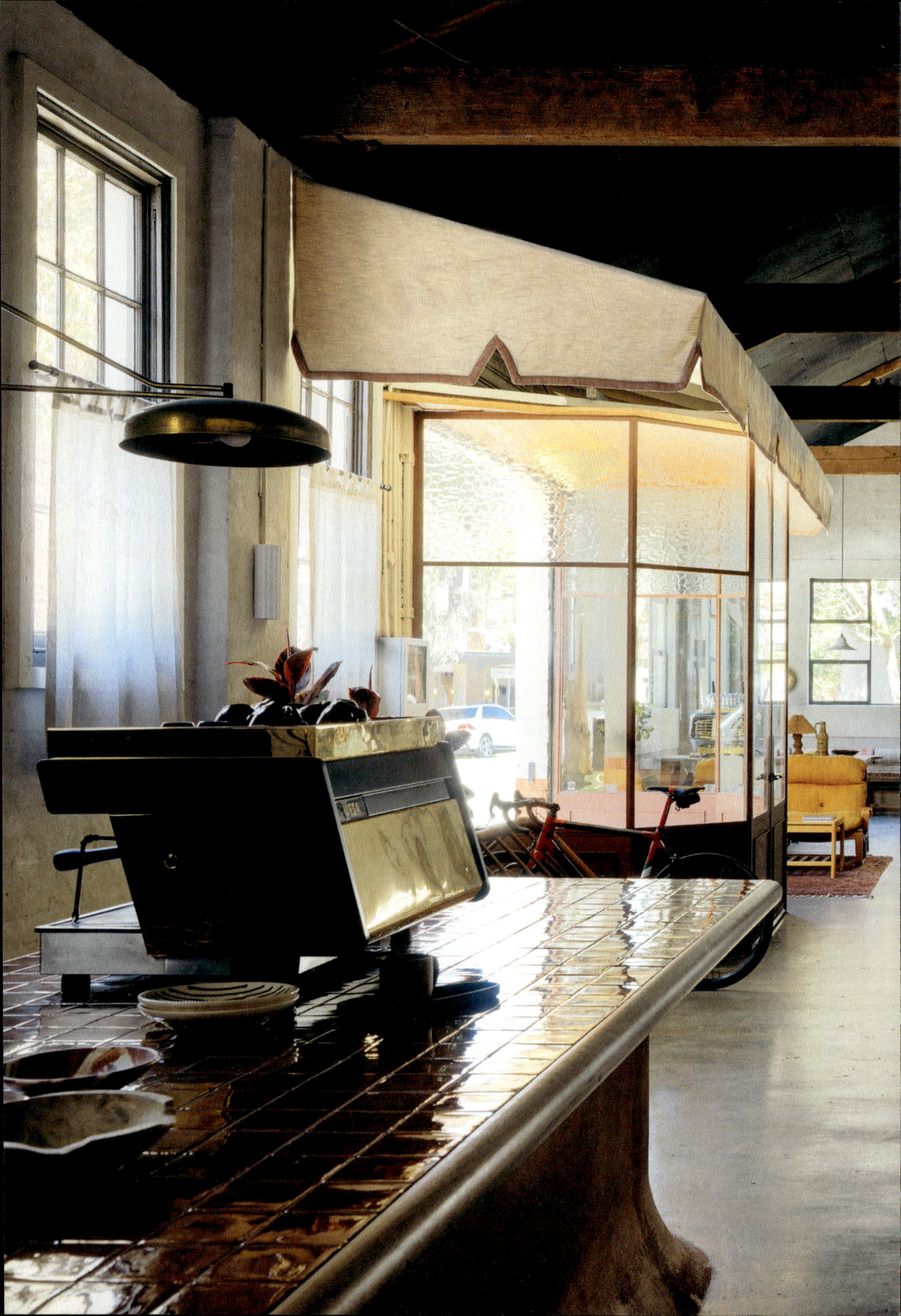

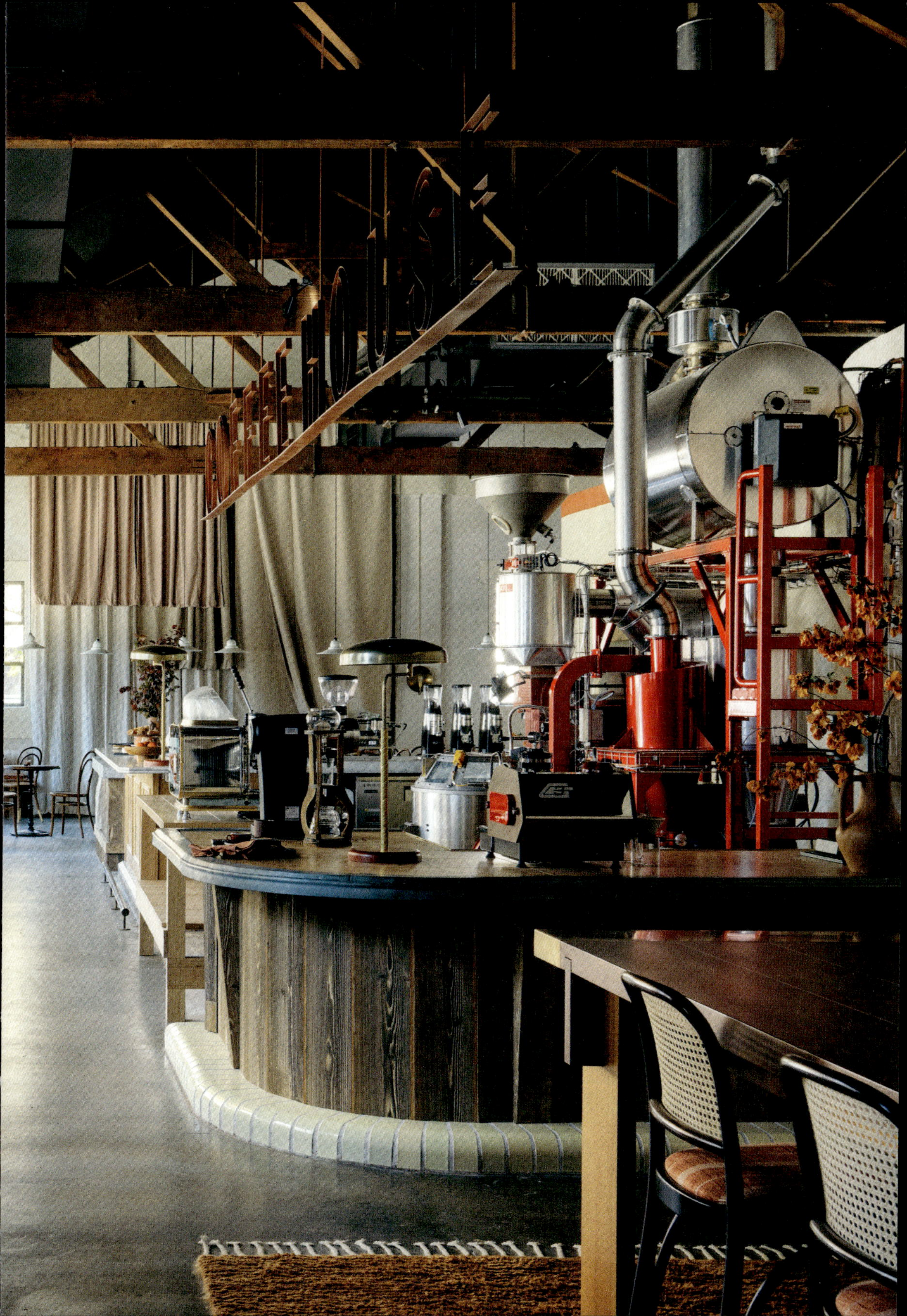
COFFEE HOUSE

147 ONA COFFEE

58/60 Smith St, Marrickville, New South Wales 2204, Australia

TO VISIT
BEFORE YOU DIE
BECAUSE

The showcase coffee bar of Australian speciality coffee roaster ONA boasts a fascinating coffee cellar full of flavoursome treasures.

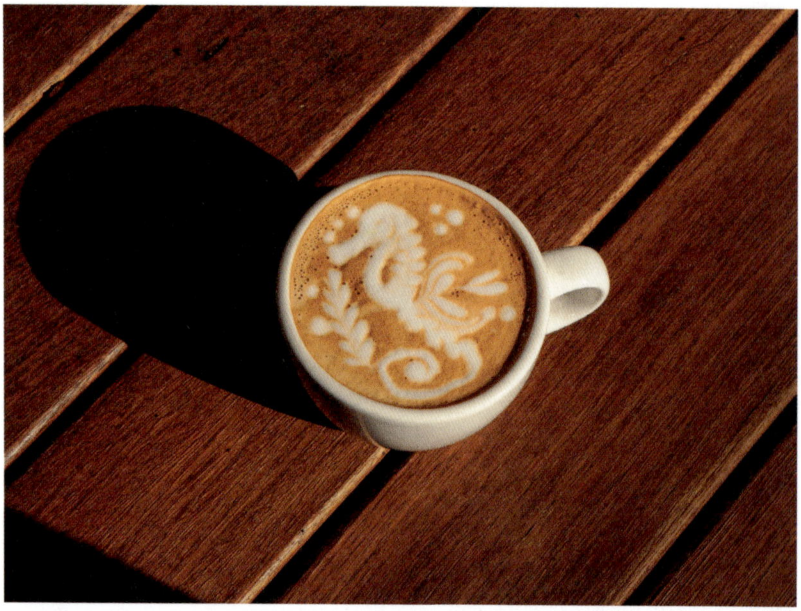

Founded in 2008 by Saša Šestic, who went on to win the 2015 World Barista Champion title, ONA Coffee is dedicated to sharing amazing coffees from around the world, as well as the incredible stories and experiences of the people who grow them. This they do at their five flagship stores, including this outpost in Marrickville, which was dubbed the region's Café of the Year 2025. 'Our approach is simple – we aim to take the best, natural characteristics of coffees from various regions of the world, and share them in the most appropriate format,' says venue manager Bora Jin. ONA's 'coffee cellar' is full of rare and special frozen coffees, while the exhaustive menu includes milk-based house blends such as Aspen Raspberry Candy along with coffees from different origins served as espresso or V60 filter coffee. 'Some of the farms we feature consistently include Panama's Finca Deborah and Iris Estate, which our founder Saša co-owns with Jamison Savage of Finca Deborah, as well as Nicaragua El Árbol, run by our close friends Claudia and Tim,' explains Bora. A French toast with a spicy Korean twist and house-made tiramisu made with ONA's Raspberry Candy espresso are the stars of Roger Peeters' food menu.

onacoffeesydney.com

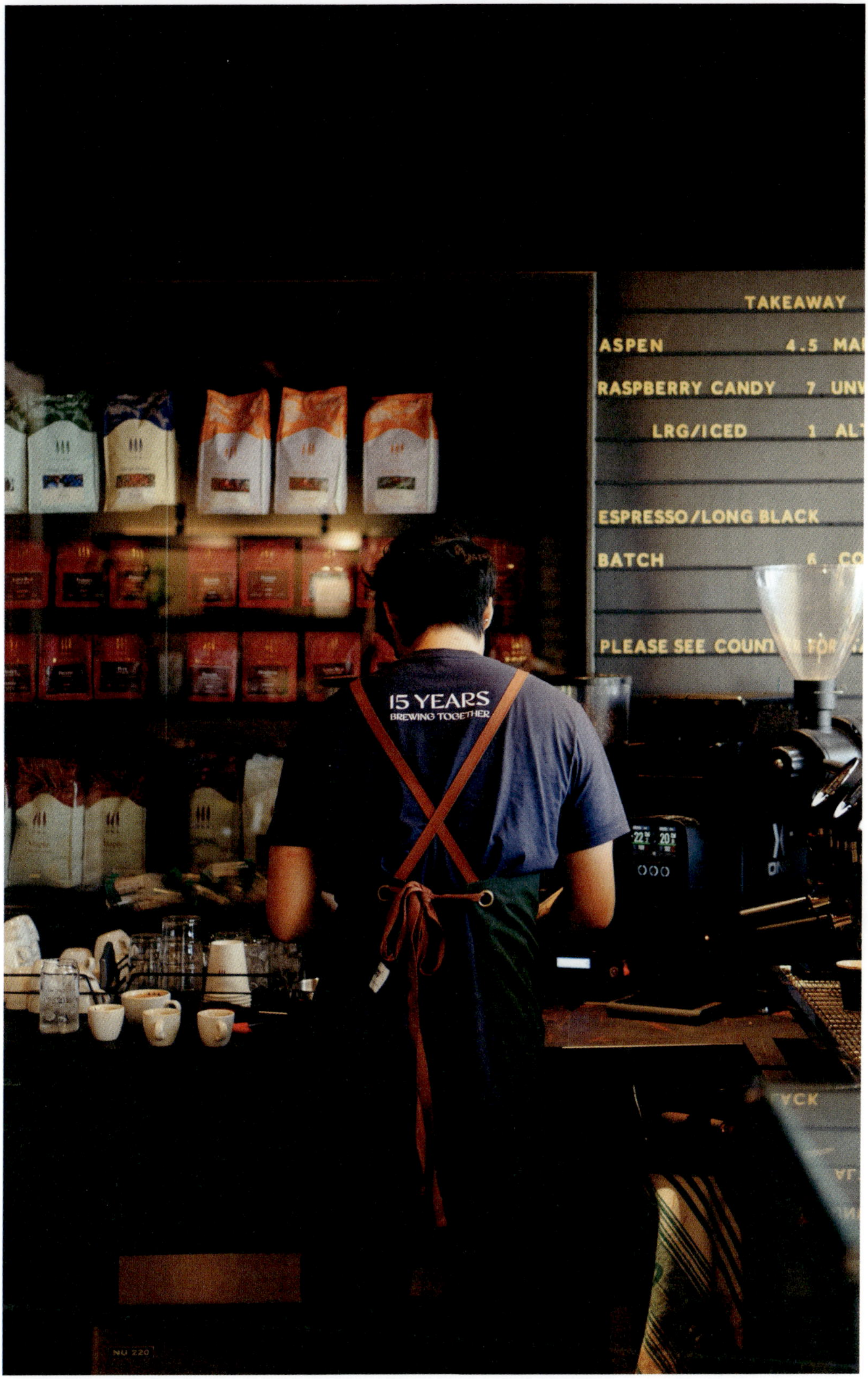
TAKEAWAY
ASPEN 4.5
RASPBERRY CANDY 7
LRG/ICED 1
ESPRESSO/LONG BLACK
BATCH
PLEASE SEE
15 YEARS
BREWING TOGETHER

148 SINGLE O SURRY HILLS

60/64 Reservoir St, Surry Hills, New South Wales 2010, Australia

TO VISIT BEFORE YOU DIE BECAUSE

Enjoy a delicious flat white with Reservoir blend at the bustling café of eco-minded Sydney coffee company Single O.

Established in 2003 by a couple of single-origin lovers escaping the corporate world, Single O's original café continues to thrive and innovate, with clever inventions such as the world's first batch brew bar, Freepour Coffee On Tap. A Certified B Corporation, Single O is embarking on the journey to achieve net zero status by 2030, with past efforts including kickstarting Sydney's largest grounds upcycling program and creating The Juggler Café Milk Tap system, saving over 100 million two-litre plastic milk bottles from the waste stream. As for the coffee itself – well, it's the cream of the crop, with daily flights including the Three Ways (espresso, mini-filter and a flattie); and rotating single-origin coffees from their producer partners. Make sure to try an espresso served in custom-made cups by Malcolm Greenwood, 'big enough to sink your nose into for extra aroma'. As the team says: 'Come for the coffee, stay for the banana bread with espresso butter…' Single O also has outposts in Brisbane and Japan.

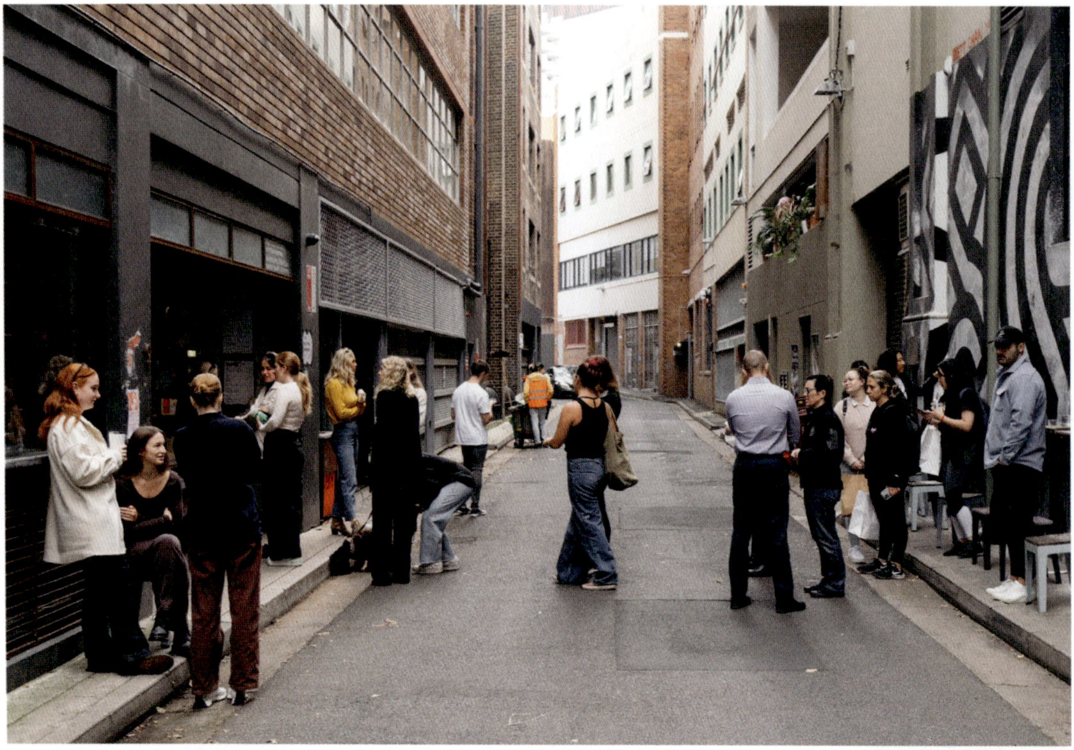

singleo.com.au

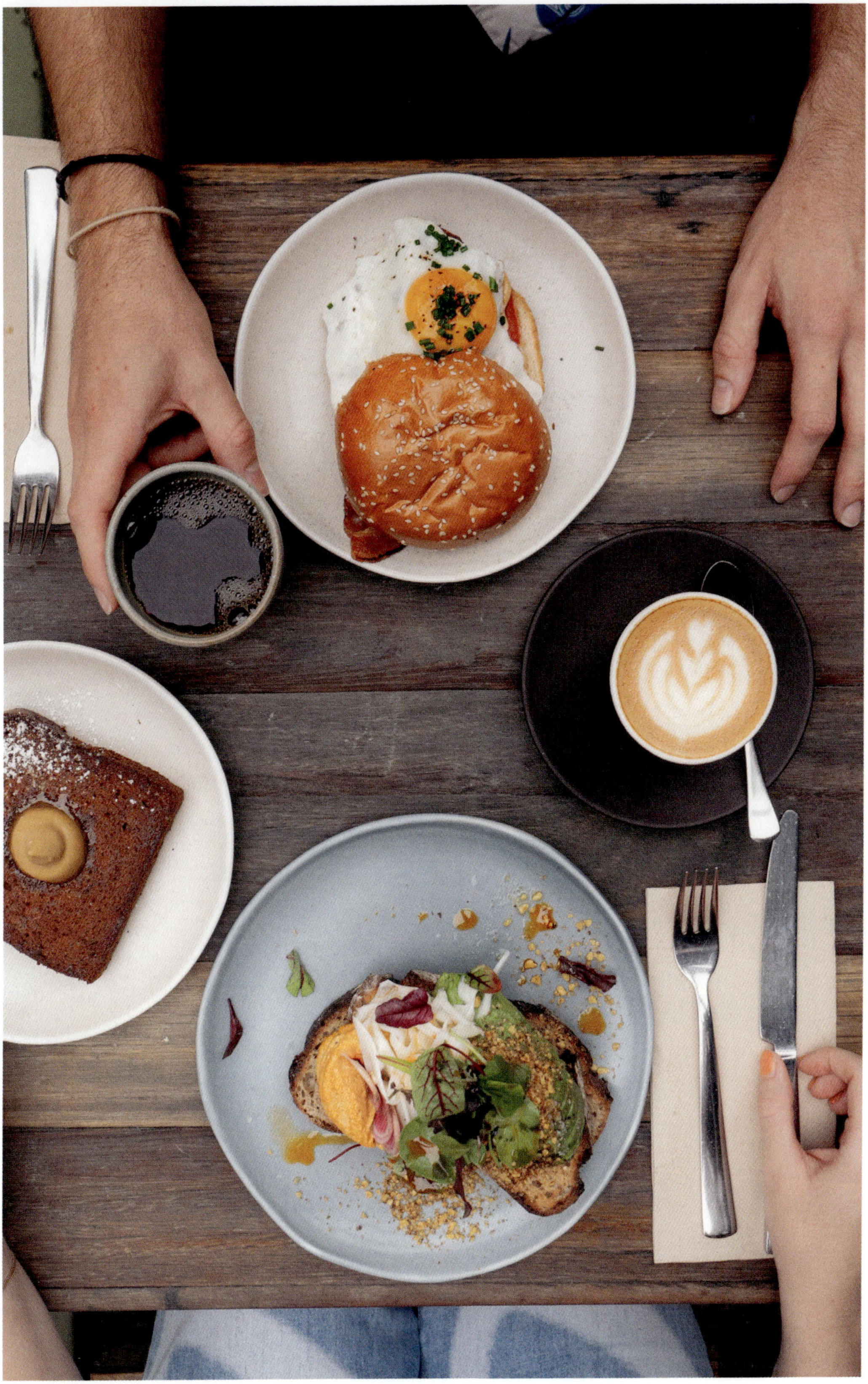

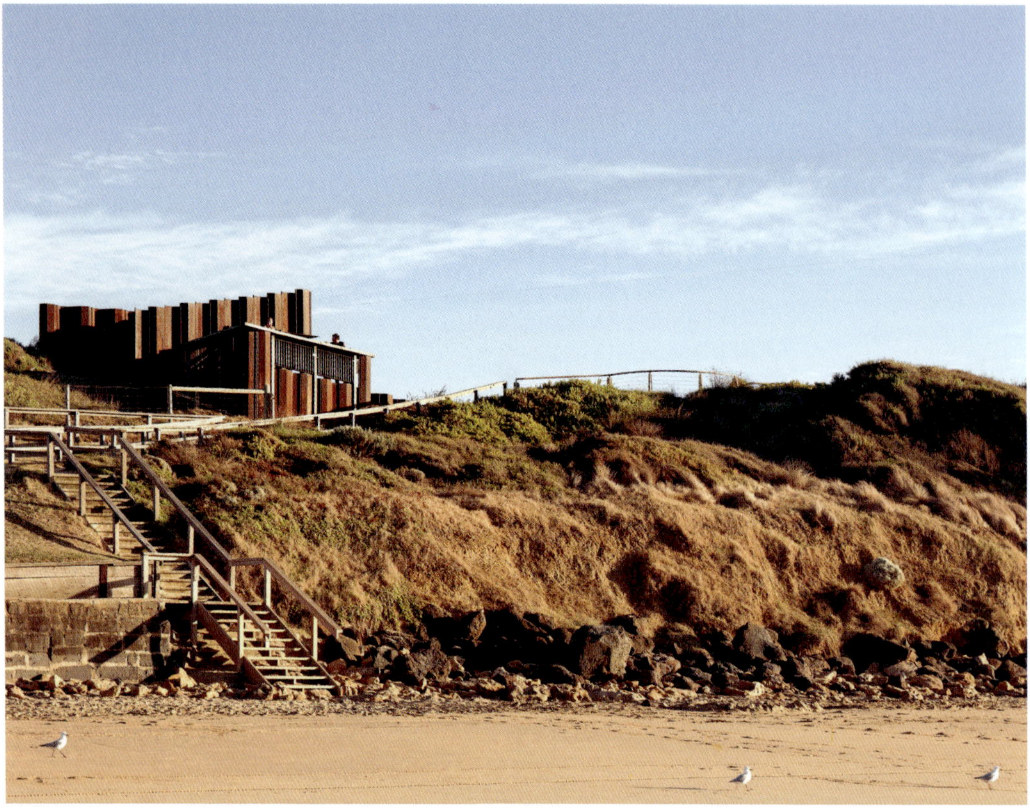

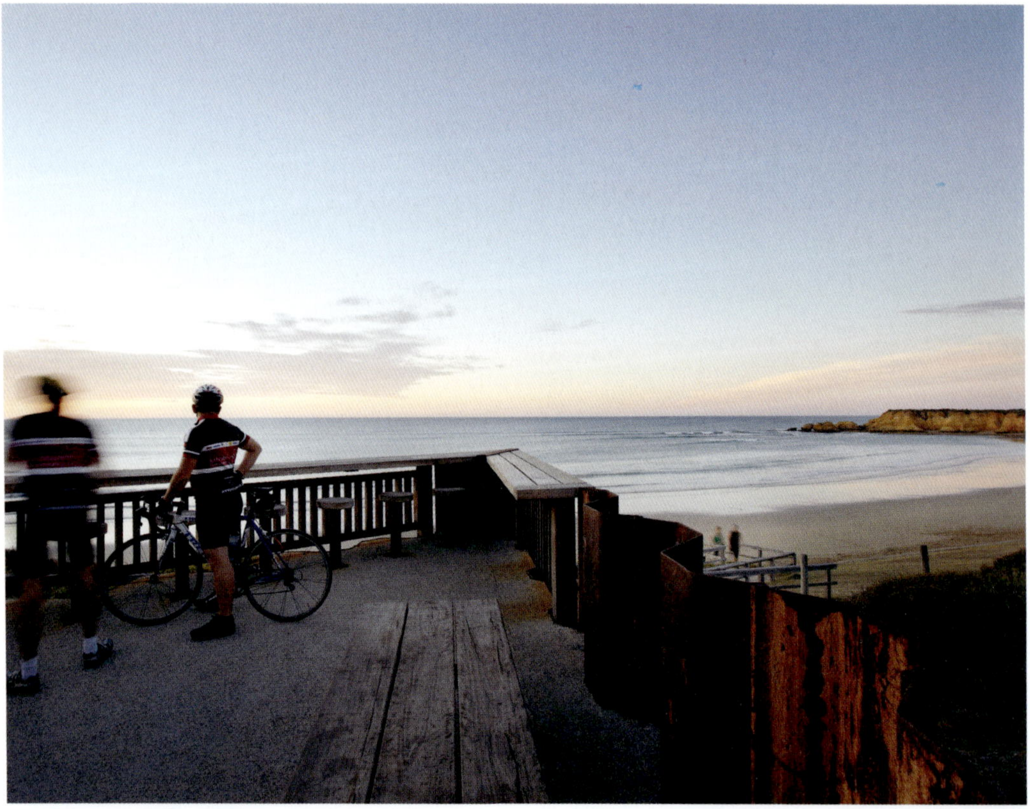

149 THIRD WAVE KIOSK

1 The Esplanade, Torquay, Victoria 3228, Australia

TO VISIT
BEFORE YOU DIE
BECAUSE

This sculptural take on the humble beach café by Tony Hobba Architects is the best place for a morning cappuccino with a view.

Most Australians would say that coffee tastes better at the beach, and who are we to argue! It is certainly true that our environment profoundly impacts taste perception, so a flat white at the Third Wave Kiosk, with its ocean views and backdrop of crashing waves, would probably be much tastier than anywhere else (and even more so after catching a few waves). Opened in 2012, the kiosk was designed by Tony Hobba Architects using recycled metal sheet piles originally used as flood protection along the Murray River. The resulting weathered façade is in perfect harmony with the surrounding cliffs and dunes, while the large terrace has become a favourite local meeting point. Perch on one of the wooden stools at the sea-facing counter and see if you can spot some southern right whales in the ocean. As well as all the classic coffee drinks, the menu includes snacks and light meals such as almond croissants, burgers and chicken schnitzel sandwiches. Closed during winter.

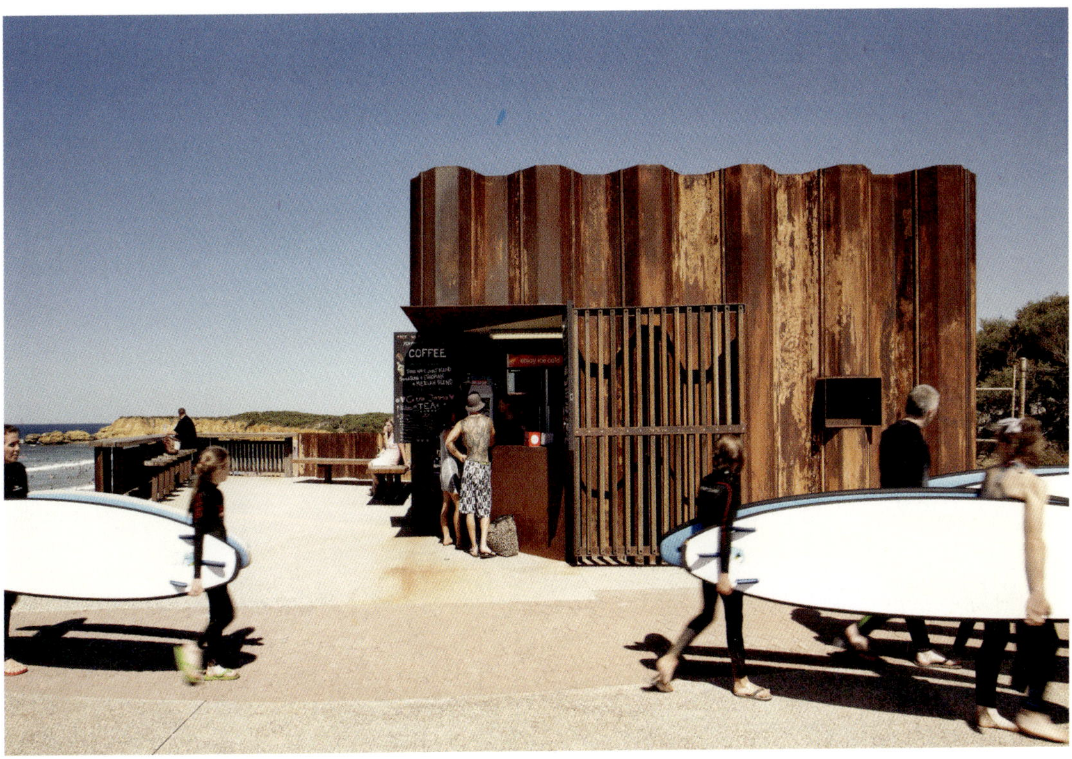

@thirdwavekiosk

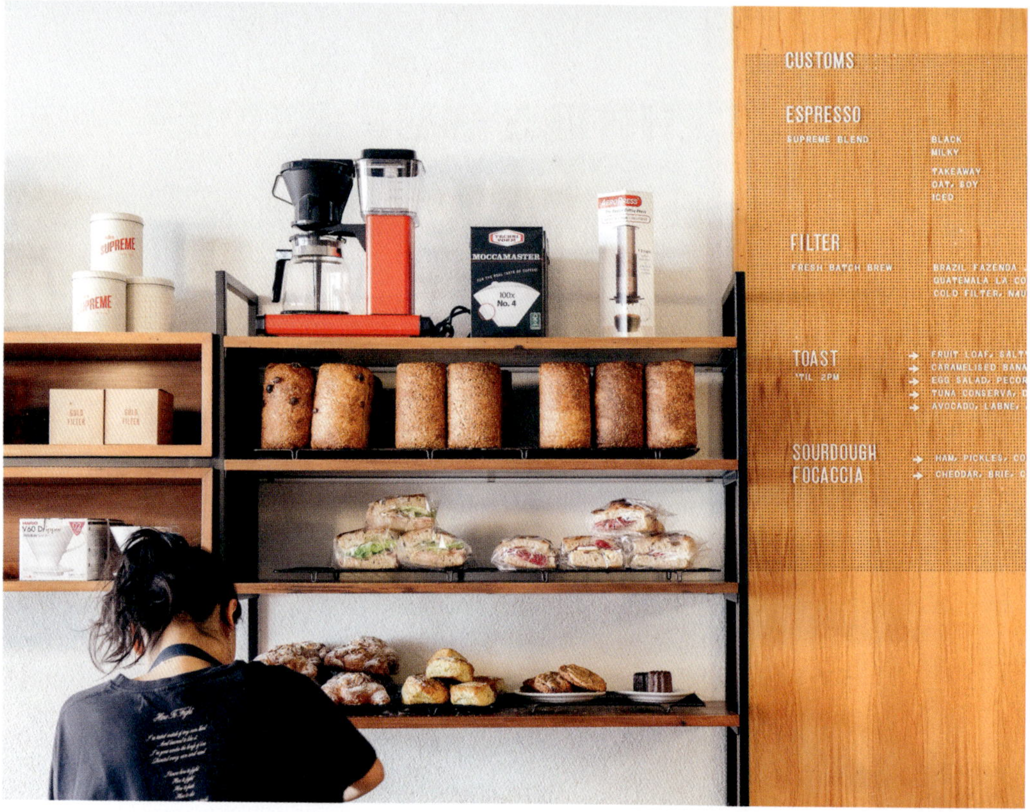

SUPREME
SUPREME
MOCCAMASTER
100x
No. 4
CUSTOMS
ESPRESSO
SUPREME BLEND
BLACK
MILKY
TAKEAWAY
OAT, SOY
ICED
FILTER
FRESH BATCH BREW
BRAZIL FAZENDA
GUATEMALA LA
COLD FILTER,
TOAST
'TIL 2PM
FRUIT LOAF,
CARAMELISED
EGG SALAD,
TUNA CONSERVA,
AVOCADO, LABNE,
SOURDOUGH
FOCACCIA
HAM, PICKLES,
CHEDDAR, BRIE,

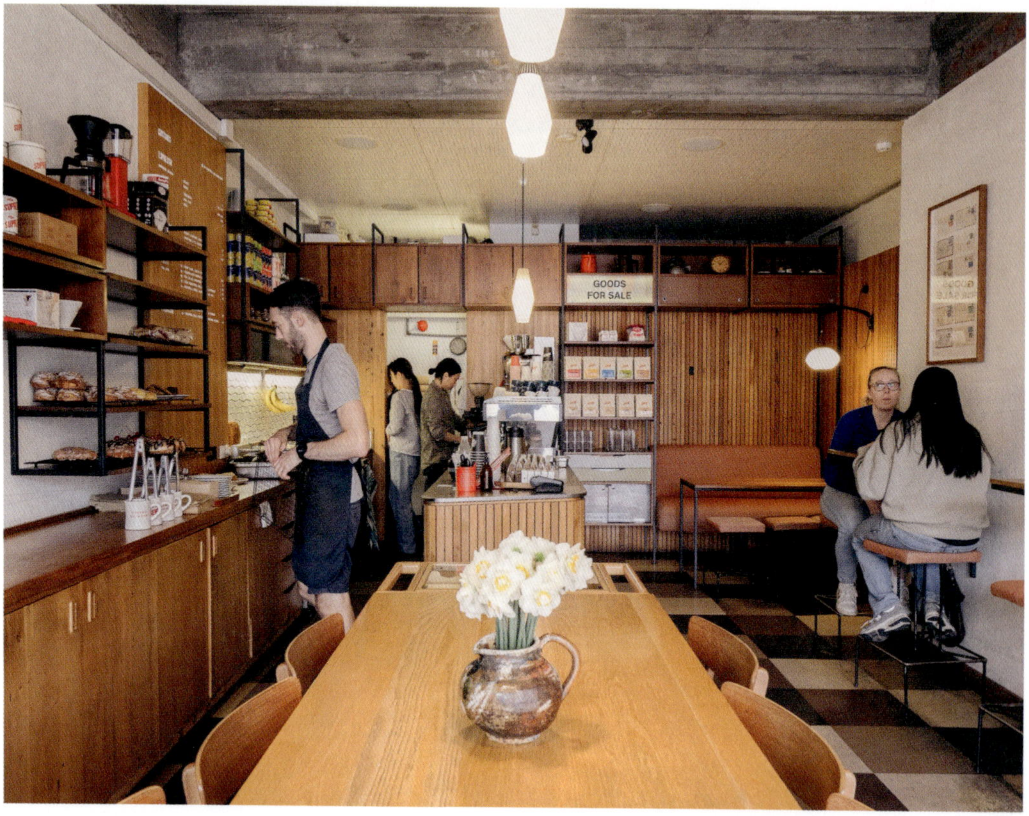

GOODS
FOR SALE

150 COFFEE SUPREME CUSTOMS

39 Ghuznee St, Te Aro, Wellington 6011, New Zealand

TO VISIT
BEFORE YOU DIE
BECAUSE

A trip to Wellington wouldn't be complete without a stop at this pioneering, community-minded café serving 'better coffee for all'.

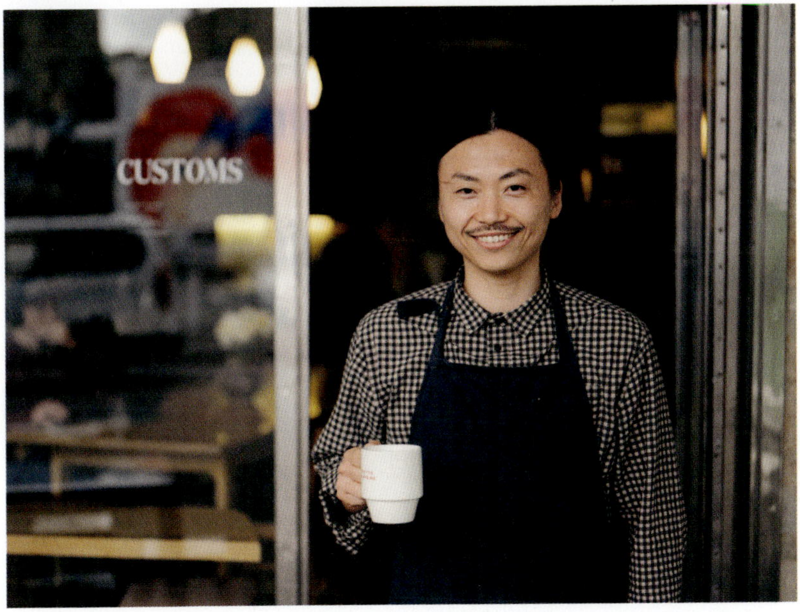

The story goes that Antipodean favourite, the flat white, was created as the result of 'a failed cappuccino' in the late 1980s, at Bar Bodega in Wellington. The delicious mistake led to the opening of many interesting cafés, including Coffee Supreme, originally opened on Woodward Street by Chris Dillon and Maggie Wells. By the time the company's Customs opened 16 years later, a new wave of cafés was reimagining what could be by championing single origins, filter brews and lighter roasts long before they were part of the mainstream. Over the years, its team of experts have built long-term relationships with producers such as the Mierisch family in Nicaragua or Azahar in Colombia, ensuring both the quality and sustainability of their coffee. Today the flagship café, known for its cosy mid-century-style interiors, serves what has been described as 'the best coffee and doughnuts in town'. Its short food menu focuses on delicious seasonal 'things on toast' – the bread is by Wellington Sourdough, while the toppings range from caramelised banana butter to avocado and chilli oil. Coffee Supreme has branches in Christchurch, Melbourne and Tokyo.

coffeesupreme.com

Index 150 Coffee shops

© Photos

Coffee shop 1: Marcel Nasr / coffee shop 02: Yohannes Ezra, Shutterstock / coffee shop 03: The Elewana Collection / coffee shop 04: Kalei Coffee Co. / coffee shop 05: 30 North / coffee shop 06: Rosetta / coffee shop 07: Truth Coffee, @CraveConcepts / coffee shop 08: Aleksandra Tokarz, iStock / coffee shop 09: JohnnyGreig, iStock / coffee shop 10: Medd Coffee Al Fayha / coffee shop 11: Bean There Coffee / coffee shop 12: Frances Marais for Father Coffee / coffee shop 13: Bacha Coffee / coffee shop 14: Kennedy Kamau / coffee shop 15: Guillermo Durán / EStudio Cuatro Santos / coffee shop 16: Colo Coffee Roasters, Bogotá, Colombia / coffee shop 17: Varietale / coffee shop 18: Eric Kitayama, iStock / coffee shop 19: Rosso / coffee shop 20: Jonathan Vega / coffee shop 21: Metric Coffee Co / coffee shop 22: tunart, iStock / coffee shop 23: Olaiya Land / coffee shop 24: Heavenly Hawaiian Farms / coffee shop 25: Hugo Cano and Joshua Clements / coffee shop 26: Coffee traders Ltd. / Clifton Mount Coffee E / coffee shop 27: Verve Coffee Roasters / coffee shop 28: Grupo Exploradores / coffee shop 29: Jonathan Jehle / coffee shop 30: Kali Coffee Roasters / coffee shop 31: David Dworkind / coffee shop 32: Victoria Quirk / coffee shop 33: Brycia James, iStock / coffee shop 34: Coffee Project New York / coffee shop 35: IKMueller Architecture PLLC / coffee shop 36: Casa Sucre / coffee shop 37: p. 66 (left) Rory Blue Browning; p. 66 (right) Alex Villeda; p. 67 Maria Orlova / coffee shop 38: Greta Rybus, Tandem Coffee Roasters / coffee shop 39: Lucia Reyes Alfranca / coffee shop 40: Café San Alberto / coffee shop 41: Bernard Barroso, Shutterstock / coffee shop 42: Onyx Coffee Lab / coffee shop 43: Seyhan Ahen, Shutterstock / coffee shop 44: Ritual Coffee Roasters / coffee shop 45: Juliana Gonzalez / coffee shop 46: Um Coffee Co / coffee shop 47: Wikimedia Commons / coffee shop 48: Pilot Coffee Roasters / coffee shop 49: Revolver Coffee / coffee shop 50: Damir Otegen / coffee shop 51: Tugu Hotels & Restaurants / coffee shop 52: Munduk Moding Plantation Nature Resort / coffee shop 53: Ballad / coffee shop 54: Nattapol Na Nakorn / coffee shop 55: Chalffy, iStock / coffee shop 56: Philocoffea / coffee shop 57: Do sy, Anh Coffee Roasters / coffee shop 58: Easy Chan - @chillifehk / coffee shop 59: Halfway Coffee / coffee shop 60: Coffee No 4 / coffee shop 61: Mandabatmaz / coffee shop 62: Montag / coffee shop 63: courtesy of Common Grounds / coffee shop 64: Roast8ry / coffee shop 65: Wikimedia Commons / coffee shop 66: Afloat Coffee Roasters / coffee shop 67: Jasonyan, Shutterstock / coffee shop 68: Weekenders Coffee / coffee shop 69: Jeff Nelson for Subko / coffee shop 70: Hu Yanyun, Yu Shuyang @HALF.HALF.PHOTOGRAPHY / coffee shop 71: Lilo Coffee Roasters / coffee shop 72: Geric Cruz / coffee shop 73: Coffee Nap Roasters / coffee shop 74: Fritz Company / coffee shop 75: blanscape, iStock / coffee shop 76: Nylon / coffee shop 77: Sanga Park, iStock / coffee shop 78: Simple Kaffa / coffee shop 79: Apollon's Gold / coffee shop 80: KOFFEE MAMEYA Kakeru / coffee shop 81: Onibus / coffee shop 82: p. 139 Paw Gissel; p. 140-141 Mathias Laustrup / coffee shop 83: Stiller's Coffee / coffee shop 84: Keng Pereira / coffee shop 85: White Turtle / coffee shop 86: Meson del Café / coffee shop 87: Salva López/Nomad Coffee / coffee shop 88: Roast Club, Mario Martinez / coffee shop 89: 19grams Coffee Roasters / coffee shop 90: Five Elephant / coffee shop 91: MOK / coffee shop 92: Corvin Cristian / coffee shop 93: Anantara New York Palace / coffee shop 94: Kross Coffee Roasters / coffee shop 95: Lasse Bech Martinussen / coffee shop 96: Noma Project / coffee shop 97: Kasper Kristoffersen / coffee shop 98: Vice Coffee Inc / coffee shop 99: p. 166 Leonardo Morfini; p. 167 (top) Leonardo Morfini; p. 167 (bottom) Federica Masciullo / coffee shop 100: Kaffa Roastery / coffee shop 101: Yevhenii Avramenko / coffee shop 102: Madmum / coffee shop 103: A Brasileira do Chiado / coffee shop 104: Stow / coffee shop 105: kelvinjay, iStock / coffee shop 106: Monmouth Coffee Company / coffee shop 107: Qima Cafe / coffee shop 108: Léa Teuscher / coffee shop 109: Hola Coffee Roasters / coffee shop 110: Cafezal / coffee shop 111: Alessandro Tortora, Shutterstock / coffee shop 112: Fuglen Coffee Roasters / coffee shop 113: Helena Krekling, Dorothée Brand/ coffee shop 114: Café Nuances / coffee shop 115: Simon Détraz / coffee shop 116: Substance Café / coffee shop 117: Starcevic, iStock / coffee shop 118: Marc Dufresne, iStock / coffee shop 119: Doubleshot / coffee shop 120: Caffé Greco / coffee shop 121: Aliena / coffee shop 122: Schot Coffee Roasters / coffee shop 123: Café Tomaselli / coffee shop 124: The Dude Specialty Coffee / coffee shop 125: Kava2 / coffee shop 126: Christian Gustavsson / coffee shop 127: Komet / coffee shop 128: Rasmus Jurkatam / coffee shop 129: Caffé San Marco / coffee shop 130: Al Bicerin / coffee shop 131: Tallat Coffee Roasters / coffee shop 132: Caffé Florian / coffee shop 133: Café Central / coffee shop 134: Ida Skovmand / coffee shop 135: Patrycja Pati Makowska, Milena Linkiewicz / coffee shop 136: Šarūnė Zurba / coffee shop 137: Luta / coffee shop 138: Mirjam Kluka / coffee shop 139: D.O.S.E ON HIGH / coffee shop 140: Espresso Studio by Fushoken / coffee shop 141: Skybury / coffee shop 142: Proud Mary - True Tribe / coffee shop 143: Manta Ray / coffee shop 144: Ben Clement / coffee shop 145: Jono Laird / coffee shop 146: Anson Smart / coffee shop 147: Heart Media / coffee shop 148: single O / coffee shop 149: Rory Gardiner / coffee shop 150: Coffee Supreme / back cover: Anson Smart for Genovese Coffee House

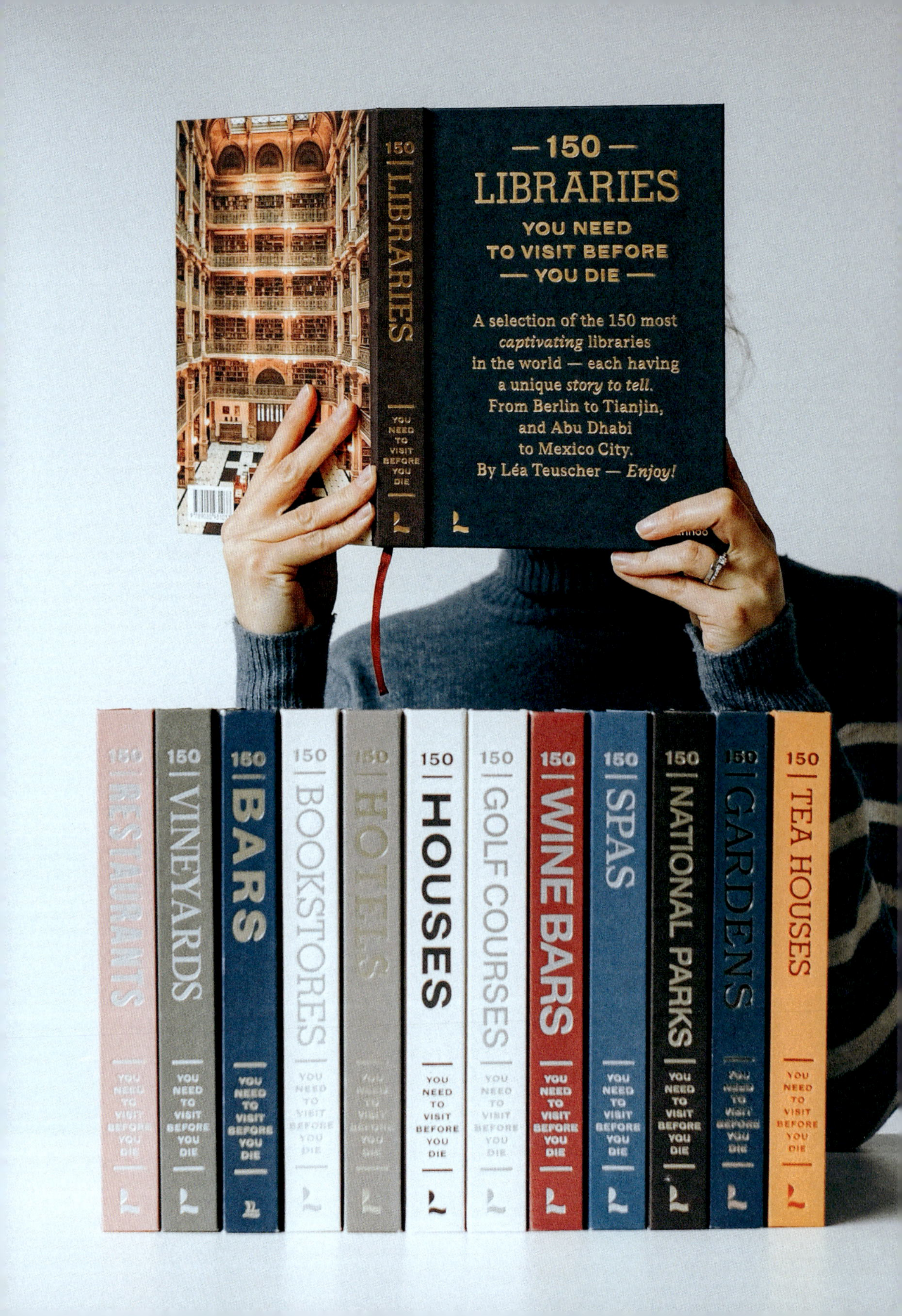

— 150 —
LIBRARIES
YOU NEED
TO VISIT BEFORE
— YOU DIE —
A selection of the 150 most
captivating libraries
in the world — each having
a unique story to tell.
From Berlin to Tianjin,
and Abu Dhabi
to Mexico City.
By Léa Teuscher — Enjoy!
150 RESTAURANTS YOU NEED TO VISIT BEFORE YOU DIE
150 VINEYARDS YOU NEED TO VISIT BEFORE YOU DIE
150 BARS YOU NEED TO VISIT BEFORE YOU DIE
150 BOOKSTORES YOU NEED TO VISIT BEFORE YOU DIE
150 HOTELS YOU NEED TO VISIT BEFORE YOU DIE
150 HOUSES YOU NEED TO VISIT BEFORE YOU DIE
150 GOLF COURSES YOU NEED TO VISIT BEFORE YOU DIE
150 WINE BARS YOU NEED TO VISIT BEFORE YOU DIE
150 SPAS YOU NEED TO VISIT BEFORE YOU DIE
150 NATIONAL PARKS YOU NEED TO VISIT BEFORE YOU DIE
150 GARDENS YOU NEED TO VISIT BEFORE YOU DIE
150 TEA HOUSES YOU NEED TO VISIT BEFORE YOU DIE

IN THE SAME — SERIES —

150 Libraries You Need to Visit Before You Die
ISBN 978 90 209 3103 7

—

150 Tea Houses You Need to Visit Before You Die
ISBN 978 90 209 2661 3

—

150 National Parks You Need to Visit Before You Die
ISBN 978 94 014 1970 3

—

150 Spas You Need to Visit Before You Die
ISBN 978 94 014 9747 3

—

150 Vineyards You Need to Visit Before You Die
ISBN 978 94 014 8546 3

—

150 Bookstores You Need to Visit Before You Die
ISBN 978 94 014 8935 5

—

150 Gardens You Need to Visit Before You Die
ISBN 978 94 014 7929 5

—

150 Bars You Need to Visit Before You Die
ISBN 978 94 014 4912 0

—

150 Wine Bars You Need to Visit Before You Die
ISBN 978 94 014 8622 4

—

150 Houses You Need to Visit Before You Die
ISBN 978 94 014 6204 4

—

150 Golf Courses You Need to Visit Before You Die
ISBN 978 94 014 8195 3

—

150 Hotels You Need to Visit Before You Die
ISBN 978 94 014 5806 1

—

150 Restaurants You Need to Visit Before You Die
ISBN 978 94 014 9570 7

Texts
Léa Teuscher

Copy-editing
Heather Sills

Book Design
ASB (Atelier Sven Beirnaert)

Typesetting
Keppie & Keppie

Back cover image
Anson Smart for Genovese Coffee House

Sign up for our newsletter with news about new and forthcoming publications on art, interior design, food & travel, photography and fashion as well as exclusive offers and events. If you have any questions or comments about the material in this book, please do not hesitate to contact our editorial team: art@lannoo.com

www.lannoo.com
BISAC: TRV036000, CKB019000
D/2026/45/12
ISBN 978-90-599-6147-0